CANADIAN TAX PAPER

NO. 105

The Income Tax Treatment of Financial Instruments: Theory and Practice

Tim Edgar

Canadian Tax Foundation
L'Association canadienne
d'études fiscales

Canadian Cataloguing in Publication Data

Edgar, Tim (Timothy), 1960-
The income tax treatment of financial instruments : theory and practice

(Canadian tax papers, ISSN 0008-512X ; 105)
Includes bibliographical references and index.
ISBN 0-88808-158-8

1. Financial instruments — Taxation. I. Canadian Tax Foundation. II. Title.
III. Series.

HJ5901.E33 2000 336.24′1 C00-932741-X

Contents

Preface

The idea for this project arose from work that I did with Brian Arnold in the early 1990s on the deductibility of interest expense. After a series of discussions with Brian, I became convinced that there was a need for a monograph that provided an accessible overview of the income tax issues presented by financial instruments. My hope for this project was to draw together much of the excellent theoretical literature on many of these issues and examine how tax-policy makers in different countries have resolved some of those issues in practice. My original intention was to keep the monograph to a manageable size so that readers might be able to take it in with a minimal commitment of time. Unfortunately, as the research proceeded and I attempted to digest the enormous volume of literature on different aspects of the subject, the comprehensive nature of the topic made it impossible to avoid a lengthy monograph. Nonetheless, I have tried to remain true to my goal of providing an accessible overview of the tax-policy issues associated with financial instruments and the related approaches to legislative design.

The monograph examines the theoretical and practical aspects associated with the treatment of financial instruments under a realization-based income tax with different effective rates for (1) interest and dividends and (2) capital and ordinary-income amounts. I argue that, within the context of such an income tax, a system of "expected-return taxation" is the preferable approach. Critical to this system is a distinction between expected gains and losses attributable to an advance of funds and unexpected gains and losses attributable to bets on specified contingencies.

The monograph focuses principally on the broad features of "expected-return taxation" as developed in some of the academic literature and implemented in certain legislative regimes. I have relied heavily on the work of other scholars, particularly certain individuals in the United States, who have provided the important theoretical ground work. As far as legislative design issues are concerned, the monograph does not purport to provide a comprehensive review of the technical details of the legislation in any particular country. Instead, various features of the regimes in New Zealand and the United States, along with proposals for legislative reform introduced in Australia, are used selectively to illustrate the details of important policy design choices that are highlighted, but not always fully developed, in the theoretical literature. These details are contrasted with the aspects of the conventional "cubbyhole system" of taxation reflected in the provisions of the Canadian Income Tax Act; they are also measured against an ideal benchmark approach to the treatment of financial instruments.

The discussion includes the treatment of the basic building-block instruments (forwards, futures, swaps, options, and fixed-payment debt obligations), as well as combinations of these instruments in sophisticated hybrids and synthetics. I have tried to emphasize the historical context within which the income tax treatment of these instruments should be seen. I am convinced that this perspective reveals clearly that in matters of taxation "everything that is old is new again." In short, many of the issues associated with the income tax treatment of the new financial instruments are longstanding issues that tax-policy makers have struggled with for decades in designing legislative responses to more conventional instruments. I believe this point is becoming much clearer than it was even five years ago when I undertook the project. More important, the common themes from the past mean that many of the features of past responses are still relevant. There is, I believe, no need to reinvent the wheel with radical legislative solutions. All that is required is a little massaging and extension of past responses. This conclusion is probably most evident in the features of the New Zealand accrual legislation and the similar regime proposed in Australia. Not surprisingly, therefore, I have drawn extensively on the experiences in those two countries.

In the five years that it took me to complete this study I have been fortunate to receive assistance in a variety of forms from many generous and talented people. I would like first to acknowledge the support of the Faculty of Law of The University of Western Ontario, which provided me with much of the time required to complete the study. I began the project while on sabbatical in Melbourne in 1995-96 and benefited greatly from an additional teaching leave on my return in the autumn of 1996. I also benefited from the assistance of my faculty secretary, Amy Jacob, who laboured tirelessly over several drafts of the manuscript and who always managed to solve the computer problems that were inevitably beyond my limited knowledge.

I received research assistance from two talented students: Jason Park and Jackson MacGillivray. They saved me endless hours tracking down citations, proofreading manuscripts, and collecting all kinds of data that did not always find its way into the final draft.

The monograph was initially a doctoral thesis written under the supervision of Rick Krever at the School of Law, Deakin University, in Melbourne. Rick is one of only a select few individuals who managed to read the manuscript from the beginning to end. In fact, he devoted far too much of his valuable time to this project. He also provided me with a series of professional opportunities for which I am eternally grateful. On a personal level, I consider him a good friend, who made my family's stay in Melbourne one of the most memorable years of our lives.

Only three other individuals read all of the manuscript. Al Warren and Eric Zolt undertook this task as thesis examiners. Tom McDonnell undertook the same task as an external reviewer for the Canadian Tax Foundation. Daniel Sandler provided detailed comments on a draft of the first chapter. Their comments and encouragement were invaluable.

Roger Paul of the Australian Taxation Office and Richard Wood of the Australian Treasury Department generously provided their time in guiding me through the proposals for an accrual regime in Australia. Rosemary Cook and her "accruals team" at New Zealand Inland Revenue provided similar guidance through the New Zealand legislation. I only hope that this monograph gains me membership in the exclusive "accruals club." I will leave that final decision to Rosemary.

Tony Rumble and the Australian Taxation Studies program at The University of New South Wales provided me with an opportunity to present a draft of one of the chapters at a conference held in Sydney. Alan Macnaughton and the School of Accounting at the University of Waterloo provided me with a similar opportunity in a seminar format. The chapters presented in these two formats benefited from comments from many of the participants.

Alex Scala and Jim Lyons undertook the daunting task of editing the manuscript. They improved both the style and substance to an extent that I cannot even begin to measure. Michael Gaughan shouldered admirably the heavy work of editing the references.

The Canadian Tax Foundation provided support that includes generous funding, but does not end there. As directors of the Foundation, Tom McDonnell and Robin MacKnight were exceedingly patient. That characteristic extends to Laurel Amalia, the Foundation's editor-in-chief. At no point did she bother me about the lengthy gestation period for this project. She organized the editing, promotion, and production of the monograph with enviable good humour and efficiency.

Finally, the highest award for patience has to go to my wife, Diane, and our two children, Wade and Rachel. For vast periods, I shirked all manner of familial responsibilities while working on this project. They never once complained, although Wade and Rachel have had considerable difficulty comprehending how and why any book could take so long to produce.

Tim Edgar
London, Ontario
August 2000

1

The Basic Building-Block Financial Instruments and the Fundamentals of Financial Innovation

Introduction

Even a casual observer of capital markets will be aware that the past 25 years have witnessed an explosion in the development of new financial instruments. Indeed, this awareness is so widespread that the idea of explosive financial innovation, presumably in response to the increasing volatility of interest rates and exchange rates, is almost as trite at this point as the idea of "globalization." Yet closer examination of the matter reveals that, in principle at least, the "explosion" is merely an acceleration of a familiar process literally hundreds of years old. In one form or another, options, forward contracts, and futures contracts, the basic financial instruments that are the foundation of financial innovation, have been traded since the 17th century.[1]

This link to the past does not mean that the recent wave of financial innovation is the inevitable outcome of past events. Most informed observers of capital markets would agree that the changes in financial institutions and instruments that have occurred in the last 25 years do constitute a major break with the past. In general, the earlier forms of forward contracts and options were limited to the provision of future delivery of commodities. The newer derivative instruments differ from their predecessors in two important respects.[2] First, they are written on both commodities and intangible financial assets and liabilities, including indices of commodities and instruments that represent a composite price mechanism. Second, the newer derivatives provide for cash settlement or commutation of their value in lieu of physical delivery of the underlying asset. These changes and the exponential growth of markets for derivatives over the past 25 years have produced an array of instruments that permit the packaging and repackaging of cash flows in many different ways and that investors can trade in standardized forms at low transaction costs. To emphasize the current importance of financial innovation, commentators invariably cite statistics on the staggering size of the financial obligations represented by derivatives and the "new financial instruments." Indeed, convention virtually requires an introductory chapter, such as this one, to quote some large numbers as evidence of the importance of the income tax treatment of financial instruments. Nevertheless, no statistics of this kind are cited here.[3] The impressive numbers merely confirm the obvious truth that new financial instruments are critical components of today's capital markets. From a tax-policy perspective (or any other policy perspective, for that matter), the statistics are essentially pointless: they reveal nothing about the relations between income tax (or regulatory) systems and capital markets. For our purposes here, it is sufficient to assume that financial innovation and its products are significant facts of life and are not about to disappear.

Survey data[4] confirm what casual empiricism suggests—namely, that financial instruments are used principally to (1) manage risk, (2) raise capital, and (3) provide an investment return.[5] A minority of instruments may be purchased and sold for speculative purposes. Whatever the intention in acquiring a financial instrument, it is clear that the treatment of financial instruments for the purposes of income taxation can have adverse effects. As a rule, these effects arise from inconsistencies in tax treatment. In some instances, for example, the treatment of an instrument that is used to hedge an exposure to risk is different from the treatment associated with the underlying position that gives rise to the exposure. The after-tax result of these offsetting positions will be different from their pre-tax result, an outcome that may adversely affect the pricing of an instrument that is used for risk-management purposes.[6] In other instances, inconsistencies in the tax system provide opportunities to repackage cash flows in a manner that reduces their after-tax cost to issuers. The tax system may even present opportunities for "pure" tax avoidance, whereby positions with offsetting cash flows are profitable solely because of an associated tax benefit.

This book does not attempt to measure the net welfare gains or losses associated with the effect of existing income tax systems on the pricing of financial instruments, nor does it attempt to measure the revenue loss that arises from the opportunities for avoidance that some financial instruments provide. It is assumed that these effects occur and that they are important enough to warrant a response from tax-policy makers.[7] In fact, the task of designing an appropriate approach to the income taxation of financial instruments is significantly easier than the task of assessing the net welfare gains or losses associated with existing income tax systems and their impact on financial innovation. The source of the problems and the range of possible solutions are both relatively clear. The tax legislation and the tax authorities in most countries maintain what is conventionally characterized as the "cubbyhole approach" to the taxation of financial instruments. As the name implies, this approach involves the definition of discrete categories for a set of standard financial instruments.[8] Distinctions in tax treatment based on these categories or cubbyholes often result in different tax treatments for equivalent cash flows—a result that, in turn, creates tax-avoidance opportunities and may distort the pricing of innovative instruments designed to reallocate risk. These problems are only aggravated by the fact that the cubbyholes are not, as a rule, very clearly defined. Past practice has resulted in a complex patchwork of legislative rules, case law, and administrative positions that makes for significant gaps and ambiguities in the taxation of both the basic building-block instruments and the more sophisticated instruments that have resulted from financial innovation. The uncertainty generated by these gaps and ambiguities can impede the use of innovative instruments for non-tax reasons and can encourage their development for tax-avoidance purposes.

The Australian and Canadian experiences described in the next chapter illustrate the cubbyhole approach to the taxation of financial instruments and the problems associated with it. The balance of the book explores the theoretical and practical aspects of various alternatives to the cubbyhole approach. In general, these alternatives attempt to broaden the capital income tax base and minimize the importance of certain key differences in tax treatment that have been the foundation of that base for decades. The principal issue in this context is the development of appropriate rules for measuring income and thus for determining the timing of the recognition of gains and losses and the character of those amounts. The argument of the book rests, at bottom, on a distinction between expected time-value returns, which provide expected gains and losses, and the bet or risk element in financial instruments, which provides unexpected gains and losses. This distinction underlies the basic features of the building-block instruments of financial innovation, which provide paradigms for the design of an appropriate approach to the taxation of financial instruments generally. In fact, the failure of most income tax systems to address the taxation of financial instruments adequately is attributable in large part to a failure to recognize (or perhaps, more accurately, to push to its logical extremes) the fundamental distinction between expected time-value returns and unexpected gains and losses as the basis for systemic design principles. These different types of financial returns present different tax-policy considerations, and the appropriate treatment of expected time-value returns is the more difficult and more critical aspect of any regime for the taxation of financial instruments.[9] The ideal regime for the taxation of these instruments would be one that required the annual recognition of all unrealized changes in value. There are practical objections to the wholesale adoption of this approach, but it would be possible to apply it selectively to a limited set of financial instruments and a limited set of taxpayers. The result would be a system that provided tight and comprehensive rules for the taxation of all expected time-value returns. Moreover, this system could be readily supplemented with provisions designed to address the more serious problems associated with unexpected gains and losses.[10] Although a system of this kind would be far from perfect, it would address many of the tax-avoidance opportunities and pricing distortions associated with the piecemeal reforms and cubbyhole regimes that constitute the status quo in most countries.[11]

In an effort to reduce the economics of financial instruments to what is relevant for tax-policy purposes, this introductory chapter emphasizes the following two points:

1) Financial innovation is nothing more than the process of combining certain basic building-block instruments with associated cash flows that provide expected gains and losses, unexpected gains and losses, or both. Consequently, the economic substance of any instrument is some combination of specified cash flows associated with these basic building-block instruments to provide expected gains and losses, unexpected gains and losses, or both.

2) The process of financial innovation has been driven primarily by a need to allocate risk among market participants in the most efficient manner. Tax-avoidance opportunities, however, are an important secondary source of innovation, one that has arisen because of a failure to recognize the equivalence of financial positions that is expressed in certain parities and pricing relationships among the basic instruments.

Chapters 2 through 7 will explore the significance of these two points for the design of a legislative approach to the income taxation of financial instruments. The first point is critical to an understanding of the tax-policy issues that are raised by both the basic instruments and the newer instruments, which are combinations of the cash flows associated with the basic instruments. As has already been noted, expected gains and losses present policy problems within the constraints of a realization-based income tax that differ from the problems presented by unexpected amounts and require different responses. The tax analysis of complex instruments involves the identification of cash flows associated with one or more of the basic instruments and the application of appropriate treatments to those cash flows. This identification requirement, however, presents considerable difficulties in the context of an income tax system that applies different tax treatments to financial instruments that are legally distinct. The second point, which is related to the first, implies that the necessary first step in any attempt to control avoidance opportunities is to ensure that the treatment of the cash flows associated with the basic building-block instruments realizes the consistent taxation of equivalent positions.

The second part of this chapter describes the general features of a distinction between the basic building-block financial instruments and the more complex instruments that are the result of the process of financial innovation. This distinction is an important element of the analytical framework used throughout the subsequent chapters. This part also reviews the essential features of the building-block financial instruments and their arbitrage pricing relationships, which constitute the conceptual foundations of the process of financial innovation. The third part of the chapter surveys the causes, benefits, and costs of financial innovation, with an emphasis on the underlying structural features of income tax systems that permit the assembly of the building-block instruments for avoidance purposes. Tax avoidance and its underlying causes explain many of the problems commonly identified with existing legislative approaches and provide a useful basis for an assessment of the strengths and weaknesses of various alternatives to the present treatment of financial instruments under an income tax.

The Conceptual Foundations of the Process of Financial Innovation

The Basic Building-Block Instruments of Financial Innovation

In its broadest sense, the term "financial instrument" includes "any evidence of the legal relationship arising from the provision of money, property, or a promise to pay money or property by one person to another in consideration for a promise by the other person to provide money or property at some future time or times, or upon the occurrence or non-occurrence of some future event or events."[12] Much of the tax literature reduces this broad definition by making a distinction between "financing transactions" and "financial instruments." The former term[13] tends to be equated with the advance of a sum of money in the expectation that the funds will be returned at some time in the future, along with an additional amount that represents a return or compensation for their use. These "capital-raising transactions" traditionally include standard forms of debt obligations, issues of shares by corporations, and leasing transactions that involve an extension of credit and whose associated cash flows are equivalent to the purchase of an asset on an instalment basis ("financial leases"). The term "financial instruments" (also "financial products" and "financial arrangements") tends to be equated with forwards, futures, swaps, and option contracts, which are collectively referred to as "derivatives" because their value derives from, or is based on, some specified asset or financial index.[14]

Despite any convenience associated with the use of this prevalent distinction, the broad categories of capital-raising and derivative instruments are not especially useful from a tax-policy perspective and are rejected here in favour of a classification that has more significance analytically. At the core of this classification is the category of "basic building-block financial instruments," which includes both capital-raising and derivative instruments. The concept of "financial innovation," as it is used in much of the finance literature, is simply the design of new financial instruments by combining these building-block instruments.[15] Indeed, the distinction between the basic building-block instruments and the newer instruments that are the product of the process of financial innovation captures roughly the aspect of this process that has caused difficulty for income tax systems based on traditional concepts and principles. In essence, the development of innovative financial instruments involves the reallocation of risk by repackaging the cash flows associated with the basic instruments in an unconventional manner.[16] For tax purposes, the result is often the conversion of a cash flow with a known tax treatment into a cash flow for which the appropriate treatment is unknown.

The process of packaging the cash flows associated with certain basic instruments to create more complex instruments is the basis of the "building-block approach" to financial innovation described by Smith, Smithson, and Wilford.[17] They identify three basic building blocks from which all financial instruments are constructed:[18]

- credit-extension instruments,
- price-fixing instruments, and
- price-insurance instruments.

Credit-extension instruments consist of traditional debt instruments that provide an expected time-value return in the form of interest. Price-fixing and price-insurance instruments are the basic derivative financial instruments (forwards, futures, swaps, and options). These instruments are in effect bets on movements in the price of the specified assets or indexes. Consequently, at least a portion of their return is unexpected and cannot be determined until resolution of the bet. The distinction between expected time-value returns and unexpected gains and losses is an essential one. It is fundamental to the relationship among financial instruments and is reflected in their arbitrage pricing and in their use for risk-allocation purposes. Moreover, the inability of income tax systems to address adequately these two different types of returns and the different policy considerations they present is the ultimate basis of the problems commonly associated with the treatment of financial instruments generally.

Credit-Extension Instruments

Credit-extension instruments involve an advance of funds ("the loan principal") by one party ("the lender") to another ("the borrower") for a defined period ("the term") in consideration of a promise to repay the funds and a return in the form of interest that compensates the lender for the forbearance of current consumption implied by the loan ("the expected time-value return"). This category of basic building-block instruments corresponds roughly to loans, deposits, bonds, debentures, notes, and other liabilities for financial-accounting purposes.[19] According to Smith and Smithson, all credit-extension instruments take one of the following basic forms, which reflect different conditions for repayment of the loan principal or for the amount and timing of the payment of the expected time-value return:[20]

- the level-coupon instrument,
- the zero-coupon or original issue discount (OID) instrument,
- the floating-rate instrument, and
- the amortizing instrument.

Level-coupon and zero-coupon instruments are fixed-payment or non-contingent obligations under which the timing and amount of all cash flows or payments are known on issue. A level-coupon instrument provides for repayment of the loan principal at the end of the term of the instrument ("maturity") and for payment of interest calculated as a fixed percentage of the principal at regular intervals over the relevant term. The label "level-coupon instrument" (also "coupon bond") refers to the fact that the interest payments are evidenced by coupons that entitle the holder to receipt in cash when they become due. The coupon expresses the rate of interest payable on the instrument as a fixed percentage of the principal. A zero-coupon or OID instrument, instead of providing for periodic payments of interest, is issued for an amount of funds that is less than the face value (or stated principal) due on maturity. The discount represents the interest return due on maturity. In the absence of periodic payments, the interest equal to the amount by which the total due on maturity exceeds the amount advanced by the lender is rolled up and compounded at specified intervals. Thus interest that is not paid periodically is effectively capitalized, and future interest becomes payable on the capitalized amount for the specified compounding periods.

A floating-rate instrument provides for periodic payments of interest that are adjusted at regular intervals over the term of the instrument in accordance with changes in a benchmark interest-rate index, such as the prime interest rate, the government treasury bill rate, or the London interbank offering rate (LIBOR). The variable return may also be based in part on some other index, such as the consumer price index (CPI), which measures inflation as the change in the level of consumer prices. Unlike the cash flows under a level-coupon or zero-coupon instrument, the cash flows under a floating-rate instrument are not known in advance. Finally, an amortizing instrument (also called a declining-principal instrument) provides for periodic payments of interest on either a fixed- or floating-rate basis and repayment of the funds advanced on an instalment or amortized basis over the term of the instrument.

The default or credit risk associated with credit-extension instruments is borne entirely by the lender. In effect, the lender extends credit to the borrower by advancing funds that the borrower is obliged to repay along with the expected time-value return. In the event of non-performance, the lender bears the risk of loss of both the loan principal and any compensating return. This return includes a pure interest element that represents compensation for the use of borrowed funds. It may also include an element of compensation to the lender for a loss in the value of the loan principal owing to inflation, some compensation for default risk and volatility risk, and a liquidity premium.[21] The pure interest element is what is left after these other elements are accounted for, and it may be viewed as the required return on a riskless security in a zero-inflationary climate. The value of any credit-extension instrument depends solely on the passage of time, the level of market interest rates, and the risk of default. The value is captured as the discounted present value of the known future cash flows,[22] given a discount rate that is determined by the prevailing market rate for similar instruments with similar default risk. The underlying proposition here is simply that an amount of funds received today is worth more than the right to receive the same amount at some time in the future.[23] Thus the discounted present value reflects the time value of money and reveals the amount that must be invested at prevailing interest rates to yield the known (and greater) cash flows payable in the future. As time passes and the time for payment arrives, the value of the instrument approaches the amount of the expected payoff.

Figures 1.1 and 1.2 illustrate the payoff profiles for a level-coupon instrument and an OID instrument, respectively.

Figure 1.1 Payoff Profile Associated with a Five-Year Level-Coupon Instrument with a Principal Amount of $10,000 and an Annual Interest Rate of 10 Percent

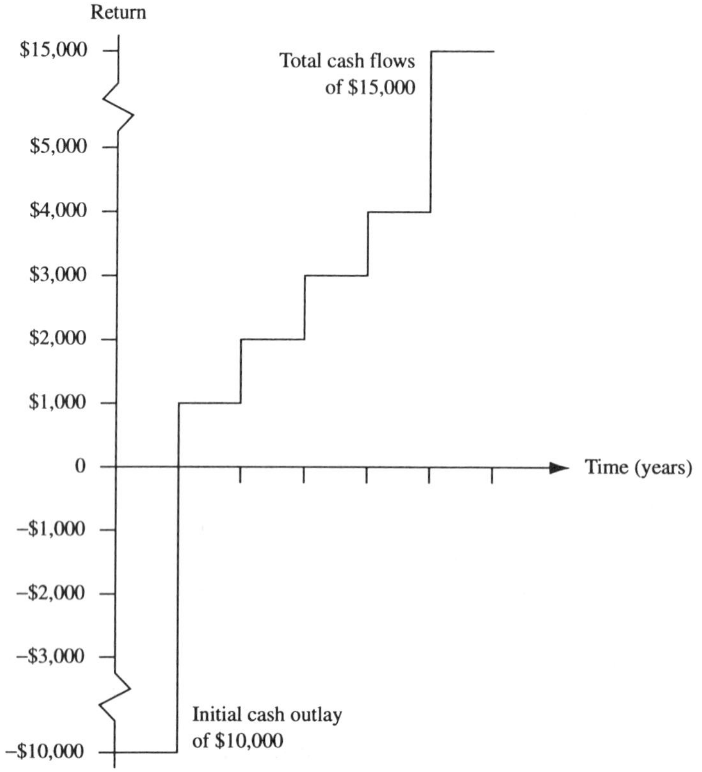

Price-Fixing Instruments[24]

Forward and Futures Contracts[25]

Price-fixing instruments fix the price of an asset by obliging one party ("the holder") to purchase the asset at a specified price ("the exercise price") on a specified future date ("the maturity date"). The standard price-fixing instrument is the forward contract. Since the holder of a forward is obliged to purchase the specified asset at the exercise price on maturity, the value of the contract depends on the relationship between the exercise price and the price of the asset in the spot market ("the spot price")[26] on maturity. If on that date the spot price exceeds the exercise price, the holder realizes a gain equal to the difference and the other party ("the seller") realizes a corresponding loss. If the spot price is lower than the exercise price, the holder suffers a loss and the seller realizes a corresponding gain. In effect, by purchasing a forward contract, the holder takes a long position in the underlying asset; that is, he agrees to purchase at the specified price. The seller takes a short position in the same underlying

Figure 1.2 Payoff Profile Associated with a Five-Year OID Instrument Issued for $10,000 with an Annual Interest Rate of 10 Percent

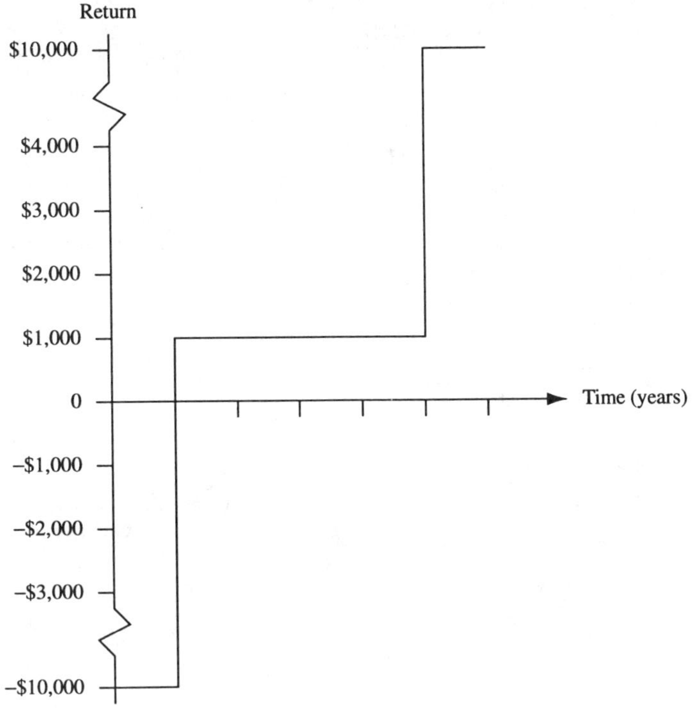

asset; that is, he agrees to sell at the specified price.[27] Figure 1.3 illustrates the payoff profile for a typical forward contract.

Since the obligations of a holder and a seller under a forward contract are mutual and offsetting, funds are not generally advanced on issue (or at any point during the contract's term) and there is no expected time-value return.[28] The value of the contract is usually commuted ("cash-settled") on maturity, when either the holder pays the seller or the seller pays the holder, depending on the difference between the exercise price and the spot price of the specified asset. A forward contract is, therefore, a pure bet, in which the amount and the direction of the payment obligation depends on the resolution of a specified contingency at a specified time. Gain or loss on the contract is unexpected and cannot be determined until resolution of the contingency.[29] The fact that the obligations of the parties are mutual also means that credit risk is two-sided; that is, each party bears the risk that the other will be unable to make any required payment on maturity. This risk increases proportionally with the term of the forward contract and the volatility of the spot price of the relevant asset, since greater volatility results in a correspondingly greater deviation between the exercise and spot prices.

Figure 1.3 Payoff Profile for a Typical Forward Contract

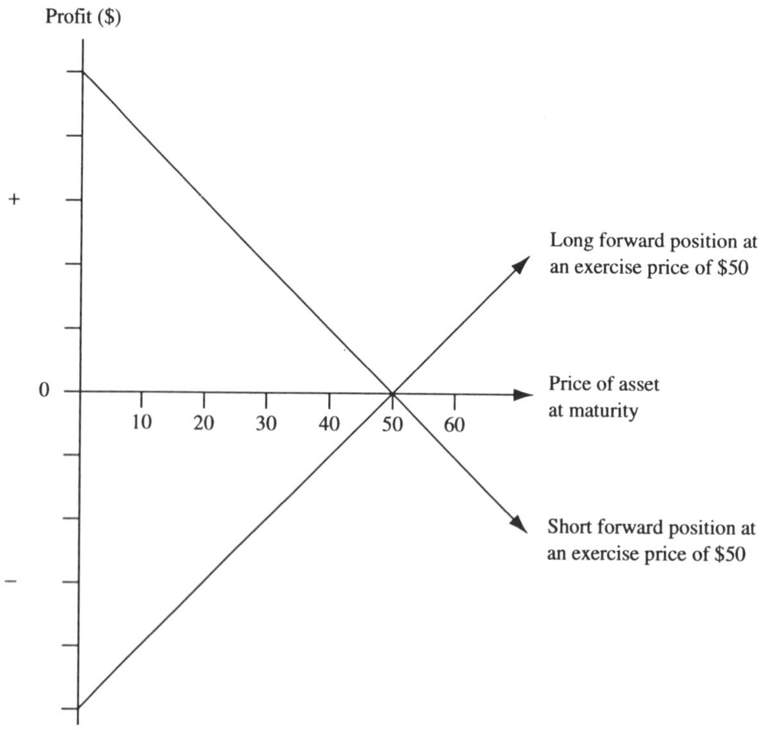

A futures contract is identical to a forward in its requirement that the holder purchase an asset at a specified price on maturity. Accordingly, the payoff profile for a futures contract is identical to the profile for a forward contract illustrated in figure 1.3. For several reasons, however, futures contracts are generally more liquid and less risky than forward contracts. A forward is an "over-the-counter" (OTC) instrument that is usually traded between dealers and financial institutions[30] and is tailored to the specific needs of the parties. Futures contracts, by contrast, are written on standardized assets, use standardized maturity dates, and come in standard sizes, factors that enhance liquidity by permitting active trading on organized exchanges. The parties need to agree only on the exercise price for the underlying asset and the number of contracts to be purchased and sold.

Futures contracts have three distinct features that make them less risky than forward contracts.[31] First, futures contracts are valued ("marked to market") at the end of each trading day, and the resulting gain or loss is cash-settled. This feature effectively reduces the performance period, and hence the duration of the risk of default, to one day. Indeed, a futures contract is equivalent to a series of forward contracts that are written at the end of one day, settled at the end of the next, and replaced with a new contract that is written immediately after settlement.[32] Second, the futures exchanges require all market participants to guarantee performance by maintaining a margin account; the margin requirement is usually in the range of 1 to 5 percent of the total value of all futures contracts. Marking to market of the futures contracts of traders means that their margin accounts are credited or debited daily ("the variation margin") by an amount equal to the difference between the preceding day's closing value of all contracts and the closing price on the current day. The variation margin is cash-settled daily, and gains and losses are realized through credits and debits to the margin account. If subsequent calls on a trader's account reduce his initial margin below a specified percentage, he must post additional sums of money to restore the guarantee. If he does not post them, his position is closed out and there is no further exposure to performance risk. Third, the exchange or clearing house acts as one of the parties to all futures contracts, which means that its capital base is available as a further guarantee of performance. Holders and sellers close out their open positions by entering into an opposite transaction with the exchange, a step that eliminates the original position. Profit or loss when a position is closed out equals the difference between the closing price of the open futures contract on the preceding day and the price of the offsetting contract. The calculation of total gain or loss on a contract takes into account the results of marking to market for all prior days on which the contract was held and the profit or loss realized when the open position is closed out. A futures contract is seldom held until maturity; the holder closes it out sometime before that date by entering into an opposite position with the exchange. As in the case of cash-settled forwards, the underlying asset is never actually acquired or sold. Forwards, by contrast, since they are not exchange-traded and are not usually assignable, can be closed out before maturity only by negotiation between the counterparties.

In principle, forward contracts are bets that can be written on any asset. In practice, those assets have been limited to commodities, such as gold, silver, oil, and agricultural products; foreign currencies; financial instruments, such as shares and debt instruments; and financial indexes, such as a share price index or a benchmark floating interest rate.[33] Forwards have been used at least since the Middle Ages to protect against commodity price risk,[34] and they are now commonly used to fix currency exchange rates and interest rates ("forward-rate agreements").[35] Commodity futures were first traded on exchanges in Chicago and now trade throughout the world on various exchanges.[36] Futures trading has more recently been extended to currencies and certain government debt instruments and similar riskless debt.[37] These "financial futures" also include trading in share price indexes.[38] Although the subject matter differs, the concept remains the same: the holder of the forward or futures contract agrees to purchase a specified amount of a commodity, currency, or financial instrument (a debt obligation or the basket of shares represented by a share index) at a specified price on a specified future date, and the seller agrees to sell that asset on the same terms.

Swaps[39]

In its most basic form, a swap contract involves an exchange of cash flows at periodic intervals by the two parties ("counterparties") to the contract. In essence, each counterparty agrees to make periodic payments to the other at specified intervals over a specified period. Swap contracts can require the exchange of interest-based cash flows in the same currency ("interest-rate swaps"), the exchange of interest-based cash flows in different currencies ("currency swaps"), or the exchange of cash flows based on movements in the prices of commodities ("commodity swaps") or share indexes ("equity swaps"). The relevant amounts are calculated on the basis of a principal amount that may be either actually exchanged or merely notional, in the sense that it exists only as a basis for calculating the amount of the relevant payments.

The original (and most familiar) type of swap is the "fixed-for-floating interest-rate swap," under which a party who has borrowed at a fixed rate of interest but wishes to borrow at a floating rate is matched with a counterparty who has borrowed at a floating rate but wishes to borrow at a fixed rate. The counterparties maintain their obligations under the original borrowings and effectively convert their loan exposures to the desired rate by agreeing to make a series of payments in which they reimburse one another in respect of interest obligations on the underlying exposures. To be more specific, the fixed-rate borrower agrees to make a series of payments calculated as a floating-rate percentage of an agreed principal amount. In return, the floating-rate borrower agrees to make a series of payments calculated as a fixed-rate percentage of the same principal amount. Each counterparty thereby incurs a series of payment obligations on the underlying borrowing equal to those incurred by the other counterparty.[40]

Since both sides of an interest-rate swap are denominated in the same currency, there is no need to exchange principal amounts on origination and re-exchange those amounts on maturity. The principal amount of an interest-rate swap, therefore, is notional—it is used only to calculate the amount of the interest payments that are to be exchanged. The typical currency swap, on the other hand, involves an exchange of principal amounts in different currencies at the spot exchange rate on origination and a re-exchange on maturity at the same spot rate, a step that reverses the initial transaction. Periodic payments, calculated on the basis of the prevailing interest rates in the relevant currencies, are exchanged throughout the period of the swap contract. The recipient of the swapped currency pays interest, at the rate applicable to loans made in that currency, on either a floating-rate or a fixed-rate basis. The exchange of payments is equivalent, therefore, to an interest-rate swap in the relevant currencies.

An equity swap is a more recent version of the basic swap contract. One counterparty ("the equity payer") agrees to make a series of payments to the other ("the equity receiver") on the basis of increases in the value of a broad share index, some form of subindex, or a specified basket of shares. In return, the equity receiver agrees to make a series of payments to the equity payer on the basis of an interest-rate index and, as well, one or more payments based on decreases in the value of the specified index or shares. Equity swaps may also include an exchange of payments based on the return on a single share owned by a counterparty in return for either interest-based payments or payments based on changes in a share index. If an equity swap involves a single share or a relatively limited basket of shares, the equity receiver will usually be entitled to payments based on the amount of dividends paid on the shares, as well as any appreciation in the share's value.[41] A commodity swap is similar to an equity swap: one counterparty agrees to pay an amount that is based on changes in the price of a specified commodity; the other counterparty agrees to pay an amount that is based on a fixed or floating interest rate. Like the counterparties to an interest-rate swap, the counterparties to an equity or commodity swap do not actually exchange a principal amount; the latter is merely a notional basis for the calculation of the series of payments.

Swap contracts are equivalent to a series of forward or futures contracts on interest rates (an interest-rate swap), currencies (a currency swap), share indexes (an equity swap), or commodities (a commodity swap).[42] Like these other price-fixing instruments, swaps are pure bets that do not involve an advance of funds by either of the counterparties; there is no expected time-value return, and the payoffs depend solely on the resolution of specified contingencies, which give rise to unexpected gains or losses.[43] For example, at each date set for the exchange of interest payments, a fixed-rate payer is effectively obliged to sell a fixed-rate cash flow for a floating-rate cash flow at the price specified when the swap was entered into. Figure 1.4 illustrates the equivalence between a series of forward contracts on interest rates and a standard interest-rate swap in the case of a counterparty who pays a series of fixed-rate cash flows and receives floating-rate cash flows.[44]

If swap payments are due at the same time, they are generally paid on a "net basis"; that is, the gross amounts of the payments due under the swap contract are offset against one another, and only the amount attributable to the difference between the relevant payment rates is paid by one of the counterparties. If the payment dates do not coincide, swap payments must generally be made on a "gross basis."[45] In terms of credit risk, the swap falls somewhere between a forward contract and a futures contract.[46] Since a swap requires periodic cash settlements over the term of the contract, the performance period for a swap is less than the performance period for a forward. A swap, therefore, involves less credit risk than does an equivalent series of forward contracts. On the other hand, a swap involves greater credit risk than does a futures contract, since it is not usual to post performance bonds for a swap. Parties who enter into a swap directly rather than through an intermediary bear the credit risk themselves as the end-users on both sides of the swap. Consequently, most swaps are entered into through a financial institution that acts as the counterparty in much the same way as a futures exchange. The institution seeks to offset its position by entering into an opposite swap with another end-user and bears the credit risk associated with default by the counterparties.

Figure 1.4 Payoff Profile for a Fixed-for-Floating Interest-Rate Swap

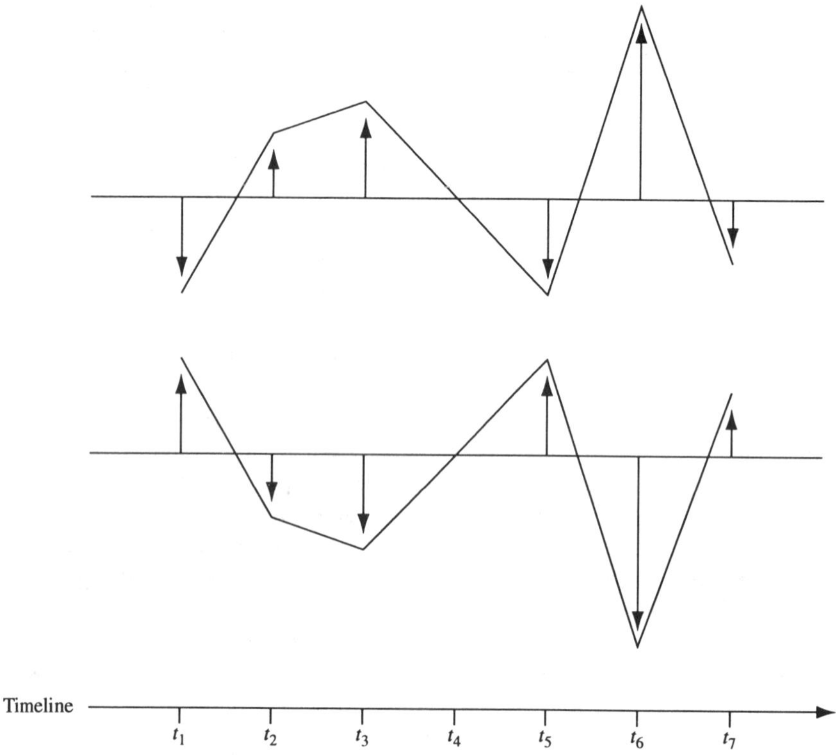

Price-Insurance Instruments: Options[47]

General

Unlike a forward, futures, or swap contract, an option gives the holder the right, but not the obligation, to purchase or sell a specified asset at a specified price ("the exercise or strike price") over a specified period. An option to purchase an asset is a "call" and an option to sell is a "put." A "European option" permits the holder to purchase (call option) or sell (put option) the specified asset at the exercise price on a particular date that is stipulated in the option contract (the maturity date of the option). An "American option" permits exercise of the right to purchase or sell at any time between the date of issue of the option and the maturity date. A "Bermudan option" permits exercise on any one of several specified dates between issue and maturity. An option is "in the money" if the exercise of the option would produce a profit for the holder. Otherwise, the option is "out of the money."

The holder of an option must pay a premium for the right to purchase or sell the specified asset. In effect, the premium represents the cost of the price insurance that the option provides in respect of the specified asset. Options, therefore, have a value on issue, unlike forwards, futures, and swaps. An option that is in the money on issue has a much higher premium than an option that is out of the money. Similarly, an American option, thanks to its flexible maturity date, has a higher premium than a European option. Even an option that is out of the money on issue, however, has a value that is reflected in the amount of the relevant premium. This amount depends, in part, on the term of the option and the volatility of the spot price of the underlying asset.[48]

Since the holder of an option advances funds, the return associated with the option includes an expected time-value element for the use of those funds. Options also provide unexpected gain or loss that arises on the resolution of a bet or contingency, in this case a bet that on maturity the spot price of the underlying asset will be greater, or less, than the specified exercise price. The return on an option, therefore, is a combination of an expected time-value return and unexpected gain or loss attributable to a bet element.[49] The value of a call option increases as the price of the underlying asset increases and is positive if on maturity the spot price of the asset is greater than the exercise price. In fact, the value of a call option on maturity equals the amount by which the spot price of the underlying asset exceeds the exercise price. If the price of the underlying asset remains or falls below the exercise price, the option is worthless, the holder loses the option premium, and the issuer realizes a corresponding gain. The exposure of the issuer is potentially unlimited, since it increases with the spot price of the underlying asset and the increase in the price is potentially unlimited. Accordingly, the holder bears the credit risk that the issuer will be able to perform his obligations under the option contract. Figure 1.5 illustrates the payoff profile for the holder of a European call option.

The value of a put option increases with decreases in the price of the underlying asset and equals the amount, if any, by which the exercise price exceeds the spot price of the asset on maturity. If the spot price exceeds the exercise price, the put is worthless and the holder loses his premium. The exposure of the issuer increases to the extent that the price of the underlying asset falls below the exercise price, and it is limited only by the value of the underlying asset. Figure 1.6 illustrates the payoff profile for the holder of a European put option.

Like forwards, futures, and swap contracts, call or put options may be written on almost any underlying asset. Most options, however, are on shares and commodities.[50] Share options have been traded for some years on recognized exchanges and may be written either on outstanding shares that trade in the secondary market or on shares that must be issued on exercise of the options (commonly referred to as "warrants"). Currency options and options on other financial instruments, including share price indexes, are now also traded over the counter and on organized exchanges. Options may provide for physical delivery of the underlying asset, but they are usually settled on a cash basis. The issuer of a cash-settled call must pay the amount by which the spot price exceeds the exercise price; the issuer of a cash-settled put must pay the amount by which the exercise price exceeds the spot price.

Figure 1.5 European Call Option Written on One Share for an Exercise Price of $50 and an Option Premium of $5

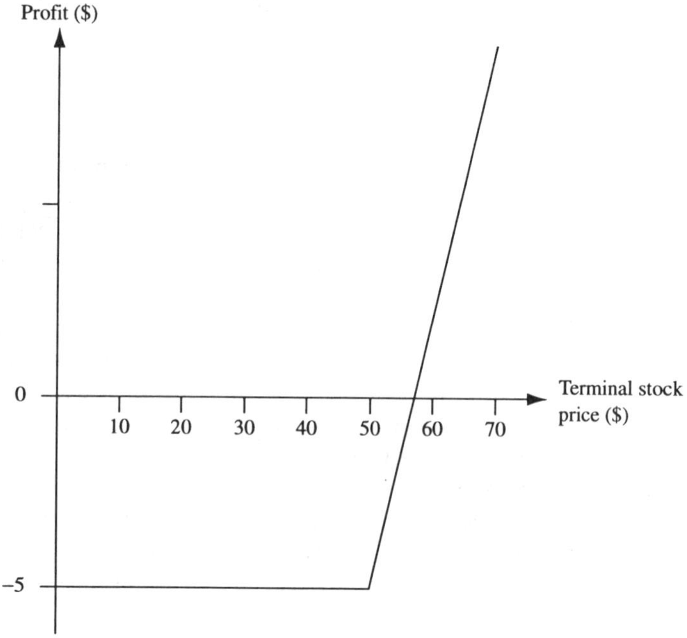

"Caps," "floors," and "collars" are options on interest rates.[51] A cap is equivalent to the purchase of a call option on an interest-rate index or the sale of a put on an interest-rate futures contract. By limiting the upper boundary on interest rates, a cap protects the holder from increases in those rates. The issuer of a cap agrees to compensate the holder for the amount, if any, by which the spot interest rate exceeds the exercise price at specified dates in the future. If this amount is negative, the option lapses and the holder loses his premium but benefits from the lower spot rate. A floor protects the holder from decreases in interest rates below the exercise price set at specified dates. The issuer of a floor agrees to compensate the holder for the amount, if any, by which the exercise price exceeds the spot rate on the specified date. If that amount is negative, the holder loses the premium but benefits from the higher spot rate. A floor is similar, therefore, to the purchase of a put option on an interest-rate futures index or the sale of a call option on an interest-rate futures contract. By simultaneously purchasing a cap and issuing a floor, it is possible to reduce the cost of a cap by the amount of the premium received on the issue of the floor. In this case, however, the holder of the cap forgoes the benefit of any decline in spot interest rates below the exercise price under the floor and, in effect, creates a combination of a cap and a floor. This combination is referred to as a "collar,"

Figure 1.6 European Put Option with an Exercise Price of $50 and an Option Premium of $5

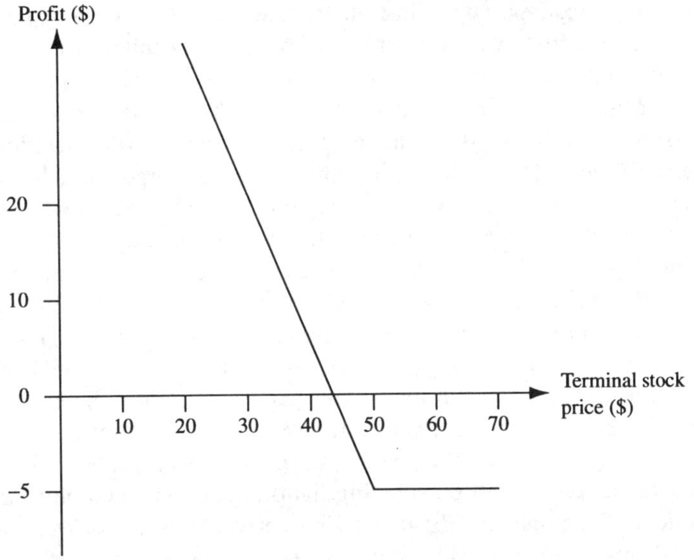

since it sets a range within which the holder of the cap and issuer of the floor is exposed to fluctuations in interest rates.

Common Shares as Options

"Common shares" are shares with an unlimited participation right in the assets of a corporation, subject only to the prior claims of debt holders and any preferred shareholders with fixed dividend and participation rights.[52] As an economic interest in the underlying assets of a corporation, common shares tend to be thought of as a standard capital market instrument with unique cash flows. Strictly speaking, however, this residual interest in corporate assets is not a basic building-block financial instrument. In the case of a corporation with only equity capital, common shares are equivalent to the direct ownership of the underlying assets. In the case of a leveraged corporation, the cash flows associated with common shares are equivalent to those associated with the purchase of either (1) a call option on the relevant shares or (2) a put option on the underlying corporate assets.[53] In other words, the conditional payment terms reflected in an option are reflected equally in the terms and conditions of the common shares of a leveraged corporation, which provide a similar combination of expected and unexpected gains and losses.[54] An expected time-value return is associated with the advance of funds; unexpected gain or loss is attributable to a bet on the value of the underlying assets of the corporation. At least in terms of their associated cash flows, therefore, common shares are nothing more than a particular type of option, and they should be considered in the context of that general category of basic building-block instrument.

Two simple examples will illustrate the equivalence of common shares and options. Consider, first, two corporations with different capital structures.[55] One corporation, Xco, owns an asset with a value of $300. Xco has outstanding a debt instrument with a principal amount of $500 that is due in one year and a number of common shares. The other corporation, Yco, owns an identical asset, but instead of encumbering the asset with an issue of corporate debt the common shareholders of Yco sell a call option on their common shares. The option is exercisable in one year on the same date as the maturity date of the debt instrument issued by Xco and for an exercise price equal to the principal amount of that debt. This call option will be worthless if the value of Yco's asset (and therefore the value of its common shares) is $500 or less on the exercise date. If the value of the underlying asset rises above $500, the call option will have a value equal to the value of the common shares minus the $500 exercise price. By comparison, if the value of Xco's asset remains below $500 on maturity of the outstanding debt, the debt holders will be entitled to the asset in satisfaction of their outstanding liability and the common shares will be worthless. If the value of the underlying corporate asset exceeds $500, the common shares will have a value equal to the difference between the value of the asset and the $500 principal amount owing on the outstanding debt. Thus the payoff for Xco's common shareholders is identical to the payoff for the holders of the call options. In other words, for any specified future value of the assets of Yco and Xco, the payoff to the holders of the call options on the common shares of Yco will equal the payoff for the common shareholders of Xco.

As was noted above, it is also possible to view the cash flows (and payoff profiles) associated with common shares of a leveraged corporation as the equivalent of (1) a borrowing by the shareholders of the principal amount of all corporate debt, (2) a purchase of the assets of the corporation, and (3) a purchase of a put option on those assets issued by the debt holders.[56] The existence of this put option is the result of the corporate law limitation of the liability of shareholders to the amount of their contributed capital. In effect, limited liability provides shareholders with an option to abandon corporate assets by defaulting on corporate debt. That option is equivalent to the purchase of a put option on the assets with an exercise price equal to the amount owed on the outstanding debt.[57] Compare, for example, the payoffs to the common shareholders of Xco and Yco, which own an identical asset with a value of $300, if Xco borrows $500 and the common shareholders of Yco purchase a put option exercisable on maturity of the debt of Xco at a price equal to its principal amount. If the value of Xco's asset remains below $500, the common shareholders will default on the outstanding debt and realize a gain equal to the difference between the principal amount owing and the value of the underlying assets. Similarly, if the value of Yco's asset remains below $500, the common shareholders of the corporation will exercise their put options and realize a gain equal to the difference between the $500 exercise price and the value of the shares (equal to the value of the underlying asset). If the value of Xco's asset increases above $500, the common shareholders will repay the debt and realize the excess value. By allowing their worthless put options to expire, the common shareholders of Yco will realize the same result if the value of the corporate asset rises above the $500 exercise price.

Arbitrage Pricing of the Building-Block Instruments

The equivalence of the cash flows associated with options and the common shares of a leveraged corporation is not unique. Indeed, there is a wide range of comparable equivalences among the payoff profiles of the basic building-block instruments and certain financial positions that consist of two or more of those instruments. This range is broad enough to ensure that positions in a particular asset, a related forward, and a related option are substantially interchangeable.[58] The equivalences are expressed in certain relationships and parities, which ensure that the relevant instruments and positions are priced equivalently. Otherwise, arbitrage profits would be available until they were traded away and price equilibrium was restored.[59] These relationships and parities are critical to the arbitrage pricing of the basic building-block instruments of financial innovation and to the process of financial innovation itself.[60] Their importance to financial innovation follows from the fact that equivalent financial positions, though they are recognized by capital markets in pricing the component instruments, are not consistently recognized for tax and regulatory purposes. As the next section of this chapter will describe, this inconsistency provides avoidance opportunities and may distort the pricing of instruments, with consequent efficiency costs.[61]

In general, there is a close relationship between the prices of the building-block instruments and the spot prices of assets, since the value of the former derives from changes in the value of the latter.[62] The prices of the building-block instruments and the prices of assets are also related in their common dependence on two factors: (1) the time value of money and (2) the uncertainty of outcomes that is captured in the price volatility or risk characteristics of an underlying asset.[63] These common factors provide the basis for certain parity pricing relationships that link the spot markets for underlying assets with those for the building-block instruments. The result of this close linkage is a high degree of substitutability between asset positions and combinations of the building-block instruments, and between the instruments themselves.[64] For pricing purposes, the most fundamental relationships are

- the relationship between the spot price for an asset and its forward price,
- interest-rate parity,
- put-call parity, and
- the relationships that underlie the pricing of options.

The General Relationship Between Spot and Forward Prices and the Specific Case of Interest-Rate Parity

The most basic pricing relationships are probably those reflected in the general relationship between spot and forward prices and in the specific case of interest-rate parity. These relationships are significant for tax and regulatory purposes, since they reveal broad equivalences between the purchase or sale of an asset in the spot market and an agreement to purchase or sell the asset some time in the future under a forward-based contract (that is, a forward, a futures contract, or a swap as the equivalent of a series of forwards). At the heart of these relationships is the fact that the forward price for an asset does not reflect the "best guess" about the future spot price of that asset.[65] Instead, the exercise price under a price-fixing instrument (forward, futures contract, or swap) is a mathematically derived rate that reflects arbitrage conditions; that is, the relationship between the spot and forward rates is characterized by the rapid elimination of riskless gains through arbitrage trading, which is the identification of price differences in different markets for the same item and the simultaneous purchase and sale of the item across those markets. Where price differences arise, arbitrage traders enter the market in an effort to realize the arbitrage gains. The result is an adjustment in the relevant prices that restores a relationship between spot and forward prices that eliminates these gains.

The relationship between spot and forward prices becomes clear when it is realized that the prospective purchaser of an asset has a simple choice: to purchase the asset now at its spot price or to take future delivery at the forward price.[66] The purchaser will acquire the same asset in either case, but there are two important differences between the cases that together determine the forward price.[67] First, since a forward purchaser does not take immediate delivery, he can earn a return on the funds that he would otherwise have used to purchase the asset at its spot price. Second, the forward purchaser forgoes any return on the asset during the period before he purchases it. Arbitrage trading ensures that there is no difference between the return available from the purchase of an asset immediately at its spot price and the return available from the asset's acquisition at some time in the future at a forward price. Accordingly, the forward price of an asset is a function of the spot price multiplied by the implicit cost of carry (or the riskless rate of return that the forward purchaser can earn) less the expected amount of the return on a long position in the asset. This relationship can be expressed as follows:[68]

$$\textit{forward price} = \textit{spot price} \times \frac{(1 + r_f)_t}{(1 + r_{pv})_t},$$

where r_f is the riskless interest rate for the term of the forward contract, represented by t, and r_{pv} is the present value of the return on an asset forgone by a forward purchaser.

The general relationship between spot and forward prices is evident in the specific cases of currency exchange rates and forward interest rates. A forward currency contract is a commitment to purchase or sell a currency in the future on a specified date at a specified price. That price is determined by a mathematically derived formula that reflects an arbitrage condition referred to as "interest-rate parity."[69] Under that condition, forward exchange rates are a function of the difference between the interest rates for borrowings in the two currencies. More particularly, the difference between the forward and spot exchange rates for two currencies must equal the difference between the interest rates for borrowings in the same currencies. This equivalence ensures that an investment in the weaker currency yields the same return as an equivalent investment in the stronger currency. Interest-rate parity is expressed as[70]

$$Ef/Es = (1 + ir)/(1 + id),$$

where *Es* is the spot exchange rate for two currencies, *Ef* is the forward exchange rate, *ir* is the interest rate for the foreign currency, and *id* is the interest rate for the domestic currency.

Comparable arbitrage conditions ensure that the relationship between spot and forward interest rates ("the forward yield curve") is such that arbitrage profits are similarly unavailable.[71] Under a forward-rate agreement, the two counterparties protect themselves against interest-rate movements in a specified currency by agreeing to exchange on the exercise date the difference between the spot rate of interest and the agreed forward rate. Like forward currency rates, the forward interest rate is set so that an investor will be indifferent between the alternative of investing his funds short term and reinvesting them for a similar term and the alternative of investing the same funds for a longer term.[72] For example, an investor who invests funds for one year at the one-year spot interest rate can lock in a forward one-year rate that will ensure a return equal to the return from a two-year investment.[73] In other words, the sum of the one-year spot rate and the one-year forward rate equals the two-year spot rate. The general relationship between spot and forward interest rates is expressed as[74]

$$\textit{forward interest rate} = \frac{(1 + \textit{longer-term spot rate})t}{(1 + \textit{shorter-term spot rate})} - 1,$$

where *t* is the number of shorter-term periods within the longer term.

Put-Call Parity and Option Pricing

The pricing relationship reflected in put-call parity reveals an even broader range of positions that are equivalent to the ownership or sale of an asset in the spot market[75] but that are often treated differently for tax and regulatory purposes. To the extent that transaction costs and other factors do not present a barrier,[76] one can use combinations of the building-block instruments and long and short positions[77] in the relevant asset to replicate the cash flows associated with the ownership or sale of that asset without attracting the same tax or regulatory treatment.[78] These equivalences begin with the following basic relationship:

$$+A +P = +B +C,$$

where $+A$ is a long position in an asset, $+P$ is the purchase of a European put option on the asset, $+B$ is a long position in a zero-coupon bond, and $+C$ is the purchase of a European call option on the asset that is exercisable at the same price as the put.

Provided that the promised payoffs on an asset and a zero-coupon bond are the same (that is, the only payoff is on maturity of the bond) and that call and put options are exercisable on maturity of the bond, put-call parity reveals that the combination of a long position in the asset and the purchase of a put option on the asset is equivalent to the combination of an investment of the spot price in a zero-coupon bond and the purchase of a call option on the asset. Assume, for example,[79] that an investor purchases an asset at a price of \$91 and covers this long position with the acquisition of a put option on the asset exercisable in one year at a price of \$100. An equivalent portfolio consists of (1) the purchase of a zero-coupon bond that pays \$100 in one year and is issued at a price equal to its present value of \$91 (annual interest rate of 10 percent) and (2) the purchase of a call option on the relevant asset exercisable in one year at a price of \$100. If the spot price of the asset declined to \$75, an investor who purchased the asset and the put option would have a net worth of \$100; that is, an asset with a value of \$75 and a put option with a value of \$25 (the \$100 exercise price minus the \$75 value of the underlying asset). An investor who purchased the zero-coupon bond and the call option would also have a net worth of \$100; that is, the bond with a value of \$100 and a call option with a value of nil (the \$75 value of the underlying asset minus the \$100 exercise price). If the spot price of the asset increased to \$125, an investor who held the asset and the put option on it would have a net worth of \$125; that is, an asset with a value of \$125 and a put option with a value of nil (the \$100 exercise price minus the \$125 value of the underlying asset). An investor who purchased the zero-coupon bond and the call option would also have a net worth of \$125; that is, the bond with a value of \$100 and a call option with a value of \$25 (the \$125 value of the underlying asset minus the \$100 exercise price). Since the positions are equivalent, investors would be indifferent between them.[80]

Rearranging the four variables in the put-call parity theorem reveals other equivalent positions. For example, the combination of a borrowing evidenced by a zero-coupon bond and a long position in an asset is equivalent to the combination of the purchase of a call option and the sale of a put on the same asset exercisable on the same date as the maturity date of the bond and for a price equal to the amount due under the bond ($-B +A = +C -P$).[81] More generally, put-call parity means that it is possible to replicate the ownership of an asset and an investment in a riskless debt obligation by entering into long and short positions on the basis of the combination of an option with either a long or a short position in the relevant asset or debt.[82]

The range of financial equivalences is broadened further by the existence of certain similarities among the payoff profiles of the basic building-block instruments. These similarities permit investors to replicate one type of basic instrument by using one or more of the other types.[83] Since a futures contract or a swap contract is equivalent to a series of forwards, it can be replicated by using forwards, which can themselves be replicated by combining call and put options.[84] In particular, the combination of the purchase of a European call option and the sale of a European put option is equivalent to the purchase of a forward contract ($+C -P = +F$) (sometimes referred to as "futures parity"), provided that the exercise price and dates are the same.[85] Conversely, the combination of the sale of a European call and the purchase of a European put is equivalent to the sale of a forward ($-C +P = -F$).[86] These equivalences mean that the purchase of a forward is equivalent to the combination of a long position in an asset and a borrowing ($+A -B = +C -P$ or $+A -B = +F$) and that the sale of a forward is equivalent to a combination of a short position in an asset and a loan ($-A +B = -C +P$ or $-A +B = -F$).[87]

The fundamental relationships and arbitrage conditions expressed in put-call parity are the foundations of modern option-pricing models, which are based on the work of Fischer Black and Myron Scholes.[88] In general, the present value of a European call option[89] on an underlying asset depends on five factors:[90] (1) the spot price of the asset, (2) the exercise price under the option, (3) the riskless interest rate, (4) the time to maturity of the option or the exercise period, and (5) the volatility of the spot price of the asset. The importance of the first two factors is obvious, since the value of a call option on maturity equals the value of the underlying asset less the exercise price.[91] Thus the value of a call increases if the value of the underlying asset increases to a point at which it exceeds the exercise price. On the other hand, the value of a call decreases if the exercise price increases, since it then becomes less likely that the value of the asset will exceed the exercise price on the exercise date. The riskless interest rate and the time to maturity are important because the holder of a call option benefits from his deferral of purchasing the underlying asset.[92] During the period of deferral, the holder has the use of an amount of money equal to the present value of the exercise price, which he can invest at the riskless interest rate to produce an amount of funds equal to the exercise price on the exercise date. Accordingly, the value of an option generally increases with increases in the riskless interest rate and the period to maturity.[93] Volatility in the price of the underlying asset is the most difficult factor to specify. The greater is the volatility, the greater is the range of possible price fluctuations over the period to maturity of a call option, and hence the greater is the range of possible values at the maturity date of the option.[94] The greater is the price volatility, in other words, the greater are the chances that the value of the underlying asset will exceed the exercise price. Consequently, the value of a call on an asset generally increases with the price volatility of the asset.[95]

If the price volatility of an asset is extremely low, the value of a European call should approximate the time value of money represented by a debt instrument that earns a return equal to the riskless rate of interest.[96] In this case, the value of holding the right to purchase the relevant asset in the future at a predetermined price is equivalent to[97] (1) borrowing the discounted present value of the exercise price on issue of the call, (2) investing the borrowed funds in a debt obligation that matures on the same date as the call and pays a return equal to the discount rate used in calculating the present value of the exercise price, (3) using the funds received on maturity of the debt to purchase the underlying asset at the exercise price on the specified exercise date of the call, (4) selling the asset in the spot market, and (5) repaying the borrowed funds. This equivalence can be written as[98]

$$+C = +A \quad -B(E),$$

where $B(E)$ denotes a debt obligation with a value equal to the present value of the exercise price discounted at the riskless rate of interest.

The obvious problem with option pricing is the price volatility of the underlying asset, which makes the option price much more than a simple product of the time value of money.[99] An option is much riskier than is ownership of the underlying asset, since the value of the option depends on the relationship between the exercise price and movements in the price of the underlying asset. If the price of the asset increases, the price of the call increases and its risk decreases. If the price of the asset decreases, the value of the option decreases and its risk increases.[100] The problem for option pricing is the incorporation of movements in the price of the underlying asset that necessarily affect the value of the option. In addressing this problem, the Black-Scholes option-pricing model and its subsequent modifications make no attempt to assess either the expected future value of an asset subject to an option or investor attitudes about risk, since these factors cannot be readily observed.[101] Instead, these models attempt to assess the value of calls and puts indirectly by equating them with combinations of purchases and sales of the underlying assets and borrowings and loans that produce a certain return from a riskless portfolio.[102] The models are based on the premise that for every combination of an asset's spot price, the riskless interest rate, an option's term to maturity, and price volatility there is an ideal combination of the purchase or sale of the asset itself and a riskless borrowing or lending of a principal amount equal to the exercise price under an option that produces a riskless return. The price of this equivalent portfolio must be the price of a particular option at a given exercise price. Otherwise, riskless arbitrage profit would be available.[103]

One can value an option, therefore, by constructing an option equivalent and valuing that equivalent, since arbitrage trading will ensure that the equivalent positions are priced equivalently.[104] Smith, Smithson, and Wilford point out that this fundamental insight of Black and Scholes follows from their adoption of a building-block approach to the pricing of options that is the foundation of the process of financial innovation generally.[105] In essence, option pricing involves a recognition of the equivalence of the cash flows associated with a call option and the common shares of a leveraged corporation. This equivalence leads to the proposition that a call written on shares can be replicated by a combination of ownership of the shares and borrowing. Similarly, the payoff profile of a call on an asset can be replicated by a combination of forward contracts on that asset and an investment in riskless government debt. Option-pricing models provide a means of calculating the value of these equivalent investment portfolios, a value that must be continuously adjusted to take into account continuous changes in the value of the underlying asset and thus in the range of possible values on the exercise date.[106] The price volatility of the underlying asset must be determined on the basis of historical price movements of an underlying asset and estimates of those movements in the future.[107]

Assembling the Building-Block Instruments: The Causes, Benefits, and Costs of Financial Innovation

Risk Allocation and the Benefits of Financial Innovation

The process of financial innovation occurs in the context of the arbitrage pricing of the basic building-block instruments. As was described above,[108] an essential element of the process of financial innovation is the recognition of financial equivalences expressed in the relationship between spot and forward prices and the different parities, which reveal arbitrage opportunities. This recognition is nothing new. From the onset of the Great Depression until the mid-1970s, the process of financial innovation was relatively slow,[109] but even this period saw the creation of some important non-traditional instruments, including preferred shares, debt with equity participation or conversion features, interest surrogates, and some combinations of the purchase or sale of an asset and the purchase or sale of a forward or futures contract on that asset.[110] Indeed, according to Miller, the recent wave of innovation is nothing more than a delayed continuation of "the long-run growth path of financial improvement,"[111] which was interrupted by the economic stagnation that plagued the world economy from the early 1930s to the early 1950s. He argues that this stagnation and the regulatory reactions that attempted to address its perceived causes tended to depress demand for financial innovation in the form of new financial instruments.[112] Whatever the causes of the latest wave of innovation, it is clear from the review in the next chapter that even in the period between the Great Depression and the mid-1970s the generation of unconventional instruments was based on the recognition of the equivalence between the cash flows associated with these instruments and conventional cash flows. The current wave of financial innovation, which began in the United States in the mid-1970s and spread from there to the rest of the world, is characterized by an overwhelming volume of new instruments; nevertheless, it involves the same identification of equivalent cash flows associated with combinations of the basic building-block instruments and their arbitrage pricing relationships.

The tax and legal literature provides a general categorization of instruments that are the product of the process of financial innovation that is useful for analytical purposes.[113] Under this categorization, which is described in somewhat different ways by Warren,[114] Goris,[115] and Paul,[116] financial innovation involves the purchase and sale of assets, the borrowing and lending of funds, and the issue of forwards and options to realize a variety of possible payoffs. All financial innovation reduces to three general techniques:[117]

1) the disaggregation of the component parts of an instrument to create separate instruments (for example, stripping the interest coupons from a bond and selling them separately from the principal portion at their discounted present value, or separating and selling the dividend rights on a share while retaining the capital appreciation component);

2) the combination of two or more separate instruments in one legally distinct instrument (for example, combining a level-coupon instrument and a call option on shares in a bond that is convertible into the shares);[118] and

3) the combination of two or more legally distinct instruments to create the payoff profile of another, legally distinct instrument (for example, converting a fixed-rate loan into a floating-rate loan by entering into a floating-for-fixed-rate swap).[119]

No attempt is made here to do what has been done elsewhere and compile a product-by-product inventory of the specific financial instruments that are the result of these three techniques. As was noted earlier, Finnerty provides a reasonably complete taxonomy of the particular instruments that were in use in the early 1990s.[120] For the purposes of either regulatory policy or tax policy, it is more important to understand the principles of the building-block theory of the general process of financial innovation and the relation of this process to the broader issue of the role of capital markets in an economy. Merton emphasizes this point in his description of financial innovation as the "engine" that drives the financial system toward its goal of improving what economists refer to as the "real economy."[121] Improvement in the real economy occurs to the extent that financial innovation makes capital markets more efficient in performing their function in the economy.[122] That function is to allocate resources among various uses by cycling funds in the form of household savings into capital investments and then back to households for consumption or further cycling as savings.[123] In other words, capital markets link sources of capital (household savings) with users of capital (businesses with needs for working capital in the form of personnel, plant, and equipment). This linkage occurs through financial instruments and intermediaries, such as institutional investors, which provide risk-pooling and risk-sharing opportunities for households and businesses.[124] Businesses provide the real investment; households provide the financial investment and bear a degree of risk associated with that investment. This separation of real investment from financial risk bearing permits specialization according to the principle of comparative advantage.[125]

A key determinant of the allocation of capital among various uses is risk in the narrow sense of the volatility of the outcomes (payoffs) associated with a financial instrument measured ex ante in terms of variance or standard deviation.[126]

Assume, for example,[127] that the possible payoffs for bets on two horses in the Kentucky Derby are as follows:

Horse one

Return	*Probability*	*Value*
$ nil	0.1	$ nil
1,000	0.8	800
2,000	0.1	200
	1.0	$1,000

Horse two

Return	*Probability*	*Value*
$ nil	0.4	$ nil
1,000	0.2	200
2,000	0.4	800
	1.0	$1,000

The value of a bet on each horse is the same ($1,000), but the risk associated with the bet on horse two is much greater than the risk associated with the bet on horse one. This is so because the dispersion in the probable returns is wider in the case of the bet on horse two, which is said to be more volatile or to involve a higher level of volatility risk than the bet on horse one. Risk in the sense of volatility is a function of an ex ante assessment of the probability of potential outcomes and the amount of the deviation of those outcomes from the average.[128] In the case of the bet on horse two, the combined probability of a return other than the average of $1,000 is 80 percent. The variance or standard deviation is much higher in this case than it is in the case of the bet on horse one, which has a combined probability of a return other than $1,000 of only 20 percent. The weighted average of all probable returns is referred to as the "expected return," which is expressed in the example as the value of the bets or the expected payoffs.

Businesses will engage in real investment if the investment has a positive net present value and the desired level of risk. There is, therefore, a need to manage the risk associated with real investment. Similarly, in providing financial capital to businesses for real investment, investors seek the highest possible return given the level of risk that they are willing to bear. If investors are risk neutral, they will require only that the expected return on a risky investment be equal to the riskless rate of return. A higher nominal return is necessary to offset the probability of loss and provide an expected return equal to the riskless rate. On the other hand, if investors are risk averse, or if the risk associated with an investment is non-unique in the sense that it cannot be diversified away, investors will demand a risk premium in the form of an expected return in excess of the riskless return otherwise available.[129]

Capital markets focus on the allocation of risk between and among the providers and users of capital. The goal is to identify real investment with a given level of risk and to find providers of financial capital who are willing to bear that level of risk.[130] In the process, both users and providers of capital can alter their risk exposure so that it accords with the level of risk they are willing to bear for the sake of the compensating return.[131] By shifting risk to the persons who are willing to bear it at the lowest cost, financial innovation enhances the risk-allocation function necessary to an economy.[132] In other words, the purpose of financial innovation is a simple one: to increase investor wealth and economic growth by reallocating risk in a more efficient manner.[133] As an underlying cause or driving force of financial innovation, risk management is equated with "real efficiency gains"[134] and the design of new financial products that improve economic performance by providing investors and issuers with greater opportunities to share and pool risk and transfer resources.[135]

In general, the development of financial instruments for risk-management purposes involves the limitation of exposure to risk by selling the source of the risk, diversifying, or purchasing insurance.[136] Forwards, futures, swaps, and options allow an investor to realize a given level of risk exposure for his portfolio without incurring transaction costs as high as those that he would incur if he realized the same level of exposure by selling or insuring the underlying assets or liabilities individually.[137] In other words, these basic building-block instruments of financial innovation permit the alteration of broad exposures at reduced costs.[138] For example,[139] an investor with a portfolio of publicly traded shares can adjust the risk exposure of that portfolio by entering into an equity swap or selling a futures contract on a share index. The more costly alternative is the sale of an appropriate portion of the shares in the portfolio.

The use of forwards, futures, swaps, and options to manage the risk associated with an asset or liability involves the effective transfer of that risk to another party who is willing to bear it, usually because this exposure hedges an inherent exposure.[140] Miller[141] cites the example of a financial institution that holds an inventory of government treasury bills available for sale to its customers. In an environment of rising interest rates, holding this inventory exposes the financial institution to the risk of a decline in the value of the bills. Instead of selling a portion of the treasury bills to manage that exposure, the financial institution can sell futures contracts on them. Any loss in value attributable to an increase in interest rates will be offset by a gain on the futures contracts. Another party may be willing to purchase the same futures contracts in order to hedge its opposite exposure to interest rates. As Miller states, the whole forward, futures, swap, and option market is analogous to a massive insurance scheme that facilitates risk sharing at the lowest possible cost.[142]

Purchases and sales of the basic derivative financial instruments constitute risk management at its simplest level. At a more sophisticated level, risk management involves the assembly of the basic building-block instruments in a search for combinations that either (1) replicate the characteristics of other, more conventional, and more obvious, assets or liabilities or (2) create risk and return payoffs that are otherwise unavailable.[143] This search is intended to uncover opportunities for both "pure arbitrage" and "risk arbitrage."[144] Pure arbitrage is the opportunity to purchase and sell equivalent financial positions at different prices.[145] For investors, risk arbitrage is the opportunity to earn higher expected returns for bearing a given level of risk;[146] for borrowers, it is the opportunity to lower the cost of funds associated with a given level of risk.

The need for the risk-management function of financial innovation is said to have increased as a result of certain factors that have increased the inherent exposure of providers and users of capital.[147] The factor that is cited most frequently is the move away from fixed currency exchange rates tied to the gold standard.[148] The consequent fluctuations in floating exchange rates introduced an unprecedented level of volatility that required management by parties exposed to the fluctuations. Forwards and futures contracts on currencies began to be traded extensively in an effort to manage the new exposure. As the volatility spread to interest rates, additional products were developed to manage that exposure. According to Merton, changes of this kind occur along the course of a "financial innovation spiral" in a process that has four steps.[149] First, the development of new trading markets in standardized instruments, such as futures, encourages the creation of new custom-designed instruments that "complete" the market.[150] Second, the volume of trading in the new markets increases as the financial intermediaries responsible for the production of the new instruments seek to hedge their exposures. Third, the increased volume results in a further reduction in transaction costs, which facilitates the creation of new instruments and trading strategies that further increase trading volume. Fourth, success in the existing markets encourages investment in the creation of new instruments and markets. This financial spiral is evident in the development of the exchange trading of currency futures and share options in the early 1970s, which led in turn to the development of more customized trading and the creation of interest-rate futures, forwards, and swaps, and also to customized and exchange trading in share indexes.[151]

Regulatory and Tax Arbitrage

The financial literature tends to emphasize the role of risk management (and risk arbitrage) in financial innovation and to downplay the role of regulatory and tax arbitrage. Miller is the most prominent proponent of these other factors as causes of the innovative process.[152] He argues that opportunities for regulatory and tax arbitrage arise from the existence of watertight compartments for identifiable legal relationships and sources of income, which can be replicated by new financial instruments that are not subject to the particular regulatory constraint or tax treatment for a particular type of income.[153] "Regulatory arbitrage" involves the design of new financial instruments to avoid the application of a regulatory constraint on the activities or structure of commercial enterprises.[154] Kane has described this process as a never-ending "regulatory dialectic" in which the regulatee seeks to avoid the application of a constraint by developing a new financial instrument, the regulator develops a response to the new instrument, and the regulatee develops a response to that response.[155] As Miller points out,[156] the process often results in the creation of an instrument that has potential beyond regulatory avoidance, which enables the instrument to survive the original reason for its creation.[157] An obvious example of this process is the development of parallel loans in the late 1970s, which became swap contracts in the early 1980s.[158]

As a stimulus to financial innovation, "tax arbitrage" refers loosely to any repackaging of cash flows in an effort to obtain a tax benefit or a lower tax burden.[159] In this loose sense, the term is tantamount to "tax avoidance" viewed broadly as the rearrangement of any transaction to minimize tax payable or otherwise obtain a tax benefit.[160] Within the narrower financial context, tax arbitrage entails a process that is very similar to regulatory arbitrage. In particular, the process depends on differences in tax treatment, which, as described by Miller[161] at a general level, encompass differences in tax rates for different sources and uses of funds. These differences in tax treatment provide taxpayers with opportunities to alter the form of cash flows in a manner that lowers the associated tax burden without altering the desired pattern of those cash flows. In some instances, the arbitrage is structured to take advantage of differences between the tax treatments for equivalent cash flows.[162] In other instances, the arbitrage is structured to take advantage of circumstances in which minor changes in the pattern of cash flows result in significant changes in tax treatment.[163] Although the repackaging and substitutability of equivalent cash flows are imperfect and not without cost when pushed to extremes,[164] constant changes in the tax rules, often in response to specific financial transactions, ensure the constant creation of new opportunities for tax arbitrage.[165] Miller concludes that changes in tax rules result in an environment comparable to Kane's regulatory dialectic, which prevents the realization of an equilibrium that would occur if the tax rules were left unchanged.[166] An equilibrium would otherwise be realized because gains from the design of new instruments that transformed high-taxed cash flows into low-taxed flows would be offset at the margin by increased transaction costs. Chapter 2 examines past examples of tax arbitrage and the tax dialectic in Canada and Australia.[167] The important general point made by Miller is that constant alteration of the tax structure has both stimulated and defined successful financial innovation by providing opportunities for tax savings through the design of new financial instruments that result in rewards for the innovator.[168] In fact, he believes that governments effectively, albeit inadvertently, subsidize the process of financial innovation. He concludes that "the role of government in producing the pearls of financial innovation over the past twenty years has been essentially that of the grain of sand in the oyster."[169]

Much of the financial literature on the role and the causes of financial innovation has been summarized by Finnerty,[170] who identifies the following 11 factors as causes of financial innovation:[171]

1) the existence of tax asymmetries that can be exploited to provide tax savings for investors or issuers without creating an offsetting liability for the other parties to a financing ("tax arbitrage");
2) the desire to reduce transaction costs;[172]
3) the desire to limit agency costs;[173]

4) the desire to reduce risk or to allocate risk to another party, who is willing to bear the risk at a lower cost;

5) the desire to increase asset liquidity;

6) the desire to avoid regulatory constraints and regulatory changes ("regulatory arbitrage");

7) the need to manage increased volatility in exchange and interest rates;

8) the need to manage increased price volatility generally;

9) advances in financial theory and in understanding of the risk-return characteristics of financial assets;

10) the desire to realize beneficial accounting treatment; and

11) technological advances.

As Finnerty notes, conventional wisdom holds that a new instrument should be characterized as "innovative" only if it allows investors and issuers to accomplish something that they could not accomplish by using existing instruments.[174] For investors, innovation may enhance the after-tax return associated with a given level of risk, provide greater liquidity, or create a more desirable pattern of cash flows.[175] For issuers, innovation may lower the after-tax cost of capital and thus facilitate the undertaking of new real investment.[176] More important, innovative instruments enable investors to realize a higher after-tax return adjusted for risk without increasing the after-tax cost of funds for the issuer; they also enable issuers to realize a lower after-tax cost of funds without adversely affecting investors.[177] Financial innovation, therefore, serves to "complete" capital markets, making them more efficient and adding value for issuers and investors.[178] According to Finnerty, this added value arises from six principal types of features of innovative instruments:[179]

1) features that reduce the required yield on a security by reallocating risk to investors who are willing to bear it,

2) features that increase liquidity and thus permit an investor to sell without incurring high transaction costs or lowering his price significantly,

3) features that reduce the agency costs attributable to information asymmetries between management and investors,

4) features that reduce transaction costs such as underwriting fees,

5) features that take advantage of existing tax rules to create a tax arbitrage that reduces the combined taxes of issuers and investors, and

6) features that avoid regulatory constraints for issuers and investors.

Like the analyses of Merton,[180] Miller,[181] and other financial economists, Finnerty's taxonomy identifies three primary motives for financial innovation: to manage risk, to reduce transaction and agency costs, and to realize opportunities for regulatory and tax arbitrage. Factors such as the progress of computer technology and the development by financial economists of influential new ideas and applications have played a significant if somewhat indeterminate role[182] in facilitating the development of new instruments for one or another of these principal purposes.[183] Some factors identified by Finnerty, such as perceived accounting benefits, are related to the pursuit of regulatory and tax arbitrage; other factors, such as increased volatility in exchange rates, interest rates, and prices, are in general related to the pursuit of more efficient risk management and risk allocation.

The role of regulatory and tax arbitrage as sources of financial innovation is often the focus of critics of the process. An early critic, Van Horne[184] emphasized the social costs of financial innovation, much of which he characterized as nothing more than innovation for the sake of realizing excessive rewards for the innovator and producing accounting profits unsupported by economic gain.[185] Innovation for its own sake, driven by competition among financial institutions, may inflate expectations of higher returns with less risk.[186] The result is the development by opportunists of a range of "innovations that have no function other than to differentiate their products superficially."[187] Activity of this kind involves the wasteful expenditure of intellectual and financial resources and may distort the allocation of capital. Moreover, the inevitable failure to realize the greater expected returns may result in excessive price volatility.[188] A somewhat different criticism is that derivatives are zero-sum instruments; for every gain to the winning party, there is an offsetting loss to the other party. Consequently, the development of new derivatives for risk-management purposes merely reallocates risk without affecting the factors that are the source of the underlying risk. In other words, they reallocate risk within the economy but do not reduce risk in the aggregate.[189]

Merton, who admits that instances of excessive innovation occur, argues that their effects are outweighed by the efficiency gains attributable to innovation's completion of capital markets.[190] These efficiency gains are, in fact, attributable to the reallocation of risk in a more cost-effective manner. The reallocation in and of itself produces the efficiency gains, even though aggregate risk is not reduced. Moreover, it is possible to argue that in a small open economy financial innovation can reduce aggregate risk itself by providing access to deeper and more mature international capital markets. In effect, financial innovation can transfer risk that arises domestically to foreign market participants.[191] The case for financial innovation as a source of social benefits thus rests on its risk-management and risk-allocation functions. The social benefits of financial innovation that is driven by regulatory constraints and inconsistent tax treatment of equivalent cash flows are much more problematic. If one takes the benefits of a particular regulatory constraint as a given, avoidance of that constraint through the development of new financial instruments presumably represents an activity that produces social costs. The obvious response is a change in the regulatory constraints to address the avoidance activity.[192] In other instances, however, a particular regulatory constraint may impose costs that outweigh any benefits. As Merton notes, financial innovation that avoids regulatory constraints of this kind may produce social benefits.[193] The resolution of this issue requires an assessment of the benefits and costs of particular regulatory constraints. Even where financial innovation that is driven by regulatory arbitrage produces social benefits sufficient to offset the costs of a regulatory constraint, the more direct (and arguably more efficient) response is the repeal of the constraint itself.

Financial innovation that is driven by tax avoidance has two related functions. First, by exploiting inconsistencies in the tax treatment of equivalent cash flows, innovation requires a response from tax-policy makers to protect the tax base.[194] This function produces no obvious social benefits and is simply one example of tax avoidance generally.[195] Second, innovation that is driven by tax avoidance tends to expose the weaknesses of existing tax structures and forces consideration of fundamental reform. Thus tax-driven financial innovation can produce social benefits and may even lead to its own elimination by encouraging the elimination of the differences in taxation that are its sources.

An Australian tax-policy maker has described the following three desirable (and ambitious) features of an income tax system applicable to financial instruments:[196]

1) For reasons of economic efficiency, the tax system should not distort the legitimate use of financial instruments as a means of allocating risk to those persons who are willing to bear it at the lowest price. In other words, the tax system should be "risk neutral"[197]—it should not distort the process of financial innovation that results in the repackaging of risk in the most efficient manner.

2) For reasons of fairness, the tax system should ensure that all equivalent financial transactions are taxed equivalently. In other words, the tax system should be "consistent"[198] in the sense that it should apply to the economic substance of financially equivalent positions in a manner that eliminates tax-driven financial innovation designed to take advantage of differences in tax treatment of equivalent cash flows on the basis of differences in legal form.[199]

3) For both of the above two reasons, the tax system should provide a rational set of general principles that is applicable to the taxation of all financial transactions. In other words, the tax system should be "universal"[200] in the sense that any particular transaction should be subject to a defined treatment that is both sensible and predictable.[201]

In the view of many tax-policy makers and practitioners, the practice in most countries fails on all three counts.[202] As was noted earlier, this practice has been characterized as the "cubbyhole approach," which requires the classification of every instrument and its associated cash flow within an established category that attracts one of a defined set of different tax treatments. In particular, the income tax systems of many countries incorporate features that result in distinctions for tax purposes between

- ordinary income and capital amounts,
- dividends and interest, and
- realization and accrual recognition of gains and losses.

Characterization of a return as a capital gain or loss is available for investors who hold instruments on capital account and not as traders. Dividend treatment is available for instruments that are considered to be shares. Treatment as interest is limited to debt-financing charges. Gain or loss (other than interest) is recognized when it is realized. Finally, specific rules for the taxation of option premiums are limited to forward-based contracts that are properly characterized as call and put options.

These distinctions are artificial in the sense that they are irrelevant in capital markets, which recognize the basic equivalences that underlie the arbitrage pricing of financial instruments. It is probably correct, if somewhat simplistic, to say that all cash flows, whatever their form, must be valued for capital-market purposes, and that differences in form affect only the valuation exercise.[203] Arbitrage pricing identifies equivalent cash flows and ensures that they are priced equivalently. Under the recognized tax cubbyholes, financial instruments that differ slightly in form may be subject to significant differences in tax treatment, differences that contradict financial theory's recognition of certain basic equivalences. These differences in tax treatment permit the replication of cash flows associated with conventional instruments in unconventional forms that attract different tax consequences. In addition to creating avoidance opportunities, the fact that new instruments must be classified on the basis of specified tax treatments also creates uncertainty, which may discourage the use of particular instruments for non-tax purposes. In particular, this uncertainty can distort the pricing of new instruments, an outcome that will generate inefficiencies and social costs if the instruments have been developed in order to reallocate risk at lower transaction costs.[204]

In essence, therefore, a tension exists between the reality of financial equivalences recognized by capital markets and the specified differences in tax treatment for certain conventional instruments on which the income tax system is based. Two aspects of the process of financial innovation described in this chapter are critical for tax-policy purposes. First, all complex financial instruments are composites of the basic building-block instruments—forwards, futures, swaps, options, and credit-extension (debt) instruments—that provide a single payoff on the occurrence of a single contingency and therefore result in expected or unexpected gains and losses.[205] Second, basic parities or financial equivalences—interest-rate parity, futures parity, put-call parity, and option pricing—underlie the arbitrage pricing of these instruments.[206] The cubbyhole approach reflected in the income tax legislation in most countries fails to recognize in any systematic sense these two fundamental aspects of the process of financial innovation and, in fact, is based on specified and often inconsistent tax treatments for a limited range of conventional instruments.

Anecdotal and survey evidence tends to confirm the problems associated with the cubbyhole approach.[207] It is argued in the following chapters, however, that radical reform of existing income tax systems is unnecessary. In principle, the challenges presented by the latest wave of financial innovation are no different from the more limited challenges that financial innovation has presented in the past, and the fundamental features of past responses require only some modification or extension to provide a workable and defensible system. The challenge for proponents of radical reform is to demonstrate that the latest wave of financial innovation has features that distinguish it fundamentally from past innovation and therefore require a radical break from past practice. To some extent, commentators have assumed both the existence of these features and the need for radical reform, without considering less ambitious reform of the core elements of existing systems. In many respects, the limited responses to the earlier challenges of financial innovation are fundamentally sound and provide a defensible paradigm for a modified approach, one that is described in some of the academic literature and that has been implemented legislatively in New Zealand and proposed in Australia. This approach, referred to here as "a comprehensive accrual regime," involves nothing more than the broad application of the following five core elements of existing income tax systems:

1) the recognition of expected gains and losses as they are expected to arise on instruments other than shares ("accrual recognition");

2) the recognition of unexpected gains as they are realized ("realization-based recognition");

3) the recognition of all gains and losses as they arise with changes in value ("accretion taxation") of a limited range of instruments (including shares) that can be traded at low transaction costs;

4) the elimination of any distinction between ordinary income and capital amounts, with the recognition in full of all gains and losses; and

5) the adoption of some form of corporate imputation system designed to impose the corporate income tax as a proxy for recognition of gains at the shareholder level.

2

Cubbyhole Taxation of Financial Instruments: Representative Lessons from the Canadian and Australian Experiences

Introduction

In order to lay the conceptual groundwork for a comprehensive legislative approach to governing the income taxation of financial instruments, this chapter reviews the Canadian and Australian experiences with the traditional "cubbyhole" approach. The choice has fallen on Canada and Australia not just because their experiences are representative but also because Australian tax-policy makers are currently considering whether to alter, in a substantial way, the traditional cubbyhole approach. The Australian treasury department and Australian Taxation Office (ATO) have proposed a comprehensive legislative approach that largely rejects the status quo.[1] As chapter 5 will argue, these proposals are the clearest expression yet offered by tax authorities anywhere of a legislative regime intended to implement the second-best approach to the income taxation of financial instruments recommended in this book.

The first three parts of the chapter following this introduction describe the existing legislative regimes and administrative practices in Canada and Australia. The first part below briefly reviews the differences among the accepted tax cubbyholes in terms of the tax treatment they imply. These differences are based in large part on perceptions of the economic substance of the cash flows associated with particular financial instruments and on an acceptance of either legal form or the purpose of a taxpayer as a proxy for the identification of that substance. The second part describes some characteristic examples of past legislative practice in Canada and Australia. This practice has focused on particular financial instruments or financing charges, sometimes in response to avoidance transactions and sometimes with an intention to address perceived anomalies. Legislation has tended to be framed in terms of an unarticulated view of the underlying economic substance of the instrument in question. The third part examines the development through administrative practice of a similar approach to the taxation of forwards, futures, swaps, and options. Administrative practice has focused on characterization and timing issues and reflects the instrument-by-instrument approach typical of past legislative practice.

With this background in place, the fourth part below explores the perceived weaknesses of the existing income tax regimes in Canada and Australia. Two principal points arise from this analysis.

The first point is that many of the legislative and administrative practices that apply to the basic building-block instruments are consistent with the comprehensive system of "expected-return taxation"[2] described in chapters 4 and 5 as a defensible second-best approach to the taxation of financial instruments. Like the existing regimes in Canada and Australia, this approach requires the accrual recognition of expected gains and losses on debt but permits the realization-based recognition of unexpected gains and losses on forwards, futures, and swaps. In these and other ways, a system of expected-return taxation would simply extend certain aspects of the existing tax regimes, at least in terms of the treatment of the building-block instruments. This extension, however, would require some important changes. In particular, it would require reform of the treatment of options and elimination of realization-based recognition for certain instruments. Moreover, an extension of expected-return taxation to shares would have profound implications for corporate income tax reform and would eliminate the distinction for tax purposes between interest and dividends. Nonetheless, any approach to the income taxation of financial instruments (other than the annual recognition of unrealized changes in value) can only be based on a cubbyhole approach with discrete treatments for expected gains and losses and unexpected gains and losses; it is simply a question of the extent to which the cubbyholes are defined and applied on the basis of criteria that are relevant from a tax-policy perspective. A comprehensive system of expected-return taxation would massage and reform the edges of the tax cubbyholes and their related treatments of the basic building-block financial instruments under existing regimes.

The second point concerns the complex financial instruments that are the result of the process of financial innovation. Much of the apparent confusion and messiness characteristic of the cubbyhole approach under existing income tax regimes arises from a failure to understand the tax-policy issues presented by financial innovation and develop any sort of consistent approach to addressing those issues. Indeed, as they are framed under existing regimes, the issues themselves are not always clear, let alone the means of dealing with them. Even so, the problems created by the cubbyhole approach are not new; nor has the process of financial innovation altered them in any fundamental sense. That process has simply exacerbated the problems to the extent that ad hoc efforts to maintain the integrity of the specified tax cubbyholes may no longer be tenable. By reducing transaction costs, financial innovation has created an expanded range of financial instruments that are based on the application of an expanded range of financial equivalences that have always existed in financial theory, but not, until now, in practice. To put the matter in another way, financial innovation is responsible for the maturation of capital markets in a manner that permits the practical application of an expanded range of financial equivalences expressed by put-call parity and the other pricing parities described in chapter 1. The new applications give taxpayers access to a broader range of financial instruments for tax avoidance and non-tax purposes, including risk management.

Subsequent chapters will argue that the issues associated with complex financial instruments become clear once the appropriate approach to the basic building-block instruments is understood and, more specifically, once the important distinction between expected gains and losses and unexpected gains and losses is clarified. That distinction is reflected, but not fully developed, in many aspects of existing regimes such as those in Canada and Australia. Second-best alternatives for reform, such as a system of expected-return taxation, are primarily attempts to rationalize existing regimes in terms of a coherent underlying theory and a legislative structure that can respond flexibly to innovative instruments. Although avoidance opportunities would remain, a system of this kind would increase consistency in the taxation of equivalent cash flows and reduce the pressure associated with the development of new instruments.

The Existing Tax Cubbyholes

The differences in tax treatment that are the source of the various tax cubbyholes appear to be based, tacitly and somewhat vaguely, on certain premises that are assumed to justify those differences. Thus the distinction for tax purposes between interest and dividends seems to be premised on a "proprietary view"[3] of the corporation that results in a superficially tidy division of the capital structure into debt obligations, which represent a limited investment of capital funds in the corporate form, and shares, which represent a proprietary or ownership interest.[4] Consistently with this view, interest on debt is considered to be a deductible expense payable to corporate outsiders and not a distribution of corporate income. Dividends are considered to be distributions of after-tax income that are not deductible at the corporate level and are subject to the corporate tax.

Similarly, the distinction for tax purposes between ordinary-income amounts and capital amounts, as well as the application of accrual recognition and realization-based recognition, appears to be based on an unarticulated discrimination between expected and unexpected cash flows. In commonwealth countries, the tax courts have tended to follow UK jurisprudence by incorporating the distinction in trust law between income beneficiaries and capital beneficiaries as a basis for the definition of income.[5] As in trust law, ordinary-income amounts are those that represent the recurrent or expected return from holding an asset.[6] Capital amounts are gains or losses attributable to changes in the value of a capital asset realized on its disposition. Unless a taxpayer is engaged in the trading of capital assets, the non-recurring or unexpected nature of the amounts is considered to be sufficient to support a characterization of the amounts as either non-taxable capital receipts or non-deductible capital losses. Even in countries that provide for the taxation of capital gains and losses under specific legislative regimes, their non-recurring nature has led the tax authorities to require recognition only on realization (that is, on disposition of the asset), when the taxpayer is considered to have the ability to pay any tax and the amount of the gain or loss has been determined (that is, it is no longer unexpected). Moreover, in an apparent effort to encourage investment in risky assets with significant unexpected gains and losses, many countries provide a preferential inclusion rate for capital gains.[7] Recognition of gain and loss in full as the amounts accrue is limited to a limited range of expected amounts (usually expected gains and losses in the form of interest).

These differences in tax treatment and their apparent underlying premises are reflected in certain general provisions of the Canadian Income Tax Act (ITA)[8] and the Australian Income Tax Assessment Act 1936 (ITAA).[9] In particular, the deductibility rules under both regimes permit taxpayers to deduct interest expense, provided that the expense can be considered to have been incurred for an income-earning purpose.[10] For corporate borrowers, this deductibility principle means that virtually all interest expense is deductible on an accrual basis.[11] All Canadian residents and all Australian financial institutions must include interest in income as it accrues.[12] Australian residents other than financial institutions must include interest income in income as it is "derived," which has been interpreted as equivalent to inclusion on receipt.[13] As a proxy for the inclusion of interest in income, both countries subject non-residents to withholding tax on the gross amount of interest paid by resident debtors.[14]

In contrast with their treatment of interest, both the ITA and the ITAA treat dividends as non-deductible distributions of after-tax profit that shareholders must include in income on receipt. The two legislative regimes differ, however, in how they provide relief for the double taxation that would otherwise apply to corporate income distributed as a dividend. Under the more fully developed imputation regime in the ITAA,[15] dividends may be "franked" if the underlying income has been subject to corporate tax. Resident individuals who receive a franked dividend may claim a tax credit for corporate tax, which is considered to have been paid on the underlying income.[16] The ITA offers similar relief for resident individuals,[17] but it provides no general mechanism to ensure that corporate tax has been paid in support of the dividend tax credit, which offsets only a portion of that tax. To prevent multiple levels of corporate tax, the legislation in each country permits dividends to be paid tax-free between resident corporations.[18] Dividends paid by resident corporations to non-resident individuals and corporations are generally subject to withholding tax on the gross amount, without any credit for tax paid on the underlying income.[19]

Both the ITA and the ITAA complicate their differential taxation of interest and dividends by making a distinction between realized gains and losses on income account and realized gains and losses on capital account. The distinction is particularly significant in Canada, which recognizes only two-thirds of realized gains and losses on capital property, including debt obligations and shares, for the purposes of inclusion and deduction.[20] Moreover, capital losses may be deducted only to the extent of realized capital gains. Although the Australian legislation generally requires the full inclusion and deduction of both income and capital amounts, the distinction remains significant for a range of assets, including shares, that are subject to a one-half recognition rate for individuals and a two-thirds recognition rate for pension funds.[21] For corporations, as well as for certain partnerships and trusts, all capital gains and losses are fully recognized, while the deductibility of capital losses by all taxpayers is subject to a limitation similar to that in Canada. In both countries, however, the provision that has perhaps the most important implications for the tax treatment of debt and shares is the requirement that instruments held by taxpayers as inventory or trading stock, and not as capital property, be carried at the lower of their cost and fair market value—a provision that effectively requires the recognition of unrealized losses.[22] Both tax regimes generally recognize on realization capital losses, capital gains, and ordinary-income gains on inventory.[23] One exception to the realization principle is the ITA's requirement that financial institutions recognize annually all unrealized gains and losses on most shares, as well as debt held as inventory in their trading accounts.[24]

The distinction between gains and losses on income account and gains and losses on capital account is not limited to financial assets. In the absence of a comprehensive statutory definition of income for tax purposes, it has been left to the Canadian and Australian courts to identify the parameters of that concept. The perceived purpose of a taxpayer in acquiring an asset is critical to the asset's characterization as either an income asset that gives rise to income amounts or a capital asset that gives rise to capital amounts. As was noted above, the gain or loss realized on the disposition of an asset that was acquired for its current yield is considered to be on capital account. This is normally the case, for example, when a taxpayer acquires debt or shares for the interest or dividend returns. If, instead, a taxpayer acquires an asset (including debt or shares) for the purpose of resale in the course of business, the gain or loss realized on a disposition is considered to be on income account. This characterization extends to gains and losses realized by taxpayers who acquire an asset not as trading stock or inventory held in the course of a business but rather for speculative purposes or as "an adventure or concern in the nature of trade."[25]

Although it is not a purpose-based distinction, the characterization of amounts as either interest or dividends for tax purposes is similarly unsatisfactory. To the extent that general definitions of debt and equity are provided in the ITA and the ITAA, they are vague and unhelpful. In the absence of comprehensive statutory definitions, the distinction for tax purposes between interest and dividends appears to have been conceived largely in terms of the "classical" forms of debt and equity. Investors who hold classical debt as evidence of their capital contributions are seen as having given up all claims to an unlimited share in corporate profits and corporate control. As compensation, they receive both a fixed return that is payable irrespective of the existence of corporate profits and a right to receive a return of their capital in whole or in part at specified times. In addition, these rights may be supported by other rights or arrangements, such as guarantees or indemnities, that reduce the risk that the promised return will not be paid. In contrast, investors who hold classical equity (usually referred to as "common shares") as evidence of their capital contributions are seen as enjoying an unlimited right to participate in corporate profits and the right to vote with respect to certain corporate matters. To receive those enhanced rights, they must bear the risk of a variable or contingent return dependent on the existence and extent of corporate profits. As well, they have no right to receive a return of their capital except on liquidation of the corporation; nor do investors receive the benefit of any rights or arrangements that might reduce the investment risk.

As a rule, the form of a security for private law purposes has been accepted for income tax purposes. The distinction between debt and equity is thus based on two premises: first, that the two types of instruments are sufficiently different from one another to merit different tax treatment; second, that the form of those instruments is a suitable proxy for the identification of the assumed difference. Even before the recent wave of financial innovation, however, it was apparent that a simplistic division of financial instruments into debt and equity does not accurately reflect the corporate capital structure. In addition to the two classical forms of debt and equity, there have always been a limited number of instruments that combine the rights and obligations conventionally associated with each of them. These instruments tend to fall into two categories: "mixed-right" instruments and "option-based" instruments.[26] The former blend rights characteristic of classical debt with rights characteristic of classical equity. Investors who hold these instruments (for example, preferred shares and "participating" or "contingent-payment" debt) are entitled to some mix of a fixed return and a contingent return, and also to priority over the holders of common shares in the return of their capital contributions. Option-based instruments usually combine a classical debt instrument with the right to acquire shares. This right may take the form of either a detachable warrant, which is separately tradable, or a conversion or exchange right, which provides the holder with the right to convert or exchange the debt into shares.

For tax purposes, the existence of mixed-right and option-based instruments makes the corporate capital structure a somewhat messy affair. Classical debt and classical equity differ from one another in respect of the allocation of profit participation, exposure to loss, and corporate control; the mixed instruments blur the differences.[27] This convergence is, in fact, a simple example of the problem of "financial equivalences," described in chapter 1—that is, the repackaging of cash flows in unconventional forms without significantly altering the pattern of those cash flows. Since the purpose of the repackaging may be to obtain a tax benefit that is available for classical debt or equity, some apparent equivalences provoke responses from tax-policy makers. In general, these responses attempt to alter the tax treatment of particular financing costs or the return on particular instruments in a manner that accords with the costs' or the instruments' perceived "economic substance." They tend to focus on maintaining the distinction for tax purposes between interest and dividends and the necessary distinction between debt and equity. Virtually no legislative attention has been paid to the tax treatment of forwards, futures, or swaps, though they are the basic instruments from which new instruments are built. For the most part, Revenue Canada (now the Canada Customs and Revenue Agency) and the ATO have been left with the task of categorizing the new instruments within the general tax regime for business income and expense, the general regime for capital gains and losses, and some specific provisions applicable to options.

Past Legislative Practice in Canada and Australia: Transactional Approach Intended To Maintain the Integrity of the Tax Cubbyholes

One can characterize past legislative practice in Canada and Australia as an attempt to maintain the integrity of the tax cubbyholes when the premises that underlie the cubbyholes fail to accord with perceptions of economic substance. The result is a limited set of legislative responses that effectively reclassify particular instruments and financing charges on the basis of these perceptions of economic substance, rather than on the basis of legal form. The responses fall into three broad categories:

1) responses that recharacterize certain debt-financing charges affected by the restrictive concept of interest developed by the courts,

2) responses that classify preferred shares and convertible debt as either debt or equity, and

3) responses that identify disguised debt and equity.

In each of these instances, the legislative responses have attempted to maintain different tax treatments for interest and dividends while recognizing a limited set of financial equivalences that permit the replication of conventional instruments in alternative and, for tax purposes, more advantageous forms. Some of the legislative responses also recognize that there are basic equivalences whose packaging in different legal forms produces tax consequences that are unduly harsh for taxpayers. Thus Canadian and Australian policy makers have pursued two distinct types of legislative response. One type is anti-avoidance legislation—legislation that attempts to foreclose the tax-avoidance opportunities offered by particular financial instruments. These instruments attempt to take advantage of the realization-based recognition of certain gains and losses, the differential taxation of interest and dividends, and the existence of different regimes for capital income and ordinary income. The other type of legislation is relieving or enabling—it attempts to alleviate apparently inappropriate differences in tax treatment for functionally similar financing charges.

Restrictive Concept of Interest and the Tax Treatment of Debt-Financing Charges

The need for definitional responses to some debt-financing charges arises because neither the ITA nor the ITAA provides a general definition of the term "interest" in its monetary sense. In the absence of a statutory definition, the courts in tax cases have adopted a fairly restrictive concept of interest, one that has been developed and applied for private law purposes. This concept of interest, which is sometimes referred to as the "legal" or "common law" definition,[28] specifies three requirements that an amount must satisfy to be considered interest:[29]

1) the amount must be compensation for the use of money;

2) the amount must be referable to a principal sum; and

3) the amount must be calculated by reference to the time during which the principal is outstanding; that is, it must accrue on a daily basis or be apportionable in time on that basis.

The first two requirements find their clearest expression in the constitutional decision of the Supreme Court of Canada in *Reference Re Saskatchewan Farm Security Act*[30] and a number of UK non-tax and tax cases.[31] The third requirement of daily accrual follows from some older UK trust law cases in which the courts held that interest may be apportioned in time for the purposes of determining any entitlement to accrued but unpaid amounts.[32] The requirement of daily accrual articulated in these cases is also codified in the apportionment statutes of several Australian states and Canadian provinces on the basis of the UK model. In general, these statutes provide that rents, annuities, dividends, and other periodic payments in the nature of income "shall be considered to accrue from day to day and are apportionable in respect of time like interest on money lent."[33]

For the most part, the requirement that an amount must be compensation for the use of borrowed money has not been problematic. In effect, the form of a security as indebtedness is accepted as determinative of the character of an advance of funds as debt and not equity. The only issue is whether particular debt-financing charges that form part of the cost of credit should be considered to be compensation for the use of the creditor's funds or compensation for some other service.

In contrast, the precise nature of the requirement that an amount be referable to a principal sum is unclear.[34] It may mean that particular amounts must be calculated as a fixed percentage of the principal sum of a debt obligation, or it may mean that there must be an advance of borrowed funds in respect of which the relevant amounts are paid as compensation and not just a notional principal sum. The ambiguity is compounded by the requirement that an amount must accrue on a daily basis, which is the most restrictive of the three characteristics of the legal definition of interest. This requirement effectively means that any amount must be fixed from the outset of a borrowing (or calculable on a daily basis) and payable solely with the passage of time for the use of borrowed money. Only in that case can the amount be apportioned prospectively over the term of a borrowing and be said to accrue on a daily basis in the sense that it can be apportioned between two creditors in succession at any time. In most instances, the requirement of daily accrual means that an amount must be calculated as a fixed percentage of the stated principal sum and payable at periodic intervals. Indeed, it would seem that only interest in this strict sense of an amount calculated as a percentage of the principal and payable solely with the passage of time can satisfy the requirement of daily accrual under the legal definition of interest. The presence of any contingencies regarding the amount or timing of payments often means that the payments are not determinable on a daily basis from the outset of a borrowing and cannot be considered to accrue on that basis.

As has already been noted, Canadian and Australian courts have tended to adopt the legal definition of interest for income tax purposes. In particular, the courts in both countries have sometimes cited the characteristic of interest as an amount that accrues daily in support of its recognition on an accrual basis rather than a cash or payable/receivable basis.[35] Application of the legal definition is also evident in several cases in which the courts have considered particular characterization problems associated with fees and expenses incurred in the process of borrowing funds; penalty payments due on the occurrence of certain events such as the early maturity of a debt obligation; lump-sum amounts paid as bonuses or premiums for default risk assumed by lenders; discounts equal to the difference between the stated principal amount of debt obligations that must be repaid on maturity and the amount of funds advanced on the issue of the obligations ("original issue discount" or "OID"); payments based on indicators of a borrower's performance such as gross revenue or cash flow ("participating payments"); amounts based on movements in an index such as the consumer price index, a commodity index, or a share exchange ("indexed payments"); and late payment charges due on the failure to pay the purchase price of goods or services in a timely manner. In each of these instances, the question has arisen whether the relevant payments should be treated as compensation for the use of borrowed money referred to a principal sum in the strict sense of being calculated as a fixed percentage of that sum or calculated on a daily basis and apportioned over the term of a borrowing on that basis. Both Revenue Canada and the ATO have expressed the opinion in connection with certain of these problematic amounts that in the absence of a statutory definition of interest all three requirements of the restrictive legal definition must govern the characterization of the amounts.[36]

One result of the application of the restrictive legal definition of interest, and in particular the requirement of daily accrual, is a relatively narrow application of the general tax provisions applicable to interest expense and income. In particular, many amounts that would otherwise be considered costs within a broad concept of the cost of credit are neither deductible as interest expense nor taxable as interest income. Instead, they are considered to be non-deductible capital payments for borrowers and tax-preferred capital receipts for lenders. Yet they are functionally equivalent to interest if interest is viewed from a broader perspective—one that includes all financial charges representing compensation for the use of borrowed funds or the cost of credit. In effect, application of the restrictive concept of interest has created "discontinuities" and "inconsistencies" in the tax treatment of debt-financing charges.[37] A discontinuity arises when small changes in the nature of debt payments result in a disproportionately significant change in tax treatment; that is, in characterization for tax purposes as non-deductible capital amounts rather than as deductible interest.

Changes of this kind alter the risk characteristics of debt payments by introducing a contingency, other than the passage of time, that affects the amount or the timing of the payments. An inconsistency in tax treatment arises when equivalent cash flows are taxed differently solely because they are packaged in different legal forms.

An obvious example of a discontinuity attributable to the application of the legal definition of interest is the deductibility under the ITA of participating payments. Considerable doubt has surrounded the characterization of these payments as deductible interest expense, largely because their contingent nature makes it impossible to conclude that they accrue on a daily basis. Moreover, since the amount of a participating payment is often unlimited and not calculated as a percentage of the outstanding principal, it is difficult to conclude that these payments satisfy the required relation between interest and principal under the legal definition of interest. These interpretive difficulties have led Canadian courts to define three types of payments that represent the cost of borrowed funds and to assign a different treatment to each of them. The first type is non-contingent or fixed interest payments within the legal definition of interest, which are deductible on an accrual basis.[38] The second is participating payments that are theoretically unlimited in amount, which are not considered interest and which taxpayers may deduct on a five-year amortized basis as a cost incurred in the course of borrowing funds.[39] The third is participating payments limited in amount to a fixed percentage of the loan principal, which are deductible as interest but only once the relevant contingency is satisfied and the amount of the payment is certain.[40] For non-tax purposes, these differences in the nature of the cash flows affect the valuation of the particular instruments.[41] Under an ideal income tax that recognized annual changes in value, they would result in tax treatments that differed in degree but not in kind. Under the tax-cubbyhole system, defined in part by the legal definition of interest, small differences in cash flows, with consequent changes in value, can result in tax treatments that differ significantly in kind and not just in degree.[42] Similar discontinuities arise with indexed payments.[43]

An obvious example of an inconsistency in the taxation of debt cash flows is the exclusion of OID from the legal definition of interest. This exclusion apparently follows from the fact that the amount of the OID takes the legal form of a payment of the nominal principal or face amount of a debt obligation and does not, therefore, satisfy the required relation between interest and principal under the restrictive legal definition.[44] In short, the amount of the OID is part of the principal itself and is not, in form, compensation for the use of the principal; moreover, the amount cannot be said to be calculated as a percentage of the outstanding principal. This formalistic approach ignores the fact that an OID obligation provides cash flows that are equivalent to the payment and reinvestment of periodic interest at the same rate as the rate of return on the OID obligation.[45]

Over the years, both Canada and Australia have amended their legislation in order to modify the application of the restrictive legal definition of interest to particular payments that constitute the cost of credit. The relevant amendments under the ITA and the ITAA are surprisingly similar in structure and purpose. In general, they consist of two broad sets of provisions that are both based on an acceptance of the label or legal form of a security as indebtedness. Assuming that such an acceptance is appropriate, the goal of one set of provisions has been the similar treatment of interest within the restrictive legal definition and other debt-financing charges that are considered functionally equivalent. The basis for this similarity of treatment is a broader concept of interest that includes all charges for the provision of credit, whether in the form of a fee, fine, penalty, commission, or other, similar charge.

In both countries, for example, certain costs incurred in the course of borrowing funds used for an income-earning purpose are expressly deductible on a five-year amortized basis.[46] These costs include loan commitment fees, finder's fees, sales commissions, legal and accounting fees, advertising and valuation costs, guarantee fees, and premiums on an insurance policy required as security for a loan. Although these amounts are part of the cost of borrowing funds, they are not deductible as interest, since they are provided for services related to the borrowing and not as compensation for the use of the borrowed funds. It is possible to argue, however, that if there were no separate provision for these costs they would be hidden in the form of an increased amount of nominal interest payments, which would be treated as interest within the legal definition.

Similarly, specific provisions in both Canada and Australia allow borrowers to deduct certain amounts paid as a bonus or penalty on the early maturity of a debt obligation, and also amounts paid as consideration for a reduction in the rate of interest on a borrowing.[47] In general, these provisions permit a deduction on the premise that the relevant amounts are surrogates for interest obligations and are therefore part of the cost of borrowing. These amounts would not otherwise be deductible as interest, since they compensate the lender for the loss of the right to interest and not for the use of borrowed money. The amounts would also not be deductible as the cost of borrowing new funds, since they are normally paid as a cost of extinguishing an old borrowing. Nonetheless, the cash flows that arise from these contingencies are equivalent to the cash flows that would arise if the obligation were held to its original maturity, which would be treated as interest.

The second set of provisions consists of anti-avoidance rules designed to eliminate the cash-basis recognition of various interest surrogates such as tax-preferred capital receipts. This recognition might otherwise follow from the form of the relevant amounts as payments of the nominal principal under a debt obligation (that is, the stated face value) or as proceeds from the disposition of the obligation. Moreover, in the absence of specific provisions that require full inclusion on an accrual basis, these amounts may not be taxable until they are received, even though they represent compensation for the use of borrowed funds that is equivalent to periodic interest within the legal definition. The more important of these rules under the ITA require the holders of certain debt obligations to include a specified return in income on an annual accrual basis.

The specified return must be calculated by using actuarial principles and a compounding period of not less than one year that produce a present value for all payments equal to the cost of the obligation.[48] The rules apply to four general types of "prescribed debt obligations":

1) debt obligations with no stipulated interest (OID obligations under which the stated principal amount exceeds the amount advanced by the lender),

2) debt obligations under which the proportion of principal payments for a holder does not equal the proportion of interest payments ("stripped obligations," whereby the interest coupons on a debt obligation are stripped from the principal amount and sold separately),

3) debt obligations under which the maximum amount of interest payable in a year is less than the maximum amount of interest payable in a subsequent year ("deferred interest obligations" with accelerated or "balloon" interest), and

4) debt obligations with contingent interest payments (participating or contingent debt).

A similar set of provisions under the ITAA is designed to isolate the interest element in payments that take the form of capital amounts, and to require the accrual recognition of amounts that have the form of interest but whose payment is deferred under a debt obligation. These rules require full inclusion by lenders (while permitting deduction by borrowers) of certain deferred amounts (balloon interest), inflation-indexed amounts, and deep discounts (including the discount that arises on the stripping and separate sale of interest coupons and the principal portion of debt obligations) on "qualifying securities."[49] These securities are defined generally as debt obligations with a term in excess of 12 months for which the sum of all payments other than periodic interest exceeds the issue price and the deferred yield is greater than 1.5 percent annually. Recognition of the fixed return on a qualifying security must use the yield-to-maturity (YTM) method and apply it under an assumption of semi-annual compounding;[50] recognition of variable amounts must occur on an annual accrual basis and use reasonable estimates of the particular contingencies.[51]

Finally, the accrual rules in the ITA and the ITAA are also overlaid with a separate series of eclectic provisions that are designed to address similar kinds of financial equivalences in other limited circumstances. Some of the more significant provisions of this kind apply in the following circumstances and with the following results:

- On the transfer of a debt obligation, the amount of any accrued but unpaid interest may be deemed to be realized as interest income paid to the transferor by the transferee and not as proceeds of disposition giving rise to a capital gain.[52]
- On an instalment sale of property, a portion of the outstanding sale price may be deemed to be interest income of the vendor and not proceeds of disposition of the property.[53] These deeming rules usually apply when there is no stipulated interest and the sale price exceeds the value of the property at the time of sale. Indeed, the case law has established that in

these circumstances it may be assumed that a portion of the proceeds is disguised interest.[54]

- The ITA treats indexed amounts on "inflation-indexed debt" (defined as any debt obligation whose terms provide for an adjustment to an amount payable that is determined by reference to any change in the purchasing power of money) as interest income for the holder and interest expense for the issuer, despite the legal form of the payments as additions to the face amount of the obligation.[55] These indexed amounts are treated in the same way as the portion of nominal interest payments that compensates lenders for depreciation in the value of loan principal attributable to inflation.
- Under the ITA, a prepayment of interest expense may be treated as a repayment of loan principal in order to ensure that debt obligations that provide for prepayments are treated consistently with equivalent OID obligations.[56]
- Under ITA, the amount of otherwise deductible interest expense on certain weak-currency borrowings is limited to the amount of interest that would have been payable on an equivalent borrowing in another currency. Disallowed interest is deducted in computing the amount of foreign exchange gain or loss realized on repayment of the borrowing. Such gain or loss, as well as any gain or loss on a related hedge, is deemed to be on ordinary-income account.[57]

The Classification of Preferred Shares and Convertible Debt

In general, the classification of a financial instrument as debt or equity for the purposes of the ITA and the ITA depends on its form for private law purposes.[58] If that form is debt, related financing charges are treated as "interest," provided they satisfy the legal definition of that term. Payments on instruments that have the legal form of equity are generally treated as dividends.[59] In some instances, however, specific legislative provisions overturn the classification implied by an instrument's private law form. Thus legislation in Australia has reclassified some types of preferred shares and convertible debt. Canadian legislation has addressed only the treatment of preferred shares.

Preferred Shares and After-Tax Financing[60]

Preferred shares take the form of share capital for private law purposes, and as a general proposition they are considered for income tax purposes to be equity. Preferred-share dividends are generally calculated as a fixed percentage of the amount of capital contributed by the original holder, but since they are payable at the discretion of the board of directors they do not fall within the restrictive legal definition of interest. Moreover, the exercise of the board's discretion is subject to certain private law restrictions whose purpose is to ensure that preferred shareholders rank behind debt holders. These contingencies imply that preferred-share dividends are not payable solely with the passage of time and cannot be said to accrue daily. Nevertheless, preferred shares can sometimes be structured as functional equivalents to debt and used as more "tax-effective" debt substitutes. Not surprisingly, policy makers in both Canada and Australia have responded to this tax-driven use of preferred shares by departing from the straightforward formalistic classification of all preferred shares as equity.

In Canada in particular, preferred shares have long been used in "after-tax financing" transactions.[61] Defined broadly, a transaction of this kind is any tax-avoidance arrangement that uses a particular financial instrument to replicate the cash flows associated with another instrument that is subject to a different tax treatment solely because it has a different legal form. In the case of preferred shares, after-tax financing involves the substitution of tax-free intercorporate dividends for interest in order to reduce the cost of capital for issuers and to increase the after-tax return for investors. The success of this financing technique depends on a discontinuity that arises from the fact that debt and preferred shares with similar risk characteristics receive different tax treatment.

A simple example will illustrate this point. Assume that a corporation is financially strong but in a non-taxable position, either because of loss carry-overs or because of the availability of tax expenditures such as accelerated depreciation or investment tax credits. The cost of borrowing for a non-taxpaying corporation equals the before-tax amount of interest expense, since any deduction for the expense produces no tax saving. The return for a fully taxable lender, on the other hand, must be calculated on an after-tax basis, since interest income on the loan will be taxable. Instead of structuring the investment as a loan, the two parties can use preferred shares. Because of its non-taxable status, the issuer will be insensitive to the non-deductibility of dividend payments, and the lender will prefer tax-free intercorporate dividends. By adjusting the dividend rate, the parties can effectively trade the benefit of any tax saving that would otherwise be available to a taxable issuer that is paying deductible interest expense. For example, instead of $100 of interest expense that would be fully taxable to the lender at a rate of 40 percent, both parties would prefer a $70 dividend on preferred shares. In that case, the issuer lowers its cost of funds by $30 ($100 interest expense less $70 dividend) and the lender increases its after-tax return by $10 (a $70 tax-free intercorporate dividend instead of $60 in after-tax interest income). The government forgoes $40 in tax that it would have collected had the investment been structured as a loan. Because they provide a fixed income stream that will be paid periodically, preferred shares are an effective loan substitute if they are issued by a financially strong, non-taxpaying corporation. Furthermore, the shares can be given redemption and retraction rights that provide a term to maturity similar to the term of a loan. They can also be supported by shareholder guarantees or rights of conversion into debt of the issuer that will protect the investment in much the same way as a loan.

An alarming growth in after-tax financing on the basis of preferred shares in the 1970s forced the Canadian government to respond in 1978.[62] That response initially took the form of a denial of the deductibility of intercorporate dividends received by a financial institution on "term preferred shares" acquired in the ordinary course of its business. These instruments, which the tax authorities considered to be tax-driven loan substitutes, were defined to include any share with redemption and retraction features or any guarantee protection or right of conversion into a term preferred share or debt. The government limited its initial response to financial institutions on the assumption that they were the principal providers of after-tax financing. It soon became apparent, however, that the response was too limited. Preferred shares had other debt-like features that made them attractive as debt substitutes, and there were investors other than financial institutions willing to lend funds on the basis of preferred shares. After several attempts to deal with particular types of preferred shares, the Department of Finance introduced a comprehensive set of rules in 1987. These rules apply to "taxable preferred shares," which are defined broadly to include almost any preferred share with a fixed dividend entitlement, guarantee protection, or right of conversion into taxable preferred shares or debt.[63] Along with this change in definitional approach, the government legislated a series of special distributions taxes for taxable preferred-share dividends.[64] The taxes are imposed at different rates in order to ensure that some corporate tax is paid on the underlying income distributed as a tax-free intercorporate dividend.[65]

Australia introduced a similar provision, applicable to "debt dividends," in 1987. The provision denies the intercorporate dividend rebate and, since 1990, the ability to "frank" debt dividends, which are defined as any dividends paid as part of a financing arrangement that may reasonably be considered to be equivalent to the payment of interest on a loan.[66] Like the Canadian preferred-share rules, this provision has the obvious intent of preventing the substitution of tax-free dividends for taxable interest income. This substitution is most likely to involve preferred shares that have the form of equity but debt-like features, such as redemption and retraction rights and guarantee protection or a right of conversion into debt. Since the status of dividends as debt dividends is to be determined on the basis of the circumstances surrounding their payment and the issue of the particular shares, the definitional features specified in the Canadian taxable-preferred-share rules are generally relevant here. The denial of the intercorporate dividend rebate and of the ability to frank debt dividends ensures that the dividends are effectively taxable to the holders as interest. The dividends remain non-deductible distributions to the issuer, however, on the assumption that they are non-taxable.

Convertible Debt

Convertible debt is the formal coupling of a classical debt obligation with a call or put option on shares of the corporate borrower that is exercisable at a specified price and may be satisfied by converting the debt obligation at the specified ratio of shares to the stated principal amount.[67] The conversion right may be at the option of either the holder (call option) or the issuer (put option), and it is normally set at a predetermined ratio. The holder thus receives a fixed return with an equity upside in the form of either the conversion feature (call option) or an embedded option premium (put option). Conventional wisdom posits that the issuer is able to raise a deferred amount of equity capital and receives a concessionary interest rate or a premium on the issue of the debt obligation in recognition of an equity call option.

Convertible debt is equivalent to the separate acquisition of a corporate debt obligation and an option or warrant written on shares of the debtor.[68] Unlike the holder of a separate warrant, however, the holder of a convertible obligation must surrender the obligation on exercise of the equity option.[69] Under the ITA and the ITAA, the tax treatment of a convertible debt obligation generally follows its legal form, and the obligation is treated as debt until exercise of the conversion feature. Accordingly, the associated cash flows are treated as deductible interest expense for the issuer and interest income for the holder. Moreover, there is no general requirement to apportion the cost of the obligation between its principal amount and the equity option.[70] This treatment is subject to the denial of a deduction under the ITAA for interest expense on a convertible debt obligation that is considered to have predominant equity features.[71] More particularly, interest on a convertible debt obligation is not deductible unless certain conditions are satisfied. Failure to satisfy these conditions is taken as an indication that the obligation is a substitute for shares, presumably in an effort to provide a corporate interest deduction as a means of avoiding the corporate tax on underlying income that would otherwise be distributed as non-deductible dividends.[72]

Disguised Debt and Equity

In some instances, factors other than the formal rights and obligations associated with an instrument indicate that what appears to be equity is, in fact, disguised debt, and what appears to be debt is, in fact, disguised equity. The tax treatment of the associated cash flows may disregard the legal form of the instrument on the ground of its inconsistency with the perceived economic substance of the cash flows. Preferred shares issued as debt substitutes are a type of disguised debt, although the legislative responses in the ITA and the ITAA do not, strictly speaking, classify them as disguised debt. The legislative responses define the shares in terms of their formal rights and obligations, which combine elements of classical debt and classical equity. It is this hybrid nature that makes preferred shares useful as debt substitutes. Disguised debt is classical equity that is more properly regarded as debt because of the presence of factors other than the formal rights and obligations provided in the terms and conditions of the shares. Thus the Canadian preferred-share legislation recognizes that firms can effect after-tax financing by issuing shares that exhibit all of the formal features of classical equity but are, in fact, disguised debt. To prevent this type of avoidance, the ITA defines preferred shares that are considered to be debt substitutes as any shares for which the risk borne by the holder is reduced by providing, in collateral arrangements, the relevant retraction, redemption or conversion, loss protection, and fixed-dividend or liquidation entitlements. Under the ITAA, the existence of debt disguised as equity—a so-called debt dividend—must be determined by reference to the circumstances that surround the issue of the related share and the payment of any dividends; the presence of arrangements beyond the formal terms and conditions of the shares should be relevant to this determination.[73]

The most obvious examples of legislative attempts to address the tax-driven use of disguised equity are the thin capitalization provisions in the ITA and the ITAA, which apply to interest on debt of a resident corporation held by non-residents with a direct investment or controlling interest in the corporation.[74] In an effort to limit avoidance of the corporate tax by non-residents on domestic-source income, these provisions deny the deduction of interest and, in a limited sense, effectively treat the relevant obligations as equity despite their formal terms and conditions. This effective reclassification occurs if the equity capital base of a corporation held by certain non-resident shareholders is minimal (in terms of a specified debt-equity ratio). Debt of the thinly capitalized corporation is assumed to serve as equity despite its legal form. This conclusion follows from an assumption that all corporations must have a certain equity capital base that for tax reasons may effectively be provided in the form of debt. The legislation targets non-resident shareholders with a direct investment or controlling interest because they are more likely than other shareholders to neglect their ostensible rights as creditors and treat what appears to be debt as equity.

Extension of a Transactional Approach to the Tax Treatment of Forwards, Futures, Swaps, and Options[75]

Canadian and Australian tax-policy makers have largely neglected the tax treatment of the basic price-fixing instruments (forwards, futures, and swaps) and price-insurance instruments (options). Like the tax treatment of debt-financing charges, the taxation of these basic financial instruments (collectively referred to as "building-block derivatives")[76] is governed by general statutory provisions. Unlike the treatment of debt-financing charges, however, these general provisions have no obvious relation to any of the unique issues presented by derivatives. In other words, there are general provisions that apply to interest income and expense, and these provisions have been supplemented with specific provisions designed to ensure appropriate treatment of debt-financing charges that are considered to be functionally equivalent to interest. Except in the case of options held as capital assets, no general provisions apply to the building-block derivatives.

In the absence of statutory provisions and case law that address the taxation of derivatives, taxpayers have been left with the application of analogous case law and the administrative pronouncements of Revenue Canada and the ATO. Since the applicability of the reasoning in the analogous case law is often uncertain, the onus has been on the two tax administrations, which have responded in a less than comprehensive manner. The result is that uncertainty surrounds the tax treatment of the basic derivative financial instruments. This uncertainty affects the use of derivatives for either risk-management or tax-avoidance purposes. Like the formalistic distinction between debt and equity, the legal form of a derivative instrument may attract tax consequences that are inconsistent with the tax treatment of equivalent cash flows associated with another instrument. In keeping with their general approach to the taxation of derivatives, however, Australian and Canadian policy makers have made no attempt to address these instances with specific legislative responses comparable to those enacted in order to maintain the distinction between interest and dividends. In the absence of legislation, Revenue Canada and the ATO have relied on a transactional approach to the application of basic tax principles to particular derivatives. Out of necessity, this approach has developed in the context of the broad statutory provisions that govern the computation of capital gains and losses and business income generally.

From a strictly domestic perspective,[77] forwards, futures, swaps, and options present two principal tax issues under the ITA and the ITAA. The first issue is the characterization of gains and losses and any payment obligations as either ordinary income or capital amounts. The second issue is the timing of the recognition of these amounts.

Characterization

Since derivative instruments do not generate a current yield, they cannot be a source of income in the classical sense of a capital asset that a taxpayer acquires in order to obtain a current yield and that may, as an incidental matter, produce gain or loss on a disposition.[78] Instead, derivatives provide gain or loss only through fluctuations in their market value, which is realized on maturity of the instrument, its closing out, or its transfer to another party. The nature of the gains and losses on derivatives should lead to the characterization of the latter as assets on income account. The conventional approach to the characterization issue, however, focuses instead on the nature of the acquisition of the derivative; that is, on whether its acquisition is an independent transaction or a transaction that is linked to another, underlying one. In effect, the distinction between ordinary-income amounts and capital amounts takes the form in the case of derivatives of a distinction between (1) derivatives that are acquired as independent instruments and (2) derivatives that are acquired as a "hedge"; that is, derivatives characterized by a risk exposure that offsets the risk exposure associated with an underlying transaction.

A derivative is normally characterized as an independent transaction on income account if it is acquired by a taxpayer as part of the business of trading in financial instruments.[79] The relevant category of taxpayers includes market makers, such as investment bankers, banks, and other financial institutions, that acquire derivatives as part of their trading operations. A derivative may also be considered to be an independent transaction on income account if the taxpayer acquires it for the purpose of realizing a profit from speculation. As noted above, the ITA treats speculative transactions as adventures in the nature of trade and specifically includes them in the definition of a business.[80] The ITAA contains no specific provision governing speculative activities, but the ATO, supported by some case law, takes a similar view—namely, that gains and losses from speculative activities must be recognized under the relevant provisions for business income.[81] Characterization as a capital asset is generally reserved for derivatives that are linked to an underlying transaction on capital account.[82] In both Canada and Australia, however, the legal basis and rationale for this "linkage approach" is unclear. There are no statutory provisions that explicitly require the linkage approach; nor is there a large body of cases that expressly approve this approach. Apart from the handful of cases[83] that do imply an acceptance of the characterization of a derivative on the basis of a related underlying transaction, the strongest support for the linkage approach is the analogous case law that characterizes foreign exchange gains and losses as either income amounts or capital amounts on the basis of the character of a related transaction.[84]

In general, the case for the linkage approach seems to be based on the intuitively appealing proposition that, since risk exposure on the hedge is closely correlated with risk exposure on the underlying transaction, gains and losses on the hedge should be netted against gains and losses on the underlying.[85] In other words, the linkage approach attempts to treat the two transactions as one transaction, and to take the risk and return characteristics of the two transactions together. The alternative is to respect the formal independence of the transactions, but this approach can lead to "tax fragmentation"; that is, to one tax treatment for the hedge and another for the underlying transaction.[86]

What makes the linkage approach to the characterization of gains and losses on derivatives difficult is the problem of identifying the circumstances in which two transactions are related closely enough to be considered one transaction. Neither the courts nor Revenue Canada and the ATO have provided much guidance here,[87] and it remains unclear what degree of correlation there must be between an underlying transaction and its purported hedge to justify their treatment as a single entity. The problem is compounded by the fact that the purpose for which a derivative has been acquired does not depend on the character of the taxpayer. Traders and speculators commonly acquire some derivatives for trading and speculative purposes and other derivatives for hedging purposes. Other taxpayers, who normally acquire derivatives for hedging purposes, may occasionally acquire derivatives for speculative purposes.

What is needed is a set of identification criteria that taxpayers and the tax administration can apply on a transactional basis. In some cases, the courts have suggested that accounting treatment may be relevant, and a transaction that is treated as a hedge for accounting purposes will be treated as a hedge for tax purposes.[88] In other cases, the courts have ignored accounting evidence and examined particular factors such as[89]

- the quantum of the relevant items under the purported hedge and the underlying transaction,
- the comparative maturity dates of the two transactions,
- the degree of contemporaneousness in entering into the purported hedge and the underlying transaction, and
- the presence of an existing risk exposure (that is, not an anticipated exposure).

None of these factors appears to be determinative, and questions of form are often critical, such as some clear formal indication that a purported hedge was entered into for the purpose of hedging.[90] Moreover, the few cases in which hedging has been addressed through the linkage approach have all concerned simple instances of specific hedges, in which one transaction is entered into in contemplation of another identifiable transaction and is closely integrated with it.[91] These instances contrast with "general hedges," in which the purpose of a transaction is to alter the overall risk exposure of a business.[92] In the few Canadian cases that address transactions of this type, the courts have rejected the possibility of any link with identifiable transactions and characterized the purported hedges as independent transactions.[93]

The difficulties that surround the linkage approach occur with all of the basic derivative instruments used for hedging purposes. Revenue Canada and the ATO, however, have limited statements of their administrative positions on this issue to interest-rate swaps.[94] These few pronouncements have supported a linkage approach that characterizes swap payments as ordinary income, a result that mirrors the characterization of the underlying interest obligations to which the payments relate.[95] Indeed, both tax administrations have stated that they will link the particular swap to the relevant underlying borrowing and treat periodic swap payments in the same manner as interest on that borrowing.[96] Because currency swaps are comparable in structure to interest-rate swaps, this administrative position may apply to them as well.[97] If this is so, then periodic payments related to interest on swapped currency loans should be treated on revenue account to match the treatment of interest expense on the underlying borrowings.[98] Reasoning by analogy may similarly support an extension of the linkage approach to forward and futures contracts[99] and options. In fact, there is some support in the case law for characterizing gain or loss on options on the basis of the nature of the underlying asset.[100]

Extension of the linkage approach to forward-based contracts and options would mean that gains and losses on forward-rate agreements and interest-rate futures, and on caps, floors, and collars as well, should normally be on income account. Each of these instruments alters the taxpayer's exposure to interest rates, which produce fully taxable or deductible interest income and expense.[101] Ordinary-income treatment should also apply to commodity forwards, futures, and options that are acquired or sold for the purpose of hedging the price exposure of a trader in the underlying commodity. Capital-account treatment is probably properly limited to forwards, futures, and options on foreign currencies and shares or share price indexes, where the derivative instrument is used to hedge the price exposure associated with foreign currency assets or liabilities or shares held as capital assets.[102]

Timing

Forwards, Futures, and Swaps

In contrast to the characterization of gains and losses on derivative instruments, the timing of the recognition of these gains and losses is based on the assumption that individual instruments represent independent transactions.[103] Accounting practice, which attempts to match the timing of the recognition of gains and losses on a derivative acquired as a hedge with the recognition of gains and losses on the underlying transaction, has been ignored. Indeed, accounting practice is considered to be subject to specific statutory provisions and case law principles that have incorporated the realization principle as a basis for the recognition of capital gains and losses on all assets and liabilities, and for the computation of business income generally.

There are three broad timing principles that can be applied to gain or loss on derivatives:[104] (1) the cash basis, (2) the payable/receivable or realization basis, and (3) the accretion basis. Under the cash basis, revenue is recognized when it is received in cash (or an equivalent to cash) and expenses are recognized when they are paid. Under the realization basis, revenue is recognized when it becomes "receivable" and expenses are recognized when they are "payable." An amount is considered to be receivable when the taxpayer has an unconditional legal right to the amount (that is, the amount is "earned"). An expense is considered to be payable when the taxpayer is subject to an unconditional legal obligation and the amount is determinable (that is, the amount is "incurred"). The accretion basis requires the recognition of unrealized gains and losses as they are reflected in changes in the value of an asset.[105]

For the most part, Canadian and Australian courts have adopted the receivable/payable basis as the basic timing rule for the calculation of business income.[106] Similarly, as has already been noted, the legislation that governs capital gains and losses explicitly incorporates the realization principle as the principal timing rule. Perhaps not surprisingly, realization-based recognition has been extended generally to gains and losses on derivatives held on capital or income account.[107]

In the case of cash-settled forward and futures contracts, the realization principle requires that gains and losses be recognized when the contracts mature, which is normally the time for settlement in cash through the closeout procedure.[108] Realization may occur earlier if a contract is closed out before maturity by entry into an opposite contract with the futures clearing house or with the counterparty to an OTC forward.[109] At any of these times, the holder of the contract has an unconditional legal right or obligation with respect to any gain or loss represented by the value of the contract.[110] The gain or loss must be recognized as it is realized, and the fact that the contract may hedge an open position in an underlying asset or liability is irrelevant.[111]

In the case of interest-rate and currency swaps, the realization principle requires the recognition of periodic payments as they become receivable or payable at the end of each payment period.[112] This position follows from the fact that periodic payments under a swap cannot be considered to be interest and are not subject to the required accrual recognition of interest income and expense. The ATO initially accepted the realization principle for periodic payments on an interest-rate swap,[113] but it has since taken the position that the payments must be spread on a straightline accruals basis[114] over the relevant payment periods, particularly if the payments are made in arrears (that is, if the payments are due at the end of a calculation period).[115] This requirement applies to all taxpayers, whether or not the particular swap is acquired as a hedge of an underlying borrowing.[116]

It is not clear, however, that the ATO would seek to apply the straightline accruals basis beyond periodic payments on an interest-rate or currency swap. For example, the realization principle requires that any foreign exchange gain or loss on a currency swap be recognized when the gain or loss is realized on the re-exchange of the principal amounts and the repayment of the underlying borrowing. Similarly, if future swap receipts and payment obligations are monetized on the early termination of a swap, gain or loss equal to the amount of the payments is realized, and should be recognized, at that time.[117] Neither Revenue Canada nor the ATO has disputed this treatment and attempted to require counterparties to spread the realized gain or loss over the remaining term of the terminated swap or an underlying borrowing hedged by the swap. Indeed, the ATO has stated that it will apply the realization principle both to upfront payments made to induce a counterparty to enter into a swap and to prepayments by a counterparty of future periodic obligations (that is, the payment of periodic swap obligations before the beginning of a calculation period).[118] In these instances, the ATO will normally permit the payer to deduct the upfront or accelerated amounts as they become due or are incurred and will require inclusion by the payee at the same time.[119]

The recognition of periodic swap payments on a straightline accruals basis is an obvious exception to the application of the realization principle to gain or loss on derivatives. Another possible exception arises under both the ITA and the ITAA from the potential application of the lower of cost and fair market value rule to forward and futures contracts held for speculative and trading purposes. There is considerable uncertainty about the appropriate characterization of these instruments as "inventory" under the ITA and as "trading stock" under the ITAA. As was noted earlier, recognition of accrued losses through the application of the lower of cost and fair market value rule is limited to property that falls within the concepts of inventory and trading stock as defined in the respective legislation. The ATO has taken the position that both exchange-traded futures contracts and OTC forwards are not generally considered to be trading stock even when they are held by traders.[120] The basis for this position is that contracts of this kind are not acquired for resale to another party in the same manner as physical assets but are instead closed out with a clearing house, in the case of futures contracts, or with the other counterparty, in the case of an OTC forward.[121] The ITA specifically requires that all property, including derivatives, held by speculators as an adventure in the nature of trade be valued at its cost; thus it excludes property of this kind from the application of the lower of cost and fair market value rule.[122]

For traders who hold derivatives as inventory in the course of their business, there is some support for the application of the lower of cost and fair market value rule and the recognition of unrealized losses.[123] This support follows from a fairly simplistic view of inventory as all property relevant to the computation of business income.[124] Given this concept, gains and losses on forwards and futures, and receipts and payments on swaps as well, are relevant to the computation of income from a business if the instruments are held on income account.[125] The ITA, however, defines inventory as property whose cost or value is relevant to the computation of income from a business.[126] Although property includes both tangible items and intangible items such as the contractual rights under derivative instruments,[127] forwards, futures, and swaps provide for mutual obligations that usually make them zero-present-value instruments with no cost that could be relevant to the computation of business income. Obligations represented by any accrued loss that subsequently arises on a forward, future, or swap because of adverse price movements may be characterized as a contingent liability that is not deductible until the time arrives for satisfaction of the payment obligation itself.[128] In effect, the accrued loss is not attributable to any difference between the value and the cost of a forward, futures, or swap contract; it is instead an unanticipated loss that cannot be deducted until it is realized.[129]

The Special Case of Option Premium

The timing issues associated with the exercise, cash settlement, or expiry of call and put options are basically the same as those associated with forward and futures contracts. If the underlying property is physically delivered, the property is acquired and disposed of for an amount at least equal to the exercise price under the option.[130] Cash settlement gives rise to an income inclusion for the payer and an ordinary-income deduction for the payee, provided the option is on income account.[131] If the option is on capital account, cash settlement constitutes a disposition of the option.[132] The holder recognizes a capital gain equal to the amount owing on settlement in excess of the cost of the option (that is, the option premium). The issuer realizes a capital loss equal to the amount owing on settlement, which offsets the recognition of any gain represented by the premium received on the issue of the option.[133]

The unique timing problem that arises in the case of options is associated with the treatment of premium payments, which is determined in large measure by the distinction between income and capital amounts. For options that are held or sold as capital assets, the timing rules are set out in specific capital gains provisions in the ITA[134] and the ITAA.[135] These provisions generally deem the grant of an option to be the disposition of a property with a cost base of nil.

Consequently, the issuer of either a call option or a put option on capital account is required to recognize the amount of any premium as proceeds of disposition. Because the option has a nil cost base, the premium is effectively taxed as a capital gain on receipt.[136] If an option held on capital account expires unexercised, the holder realizes a capital loss equal to the amount of the premium paid to acquire it.[137] If the option is exercised and physically settled, specific capital gain provisions in the ITA[138] and the ITAA[139] apply to recharacterize the grant of the option as part of the subsequent transaction. In the case of a call option, the premium becomes part of the cost of the underlying property to the option holder and part of the proceeds of disposition for the issuer. In the case of a put option, the premium reduces both the proceeds of disposition of the underlying property for the holder and the cost of the property for the issuer.[140]

Premiums for options held on income account are not subject to any specific legislation. Under the general provisions that govern the computation of business income,[141] any such premium should be recognized as income by the issuer and may be deducted by the holder. The more difficult issue is the timing of the inclusion and the deduction. Although payable up front, the premium is arguably unearned until the option expires or is exercised, since until that time the issuer has an obligation to perform under the option and the latter may result in a loss.[142] Receipt of the premium is thereby subject to a contingency, and it should not be recognized until the contingency is resolved. The ATO, however, apparently rejects this argument and treats the issue of an option as a transaction separate from any liability that may arise when the option is exercised.[143] Under this characterization, the issuer is required to include the option premium in income as received on the theory that there is an unconditional right to retain it.[144] Revenue Canada, on the other hand, has stated that it will not require the inclusion of any option premium on receipt, at least in the case of publicly traded puts and calls written on instruments held on income account.[145] If the option is physically settled, Revenue Canada apparently treats the premium in the same manner as the premium received for an option on capital account.[146]

The recognition of option premium by a holder on income account is equally unclear. As an initial proposition, the premium may be deductible as it is paid.[147] Difficulties arise because of the possible application of the general prepaid expense provisions under the ITA[148] and the ITAA,[149] which might defer recognition of the premium on an amortized basis over the term of the particular option. Alternatively, for option traders, premiums might be considered to be the cost of inventory that is not deductible until a disposition on either exercise or expiry.[150] In this connection, Revenue Canada has stated that a financial institution must recognize the premium paid for a cap, floor, or collar over the term of the option in the future periods to which the premium can reasonably be considered to relate.[151] The basis for this position would seem to be that the premium is paid as consideration for services to be provided by the issuer in the future (that is, protection against adverse interest rate movements).[152] The same approach could, in theory, be extended to other options held by all taxpayers on income account. In the case of calls and puts on publicly traded instruments, however, Revenue Canada has stated that the holder may deduct premiums only on expiry, when the relevant amounts presumably become payable.[153]

The Apparent Limitations of Past Legislative Practice in a World of Financial Innovation

Grafting Piecemeal Amendments onto the Status Quo

The above account is not intended to be an exhaustive technical discussion; it has drawn on Canadian and Australian legislative experience to illustrate broadly the cubbyhole taxation of financial instruments and the transactional approach that tax-policy makers often adopt in an effort to maintain the cubbyholes' integrity. It is important to emphasize again that the income tax systems in these two countries (and most other OECD countries) are based on the following features:

- different tax treatments for ordinary-income amounts and capital amounts,
- different tax treatments for interest and dividends, and
- realization-based recognition of gains and losses other than interest.

In general, Canadian and Australian policy makers have relied on basic legislative provisions that prescribe the tax treatment of the return on certain standard debt and equity instruments. When an unconventional instrument is developed, the initial response is to fit its associated cash flows somehow within the general legislative provisions for debt and equity. This response may be administrative, judicial, or legislative. It may involve the development of new administrative practice, or recourse to analogous case law that is relevant to the interpretation and application of the general provisions, or the enactment of specific legislation—provided that the stakes are high enough and the tax consequences uncertain enough to preclude reliance on administrative practice or the courts.

It is in this manner that policy makers in the two countries have approached the tax treatment of forwards, futures, swaps, and options. Largely through administrative practice, the tax treatment of the cash flows associated with these building-block derivatives has developed independently in the context of the general provisions that govern the computation of business income and capital gains and losses. Virtually no attention has been given to the more sophisticated combinations of these basic instruments that have been developed for either risk-management or tax-avoidance purposes.

The result of this approach is a series of ad hoc responses—administrative, judicial, or legislative—to particular financial instruments, responses that are grafted onto a core set of provisions that provide for the basic tax treatment of classical debt and equity instruments. For the most part, this transactional approach lacks any underlying theoretical principles; it is formulated, instead, as a series of reactions intended to maintain the different tax regimes that apply to specified categories of instruments and returns. Although there is often some vague attempt to transcend these categories, with their basis in legal form, in order to develop a tax rule based on perceived economic substance, for a broad range of financial instruments there is no clear view of what that substance is. In fact, the reliance on legal form is predominant; it is interrupted only occasionally by government responses to apparent financial equivalences that have different tax results.

In spite of the glaring gaps and anomalies in the tax regimes in Canada and Australia, it is possible to argue that the current provisions in the ITA and the ITAA are effective in limited respects. In particular, they ensure that almost all basic financing charges are deductible in much the same manner as interest even though they do not fall within the legal definition of interest. They also ensure that holders recognize as interest, on an annual accrual basis, many types of common financial returns that are equivalent to interest. It is interesting to note in this connection that tax practitioners in Canada have long advocated the adoption of a wider concept of the cost of borrowed funds that is deductible on the same basis as business expenses generally.[154] Their position assumes that the courts have adopted the legal definition of interest for tax purposes and that this definition is, in fact, too restrictive. Although a close analysis of the case law casts some doubt on the first assumption, there is also some support for it.[155] The second assumption is somewhat misleading. The current transactional approach under the ITA and the ITAA provides for the inclusion and deduction of a broad range of basic debt-financing charges that are equivalent to interest in a manner similar to interest in its strict sense under the legal definition. These provisions are usefully supplemented with some specific anti-avoidance measures intended to eliminate a limited range of tax-driven financings that use preferred shares, convertible debt, and disguised equity of thinly capitalized corporations.

Admittedly, it would be useful to amend the core provisions that prescribe the tax treatment of interest income and expense to correct perceived anomalies. In the Canadian context, an obvious amendment would be an extension of the accrual rules for prescribed debt obligations to provide an annual accrual deduction that parallels the recognition of income by holders. In the Australian context, it would make sense to clarify the application of the accrual principle established in the legislation and to extend it to obligations outside of the existing rules. In particular, accrual recognition should be extended to individuals and non-financial corporations in respect of debt obligations that are not "qualified securities" otherwise subject to the accrual rules. If amendments of this kind were made to rationalize the tax treatment of all charges that represent the cost of credit, a reasonable case could be made for the present treatment, at least in a general sense, of basic debt-financing charges and simple financial equivalences.

Limited amendments of this kind would be generally consistent with past legislative practice in Canada and Australia. It would be possible, moreover, to extend the transactional approach to legislation that governs the taxation of forwards, futures, swaps, and options. The result would be a series of self-contained provisions like those that currently govern the taxation of options held or issued on capital account; these provisions would reflect and clarify current administrative practice and extend it to all of these basic instruments. Like the provisions intended to equate the tax treatment of certain costs of credit with the treatment of interest within the restrictive legal definition, legislation that governed the taxation of the building-block instruments would generally be enabling in nature; that is, its purpose would be to clarify the fundamental tax treatment of these instruments in order to remove any tax barriers to their use for risk-management purposes. As will be discussed in chapters 5 and 6, avoidance arrangements, such as commodity straddles and loans disguised as accelerated swap payments or deep-in-the-money options, could be dealt with specifically.[156] A more difficult problem, one that will be discussed in chapter 7,[157] would be the design of a statutory test to determine whether it is appropriate to treat a particular derivative as a hedge of another, underlying transaction. Even this problem is not insurmountable, at least in some circumstances. In particular, the purported hedge would have to provide a payoff profile that varied inversely with an identified underlying transaction; it would also have to be acquired at the same time as the underlying asset and held for the same period. In these circumstances, it would be reasonable to conclude that the derivative was closely correlated with the underlying transaction and therefore intended to hedge the associated risk.

This continued transactional approach to the taxation of financial instruments has been characterized by an Australian tax practitioner as "the status quo," involving "more rulings and determinations and occasional ad hoc pieces of legislation devoted to particular situations (usually of an anti-avoidance nature)."[158] As the above review has shown, the current law in Canada and Australia is a patchwork of general and specific legislative provisions, case law, and administrative positions that arguably requires an overhaul. Superficially at least, a continued transactional approach appears only to compound the problems associated with the current patchwork of rules. The same tax practitioner has compared the Australian legislation to

> a very badly constructed jigsaw puzzle. Many of the pieces are missing, pieces are forced into the wrong spots, pieces from other puzzles have been mixed in and, perhaps most importantly, the puzzle came without a picture of the completed work, so nobody is quite sure what it is supposed to look like, even assuming it is possible to find enough pieces to "finish" it.[159]

The state of affairs captured in this comparison, which applies with equal force to the legislative approach in Canada, is often criticized by taxpayers, practitioners, and tax administrators as the cause of (1) too much uncertainty in the tax consequences associated with many financial instruments, (2) non-neutralities in tax treatment that affect the pricing of financial instruments, (3) tax-avoidance opportunities, and (4) excessive administrative and compliance costs. These shortcomings, however, are merely symptomatic of the deeper problems that afflict the status quo. The more fundamental search must be for the cause of the symptoms. In other words, tax-policy makers must identify the characteristics of financial innovation that make it difficult to maintain the existing tax cubby-holes and the associated differences between the taxation of capital income and the taxation of ordinary income, between the taxation of interest and the taxation of dividends, and between accrual and realization-based recognition of gains and losses. This identification process produces some important insights into why a transactional approach to the taxation of financial instruments may be inadequate.

The process also suggests some of the desirable design features of alternative approaches that in some respects are not radically different from past legislative practice and the extension of a piecemeal legislative agenda. In fact, once the underlying problems presented by financial innovation have been identified, governments can address them under either a comprehensive legislative regime or further piecemeal reforms that build on selected aspects of the status quo. The choice of a legislative approach is an irrelevant matter of form. Indeed, as will be argued in the following chapters, much past legislative practice needs only to be massaged in several important respects, a task that can be achieved on an ad hoc basis. As a practical matter, the design of a comprehensive legislative regime may be desirable largely because it would provide a convenient occasion for implementing necessary structural reforms in a manner that integrated all of the required pieces into a coherent whole.

Structural Reform and a Comprehensive Legislative Regime

A major problem with the tinkering characteristic of the transactional approach is that in the new financial environment the status quo it seeks to sustain is no longer sustainable. Any legislative agenda, piecemeal or comprehensive, must overturn certain fundamental aspects of the status quo. This fact manifests itself in a characteristic of the current state of the law in both Canada and Australia—the absence of one overriding tax treatment potentially applicable to all relationships that take a specified legal form or some economic equivalent. Instead, several different treatments apply to various types of financial instruments that combine the characteristics of two or more other instruments. A more suitable legislative regime would be based on a rational set of guiding principles that would apply to all financial instruments and therefore would realize a measure of consistent taxation of equivalent cash flows. Continued acceptance of the distinctions between ordinary income and capital amounts and between interest and dividends would make achievement of this goal difficult, if not impossible. On the other hand, it would be possible to construct a defensible approach to the taxation of financial instruments around the distinction between accrual-based and realization-based recognition of gains and losses.

As an example of the problems that arise from the inconsistency of the current tax regime, consider the simple case of a convertible debt obligation.[160] As was noted earlier, one may view an obligation of this kind as the equivalent of both a debt obligation and an option to acquire the relevant shares at a specified exercise price. Under a convertible obligation, the holder pays for this option by accepting a reduced interest rate for the term of the debt obligation. Option premium that might not otherwise be deductible to the holder on income account is effectively amortized over the term of the obligation and deducted in full in the form of a reduced amount of taxable interest income. To reverse this result, it is necessary only to break down a convertible debt obligation into its equivalent of (1) a straight debt obligation with a market interest rate and (2) a call option on shares of the issuer with an appropriate premium payment. The holder will recognize interest income at the higher market rate, and the excess above the actual rate will be treated as non-deductible option premium. This situation, which is based on an identification of financial equivalences, becomes problematic, however, when it is realized that the result for the holder of a convertible bond can also be achieved through the combination of (1) a purchase of shares of the issuer and (2) the acquisition of a put option exercisable at the same price and over the same term as the call option embedded in a convertible obligation. This financial position is equivalent to a convertible debt obligation or to the combination of a straight debt obligation and the acquisition of a call option on shares of the issuer, but because of the substitution of shares for debt it is taxed very differently. The simple equivalences and apparent economic substance of a convertible obligation are no longer so obvious when it is so easy to replicate the risk and return mix by using other financial instruments with specified tax treatments different from those implied by the perceived paradigm.

The fact that it is possible to alter the tax treatment of the cash flows associated with a particular financial instrument by altering the instrument's legal form is the cause of tax-driven financial innovation. In essence, the arbitrage pricing relationships among the basic building-block instruments of financial innovation permit the replication of equivalent cash flows in a variety of forms, to which a variety of tax treatments apply. Reasonably enough, this state of affairs offends an intuitive sense that equivalent financial instruments or positions should be taxed consistently.

Although the problems presented by the varying tax treatments of equivalent cash flows seem self-evident, the system is reasonably clear and workable when the range of financial instruments that must be categorized is limited.[161] Problems begin to arise as some instances of financial equivalences occur that expose the arbitrariness of the differences in tax treatments across financial instruments. Yet as long as these instances are not numerous, they can be addressed and the system held together by a limited number of ad hoc responses. In the end, however, this transactional approach only papers over the system's lack of rational guiding principles. As the instances of financial equivalences that receive differing tax treatments multiply, the system becomes confused and, ultimately, untenable.

In effect, there are now four general types of financial instruments: classical debt, classical equity, the building-block derivatives, and a residual category of new financial instruments that combine elements of the other types. Classical debt and equity, and many of the new financial instruments as well, involve an initial transfer of funds made in the expectation that the issuer will return to the holder an amount greater than the initial amount. The return on these instruments compensates the investor for the use of the transferred funds; the instruments differ only in the degree of certainty they provide about the amount that will be returned to the investor. As to derivatives, it is important to note that they are not "radically different"[162] from traditional financing instruments and risk management techniques that use conventional insurance. In this connection, it is also important to emphasize again that the building-block derivatives come in only two basic types:[163] forward-based contracts (including futures and swaps) and options (including caps, floors, and interest-rate collars). Forward contracts are price-fixing instruments; they are analogous to annuity contracts in that the counterparties provide for payment to be made unconditionally on a specified future date.[164] Unlike an option or an annuity, a forward provides for offsetting mutual obligations. No premium or fee is paid upfront, since movements in the underlying transaction may cause either of the counterparties to realize gain or loss on the specified date. Options are price-insurance instruments; they are analogous to standard insurance contracts in that payment is to be made by the issuer (the insurer) on the occurrence of a specified contingency.[165] The holder (the policy holder) must pay a premium or fee to acquire the right to require payment on the occurrence of the contingency.[166]

Despite their straightforwardness (at least in their basic forms), derivatives lie at the root of many of the problems associated with the taxation of financial instruments; their use as the basic building blocks of financial innovation challenges the accepted tax treatments and their related cubbyholes. Indeed, this challenge arises from the nature of the returns on financial instruments of any kind. These returns consist of one or more of three basic elements.[167] The first element is a pure "time value of money return," or the expected gain that compensates a person for the use of his money ("the riskless rate of return"). The second element is the unexpected gain or loss realized on winning or losing a bet on a specified outcome. The third element is compensation for the assumption of undiversifiable risk[168] ("risk premium"); it often takes the form of expected gain in excess of the riskless rate of return. The portion of a return that is attributable to the time-value element depends on the amount of funds or capital provided by the investor and on how long the funds are made available to the user. The portion of the return that is attributable to the bet element depends on the investor's success or failure in assuming a given risk, and the portion that is attributable to the risk premium depends on his or her willingness to assume that risk.

As was described in chapter 1, the return on financial instruments (and the instruments themselves) may be viewed as a continuum of possibilities. At one end, there is the pure time-value return, represented by riskless government debt that pays interest at a floating rate. This type of instrument provides the holder solely with a return that compensates for the use of the funds borrowed by the government. At the other end of the continuum is the pure bet provided by forward, futures, and swap contracts, which require no upfront payment by either counterparty. In the case of these instruments, the parties specify an outcome that will pay off for one of them, and since the chances that the outcome will occur or not occur are equal, there is no initial transfer of funds. The only return to either party is the gain or loss that results when the specified outcome occurs or fails to occur. Between these two extremes, there are returns based on both the time value of money and a bet on specified outcomes.

In fact, the return on most financial instruments is a combination of the conceptually distinct time-value and risk or bet elements. Obvious examples of instruments that produce mixed returns of this kind are the standard capital-raising financial instruments and the cash-settled option. For example, a debt obligation with a fixed interest rate provides the holder with compensation for the use of the borrowed funds, but it also contains (1) a bet on future fluctuations in interest rates and (2) compensation for the assumption of credit risk. If rates increase, the value of the fixed-rate obligation decreases; conversely, a decrease in rates increases the value of the obligation. The lender also assumes some risk that the borrower will be unable to fulfill the specified payment obligations. Similarly, the relation between the amount of an option premium and the exercise price reflects both (1) a time-value element, which compensates the holder for the use of the option premium by the issuer, and (2) a risk element, which is reflected in the possibility that the price of the underlying asset will exceed or be exceeded by the exercise price.[169] Common shares also provide both a time-value return and a risk element; the latter is reflected in the possibility that the shares will produce a return in excess of the riskless rate.[170] Preferred shares provide a fixed return that compensates the holder for the use of his funds, but there is also a risk that the return will not be paid or will exceed the market rate. Convertible debt is a combination of the time-value return associated with a fixed-payment debt instrument and the risk associated with an embedded option that permits conversion of the debt into shares of the issuer.

The distinctions for tax purposes between capital amounts and ordinary-income amounts, between interest and dividends, and between realization-based recognition and accrual recognition are loosely based on the distinction between expected time-value returns and the unexpected gains and losses associated with risk. Accrual recognition on ordinary-income account is limited to the expected time-value return on debt, which is considered to be predominant. Returns on shares and derivatives are assumed to be primarily attributable to the assumption of risk and are taxed on realization; depending on the holder's purpose in acquiring the instrument, they may even be considered to be on capital account.[171] These differences in tax treatment and the distinctions on which they depend have proved difficult to maintain in the face of the recent multiplication of sophisticated new instruments that combine time-value and risk elements in different proportions.

These new instruments exploit the equivalences among debt, shares, and derivatives that are expressed by put-call parity and the other parities described in chapter 1.[172] In effect, it is possible to combine the basic building-block instruments in ways that replicate the cash flows associated with other instruments or combinations of instruments with different tax consequences. Indeed, a review of the tax literature over the past 15 years yields a large inventory of specific instruments and combinations that have been constructed as financial equivalents for various purposes, including tax avoidance.[173] This literature illustrates a fact that tax practitioners, administrators, and policy makers have been aware of (albeit anecdotally) for some time—that the opportunities for tax avoidance implicit in these financial equivalences are no longer just theoretical possibilities. Capital markets have matured to the extent that taxpayers can now implement many avoidance strategies at relatively low transaction costs.

Warren has made much the same point in considerable detail.[174] He argues that accepted principles of financial theory render meaningless the current practice of imposing accrual recognition of fixed-payment obligations and realization-based recognition of contingent returns, given the availability of sophisticated financial equivalences, based on derivative financial instruments, that permit the replication of assets of either type by assets of the other type. As Warren points out, there are two equivalences of this kind, put/call parity and dynamic hedging;[175] they both permit the creation of simple and complex identical positions that are taxed differently. These equivalences undermine the tax system by effectively allowing taxpayers to elect taxation on either an accrual basis or a realization basis. Moreover, the fact that different taxpayers face different tax rates makes it unlikely that any benefit for one taxpayer is offset by a detriment to another.[176] The differences between the tax treatment of ordinary income and the tax treatment of capital amounts, and between the treatment of interest and the treatment of dividends, are permanent differences that overlay and exacerbate the timing problem. In effect, taxpayers can substitute one type of receipt or expense for the other, without altering the pattern of cash flows.

Chapters 6 and 7 will discuss the particulars of complex financial instruments, including the specifics of their construction and the challenges they present for an income tax system. Although the distinction is not necessarily of any analytical significance,[177] it is useful to sort the more sophisticated financial instruments that have appeared over the past 15 years into two categories, "hybrids" and "synthetics." Hybrids combine an expected time-value return with an unexpected gain or loss attributable to a bet element. They fold two or more separate instruments into one legally distinct instrument ("internal financial engineering").[178] Synthetics combine two or more legally distinct instruments in order to replicate the cash flow pattern associated with another legally distinct instrument ("external financial engineering").[179] Whatever the significance of the labels, both categories include combinations of (1) rights and obligations normally associated with classical debt and classical equity, (2) debt and derivatives, (3) equity and derivatives, and (4) different types of derivatives. The result is an array of new instruments with a range of risk and return characteristics broad enough to provide for every type of financial equivalence.

The emergence of these new instruments has not created new problems; it has simply exacerbated old ones. As this chapter has described, the restrictive concept of interest and a reliance on the form of instruments as debt or equity have long allowed taxpayers to exploit differences in tax treatment by substituting deferred amounts realized as capital gains for periodic interest income, tax-exempt intercorporate dividends for taxable interest income, and tax-deductible interest expense for non-deductible dividends. These substitutions are accomplished by altering the form of the investment to realize a particular tax treatment without substantially altering the pattern of cash flows. By broadening the range of possible financial equivalences, the development of derivatives has broadened the range of possible manipulations of tax systems on the basis of untenable differences in tax treatment. In theory, therefore, derivatives present a general tax issue that tax-policy makers have faced in the past. The multiplication of derivatives has simply exposed the longstanding fundamental weaknesses of income tax systems in a much starker fashion.

Another important problem is that the tax system's lack of certainty in dealing with complex financial instruments may create tax barriers to the efficient use of these instruments for non-tax purposes. This problem is most especially likely to arise when taxpayers use complex combinations of derivatives in order to manage risk. Like the tax-driven use of derivatives, the use of derivatives to manage risk is often based on sophisticated combinations that recognize financial equivalences and take advantage of arbitrage opportunities.[180] Again, however, the significance of these equivalences for tax purposes is nothing new. As was noted above, the appropriate recognition of two or more transactions as composite transactions is an issue that the tax systems in Canada, Australia, and other countries have long sought to address, albeit with limited success. The same issue presents itself in the case of very crude and simplistic uses of the basic forward, futures, swap, and option contracts for hedging purposes. More sophisticated combinations of derivatives intended to alter the risk exposure of taxpayers are simply more sophisticated hedging techniques that may be extremely difficult to identify and treat appropriately on the basis of some other linked transaction. Under the more sophisticated risk-management techniques, there is usually no obvious single transaction or set of transactions that it is possible to link with particular positions in derivative instruments or combinations of them. Similarly, forwards, futures, and options may be combined and embedded in a single financial instrument that is more sophisticated than a convertible debt obligation. Neither the ITA nor the ITAA provides explicit rules for the taxation of the building-block derivative instruments, let alone combinations of such derivatives held separately within a portfolio or combined within a single instrument. The result is a problem of "universality," whereby it is often difficult to determine the appropriate tax treatment for a particular instrument.[181]

Ideally, tax-avoidance opportunities and pricing distortions created by uncertainty in tax treatment would be corrected by addressing the incongruence of the cubbyhole approach and the underlying economics of financial equivalences. The significant policy question is how best to correct that incongruence in a second-best world of practical policy constraints. The search should be for an alternative approach that provides some measure of comprehensiveness, at least at the level of principle. Given a set of sensible general principles that attempt to minimize differences in tax treatment (and the attendant tax cubbyholes), it should then be possible to develop coherently appropriate tax treatments for particular financial instruments. The new system should be designed to realize greater consistency in taxation among the building-block derivative instruments, an outcome that would help to address the tax-avoidance opportunities presented by hybrid and synthetic instruments and go some way toward ensuring that derivatives used for risk-management purposes were used efficiently.[182]

Any effort to address the results of financial innovation systematically must give some consideration to the costs and benefits associated with comprehensive legislative approaches. A useful starting point would be to measure both various second-best approaches of this kind and the ad hoc responses characteristic of past legislative practice against the theoretical first-best approach—the annual recognition of all unrealized changes in the value of financial instruments. This benchmark of market-value accounting ("accretion taxation")[183] eliminates all of the differences in tax treatment of functionally equivalent cash flows that are the source of avoidance opportunities and non-neutralities. There is little doubt, however, that certain practical policy constraints would prevent the adoption of this first-best response. The alternative is to consider the various second-best solutions on the basis of how closely they approximate the theoretical benchmark.

Given this alternative, the distinction between expected gains and losses and unexpected gains and losses is critical. Any benchmark approach to the taxation of financial instruments (and any comprehensive legislative regime that attempts to implement some of its dictates) must begin by addressing the appropriate taxation of the basic building-block instruments of financial innovation. Indeed, many commentators attribute the inadequacy of the status quo, as reflected in past legislative practice, to a failure to design appropriate rules for the taxation of the building-block instruments, whether the use of these instruments is driven by tax avoidance or by risk management. In turn, however, much of that failure is attributable to an apparent failure to appreciate fully the implications for tax policy of the critical distinction between expected time-value returns and unexpected gains and losses attributable to a bet element. In essence, ad hoc responses fail to address in a comprehensive and fundamental manner the fact that opportunities exist to disguise expected time-value gains as unexpected amounts, or vice versa. Once the policy implications of this fact are fully understood, it becomes possible to implement appropriate rules for the basic building-block instruments.

In fact, a review of the basic tax-policy issues that centres on a distinction between expected and unexpected gains and losses reveals that many aspects of the existing cubbyhole approach to the taxation of the building-block financial instruments are consistent with certain comprehensive second-best approaches. In particular, the approach recommended in this book, referred to as "expected-return taxation,"[184] is based on a general acceptance of the realization basis for unexpected gains and losses and the implementation of accrual recognition for expected gains and losses. Expected-return taxation reflects many aspects of existing legislative regimes, including

- realization-based recognition of unexpected gains and losses associated with forwards, futures, and swap contracts; and
- accrual recognition of the expected gains and losses on fixed-payment debt.

Fully realized expected-return taxation, however, would require some substantial modifications of existing regimes, including

- the elimination of the distinction between ordinary income and capital amounts;
- the extension of accrual recognition to the expected return attributable to the embedded debt in options and prepaid forward and swap contracts;
- the extension of accrual recognition to the expected return associated with the fixed-payment debt element in all contingent-payment debt instruments with embedded derivatives; and
- the application of accretion recognition to unexpected gains and losses on certain instruments that give rise to problems of "selective realization."

Moreover, although any approach to the taxation of financial instruments other than accretion taxation cannot address completely the more problematic complex instruments, some of the challenges presented by these instruments disappear under a comprehensive system of expected-return taxation. To be brief, because complex instruments are composites of the basic building blocks, the development of appropriate rules for the taxation of the more fundamental instruments would eliminate many tax-avoidance opportunities that depend on differences between the separate taxation of the component parts of a synthetic and the taxation of the whole. In order to achieve this elimination, it would be necessary to distinguish the expected gains and losses generated by a financial instrument from the unexpected gains and losses and treat them differently. In other words, it should be possible to provide consistent tax treatment of equivalent cash flows, defined in terms of the distinction between expected and unexpected amounts, in a manner that encompasses all of the basic building-block instruments and, therefore, all hybrid and synthetic instruments as well.

Thus an understanding of the challenges presented by hybrids and synthetics, and hence the effectiveness of various responses to their use, depends upon an understanding of the policy problems raised by the building-block instruments and the rules that establish their tax treatment. The following chapter attempts to frame these policy issues in terms of (1) the structural features of a benchmark approach to the taxation of financial instruments and (2) a system of expected-return taxation that provides a defensible second-best alternative.

3

The Elements of a Benchmark Approach to Financial Instruments Under an Income Tax

Introduction

The conclusions set out at the end of chapter 2 have also appeared in the relevant tax literature in the United States.[1] Although the US writers vary in their views of some aspects of the tax treatment of financial instruments, they tend to agree on one point: the use of derivative instruments to create new risk and return combinations complicates the attempt to design a satisfactory set of comprehensive tax rules. In other words, any comprehensive attempt to classify and tax financial instruments must take into account the infinite combinations of risk and return available with the creative use of derivatives. Yet unless there is some fundamental rethinking of the realization-based recognition of gains and losses, the use of different tax treatments for interest and dividends, and the distinction between ordinary income and capital amounts, any such attempt may be futile.

This general conclusion is developed at a sophisticated conceptual level by Strnad,[2] who cites these three structural features of most income tax systems as sources of inconsistencies and discontinuities that taxpayers can exploit. He defines "inconsistencies" to include instances in which identical cash flows are taxed differently because they are packaged in different legal forms. His definition of "discontinuities" includes instances in which a small change in the risk characteristics associated with a cash flow results in a disproportionately significant change in the tax treatment of the cash flow. Taxpayers exploit inconsistencies by packaging the cash flows associated with a traditional instrument in a new instrument that receives a different tax treatment, even though the sum of the components of the new instrument is equivalent to that associated with a conventional instrument. Discontinuities can be exploited by designing new instruments that permit taxpayers to approach the boundary between two distinct tax treatments as closely as possible without actually crossing it.

Chapter 2's discussion of experience in Canada and Australia provided examples of these two tax-avoidance techniques and made the point that the principal source of inconsistencies and discontinuities is a reliance on differences in risk as the basis for much of the variation in the tax treatment of financial instruments.[3] Perceptions about risk underlie (1) the adoption of accrual recognition for fixed returns and realization-based recognition for contingent returns, (2) the distinction for tax purposes between interest and dividends, and (3) the tax-subsidy arguments in favour of a capital gains preference for shares.[4] Instead of indicating differences in degree and thus having only a limited effect on the valuation of financial assets, perceptions regarding risk underlie the maintenance of the tax cubbyholes, which provide tax treatments that differ in kind. These differences are the focal points for "jumps" in tax treatment and the associated discontinuities.

Strnad emphasizes the need for fundamental reform to eliminate the variations in tax treatment that are the source of inconsistencies and discontinuities.[5] In the absence of fundamental reform, he argues that any attempt to design a comprehensive regime for the taxation of financial instruments will fail to provide consistent tax treatment for all instruments.[6] Brooks and Head[7] make much the same point in developing their model of tax avoidance, which they define broadly as any behavioural adjustment to differences in taxation. They describe capital-income taxation as "a major disaster area in the income tax systems of industrial countries"[8]—a state of affairs that they attribute to the high substitutability of various sources of capital income. This substitutability, which provides opportunities for tax avoidance whenever a given source and its substitute are taxed differently, may result in revenue losses and efficiency costs; it may also have equity effects.[9]

Brooks and Head observe that these perceived costs and effects depend on a distinction made in the economics literature between "pure" and "approximate" tax avoidance. Pure tax avoidance attempts to take advantage of inconsistent taxation of equivalent cash flows; it involves "purely paper transactions"[10] that attempt to arbitrage differences in tax treatment without altering the cash flow pattern.[11] This type of avoidance does not directly entail any efficiency costs.[12] It does, however, entail revenue loss (and savings for the taxpayer) that the government must recover by either taxing other sources of income at higher rates or reducing spending. Increased taxes on other sources may entail efficiency losses, and reductions in spending may have significant distributional consequences.[13] All other types of tax avoidance attempt to take advantage of discontinuities in the taxation of cash flows. These instances of approximate tax avoidance[14] involve the substitution of one type of transaction for another with a slightly different cash flow pattern; as a result, they involve direct efficiency costs[15] as well as revenue loss.[16]

Brooks and Head argue that capital income taxation provides a broad range of opportunities for avoidance because increasingly mature capital markets have developed an ever-increasing number of financial instruments that are close or even perfect substitutes for other instruments. The fact that it is possible to arbitrage the differences in tax treatment between the cash flows associated with instruments that are substitutable for one another makes these differences in tax treatment untenable.[17] Thus Brooks and Head reach much the same conclusion as Strnad reaches. They argue that the most effective strategy for reform of the taxation of capital income is an expansion of the tax base to eliminate the differences in tax treatment that are the sources of avoidance opportunities.[18] This expansion must approximate as closely as possible the Haig-Simons income base[19] and its two fundamental prescriptions:

1) the equivalent tax treatment of different sources of income and

2) the recognition of gains and losses as they arise with changes in the value of assets and liabilities.[20]

Indeed, many writers have concluded that the best way to eliminate tax-avoidance opportunities in capital markets would be to adopt a benchmark income tax system, modelled on the Haig-Simons ideal, that incorporated three fundamental principles for the taxation of all financial instruments, including shares:

1) recognition of changes in value by marking to market all financial instruments ("accretion taxation"),[21]

2) elimination of the corporate income tax and its replacement with a tax at the investor level on changes in the value of all financial instruments, and

3) inclusion and deduction of the full amount of all gains and losses.

The next two parts of this chapter examine the first two of these three fundamental principles. Deviation from the first principle has led to the problems associated with realization-based recognition of gains and losses; failure to observe the second principle has led to the problems associated with the distinction for tax purposes between interest and dividends. The fourth part briefly considers the third principle in relation to the preferential tax treatment of capital gains. It argues that elimination of the distinction between ordinary income and capital amounts is a basic premise of both the benchmark approach to the taxation of financial instruments and any approach that attempts to approximate that benchmark.

The fifth part reviews the problems associated with cross-border cash flows. Like some of the tax literature, it argues that the application of non-resident withholding tax is the only issue unique to the taxation of financial cash flows.[22] All other issues involve either (1) the application of the same income measurement principles as apply in a purely domestic context or (2) specific applications of general approaches developed in the context of income from services, manufacturing, and trade. The imposition of non-resident withholding tax is especially problematic, owing to a lack of explicit normative principles that has led to the application of different tax rates to equivalent cash flows. The obvious solution would be consistent taxation of these flows, but its achievement is impeded by the absence of any clear concept of the role of withholding taxes and by an apparent acceptance of certain features of the status quo as immutable.

Each part of the chapter discusses the relevant policy concerns in terms of either (1) the revenue loss that arises from pure avoidance or (2) the perceived inefficiencies that arise from approximate avoidance. For illustrative purposes and the sake of simplicity, the focus throughout this chapter is on the problems presented by the cash flows associated with the basic building-block financial instruments described in chapter 1 (including common shares of leveraged corporations). Chapters 6 and 7 will address the same problems in the context of complex instruments that are combinations of the building blocks. These instruments present unique issues, including the problem of identifying the basic building-block instruments that constitute a particular "hybrid instrument" or "synthetic."[23]

To a considerable extent, the discussion in this chapter presents the conventional case in support of accretion taxation modelled on the Haig-Simons ideal as the most effective means of eliminating the variations in tax treatment and the other distinctions that are the sources of pure and approximate tax avoidance. The recognition of all changes in value on an annual basis, however, presents practical problems that require consideration of alternative approaches to the accretion ideal (at least in the short to medium term). This chapter is intended, therefore, to present the relevant issues in general terms and to provide a framework for the assessment of the various alternatives for reform. This framework draws on Strnad's much broader and more ambitious work; in particular, it shares his emphasis on the value of incremental reforms in the absence of realistic opportunities for fundamental changes.[24] The framework attempts to provide a context for the assessment of incremental reform strategies that address, to varying degrees, the differences in tax treatment responsible for inconsistencies and discontinuities. It rests on the basic distinction, emphasized in chapters 1 and 2, between expected time-value returns and unexpected gains or losses attributable to a bet element.[25] This distinction is the rationale for the application of accretion taxation to all financial instruments, for the elimination of the differences between the taxation of interest and the taxation of dividends, and for the elimination of the differences between the taxation of ordinary income and the taxation of capital amounts. Moreover, the distinction provides an important conceptual basis for the assessment of second-best reform alternatives. Some of those alternatives receive brief discussion at the end of this chapter and detailed assessment in chapter 4.

The Problem of Deferral Created by the Realization Requirement

The variation in types of deferral associated with the realization-based recognition of gains and losses presents some of the more difficult policy problems for the income taxation of financial instruments. To some extent, these problems arise from a failure to identify clearly the different issues presented by expected and unexpected amounts and to design alternatives to accretion taxation on the basis of that distinction.[26] Even when the issues are clarified, however, the fact remains that all second-best approaches in this area depend in part on an acceptance of the realization requirement and are ultimately flawed.

The application of accretion taxation to financial instruments is routinely cited as the ideal approach to the recognition of the cash flows associated with these instruments.[27] This conclusion depends on two related premises: first, that an accretion-based income tax is normatively desirable;[28] second, that the application of accretion taxation to financial instruments is defensible even in the context of a realization-based income tax for non-financial assets. The first premise obviously does not apply only to financial instruments. The premise is important, however, since it establishes an accretion-based income tax as a benchmark for income taxation generally. The second premise is important because it implies a recognition that in practice accretion taxation is difficult to achieve. Even in a decidedly second-best world, however, financial instruments have characteristics that support the application of accretion taxation in their case. These characteristics are largely the product of the distinction between expected gains and losses and unexpected gains and losses, and of the different types of deferral associated with this distinction.

Realization-Based Income Taxation and the Accretion Ideal

The issues and policy options associated with the taxation of financial instruments are determined, at a general level, by resolution of the broader debate over the alternatives of an accretion-based income tax and a cash flow consumption tax. Decisions made in the context of this broader debate necessarily limit the range of options for the taxation of financial instruments. Acceptance of an accretion-based income tax as the ideal approach to the taxation of financial instruments is based on the assumptions that an income tax is normatively desirable and that an accretion model is the first-best version of an income tax base.[29] In fact, however, all of the problems commonly associated with the treatment of financial instruments under a realization-based income tax can also be addressed by a cash flow consumption tax.[30] The problem is that neither ideal is about to be adopted in either the short term or the medium term. For the reasons discussed briefly below, tax-policy makers have tended to favour an income tax over a personal consumption tax and have adopted a realization-based income tax as a compromised version of the accretion ideal.[31] Acceptance of this status quo means that an appropriate treatment of financial instruments must be designed in the context of a realization-based income tax. This task is much more difficult than would be a simple application of either the accretion ideal or a cash flow consumption tax. In essence, the challenge is to design a theoretically defensible and workable approach to the taxation of financial instruments in the second-best setting provided by a realization-based income tax. Two of the critical issues in that context are the articulation of a defensible role for accretion taxation of financial instruments and the design of effective alternatives to an accretion approach under a realization-based system.

The status quo is the outcome of a long debate over the relative merits of an accretion-based income tax and a personal cash flow or consumption tax. In general, an accretion-based income tax is equivalent to market-value accounting and involves the recognition of gains and losses on an asset on the basis of changes in its value during the period in which it is held. Tax must be paid on the basis of the changes in value, whether or not they are realized in the form of cash or its equivalent.[32] Advocates of this tax base draw on a long intellectual tradition in the tax-policy literature that does not refer only to the taxation of financial instruments.[33] To be more particular, the recognition of changes in the value of assets and liabilities on an accretion basis as the theoretically preferable timing principle under an income tax follows from the second element of the Haig-Simons concept of income; that is, net accretions to wealth arising in a taxation period.[34]

Advocates of a cash flow tax, by contrast, focus on the consumption component of Haig-Simons income.[35] Under a cash flow base, all receipts must be included in income and all non-consumption expenses may be deducted as paid. Deductibility extends to the savings component (that is, accumulated wealth) of Haig-Simons income, which is not taxed until it is consumed.[36] Exemption through deductibility also extends to the return on savings that is reinvested. The essence of a cash flow tax, therefore, is the recognition of cash receipts and the provision of a deduction for savings.[37] The difference between cash receipts and savings (including the return on savings that is reinvested) represents current consumption that is taxed on a cash flow basis. In an important sense, therefore, savings (as a form of deferred consumption) are not taxed until a taxpayer consumes them.[38] In its application of progressive rates to the amount of taxable consumption, however, a cash flow tax differs from a flat rate consumption tax imposed on value added. The incorporation of progression requires that the tax be imposed as a personal expenditure tax on the basis of personal tax returns.

The difference between the results under an accretion-based income tax and the results under a cash flow tax highlights a perceived distortion in the choice between present consumption and deferred consumption under an income tax. The distortion arises because of the well-known double tax on savings under an income tax.[39] In effect, savings are taxed as they are accumulated, and any return generated by the after-tax amount is also taxed.[40] An income tax, therefore, upsets the pre- and post-tax discount rate and leaves the taxpayer with a reduced value for deferred consumption.[41] A consumption tax maintains the same pre- and post-tax discount rates by taxing wealth in the same proportion (equal to the relevant tax rate)[42] whether that wealth is consumed immediately or in the future.[43] Thus the after-tax return to savings is greater under a cash flow tax than it is under an income tax. Provided that the level of private savings increases[44] and that an increase in private investment is desirable, the increased return will result in efficiency gains.

Although the double taxation of savings under an accretion-based income tax tends to be defended, almost as a prescriptive matter, on the basis of the Haig-Simons concept of income,[45] it is also defended on the basis of distributive justice, or the allocation of benefits and burdens within society.[46] This defense reduces to two arguments.[47] First, advocates of an income tax argue that the double taxation of savings is necessary if taxation is to reach intangible benefits from holding wealth, such as security and prestige.[48] Second, they argue that the clear superiority of an income tax over a cash flow tax as a means of reducing disparities in wealth justifies its use in a world in which the only alternative is a cash flow tax.[49]

Advocates of a cash flow tax point out that it is possible to tax the intangible benefits associated with wealth accumulation directly under a wealth tax, which through the use of progressive rates can effect whatever degree of wealth redistribution one considers to be desirable.[50] An income tax, they argue, is only a poor proxy for a wealth tax. The wealth base includes the whole stock of a taxpayer's wealth, whereas the income base includes only accretions to wealth.[51] Since the intangible benefits flow from the holding of the total stock itself, the wealth base is more appropriate than the income base for the purpose of taxing those benefits. Moreover, the usefulness of progressive rates as a redistributive mechanism is seriously diminished if the tax base is limited to net accretions.[52] The prevailing view, however, is that practical implementation problems and political considerations preclude the use of a wealth tax and limit the choice of tax bases to the existing income tax, which has some redistributive effect, and a cash flow tax, which would have none.[53]

Thus wealth-distribution imperatives and mundane practical considerations conspire to entrench the income tax as a second-best alternative to a cash flow tax supplemented by a wealth base.[54] Acceptance of this imperfect rationale is reflected in an apparent assumption of policy makers that the important choice is between an accretion-based income tax and a realization-based income tax. The latter is seen to lie somewhere between an accretion-based income tax and a cash flow tax in its ability to reach the intangible benefits associated with the holding of wealth.[55] Despite opposition in the tax-policy literature,[56] policy makers continue to invoke liquidity and valuation concerns to support the use of a realization-based income tax as a compromised version of an accretion tax, though they have afforded cash flow tax treatment to certain types of savings (in particular retirement savings) and provided for accretion treatment in selected circumstances.[57] The interesting question is why the return on financial instruments should be singled out for accretion treatment. Given the acceptance of realization-based recognition generally, how does the selective application of accretion taxation to financial assets and liabilities both promote the normative goals of an income tax and prevent the distortions and inequities associated with the realization basis?

Much of the answer to this question can be found in the literature on the concept of deferral and the supposed significance of that concept for the taxation of financial instruments. This literature is premised on an acceptance of an accretion-based income tax as a normatively desirable proxy for a combination of a cash flow tax and a wealth tax. On the basis of this premise, recognition of increments to wealth on an accretion basis is accepted as the benchmark treatment. More particularly, the recognition of income (or accretions to wealth) as it arises is closely linked with the perceived benefit of tax deferral that is attributable to the adoption of realization-based recognition as a deviation from an accretion-based benchmark. In other words, the concept of deferral depends critically on an assumption that all increments in wealth, as reflected in changes in the value of an asset, should be taxed as they arise during a taxation year. A realization-based income tax brings gains or losses into account only as they are realized by a taxpayer in the form of cash or an equivalent to cash.

Different Concepts of Deferral Associated with the Different Types of Financial Returns

The tax-policy literature has for some time recognized the concept of deferral and its associated efficiency and equity costs. As a benchmark for the assessment of deferral, the accretion ideal applies to all revenue and all expenses associated with all assets and liabilities.[58] In the context of an analysis of the tax treatment of financial instruments, however, the significance of deferral (and therefore the appropriateness of accretion taxation as the accepted benchmark) depends on a distinction among the types of returns associated with various instruments and a distinction among the types of deferral applicable to those returns. The more specific rationale for the application of accretion taxation to financial instruments, which arises from these distinctions, assumes that a realization-based income tax will be maintained for the distributional and practical reasons discussed above.[59] The literature largely ignores the distributional effects that motivate the larger debate over the respective merits of income taxation and cash flow taxation.[60] Instead, it emphasizes efficiency considerations and the revenue loss occasioned by the tax-avoidance opportunities presented by the use of realization-based recognition of gains and losses on financial instruments.[61]

Deferral under a realization-based income tax is the recognition of gain or loss after the period during which it has arisen.[62] It is common to describe the benefit of deferral under a realization-based income tax as the equivalent of an interest-free loan from the government that reduces the effective tax rate below the nominal rate.[63] The amount of the loan is equal to the tax that would be paid under an accretion system whenever a gain arose.[64] Much of the literature on timing issues uses the interest-free loan analogy without distinguishing the types of gains; in particular, it fails to distinguish between expected gains and unexpected gains.[65] Shuldiner,[66] however, does distinguish between (1) expected gains and losses attributable to the time-value-of-money element in financial instruments and (2) unexpected gains and losses attributable to the assumption of risk associated with a bet element in financial instruments. He calls deferral associated with the first type of gains "anticipated deferral"[67] and deferral associated with the second type "unanticipated deferral."[68]

As was discussed in chapter 1, all financial instruments, other than pure bets, provide an expected payoff that is determined ex ante on the acquisition of the instrument (or the initiation of a financial contract). The expected payoff is the weighted average of all of the possible payoffs associated with a specified outcome. The concept of risk expresses the degree of variance in the possible payoffs. The difference between the actual payoff determined ex post and the expected payoff determined ex ante represents a gain or a loss that is either higher or lower than the market rate of return and is, in essence, the outcome of a bet that reflects the risk associated with the financial instrument. The amount by which a payoff exceeds the expected return represents compensation for successfully assuming risk.[69] The amount by which a payoff falls short of the expected return is a measure of the extent to which the assumption of risk has been unsuccessful. Expected gain represents the time-value return associated with a particular financial instrument plus any premium demanded for assuming risk.[70] This gain may be allocated systematically over the entire term of the instrument. In a sense, the expected gain is considered to arise over time in the form of increments to the value of the instrument.[71]

Anticipated deferral arises when the expected gain on a financial instrument is recognized on realization (normally a sale, transfer, or other disposition); that is, after the period during which the expected gain has arisen. The deferral is said to be "anticipated" because it is anticipated when the financial instrument is issued (or the financial contract is initiated) that recognition of the expected gain will occur after the time of accrual.[72] Unanticipated deferral arises when the specified contingency on which a cash flow depends is resolved and there is an unexpected gain in excess of the expected return. Deferral in this case is "unanticipated" because the gain was not anticipated ex ante. At the outset, therefore, the value of any unanticipated deferral is nil.[73] The benefit of deferral may still arise, however, if the factors that affect the outcome are resolved yet recognition is deferred until a subsequent period. In this case, although there can be no deferral ex ante, there may be deferral ex post.[74]

Shuldiner illustrates the distinction between anticipated and unanticipated deferral with a series of examples that highlight the difference between expected time-value returns and unexpected returns determined by the outcome of a coin flip.[75] Consider an investment of $30,000 at the end of period one (T(0)) in a two-year bond that provides a riskless rate of return of 10 percent, compounded annually, for periods two and three at T(1).[76] When the investment is made, at T(0), its expected return is $6,300. Assuming that the internal rate of return on the bond remains constant (10 percent market rate of return compounded annually),[77] $3,000 of the expected return is allocable to period two ($30,000 × 0.1) and $3,300 is allocable to period three ($33,000 × 0.1). Given a 40 percent tax rate, the after-tax return is $72 more under a realization-based income tax than it would be under an accretion-based income tax. The additional return arises because taxation of the $3,000 period-two return is deferred until T(2) ($3,000 × 0.4 = $1,200) instead of applying at T(1) ($1,200 × 0.1 pretax return × 0.6 after-tax return = $72). This additional amount represents the value of the deferral, which is anticipated in the sense that the return is expected at the outset of the investment but taxation of some of the return is not expected to occur until the end of a period after the period of accrual. Thus taxation on realization rather than accrual provides the holder of the two-year bond with an anticipated interest-free loan equal to the $1,200 of tax on the period-two return that would otherwise be paid at T(1).

As was noted earlier, anticipated deferral is associated with the expected time-value return on financial instruments; it arises in its extreme form in the case of a debt obligation that carries no default risk and no interest-rate risk (for example, a government bond that pays interest at a floating rate).[78] Because of the creditworthiness of the issuer, the holder of an instrument of this kind bears no risk of default; nor does the holder bear any risk that the value of the debt will increase or decrease with changes in the market rate of interest. The instrument provides a pure time-value return, and any deferral that arises from the recognition of expected increases in the value of the obligation after the time of accrual is anticipated. The antithesis of a riskless debt obligation is a pure bet with a 50/50 payoff opportunity. Because a pure-bet instrument provides no expected gain or loss at the outset, there can be no anticipated deferral. Assume, for example,[79] that a taxpayer enters into a contract at T(0) whereby he promises to pay either $30,000 or $42,600 at T(2), depending on the outcome of a coin flip. In return, he is promised a payoff of $36,300 at the same time. At the outset of the contract, there is no expected return, since the expectation of a payoff of $36,300 at T(2) is offset by the expectation of an obligation to pay $36,300. The latter value is derived from the fact that the taxpayer will be required to pay either $30,000 or $42,600, depending on the outcome of the coin flip; the value of the obligation at T(0), therefore, is $36,300 ($30,000 × 0.5 + $42,600 × 0.5). At T(2), the bet will be resolved by the coin flip and the taxpayer will receive $36,300 and pay either $30,000 or $42,600. In the former case, a gain of $6,300 will arise; in the latter case, a loss of $6,300 will arise. In either case, the result is ex post in the sense that it arises after the coin flip and cannot be expected when the contract is entered into.

Unanticipated deferral, therefore, is associated with the bet or risk element in a financial instrument. Pure forms of instruments with a bet element are forward, futures, and swap contracts with single payoffs that depend on a specified outcome. Because any gain or loss is unexpected ex ante, deferral can only be unanticipated and occurs when the gain or loss that arises on resolution is recognized in a subsequent period. Thus unanticipated deferral does not occur in the above example if any gain that arises for the taxpayer on the coin flip must be recognized at that time. In this case, the gain is taxed when it is earned, and it is earned when the value of the bet becomes a positive amount because of the resolution of the specified contingency. Unanticipated deferral arises only if it is possible to defer taxation of an unexpected gain to a period after the period in which the amount is determined or earned. Taxation in a subsequent period when cash is received provides a deferral benefit similar to the benefit that arises when deferral is anticipated and gains are expected.

Under an accretion-based income tax, therefore, a $6,300 gain in the example must be recognized at T(2) when the gain is determined by the coin flip. Given a tax rate of 40 percent, tax of $2,520 must be paid at that time even if the gain is not to be paid until the following taxation period at T(3). Assuming that the contract provides for a rate of interest on the deferred payment of 10 percent, the taxpayer will earn interest of $630 ($6,300 × 0.1) over the following taxation period. Under a realization-based income tax, which will not tax the gain until it is received in cash, no tax must be paid at T(2). The $6,300 gain plus the $630 one-year return on that gain is taxed, instead, at the end of three years ($6,930 × 0.4 = tax of $2,772). The result is a total after-tax return of $4,158 ($6,930 less $2,772). Under an accretion-based income tax, the taxpayer must forgo the pre-tax return on the $2,520 tax payment required at T(2) on the $6,300 gain ($6,300 × 0.4 = $2,520). The forgone after-tax return ($2,520 × 0.1 × 0.6 = $151.20) is the difference between the total after-tax return under a realization-based income tax and the after-tax return under an accretion tax;[80] it represents the value of the deferral benefit associated with a $2,520 interest-free loan under a realization-based income tax that permits payment of tax on the $6,300 gain at T(3) rather than T(2).[81]

As was pointed out in chapters 1 and 2, most financial instruments (including debt, shares, and options) provide a return that is a combination of an expected time-value return and unexpected amounts attributable to a bet element. Any associated deferral, accordingly, is a combination of anticipated and unanticipated deferral. Assume that a taxpayer pays $30,000 at T(0) for the right to receive either $30,000 or $42,600 at T(2) as determined by the outcome of a coin flip. This financial instrument provides an expected payoff of $36,300 ($30,000 × 0.5 + $42,600 × 0.5) and an expected gain of $6,300. The instrument also provides for unexpected gain of $6,300 if the coin flip is in the taxpayer's favour ($42,600 less the expected payoff of $36,300) and an unexpected loss of $6,300 if the coin flip is unfavourable for the taxpayer ($30,000 less the expected payoff of $36,300). To the extent of the expected return, the result for this instrument under an accretion-based income tax is no different from the result for a financial instrument that provides a pure time-value return: the taxpayer must recognize the expected increase in the instrument's value represented by the expected return. As in the case of a pure time-value instrument, one can apply accrual recognition in this case by using some sort of assumption about the expected growth in the value of the instrument. Anticipated deferral arises under a realization-based income tax that allows the taxpayer to recognize the expected gain on receipt of any payment at T(2). Moreover, under an accretion-based income tax, the unexpected gain, if any, must be recognized when the amount of the payment is resolved by the coin flip at T(2). Failure to recognize the unexpected gain at that time provides the benefit of unanticipated deferral associated with a pure bet.[82]

The Tax-Avoidance Rationale for the Application of Accretion Taxation to Financial Instruments

Shuldiner develops the distinction between anticipated and unanticipated deferral in order to articulate some principles for the design of appropriate timing rules to govern the recognition of gains and losses on financial instruments.[83] Anticipated and unanticipated deferral, he argues, have different efficiency and equity consequences.[84] In particular, anticipated deferral results in overinvestment in instruments that provide the benefit of anticipated deferral.[85] The overinvestment, and the consequent misallocation of resources, arises because these instruments yield after-tax returns greater than those that alternative investments provide.[86] The equity effects of anticipated deferral depend on the extent to which the greater after-tax returns are capitalized in the prices of financial instruments.[87] In other words, the existence of the greater after-tax returns may cause the price of instruments that provide the benefit of anticipated deferral to be bid up, with the result that the pre-tax return on these instruments will fall below the pre-tax return on alternative investments that do not provide anticipated deferral. The process is complete when the after-tax returns on the two investments are the same and investors are left indifferent between tax-preferred and fully taxable instruments. If tax capitalization is complete, there will be no equity effects; if it is incomplete, holders of instruments that provide anticipated deferral will realize a greater after-tax return than will holders of investments that provide the same pre-tax return but not the lower effective tax rate associated with anticipated deferral.

In contrast with anticipated deferral, unanticipated deferral has an expected value of zero under either an accretion-based or a realization-based income tax.[88] Thus there is no incentive on the basis of expected values to prefer instruments that provide unanticipated deferral to other instruments. The efficiency consequences of unanticipated deferral follow instead from the fact that this type of deferral reduces the effective tax rate on the unexpected gains or losses that arise from the bet element in a financial instrument. This rate reduction increases the after-tax return from unexpected gains and decreases the tax saving from unexpected losses. The latter result, which increases the after-tax amount of the losses,[89] arises because recognition of the unexpected losses is deferred until realization. This deferral postpones the taxpayer's ability to use the losses to offset other income and save tax otherwise payable.[90] By increasing the amount of the after-tax gain or loss, unanticipated deferral increases the variance of the returns on instruments that provide deferral of this kind.[91] The increased variance translates into increased risk, which can discourage investment in financial instruments that provide unanticipated deferral.[92]

The equity effects of unanticipated deferral, like the efficiency effects, differ from those of anticipated deferral because of the different natures of the gains or losses associated with the two types of deferral. Ex ante, the value of unanticipated deferral is zero, which means that the expected effective tax rate equals the statutory rate and no equity effects arise. Ex post, however, the holder of a financial instrument with unexpected gain benefits from an effective tax rate that is lower than the rate faced by a taxpayer who realizes the same gain but must pay tax on it currently. Since income tax systems generally apply to the results of an investment or income-earning activity as they are viewed ex post, the equity effects of unanticipated deferral may be considered to be inappropriate.[93]

Like much of the other general tax-policy literature on deferral, Shuldiner's analysis of the different types of deferral associated with expected and unexpected returns assumes that an accretion-based income tax is the appropriate benchmark for the measurement of income. Failure to apply this supposedly correct measure produces the distinction between anticipated and unanticipated deferral and the different efficiency and equity consequences associated with these different types of deferral. It is significant that Shuldiner does not attempt to justify the application of the accretion standard to financial instruments in the context of an income tax that taxes the returns to non-financial assets on realization. Some of the literature, however, emphasizes the opportunities for tax avoidance created by financial instruments as a justification for the application of accretion recognition to financial instruments alone.[94] This tax-avoidance rationale builds, nonetheless, on the distinction between expected time-value returns and anticipated deferral on the one hand and unexpected gains and losses and unanticipated deferral on the other. The added element in the analysis in this case is the recognition of a financial instrument as a contract between two parties that provides offsetting positions. Deferral analysis traditionally focuses on the consequences of deferral to one party, usually the party with an expected or unexpected gain. It ignores the significance of both the deductibility of the expected time-value return by a borrower and the deductibility of unexpected losses by a party to a losing bet. Yet recognition of these additional considerations is critical to the development of a tax-avoidance rationale for the application of accretion taxation to financial instruments.[95] So, too, is recognition of the circumstance that the transaction costs associated with buying and selling financial instruments are low—a circumstance that facilitates the exploitation of the avoidance opportunities presented by a realization-based income tax. In a world of risk and multirate taxpayers, accretion taxation is the alternative that addresses these opportunities most completely.

The tax-avoidance rationale for the accretion taxation of financial instruments is premised, therefore, on the basic distinction between expected and unexpected returns on financial instruments and the consequent availability under a realization-based income tax of two types of tax-avoidance opportunities:[96] (1) "timing arbitrage" and (2) "risk arbitrage." Timing arbitrage is associated with expected returns and the availability under a realization-based income tax of anticipated deferral. Risk arbitrage is associated with unexpected gains and losses and arises because of taxpayers' ability under a realization-based income tax to realize losses selectively. These two types of avoidance opportunities presented by the realization-based taxation of financial instruments are pure avoidance opportunities in the sense described above;[97] that is, they permit a taxpayer to assume offsetting positions that provide a positive cash flow only because they receive different tax treatments.

The most obvious opportunities for timing arbitrage occur under an income tax that provides different recognition rules for the offsetting sides of a financial instrument with an expected time-value return.[98] Assume, for example, that the issuer of the two-year bond described earlier[99] can deduct the expected loss on an accrual basis at T(1) and T(2), whereas the holder is not required to recognize the same return as income until realization at T(2). Under these conditions, a taxpayer can realize a pure avoidance opportunity by issuing a two-year bond and using the proceeds to acquire another bond with identical cash flows. The cash flows under the borrowing and lending transactions offset one another, which means that the net value of the two positions is zero. Owing to the asymmetry of the recognition rules, however, the taxpayer enjoys a positive cash flow. Provided that the expense on the borrowing side is fully deductible against other income, a tax benefit arises that is equal to the after-tax return on the tax saving realized through the deduction against other income.[100] Of course, this tax saving is recaptured when revenue from the lending side of the transaction is recognized at T(2); meanwhile, however, the taxpayer has enjoyed the benefit of an interest-free loan from the government in the form of the forgone tax on other income generated by the accelerated deduction of the expenses on the offsetting borrowing. The taxpayer realizes this benefit because he is able to deduct the expected amount of expense on the borrowing before he is obliged to recognize the expected amount of revenue on the offsetting loan.[101] In effect, the rate of tax on the borrowing is different from (higher than) the rate of tax on the loan; the latter benefits from a lower effective rate because of anticipated deferral under the realization requirement.[102]

In a riskless world in which a single tax rate applied to all taxpayers, one could eliminate opportunities for timing arbitrage by implementing symmetrical recognition rules—that is, by requiring the two parties to a financial instrument to recognize the expected time-value return on the instrument as expense and as revenue at the same time.[103] Since any deduction of the expense that arose from a borrowing would be offset by inclusion of the revenue that arose from the associated lending, taxpayers would be unable to realize tax-arbitrage profits by assuming two sides of the same transaction.

Symmetrical treatment of borrowing and lending transactions would not require the use of accretion-based recognition. In fact, in a single-rate world without risk, symmetrical realization-based recognition of expected time-value returns might eliminate opportunities for timing arbitrage that would otherwise be available.[104] As an effective response to timing arbitrage, however, the use of symmetrical realization-based recognition is problematic in two important respects.[105] First, taxpayers would be able to manipulate a symmetrical realization requirement to achieve much the same result as they would achieve under a system of asymmetrical recognition rules. For example, a taxpayer could accelerate the deduction of borrowing expenses by paying another party to assume the liability.[106] (He could even repurchase the obligation and hold it to maturity.) The taxpayer could realize a pure avoidance opportunity by offsetting the borrowing with an identical lending transaction that will be taxed on realization. The result would be similar to the result under an asymmetrical system that provided accrual recognition of the expense represented by the expected time-value return on a financial instrument and recognition on realization of the revenue. The only difference is that under a symmetrical system it would take some extra steps (and transaction costs) to create a homemade form of accelerated recognition of expenses on the borrowing side of the transaction.[107]

Second, and more important, symmetrical timing rules alone would not be sufficient to eliminate timing arbitrage under a system of realization-based recognition in a world in which different taxpayers were subject to different nominal or effective tax rates.[108] Assume, for example, that there are two types of taxpayers in the world, the fully taxable and the tax-exempt. In this case, even under an income tax with symmetrical recognition rules for the revenue and the expenses associated with a single instrument, taxable investors could realize avoidance opportunities if the cash flows associated with two different forms of investment were subject to different recognition rules. For example, a taxable investor who issued a coupon bond—that is, a bond that paid periodic interest—and used the proceeds to acquire a two-year bond could deduct the expense on the coupon bond at T(1) and T(2) but would not have to recognize the offsetting revenue until T(2). The accelerated recognition of the expense would provide a tax benefit similar to the benefit under an asymmetric system. Symmetrical treatment of the counterparties to the coupon bond and the two-year bond would not ensure that any tax benefit for one party would be offset by a tax detriment for the other party. This is so because tax-exempt market participants could take an offsetting position that resulted in the accelerated recognition of revenue (by holding a coupon bond, for example) and the deferred recognition of expense (by issuing a two-year bond, for example) without any tax detriment.[109] Tax-exempt market participants would be insensitive to the offsetting tax detriment and could therefore facilitate timing arbitrage opportunities for taxable investors.[110]

In order to address tax-avoidance opportunities in a world of multiple tax rates, the income tax system must incorporate recognition rules that are both symmetrical and consistent.[111] Consistency in this context means the consistent recognition of the equivalent cash flows from financial instruments that provide an expected time-value return. It requires the spreading of the expected time-value return on all financial instruments (including shares)[112] over the relevant term for the purpose of accrual recognition by issuers and holders. In a riskless world in which the only returns were time-value returns and all gains and losses were expected, this basic recognition principle would be equivalent to the required recognition of changes in value on an annual basis under an accretion-based income tax.[113] Under these conditions, the return on (and therefore the value of) any instrument is solely a function of the time-value of money.

Recognition of the return as it accrues eliminates not only the benefits of anticipated deferral itself, but also the opportunities for timing arbitrage that arise from the lower effective tax rates that anticipated deferral provides.[114] In particular, if the expected time-value return on a financial instrument must be recognized as it accrues, whatever the form of the instrument, taxpayers will not be able to generate tax arbitrage profits by accelerating recognition of expenses while deferring recognition of the revenue associated with an offsetting position. Consistency precludes these opportunities even in a world of multiple tax rates. If all taxpayers must recognize offsetting expense and revenue on a consistent basis, tax-policy makers do not have to rely on a tax disadvantage that arises for one counterparty to a financial instrument to offset a timing advantage that arises for the other party. Nor can taxpayers accelerate deductions by manipulating the realization requirement. In short, expense recognition is available under a full accrual system for expected time-value returns without the need for a realization transaction and is offset by the accrual recognition of offsetting lending transactions.

In a world in which risk is relevant, the bet element in a financial instrument presents opportunities for risk arbitrage through the selective realization of unexpected losses.[115] "Selective realization," otherwise known as the "timing option,"[116] refers to a taxpayer's ability under a realization-based income tax to control the timing of realization and hence to deduct losses associated with risky positions before he recognizes any offsetting gains. This type of strategic trading allows the taxpayer to maximize the effective tax rate on unexpected losses and minimize the effective tax rate on unexpected gains. The taxpayer realizes a tax benefit even though the expected value of unanticipated deferral associated with unexpected gains is nil. Indeed, the manipulation of the realization requirement in this context is simply another form of timing arbitrage, one that is referred to as "risk arbitrage" because of its association with financial instruments that involve a bet element. The discussion here, however, will limit its use of the term "timing arbitrage" to arbitrage opportunities associated with instruments with an expected time-value return and apply the term "risk arbitrage" to arbitrage associated with instruments that yield unexpected gains and losses.

It will clarify the tax benefit provided by the timing option under a realization-based income tax to consider again the example of a taxpayer who is promised a payoff of $36,300 in return for a promise to pay either $42,600 or $30,000 at T(2), depending on the outcome of a coin flip.[117] This instrument provides a return that is attributable solely to a bet. At the outset, the expected return is nil,[118] and the value of any deferral is also nil. The benefit of unanticipated deferral arises if the bet is resolved at T(2) but the taxpayer can defer realization of the $6,300 unexpected gain from a winning bet until T(3). Given a 40 percent tax rate and a 10 percent discount rate, the present value at T(2) of the tax payment of $2,520 at T(3) is $2,290.91 and the effective tax rate on the gain is reduced to 36 percent.[119]

This tax benefit is compounded by the taxpayer's ability to maintain the full after-tax value of an unexpected loss by realizing the loss at T(2). If the taxpayer loses the coin flip, he will have a $36,300 payment obligation and a $30,000 payment entitlement. Under a realization-based income tax, he can realize the $6,300 loss on resolution of the bet by, for example, disposing of any interest in the instrument. The loss will result in an immediate tax saving of $2,520 ($6,300 × 0.4) if the taxpayer can offset the amount in full against other taxable income. The taxpayer maintains the full after-tax value of the loss (that is, $3,780) by taking the loss early instead of deferring its recognition until T(3). Deferral would reduce the effective tax rate on the loss to 36 percent, and increase the after-tax value of the loss to $4,009.09 ($6,300 less the $2,290.91 present value at T(2) of a $2,520 tax saving realized at T(3) on realization of the loss). Accordingly, by taking any unexpected losses before any unexpected gains, the taxpayer can ensure that unexpected losses are deducted immediately at the highest possible effective tax rate. Conversely, he can reduce the effective rate on unexpected gains by deferring their realization until some time after the resolution of the bet that gives rise to them. The net result is a reduction in the effective tax rate on risky financial instruments that provide unexpected gains and losses.[120]

Although the timing option is available only with financial instruments that provide unexpected gains and losses,[121] the benefit is not restricted to instances of unanticipated deferral in which the bet element in a financial instrument has been resolved. In practice, the passage of time generally reveals information about the bet element that indicates in advance of the specified contingency which of the two parties to the instrument will win. Thus the timing option may arise immediately after the initiation of a financial instrument and persist over the term of the instrument.

In general, the timing option has a positive value for taxpayers if two conditions are met.[122] First, the income tax system must permit the immediate offset of realized losses on a financial instrument in full against other income. Second, there must be no requirement that one party to a financial instrument recognize an amount of offsetting unexpected gain if another party to the instrument has realized unexpected loss. Restrictions on loss offsets against other income eliminate the value of the timing option by increasing the effective tax rate on losses. A requirement of symmetrical recognition achieves a similar result by ensuring that unexpected gains and unexpected losses are recognized at the same time. A taxpayer will expect recognition of loss to be matched with recognition of gain and no timing option will arise.

Given the availability of full loss offsets and a lack of symmetrical recognition of unexpected gains and unexpected losses, a taxpayer can engage in risk arbitrage through "straddle" transactions.[123] In its simplest form, a straddle is the assumption of long and short positions in financial instruments that are pure bets. The passage of time reveals which position will be the winner and which the loser, and the taxpayer closes out the losing position first. Although the two positions offset one another, the early closeout of the loser and the deferred closeout of the winner produce different effective tax rates on the unexpected loss and gain, and the result is a tax-arbitrage profit.[124] This strategy ensures that the timing option has a certain deferral value for the taxpayer.[125] In the absence of a straddle, the timing option is just that: an option with an uncertain value that depends on whether the taxpayer assumes a winning position or a losing one in respect of a financial instrument with a bet element.[126]

As a response to straddle transactions, a requirement of symmetrical recognition by the counterparty to a financial instrument suffers from the same shortcomings as those associated with timing arbitrage.[127] In particular, symmetrical recognition is ineffective in a multitax rate world, since in such a world a taxable investor can find a non-taxable (or lower-rate) counterparty who will be insensitive to the accelerated recognition of unexpected gain. The more effective response is a requirement of consistency—specifically, a requirement that a taxpayer with offsetting positions treat the two positions identically for income tax purposes.[128] Under a realization-based income tax, this response requires a taxpayer who undertakes a straddle to recognize unrealized gains to the extent that he realizes offsetting losses.[129]

As was noted earlier, however, the timing option that exists even in the absence of a straddle transaction—the "bare" timing option—has value for a taxpayer and attendant revenue consequences, primarily because of the difference that it permits between effective tax rates on unexpected gains and effective tax rates on unexpected losses. In effect, the bare timing option lowers the effective tax rate on a financial instrument that provides unexpected gains and losses.[130] The uncertainty of the value of the timing option for a particular taxpayer who recognizes unexpected loss does not mitigate the revenue loss that arises because of the lack of an offsetting recognition of gain by the other party to the instrument. Arguably, therefore, one could use the method described above for eliminating the value of straddle transactions to eliminate the value of the bare timing option as well. That is, one could quarantine unexpected losses on financial instruments and not allow taxpayers to deduct them from income other than gains from financial instruments.[131] However, in the absence of an offsetting position held by the same taxpayer—a straddle—a broad loss limitation might increase the variance of after-tax returns by reducing the tax rate on unexpected losses and thus increasing the after-tax amount of those losses. Any increase in the variance of returns effectively increases the risk associated with financial instruments that provide unexpected gain or loss and hence may lead to efficiency losses.[132] The obvious alternative to the use of loss limitations is abandonment of the realization requirement in favour of accretion taxation. Under an accretion approach, a taxpayer who takes a position in a risky financial instrument knows that unexpected gains and losses must be recognized as the passage of time reveals information that affects the value of the position. As a result, the effective tax rates on unexpected gains and losses are equal to the nominal tax rate, and this outcome ensures that the expected pre-tax values are undisturbed. Thus accretion taxation eliminates the value of the bare timing option without creating adverse consequences for risk taking.

In the context of a realization-based system for non-financial assets, therefore, the case for the application of accretion-based recognition to gains and losses on financial instruments reduces to an anti-avoidance rationale. Even in a world of multiple tax rates, timing arbitrage can be addressed, in principle, by the accurate accrual recognition of all expected returns by issuers and holders. Similarly, the opportunities for risk arbitrage available through straddle transactions can be addressed by the use of loss-limitation rules that require the matching of unexpected losses and gains by a taxpayer who holds long and short positions in a financial instrument with offsetting cash flows. This approach presents difficult identification issues, however, since it is not always an easy administrative task to isolate offsetting positions within a taxpayer's portfolio.[133] Moreover, the narrow application of a loss-limitation rule to offsetting positions fails to address the bare timing option that is available with a risky instrument whose associated cash flows are not offset by those associated with another position. Use of a broader limitation rule can eliminate the problem, but it introduces the possibility of efficiency losses. Under accretion-based recognition, the identification issue and the issue of possible efficiency losses disappear. The required matching of offsetting losses and gains occurs automatically. Moreover, because the taxpayer loses the ability to control recognition of gains and losses, deductibility restrictions are unnecessary.

The discussion here of the application of accrual recognition to expected time-value returns has assumed somewhat artificially the existence of a category of financial instruments that provide only time-value returns and avoidance opportunities associated with timing arbitrage. In fact, there are very few financial instruments that do not contain some bet element and therefore some opportunity for risk arbitrage as well. For instance, a debt obligation that provides a fixed interest rate and time-value return contains an implied bet on market interest rates. If market rates increase during the term of the instrument, the value of the instrument decreases, in which case the holder can realize the resulting loss immediately by selling the instrument. If rates decrease, the value of the instrument increases, in which case the holder can defer recognition of the gain until maturity and the receipt of the benefit of the above-market interest rate. The most effective way to address the bare timing option inherent in any financial instrument with a bet element, including most instruments with a predominantly time-value return, is to apply accretion taxation to all gains and losses.

To sum up, accretion taxation of all gains and losses on financial instruments has several important advantages. First, it addresses the bare timing option associated with unexpected gains and losses that are not part of a straddle transaction. Second, it addresses the timing option associated with straddle transactions without requiring the identification of offsetting positions. Third, it provides the same result as accurate accrual-based recognition of time-value returns, which eliminates opportunities for timing arbitrage. Fourth, unlike accurate accrual taxation, accretion taxation can also address the bare timing option that may be implicit in an instrument with an expected time-value return. It may be necessary under the accrual approach to distinguish between expected returns and unexpected amounts from a single instrument and to address separately the timing arbitrage associated with the former and the risk arbitrage associated with the latter. Accretion taxation avoids this requirement by forcing the recognition of all changes in value, whether they are attributable to expected time-value returns or to unexpected gains and losses.

The Case for Similar Taxation of Interest and Dividends

Chapter 2 described some of the differences between the treatment of debt and the treatment of equity under both the Canadian and Australian income tax systems.[134] In general, the experience in these two countries is representative. Most countries permit the deduction of corporate interest expense and require the inclusion of interest income by debt holders, just as in most countries dividends are non-deductible for issuers and taxable to shareholders, with or without some credit for corporate tax paid on the underlying income. An exemption for intercorporate dividends ensures that there is only one level of corporate income tax on equity earnings. As already noted,[135] this distinction for tax purposes between interest and dividends is based on a "proprietary view"[136] of the corporation that equates the corporate enterprise with the residual interest of shareholders, who are considered to be the effective owners of the underlying assets. In keeping with the treatment of income from assets that are owned directly, dividends are considered to be non-deductible distributions of profit and the corporate income tax is applied to the return on equity.[137] Debt holders are considered to be outsiders whose required return is an expense to the proprietary shareholders and is therefore deductible in calculating corporate income.

For some time now, the legal and economics literature on corporate governance has rejected this proprietary view of the corporation. In fact, some of the legal literature rejected this view generations ago, to adopt in its place the distinction that Berle and Means drew between the interests of management and the interests of investors,[138] among whom they included both shareholders and debt holders. Subsequently, the new economic view of the firm emerged with its description of the corporation as a composite of a series of bargains or a nexus of contracts among various participants.[139] According to this view and the principal-agency analysis that it has spawned,[140] the labels attached to securities are irrelevant and there is no special distinction between debt and equity. Both forms of investment present agency problems that require pricing and compensation in the form of a higher rate of return ("agency costs").[141] The proprietary view of the corporation, which underlies much of financial accounting practice and its identification of the corporation with the interests of the shareholders, has been challenged for some time even in the theoretical accounting literature.[142]

The alternatives to the proprietary model of the corporation are all based on a premise that debt and equity capital perform much the same function, in that they both provide a specified rate of return as consideration for the use of capital committed to the corporate enterprise. This basic functional similarity of debt and equity is the apparent basis of various schemes for the integration of corporate-level and shareholder-level income taxes, such as the dividend-imputation schemes that many countries have adopted. Dividend-imputation systems, however, like other integration schemes that do not realize the identical taxation of the returns on debt and equity, are ultimately second-best approximations of accretion taxation. Indeed, the only completely effective approaches to integration are (1) accretion taxation and (2) an approach that combines realization-based recognition of unexpected gains and losses with the application of accrual recognition to the expected gains and losses on the embedded debt in shares.

The Functional Similarity of Debt and Equity

The functional similarity of debt and equity follows from the fact that in accumulating assets a corporation uses all contributed capital. Thus the wealth generated in a corporation belongs to all investors, who expect to receive compensation for the use of their funds and the risk they bear.[143] This compensation takes the form of cash flow streams that vary in amount and reflect priorities that vary with the allocation of the right to participate in profit, exposure to loss, and control. In an important sense, therefore, the investment interests represented by all outstanding corporate instruments realize a division of the cash flows from the underlying corporate assets that reflects the bargain among all corporate participants, including investors (as the providers of capital), management (as the providers of managerial expertise), employees (as the providers of labour), and suppliers (as the providers of required productive inputs). The expected rate of return demanded by investors depends on the market rate for a riskless investment and the premium required to compensate them for bearing undiversifiable risk.

In general, the expected return on shares is higher than the expected return on debt simply because the amount and the timing of the cash flows from shares are subject to a greater degree of contractual contingency than are the amount and the timing of the cash flows from debt. Apart from this difference in degree of risk and the commensurate rate of return, debt and equity serve the same function economically, and conceptually there is no fundamental difference between them.[144]

The point about risk merits some elaboration. Because the amount and the timing of debt payments are fixed, the risk that they will not be realized is less than the risk that the payment rights associated with shares of the same corporation will not be realized. The risk that debt payments will not be made or that their amount will not be consistent varies from one issuer to another and one debt obligation to another and depends on the extent of the security interests in the underlying corporate assets that any protective covenants associated with the debt provide. Since dividend cash flows determine share value, the greater variability of those flows, in timing and amount, generally means that shares are riskier than debt.[145]

In essence, then, the amount and the timing of dividend payments are linked more closely than debt payments are to the realization of profits by the issuer. Even so, the payoff and the value of a debt obligation also depend ultimately on the value of the underlying corporate assets. Debt, which is senior to equity as an investment interest, has a limited upside[146] that is predominantly a time-value return. Along with that return, there is some risk that the value of the corporate assets will be insufficient to support the required payoff.[147] Debt is senior to equity in that it generally has payment priority over equity; thus the risk of non-payment is less. Equity, the junior investment interest,[148] has a greater upside that is predominantly the unexpected return on corporate assets in excess of the time-value return. Although equity investors require a time-value return as compensation for forgoing current consumption, this embedded "bond element" tends to be de-emphasized in favour of the bet element and the unexpected returns that it represents. The de-emphasis occurs largely because that return, and the equity capital itself, is the first to be lost in the event that the value of the underlying assets is insufficient to support the time-value return on the capital of the equity investors. Thus equity investors bear a greater risk than do holders of corporate debt that the value of the underlying assets will be less than their required time-value return and that they will incur unexpected losses. In return for this downside, equity investors enjoy the right to unexpected returns in excess of the required time-value return if the value of the underlying corporate assets exceeds the value of comparable assets that provide only a time-value return.[149]

Debt and equity, therefore, may be said to differ not in kind but only in degree, as measured in terms of risk.[150] Indeed, debt and equity alike provide both an expected time-value return as compensation for the use of the investor's funds and a bet element that produces unexpected gains or losses. To put the matter in another way, all corporate investors advance funds in the expectation that they will receive a greater amount in return.[151] That expected amount has both (1) a time-value element that reflects the return required to induce an investor to forgo current consumption and (2) a bet element that depends on the value of the underlying assets and in particular on whether that value will exceed or be less than the required time-value return. The first element corresponds to the riskless rate of return. The variability of returns associated with the second element represents the risk aspect of a security. All debt and equity securities with a non-trivial bet element (and thus a non-trivial risk of loss) must provide a nominal return in excess of the riskless rate to offset the possibility of loss and equate the expected return with the riskless return.[152] If investors are risk averse and the risk associated with a particular security is non-unique—that is, if it cannot be diversified away[153]—investors must be offered an expected return in excess of the riskless rate if they are to be induced to purchase the security. This excess, or risk premium, may be found either in a debt obligation or in a share with a non-trivial bet element and the associated risk.

As chapter 1 noted, this intuitive basis for the proposition that debt and equity are functionally similar is supported by option-pricing theory.[154] The fundamental insight underlying much of this theory is the proposition that the payoffs on the outstanding securities of a corporation with a mix of debt and equity capital are a combination of long or short positions in the underlying corporate assets and call or put options on those assets.[155] The debt investors and the equity investors simply assume offsetting positions. This equivalence of payoff profiles follows from the fact that the limited liability of the shareholders provides them with an option that is embedded in the terms of a debt obligation as written by the debt holders.[156] To be more particular, one can consider the payoff associated with corporate debt to be equivalent to the combination of[157] (1) a sale by the shareholders to the debt holders of the underlying assets acquired with the borrowed funds and (2) the issue by the debt holders of a call option on the underlying assets that the shareholders can exercise at a price equal to the required payoff on the debt.

Consider, for example, a one-period asset with a cost at T(0) of $30,000 and a payoff at T(1) of either $15,000 (10 percent probability) or $36,000 (90 percent probability). Assume that the asset is acquired in corporate form with a contribution of $30,000 of debt capital. Assume also that the required payoff to the debt investor at T(1) is $33,900 (a $3,000 time-value return based on a riskless rate of 10 percent plus a $900 risk premium). Given these assumptions, one can consider the debt holders to have effectively purchased the underlying asset and to have issued a call option on the asset that the shareholders can exercise at T(1) for a price of $33,900. The shareholders, for their part, have effectively sold the asset and purchased the call option. If the specified contingency is resolved favourably, the payoff on the asset is $36,000, which is more than the required payoff to the debt holders. The shareholders, accordingly, will exercise their embedded call option and reacquire the asset from the debt holders. In effect, the shareholders capture the excess value of $2,100 over the $33,900 option price. If the contingency is resolved unfavourably, the payoff on the asset is $15,000. Since this is less than the exercise price under the call option, the shareholders will let the option expire and the debt holders will retain the asset.

One can also consider the payoff associated with this debt investment to be equivalent to the combination of[158] (1) the purchase by the debt holders from the shareholders of a riskless asset for a purchase price equal to the amount of the borrowed funds advanced and (2) the issue by the debt holders of a put option on the underlying corporate assets that the shareholders can exercise at a price equal to the payoff on the debt. Thus one can consider the debt holders in the previous example to have purchased a riskless asset from the shareholders at a cost of $30,000 (the amount of borrowed funds advanced) and to have issued a put option on the underlying corporate asset with an exercise price of $33,900 (the required one-period return on the debt). The shareholders have in effect sold a riskless asset for the advance of $30,000 and purchased the put option. If the specified contingency is resolved unfavourably at T(1), the payoff on the asset is $15,000. Since the payoff is less than the return on the debt, the shareholders will exercise their put option and the debt holders will effectively be required to purchase the underlying corporate asset with a value of $15,000 at a price of $33,900. If the contingency is resolved favourably at T(1), the payoff on the asset is $36,000. Since in this case the value of the asset is greater than the exercise price under the put option, the shareholders will allow the option to expire and will realize the $2,100 excess of that value over the exercise price.

This division of the payoffs on debt and equity as if between the owner of an asset and the holder of an option applies to corporate assets that are financed with debt. In general, the debt holders are in effect the owners of the underlying asset and the shareholders the holders of an option on the asset.[159] The debt holders earn an expected time-value return on the asset and bear a degree of risk that depends on the outcome of the specified contingencies that determine the ex post value of the underlying asset and the embedded option.[160] The shareholders hold only the call option (or the corresponding put option) and realize any unexpected gain or loss that arises because of the difference between the value of the particular asset at maturity of the debt and the exercise price under the embedded option, which is equal to the required payoff on the debt.[161] If a corporate asset is financed with equity, the shareholders retain both the expected time-value return associated with the asset and the option value, which depends on the resolution of the same contingencies as determine whether there is unexpected gain or loss ex post. In this case, then, the shareholders retain not only the bet element associated with the riskiness of the underlying corporate assets but the expected time-value return as well. Thus option-pricing theory helps to highlight the expected time-value return that is embedded in equity capital.

Avoidance Opportunities and Inefficiencies Caused by the Distinction for Tax Purposes Between Interest and Dividends

The basic functional similarity of debt and equity instruments means that they are substitutable and that differences between the tax treatments applied to them may influence an investor's choice between them. In some cases, debt and equity are perfect substitutes, in the sense that an investor faces the same level of risk with either of them but owing to their different tax treatments will realize a higher after-tax return from one than he will from the other. Instances of perfect substitutability involve only revenue loss and possible equity effects; no inefficiencies arise. Differences in the level of risk are measured, of course, in terms of differences in the chance to realize unexpected gains and losses. All forms of debt and equity have a time-value return.

Chapter 2 described two examples of perfect (or near perfect) substitutability:[162] (1) the issue of preferred shares by financially strong but non-taxpaying corporations in after-tax financing transactions and (2) the use of disguised equity by thinly capitalized corporations. The former instance involves the substitution of preferred shares for debt in loan transactions without any significant alteration in the pattern of cash flows. The only substantive change is the substitution of tax-free intercorporate dividends for fully taxable interest income. The latter instance involves the substitution of what is debt in form for what is treated in fact as an equity capital contribution by the issuer and the investor, who is a corporate insider or holder of a direct investment interest. The substitution does not alter in any way the pattern of cash flows associated with the investment, and it increases the after-tax return only by avoiding corporate-level tax on what is, in essence, equity income distributed as deductible interest expense. These instances of perfect substitutability are examples of what may be called "character arbitrage," whereby the tax treatment of an expected gain or loss is altered by changing the legal form of the transaction. In the case of after-tax financing, the expected time-value return associated with a loan transaction is disguised as tax-free intercorporate dividends. In the case of a thinly capitalized corporation, the expected time-value return associated with the embedded debt in equity capital is disguised as interest on shareholder-held debt. The perfect substitutability is possible provided that the tax law respects the legal form of the alternative transactions.

In other instances, differences in risk between debt and equity mean that their substitutability is imperfect, in which case the substitution of one for the other causes efficiency losses. The identification of tax-induced inefficiencies of this kind requires the identification of

- differences in tax treatment that create a tax bias in favour of corporate debt and
- efficiency losses that follow from that bias.

The necessary analysis of these two related effects is to be found primarily in the corporate finance literature on the theory of an "optimal capital structure" that lowers the cost of capital and maximizes shareholder wealth through the judicious use of debt. This literature begins with the work of Franco Modigliani and Merton Miller,[163] who offer a fundamental insight that may be stated as follows: in the absence of taxes, the value of a corporation is independent of its capital structure and therefore corporate debt policy is irrelevant.[164]

The irrelevance proposition follows from two simple premises: first, that the value of a corporation is equal to the present value of the expected cash flows from its real assets or investments; second, that the relative mix of debt and equity securities divides those expected cash flows among investors. Accordingly, the present value of the expected cash flows associated with the outstanding debt and equity securities of a corporation must equal the present value of the expected cash flows associated with the underlying corporate assets. Critical to this proposition is a requirement of perfect capital markets and a resultant insensitivity between the investment policy of a corporation and its borrowing policy.[165] Under these conditions, the value of two corporations with the same asset profile must be equivalent, whatever their mix of debt and equity securities.[166] This equivalence holds because investors can replicate the risk and return mix realized by any alteration of the relative mix of corporate-level debt and equity by substituting personal debt for corporate-level debt. This means that investors will not pay a premium for shares of corporations whose capital structures are a mix of debt and equity.[167] Changes in the mix of corporate-level debt and equity securities are, therefore, only changes in the composition of investors' portfolios and do not entail any efficiency losses.[168]

As Modigliani and Miller emphasize, the introduction of taxes alters the analysis. This is so primarily because of the existence of a tax bias in favour of corporate debt that investors can use to reduce the after-tax cost of capital and increase the value of a corporation. In particular, the deductibility of interest expense permits the distribution of corporate income free of the corporate-level tax. Thanks to this "shield" from the corporate income tax provided by the interest deduction, corporate debt generates a higher after-tax return and a lower cost of capital than equity does.[169] The tax shield, therefore, is an asset that adds value to a corporation[170] and induces it to issue more debt than it would issue in a world without taxes. An extensive literature,[171] including revisions by Miller of the original Modigliani-Miller propositions,[172] has followed the seminal work of Modigliani and Miller. The later literature emphasizes the more complex rate relationships that determine whether, in the aggregate, there is a tax bias in favour of either debt or equity and whether there is an optimal capital structure for particular corporations.[173] In general, the literature has expanded on the original Modigliani-Miller analysis in order to take into account the effect on corporate capital structure of investor-level taxes on debt and equity returns,[174] as well as the impact of differences in effective corporate tax rates.[175] To some extent, these additional factors reduce or offset the present value of the tax shield from the corporate interest deduction and thus reduce the tax bias in favour of debt.

Studies of the US classical corporate tax system, with its unintegrated corporate-level and shareholder-level taxes, have concluded that there is a general tax bias in favour of debt, although the size of this bias is a matter of debate. The bias persists even after one accounts for differences between corporate tax rates and investor-level tax rates on debt income and equity income.[176] It arises largely because for the majority of investors the investor-level tax on interest income is less than the double tax on equity income.[177] The US studies highlight the fact that the present value of the tax shield provided by the corporate interest deduction is sufficient to induce corporations to issue more debt than they would issue in the absence of income taxes. The equilibrium point at which the present value of the tax shield equals the tax rate of the marginal investor indicates the point at which a tax advantage arises for corporate debt.[178]

This bias in favour of debt persists even in countries that have imputation systems designed to reduce the tax burden on equity income. That is, it holds even where the corporate income tax rate and the highest marginal personal income tax rate are equivalent and shareholders receive full imputation credits for actual corporate tax on underlying income from which dividends are paid. Under these conditions, an imputation system ensures that the corporate income tax operates as a withholding tax on dividend distributions, and investors should have no preference between debt and equity. Nevertheless, a tax bias in favour of debt often remains. This is so because of two features of the imputation systems that most countries have adopted:[179]

1) the non-refundability of imputation credits for investors, including tax-exempt pension funds, who are subject to tax rates that are less than the corporate rate on distributed equity income;

2) the failure to provide imputation credits for investors who realize distributions of corporate income in the form of capital gains on the sale of their shares.

These features result in a combined corporate and shareholder tax that is higher than the investor-level tax on interest and ensure that for a large number of investors debt is preferable to equity. Taxable corporations will issue tax-preferred debt until the present value of the tax shield equals the tax payable on interest income for the marginal investor who is subject to a personal tax rate equal to the corporate rate.

Given a tax bias in favour of debt finance, the substitution of debt for equity is inefficient only if it is imperfect; that is, if in the absence of taxes equity would be preferable to debt. To put the matter in another way, the tax advantage associated with the deductibility of corporate interest expense induces a substitution of debt for equity that continues until the instruments are no longer perfect substitutes. At that point, the substitution begins to generate non-tax costs and so becomes, by definition, inefficient.

Several kinds of efficiency losses arise from the tax-induced substitution of debt for equity, but most observers emphasize the costs of financial distress caused by an excessive reliance on debt. Financial economists distinguish between "direct" and "indirect" costs of financial distress.[180] Direct costs are the administrative and legal costs incurred in any legal proceeding, including bankruptcy, that governs the orderly breakup or reorganization of an insolvent corporation.[181] Indirect costs are the less tangible costs associated with financial distress short of bankruptcy. Thus suppliers, employees, and customers may become reluctant to deal with a corporation that is in financial difficulty, since they cannot rely on the corporation to perform its obligations. This reluctance may choke off necessary suppliers and purchasers, and thereby force the corporation to forgo favourable investment opportunities.[182]

A second inefficiency identified in some of the literature[183] arises from the effect of the tax bias in favour of debt on investment decisions. In general, debt is the preferred source of capital for relatively safe projects that involve the acquisition of tangible assets, such as real estate or equipment. Similarly, debt investors prefer mature corporations with established credit records. The preference arises in each case because in each case the likelihood that the fixed stream of payment obligations on debt will not be serviced is relatively small. Moreover, if default and bankruptcy proceedings do occur, tangible assets are more likely than intangible assets to retain their value and, therefore, to support the value of the outstanding debt. In contrast, risky investment projects and new businesses tend to involve a relatively high variance of returns and a relatively high chance of unexpected loss and therefore a relatively high risk that default on outstanding debt will occur. Furthermore, the value of the intangible assets, such as human capital and property rights in technology, that are often associated with risky projects and new businesses tends to be more difficult to realize than the value of assets that are part of a going concern. Thus a tax bias in favour of debt may favour investment in relatively riskless projects and more mature corporations. The result is that the cost of capital will be higher for risky projects and new businesses than it is for other projects and businesses. In short, a tax bias in favour of debt reduces economic efficiency by distorting investment decisions.

This efficiency loss is all the greater if, as is likely, investment in risky projects and new businesses with extensive requirements for human capital and technological development generates social returns in excess of the private returns to entrepreneurs ("positive externalities"). Indeed, conventional economic wisdom posits that the government should provide subsidies to ensure that there is a socially optimal level of investment in research and development, new technologies, and human capital. A tax bias in favour of debt may not only discourage this desirable type of investment but even counteract the effect of government subsidies designed to encourage it.

The obvious response to opportunities for both pure tax avoidance and approximate tax avoidance that occur because of the substitutability of debt and equity is an explicit recognition of the functional similarity of debt and equity and the identical taxation of the returns on all financial instruments in either category. If interest and dividends are taxed in the same way, the incentive to choose one over the other in instances of pure tax avoidance will disappear, and so will the revenue loss associated with avoidance strategies. The identical tax treatment of interest and dividends also introduces a desirable degree of neutrality into the choice between debt and equity capital. If suitable non-tax factors are left to govern this choice, instances of approximate avoidance will be greatly reduced and the associated efficiency losses will be minimized. The extent of this result depends directly on the extent to which the significance of the value of the tax shield provided by the corporate interest deduction is minimized.

For the reasons cited briefly above, imputation systems do not realize the consistent taxation of interest and dividends, let alone the consistent taxation of the returns on debt and equity generally. Most imputation systems reduce the burden of a classical corporate income tax on the return on equity, which nevertheless remains subject to a greater tax burden overall than does the return on debt. By contrast, accretion taxation, by recognizing annually the changes in value of both debt instruments and equity instruments, would realize the identical treatment of the returns on both. Under accretion taxation, in effect, expected, as well as unexpected, gains and losses on debt and equity would be subject to recognition annually.[184]

The interesting question, one that chapter 6 will take up in detail, is whether this approach is the only solution to the problem of pure and approximate tax avoidance presented by the differential taxation of the returns on debt and equity. In fact, chapter 6 will argue that accretion taxation is not necessary in this context, and that there is another way in which to realize the desirable goal of consistent taxation. This alternative is less defensible in theory than is accretion taxation. It consists in accrual recognition of expected gains and losses on debt instruments and the embedded debt in all shares and realization-based recognition of unexpected gains and losses, with all of the tax-avoidance problems attributable to the latter approach. As was noted earlier, accretion taxation is a first-best regime largely because it is the alternative that best addresses the problems associated with timing arbitrage, risk arbitrage, and the bare timing option in the context of expected and unexpected gains and losses. It is only incidentally that accretion taxation also addresses the problems associated with the existing distinction between debt and equity for tax purposes.

Elimination of the Distinction Between Ordinary Income and Capital Amounts

The third element of a benchmark approach to the taxation of financial instruments is elimination of the distinction between ordinary income and capital amounts. The need for this element is based on two premises. First, the distinction between expected and unexpected amounts provides no obvious insight that supports the distinction for tax purposes between ordinary income and capital amounts. Second, although the distinction between expected and unexpected gains and losses may support a capital gains preference on subsidy grounds,[185] the supposed benefits from a capital gains preference are too problematic when the preference is applied to financial instruments to offset the revenue loss and the inefficiencies that it generates. Accordingly, all returns on financial instruments, whether expected or unexpected, should be recognized in full as income or expense.

This brief and unequivocal expression of the two premises glosses over the contentious treatment of this subject in the tax literature. In the absence of anything new to add, the present discussion makes no attempt to review the enormous volume of literature concerned with the preferential taxation of capital gains.[186] It limits itself instead to a few select points that are relevant to the taxation of financial instruments. In general, these points indicate that the application of a capital gains tax preference to financial instruments creates opportunities for pure and approximate tax avoidance. The effect of a capital gains preference is not much different, therefore, from the effects of realization-based recognition of gains and losses and the distinction for tax purposes between interest and dividends. To eliminate the inconsistencies and discontinuities that are the sources of both types of tax avoidance, all three of these features of the existing tax system must be eliminated. In one important respect, however, the issue of the capital gains preference is distinct from the other two issues: practical policy constraints require consideration of second-best alternatives to accretion taxation and the identical treatment of interest and dividends, but there is no need to consider any second-best alternative to the elimination of the preferential treatment of capital gains.

Chapter 2 made the point that a capital gain is a special type of gain created and recognized for income tax purposes.[187] Capital gains (and losses) have two principal characteristics. First, the amount of the gain (loss) is the appreciation (depreciation) in the value of an asset realized on a sale or other disposition. Second, a gain (or loss) is capital in nature only if the taxpayer acquired the asset for its current yield and not for a trading purpose. The proposition that all cash flows associated with financial instruments should be recognized as non capital amounts rests on the following intuition: given a concept of income that is equivalent to realized gains, there is nothing special about capital gains to justify taxing them at a rate lower than the rate applicable to other income.[188] Appreciation in the value of a financial instrument over its cost is a gain; conversely, any depreciation is a loss. The gain or loss is determined by discounting the expected cash flows associated with the instrument at an appropriate risk-adjusted rate. The passage of time reveals changes in expectations that affect the cash flows and, with them, the value of the instrument. The fact that cash flows may be realized on disposition of a financial instrument, producing a gain or loss, seems an arbitrary basis for recognizing these cash flows at a rate lower than the rate that applies to the same cash flows if the taxpayer recognizes them while he is holding the instrument.[189] Moreover, the fact that a taxpayer acquires an asset for trading purposes rather than investment purposes does nothing to alter the nature of the associated cash flows in a manner that should alter their tax treatment.

Preferential tax regimes for capital gains violate the intuition that any differences between capital gains and losses and other gains and losses are insufficient to justify treating the former differently from the latter. Not surprisingly, the existence of these regimes has led to instances of pure tax avoidance in which taxpayers attempt to convert expected gains that are equivalent to fully taxable interest into tax-preferred appreciation in the value of a debt instrument realized on a disposition.[190] Chapter 2 described the legislative responses to certain simplistic instances of pure avoidance, including the issue of original issue discount (OID) obligations and the transfer of debt with accrued, but unpaid, interest.[191] Conceptually, these instances of transactions structured to exploit inconsistencies created by the distinction between ordinary income and capital amounts[192] are identical to the "dividend-stripping" transactions intended to convert costlessly[193] what would otherwise be a fully taxable dividend distribution of retained earnings into a tax-preferred capital gain realized on the sale of shares. Various legislative responses have been required to override the legal form of pure avoidance transactions of this kind and the attendant characterization of the relevant cash flows as the realization of appreciation in the value of shares.[194] Other, more complex transactions, described in chapter 7,[195] involve combinations of financial instruments, including derivatives, to provide an expected time-value return in the form of a capital gain realized as appreciation in value.[196]

The preferential taxation of capital gains also leads to instances of approximate tax avoidance and misallocation of resources. In particular, conventional wisdom holds that taxpayers respond to a capital gains preference by shifting their savings into assets, such as real estate, that provide cash flow patterns in the form of capital appreciation. Thus the result of a capital gains preference is overinvestment in assets of this kind.[197] In the case of financial instruments, the misallocation is more difficult to observe, since it is easy to alter cash flow patterns costlessly to provide capital gain treatment in instances of pure avoidance. Nonetheless, some obvious forms of approximate avoidance are possible.

For example, a capital gains preference creates a bias in favour of the retention of equity income and the provision of returns in the form of capital gains rather than dividends. Efficiency losses will result if a corporation retains earnings for tax purposes when investors would be better off if they received the earnings in the form of dividends and reinvested the after-tax amount in projects with higher expected returns.[198] From an efficiency perspective, however, the least desirable consequence of a capital gains preference is an indirect one that is unrelated to approximate tax avoidance. This consequence follows from the inevitable need under preferential regimes to (1) reduce the recognition rate for capital losses so that it reflects the reduced inclusion rate for capital gains and (2) restrict the deductibility of capital losses to the amount of realized capital gains. The former reduction follows from a perceived need for symmetrical recognition rates; the latter restriction is intended to address the problem of selective realization, whereby taxpayers accelerate the realization of their capital losses and defer the realization of offsetting gains.[199] Both restrictions effectively increase the after-tax value of capital losses in a way that increases deviation from the expected return associated with an asset, and hence increases the associated risk as well.[200] This outcome may reduce the attractiveness of risky investments and thus lead to a suboptimal level of risk taking.[201]

It is possible to argue that the application of a capital gains preference generates benefits that offset the revenue losses and inefficiencies that arise from pure and approximate tax avoidance. There are, in fact, several fairly well-known arguments that are persistently cited in support of a general capital gains preference on subsidy and efficiency grounds.[202] Only three of these arguments, however, warrant serious consideration.[203] The first is that a capital gains preference is a necessary stimulus to savings, growth, and investment generally. According to this argument, a preferential capital gains tax rate, by increasing after-tax returns, encourages taxpayers to save and invest more than they would in the absence of the preferential rate. The additional savings and investment, in turn, encourage economic growth by lowering the after-tax cost of capital and thus making marginal projects feasible.

A second argument on subsidy grounds is that a capital gains preference is necessary as a stimulus to risk taking. This position, obviously, presumes that risk taking is desirable and that the prospect of a higher after-tax return induces taxpayers to invest more of their savings in risky projects than they otherwise would. It also presumes that a capital gain is an accurate proxy for the realization of unexpected gains that arise from the assumption of risk.[204]

The third argument is that a capital gains preference is necessary as an offset to the "lock-in effect" and the inefficiencies it entails.[205] This term refers to the tax-induced incentive under a realization-based income tax to continue to hold an asset and avoid realization. Inefficiencies arise if the optimal choice for a taxpayer in the absence of taxes would be to sell the asset and reinvest in another asset but tax considerations induce him to continue to hold the asset. A preferential tax rate on capital gains, according to its advocates, is a means of inducing taxpayers to realize accrued gains. In essence, the argument is that a reduction in the tax cost of a sale and reinvestment can offset the welfare loss arising because of the decision to continue to hold capital assets. An additional supposed benefit of a preferential capital gains rate is that by increasing the incidence of realizations it increases revenue as well.[206]

All of these arguments are problematic, particularly in the context of the design of a system for the taxation of income from financial instruments. They have two general shortcomings.[207] One is that they may seriously overstate the problems that a preference is designed to address. In this connection, it is important to distinguish between the impact of a capital gains preference on the overall level of savings and investment and its impact on the choice of investments, given the reflection of this choice in the pattern of ownership of financial assets.[208] As a stimulus to economic growth generally, a capital gains preference is intended to increase the overall level of savings and investment in much the same way as would a lower rate of tax on all forms of capital income under a cash flow consumption tax. This line of reasoning rests on two propositions:

1) that an increased level of savings and investment is necessary as an economic stimulus, and

2) that a reduced capital gains tax rate results in an increased level of savings and investment.

Even if one accepts the second proposition, which is questionable in its own right, the first proposition has proved to be extremely contentious. In particular, serious concerns about distributional consequences continue to prevent the wholesale substitution of a consumption tax for an income tax and thus the reduction in the rate of tax on capital income that such a substitution would entail. Indeed, it is probably accurate to say that the evidence in favour of a causal link between an increased level of savings, economic growth, and a lower tax rate on capital income must be much stronger before concerns about the distributional consequences of such a shift in the tax burden can be overcome.[209]

The argument that the capital gains preference is useful as a stimulus to risk taking rests on the assumptions that the economy lacks an adequate pool of risk capital and that a capital gains preference will increase the overall level of that type of capital. Similarly, the argument that a capital gains preference is useful as a response to the lock-in effect rests on the assumption that investors' inability to diversify their portfolios results in welfare losses for the economy as a whole. Lowering the tax rate on capital gains and thereby inducing realizations alleviates the welfare loss by encouraging investors to switch to financial assets that they value more highly. In both contexts, however, the operation of the tax system may in general affect only the pattern of ownership or allocation of financial assets and not the overall level of investment, and thus may produce no serious inefficiencies in the economy as a whole.[210]

To be more specific, there is no clear evidence that the level of risk capital is deficient or that any discrimination in the tax system against risky investment by taxable investors causes a shortfall in this kind of investment.[211] Any adverse effects of the tax system on risk taking may, in fact, be offset by the substantial presence of tax-exempt investors, such as pension funds, and venture capital corporations, which benefit from significant tax preferences and provide risk capital at prices that do not exceed the opportunity cost of capital.[212] As well, the lock-in effect primarily influences the pattern of ownership of financial assets rather than the overall level of investment. This is true provided that another investor is willing to acquire an asset (asset B) that an investor who is locked into an investment (asset A) because of the tax payable on realization of an accrued gain would otherwise prefer.[213] In other words, the tax on realized gains on asset A imposes a transaction cost that may prevent the holder from acquiring asset B at a specified price; yet provided that another investor is willing to acquire asset B at that price, the only welfare loss is the one sustained by the investor who owns asset A and would prefer asset B in the absence of taxes.[214] The only thing that the lock-in effect may affect is the identity of the investors who are willing to hold asset B.[215]

The arguments in support of a capital gains preference may also overstate the effectiveness of a preference in realizing its intended results. As many commentators have pointed out, in almost every instance in which a case is made for a capital gains preference it would be possible to adopt a more direct policy response. In particular, it is not at all obvious why a tax preference that is intended to stimulate savings, investment, and growth should be limited to capital gains. If a subsidy of this kind is desirable, it should presumably be extended to all forms of capital, in which case the adoption of a cash flow consumption tax would be the appropriate policy response.[216] Similarly, even if one agrees that there is a need for more risk capital, the additional after-tax reward for risk taking that a capital gains preference provides may not be sufficient to offset the reduced attractiveness of risky investments caused by the preference's attendant restrictions on loss recognition.[217] The obvious alternative is to reduce the risk associated with certain financial instruments by lowering the after-tax cost of losses through the provision of full loss offsets against other income. Arguments for using a capital gains preference to increase the after-tax return to risky investments may, at best, support the provision of a limited subsidy for certain types of financial instruments (usually shares of closely held corporations) that is a common practice in some countries.[218] Even the case for these more restrictive preferences is doubtful, given the difficulty of targeting them accurately and the failure of the empirical data to demonstrate clearly that they do in fact provide the benefits they are intended to provide.[219]

As to the perceived welfare losses attributable to the lock-in effect, the obvious first-best response is elimination of the realization basis that gives rise to the problem in the first place. Accretion taxation of all gains and losses on all assets would eliminate taxpayer sensitivity to the tax costs otherwise associated with sale and reinvestment strategies.[220] Even if a general application of this approach is considered to be infeasible because of liquidity and valuation concerns,[221] it would be possible to apply accretion taxation to a range of financial instruments that can be traded at low transaction costs and, therefore, do not present these concerns. This point is taken up in more detail in the next two chapters.[222] In the present context, the important general point is that it is possible to address many of the timing issues presented by the realization requirement by applying accretion taxation to a limited range of financial instruments and requiring accrual recognition of expected gains and losses on other financial instruments. The interesting thing is that this approach might also address many of the perceived problems associated with the lock-in effect and the supposed adverse impact of the tax system on risk taking.[223]

Even if one believes that none of the objections to the arguments in support of a capital gains preference is sufficient by itself to refute them, the cumulative effect of these objections makes the case for a preference tenuous. That case is especially problematic in the context of the taxation of financial instruments, where more direct policy alternatives are readily available. The desirability of these alternatives is enhanced by the fact that the introduction of a capital gains preference creates tax-avoidance opportunities, whose attendant costs in the form of revenue loss tend to negate any benefits that the preference may produce.[224] As described already, avoidance opportunities are of particular concern in the case of financial instruments that are easily substitutable—that is, instruments whose cash flows taxpayers can repackage in a legal form that benefits from the preference. It is extremely difficult, therefore, to build a convincing case for the maintenance of a distinction between ordinary income and capital amounts as the basis for preferential taxation of financial instruments. At best, there may be a case for applying a reduced tax rate to income from capital generally (or all forms of financial capital) in order to stimulate savings, investment, and economic growth.[225]

Non-Resident Withholding Tax and the International Dimension

As was noted in chapter 1, the income taxation of financial instruments centres on the treatment of their associated cash flows. These cash flows raise both issues of timing, which centre on the choice between accrual and realization-based recognition of gains and losses, and issues of characterization, which centre on the distinctions under existing income tax systems between interest and dividends and between ordinary income and capital amounts. In each of these areas, tax-policy makers must attempt to suppress inconsistencies and discontinuities that arise from a reliance on legal form as the basis for differences in treatment under the traditional tax cubbyholes. The only distinction between types of cash flows that should have any policy significance is the distinction between expected and unexpected gains and losses, and the accretion ideal, by requiring the recognition of changes in value as they arise, eliminates the need for even this distinction. Differences in the taxation of cash flows that depend on their classification as interest or dividends or ordinary income or capital amounts give rise to avoidance opportunities and inefficiencies that are not necessarily offset by efficiency gains. As a result, the benchmark approach to the taxation of financial instruments consists of a simple policy prescription: the recognition of all amounts of income or expense in full as they arise with changes in the value of the instrument.

The discussion to this point has developed these basic insights in an exclusively domestic context. It has assumed (1) that the cash flows associated with a financial instrument occur between taxpayers resident in the same country and (2) that one can properly characterize these flows as being sourced in the country of residence. The present part considers what distinct issues, if any, arise in the context of cross-border transactions. The discussion will be relatively brief, since it will argue that in fact this context has very few distinct implications for the issue of the appropriate tax treatment of the cash flows associated with financial instruments.[226] Central to this issue are problems of income measurement that are identical in the domestic context and the cross-border context.[227] The sourcing of the cash flows associated with financial instruments for the purpose of determining jurisdiction to tax is a largely unrelated issue. Indeed, except in one respect, there is nothing about these cash flows that distinguishes the resolution of jurisdictional issues in their case from the resolution of these issues in the context of the provision of goods or services across borders.

The exception is the application of non-resident withholding tax to cross-border financial flows. In this area, application of the traditional tax cubbyholes results in differences in tax treatment based on legal form, and financial innovation presents familiar opportunities for character arbitrage designed to avoid or reduce non-resident withholding tax.[228] As in the domestic context, the obvious response to these avoidance opportunities is the consistent taxation of equivalent cash flows.[229] This does not necessarily mean the absence of withholding taxes; rather it means the application of the same tax rate to equivalent cash flows.[230] However, unlike approaches to income measurement in the domestic context, it is difficult to identify a basis for the application of consistent taxation in the context of withholding taxes. In other words, the role of withholding taxes is too unclear to indicate which cash flows should be considered equivalent and, therefore, taxed consistently.

It is not suggested here that a new international order is required to address the cross-border issues presented by the taxation of financial instruments. Since the cross-border issues associated with financial flows are limited primarily to the application of withholding taxes, it is possible to frame adequate policy responses within the status quo.[231] Any attempt to alter the status quo must focus on wider issues that concern equally the cross-border provision of goods and services and the questionable normative bases for the current division of taxing power and the attendant revenue from cross-border transactions. Consideration of these wider issues is beyond the scope of this book.[232] It is accepted here, therefore, that the country in which income is earned or sourced ("the source country") enjoys the primary taxing right and that the taxpayer's country of residence ("the residence country") has only a secondary or residual right. The nature of the latter right is reflected in the fact that the country of residence usually either provides a credit for foreign tax paid on the foreign-source income of a resident or grants an exemption. Since the principle of taxation at source applies largely to active business income,[233] one possible explanation for its use is acceptance of a vaguely framed "benefits theory" to the effect that the country in which income is earned is entitled to tax it in return for the provision of the infrastructure and other conditions necessary for the income-earning process.[234] In the case of investment income, the taxing right of the source country is reduced to the imposition of minimal withholding taxes[235] and the principal tax is the residence-based tax. The apparent assumption in this case is that most investment income is earned by individuals, who should be taxed on their wealth increments from all sources. Only the country of residence is in a position to impose such a tax.[236]

Given this status quo, the issues associated with the taxation of cross-border financial flows are relatively clear.[237] To the extent that residence-based and source-based taxation are applied on a net basis (income less related expense), the income measurement issues are identical to those that arise in the case of a resident taxpayer and domestic-source income. In particular, a resident who earns foreign-source income from financial instruments must calculate that income on a net basis, using rules that resolve the issues already described. The same requirement holds for a non-resident who is taxable on net income from financial instruments subject to tax in the source country. This similarity in income measurement principles leaves three principal jurisdictional issues, which are unrelated to the determination of net income.

The first issue concerns the relationship between particular financial instruments and the activities of a non-resident in a source country. If these activities constitute the carrying on of a business, the source country conventionally asserts the right to tax the associated income. If a tax treaty is in force between the taxpayer's country of residence and the country of source, the business must generally be conducted through a permanent establishment in order for the source country to assert its prior taxing right.[238] Any income and expense from financial flows that constitute the required business presence, or that are connected with such a presence, are subject to taxation in the source country. It must be determined, therefore, whether any income or expense is allocable to a business or a permanent establishment in the source country.

The second jurisdictional issue concerns the application of the anti-deferral legislation of certain countries to income from financial instruments. In general, this legislation requires resident shareholders of certain non-resident corporations, and resident beneficiaries of certain non-resident trusts as well, to recognize their pro rata share of foreign-source investment income earned in the offshore entity. Residence-country tax is imposed on the "tainted" income, which is attributed to particular resident taxpayers as it accrues rather than being deferred until distribution. For the purposes of the anti-deferral legislation, it must be determined whether income or expense from financial flows has a foreign source and, under some legislative regimes, whether these amounts are passive in character.

The third jurisdictional issue concerns the allocation of income or expense from financial flows to the operations of a multinational enterprise located in several jurisdictions. The allocation is necessary for the calculation of the net income or loss attributable to each location, and it may also determine the source of income or expense for the purposes of foreign tax credits.

Rosenbloom argues that the resolution of these jurisdictional issues involves the application to financial instruments of the same general approaches as apply in the context of the provision of goods and services, and that there is nothing unique about the cash flows associated with financial instruments to indicate how the issues should be resolved.[239] Determination of the source and character of income or expense depends on the characterization of a financial instrument as either an isolated transaction or an integral part of a business carried on by a taxpayer.[240] This determination is a factual one; that is, certain factors must be assessed to determine whether or not there is a sufficient connection between a particular financial instrument and a business carried on by the taxpayer in a particular country. Many of these factors are the same as the factors that are assessed in the case of a taxpayer who is engaged in the provision of goods and services.[241] Some factors may be unique to the case of financial instruments,[242] but the overall determination is no different in kind from the determination made in respect of the provision of goods and services. Since no one factor is determinative, the process entails some arbitrariness and uncertainty. For the purposes of anti-deferral legislation that is based on a tainted-income approach, it must similarly be determined on the facts whether a given financial instrument is or is not connected with an active foreign business that is not subject to the legislation. If it is not, the income or loss is deemed to be from an investment source and therefore within the scope of the legislation.

The allocation of income and expense among the various units of a multinational enterprise depends on another factual determination. In the case of branch operations, this determination requires the attribution of particular financial instruments to the different branches as if the latter were separate entities. In the case of operations conducted through affiliated corporations, the allocation issue involves a factual determination that the pricing of instruments between two legally distinct affiliates reflects arm's-length terms. In resolving these issues, it may be necessary to take into account some factors that arise only in the context of financial instruments,[243] but the assessment is no different in kind from the assessment that is undertaken in the context of the provision of goods and services. In particular, it must be determined what items of income and expense are properly attributable to particular branches in different countries. Policy makers must decide to what extent internal dealings between branches are to be treated as transactions between separate entities with attendant consequences for the allocation of income and expense between taxing jurisdictions.[244] To the extent that dealings between affiliates are respected as transactions between distinct entities, application of the arm's-length standard requires the development of pricing techniques to assess the adequacy of the internal prices. If the operations of a multinational enterprise are highly integrated, the application of these pricing techniques may take the form of a "functional approach,"[245] under which the aggregate income or loss of the enterprise is allocated among affiliates on the basis of their relative contributions. The nature of the cash flows associated with financial instruments provides nothing in the way of unique insights for the resolution of these issues.

None of the above observations should be interpreted to mean that jurisdictional and transfer-pricing issues are unimportant; they have legitimately occupied the efforts of a vast army of tax-policy makers, tax practitioners, and academics. The simple point made here is that the resolution of these issues in the context of the taxation of financial instruments depends on the same factors and considerations as apply to their resolution in the context of the provision of goods and services and does not depend in any appreciable sense on the nature of the cash flows associated with financial instruments. In contrast, the resolution of income-measurement issues in the context of the taxation of financial instruments does depend uniquely on the nature of financial flows. The income-measurement principles are taken as a given, and the resulting amounts are then allocated among taxing jurisdictions in much the same manner as amounts that arise in the case of the cross-border provision of goods and services.

The unique issues presented by the application of withholding tax by a source country arise when a resident makes payments to a non-resident and the relevant financial instrument is not connected with a business or permanent establishment of the non-resident in the source country.[246] In this case, the nature of the cash flow determines the application of withholding tax. Because the tax is essentially an excise tax on the gross amount of financial flows, the timing issues discussed earlier do not arise and the sole issue is the character of the cash flow. The legislation in most countries divides financial flows among tax cubbyholes for (1) dividends, (2) interest, and (3) payments on derivatives.[247] Dividends are generally not deductible in calculating the income of a corporate payer, and the underlying income is subject to corporate tax in the source country. Dividends too are generally subject to withholding tax on payments to a non-resident shareholder, though some countries forgo the tax (by treaty or unilaterally under domestic legislation) by providing an imputation credit for corporate tax paid. Interest paid by a resident debtor to a non-resident creditor is generally deductible in calculating income of the debtor, and it is subject only to withholding tax in the source country (the debtor's country of residence). In the case of interest on portfolio debt, withholding tax is often waived by the source country under its domestic legislation.[248] Payments on derivatives are generally free of non-resident withholding tax, usually because of the absence of a specific charge in the domestic legislation that covers payments of this kind.[249] To the extent that the payments are deductible in calculating the income of the payer, source-country tax is nil and the payee's country of residence is the sole taxing jurisdiction.

The problems with this status quo are well known and will be described in detail in chapter 7.[250] For present purposes, it is enough to say that differences in withholding rates present opportunities for pure tax avoidance through the combination of derivatives and long positions in debt or shares that replicate the cash flows associated with either of the latter two instruments.[251] These opportunities are attributable, in large part, to the exempt status of payments on derivatives and interest on portfolio debt. For example,[252] the paradigm case of synthetic replication in this context is the so-called total-return equity swap,[253] which allows a non-resident to realize the exposure associated with the leveraged acquisition of shares without the application of withholding tax.[254] A non-resident can achieve this result by taking advantage of the exempt status of payments under the swap while receiving interest on an underlying position in portfolio debt. Comparable avoidance opportunities arise from various applications of the put-call parity theorem described in chapter 1[255] and from the combination of a long position in portfolio debt and the forward purchase of shares.[256]

The first-best response to these instances of pure avoidance is a withholding tax system that taxes equivalent cash flows consistently. A system of this kind will ensure that the sum of the taxes on the cash flows associated with the basic building-block instruments that are combined to create a synthetic instrument equals the tax on the cash flow replicated by the synthetic. Realization of this result, however, requires a clear concept of the application of non-resident withholding tax to the basic instruments; yet it is not apparent how consistency should be defined for this purpose. Indeed, although both the general status quo for the application of non-resident withholding tax and the problems associated with it are relatively clear, it is difficult to define a benchmark in the absence of an obvious normative basis for the tax.

The tax literature identifies three possible approaches to the design of a consistent withholding tax system for financial flows. One approach distinguishes cash flows in terms of expected and unexpected gains and losses. This distinction, which has some policy relevance for timing purposes, is applicable in the context of non-resident withholding tax largely on the basis of two categories of payments: (1) payments associated with capital-raising debt and equity instruments and (2) payments associated with risk-shifting derivatives.[257] The first category of payments corresponds roughly to the payments associated with any instrument that involves an advance of funds in return for an expected payoff that provides an expected time-value return. The second category corresponds roughly to the payments associated with forwards, futures, and swaps that are pure bets and therefore substitute mutual promises for an advance of funds. The latter instruments provide only unexpected gains and losses that arise on the resolution of a specified contingency. On the theory that the provision of capital by a non-resident constitutes a sufficient connection to the source country, one could, conceivably, limit the application of withholding tax to expected gains on capital-raising instruments. Since options involve an advance of funds and an expected gain, payments made on maturity of a cash-settled option should be subject to withholding tax to the extent that they represent payment of the expected return.[258] Similarly, any bet element of a forward or swap that is prepaid wholly or in part provides an expected gain that should be taxed as an interest equivalent.[259]

As the basis for a benchmark withholding tax system, the distinction between expected and unexpected amounts is inconsistent with the status quo, which imposes withholding tax on dividends without distinguishing between an expected time-value return and an unexpected return in excess of the riskless interest rate. In many countries, moreover, the expected gain on portfolio debt is usually exempt from withholding tax. Obviously, the direct response to this inconsistency is to implement the distinction between expected and unexpected returns in all cases as a basis for the application of non-resident withholding tax.

The problem with this response is the fact that the distinction itself has no clear policy relevance. A commonly suggested rationale for the distinction is that since withholding tax is applied as a proxy for a tax on net income it should be limited to payments that can be assumed to "have a high content of net income."[260] The relatively thin margins associated with payments on derivatives means that these payments may not have the requisite content and should be exempt from withholding tax.[261] This rationale does not necessarily hold up as a basis for the application of withholding tax, since expected time-value returns in the form of interest, royalties, or even dividends are often associated with thin investor margins and may not have an especially high content of net income.[262] More important, there is nothing about the nature of gains as expected or unexpected that indicates whether they tend to be paid "gross" or "net" to a non-resident payee. At best, therefore, any assumptions about high content of net income should probably be made for all financial flows generally; that is, on some basis other than a distinction between expected and unexpected returns.[263]

The second possible benchmark approach to the application of withholding tax begins with the premise that also underlies the case for the elimination of the distinction between ordinary income and capital amounts. Under this premise, any payment from a resident to a non-resident should be subject to withholding tax in the source country to the extent that the payment represents a gain to the payee in the sense of a return in excess of any advance of funds. Whether the gain is expected or unexpected is irrelevant, and characterization of the gain as interest or dividends or a payment on a derivative is no justification for differences in withholding tax rates. In effect, it is assumed that the payment of a gain by a resident payer to a non-resident payee provides sufficient justification for assertion of the taxing right of the source country.[264] Limitation of a single withholding tax rate to the gain element in a payment ensures that the tax is applied exclusively as a proxy for what would otherwise be a tax on net income of the non-resident.

This approach is roughly comparable, therefore, to the recognition of all income and expense in full in the domestic context. The basic starting point is the application of withholding tax to all payments that represent gain to a non-resident, unless exemption can be justified on a defensible policy basis. As in the domestic context, the important policy issues involve consideration of the case for exceptions to the identical tax treatment of all cash flows. In the cross-border context, this process requires a determination whether the payment of a particular gain differs from the payment of other gains sufficiently to justify its exemption from non-resident withholding tax. Thus the exemption of interest on portfolio debt is usually justified on the ground that the mobility of portfolio debt results in the shifting forward of withholding tax to resident debtors. If it were not exempt, portfolio investors would move their debt investments to source countries that did not impose withholding tax.[265] An exemption allows resident debtors access to international debt capital markets at a lower cost.

Although the connection is not entirely clear, much the same rationale is the apparent basis for the continued exemption of payments on derivatives from withholding tax. However, the rationale is extended to all derivative instruments on the assumption that they are equivalent to portfolio debt. No special exemption is provided for portfolio equity, but as was noted above some countries provide an effective exemption either by extending imputation credits to all dividends paid to non-residents or by applying a lower rate of withholding tax to dividends from foreign direct investment. A consistent application of non-resident withholding tax to all cross-border financial flows subject to an exemption for portfolio investment requires consistent treatment of debt and equity and an extension of the same treatment to payments on derivatives, on the assumption that they are analogous to portfolio investments.

One obvious design problem with exemption on the basis of a distinction between foreign direct investors and foreign portfolio investors[266] is that it would require the development of a definition of portfolio investment for debt, equity, and derivative instruments.[267] The result would be a significant discontinuity between the tax treatment of investment that satisfied the definition and the tax treatment of investment that did not. Thus a small change in the level of non-resident investment would result in significantly different tax consequences. The discontinuity would be the focus of considerable tax planning centred on the level of investment that was considered to constitute a foreign direct interest. Although this problem is no different in kind from the definitional problem associated with portfolio debt, its magnitude increases significantly if one extends the same rationale for exemption to equity investment and payments on derivatives. More fundamentally, it is unclear whether the rationale for the exemption of interest on portfolio debt applies equally to international equity markets and the market for derivative instruments.[268] In particular, it is unclear whether the application of withholding tax to portfolio dividends has resulted in an increased cost of capital or a flight of equity capital to jurisdictions without a comparable tax.[269] Advocates of exemption from withholding tax for all payments on derivatives have not shown clearly that derivatives markets operate similarly to debt or equity markets or what differences between the latter two markets justify the application of withholding tax to portfolio dividends but not to interest on portfolio debt.

The third possible benchmark approach, suggested by Avi-Yonah,[270] incorporates a distinction between deductible and non-deductible payments as the basis for the application of withholding tax to all cross-border cash flows. The basis of this approach is a concept of withholding taxes as a backup for residence-based taxation of investment income, under which payments are deductible in calculating the income of the payer.[271] One can exempt non-deductible payments from withholding tax because they are already subject to tax in the source country as part of the net income of a resident payer. To be more specific, the country of residence has the primary taxing right if financial flows are unrelated to a business carried on in the source country, but a source country can impose a withholding tax as a means of preventing non-taxation through the routing of cash flows to entities established in tax-haven jurisdictions as the country of residence. In theory, it would be possible to implement this supporting role relatively easily by applying non-resident withholding tax to payments that are tax-deductible in the source country and therefore not otherwise subject to tax in that country. In practice, adoption of this approach as the basis for the consistent taxation of cross-border financial flows would require a substantial alteration of the status quo, including the imposition of withholding tax on tax-deductible payments on portfolio investments. The latter requirement is especially problematic for small open economies that are net capital importers or for which the possibility of capital flight is a serious problem.[272] Opportunities for tax avoidance would also arise to the extent that the effective source-country tax was applied on a net basis to non-deductible payments, such as dividends, at a rate that was higher than the withholding tax rates applied on a gross basis to tax-deductible payments. Indeed, it is possible to realize consistent taxation in all respects only by levying source-country tax at the same effective rate on all cross-border financial flows, whether they are tax-deductible or not. Nonetheless, one could realize an important measure of consistent taxation of cross-border cash flows, which is lacking under the status quo, by implementing withholding tax on the basis of either a distinction between deductible and non-deductible payments or a distinction between portfolio and direct foreign investments.[273] It is simply not clear, however, whether governments (particularly those of capital-exporting countries) are sufficiently committed to source-country taxation, even as a backup for residence-based taxation, to undertake the necessary changes in the status quo.[274]

The Significance of Practical Constraints and the Promise of Expected-Return Taxation

The theoretical purity of accretion taxation and the case for its application to all financial instruments, including debt, shares, and derivatives, has an obvious appeal. The accretion approach appears to address completely both avoidance opportunities and any perceived efficiency losses created by the realization requirement and the application of different tax treatments to interest and dividends. In fact, provided that the distinction between ordinary income and capital amounts is eliminated, accretion taxation realizes a measure of consistency that no other approach to the taxation of financial instruments can provide. In the most complete sense, the problematic tax boundaries created by the realization requirement, the distinction for tax purposes between interest and dividends, and the preferential taxation of capital gains all disappear under accretion taxation and are no longer sources of pure and approximate tax avoidance. Moreover, by eliminating the difficult legal distinctions required under any income tax system that treats equivalent cash flows differently, accretion taxation eliminates the waste of administrative and taxpayer resources on

- defining a realization transaction,[275]
- classifying instruments as debt or equity,[276] and
- characterizing gains and losses as either ordinary amounts arising from trading activities or capital amounts arising from investment transactions.[277]

Finally, accretion taxation even eliminates the need for a corporate income tax.

Despite its theoretical appeal, the comprehensive application of accretion taxation is invariably rejected because of perceived practical constraints. This chapter has already alluded to the principal constraints conventionally associated with accretion taxation in its discussion of the longstanding debate over the relative merits of an accretion-based income tax and a cash flow tax.[278] As one commentator has observed, the accretion ideal and all approaches that attempt to approximate its results[279] tend to substitute difficult problems of "factual uncertainty" for problems associated with "legal uncertainty" and the distinctions described above.[280] In particular, the principle of taxing changes in value as they accrue annually is much easier to state than it is to apply in practice, since application of the principle depends critically on an accurate assessment of the underlying factors that determine value. In the light of this factual uncertainty, it is perhaps not surprising that no OECD country has yet adopted this theoretically pure approach to the taxation of financial instruments generally. The three most widely cited and accepted reasons for this failure are

- the difficulty of establishing values for financial instruments and other, non-financial assets that do not trade publicly,
- the liquidity problems that accretion taxation would raise for taxpayers by forcing them to pay tax on unrealized gains, and
- the unevenness in the recognition of unrealized gains and losses that would occur under accretion taxation owing to wide fluctuations in value.

Although various contributions to the academic literature[281] have made a forceful case for the feasibility of the comprehensive application of the accretion ideal, the accepted significance of these practical constraints suggests that the corporate income tax is not about to be eliminated in its favour. In fact, in the absence of comprehensive accretion taxation or the conduit treatment of all legal entities, the corporate income tax must be maintained as a withholding tax on the unrealized capital gains of shareholders.

Given the accepted significance of practical obstacles to the adoption of accretion taxation, there is an obvious need for second-best reform options in the short to medium term.[282] In other words, if the comprehensive application of accretion taxation is impractical, one must attempt instead to approximate its results within the constraints of a realization-based income tax. As has been noted already,[283] one minimal measure in the context of the returns on financial instruments is the elimination of the distinction between ordinary income and capital gains and losses. The question of the timing of the recognition of gains and losses is a much more difficult issue, one that in practice is closely linked with the debt-equity distinction and the distinction for tax purposes between interest and dividends.

Three principal reform options designed to realize the identical taxation of interest and dividends have been put forward. The first two involve the extension of dividend tax treatment to interest. In the context of an imputation system for dividends, one could realize this extension by not allowing corporate borrowers to deduct interest. Lenders would remain taxable on interest payments, but they would receive a tax credit to compensate them for corporate tax on the underlying income from which the interest was paid.[284] An alternative recommended by the US treasury department,[285] the so-called comprehensive business income tax (CBIT), would both deny the deduction of dividends and interest by corporate issuers and exempt them from taxation in the hands of shareholders and lenders. Thus the corporate income tax would effectively become a flat tax on interest and dividends as forms of capital income. The third reform option is the extension of the tax treatment of interest to dividends. One could realize this extension by providing a deduction for either dividends paid or the imputed cost of equity capital.[286]

The need for reform and the respective merits and design details of these three reform options have been the subject of extensive debate. Notably absent from this debate is consideration of the question whether any of the reform options adequately address the problems that the development of sophisticated financial instruments has created for corporate income tax systems.[287] The debate has been joined, instead, on the unrealistic premise that corporate capital takes the form of traditional debt and equity. Continued developments in financial markets may ultimately force policy makers to recognize the basic functional similarity of all corporate investment instruments and adopt income tax systems that treat all of these instruments identically. A system of this kind would obviously eliminate the need for artificial distinctions based on the private law rights and obligations associated with particular financial instruments. For a variety of reasons, not the least of which is its implications for the taxation of cross-border financial flows,[288] this sensible approach to tax policy is unlikely to be taken up soon. In the meantime, policy makers struggle to maintain the traditional classifications in a world in which those classifications have become largely irrelevant.

This conclusion leads back to the timing question and Strnad's troubling suggestion that in the absence of fundamental reform of the taxation of capital income any attempt to comprehensively address the tax treatment of financial instruments is pointless. In a world of limited reform options, he argues, the only viable solution may be the conventional approach of analyzing each type of transaction "and then crafting a detailed response depending on the 'normative stakes' that they present."[289] This approach accepts the inevitability of "loose ends in the form of inconsistencies, discontinuities, or lack of universality."[290]

Similarly, Brooks and Head conclude that it is possible to address pure tax avoidance fairly effectively by supplementing specific anti-avoidance rules with computerized matching and comprehensive information reporting. Responses of this kind would be easy to implement in the context of perfect capital markets;[291] they become much more problematic, and the social costs much higher, in the context of high substitutability and approximate tax avoidance. In other words, specific responses targeted to particular instances of tax avoidance fail to address many highly substitutable alternatives and the efficiency costs and revenue loss they entail. More comprehensive responses designed to address a wider range of substitutable instruments inevitably involve reform of certain fundamental aspects of the income tax system.[292]

It is perhaps significant that Strnad develops his conclusion in the context of the US classical corporate tax and its double taxation of equity income. The imputation systems adopted in other OECD countries alleviate the double taxation of equity income distributed as dividends and reduce, to some extent, the differences between the tax treatment of debt and the tax treatment of shares. In theory, the corporate income tax serves as a withholding tax on shareholder income; interest received by debt holders, meanwhile, is taxed currently on an accrual basis. If the general corporate rate and the highest marginal rate for individuals are properly aligned, there is only one level of tax on corporate income. An interesting question is whether this rough similarity between the tax treatment of interest and the tax treatment of dividends is a sufficient precondition for the successful design of a comprehensive regime for the taxation of all financial instruments other than shares. It may be that the implementation of some sort of accrual regime for the taxation of the returns on all financial instruments other than shares is a necessary corollary to an imputation system.

In this connection, Warren concludes that the goal for tax-policy makers must be a reduction in the reliance on a distinction between fixed returns that are taxed on an accrual basis and contingent returns that are taxed on a realization basis.[293] As a paradigm for the tax treatment of financial instruments—and, by implication, for the distinction between debt investments and equity investments, including options—this distinction appears to have become untenable in the face of the development of mature markets for derivatives and the financial equivalences that these instruments can be used to create.[294] Interestingly, it might be possible to realize Warren's stated goal more easily in countries that have adopted an imputation system. In this context, the return to holders from all financial instruments other than shares would be subject to one level of tax on an accrual basis. The return on shares too would be subject to just one level of tax—in this case, a corporate withholding tax on retained earnings, which would be creditable against the shareholder-level tax on dividend distributions.

Admittedly, this system does not adequately address avoidance opportunities that arise because of rate differences among taxable corporations, loss corporations, and tax-preferred holders of financial instruments such as pension funds. Only a system that taxes all financial returns identically in all respects can eliminate opportunities of this kind. Nonetheless, the complementary roles of an imputation system for shares and the accrual taxation of all other financial instruments provide an attractive basis for an alternative to a transactional approach to the classification and taxation of financial transactions. It is, in fact, the basis for the comprehensive approaches enacted in New Zealand and proposed in Australia. Given that more fundamental approaches to the problems presented by sophisticated instruments involve structural reform of the corporate income tax system and capital-income taxation generally, it is not surprising that some countries have adopted this less radical approach.

The obvious basis for second-best approaches of this kind is the assumption that the practical barriers to universal accretion taxation of financial instruments are insurmountable. In a second-best world, however, one must make difficult choices among second-best alternatives. Gergen, for instance, argues that transaction costs, credit risk, and legal risk present substantial constraints that limit the scope of tax avoidance in capital markets.[295] In effect, these constraints mean that there is a limit to the substitutability of financial instruments for tax-avoidance purposes. As a result, Gergen suggests that it may not be necessary to abandon the essential features of current income tax systems, which provide different tax treatments for different categories of cash flows. It may be possible, instead, to minimize the differences in tax treatment by providing systematically rational treatment of certain basic financial instruments. This treatment would be rational in the sense that it recognized the similarity of the cash flow patterns associated with these instruments. Differences in treatment that for practical policy reasons cannot be eliminated can be maintained by adopting certain approaches that provide sufficient friction to deter tax-avoidance arrangements.

In Gergen's view, therefore, the constraints on avoidance that he describes make it possible to develop second-best policies that will maintain capital income as a significant tax base. Yet difficulties surround the determination of the type of incremental reform that is most desirable. Gergen believes that the goal for tax-policy makers should be a set of rules and principles that "governs the existing set of securities tolerably well"[296] and does not impose a "socially harmful level of uncertainty regarding the tax treatment of novel securities."[297] One can realize this modest goal by focusing on "sharp discontinuities"[298] and blatant inconsistencies that give rise to obvious opportunities for tax avoidance.[299] Difficult issues concerning welfare gains and losses can be finessed, since it is often safe to assume that the harmful effects of tax avoidance outweigh any distortions that incremental reform may introduce. The problem is to identify the sharp discontinuities and blatant inconsistencies with reasonable confidence and then craft an appropriately targeted response. As Brooks and Head suggest, these responses can take the form of either narrowly targeted anti-avoidance rules or more broadly focused measures that expand the capital-income tax base, if only incrementally.[300] In general, either type of response seeks to

- extend accrual recognition to gain and losses on a wide range of financial instruments,

- reduce the significance of the distinction between the tax treatment of interest and the tax treatment of dividends and hence the significance of the distinction between debt and equity, and
- eliminate the distinction between ordinary income and capital amounts.

Brooks and Head, and Gergen as well, suggest that the possibility of imposing accretion taxation on a wide range of financial instruments will actually increase as capital markets develop new instruments that reduce transaction costs. As these instruments expand the range of tax-avoidance opportunities, they paradoxically reduce the practical policy constraints that otherwise prevent the imposition of accretion taxation as a first-best approach.[301]

As an alternative to accretion taxation, a possible paradigm for fundamental reform is the distinction between expected and unexpected gains and losses.[302] Indeed, as was emphasized above, both pure avoidance opportunities and much of the efficiency loss associated with approximate tax avoidance are attributable to the adoption of the realization requirement and the distinction for tax purposes between debt and equity. These structural features of most income tax systems highlight the need for appropriate tax treatment of both expected gains and losses and unexpected gains and losses. As a means of eliminating avoidance opportunities, accretion taxation is arguably overbroad in requiring annual recognition of all unrealized gains and losses. From a normative perspective, one can justify this requirement only on the basis of distributive considerations and the consequent need to adopt accretion recognition of all gains and losses as a second-best form of wealth tax. In the context of a realization-based income tax system applicable to non-financial assets, the distinction between expected and unexpected gains and losses is critical to the design of any approach to the taxation of financial instruments that must stop short of accretion recognition. This is true both for normative reasons and for considerations of administration and compliance costs.

Although the distinction between the expected time-value return and the bet element in financial instruments resembles the distinction that Warren stresses between fixed and contingent payments, it differs from the latter in some important respects that make it the basis for a workable regime. As a basis for the application of accrual rather than realization-based recognition and for the distinction for tax purposes between interest and dividends, the traditional distinction between fixed returns and contingent returns is premised on an "all or nothing" approach under which a cash flow stream must be characterized in its entirety as being either fixed or contingent. The form of recognition, accrual or realization, applicable to that characterization is then applied to the whole of the cash flow, including any elements that are inconsistent with that treatment. Similarly, interest or dividend treatment is applied to the whole of a cash flow on the basis of its perceived risk attributes. Traditional efforts to apply a more substantive approach to the characterization of financial instruments as either debt or equity and the associated returns as either interest or dividends have used a qualitative determination that focuses on an assessment of legal rights, which are used as proxies for the identification of risk as the basis for the distinction between fixed and contingent returns. No attempt is made to measure risk quantitatively and thus to characterize a return as being neither entirely fixed nor entirely contingent.[303]

The traditional approach, in other words, ignores the fact that most financial returns are a combination of expected time-value elements and bet elements that one can justifiably subject to different tax treatments once they are adequately identified. The conceptual framework described here depends on a characterization of this kind. This characterization requires the identification of the time-value element (the expected return) and its separation from the bet element (the unexpected return or risk element) that is present in most financial instruments. One can then apply accrual recognition to the expected return as distinct from the unexpected gain or loss. Moreover, it is possible to extend a similar separation of the different types of returns implicit in all financial instruments to the tax treatment of interest and dividends, without having to provide a specified treatment to the whole of a cash flow on the basis of its predominant characteristics. In all cases, one can make the required identification of the time-value return and bet elements quantitatively by using concepts and risk-measurement approaches that are commonly used in financial analysis, whereby expectations are determined ex ante at the outset of an investment or the initiation of a financial contract.

The literature on expected-return taxation has already developed much of this framework,[304] which underlies the accrual regime in New Zealand and the accrual regimes applicable to contingent debt in Canada and Australia.[305] Perhaps of necessity, analysis of the theoretical insights on which expected-return taxation is based and the practical implementation of this approach have both been limited to debt instruments and derivatives. As the following three chapters will demonstrate, however, these insights are also applicable to the related issue of the distinction for tax purposes between interest and dividends; in addition, they provide a conceptual basis for certain responses to the use of complex hybrid and synthetic instruments. Indeed, the insights provided by expected-return taxation provide a basis for a comprehensive second-best approach to the taxation of financial instruments that appropriately links the tax treatment of debt and derivatives with the broader issues of corporate income tax reform and the debt-equity distinction. That link is suggested, but not sufficiently explored, in the existing literature on cost-of-capital approaches to corporate income tax reform.[306] Chapters 4 and 5 follow, therefore, with a more detailed examination of the policy and technical design issues that surround the comprehensive application of expected-return taxation as a preferable second-best alternative to the accretion taxation of financial instruments.

4

The Case for Expected-Return Taxation in a Second-Best World

Introduction

Chapter 3 described the essential features of accretion taxation and their incorporation in a benchmark approach to the income tax treatment of financial instruments. It also compared that benchmark with expected-return taxation as a second-best approximation of the accretion ideal, whose implementation is generally considered to be impractical. To reiterate, both approaches eliminate the distinction between ordinary income and capital amounts and recognize all financial returns in full as either income or expense. They differ principally in their treatment of unrealized gains and losses. Accretion taxation requires the recognition of both expected and unexpected gains and losses as they arise with changes in the value of a financial instrument. Expected-return taxation limits accrual recognition to expected gains and losses; it has three core elements:[1]

1) inclusion and deduction of the full amount of all returns on financial instruments,
2) recognition of expected gains and losses annually as they are expected to arise ("accrual recognition"), and
3) recognition of unexpected gains and losses on realization.

Accrual recognition is achieved by requiring that expected gains and losses be spread systematically over the term of an instrument. With its strictly ex ante focus, expected-return taxation attempts to address the problems of anticipated deferral and timing arbitrage;[2] it cannot address the problems of unanticipated deferral and selective realization (which is also referred to as "risk arbitrage," "selective realization," or "adverse selection").[3] Expected-return taxation fails to address these problems largely because they are the product of strategies that involve manipulation of the realization requirement to accelerate the recognition of unexpected losses while deferring the recognition of unexpected gains. In order to address these problems and maintain the integrity of a system of expected-return taxation, it is necessary to adopt special provisions that attempt to refine the scope of a realization transaction and limit the recognition of unexpected losses.[4]

This chapter reviews the case for expected-return taxation as the preferable second-best approach to the taxation of financial instruments. The critical point made here is simply that the core elements of expected-return taxation provide a defensible paradigm for the taxation of the building-block financial instruments described in chapter 1 (fixed-payment debt, forwards, futures, swaps, and options). As discussed in chapters 6 and 7, this paradigm can also be applied to more complex combinations of the building-block instruments (hybrids and synthetics) in an attempt to alleviate many of the problems associated with those combinations.

The next three parts of this chapter review the general principles that underlie various second-best alternatives to accretion taxation as a comprehensive approach to the taxation of financial instruments. The discussion attempts to determine which alternatives are preferable from both a theoretical and a practical perspective. Some of these alternatives are described in the academic literature but have not been adopted legislatively. Expected-return taxation is preferable to other second-best alternatives primarily because it is consistent with several aspects of existing legislative regimes. Expected-return taxation also has an important theoretical dimension that makes it preferable to another alternative with some practical appeal: the "dual income tax" (DIT) approach that the Nordic countries (Denmark, Finland, Norway, and Sweden) have all adopted to one extent or another.

The last part of the chapter briefly discusses the incorporation of certain elements of expected-return taxation in many existing legislative regimes. The existence of a relationship between the design features of expected-return taxation and existing legislative regimes is significant; indeed, it provides an important basis of support for expected-return taxation as the preferable second-best alternative to the accretion taxation of financial instruments. Since existing legislative regimes have already adopted some measure of expected-return taxation, its adoption in full would raise fewer administrative, compliance, and transitional concerns than would the adoption of any other reform alternative. For these and other reasons, it is argued here that expected-return taxation is the preferable second-best alternative to accretion taxation, provided that it includes the application of accretion taxation to a limited range of financial instruments as the most efficient means of addressing the problem of selective realization.[5] At present, the most complete expressions of this modified form of expected-return taxation are the comprehensive accrual regimes embodied in legislation in New Zealand and in reform proposals under consideration in Australia. Chapter 5 will describe the principal design features of a regime of this kind.

A General Assessment of Second-Best Alternatives

Several commentators have summarized the general case for some form of comprehensive legislative regime to govern the income taxation of financial instruments.[6] In arguing for a regime of this kind, they tend to assume that the taxation of financial instruments involves two paramount policy goals. The first goal is to eliminate the avoidance opportunities and pricing distortions that arise from the inconsistent tax treatment of different instruments and different taxpayers. The second is to realize consistent taxation through measures that are relatively easy for taxpayers and administrators to understand and apply.

Chapter 2 made the point that these general policy goals cannot be realized under the existing system of cubbyhole taxation of the cash flows associated with financial instruments. In particular, the combination of accrual and realization-based taxation, the distinction for tax purposes between interest and dividends, and the distinction between ordinary income and capital amounts under the cubbyhole system all give rise to inconsistency in the tax treatment of different financial instruments and to uncertainty about how particular instruments should be classified for tax purposes. The inconsistency and uncertainty follow largely from a failure to identify the expected gains and losses that arise from the embedded debt in options, shares, and prepaid forwards and swaps, and to tax them in the same manner as gains and losses on conventional debt. Remedying this failure requires reform of the existing tax cubbyholes and corporate income tax systems. Piecemeal reform intended to minimize avoidance opportunities and the distortions that arise from particular inconsistencies in the tax treatment of financial instruments may only create other inconsistencies and hence other avoidance opportunities and distortions.

The development of consistent and understandable rules for the taxation of all financial instruments is easy to state as a general policy goal, but it is extremely difficult to realize other than through the first-best approach of accretion taxation. Given that valuation and liquidity difficulties make the comprehensive application of accretion taxation impractical, it is necessary to make difficult choices among various second-best alternatives to the status quo.[7] These alternatives are "second-best" in the sense that they are imposed on a differentiated income tax; that is, they are all based, to one degree or another, on an acceptance of the realization-based recognition of some gains and losses but not others, on a distinction for tax purposes between interest and dividends, and on a distinction between ordinary income and capital amounts. The tax literature and the legislation in various countries offer an array of second-best approaches that fall into three general categories:[8]

1) use of the techniques of bifurcation and integration,
2) non-statutory approaches, and
3) comprehensive legislative approaches.

The second category includes two alternatives that will be referred to here as "reliance on financial-accounting practices" and "interpretive activism." The third category includes three alternatives that will be referred to here as "expected-return taxation," "retrospective taxation," and a "dual income tax" (DIT).

Since all of the approaches within these categories are second-best approaches, the case for a comprehensive system of expected-return taxation can only be a relative one; that is, it must show that expected-return taxation has fewer weaknesses than do the other approaches. An effective second-best response must, arguably, incorporate three minimal features. First, it must be based on a clear set of general principles that respond to specified policy concerns. Second, these general principles must address inconsistencies in the tax treatment of the basic building-block financial instruments that are the source of tax-avoidance opportunities. Third, a second-best approach must also address the taxation of the more complex instruments that are the product of financial innovation.

As approaches to the taxation of financial instruments, the techniques of bifurcation and integration are the subject of a fairly extensive literature[9] and are reflected selectively in the legislation of some countries (most notably the United States).[10] In general, these two techniques fail to satisfy the first and second criteria for a desirable second-best approach. To be more particular, bifurcation and integration are limited approaches that accept the existing tax cubbyholes for the basic building-block financial instruments. They are not invoked, therefore, as a basis for the elimination of fundamental inconsistencies in tax treatment; they are applied instead as specific responses to the use of particular complex instruments in limited instances (often in tax-avoidance transactions). Indeed, they tend to be the basis of specific legislative responses to the use of instruments of this kind. Given their limited scope, bifurcation and integration cannot be regarded as comprehensive alternatives to accretion taxation.

Only the approaches in the second and third categories above can potentially serve as comprehensive alternatives to accretion taxation. The two approaches in the second category, a reliance on financial-accounting practices and interpretive activism, resemble bifurcation and integration in their acceptance of the status quo and the significant variation in tax treatment that it imposes on the basic building-block instruments. These approaches are unique, however, in their use of non-statutory responses to problems presented by a tax system that treats different financial instruments differently. These responses are non-statutory in that they do not depend on the development of detailed legislative rules for the treatment of particular financial instruments. They involve, instead, the development of appropriate principles by the accounting profession and the courts within the framework of the general legislative provisions that govern the computation of business income. As will be argued below, reliance on financial-accounting practices and interpretive activism are both potentially comprehensive in scope but suffer from weaknesses that, at the level of principle, make them unsatisfactory approaches to the taxation of financial instruments. Like bifurcation and integration, these two approaches to reform can at best play only a supporting role within a comprehensive legislative regime.

The approaches in the third category differ from those in the other two categories by focusing on the taxation of a broad range of financial instruments and capital income generally. Two of these approaches, expected-return taxation and retrospective taxation, attempt to eliminate, to the greatest extent possible, the differences in tax treatment that create the difficulties associated with the taxation of financial instruments. The other approach, a DIT, attempts to address the same difficulties by reducing the tax rate on capital income and imposing a schedular system of taxation. Together, these measures make the substitutability of financial instruments for tax-avoidance purposes unattractive. Each of these alternatives satisfies, at least to some extent, the criteria for a defensible second-best approach and provides a comprehensive legislative response that merits serious consideration. Thus both retrospective taxation and the DIT present significant challenges to expected-return taxation. Yet closer reflection reveals theoretical and practical considerations that sustain a case for comprehensive expected-return taxation as the preferable second-best approach to the taxation of financial instruments. In particular, a system of retrospective taxation is theoretically appealing but unattractive from a practical perspective that takes into account possible compliance and administrative costs and transitional problems. In contrast, the DIT has a definite practical appeal because of the real-world experience with this approach in the Nordic countries. Even so, a DIT is not really an alternative to a system of expected-return taxation, at least not in the context of the income-measurement issues presented by the cash flows associated with various financial instruments. Indeed, the unique dual-rate feature of a DIT is intended to address an issue that is entirely distinct from the concerns addressed by a system of expected-return taxation, and the two approaches are not at all incompatible.

Incomplete Approaches

Bifurcation and Integration

The label "bifurcation" (also "disaggregation"[11] or "deconstruction"[12]) refers to the process of breaking down a financial instrument into its component parts (the basic building-block instruments) and applying a specified tax treatment separately to each of the parts. In other words, bifurcation is the recharacterization of a financial instrument that is, in form, a single instrument as two or more fundamental financial instruments, and the sum of the taxes on the component instruments is equal to the tax treatment of the single instrument. "Integration" refers to any technique that determines the tax treatment of legally distinct instruments by combining those instruments and accounting for their offsetting cash flows as a single instrument.[13] In other words, the relevant instruments are treated for income tax purposes as one indivisible instrument, which is subject to a specified treatment for a cash flow that is the aggregate of the offsetting cash flows associated with the otherwise legally distinct instruments.

Bifurcation is a technique that is conventionally associated with "hybrid instruments,"[14] or instruments that combine an expected time-value return with unexpected gain or loss attributable to a bet element. These instruments are of two general types. One type consists of certain basic instruments (for example, options, shares, and prepaid forwards and swaps) that involve an advance of funds and, as a result, have an embedded debt element in addition to a bet on the price of an underlying asset. The other type consists of "compound" instruments, which package together, in form, two or more basic instruments as one instrument (for, example, contingent-payment, convertible, and exchangeable debt).[15] Both types present problems under the tax-cubbyhole approach to the taxation of financial instruments, since there is no recognized cubbyhole that provides a tax treatment appropriate to the unique combination of instruments packaged together in the form of a single instrument. In the case of hybrids of the first type, the particular instrument does correspond to a recognized tax cubbyhole, but the tax treatment for instruments within that cubbyhole fails to tax the expected gain or loss on the embedded debt element in the same manner as expected gain or loss on conventional debt with fixed-payment obligations.[16] In the case of compound instruments, there is often no recognized cubbyhole, and the appropriate tax treatment is unknown or uncertain.[17] The failure to fit the cash flows within a recognized cubbyhole that provides appropriate treatment may lead to the use of hybrids for tax-avoidance purposes and deter their legitimate non-tax use.

Integration is a technique that is conventionally associated with "synthetic" instruments,[18] which result from the combination of long and short positions in separate financial instruments whose offsetting cash flows, in the aggregate, replicate the cash flow associated with a single instrument within one of the tax cubbyholes.[19] Synthetics present a problem under the tax-cubbyhole approach if the sum of the tax treatments applied to the relevant instruments within recognized cubbyholes does not equal the tax treatment applied to the single instrument that the synthetic replicates. Thus it is possible to use synthetics to take advantage of tax-avoidance opportunities available under the tax-cubbyhole approach.

Integration is also associated with hedging transactions and the attempt to match the character and timing rules for gains and losses on a financial instrument with the underlying asset that the instrument is used to hedge.[20] In these instances, the cash flows associated with the financial instrument are netted against those associated with the underlying asset that the instrument hedges. The result is a net tax treatment for the hedge and the hedged asset that would not necessarily follow if the tax treatment specified by the tax cubbyholes were applied to the hedge independently of the hedged asset. The matching and netting of the cash flows may eliminate additional tax that would be payable if the hedge and the hedged asset were treated separately.[21]

It will clarify the uses of bifurcation and integration to consider some examples.[22] To begin with bifurcation, assume that the world consists of instrument C, which is a combination of two instruments, A and B, for which there are defined tax treatments. As a taxation technique, bifurcation takes instrument C as its starting point, but since there is no known cubbyhole with a known tax treatment for instrument C it is broken down into its component parts, instruments A and B, which are taxed separately under recognized cubbyholes. In short, the tax treatment of instrument C is the sum of the tax treatments accorded to instruments A and B. Alternatively, even though instrument C is a combination of instruments A and B, its legal form and predominant attributes may be sufficient to support a characterization of it as instrument B, so that it will attract the tax treatment for instruments within that recognized cubbyhole. Bifurcation accepts the legal form of instrument C as a single security, but since a characterization of it as instrument B would ignore the attributes of instrument A and tax those attributes inappropriately, instrument C is broken down into its component parts, instruments A and B, which again are taxed separately.

In contrast to bifurcation, integration takes instruments A and B as its starting point. In the case of a synthetic, the sum of the cash flows associated with instruments A and B is equal to the cash flows associated with instrument C. Accordingly, integration uses a known tax treatment under the cubbyhole system to tax instruments A and B as a single instrument C. This is done even though the sum of the taxes applied to instruments A and B under their own cubbyholes would not equal the taxes applied to instrument C. In the case of a hedge of asset X by instruments A and B, the cash flows associated with the two instruments are matched with those associated with asset X. As a result, the character and the timing of the recognition of gains and losses on instruments A and B are determined by reference to the gain or loss on asset X, which provides a net cash flow that is equivalent to the net cash flow from a single position consisting of the hedge and the hedged asset.

Bifurcation and integration have a powerful intuitive appeal as approaches to what appear to be two separate and unrelated issues, the appropriate taxation of hybrids and the appropriate taxation of synthetics and hedge transactions.[23] This intuitive appeal, however, disguises important weaknesses that make both approaches problematic under income tax systems that apply significantly different tax treatments to interest and dividends, provide preferential treatment for capital gains, and use both accrual-based and realization-based recognition of gains and losses. Thus there has been considerable debate in the tax literature about the relative merits of bifurcation and integration—or, perhaps more accurately, about which approach is more problematic.[24] Bifurcation originally had a broad appeal by virtue of its apparent applicability to the building-block approach to financial innovation. An income tax system that breaks down all financial instruments into their component parts seems to be consistent with a process of financial innovation that uses the basic building-block instruments to construct the complex risk and return profiles associated with hybrid instruments. The apparent promise of this approach, however, has faded with the recognition that the conventional cubbyholes on which existing income tax systems are based do not necessarily correspond to the basic building-block financial instruments—shares, for example, are not a building-block instrument. This incongruence is a source of difficulty largely because there is often more than one way to bifurcate a financial instrument and the different bifurcations do not necessarily produce equivalent tax treatments under the cubbyhole system.[25] Criticism of bifurcation almost always focuses on this problem and has led to an emphasis on integration as the preferable approach.[26]

This debate over the general merits and faults of bifurcation and integration is somewhat curious. In fact, in the context of an income tax system based on the standard cubbyholes, the debate is meaningless.[27] Under a system of this kind, with its reliance on legal form as a proxy for the distinction between expected and unexpected gains and losses that underlies the inconsistent taxation of the various building-block financial instruments, avoidance opportunities and uncertainties about the tax consequences of a given instrument are inevitable. In other words, under an income tax system that varies significantly in its treatment of instruments within the recognized cubbyholes, there will always be opportunities for (1) the combination of two or more basic instruments in the form of a single hybrid instrument; (2) the provision of expected time-value returns through instruments that do not take the form of debt; and (3) the replication of single instruments with recognized tax treatments through various combinations of other instruments. In addressing these combinations of basic instruments, there is nothing to choose from between bifurcation and integration. They are, in fact, complementary techniques that differ in form but address the same issues. The analysis of avoidance opportunities (or uncertain tax consequences) under a bifurcation approach focuses on a single instrument that, in form, consists of two subinstruments (thus one can bifurcate instrument C into instruments A and B).[28] Under integration, the focus shifts to the two subinstruments, which are separate in form but whose associated cash flows together add up to the cash flows associated with a single instrument (thus one can integrate instruments A and B into instrument C). If one views the matter in the context of a taxpayer's entire portfolio,[29] bifurcation involves an implicit prior integration, in which the taxpayer selected elements of the portfolio to integrate in the form of a single instrument.[30] By the same reckoning, integration involves an implicit prior bifurcation, in which the taxpayer identified the instruments to be integrated and separated them from the portfolio as a whole.[31]

The complementary nature of bifurcation and integration has some practical relevance beyond the debate in the tax literature over their relative merits and defects. Since the apparent differences between the two approaches are matters of form only, bifurcation and integration suffer from much the same shortcomings, which make both of them problematic.[32] Their principal shortcoming is the one already noted here—and already widely recognized—in connection with bifurcation alone: an inability to deal with the fact that the tax cubbyholes do not in all cases accurately distinguish between expected and unexpected gains and losses associated with the basic building-block instruments. For example, options and shares combine expected time-value returns with unexpected gains and losses attributable to a bet element, but existing income tax systems do not bifurcate either options or shares into these two elements and tax the two elements differently. Instead, the expected gain or loss on the debt element embedded in an option or a share is taxed differently from the expected gain or loss on conventional debt.

Given this state of affairs, problems of identification inevitably arise; that is, it is often uncertain how a particular instrument should be bifurcated, since alternative bifurcations of the same instrument will have significantly different tax consequences. Two examples will clarify this point:

> **Example 1:** On January 1, 1996, taxpayer A paid $100 for an original issue discount (OID) bond of Xco that pays $133 in three years (10 percent discount rate compounded annually). The bond is convertible on maturity (January 1, 1999) into 50 shares of Xco for a price equal to the amount payable.
>
> **Example 2:** On January 1, 1996, taxpayer B acquired 50 shares of Xco for $100. The shares are subject to a put option that allows B to require Xco to redeem them for $133 on January 1, 1999.

If one ignores credit risk, taxpayers A and B are in identical positions in the sense that they will realize identical cash flows on their simple portfolios.[33] Bifurcation of each of the two positions, however, does not yield identical tax results under most tax systems. It is possible to bifurcate the OID bond in example 1 into a fixed-payment debt instrument and a call option on the shares of Xco. To realize this result, one would discount the $133 expected payment, using the appropriate market rate, to arrive at a present value for the debt component that represented its acquisition price and subject the difference between the acquisition price and the expected payment to the accrual recognition otherwise applicable to fixed-payment debt. The balance of the $100 issue price would be allocated to the cost of the option, and the expected gain associated with the option would be ignored.[34]

Alternatively, it is possible to treat taxpayer A in the same manner as taxpayer B in example 2 by regarding him as the holder of the shares of Xco with a put option. In this case, one would allocate the $100 purchase price between the shares and the option, and the expected gain of $33 would not be taxed until the shares were sold. Finally, it is possible to treat the OID bond and the shares as a single instrument and ignore the option.[35] This rejection of the application of bifurcation results in the accrual recognition of $33 of expected gain on the OID bond[36] and the realization-based recognition of an equivalent gain on the shares. The two different bifurcations and the refusal to bifurcate are all equally plausible characterizations of the cash flows associated with the alternative positions,[37] yet each characterization attracts a tax treatment that is significantly different from the tax treatments that the other two attract. This outcome occurs because the tax system does not tax the debt embedded in options and shares in the same way as it taxes the expected gain or loss on conventional debt.[38] If bifurcation is to be applied, the choice among alternative bifurcations is unclear. It is not always readily apparent how a given instrument should be broken down for tax purposes.

By emphasizing the identification problems associated with bifurcation and extolling the apparent virtues of integration, some commentators[39] appear to suggest that problems of this kind do not arise under integration. This position is misleading, since it ignores the fundamental similarity between bifurcation and integration as tax techniques. In fact, problems of identification arise as inevitably under integration as they do under bifurcation. Consider the following example:

> **Example 3:** On January 1, 1996, taxpayer C acquired 50 shares of Xco for $100. This acquisition was combined with the issue of a call option and the acquisition of a put option on the shares exercisable on January 1, 1999 at a price of $133.

This example is the standard case of a synthetic OID bond revealed by put-call parity.[40] By writing and purchasing the offsetting options (with offsetting premiums), taxpayer C has ensured an expected gain of $33, which equals the discount on a comparable OID bond with a three-year maturity. Under integration, the call and put options are combined with the long position in the shares, and the offsetting cash flows (option premiums and unexpected gain and loss realized on maturity) are netted. The remaining gain of $33 should be taxed in the same way as the OID bond that the synthetic instrument replicates.[41] This result, however, is much easier to state in principle than it is to realize in practice. Taxpayer C may have a portfolio that consists of more than just these three simple instruments. As well, the call and put options may differ in their maturity dates or their exercise prices and thus may provide cash flows that partially offset one another. The net result may approximate, but it is not likely to replicate, the expected gain on an OID bond.

These considerations raise obvious identification issues that make it difficult to conclude that taxpayer C has, in fact, created a synthetic OID bond. The need to define and identify the offsetting or component parts within taxpayer C's portfolio necessarily limits the usefulness of integration as a tax technique. In the context of a tax system that is inconsistent in its treatment of some basic instruments, the possible range of full and partially offsetting positions, with inconsistent tax results that must somehow be identified, is almost infinite.[42]

From the discussion to this point, it would appear that the problems of identification associated with integration are different from those associated with bifurcation, and indeed this apparent difference may explain many commentators' evident preference for integration. To be specific, since bifurcation assumes an acceptance of the taxpayer's choice to integrate two or more instruments in the form of a single instrument, it does not raise the practical problem of identifying the relevant instruments in a taxpayer's portfolio. The identification problem appears, instead, to be a substantive one that arises from the attempt to apply bifurcation in the context of income tax systems that rely on the standard cubbyholes. It is possible to apply bifurcation effectively only if the basic building-block instruments are treated consistently. Unfortunately, however, consistency in tax treatment is not, in general, a characteristic of existing legislative regimes, most of which fail to distinguish expected gains and losses from unexpected gains and losses in the case of the basic instruments that combine such amounts (for example, options and shares as option equivalents). In the absence of consistent taxation of these instruments, bifurcation can accomplish very little, particularly where there are two or more possible bifurcations and they result in different tax treatments of the same gains and losses. What is required, therefore, is sufficient consistency in tax treatment to permit the application of bifurcation for the purpose of identifying and taxing appropriately the expected gain or loss associated with the embedded debt element in all financial instruments, other than the basic instruments (forwards, futures, and swaps) that are pure bets and therefore provide only unexpected gains and losses.[43]

In the case of integration, the identification issue appears to be a practical administrative concern rather than a substantive one. If the cash flows associated with a combination of two or more instruments are identical (or closely similar) to those associated with a single identifiable instrument, it seems all too obvious that the combination should be taxed in the same manner as the single instrument. This apparent obviousness, however, obscures the fact that there must be some justifiable basis for integrating the separate positions rather than leaving them to be taxed separately. The result of taxing them separately would be inconsistent with the result of taxing a comparable instrument that combined the cash flows associated with the separate instruments; nevertheless, existing tax systems are generally based on an acceptance of the form of an instrument that fits within an accepted cubbyhole with a known tax treatment. Accordingly, the identification issue associated with integration is not just an administrative problem. In effect, the initial bifurcation step that is implicit in integration techniques (that is, the separation of a defined set of instruments from a taxpayer's whole portfolio and their taxation as a single instrument) must somehow be justified substantively.

The identification problems associated with bifurcation and integration mean that both approaches lack any basis in principle for their application under existing income tax systems. At a general level, this characteristic of the two approaches is evident in the simple fact that the rationale for the application of either of them in a given set of circumstances is not always clear. It is not always clear, that is, why one identification of a combination of instruments rather than another should be regarded as determinative for tax purposes. Tax-policy makers and administrators must either choose the bifurcation that seems somehow to most accurately reflect the underlying economics of the hybrid instrument or simply refuse to bifurcate when refusal seems somehow to be the more appropriate course.[44] Similarly, integration is based on the uneasy premise that the taxpayer's purpose in entering into a combination of instruments somehow justifies the instruments' treatment as a single unit.[45] Tax-policy makers must somehow find proxies that accurately reflect the underlying purpose-based premises for integration, and tax administrators must simply live with the practical problem of identifying those proxies in the real world of large taxpayer portfolios.[46] As chapters 6 and 7 will describe more fully, the lack of any basis in principle for the application of bifurcation and integration often manifests itself in legislation that is inordinately complex. The complexity arises largely because of the need to draw defensible lines that define which combinations of instruments are to be chosen as determinative in which circumstances. This legislative complexity and the uncertainty that it engenders are significant concerns from an administrative and compliance perspective.

The lack of a basis in principle for the application of bifurcation and integration reduces these techniques to, at best, short-term responses to the challenge of financial innovation.[47] In other words, in an imperfect world of inconsistent tax treatments based on the standard cubbyholes, bifurcation and integration should only be used selectively to address the worst of the tax-avoidance opportunities and uncertainties created by the tax-cubbyhole approach. They should be limited to narrowly defined attempts to supplement differentiated income tax systems by providing a set of known tax treatments for a limited range of hybrid and synthetic instruments.[48]

For the longer term, as chapter 6 will argue, the more promising approach is the use of bifurcation to identify the embedded debt in options and shares and require the taxation of the associated expected return on a yield-to-maturity

(YTM) basis as ordinary income or loss.[49] This technique is a logical extension of the concept of expected-return taxation that underlies the design features of a comprehensive accrual regime. It is already a feature of legislative provisions that apply to the embedded debt in certain forward and swap contracts. Bifurcation remains important, therefore, as a technique for the identification of embedded debt in the basic building-block financial instruments, for which the problem of multiple bifurcations does not arise. By eliminating many of the worst inconsistencies and discontinuities associated with the cubbyhole system, the extension of expected-return taxation to the embedded debt in options and shares would eliminate much of the need to apply bifurcation to compound instruments.

On the other hand, chapter 7 will argue that, even under a regime of expected-return taxation, integration would continue to be necessary as a means of addressing avoidance opportunities that do not depend on the inappropriate taxation of the expected gain or loss on options. It would be possible, however, to reduce the importance of integration, particularly if expected-return taxation were extended to the embedded debt in shares. In this case, it would even be possible to eliminate the application of integration as the basis of a separate hedge accounting regime. Thus the extension of expected-return taxation holds out the promise of a substantial reduction in the legislative complexity that has arisen because of the difficult problems of identification associated with integration. Any reduction in complexity can only enhance the compliance efforts of both tax administrators and taxpayers.

Non-Statutory Approaches

Reliance on Financial-Accounting Practices

Unlike bifurcation and integration, reliance on financial-accounting practices can, in theory, provide a comprehensive approach to the tax treatment of both the basic building-block instruments and sophisticated hybrid and synthetic instruments. The weaknesses of this alternative arise from the fact that it effectively transfers part of the function of making tax policy to the accounting profession. The problems that any extensive transfer of this function would create are serious enough to relegate reliance on financial-accounting practices to a supporting role in the development and application of a comprehensive legislative regime for the taxation of financial instruments.

Close conformity of financial-accounting and tax-accounting standards for financial instruments is an approach that several tax practitioners have strongly advocated.[50] The rationale that underlies this advocacy should be familiar to Canadians who can recall the recommendation of the joint committee on taxation[51] for the repeal of paragraph 20(1)(c) (and related provisions) of the Income Tax Act (ITA)[52] in favour of the deductibility of interest expense under section 9 of the ITA and the incorporation of commercial accounting practices under that provision. In fact, the use of financial-accounting practices for income measurement purposes has enjoyed a longstanding appeal in the context of the computation of business income generally.[53] Since income and expense from financial instruments must be accounted for in the financial statements of an enterprise, the accounting profession has been forced for some time to develop practices unique to that area.[54] It is not surprising, therefore, that tax practitioners should advocate the acceptance of financial-accounting practices as a means of determining the appropriate tax treatment of the cash flows associated with particular financial instruments.

The perceived advantage of a reliance on this body of developed practices is that it would reduce the compliance burden associated with detailed, and independent, income tax rules.[55] This perceived advantage is enhanced by the consideration that financial-accounting practices are developed on the premise that they should reflect the perceived economic substance of a particular instrument.[56] Since this search for economic substance is presumably also the goal of any set of rational tax rules that governs financial instruments, reliance on financial-accounting practices has an obvious intuitive appeal. In its more rigorous form, this reliance would involve an unqualified acceptance of financial-accounting practices as determinative for income tax purposes.[57] A more permissive version of the approach would require very close conformity between financial accounting and tax accounting but permit deviations where they were appropriate.[58]

Despite its superficial appeal, an uncritical reliance on accounting practices would present serious problems.[59] For one thing, accounting standards are notoriously vague and flexible, and they leave much to the judgment of the particular professional.[60] Although there has been substantial progress in the development of appropriate accounting practices for financial instruments, many difficult issues have not been resolved and remain the subject of some judgment. The vagueness of accounting standards is especially pronounced in the very areas that are most troublesome for income tax purposes. For instance, accounting standards for the classification of particular instruments as either debt or equity are not entirely clear.[61] In addition, the appropriate application of bifurcation and integration techniques to hybrid and synthetic instruments, including hedging strategies, is still the subject of considerable debate in the accounting field.[62]

A more important problem is that, even where accounting practices are relatively clear and consistent, such as in their application of accrual recognition to the expected returns on some instruments and their use of market-value reporting of gain and loss on others,[63] they are not necessarily appropriate for income tax purposes. In the context of measurement rules for business income generally, it has long been recognized that the goals of financial reporting and tax reporting are different, and that the former should not be accepted unquestioningly for the purposes of the latter.[64] This recognition is conventionally expressed in the caution that the principle of accounting conservatism can lead to deferral of the recognition of revenue and acceleration of the recognition of expenses, which, either alone or together, can produce an understatement of income for tax purposes. These concerns are not limited to the recognition of gains and losses on financial instruments; they are simply much more complex when they arise in the context of the debt-equity distinction and the appropriate recognition rules for sophisticated financial instruments and hedging strategies than they are in other contexts. It was explained in chapter 3 that the general goal of accounting for tax purposes is the measurement of changes in the value of instruments in a manner that addresses opportunities for anticipated deferral, timing arbitrage, selective realization, and character arbitrage. There is absolutely no reason to believe that financial-accounting practices, with their focus on the matching of revenue and expenses, realize this goal.[65] Moreover, the classification of an instrument as debt, equity, or a derivative for financial-accounting purposes is no more relevant from a tax-policy perspective than is an uncritical reliance on the instrument's legal form for private law purposes.

As a general proposition, therefore, it is probably true that any correlation between financial-accounting practices and the tax-policy concerns outlined in chapter 3 is entirely fortuitous. The development of a rational tax-accounting regime for the purpose of addressing those concerns should be the task of tax-policy makers and legislators charged with that responsibility. Perceived compliance savings cannot justify the delegation of tax-policy making to accounting bodies, which have no concern with that role. There is also the unique concern in the area of financial instruments that the rapid process of financial innovation and the complexities that it entails might cause tax administrators to rely excessively on accounting practice in the absence of specific legislation. This reliance might undermine one of the major advantages of a comprehensive legislative regime: the provision of broad norms that allow tax administrators to respond rapidly and flexibly to the development of specific financial instruments in a manner that is suitable to the goals of an income tax.[66]

The general problems associated with a reliance on accounting practices for income tax purposes do not mean that these practices should be ignored entirely.[67] Since the development of new financial instruments presents the accounting profession and tax-policy makers with similar problems, financial-accounting practices are a convenient starting point for the development of appropriate income measurement rules. Where these practices are consistent with income tax responses that appropriately address policy concerns, it is appropriate to adopt accounting practice for income measurement purposes in order to minimize the burden of compliance.[68] Indeed, many financial-accounting practices are often consistent with a comprehensive system of expected-return taxation and could be incorporated usefully in tax legislation in order to reduce compliance costs. Nonetheless, tax-policy makers, legislatures, and the courts must retain sole responsibility for assessing the appropriateness of accounting practices and for developing independent tax-accounting standards when tax-policy concerns require a different response. In short, adherence to accounting practices can reduce compliance and administrative problems, but these practices should be followed only when they are both reasonably clear and consistent with the principles that underlie the relevant income tax legislation.[69]

As chapter 5 will describe in more detail,[70] a relatively limited role for financial-accounting practices is evident in the New Zealand accrual legislation and the comparable Australian proposals.[71] In general, these comprehensive regimes attempt to implement a general statutory framework that clearly expresses the accrual principle and provides a suitable interpretive context for taxpayers and tax administrators. The necessary details of the recognition rules are left to be developed flexibly over time through administrative practice and regulation. In both the New Zealand regime and the evolving Australian proposals, this development has tended to mirror recent developments in accounting practice[72] that are relevant to, but not determinative of, the treatment of specific instruments. In particular, the New Zealand rules attempt to address the possibility of excessive reliance on accounting practice by providing that commercially acceptable reporting methods are to be followed as an alternative to specified tax methods, such as the YTM method, only when these alternatives result in an allocation of amounts to taxation years that is not materially different from the allocation under the specified method.[73] The Australian proposals similarly require that the results under an accrual method used for non-traded debt comply with either a benchmark safe harbour or a reasonableness standard.[74] Estimation methods used for instruments that are subject to market-value accounting must also conform with industry-accepted pricing techniques and the criteria for arm's-length transactions.[75]

Interpretive Activism

In another apparent effort to reduce the compliance burden associated with detailed legislative provisions, some tax practitioners[76] have advocated an acceptance of the status quo and a moratorium on further legislative responses. The taxation of financial instruments would be addressed, instead, through administrative practice and the courts, which would take an activist approach to the application and interpretation of existing provisions.[77] Under this "interpretive activism," the perceived substance of a particular financial instrument would be determined, and the instrument would be taxed accordingly under the existing cubbyholes applicable to interest and dividends, capital gains and losses, and business income generally. The apparent premise for this approach is the notion that the development of detailed rules entails "approaches to law that try to make most or nearly all legal judgments under the governing provision in advance of actual cases."[78] As Gergen has noted,[79] the "logical corollary" of this premise is that detailed rules cannot effectively address areas of law that are in a "state of flux," since in these circumstances legislators cannot anticipate every case that the system of rules will have to address. The alternative is to leave resolution of unanticipated problems to an ad hoc, case-by-case analysis that is based on the application of general principles.

The basic premise underlying interpretive activism is sound. As in the case of a reliance on financial-accounting practices, the principal problem with this approach to the taxation of financial instruments has to do with matters of process.

To be specific, it is doubtful whether interpretive activism is more efficient as a process for the resolution of specific cases than the process it proposes to replace. Advocates of interpretive activism reject, without sufficient justification, the use of a comprehensive legislative regime as the basis for the development of appropriate general principles to provide the context necessary for resolving specific cases. In effect, just as a reliance on financial accounting involves a transfer of the function of making tax policy from the legislature to the accounting profession, interpretive activism involves a transfer of this function from the legislature to the courts. In this case, however, the transfer is not especially problematic, at least as an initial proposition, since the courts are charged with the responsibility of formulating appropriate taxation rules and are free to focus exclusively on relevant tax-policy considerations. Indeed, because judges are free to develop principles that are appropriate in the context of a given legislative framework, there should be a close correlation between particular judge-made rules and the underlying tax-policy concerns. It is doubtful, however, whether in practice courts have the ability to craft either rules that are general enough to establish broad principles or rules that are detailed enough to apply to particular instruments. In fact, in the absence of a specifically defined legislative context, the courts could well end up relying heavily on financial-accounting practices, with the possible consequences noted above. These difficulties mean that interpretive activism is useful only as a complement to a well-developed legislative regime that provides clear general principles for the taxation of the broadest possible range of financial instruments.[80]

The inability of the courts to develop adequate principles for governing the taxation of financial instruments is attributable to three general problems. First, the judicial process in most countries does not lend itself easily to either the efficient resolution of large numbers of specific cases or the development of necessary general principles for the taxation of financial instruments. It takes considerable time for a given issue to work its way through the audit, assessment, and appeals process, which must be exhausted before the formalistic and time-consuming procedures of a court can begin.[81] In the absence of specific legislative responses, the need to resolve cases in a timely manner would probably lead to an even greater reliance on administrative rulings and the judgment of tax practitioners at the expense of the judicial process. For that matter, the rulings process itself would probably require considerable streamlining before it could ensure that "appropriate cases [got] presented . . . in a timely fashion for a ruling."[82] In addition, the environment of perpetual "legal uncertainty" in which interpretive activism would operate would put extreme pressure on tax practitioners. Some tax practitioners might attempt to take advantage of the uncertainty by resolving all doubts in favour of their clients.[83] It might be necessary therefore to issue retrospective rulings to deter behaviour of this kind,[84] since in the worst instances disclosure requirements and threats of penalties would probably not be enough.

A second problem with interpretive activism is that it places excessively high expectations on judicial performance. In many countries, quite frankly, the past performance of the courts makes it difficult to have confidence in their ability to produce sensible results in an area as complex as the taxation of financial instruments. Indeed, there is simply no reason to wait for lengthy administrative or judicial resolution of matters that legislation can resolve effectively and immediately. Interpretive activism appears, in reality, to be a counsel of despair; it assumes implicitly that it is impossible to implement a satisfactory legislative regime. If this is true, then the only solution is, in fact, to leave it to the courts, tax administrators, and tax practitioners to do the best they can to reach results in specific cases on the basis of vaguely articulated notions of economic substance.

A third problem is the inadequacy of most existing legislative frameworks, rather than the inadequacy of the courts themselves. Those frameworks and the tax cubbyholes they create severely constrain the promise of interpretive activism. Instead of one overriding tax treatment applicable to all relationships that take a specified legal form or some economic equivalent, there are several different treatments applicable to different types of financial instruments that often combine characteristics of one another. The result is a lack of overriding or guiding principles to provide a useful picture of what the completed legislative puzzle governing financial instruments should look like.[85] In the absence of guiding principles, it is impossible to realize consistent taxation of financial instruments that provide equivalent cash flows and differ only in form.[86] It is expecting too much of tax administrators, practitioners, and the courts to make sense of what is, in essence, a nonsensical legislative scheme that flies in the face of the reality of financial equivalences. If the courts and tax administrators cannot make sense of the existing legislation, then the only way in which they can realize the consistent taxation of financial instruments on the basis of their associated cash flows is to disregard the legislation—and this option is not one that is available to them.

The obvious response to the problems associated with interpretive activism is the same as the obvious response to the problems associated with reliance on financial-accounting practices: the development of a sensible and comprehensive legislative framework that allows tax administrators, tax practitioners, and the courts to fill in the inevitable gaps in an appropriate way.[87] Not even a well-thought-out legislative regime can anticipate every circumstance that might arise; consequently, tax administrators, practitioners, and the courts can serve a useful supporting role, especially if the legislative framework is, of necessity, a second-best one. For this support to be effective, however, there must be a clear legislative expression of general principles to provide a focus for tax administrators, practitioners, and the courts when they are working out the details of appropriate treatment for specific instruments.[88] As chapter 7 will show, support of this kind would be especially important when it came to developing the purpose-based rules that are required to address the use of synthetic instruments. Ideally, these rules would be layered on top of relatively straightforward provisions that governed the taxation of the basic building-block financial instruments. This approach would provide tax administrators, practitioners, and the courts with a clear view of the relevant issues raised by synthetics and of the range of responses that were consistent with certain basic provisions.

Comprehensive Legislative Approaches

Retrospective Taxation and Expected-Return Taxation

Retrospective taxation and expected-return taxation are the only comprehensive second-best alternatives to the accretion ideal. They are comprehensive in the sense that they express a clearly defined set of general principles from which it is possible to derive a detailed set of rules governing the taxation of all gains and losses on all financial instruments. Although retrospective taxation and expected-return taxation have common intellectual roots, they differ in their underlying rationales and, consequently, in their emphasis and some of their design features as well. Even so, it is possible to design either system of taxation so that it addresses the principal policy problems associated with the traditional cubbyhole taxation of financial instruments. Indeed, it is extremely difficult to conclude with any certainty that one approach is preferable to the other, at least in terms of its substantive features. Expected-return taxation, however, does have the advantage that it is generally consistent with many aspects of the existing legislation in most countries. In fact, it simply extends those aspects in some significant respects. Thus the adoption of a comprehensive system of expected-return taxation would involve fewer administrative, compliance, and transitional costs than would the more radical change of a shift to a system of retrospective taxation. A more pedestrian, but not insignificant, consideration is the fact that policy makers and legislators who face two policy options of roughly comparable merit will obviously tend to prefer the one that is easier to implement.[89]

The common intellectual roots of retrospective taxation and expected-return taxation are apparent in some of the academic literature[90] that considers two general policy problems created by a realization-based capital gains tax: (1) the lock-in effect and (2) selective realization. Chapter 3 made the point that a realization-based capital gains tax allows taxpayers to defer tax on accrued gains represented by increases in value or accretions to wealth.[91] The taxpayer defers the tax, obviously enough, by deciding to continue to hold the relevant capital asset rather than sell it or otherwise dispose of it. The deferral benefit provided by the realization-based tax system can "lock" taxpayers into holding assets with accrued gains when it might be more efficient to sell the assets and put the proceeds to a new use. Selective realization occurs when a taxpayer realizes accrued losses by selling "losing assets" and defers realization of offsetting accrued gains by continuing to hold "winning assets." If the taxpayer can deduct the losses against other income, accelerated recognition provides an immediate tax saving that is not recaptured until the offsetting gains are realized when the winning assets are sold. The after-tax return on the tax savings provides an immediate benefit that is the equivalent of an interest-free loan from the government.[92]

By taxing all changes in value annually as they arise, an accretion-based income tax eliminates the realization-based recognition that is the source of the lock-in effect and selective realization. As alternatives to an accretion-based income tax, retrospective taxation and expected-return taxation have been described in the academic literature[93] as comprehensive approaches that attempt to approximate the results of an accretion tax but avoid the compliance burden, valuation difficulties, and liquidity problems that accretion taxation entails.[94] It is possible to trace both the concept of retrospective taxation and its underlying rationale to the early work of William Vickrey[95] and the proposed system of cumulative averaging that he developed in the context of a realization-based capital gains tax.[96] The following fundamental features of Vickrey's system are the basis of retrospective taxation:

1) the realization-based recognition of all gains and losses,

2) the retrospective allocation of realized gains and losses to prior taxation years in the period during which an asset was held (hence "retrospective taxation"), and

3) the imposition of a tax-deductible interest charge to compensate for the failure to tax the realized gains and losses in the years in which they can be considered to have arisen.

The combination of these three features is intended to address the benefit of deferral and the problem of selective realization by imposing a higher effective tax rate on gains realized on assets with longer holding periods.[97] The valuation and liquidity problems associated with accretion taxation are avoided by waiting until realization to collect the tax.[98]

Subsequent works have developed the technical details and design features of Vickrey's system of cumulative averaging.[99] The most complete system is that of Mary Fellows,[100] who describes the detailed features of a "time-adjusted-realization-event tax" (TARET) applied to a wide range of assets. In essence, a TARET, like other, similar forms of retrospective taxation, follows Vickrey's approach by requiring a retrospective allocation of realized gains and losses (both expected and unexpected) over the term of an asset and imposing an interest charge to compensate for the deferred recognition of the relevant amounts. As a legislative approach, a TARET involves five discrete steps. The first is recognition of the gain or loss on an asset when it is realized. The second is retrospective allocation of a portion of this gain or loss to each taxation year during which the taxpayer held or issued the asset. The allocation effectively estimates, on the basis of the asset's realized value, the increase or decrease in value of the asset that occurred in each taxation year, and it uses a specified assumption about the rate at which the gain or loss accrued in each of the years that constitute the holding or issue period. The third step is the calculation of a tax liability (in the case of a gain) or a refund (in the case of a loss) for each year to which a portion of the gain or loss is allocated. The fourth step is to adjust the tax liability or refund by imposing an additional charge or additional compensation to reflect the time value of money associated with the delay in recognition of the gain or loss to the point of realization. The final step is to aggregate the time-adjusted tax liabilities or refunds to arrive at a total amount owing in respect of the realized gain or loss.

The analytical insights that are the basis of a comprehensive system of retrospective taxation are also the basis of expected-return taxation. The two systems' common conceptual bases and differences in approach are most clearly evident in the work of Auerbach.[101] Like a TARET or Vickrey's earlier system of cumulative averaging, Auerbach's suggested approach involves the taxation of capital gains on a retrospective basis. Auerbach, however, describes a system that does not attempt to calculate and tax all realized gains or losses on the basis of ex post results. Instead, his system ignores the taxpayer's cost of an asset and uses only the amount of realized proceeds. That amount is considered to be the result of investing at the risk-free rate of return over the holding period of the asset. In effect, the amount of proceeds is allocated among the taxation years that occur during the holding period, on the assumption that the allocated amounts were reinvested at the end of each year at the riskless rate of return. Tax is calculated on the allocated amount for each taxation year on the basis of the taxpayer's marginal rate for that year, and a tax-deductible interest charge is imposed at the riskless rate to compensate for the benefit of deferred payment on realization. Although its allocation and interest features are identical to those of a TARET, Auerbach's system of retrospective taxation attempts to avoid the "informational requirements"[102] of a time-adjusted tax imposed on realized gain or loss measured ex post. To be specific, Auerbach's system does not require knowledge of the pattern of accrual of gain or loss on an asset, since it assumes that all investors choose an optimal portfolio that can be expected to earn the market interest rate.[103] Given this assumption, Auerbach's system imposes a uniform tax rate on the expected gain or loss viewed ex ante and makes no attempt to tax gains or losses viewed ex post. In a sense, the system views unexpected gains and losses as the outcome of implicit bets with an equal chance, viewed ex ante, of a positive or negative payoff.[104] The lock-in effect and the problem of selective realization attributable to the realization-based recognition of unexpected gains and losses are eliminated by eliminating the recognition of unexpected gains and unexpected losses equally.[105]

Bradford has demonstrated[106] that it is relatively easy to convert Auerbach's retrospective focus on expected returns into a system of expected-return taxation with a prospective focus. Under Bradford's system, the difference between an asset's cost and its expected payoff on maturity, which represents the expected return on the asset, is allocated prospectively on acquisition among the taxation years that occur during the expected holding period. The portion of this difference that is allocated to a given year must be recognized and taxed in that year, whether it is realized in that year or not. Unexpected gain or loss, represented by the difference between an asset's sale proceeds and its cost (increased by expected amounts previously recognized), is recognized on realization (sale or other disposition). On the acquisition of an asset, however, the taxpayer must specify both a "gain reference date" and a "gain tax rate." If realization occurs after the gain reference date, the realized gain is discounted by the riskless rate of return in order to convert it into its present value as of the gain reference date. The gain tax rate is applied to the resulting amount, and an interest deferral charge is imposed to compensate for deferral of the tax for the period from the gain reference date to the realization event. If realization occurs before the gain reference date, the taxpayer receives an interest credit for prepayment of the tax and a comparable credit to compensate him for the deferred recognition of an unexpected loss realized after the gain reference date. If the taxpayer realizes an unexpected loss before the gain reference date, an interest charge on the tax saved for the period from realization to the gain reference date compensates for the accelerated recognition.

Since a taxpayer must specify both the gain reference date and the tax rate when he acquires an asset, Bradford's system of expected-return taxation eliminates the lock-in effect and the problem of selective realization. The system assumes that unexpected gains and losses arise on the gain reference date, and the imposition of deferral charges or credits appropriately accounts for deferred or accelerated recognition. Given equal opportunity for a positive or a negative payoff, viewed ex ante, specification of the gain reference date and the gain tax rate is entirely arbitrary. Taxpayers obtain no advantage from setting either variable and can even choose a zero rate, since it will have the same effect as a positive tax rate. In fact, the specification of a zero tax rate provides Bradford's system with the attribute that defines expected-return taxation in its pure form—namely, taxation of expected gains and losses only. If the tax rate on unexpected gains and losses means is zero, then ex post results, measured as the difference between realized proceeds and the cost of an asset, are effectively ignored.[107] Thus expected-return taxation in its pure form addresses the problem of anticipated deferral,[108] which is associated with the taxation of expected gains on realization, by requiring accrual recognition of those amounts as they are determined prospectively. It addresses both the problem of unanticipated deferral, which is associated with the taxation of unexpected gains on realization, and the problem of selective realization of unexpected losses by ignoring this type of gain and loss.[109]

Expected-return taxation in its pure form, as described by Bradford, is preferable to a system of retrospective taxation. From a strictly theoretical perspective, the basis for this preference is the fact that retrospective taxation attempts to approximate the results of an accretion-based income tax by taking into account both expected and unexpected gains and losses measured ex post. In order to realize the results of accretion taxation and yet avoid the practical problems associated with an accretion-based system, a system of retrospective taxation must require the collection of tax on realization and levy a deferral charge that is based on assumptions about the pattern of accrual of all gains and losses over the period in which a particular asset is held. The principal weakness of retrospective taxation, therefore, is its need for a statutory assumption about the rate or pattern at which realized gain or loss has accrued. Since this assumption will rarely accord with the actual pattern of accrual, it will fail to produce the same tax result as would accretion taxation.[110]

To put the matter in another way, it is not possible under retrospective taxation to know the actual pattern of accrual on realization, which means that the present value of the tax payable will not equal the tax payable under an accretion tax other than by accident. If the actual pattern of accrual produces increases in value during the earlier portions of the holding period that are greater than the assumed rate, the taxpayer enjoys the benefit of unanticipated deferral and has an incentive to continue to hold the relevant assets. In effect, by continuing to hold the asset, the taxpayer can spread unanticipated gain over the later years of the asset's holding period.[111] If an asset declines in value, the taxpayer has an incentive to sell the asset and realize the full amount of the unexpected loss immediately, and to defer taxation of unexpected gain on assets whose pattern of accrual allows him to spread this gain retrospectively over later years of the holding period.[112] Several commentators have pointed out this failure to replicate the results of an accretion tax;[113] they have concluded that a system of retrospective taxation only alleviates, without eliminating, the problems of unanticipated deferral (including the lock-in effect) and selective realization. A pure system of expected-return taxation eliminates these problems by applying an effective tax rate of zero to both unexpected gains and unexpected losses.[114]

The principal difficulty with a pure system of expected-return taxation is the practical one of gaining popular acceptance for its exclusively ex ante focus.[115] Once again, the application of a zero rate of tax to unexpected gains and losses avoids the efficiency and avoidance problems associated with the lock-in effect and selective realization. A zero rate is not inappropriate, since from a strictly ex ante perspective unexpected gains and unexpected losses are equally likely to occur and therefore both can be ignored. The obstacle to this approach is a prevalent belief that a failure to tax realized gains and permit the deduction of realized losses is inequitable, even if the gains and losses are unexpected.[116] Income tax systems are invariably predicated on the recognition of gains and losses as they are viewed and measured from an ex post perspective. Most countries' income tax systems reflect this apparently deeply held principle. In particular, as was noted earlier,[117] several countries apply expected-return taxation to a limited range of financial instruments, including debt obligations with fixed payments that provide compensation for the time-value of money. This approach requires the allocation of a portion of the expected gains and losses associated with a financial instrument to each taxation year that occurs while the instrument is outstanding. The allocation is made prospectively when the instrument is issued on the basis of certain assumptions about the internal rate of return that are embodied in a specified convention or formula.[118] The allocated amounts must be recognized as income or expense in the years to which they are allocated. Expected gains and losses, therefore, are recognized for income tax purposes as they accrue; that is, as they are assumed to arise with expected increases in value of a financial instrument. Because existing income tax systems recognize unexpected gains and losses on realization at positive tax rates, they differ significantly from a system of expected-return taxation in its pure form.

The result of this difference between a pure system of expected-return taxation and the existing income tax systems in most countries is that the latter generally fail to deal adequately with manipulation of the realization requirement in order to defer recognition of unexpected gains (unanticipated deferral) and accelerate the recognition of unexpected losses (selective realization).[119]

Indeed, if the comparison is between a system of retrospective taxation and a system of expected-return taxation that recognizes unexpected gains and losses at positive tax rates, the former is clearly preferable by virtue of its ability to address, at least to some extent, the problems of unanticipated deferral and selective realization.

As was noted previously, however, it is possible to modify the existing systems that govern the taxation of financial instruments to permit the recognition of unexpected gains and losses on realization at positive tax rates and yet address the problems of unanticipated deferral and selective realization. The most important modification would be the application of accretion taxation to a limited range of financial instruments as a response to the problem of selective realization.[120] Given this modification, a system of expected-return taxation would comprise the following features—features that characterize the comprehensive accrual regimes that a handful of countries have already adopted or proposed:[121]

- the accrual recognition of expected gains and losses on most non-traded instruments,
- the accretion taxation of all gains and losses on a wide range of traded instruments, and
- the realization-based recognition of unexpected gains and losses on non-traded instruments.

Properly speaking, therefore, the comparison of comprehensive second-best approaches should be between a system of retrospective taxation and a system of expected-return taxation that combines accrual recognition of expected gains and losses with accretion taxation of a limited range of financial instruments. Once the policy stakes are framed in this manner, the choice becomes much more difficult. It involves difficult judgments about the two approaches' relative strengths and weaknesses, including a judgment about the ability (or inability) of either approach to address completely the problem of selective realization. One study indicates that a system of retrospective taxation may generally be more effective in this respect than a system of expected-return taxation.[122] This study, however, compares a system of retrospective taxation with a system of expected-return taxation that does not include the limited application of accretion taxation to a range of instruments that can be traded at low transaction costs and are therefore the principal sources of trading strategies that attempt to maximize the benefit of selective realization. Obviously, a system of expected-return taxation that included limited accretion taxation would be more effective in this context than a system of expected-return taxation that included the recognition of all unexpected gains and losses on realization at positive tax rates.

The more difficult question is whether a system of expected-return taxation modified by the introduction of limited accretion taxation would be more effective than a system of retrospective taxation in addressing the problems of unanticipated deferral and selective realization. In the absence of empirical data or theoretical modelling that addresses the point, it is at least arguable that there is little to choose from between the two approaches in this respect. By limiting the application of realization-based recognition to the unexpected gains and losses on non-traded financial instruments, a modified system of expected-return taxation would constrain trading strategies designed to access the benefit of selective realization.[123] The problem of unanticipated deferral reduces to the problem presented by attempts to manipulate the realization requirement to effect an economic disposition without also effecting a legal disposition that attracts tax. As to a system of retrospective taxation, its dependence on an assumption about the pattern of accrual of gains and losses means that it, too, constrains but does not eliminate the problems of selective realization and unanticipated deferral.[124]

It was suggested earlier that the most compelling argument for a modified system of expected-return taxation is a practical one. Indeed, from a practical perspective, a system of retrospective taxation suffers from much the same problem as does a pure system of expected-return taxation, with its strictly ex ante focus that justifies a zero tax rate on unexpected gains and losses. A system of retrospective taxation would be an equally radical departure from the status quo, which is a combination of accrual recognition of expected gains and losses and realization-based taxation of unexpected gains and losses. The radical nature of retrospective taxation is reflected in its use of interest-deferral charges, with which tax-policy makers and administrators have had only limited experience.[125] A more general use of this approach would raise concerns about the choice of an appropriate rate and the prospect of liquidity problems for taxpayers who reinvested their deferred taxes at a rate of return that was less than the deferral rate.[126] What is perhaps most important, the application of retrospective taxation to financial instruments for deductibility purposes implies the provision of an interest credit to compensate taxpayers for the deferral of a deduction until realization. No tax authority has had any practical experience with a tax credit of this kind, which would be especially important in the case of the application of retrospective taxation to financial instruments.

This lack of experience highlights the practical problems that retrospective taxation presents; it simply does not fit easily with the predominantly ex ante approach to the taxation of the expected gains and losses on financial instruments that characterizes the existing legislation in many countries. By contrast, the application of a combination of expected-return and accretion taxation to financial instruments is generally consistent with the combination of ex ante and ex post perspectives that underlie the taxation of returns on other assets. In other words, although there is no compelling theoretical objection to the adoption of retrospective taxation and the change in focus that it would entail, the reality of tax reform is that both policy makers and taxpayers are reluctant to accept approaches that depart radically from familiar concepts. This reluctance often justifies itself by invoking concerns about the increases in compliance and administrative costs that accompany radical change, though the increases might be only temporary and costs might actually decline in the long run. Nevertheless, in the absence of any clear evidence that a system of retrospective taxation would be more effective than a modified system of expected-return taxation in addressing the problems of unanticipated deferral and selective realization, these practical considerations provide important support for the adoption of the latter alternative.[127]

Both retrospective and expected-return taxation are second-best approaches to accretion taxation because they both focus exclusively on the timing of the recognition of gains and losses on all assets. Neither approach, as it has been developed in the academic literature, is intended to be limited in application to financial instruments; nor does either approach provide an obvious response to the issues associated with the distinctions for tax purposes between interest and dividends and between ordinary income and capital amounts. Either approach, however, can be modified and limited in its application to address the whole range of issues associated with the taxation of gains and losses on financial instruments. Thus it is possible under either system to eliminate the distinction between income and capital amounts by simply requiring the recognition of all gains and losses on financial instruments in full as income or expense. It is also possible under either retrospective or expected-return taxation to treat interest and dividends identically, though in this case the two systems would use different means to achieve comparable results.

As a general proposition, only the identical treatment of interest and dividends can eliminate opportunities for pure and approximate tax avoidance provided by the substitutability of debt and equity. Under retrospective taxation, realization of this policy goal is a matter of eliminating the corporate income tax and applying the system of interest-deferral charges equally to all realized returns on debt and shares. For either type of instrument, in effect, the difference between the proceeds of disposition and the instrument's cost is allocated over the taxpayer's holding period for the purposes of calculating and collecting the tax payable and interest-deferral charges on disposition. The result is a tax system that treats all distributions on debt and shares as if they had been made in years before the disposition of the instrument and reinvested by the holder at the rate of return reflected in the assumed pattern of accrual of both expected and unexpected gains and losses. If expected returns allocable to a particular taxation year are paid as interest in that year, no interest deferral charge is necessary and the retrospective tax calculation is ignored.[128] Similarly, if dividends are paid pro rata to shareholders, these distributions are taxed currently without reference to the taxpayer's cost.[129] This approach avoids the computational difficulties that would arise if each distribution were treated as a partial disposition.[130] If the distribution involves a disposition of the shares or constitutes a substantial portion of their value (the economic equivalent of a disposition), it is deemed that a realization event has occurred and retrospective taxation is applied to the resultant gain.[131]

It is possible to realize much the same result under a system of expected-return taxation by distinguishing expected gains and losses associated with debt or equity from unexpected gains and losses. Given this distinction, the treatment of the expected gain or loss attributable to the embedded debt in shares must be identical to the treatment of expected gain or loss on conventional debt. The consequence of this simple policy prescription is a requirement that corporate issuers and holders of debt or shares apply the relevant deductibility and income-inclusion provisions equally to the expected gain or loss on either type of instrument. Expected amounts recognized by a holder are added to the cost of the instrument (either debt or shares), and distributions made during the holding period are considered to be a non-taxable recovery of cost.

Since it is possible to design either a system of retrospective or a system of expected-return taxation to realize the identical taxation of interest and dividends, there may not be much reason to prefer one approach to the other in this respect, at least in theory. The requirement under retrospective taxation of payment of tax on gains during the holding period would involve some computational complexity and some difficult qualitative distinctions.[132] In the case of expected-return taxation, difficulties would arise from the need to identify the expected return on financial instruments with contingent payments, such as shares and options.[133] It would also be difficult, but necessary, to identify expected gains and losses associated with the embedded debt in certain derivative instruments and embedded options in debt obligations with contingent payments.

Chapter 6 will discuss the design problems presented by the extension of expected-return taxation in more detail. Expected-return taxation may have, at best, a marginal advantage over retrospective taxation as a response to the problems associated with the existing distinction for tax purposes between interest and dividends. Its advantage in this context, as in others, is its apparent consistency with existing income tax systems. Taxpayers and tax administrators are already somewhat familiar with the imputation of expected gains and losses on debt obligations and the accrual recognition of those amounts. It should be relatively easy, therefore, to identify the embedded debt in shares and extend accrual treatment to the associated expected return. Given this alternative, it seems somewhat cumbersome and unnecessary to wait until realization to tax the same expected gains and losses, with additional interest-deferral charges, on the basis of a retrospective allocation over the instrument's holding period. In fact, retrospective taxation is useful primarily as a substitute for the accretion taxation of unexpected gains and losses. As was argued in chapter 3 and will be argued more fully in chapter 6, however, it is not necessary to tax unexpected returns on debt and unexpected returns on shares identically, let alone on an accretion basis. The tax-avoidance opportunities attributable to the substitutability of debt and equity can be minimized without the identical taxation of all unexpected gains and losses. The policy concerns associated with unexpected gains and losses centre on the problems of unanticipated deferral and selective realization, which can be addressed under a system of expected-return taxation.

From a policy perspective, therefore, a comprehensive system of retrospective taxation has no conspicuous advantages over a system of modified expected-return taxation. It is not superior to its rival either in its ability to resolve timing issues (realization-based recognition versus accrual recognition) or its ability to resolve character issues (the distinction for tax purposes between interest and dividends). A modified system of expected-return taxation would avoid the radical changes that the introduction of a system of retrospective taxation would inevitably involve without significantly compromising the substantive policy goals associated with the taxation of financial instruments.[134]

Dual Income Tax

Another, apparently different, approach to the taxation of financial instruments is the dual income tax (DIT) system that has been implemented in various forms by the Nordic countries (Denmark, Finland, Norway, and Sweden).[135] The radical feature of this approach is its application of progressive marginal tax rates to labour income and a lower flat rate of tax to capital income generally. The Nordic DITs are therefore another second-best approach to the taxation of financial instruments and capital income that is both comprehensive in scope and different in concept from traditional approaches that require the equivalent treatment of different income sources.[136] Moreover, the evident success of the DIT approach in the Nordic countries gives it some credibility from a purely practical perspective. Nonetheless, closer inspection of the design features of the Nordic DITs shows that these systems are not competing alternatives to a system of expected-return taxation, at least in a strictly domestic context. It is probably more accurate to describe them as somewhat incomplete versions of expected-return taxation, with the addition of a dual-rate structure for capital and labour income as a means of addressing the separate tax-policy issues of international capital mobility and the "competitiveness" of a country's tax system.

Before the enactment of DIT systems in the early 1990s,[137] the taxation of capital income in the Nordic countries was plagued by the same general problems as precipitated tax reform in the United States and other OECD countries in the 1980s.[138] In general, the income tax systems in the Nordic countries were characterized by high marginal tax rates applied to narrow tax bases. The combination of these two general features gave rise to a significant tax-avoidance and tax-shelter industry.[139] Problems were particularly prevalent in the area of capital income taxation, where taxpayers could exploit differences between the taxation of interest and the taxation of dividends, preferential capital gains tax rates, and realization-based recognition of many gains and losses in instances of pure and approximate tax avoidance similar to those described in chapters 2 and 3. The courts generally gave credence to tax-avoidance techniques by adopting formalistic approaches to the application and interpretation of the relevant legislative provisions.

The general response to this state of affairs is reflected in the broad features of the Nordic DIT systems, which are identical to the two features characteristic of the tax-reform experience in other countries in the 1980s; that is, (1) the elimination of various tax preferences in order to broaden the income tax base and (2) the lowering of income tax rates as a quid pro quo for the broader base. The novel feature of the DIT approach is its imposition of personal tax on all forms of capital income at a flat or proportional rate that is significantly lower than the progressive rates applied to labour income. In other words, it rejects the traditional global income tax under which income and losses from all sources are aggregated and progressive personal rates are applied to the resultant sum. Under the Nordic DITs, capital income is taxed under a schedular system that separates it from other income. The separation is reflected not only in the different rate structure but also in a prohibition of the deduction of losses from capital sources against business and labour income. In its purest form, the DIT rate on capital income is set at a level equal to the lowest marginal rate on labour income, which is equal to the corporate income tax rate. The identical treatment of interest and dividends is realized by effectively exempting the dividend return on shares from the personal tax[140] and permitting the deduction of corporate interest expense, which is taxed as interest income to individuals who hold corporate debt. Capital income for the purposes of the DIT systems generally includes interest, dividends, capital gains, rent, and the imputed investment return to business assets of sole proprietors. All other income is considered "personal" or "earned" income.

The rationale for the different tax rates under a DIT appears to derive from the insights of optimal tax theory and its general challenge to the accepted dogma of the Haig-Simons/comprehensive tax base, which dictates the equal taxation of all forms of income.[141] Stated simply, optimal tax theory is concerned with the design of a tax system that is efficient in the sense that it does not affect the pre-tax allocation of resources. In other words, the tax system should be designed to minimize the deadweight loss to society that results from a reallocation of resources in response to taxation. The fundamental insight of optimal taxation is that it is possible to realize this policy goal by applying different tax treatments to different activities on the basis of their relative "elasticities." In effect, activities that are relatively sensitive to taxation should be lightly taxed, and activities that are relatively insensitive to taxation should be taxed more heavily. Sensitivity to taxation is defined largely in terms of the alteration of the pre-tax ratio of supply and demand of a particular activity in response to tax changes. In the case of the Nordic DITs, this basic insight was applied in the context of the perceived mobility of capital flows across national borders. To be more specific, a reduction in the rate of tax on capital income was apparently justified as a response to the increasing mobility of capital internationally and the need to maintain the competitiveness of the tax systems of the Nordic countries.[142] In other words, a low rate on capital income was seen as necessary to prevent both the flight of the financial capital of resident taxpayers to low-taxed foreign jurisdictions and the loss of non-resident investment to the same jurisdictions.[143] Since labour was perceived to be much less mobile than capital, higher tax rates were maintained for employment income.[144]

Apart from this dual-rate structure and its unique rationale, the Nordic DITs are strikingly unremarkable. Much of their treatment of income from financial capital is identical to its treatment under the benchmark approach outlined in chapter 3 and the modified system of expected-return taxation described here as the preferable alternative to a first-best system of comprehensive accretion taxation. In particular, the Nordic DITs respond to the tax-avoidance opportunities associated with the preferential taxation of capital gains by eliminating the distinction between ordinary income and capital amounts and requiring the recognition of the full amount of all gains and losses on financial instruments at the same proportional tax rate as applies to capital income generally. They eliminate the tax-avoidance opportunities associated with the application of different tax treatments to interest and dividends by aligning the corporate income tax rate with the personal tax rate on capital income and effectively exempting dividend income from personal income taxation. This arrangement subjects the underlying income distributed as a non-deductible dividend payment to a corporate tax rate that is equal to the investor-level tax on deductible interest payments (which is the same for resident individuals and corporations). Since capital gains, interest, and dividends are generally subject to the same proportional tax rate, taxpayers are largely indifferent to the characterization of the cash flows on financial instruments for tax purposes.

As was noted already, it is possible to incorporate these features of a DIT in an ideal system of expected-return taxation. Two important characteristics of an ideal system of this kind are the elimination of the distinction between ordinary income and capital amounts and the recognition of the full amount of all gains and losses on financial instruments at the general tax rates. In addition, the system would be extended by an application of accrual recognition to both the expected return on debt and the embedded debt in all shares. The details of this extension are developed fully in chapter 6; at this point, it is sufficient to note that application of identical tax treatment to the expected return on debt and the expected return on shares could ensure the identical treatment of a significant element of interest and dividends and thereby eliminate the tax-avoidance opportunities associated with the application of different tax treatments to these cash flows. Elimination of the distinction between ordinary income and capital amounts would similarly eliminate tax-avoidance opportunities that are premised on the repackaging of cash flows in the form of tax-preferred capital gains.

In its approach to tax-base issues, expected-return taxation differs from the Nordic DITs primarily in the area of timing. In general, both expected-return taxation and the DITs accept the realization basis for the recognition of gains and losses, but important differences in approach result in a more limited availability of that basis under a comprehensive system of expected-return taxation supplemented by the application of accretion recognition to certain financial instruments. This more limited availability makes expected-return taxation more effective than a DIT as a means of minimizing tax-avoidance opportunities of the kinds described in chapter 3.

Expected-return taxation and the DIT systems differ in their approaches to timing issues in two principal ways. To begin with, they differ in how they deal with the problem of selective realization associated with the realization-based recognition of unexpected gains and losses. A system of expected-return taxation attempts to address this problem by imposing accretion-based recognition on a limited range of financial instruments that are susceptible to trading strategies designed to accelerate recognition of unrealized losses and defer the recognition of offsetting gains. To the extent that the Nordic DIT systems address selective realization, they do it by quarantining losses and expenses that are related to the earning of capital income by resident individuals. As was noted earlier, this quarantining is a result of the DITs' schedular approach, which limits the deduction of realized losses and expenses associated with the earning of capital income to the amount of realized revenue from that source. This schedular approach was attractive to tax-policy makers in the Nordic countries as a means of addressing revenue erosion caused by the effective deductibility by individuals of interest expense against their labour income.[145] Because of the general quarantining of capital income under a schedular DIT, any excess of personal interest expense related to the earning of capital income cannot be deducted against other income sources.[146] In a sense, therefore, the general quarantining operates as a simpler version of the US passive loss restrictions enacted as part of the 1986 tax reform.[147] In addition, the Nordic DIT systems contain specific limitations, similar to those in many other countries, that restrict the deduction of realized capital losses to the amount of realized capital gains.

The second difference between the approaches to timing issues under the Nordic DIT systems and a system of expected-return taxation concerns the accrual recognition of expected gains and losses. A comprehensive system of expected-return taxation applies accrual recognition to expected gains and losses on all financial instruments for all taxpayers. This approach addresses the problem of anticipated deferral described in chapter 3, whereby taxpayers can reduce the effective tax rate on financial instruments that provide expected gains and losses by deferring recognition until realization. Comprehensive recognition of all expected gains and losses also addresses avoidance opportunities that arise when either (1) different instruments that provide comparable expected gains and losses are subject to different recognition rules or (2) different taxpayers are subject to different recognition rules on the same financial instrument. In the first case, a taxpayer can realize tax savings by assuming offsetting long (lending transaction) and short (borrowing transaction) positions in identical instruments, recognizing expense (expected loss on the borrowing transaction) on an accrual basis, and deferring recognition of revenue (expected gain on the lending transaction) to realization. In the second case, tax savings arise from the accelerated recognition of expense by an accrual-based taxpayer (who assumes a short position in a borrowing transaction) and the deferred recognition of revenue by a realization-based taxpayer (who assumes a long position in a lending transaction). Neither trading strategy produces tax savings under a comprehensive system of expected-return taxation, which subjects the expected gain and loss on all financial instruments to accrual recognition by all taxpayers.

In contrast to expected-return taxation, the Nordic DITs reflect a mix of accrual and realization-based recognition of expected gains and losses by different taxpayers. What is most important, interest income of resident individuals is generally taxed on a cash basis, sometimes under a domestic withholding system.[148] This timing rule provides the benefit of anticipated deferral for interest-bearing securities held by individuals and permits avoidance opportunities of the second type described above, since corporate borrowers may deduct interest expense generally on an accrual basis. Application of cash-basis recognition to the interest expense of individuals[149] alleviates the worst avoidance opportunities associated with the accrual recognition of interest expense and the realization-based recognition of interest income on offsetting positions assumed by a taxpayer. It is still possible, however, to manipulate the realization basis in order to accelerate the recognition of interest expense while deferring the recognition of interest income.[150] The tax savings that individuals can realize through these timing strategies are limited by the fact that an individual can deduct only a limited amount of personal interest expense against non-capital income sources.[151]

These differences between the approaches to timing issues under the Nordic DITs and a comprehensive system of expected-return taxation mean that the DIT systems are generally more susceptible to avoidance opportunities; in addition, the limitations they place on the deductibility of losses may cause some inefficiencies.[152] Indeed, apart from their extended quarantining of losses and expenses associated with capital income sources, along the lines of the US passive loss rules, the Nordic DIT systems are familiar versions of the dividend imputation systems that many countries have adopted in order to mitigate differences between the effective tax burden on interest and the burden on dividends. Expected-return taxation appears to be the more desirable alternative, primarily because of its superiority as a means of addressing timing arbitrage.

This conclusion, however, misses the essential point about the DIT and expected-return taxation as second-best approaches to the taxation of financial instruments. As was emphasized earlier, the tax base issues under the Nordic DIT systems are exactly the same as those under a system of expected-return taxation. Both attempt to address the avoidance opportunities associated with the application of different tax treatments to interest and dividends, the distinction between ordinary income and capital amounts, and the realization-based recognition of certain gains and losses. The general thrust of both responses to these avoidance opportunities is to broaden the capital income tax base by eliminating differences in the taxation of financial cash flows and restricting the realization-based recognition of gains and losses. Both responses recognize that cash flows are often substitutable, and that financial markets are extremely sensitive to tax-avoidance opportunities presented by differences in taxation. The basic insights of optimal tax theory and the dogma of a comprehensive tax base thus come together to support base-broadening measures for capital income taxation in a domestic context. It would be easy to alter the Nordic DITs by substituting the limited application of accretion taxation for the use of loss limitations as a response to the problem of selective realization. Similarly, the DITs could easily extend accrual recognition of expected gains and losses on all financial instruments to all taxpayers. The result would be a system of comprehensive expected-return taxation for all financial instruments much like the one described here.

Ultimately, therefore, the only unique feature of the Nordic DIT systems is their application of different tax rates to the capital income and labour income of individuals, which they have adopted for reasons that have absolutely nothing to do with the elimination of avoidance opportunities of the kind that a system of expected-return taxation is designed to address. Even if one accepts the goals that underlie adoption of a dual-rate structure, it is debatable whether this rate structure is either effective or necessary as a means to those ends.[153] Moreover, the dual-rate approach causes problems in the domestic context, particularly by requiring small businesses to separate the capital-return and labour-return components of the proprietor's income so that different tax rates may be applied to them.[154] This consequence of the dual-rate structure has created an intractable problem, one that has been addressed with only limited success by the use of rough proxies to measure the different returns.

The simple point made here is that there is nothing to prevent the application under a system of expected-return taxation of a separate rate to the tax base for all financial income. Conversely, there is nothing to prevent the Nordic dual-rate systems from adopting an expected-return tax base for financial instruments. In the former case, the result would be a system of expected-return taxation with a DIT rate structure; in the latter case, the result would be a DIT rate structure with a tax base equivalent to a system of expected-return taxation. This identical result is attributable to the fact that the Nordic DIT systems and a comprehensive system of expected-return taxation are in no sense incompatible; they are simply different responses to very different issues.

Expected-Return Taxation and Existing Legislative Approaches

To varying degrees, many existing legislative regimes reflect the core elements of expected-return taxation and differ only in the range of particular financial instruments that they subject to the recognition of unrealized gains and losses. Thus the adoption of expected-return taxation would be a natural progression consistent in principle with many aspects of existing legislative regimes for the taxation of financial instruments. One can obtain an idea of the extent to which existing legislative regimes have incorporated the core elements of expected-return taxation by placing the general design features of those regimes on a continuum. At one extreme are regimes that apply expected-return taxation in its broadest form to debt and the embedded debt in other financial instruments, including shares. At the other extreme are legislative regimes that limit the application of expected-return taxation to periodic interest on fixed-payment debt and comparable returns on a narrow set of debt equivalents. Between these extremes are legislative approaches that apply expected-return taxation to expected gains and losses on a range of financial instruments beyond a limited set of debt and debt equivalents. By failing to extend accrual treatment to shares and some of the standard derivative instruments (especially options), these regimes stop short of the implementation of expected-return taxation in its broadest form.

The transactional approach to the taxation of financial instruments described in chapter 2 exemplifies the most limited legislative form of expected-return taxation and continues to be the predominant approach in most countries, including Canada.[155] In fact, only a handful of countries have extended their legislation beyond this approach. Frost has usefully described the various alternatives to a transactional approach evident in the legislation of some of these countries;[156] his list includes the following:[157]

1) "half-page amendments," which consist of the extension of accretion taxation to gains and losses of financial institutions on a limited class of financial instruments, including debt obligations, swaps, options, and foreign currency contracts;

2) "concerted piecemeal amendments," which attempt to preserve the integrity of existing core provisions that govern the deductibility and taxability of basic financing charges but do it by adding a broad set of new provisions designed to address new financial instruments on a piecemeal basis;

3) "a comprehensive legislative code for financial institutions," which applies a set of provisions that governs the taxation of all financial instruments held or issued by financial institutions; and

4) "a comprehensive legislative code applicable to most taxpayers," which extends a comprehensive code for financial instruments held or issued by financial institutions to most taxpayers, with limited exceptions for individuals and small businesses.[158]

To an important extent, many of the differences in approach that Frost's categories suggest are really no more than differences in degree.[159] Indeed, any greater emphasis on these differences may be misleading. Although a comprehensive code can be expressed clearly and simply at a level of general principle, the application of the principles to specific instruments or categories of instruments inevitably requires the development of detailed accounting methods. As these methods are developed, however, the comprehensive code may gradually assume the aspect of an instrument-specific approach characteristic of "half-page amendments" and "concerted piecemeal amendments." Concerted piecemeal amendments, conversely, begin at the level of detailed recognition rules for gains and losses on particular instruments. The adoption of these amendments is, therefore, no more than a logical extension of the transactional approach to the taxation of financial instruments. In particular, the transactional approach tends to involve the ad hoc development of rules through administrative application of general legislative provisions to specific instruments, as well as through the adoption of specialized legislative regimes for specific instruments used for tax-avoidance purposes. An approach that uses concerted piecemeal amendments tends to be characterized by the ad hoc development of specialized legislative regimes for broader categories of debt obligations and derivative instruments used for tax-avoidance and risk-management purposes.

If the recognition methods are consistent enough, the piecemeal amendments may become a set of rules that is applicable to a wide range of instruments and thus end by resembling a comprehensive regime that began at a level of broad principle but inevitably sank into the form of an array of specific recognition methods. In other words, given a sufficient number of self-contained pieces of legislation applicable to particular financial instruments, the scope of concerted piecemeal amendments begins to resemble the scope of a purportedly comprehensive code.[160]

The adoption of concerted piecemeal amendments has probably been pushed to its greatest extent in the United States. Because that country has the world's deepest and most mature capital markets, US tax-policy makers were forced to react to the consequences of financial innovation long before policy makers in other countries. A series of piecemeal amendments applicable to specified categories of instruments began in earnest with the introduction in the early 1980s of three sets of rules. The first was intended to correct flaws in the tax treatment of original issue discount (OID) bonds,[161] the second addressed straddle transactions,[162] and the third imposed mark-to-market reporting for gains and losses on futures contracts and certain exchange-traded options.[163] This legislation was followed by the introduction of self-contained regimes for foreign currency transactions[164] and OID obligations.[165] The late 1980s and early 1990s saw the introduction (and protracted adoption) of (1) rules applicable to debt with contingent payments ("contingent debt");[166] (2) mark-to-market reporting for gain or loss on most securities held by traders and dealers;[167] (3) regulations that govern the recognition of payments under notional principal contracts (NPCs), including swaps, caps, floors, and collars;[168] and (4) regulations that provide for hedge accounting of eligible financial instruments.[169] Even now, this process of piecemeal amendment is far from complete. In the last few years, the US Treasury department has switched its focus to synthetic instruments, whose tax consequences have been addressed, in part, through legislation applicable to "conversion transactions"[170] and "constructive sales."[171]

In apparent contrast with the US approach, the New Zealand government adopted a comprehensive legislative code in March 1987.[172] This legislation imposes accrual recognition of expected gains and losses on a wide range of financial instruments. Although the legislation was originally intended to address debt instruments and debt equivalents, it has since been applied as well to derivatives in their basic forms and some complex instruments that combine the cash flows normally associated with debt and derivatives. This extension of the New Zealand legislation has been possible because the legislation adopted a definition of "financial arrangements" that was potentially broad enough to include more than debt instruments and debt equivalents alone. In discussion papers released three years apart, the Australian Taxation Office (ATO) and Australia's Treasury department have proposed a comprehensive regime for the taxation of financial arrangements that is loosely patterned on the New Zealand legislation.[173]

The legislation in the United States and New Zealand and the reform proposals in Australia have three features in common:

1) They all define the types of financial instruments that are subject to the legislation.

2) They all develop tax-accounting methods for the recognition of gain or loss on the relevant instruments.

3) They all apply certain techniques that attempt to tax complex financial instruments or positions on the basis of their perceived substance.

Characterization of each country's particular legislative approach as "concerted piecemeal amendments" or "a comprehensive code applicable to financial instruments held or issued by most taxpayers" does not reveal much that is instructive. Where the three approaches do differ significantly is at the level of the specific rules and concepts that they have developed in each of the three areas listed above. As the following chapter will attempt to show, the most important differences are those that concern tax-accounting methods, and in particular the methods used to distinguish expected gains and losses from unexpected gains and losses for recognition purposes. To a large extent, the general definitional issue of which financial instruments should be subject to which legislative regime is determined by the choice of tax-accounting methods. Legislation that contemplates accrual recognition of expected gains and losses is inevitably limited to debt instruments and a limited set of debt equivalents. On the other hand, it is possible to apply legislation successfully to a broad range of instruments if the tax-accounting methods incorporate a combination of accrual recognition of expected gains and losses and realization-based and accretion recognition of unexpected amounts.[174]

The next chapter will develop these general points fully as it examines in detail the core elements of expected-return taxation, as it is implemented in the form of a comprehensive accrual regime, and its three principal design features:

1) the definition of the types of financial instruments and taxpayers subject to the regime;

2) the development of tax-accounting methods for the recognition of expected gains and losses associated with the basic building-block financial instruments; and

3) the use of loss limitations or accretion taxation as a response to the problem of selective realization associated with unexpected losses under a realization-based approach to the recognition of unexpected amounts.

5

A Comprehensive Accrual Regime as the Legislative Expression of Expected-Return Taxation

Introduction

Chapter 4 presented the policy arguments in support of expected-return taxation as the preferable approach to the taxation of financial instruments under a realization-based income tax. This "second-best" alternative to accretion taxation focuses on the timing issues associated with expected gains and losses; in particular, it addresses the problem of anticipated deferral created by the realization-based recognition of these amounts. As was argued in chapter 4, a more complete approach requires the addition of other elements that attempt to address

- the issues of character arbitrage associated with the distinctions for tax purposes between capital amounts and ordinary-income amounts and between interest and dividends, and
- the problems of unanticipated deferral and selective realization associated with the realization-based recognition of unexpected gains and losses.

This chapter explores the design features of a system of "comprehensive accrual rules" as a legislative regime that attempts to implement the core elements of expected-return taxation but goes beyond those elements to address the important problems of unanticipated deferral and selective realization. It eliminates the problems of character arbitrage associated with the distinction between capital amounts and ordinary-income amounts by requiring the recognition of all gains and losses in full as income and expense. For the reasons that were outlined in chapter 3,[1] it is assumed that this approach is adopted as a critical part of a comprehensive accrual regime applicable to financial instruments. Chapters 6 and 7 examine the more difficult problem of character arbitrage associated with the distinction for tax purposes between interest and dividends.

The labels "comprehensive accrual rules" and "comprehensive accrual regime" are used here for convenience, without equating them with the specific legislation in any country. In fact, as was emphasized at the end of chapter 4, the legislation in many countries reflects, to varying degrees, certain elements of expected-return taxation and the limited application of accretion recognition, which are the fundamental features of a comprehensive accrual regime. Nonetheless, since these rules are reflected most clearly in the New Zealand accrual legislation[2] and the comparable Australian proposals,[3] the discussion will draw extensively on the experience in those two countries. Indeed, the New Zealand regime and the proposed Australian regime are the most comprehensive attempts to implement the core elements of expected-return taxation for the broadest possible range of basic building-block financial instruments (hence the label "comprehensive accrual rules"). The two regimes come closer than any others to the implementation of expected-return taxation in its broadest sense; nevertheless they stop short of this result in some significant respects, such as by failing to extend accrual recognition to the expected return associated with the embedded debt in options and shares.

In addition to the recognition of all gains and losses on financial instruments as ordinary income or expense, a comprehensive accrual regime intended to implement the dictates of expected-return taxation must include

- a definition of financial instruments and taxpayers that are subject to the regime,
- the accrual recognition of expected gains and losses on non-traded instruments,
- the realization-based recognition of unexpected gains and losses on non-traded instruments,
- the accretion taxation of all gains and losses on traded instruments, and
- some limitations on the realization-based recognition of unexpected losses.

The second part of this chapter begins with a discussion of the issues of scope associated with the determination of the types of financial instruments and taxpayers that should be subject to an accrual regime. This discussion uses the New Zealand and Australian experiences as examples in arguing that the definition of eligible instruments should be as inclusive as possible. Shares are commonly excluded from the application of comprehensive accrual rules, and as chapter 6 will argue, there are significant practical and theoretically defensible rationales for this exception. Otherwise, the definition should include all financial instruments that provide expected time-value returns, all instruments that provide only unexpected gains and losses, and all instruments that combine these two elements. This wide definition encompasses all of the basic building-block instruments, and all of the more complex hybrid and synthetic instruments that are the subject of chapters 6 and 7. A wide scope is necessary to ensure that expected gains and losses are subject to accrual recognition and that unexpected gains and losses are subject to realization-based recognition or accretion taxation as ordinary income and expense.

The definition of eligible taxpayers should be even more inclusive. Comprehensive accrual rules often provide specific exclusions for individuals and small businesses, but although exceptions of this kind have an intuitive appeal they are almost always indefensible and should be rejected. In particular, these exceptions tend to create a "two-code approach," under which some taxpayers are subject to a comprehensive accrual regime and other taxpayers are subject to taxation under the traditional tax cubbyholes. This approach gives rise to timing and character mismatches between taxpayers and thus to potential tax-avoidance opportunities that are difficult to justify on the basis of any perceived saving in compliance costs. Indeed, a two-code approach presents its own unique administrative complexities, which may limit the benefit of any compliance savings that arise from providing exceptions for certain issuers and holders of financial instruments. The only defensible application of an accounting method based on the status of a taxpayer is the application of accretion taxation to traders or dealers in financial instruments.

The third part of the chapter describes the basic tax-accounting methods for gains and losses associated with fixed-payment debt and the price-fixing building-block instruments (forwards, futures, and swaps). In general, any attempt to implement expected-return taxation must use three different methods of tax accounting. The first method attempts to approximate an instrument's expected increases in value over its term, which must be recognized annually as they are expected to arise. The standard methodology used for this accrual recognition of expected gains and losses is the yield-to-maturity (YTM) method commonly associated with fixed-payment debt and original issue discount (OID) bonds. Administrative and compliance considerations require modifications of the ideal YTM method that result in some mismeasurement of the pattern of accrual of expected amounts. These modifications do not, however, undermine the basic integrity of the YTM methodology, which is preferable to other approaches. The most difficult problems associated with use of the YTM method arise in the case of hybrid instruments, or instruments that provide both expected returns and contingent payments attributable to a bet element; these unique problems are the subject of chapter 6. The second and third methods of tax accounting apply to unexpected gains and losses. The second method is the realization basis for the recognition of gains and losses, which is the only alternative for unexpected gains and losses in the absence of accretion taxation. Realization-based recognition, however, creates the problems of unanticipated deferral and selective realization, which require certain modifications of the realization requirement to ensure that a taxable event is equated with an unconditional legal right to an amount and not to the receipt of cash. The third method, accretion taxation (or "mark-to-market" reporting) of all gains and losses, is required to address the problem of selective realization. For efficiency reasons, this method is generally preferable to loss limitations, and it is possible to target it to financial instruments that may be traded at low transaction costs.

The chapter concludes with a brief review of the limitations of a comprehensive accrual regime. The discussion argues that the New Zealand legislation and the Australian accrual proposals provide a useful model for the design of a modified system of expected-return taxation, one that effectively balances theory and practical administrative constraints. The general approach represented by the New Zealand and Australian regimes is consistent with incremental reform undertaken in many other countries; it differs from the ad hoc responses of past legislative practice primarily in the degree to which it suppresses problematic inconsistencies and discontinuities. This chapter limits its discussion of the design principles of a comprehensive accrual regime to the appropriate tax treatment of certain of the basic building-block instruments of financial innovation. A complete accrual regime must also address the more complex hybrid and synthetic instruments that are the products of various combinations of those basic instruments. The various tax-accounting methods described in this chapter provide sound fundamentals that can readily be extended to the more complex instruments. Even a comprehensive accrual regime, however, has certain important weaknesses. These weaknesses result from the regime's use of realization-based recognition of unexpected gains and losses, its exclusion of shares, and the imposition of non-resident withholding tax. As chapters 6 and 7 will discuss in detail, hybrid instruments, synthetics, and hedge transactions pose challenges in these areas that require unique responses, notably the techniques of bifurcation and integration, as complements to the application of a comprehensive accrual regime.

The Scope of a Comprehensive Accrual Regime

In designing any legislative regime for the taxation of financial instruments, it is necessary to determine the scope of the regime. It is necessary, that is, to determine both which instruments are to be subject to the regime and which taxpayers, as parties to these instruments, must apply specified tax-accounting methods for the recognition of income and expense. The designation of affected instruments is a direct function of the policy concerns outlined in chapter 3 and lies at the heart of the design of a legislative regime. As will be emphasized below, there is a necessary link between the regime's choice of tax-accounting methods and its definition of financial instruments whose associated cash flows will be subject to those methods. In contrast, there is no obvious correlation between the identity of taxpayers and the choice of tax-accounting methods for the recognition of income and expense. As an initial proposition at least, all returns on affected financial instruments should be recognized, by means of a specified accounting method, regardless of the identity of the parties. Administrative and compliance concerns are often invoked to justify exceptions for certain types of taxpayers, but these limitations on the scope of a legislative regime are almost always indefensible. A defensible case can be made, however, for the application of accretion taxation to instruments held or issued by traders or dealers and other financial institutions.

Types of Instruments Subject to Accrual Rules

The Concept of a "Financial Instrument" as a Function of Tax-Accounting Methods

In principle, development of a definition of the types of financial instruments that are to be subject to a legislative regime is a straightforward matter. It is impossible to separate the policy that underlies an accrual regime from the choice of tax-accounting methods and, in turn, the range of financial instruments that should be subject to the regime. It seems fairly obvious, therefore, that any definition of affected instruments should reflect general characteristics of financial instruments that are consistent with the perceived underlying policy. In other words, the definitional issue must be treated as a function of the more fundamental policy decision about the scope of the application of accrual treatment, which is defined by the choice of tax-accounting methods.[4] Otherwise, the definition is likely to be either underinclusive or overinclusive. It may be difficult, however, to articulate a clear underlying policy to which one can refer in order to ensure that the definition of affected instruments is targeted appropriately. The significant policy questions in this context are the following:

- Which types of gains and losses should the accrual regime address?
- Which types of accounting methods should be used to address these types of gains and losses?

A broad definition of financial instruments should ideally reflect a policy choice to apply accretion taxation to all gains and losses. Given a regime of this kind, the only issue of scope is whether accretion taxation should be extended to shares—an issue that has significant implications for reform of the corporate income tax system in most countries.[5] In contrast with accretion taxation, a system of expected-return taxation attempts to spread expected gains and losses over the term of an instrument by using the YTM method and comparable techniques.[6] As will be described below,[7] this narrow focus on expected gains and losses makes it possible, in general, to limit the definition of affected financial instruments to debt and debt equivalents; that is, to instruments whose returns are predominantly a reflection of the time-value of money. In effect, when it is assessed in terms of the basic building-block financial instruments described in chapter 1, the policy that underlies an accrual regime of this kind does not require the unqualified inclusion of price-fixing derivatives (forwards, futures, and swaps)[8] whose returns reflect a pure bet. Since these instruments provide only unexpected gains and losses, the core tax-accounting methods adopted to require the accrual recognition of expected returns are irrelevant in their case.

There are grounds, however, for extending even a legislative regime of expected-return taxation to financial instruments that provide unexpected gains and losses. As was noted above, an extension of this kind is required for three principal reasons. First, one of the core elements of a system of expected-return taxation is the required recognition of unexpected gains and losses on realization. Inclusion of financial instruments with both expected and unexpected gains and losses may be necessary to ensure that the recognition of unexpected amounts occurs on realization. Second, it may be necessary to supplement a system of expected-return taxation with either loss-limitation rules or a limited application of accretion taxation in order to address the selective realization of unexpected gains and losses. If the accretion alternative is chosen, it becomes a supporting element of a system of expected-return taxation and the definition of affected financial instruments must be broad enough to include any instrument with a bet element. Third, a focus on expected gains and losses associated with debt instruments requires the specific inclusion of debt equivalents, which can range from the embedded debt in options and prepaid forwards and swaps to more sophisticated combinations of derivatives and long and short positions in assets.

The need to supplement the application of expected-return taxation means that a broad definition of financial instruments subject to accrual treatment is an appropriate starting point under either a system of accretion taxation or a system of expected-return taxation. For all practical purposes, the scope of any legislative regime is effectively defined by the tax-accounting methods that it applies to specific instruments. This fact is apparent in the two contrasting legislative approaches used in countries whose tax regimes define the scope of their application of accrual taxation.[9] One approach, characteristic of legislative practice in the United States, is what Frost has called the "concerted piecemeal amendment" of existing legislation.[10] This approach accepts the traditional cubbyholes for interest and dividends, which are based on longstanding judicial concepts of interest and an acceptance of the legal form of an instrument as a share. It involves the adoption of a series of specific legislative responses intended to (1) modify the traditional cubbyholes in limited circumstances and (2) create new cubbyholes for new categories of financial instruments or transactions. The concerted piecemeal approach differs from the traditional transactional approach to the taxation of financial instruments in two respects: its legislative responses are systematic rather than scattered and ad hoc, and they apply to wider categories of financial instruments, categories that often include derivatives. Its effect is similar to that of a listing of specific financial instruments and their characteristics for the purposes of the application of particular tax-accounting methods.[11] Newer instruments, including the basic building-block derivatives, must be slotted in newly created cubbyholes that are reflected in self-contained legislation.[12]

The second approach, characteristic of the legislation in New Zealand and the reform proposals in Australia, is to apply comprehensive accrual rules. This approach, like the first, accepts the traditional tax cubbyholes for interest and dividends. Instead of introducing new rules on a piecemeal basis, however, it develops a singular definition of the types of financial instruments to which accrual treatment will apply. This definition attempts to identify the general characteristics of financial instruments for which the application of accrual treatment is appropriate.[13] In fact, however, the inevitable link between definitional issues and tax-accounting methods eliminates much of the difference between a piecemeal approach to the definition of affected instruments and a comprehensive one. To be more specific, it is always necessary to assess the unique features of a particular instrument on a transactional basis in order to determine whether the relevant accrual rules should apply and, if so, in what manner under different tax-accounting methods. Perhaps the only important difference between the two approaches is that the piecemeal approach makes this assessment at the level of the application of the necessary recognition rules and the comprehensive approach treats it as an initial question about the appropriate scope of an accrual regime generally. By reducing a transactional assessment to the level of the application of accrual recognition, the comprehensive approach may avoid gaps in the scope of the legislation that might occur under piecemeal amendments.[14] Since the latter approach requires a transactional assessment to determine the scope of particular legislation, new instruments may be created that do not fit easily within the resulting series of narrowly focused legislative regimes.[15] This uncertainty in application may occur even if the instruments are functionally equivalent to older instruments within the particular rules. If it does occur, new definitions and new legislative responses may be required in order to address tax-avoidance opportunities or to alleviate the uncertainty that otherwise inhibits the use of new instruments. The comprehensive approach, which is based on the identification of general characteristics of financial instruments, accommodates the development of new instruments by avoiding this endless dialectic and ensuring that the relevant accrual principle applies to the widest range of financial instruments.[16]

New Zealand's experience with its accrual legislation illustrates the importance of an appropriate link between the definition of affected instruments and the underlying policy reflected in tax-accounting methods. One prominent source of contention under that legislation is a perceived inconsistency between the legislation's broad definition of a "financial arrangement" and an underlying policy, reflected in the legislative history, that is much narrower.[17] In particular, considerable confusion has arisen over whether under the legislation accretion taxation is a supplement to an expected-return system or the principal recognition method that is supplemented with alternative methods when valuation and liquidity problems make accretion recognition impractical. This confusion and the tension evident in the New Zealand legislation are less pronounced in the Australian accrual proposals, which appear to reflect a clearer policy choice to impose accretion taxation on a range of unexpected gains or losses and require the accrual recognition of the expected returns associated with debt instruments and debt equivalents.

Comprehensive Definitions Reflected in the New Zealand Legislation and the Australian Accrual Proposals

The concept of a comprehensive accrual regime implies the application of accrual treatment to a broad range of financial instruments within one legislative framework. As examples of this approach, both the New Zealand accrual legislation and the comparable Australian proposals incorporate comprehensive definitions of a "financial arrangement," the return on which is subject to specified tax-accounting methods. In general, this concept of a financial arrangement consists of two elements. The first focuses on debt obligations and debt equivalents in an attempt to require accrual recognition of expected gains and losses associated with these instruments. The second focuses on non-debt instruments in an attempt to require accretion taxation of unexpected gains and losses represented by the bet element in certain of the basic derivative instruments. The inclusion of the first element reflects a definitional approach that is somewhat conventional and arguably represents no more than a repackaging, consolidation, and extension of existing legislative regimes that attempt to modify the results of the application of a restrictive concept of interest developed by the courts.[18] The inclusion of the second element gives an accrual regime a more comprehensive focus that differs significantly from the status quo reflected in the transactional approach characteristic of legislative practice in many countries.

The New Zealand legislation provides a general set of rules that govern the accrual recognition of income and expense in respect of "financial arrangements," which are defined broadly to include two principal elements:[19]

- any debt or debt instrument;[20] and
- any arrangement whereby a person obtains money (or money's worth)[21] in consideration for a promise by any person to provide money (or money's worth) to any person at some future time or times, or upon the occurrence or non-occurrence of some future event or events.

Perhaps not surprisingly, some ambiguity surrounds the relationship between these two elements of the definition.[22] In particular, the question has arisen whether the wider second element should be read down in the light of the more restrictive first element, which appears to include only "unconditional promises to pay money."[23] The second element extends to mutual promises, whether they are conditional or not, and whether or not they involve any initial transfer of consideration from one party to the other.[24] Although it is not entirely free of doubt, the prevailing view seems to be that owing to its much wider scope the second element should be regarded as the primary test under the definition of a financial arrangement.[25] In fact, the legislative wording of the second element encompasses debt and debt instruments; it also encompasses (1) options; and (2) forwards, futures, and swaps.[26]

The Australian proposals, too, define the scope of accrual treatment in terms of the concept of a "financial arrangement," which includes three classes of transactions:[27]

- debt arrangements and arrangements that are in substance debt;
- the debt component of certain hybrid transactions; and
- all derivatives, including debt derivatives and non-debt derivatives, whether based on the value of a group of commodities or equities or a single commodity or equity.

The Australian proposals describe the central feature of a debt arrangement as "the payment of an amount that gives rise to a right to receive, or an obligation to pay, another amount that is reasonably likely to equal or exceed the first-mentioned amount."[28] The term "derivative" follows the concept generally used in financial markets, and refers to "arrangements under which there is a right or obligation in relation to an underlying interest or measured by reference to a variable."[29] Derivatives based on the value of a debt obligation, foreign currency arrangement, or an interest or foreign exchange rate are referred to as "debt derivatives."[30] "Non-debt derivatives" include all other derivative arrangements, most notably derivatives based on either (1) an index made up of a number of commodities or equities or (2) a single commodity or equity.[31]

In large part, the New Zealand legislation and the Australian proposals use these broad concepts of a financial arrangement in order to counteract the effect of the restrictive legal definition of interest. This restrictive definition applies only to fixed amounts that represent compensation for the use of borrowed funds and accrue on a daily basis, so that they can be allocated prospectively over the term of a borrowing. It is suited to basic statutory rules that provide for the recognition of fixed interest obligations on an annual accrual basis, but it has created considerable difficulties for the treatment of debt with contingent returns. The New Zealand legislation and the Australian accrual proposals attempt to negate the significance of the restrictive legal definition of interest by subjecting all returns on all forms of financial instruments, other than shares, to some form of accrual treatment. In this connection, the use of a wide concept of a financial arrangement permits the implementation of two critical features of both regimes. First, in the case of capital-raising instruments (other than shares) that involve an advance of funds, both regimes eliminate the distinction between gains and losses on capital account and gains and losses on income account and treat all instruments of this kind essentially as debt. The basis of this categorization is an apparent ideal income tax under which all financing charges are recognized annually as income and expense on an accrual basis. The inclusion principle ensures that all amounts that increase the wealth of providers of capital are taxed. Deductibility reflects the fact that all financing charges incurred by users of capital for an income-earning purpose reduce their wealth and should not be recognized as income. Recognition on an annual accrual basis minimizes the ability of taxpayers to manipulate the timing of deductions and income inclusions and approximates an income tax imposed annually on the expected changes in wealth of taxpayers.[32] Although these fundamental principles should apply generally to all amounts that represent the cost of capital, the New Zealand accrual regime and the Australian proposals recognize the traditional exception made for corporate equity, the return on which is subject to the corporate income tax as a proxy for accrual taxation in the hands of shareholders. The accrual regimes are thus left to apply to the expected return on all capital-raising instruments other than equity. In effect, this arrangement applies the theoretical ideal for the tax treatment of the cost of capital to classical debt obligations and everything else that is not considered corporate equity.[33]

Second, as has been noted already, both the New Zealand legislation and the Australian proposals extend the application of the accrual regimes to derivative instruments. In New Zealand's case, the broad language of the definition of a "financial arrangement" in the legislation has led to this extension almost as an afterthought.[34] The Australian proposals extend much more deliberately to both debt-financing charges and the return on derivatives.[35] Whether deliberate or not, this extension ensures that an accrual regime is not limited to the recognition of expected gains and losses on fixed-payment debt instruments. It recognizes that taxpayers can use derivatives to create debt with contingent returns, as well as other financial equivalents with fixed returns, and that the expected returns associated with these instruments should be subject to the same treatment as the periodic returns on fixed-payment debt.

In effect, therefore, the broadness of the definition of a financial arrangement in the New Zealand legislation and the Australian proposals serves to deem both the fixed and contingent returns on many instruments to be interest. The solution to problems of definition, apparently, is to define most instruments as financial arrangements and treat the returns as interest in the strict sense of the legal definition. This solution, however, is only at the initial level of the determination of the scope of the accrual rules. The definitional problems that the application of a restrictive concept of interest creates must be dealt with again in the application of the relevant recognition rules, and again the issue turns on the distinction between fixed and contingent returns. One general set of recognition rules must be developed for financial instruments with fixed returns. Another set must be developed for financial instruments with contingent returns, and these rules must include specialized provisions for derivatives. In other words, the appropriateness of the inclusion of all forms of instruments, other than shares, depends ultimately on the appropriateness of the various tax-accounting methods adopted for the treatment of income and expense. Consideration of the important definitional issues related to the distinction between fixed and contingent amounts is only subsumed in the development of the tax-accounting methods.

Limited Focus on Debt and Debt Equivalents

The wide definitional approach reflected in the New Zealand legislation and the Australian accrual proposals stands in contrast with the narrow focus on debt and debt equivalents that characterizes other legislative regimes. The case for this narrower approach was expressed clearly and forcefully by the Valabh consultative committee,[36] which was established shortly after the introduction of the accrual regime in New Zealand. The committee's recommendations illustrate the problems associated with the failure to adopt accretion taxation as a necessary supplement to a system of expected-return taxation. In fact, the application of accretion taxation to a limited range of instruments requires a broad definition of the types of instruments that are subject to the accrual regime. Attempts to limit this definition to debt and debt equivalents may result in both overinclusiveness and underinclusiveness. To avoid this difficulty, the exclusive focus of an accrual regime must be the accrual recognition of all expected gains and losses.

The general thrust of a number of the Valabh committee's recommendations was to ensure that the New Zealand legislation implemented a system of expected-return taxation focused on debt and debt equivalents, which were perceived to be the original subject matter of that legislation.[37] The mechanism for realization of this goal was the amendment of the definition of a financial arrangement to include within a primary debt category only transactions that involved the acquisition of money by one person in return for a promise to provide money at some future time to another person, where it could reasonably be anticipated, at the time that the arrangement was entered into, that the amount of money to be provided to the second person would exceed the amount obtained by the first.[38] The definition was considered to reflect the following elements that the committee believed were characteristic of debt:[39]

- a present cash flow linked to a future cash flow and
- a time value of money return that was relatively systematic.[40]

The committee recognized, however, that this limited definition provided an opportunity to use debt with contingent payments, and combinations of derivative instruments as well, to create debt equivalences outside the accrual rules.[41] Moreover, certain instruments could be used to hedge or alter the return on a financial arrangement that was within the accrual regime and should therefore be within the regime themselves.[42] These possibilities were to be addressed, first, by excepting foreign currency transactions from the requirement that a future sum exceed a present advance. These transactions would be included within the primary debt category provided that there was an advance of money or money's worth in return for a promise to provide the same. In addition, the proposed definition of a financial arrangement specifically included[43]

- forward contracts for foreign exchange;
- interest-rate swaps;
- any arrangement involving money lent that would satisfy the debt test but for the fact that all, or some portion, of the money to be provided in the future was payable only on the occurrence or non-occurrence of a future event or events;[44] and
- options (whether providing for cash settlement or physical delivery) to acquire or dispose of a financial instrument that otherwise falls within the definition of a financial arrangement.

Some commentators have argued that a critical deficiency of the Valabh recommendation (and, by extension, of the concept of a debt arrangement under the Australian accrual proposals) is its introduction of an unnecessary element of uncertainty in the form of a vague debt test, which requires a determination that the amount to be paid by a user of capital will exceed or equal the amount provided.[45] These commentators' stated preference is for a wide definitional approach that is said to be consistent with the apparent anti-avoidance nature of the New Zealand rules, and in particular with the attempt to ensure "the consistent taxation of all debt-related—or equivalent—cashflows and non-money equivalents."[46] According to this view, the appropriate exclusion of transactions is best tested in the application of the relevant recognition rules. If there is no time-value-of-money element, these rules will apply but with no effect. The Valabh recommendation elevates the same determination to an initial question about the scope of the accrual rules. The perceived weakness of this approach is that some transactions that should be subject to the rules might be excluded because of the vagueness of the debt test. In other words, the test provides a focus for tax-planning attempts that are intended to avoid the application of the accrual rules. This possibility is said to be a potentially high price to pay for the exclusion of certain items cited by the Valabh committee,[47] such as dry-cleaning contracts and bus tickets, not to mention more significant items such as guarantees and indemnities, which would otherwise fall within the broad second element of the definition of a financial arrangement under the New Zealand legislation. The price may also be an unnecessary one, since it would be easy to exclude transactions of this kind through specific exemptions under the definition of a financial arrangement.[48]

Although accurate in a general sense, this critique of the limited definitional approach recommended by the Valabh committee fails to articulate specific problems and the reasons for them. At least as an initial proposition, the focus of the Valabh definition on debt instruments and debt equivalents is entirely appropriate, assuming that the underlying policy of an accrual regime is the implementation of a system of expected-return taxation. The committee obviously believed that the wide definition of a financial arrangement under the legislation had led to the inappropriate adoption of market-value accounting methods consistent with a system of accretion taxation. In the light of the considerable support for this belief evident in the legislative history, the principal shortcomings of the committee's recommended definition are its unduly restrictive application of the primary debt test to instruments with embedded debt and an overinclusiveness attributable to a failure to articulate and apply a clear and consistent policy for the specific inclusion of derivatives.[49] The undue restrictiveness of the proposed debt test leads to inappropriate characterization of (1) instruments that are debt in form but that provide contingent returns associated with embedded derivatives ("contingent debt") and (2) instruments that are derivatives in form but that have an embedded loan attributable to the prepayment of a specified bet.[50] Under the Valabh committee's recommended definition of a financial arrangement, it would be necessary to assess the amount of the cash flows under these instruments at the outset on an expected-value basis in order to determine whether the expected future amounts were likely to exceed the present amount advanced. As chapter 6 will discuss in detail, a test of this kind creates problematic discontinuities in the characterization of hybrid instruments, or instruments that combine an advance of funds with a bet element and therefore straddle the boundary between debt and derivatives. Despite features that seem to make these instruments, in substance, something other than fixed-payment debt, there is an expected return associated with all contingent-debt instruments and prepaid derivatives that should be taxed in the same manner as the expected return on conventional debt. A primary debt test, by creating the possibility of a different tax treatment for the expected gains and losses on these instruments, fails to realize consistent results in all cases and thereby creates potential avoidance opportunities.[51]

It is equally difficult to justify the Valabh committee's unqualified inclusions of forward currency contracts, interest-rate swaps, and options on financial arrangements. Given a limited policy focus on expected gains and losses, the inclusion of these instruments is justifiable only to the extent that they are used to construct debt substitutes and alter interest-rate exposure.[52] The assumptions that underlie the committee's proposed inclusions of specific derivatives reflect a failure to understand the policy significance of the distinction between expected and unexpected gains and losses in the design of a comprehensive regime for the taxation of financial instruments. The significant policy issues are the choice of tax-accounting methods that are appropriate for the returns associated with the basic derivative instruments and the appropriateness of the inclusion of these instruments in a definition of a financial arrangement that is subject to accrual treatment. Since the Valabh committee lacks a clear concept of these accounting methods and how they should apply to the gains and losses on derivatives, its proposals are overinclusive in some respects and underinclusive in others.

The overinclusiveness results from the committee's stated intention to limit inclusion of derivative instruments to circumstances in which these instruments are used as debt substitutes. Given that intention, the Valabh committee's specific inclusions of foreign exchange transactions, forward currency contracts, interest-rate swaps, and options on financial arrangements are overinclusive to the extent that they purport to require the accrual recognition of all gains and losses on the relevant instruments. Forward currency contracts and interest-rate swaps are forward contracts that provide single payoffs on the occurrence of a specified contingency; they are pure bets, which at the outset of a contract have a zero present value represented by the offsetting obligations of the counterparties. As time passes and reveals movements in the price of the underlying, the position of one of the parties acquires value. The resulting gains and losses are wholly unexpected and are not attributable to the time value of money. The fact that interest-rate swaps are often used to construct debt equivalents or alter the payoff on a debt instrument does not mean that gains and losses on a swap should be subject to accrual treatment.[53]

Similarly, the fact that there is a causal relationship between forward exchange rates and interest-rate differentials in two currencies does not reduce all foreign currency transactions to substitutes for domestic debt.[54] Even the fact that an option is written on an underlying asset that is a financial arrangement does not, of itself, provide the holder with a synthetically created return that is expected in the same way as the return on the underlying debt is expected.[55] Given a regime that is designed to address only expected gains and losses on debt instruments with a return that reflects the time value of money, foreign currency transactions and derivatives should be included only to the extent that they are combined in a manner that provides a time-value return and thus approximates the return on a debt instrument. As will be discussed in chapters 6 and 7, this approximation may be realized by (1) combining derivative instruments that are pure bets in a manner that creates synthetic debt, (2) prepaying the bet element in a derivative, or (3) combining derivatives with a debt instrument to modify the cost of funds in a hedge transaction. If one ignores the significant identification problems that are associated with these combinations, then given an accrual regime that focuses on the expected returns associated with debt instruments the policy choice is a simple one: either to exclude all derivatives or to include all derivatives to the extent that they synthetically replicate returns of this kind. By this reckoning, the committee's recommended definition is also underinclusive, since it fails to include all derivative instruments that may be used to replicate debt synthetically or hedge a debt instrument. An accrual regime that is focused on the expected gains and losses on debt instruments and debt equivalents should include forward and futures contracts, and options over any underlying asset as well, to the extent that they are used for these purposes. There is nothing unique about forward contracts on foreign currency, interest-rate swaps, or options on financial arrangements that should limit the scope of an accrual regime to these particular instruments used to create synthetic debt or to modify the cash flows on a debt instrument.

Inconsistencies of this kind between the policy that underlies an accrual regime and the definition of affected instruments are not unique to the Valabh committee's recommendations and are reflected, to some extent, in the New Zealand legislation.[56] As was argued earlier, the wide scope of a definition of a financial arrangement that includes foreign currency transactions and all derivative instruments, however they are used, is defensible if the underlying policy is the application of accretion taxation to all gains and losses on financial instruments. Even where the underlying policy is limited to the implementation of expected-return taxation for debt and debt equivalents, a wide definition is appropriate if the intent is to supplement the core elements of such a system with

- realization-based recognition of unexpected gains and losses on all other instruments, and
- accretion taxation as a response to a limited range of instruments that are susceptible to the selective realization of unexpected losses.

Even though it closely follows the description of a primary debt category recommended by the Valabh committee, the proposed definition of a "financial arrangement" under the Australian accrual proposals[57] provides a measure of consistency between the specified tax-accounting methods and a wide definitional approach. It realizes this result, first, by including in the debt category all arrangements that are debt in substance, irrespective of their form. This category presumably includes all types of derivatives that are combined or altered to provide an expected return similar to interest.[58] It is possible to apply tax-accounting methods that implement accrual recognition to the expected gains and losses on these instruments. The second general category of financial arrangements under the Australian definition includes all derivatives. The tax-accounting methods that the proposals apply to these instruments reflect a reliance on market-value techniques that attempt to require recognition of unexpected gains and losses as they arise with changes in value of the instruments. This focus is consistent with a definition of financial arrangements that includes debt instruments and debt equivalents with expected returns, and also foreign currency transactions and derivatives with unexpected amounts.

Exclusions for Specific Instruments and Taxpayers

Even an expansive accrual regime that includes debt and derivatives must provide specific exclusions that refine the scope of application. The refinement may take any one of three general forms. The first is the grafting of a list of specifically excluded instruments onto the core definition of affected instruments. For example, the New Zealand legislation includes specific exclusions for life annuity contracts, insurance contracts and pension plans, short-term agreements for the purchase and sale of property, leases, gaming or lottery contracts, and security arrangements that insure against credit risk.[59] The Australian proposals provide a similar set of exclusions,[60] which are generally defensible either because of compliance considerations or because the particular instruments are subject to self-contained legislation that imposes accrual recognition of expected gains and losses.[61] The need for the latter category of exclusions largely involves considerations of legislative drafting style.[62] The policy that underlies the particular legislation is often consistent with the policy that underlies an accrual regime, and in these instances the ideal policy would be to incorporate the parallel legislation in the wider regime, along with the details of the tax-accounting methods. Nevertheless, a legislative regime of this kind can coexist comfortably outside of accrual rules applicable to other financial instruments generally.[63] The provision of a category of exclusions because of compliance considerations is much more problematic; this issue is discussed below.[64]

The second type of refinement is the determination of boundaries between included and excluded instruments under a differentiated income tax system that stops short of accretion taxation of all returns on all financial instruments. In particular, if it is decided to permit realization-based recognition of unexpected gains and losses on certain instruments, it becomes necessary to devise appropriate responses to the use of these instruments for the synthetic replication of other instruments that are subject to expected-return taxation. Similarly, if shares are specifically excluded from the legislative regime, measures must be adopted to maintain the integrity of the boundary between debt and equity. The important question in this context is whether the form of instruments should be determinative or whether some instruments that are shares in form should be treated as debt that is subject to an accrual regime. Other difficult issues are the identification of synthetic debt and debt equivalents that blur the boundary between debt and derivatives and the concept of the disposition of an asset as a realization event that should result in the recognition of unexpected gains and losses. These issues are examined in chapters 6 and 7.

The third form of refinement is limitation of the range of taxpayers to whom the comprehensive accrual regime applies. In this case, policy makers cite a perceived compliance burden to justify the exclusion of all financial instruments issued or held by certain taxpayers.[65] Exclusions of this kind effectively create two different "codes" for the tax treatment of gains and losses on financial instruments. One code consists of the traditional tax cubbyholes applied on a transactional basis. The other code consists of a comprehensive accrual regime applied to a wide range of instruments held or issued by a limited range of taxpayers. In general, two principal types of two-code approaches are evident in the tax literature and certain legislative regimes. Although both approaches are superficially attractive, the case for either of them is problematic.

The first type of two-code approach accepts the application of a comprehensive accrual regime to all taxpayers except "small investors" and "small businesses." In essence, the argument for this approach is that the costs of complying with a regime of this kind are more or less fixed and therefore disproportionately high for these taxpayers. Thus it is difficult to justify these costs in their case, regardless of the avoidance opportunities and the uncertainties that the inconsistent taxation of cash flows under the traditional tax cubbyholes creates. The New Zealand accrual legislation adopts this approach in permitting individuals to account for income and expense from financial instruments on a cash basis if the face value of the instruments does not exceed $1,000,000, the absolute value of income and expense for the year from financial instruments does not exceed $100,000, and the difference between the amount reported on a cash, as opposed to an accrual, basis does not exceed $40,000.[66] In addition, all taxpayers may use a simplified straightline accrual methodology if the value of their financial instruments does not exceed $1,500,000.[67] The first version of the Australian accrual proposals included a similar exemption,[68] but administrative and compliance problems associated with the application of the exemption to fluctuating holdings led to its subsequent rejection.[69] The exemption was replaced with a broader exclusion for all individuals and a limited exclusion for unincorporated small businesses.[70] In effect, the revised proposals assume that taxpayers who carry on a business in corporate form have sufficient sophistication to comply with an accrual regime, and that the fixed nature of the costs of compliance is not a sufficient justification for an exemption based on amounts. The corporate form serves as a rough proxy for these assumptions.

The obvious problem with exemptions for small investors and small businesses is that they create opportunities for avoidance transactions between cash-basis investors and accrual-basis issuers.[71] The revenue loss attributable to these opportunities has not been the subject of any published study[72] and may not actually be all that significant, particularly given the fact that many individuals hold interests in financial instruments through intermediaries such as financial institutions and pension funds. Indeed, the revenue problem, if there is one, is probably a small matter in comparison with the tax planning opportunities that the tax-preferred status of pension funds in most countries creates. Nonetheless, it is somewhat unsettling to find oneself considering whether the revenue loss from exemptions is worth the supposed compliance and administrative gains. At the very least, any exemption should be limited to the direct holdings of individuals. Where interests in financial instruments are held through intermediaries that are treated as conduits for tax purposes, any justification for exemption based on the perceived compliance burden disappears. The managers of the intermediary would presumably have the sophistication necessary for compliance and the ability to determine the relevant amount of gain or loss to be allocated among their investors,[73] and the fixed costs of compliance would be spread over the large number of individuals who pooled their holdings through the intermediary. Even individuals who hold direct interests in financial instruments may reasonably be presumed to have sufficient ability to comply with basic accrual rules. The imposition of information-reporting requirements on issuers would alleviate the compliance burden on individuals without incurring the revenue cost of exempt status. Issuers of sophisticated instruments would presumably have the sophistication necessary for compliance on behalf of investors, who would be required to report the amount stipulated on a prescribed form.[74]

The case for exemption is even more problematic in the context of the second type of two-code approach, which limits the compliance burden associated with a comprehensive accrual regime to financial institutions.[75] The apparent assumption is that these taxpayers, but not others, would be able to manage the compliance burden associated with consistent application of the accounting measures necessary for the accrual recognition of the expected gain or loss on all financial instruments except shares. For other taxpayers, the traditional tax cubbyholes under existing legislative structures would continue to apply, on the apparent assumption that these taxpayers' level of sophistication is not high enough to require imposition of a comprehensive accrual regime in their case. In general, accrual treatment would be limited to the fixed return on conventional debt instruments and other substitutable instruments. Realization-based recognition and the distinction between ordinary income and capital amounts would continue to be relevant for contingent returns.

This approach is difficult to take seriously. Except in the case of small investors and small businesses, any perpetuation of the inconsistent taxation of equivalent cash flows under the traditional tax cubbyholes is extremely difficult to justify on the basis of perceived compliance costs. Non-financial corporate taxpayers are significant issuers and holders of financial instruments whose familiarity with financial reporting requirements should make compliance with a comprehensive accrual regime a relatively easy matter for them.

There is, however, a defensible case for a third type of two-code approach that is a version of the second type. This approach is probably more accurately described as the application of a specialized code within a comprehensive accrual regime. It has two principal elements, which are reflected to some extent in the Canadian mark-to-market legislation.[76] The first element is repeal, in the case of financial instruments, of the rule that allows taxpayers to value their closing inventory at the lower of its cost and fair market value.[77] This rule is nothing more than an indefensible form of statutory selective realization that permits taxpayers to recognize accrued losses on inventory and defer accrued gain until realization. The second element is accretion taxation of all gain or loss on all financial instruments of traders or dealers in securities. Applied to these taxpayers, who regularly assume offsetting positions in financial instruments, a system of accretion taxation substitutes for a hedging regime and its elimination of mismatches in the character and timing of the recognition of offsetting amounts.[78] The difficulty is to define the range of taxpayers who would be subject to this narrowly drawn code within what was otherwise a system of expected-return taxation for financial instruments.[79] A wide definition would include financial institutions that engaged in both trading and investment activities and were not necessarily hedged.[80] A narrower definition would limit the application of accretion taxation to traders and dealers who assumed positions solely for trading purposes.[81]

This definitional problem and the need for a specialized code for traders and dealers are largely eliminated by the broad approach to the application of accretion taxation that is proposed later in this chapter.[82] If traded instruments are subjected to this recognition method and are defined widely on the basis of a functional approach, securities dealers are generally subject to accretion taxation in any event. Instruments held in the trading accounts of financial institutions are similarly subject to accretion taxation, and non-traded instruments are subject to a system of expected-return taxation. Use of a very limited hedge-accounting regime would provide a measure of appropriate taxation for traded instruments that were acquired as a hedge of non-traded instruments and non-financial assets subject to realization-based recognition.[83]

Tax-Accounting Methods for the Basic Building-Block Financial Instruments

It was emphasized above that the definition of the types of instruments subject to an accrual regime is related to the development of tax-accounting methods for the recognition of gains and losses. The Australian accrual proposals incorporate three general principles that are fundamental elements of any comprehensive regime intended to implement a system of expected-return taxation. The first principle is the elimination of the distinction between gains and losses on capital and gains and losses on ordinary-income account: all amounts are recognized in full as income or expense provided that other deductibility tests, such as an income-earning purpose requirement, are satisfied. The second principle is the recognition of expected gains and losses on fixed-payment debt acquired for investment purposes on an accrual basis. The third principle is the application of accretion taxation to all gains and losses on debt and derivative instruments acquired for trading purposes. Implicit in these three principles is the realization-based recognition of gains and losses on derivatives that are not acquired for trading purposes or as a hedge of another position.

Each of these principles is reflected to one extent or another in the New Zealand accrual legislation and certain provisions in the legislation of other countries, including Canada, the United States, and the United Kingdom. This legislation, however, does not always clearly articulate the rationale for the adoption of these principles or the relationship among the different provisions that incorporate them. In fact, each tax-accounting principle has a unique rationale that is linked closely to specific policy problems associated with the basic building-block financial instruments. Accrual recognition of the expected return on debt (and debt equivalents) is required to eliminate the benefit of anticipated deferral. Realization-based recognition is limited to the unexpected gains and losses associated with pure bets, which do not provide expected returns, and to the bet element in hybrid instruments, which include an expected time-value return. As a response to selective realization, accretion taxation is applied to traded instruments that can be marked to market.

A primary feature of a comprehensive accrual regime is the expression of these basic tax-accounting methods at the general level of principle. Indeed, the comprehensiveness of a regime of this kind is attributable to the range of accounting methods that must be employed as an appropriate policy response in the context of a realization-based income tax. A wide definitional approach follows logically from the incorporation of diverse accounting methods that are suitable for both expected and unexpected gains and losses. As will be described in more detail below, refinements of the definition of affected instruments must be based on the nature of the gains and losses associated with a given type of instrument and the application of accounting methods that are suitable for those gains and losses. Ideally, however, the legislation will express a set of tax-accounting methods only at the general level of principle, though it will also be necessary to legislate some supporting rules that resolve basic design issues common to all instruments in a particular category. Apart from these design issues, the details of the application of the accounting methods to specific instruments are best left to a regulatory process, such as the one embodied in the New Zealand legislation.[84] Under this process, the technical details necessary for the application of the principles described in the legislation are developed on a transactional basis for various instruments (including the basic building-block instruments) in a series of regulations referred to as "determinations."[85] Use of the determinations allows the New Zealand Inland Revenue to develop the general principles of the basic tax-accounting methods in a flexible manner that accommodates the specifics of new financial instruments and addresses the possibility of inappropriate revenue loss.[86] Although financial-accounting practice can be an important source of information, it is argued here that tax-policy makers must be able to deviate from this practice and adopt particular methods that are appropriate in terms of the distinct policy problems presented by expected gains and losses on the one hand and unexpected gains and losses on the other. Maintenance of this independence requires the rejection of an uncritical acceptance of financial-accounting practices, despite the appeal of the reduction in administrative and compliance costs that acceptance of these practices appears to imply.

Accrual Recognition of Expected Gains and Losses

Chapter 3[87] made the point that the accrual recognition of expected gains is a response to the problem of anticipated deferral. To be brief, deferral of the recognition of expected gains until they are realized reduces the effective tax rate on these gains relative to the effective tax rate on gains that are recognized as they accrue. Taxpayers therefore have an incentive to overinvest in instruments that provide the benefit of anticipated deferral, and this overinvestment may result in efficiency losses. The deferral is "anticipated" in the sense that the holder knows that the gain will be recognized after the period in which it is expected to arise. To the extent that the expected loss for an issuer is also subject to realization-based recognition, the benefit of anticipated deferral for the holder is offset by a corresponding detriment. This offset is incomplete or non-existent, however, if the holder's tax rate is higher than the issuer's, or if the holder is taxable and the issuer is not. In this case, the benefit of anticipated deferral for the holder is greater than any detriment attributable to a deferred deduction for the issuer. In a world of different tax rates for different taxpayers, accrual recognition of expected gains and losses is the only effective response to the problem of anticipated deferral.

Any system of expected-return taxation requires the development of at least one method for the recognition of expected gain and loss on an accrual basis. The essence of any such method is an attempt to measure ex ante the pattern of expected increases in value over the term of a particular financial instrument. Accordingly, all accrual methods involve a determination of the amount of the expected gain or loss associated with a particular instrument, which is spread on an ex ante basis over the relevant term to reflect the expected pattern of accrual. To eliminate the benefit of the recognition of expected returns at a point after the period in which they are expected to arise, any particular method should produce an accrual pattern that is consistent with the pattern anticipated by market participants.[88] For fixed-payment instruments, the standard spreading method used for financial-accounting purposes is the yield-to-maturity (YTM) method. Although far from perfect, the YTM method is a familiar accrual method that has been incorporated in the income tax legislation of many countries.[89] More important, the YTM method is defensible from a tax-policy perspective, since it assumes that accrued, but unpaid, amounts are continuously reinvested by holders. This assumption provides an accrual pattern that closely approximates the anticipated accrual of expected gains and losses.

For practical administrative and compliance reasons, however, it is often necessary to deviate from a theoretical ideal. A difficult policy question is the extent to which practical considerations require deviation from a benchmark accrual pattern based on the YTM method.

The Fundamentals of Yield to Maturity

The YTM method allocates expected gain and loss over the term of a financial instrument on the basis of the instrument's yield to maturity or internal rate of return. For the holder, the expected gain is equal to the excess of the total of all expected cash flows (whether in the form of interest or some other amount)[90] over the cost of the instrument.[91] For the issuer, the expected loss is equal to the excess of the total of the same expected cash flows over the amount received on issue. The yield to maturity is the discount rate at which the present value of the expected cash flows equals the cost or issue price. In other words, the yield to maturity provides a discount rate that determines for any particular taxation year after issue the present value of the expected cash flows arising after the beginning of that year.[92] The difference between this present value and the present value of the expected cash flows arising after the beginning of the immediately succeeding year represents the expected increase in value allocable to the current year that must be recognized on an accrual basis. In order to calculate the amount of the expected increases in value allocable to a particular period as accrued income (for the holder) and accrued expense (for the issuer), it is necessary to

1) determine the period in which accrued but unpaid amounts must be compounded;

2) calculate the yield to maturity on the basis of the specified period of compounding;

3) determine the accrued income and expense for the first period of compounding on the basis of the yield to maturity;

4) calculate the amount of principal outstanding at the end of the first period of compounding as the sum of the initial principal plus accrued income less any payments in the period;

5) determine the accrued income and expense, and the outstanding principal amounts, for subsequent compounding periods by repeating steps (3) and (4); and

6) allocate income and expense pro rata over the days in the specified compounding periods.[93]

Table 5.1 illustrates the application of each of these steps to the cash flows associated with (1) an OID obligation without periodic payments—that is, with only a single payment due on maturity ("zero-coupon bond"); (2) a debt instrument with fixed periodic payments evidenced by coupons ("coupon bond"); (3) a coupon bond issued at a discount—that is, the excess of the amount due on maturity over the amount advanced; and (4) a coupon bond issued at a premium—that is, the excess of the amount advanced over the amount due on maturity.[94]

Table 5.1 Application of the YTM Method to Fixed-Payment Debt

Period	Cash flow[a]	Opening cost base/ principal owing[b]	Accrued gain[c]
Scenario 1			
Zero-coupon bond		Issued January 1, 1999	
Face amount = $1,000,000		Maturity January 1, 2004	
5-year term		YTM = 8% discount rate with annual compounding	
0	$ (680,583)[d]		
1	nil	$680,583	$ 54,447
2	nil	735,030	58,802
3	nil	793,832	63,507
4	nil	857,339	68,587
5	1,000,000	925,926	74,074
			$319,417
Scenario 2			
Coupon bond issued at face amount		Issued January 1, 1999	
Face amount = $1,000,000		Maturity January 1, 2004	
Coupon rate payable annually = 8%		YTM = 8% discount rate with annual compounding	
5-year term			
0	$(1,000,000)		
1	80,000	$1,000,000	$80,000
2	80,000	1,000,000	80,000
3	80,000	1,000,000	80,000
4	80,000	1,000,000	80,000
5	1,080,000	1,000,000	80,000
Scenario 3			
Coupon bond issued at discount		Issued January 1, 1999	
Face amount = $1,000,000		Maturity January 1, 2004	
Coupon rate payable annually = 8%		YTM = 10% discount rate with annual compounding	
5-year term			
0	$(924,184)[d]		
1	80,000	$924,184	$92,418
2	80,000	936,602	93,660
3	80,000	950,262	95,026
4	80,000	965,288	96,529
5	1,080,000	981,817	98,183
Scenario 4			
Coupon bond issued at premium		Issued January 1, 1999	
Face amount = $1,000,000		Maturity January 1, 2004	
Coupon rate payable annually = 8%		YTM = 6% discount rate with annual compounding	
5-year term			
0	$(1,084,244)[d]		
1	80,000	$1,084,244	$65,055
2	80,000	1,069,299	64,158
3	80,000	1,053,457	63,208
4	80,000	1,036,665	62,200
5	1,080,000	1,018,865	61,132

(Table 5.1 is concluded on the next page.)

Table 5.1 Concluded

Scenario 1: [a] All cash flows are reversed for a borrower and accrued gains equal accrued losses. [b] Opening cost base/principal owing from the previous period + accrued gain – cash flows received. [c] Opening cost base/principal owing × YTM. [d] $680,583 = present value of $1,000,000 at the end of year 5.

Scenario 2: [a] All cash flows are reversed for a borrower and accrued gains equal accrued losses. [b] Opening cost base/principal owing from the previous period + accrued gain – cash flows received. [c] Opening cost base/principal owing × YTM.

Scenario 3: [a] All cash flows are reversed for a borrower and accrued gains equal accrued losses. [b] Opening cost base/principal owing from the previous period + accrued gain – cash flows received. [c] Opening cost base/principal owing × YTM. [d] Present value of expected cash flows for periods 1-5 discounted at 10 percent rate.

Scenario 4: [a] All cash flows are reversed for a borrower and accrued gains equal accrued losses. [b] Opening cost base/principal owing from the previous period + accrued gain – cash flows received. [c] Opening cost base/principal owing × YTM. [d] Present value of expected cash flows discounted at 6 percent rate.

Application of the YTM method presupposes the resolution of two basic design issues that are addressed in the legislation of those countries with accrual rules for expected gains and losses. The first issue is the definition of the types of instruments that should be subject to a YTM calculation. It is conventional to think of the YTM method only in relation to "fixed-payment debt," which is defined generally as any instrument under which the amount and the timing of each payment are fixed at the time of acquisition by the holder.[95] The YTM method tends to be limited to fixed-payment debt because under fixed-payment debt the expected gain (or loss for the issuer) is clearly defined as the difference between the cost of the instrument and all fixed-payment obligations. It is easy to reduce the gain to a yield-to-maturity rate and spread it over the relevant term in accordance with the timing of the payments under the specified schedule. The contentious question is, to what extent can one apply the YTM method to instruments other than fixed-payment debt? In principle, application of the YTM method is impossible only in the case of the basic building-block instruments that are pure bets (forwards, futures, and swaps) and therefore provide only unexpected gain and loss.[96] Any other instrument that involves an advance of funds for a right to receive an amount in the future has an expected time-value return, even if the amount or timing of the future payments is based on a specified contingency.[97] That return is simply the excess of the expected values of all payments over the issue price. As an initial proposition, accrual recognition based on the YTM method should apply to all instruments that provide expected gains and losses.[98] Otherwise, there will be opportunities for pure and approximate tax avoidance[99] designed to provide the benefit of anticipated deferral by substituting the expected return on a contingent-payment instrument for the expected return on a fixed-payment instrument. In other words, taxpayers can realize arbitrage profits by borrowing funds under a fixed-payment instrument that is subject to accrual treatment and using the funds to acquire a contingent-payment instrument that is subject to realization-based recognition.[100] The difficulties associated with the determination of an expected return on contingent-payment instruments and the extent to which accrual treatment can realistically be extended to these instruments are the subjects of chapter 6. The simple point made here is that some extension of the YTM method to contingent-payment instruments is required.

The other basic design issue concerns the calculation of a yield to maturity as the basis for the determination of the pattern of accrual of expected gains and losses.[101] In this connection, it is important to emphasize that payments made under an instrument do not directly affect the recognition of accrued income and expense. The timing of the cash flows is relevant only to the extent that the cash flows affect the calculation of the yield to maturity.[102] Accrued amounts are determined, in effect, on an ex ante basis by calculating the yield to maturity at the time of issue or other acquisition, taking into account the specified time for payment of the expected cash flows. As was noted above, implementation of this ex ante approach requires the addition of accrued amounts to the cost of an instrument in the period of accrual; any payments reduce that cost when they are made, irrespective of their legal form[103] (that is, whether the amounts are considered to be principal repayments, payments of periodic interest as they become due, or prepayments of interest allocable to a subsequent period).[104] Table 5.2 illustrates the significance of this irrelevance of the legal form of the cash flows.[105] It shows that the YTM method requires only that all cash flows are accounted for ex post as a recovery of the cost of the instrument (including accrued amounts).[106] Accrued amounts for subsequent periods are determined by applying the yield to maturity to the remaining cost of the instrument.

Determination of the yield to maturity depends primarily on the specification of a compounding period for accrued but unpaid amounts. The fundamental premise underlying an assumption of compounding is that expected gain or loss accrues throughout the relevant term, even if the return is paid at some time after the time of accrual.[107] If accrued gain or loss is not paid as it accrues, the accrued amount is considered to be reinvested by the holder at the compounding intervals. The YTM on a particular instrument is the rate of return expressed for the compounding period that provides the expected gain or loss on maturity. In theory, the appropriate assumption about the period of compounding is one of "continuous compounding," under which income is considered to be earned and reinvested by the holder of a debt instrument continuously with every passing nanosecond.[108] Although this assumption is used in financial economics, accounting practice has generally rejected it in favour of some form of discrete compounding period, such as monthly, half-yearly, or annual compounding. An assumption of daily compounding is more precise and, therefore, more desirable, in the sense that it approximates most closely the results under continuous compounding.[109] Longer compounding periods result in the recognition of greater amounts of expected gain or loss in the earlier portions of the relevant period and lesser amounts in the later portions. This

Table 5.2 Prepaid Interest and the Irrelevance of the Form of Cash Flows as Interest or Principal

Scenario 1

Coupon bond issued at face amount	YTM = 10% with annual compounding
Face amount = $100,000	Issued January 1, 1999
10-year term	Maturity January 1, 2009
Coupon rate payable annually = 10%	Interest for years 6-10 prepaid on January 1, 2002

Interest for	Number of years discounted	Amount
2004	3	$ 7,513
2005	4	6,830
2006	5	6,209
2007	6	5,645
2008	7	5,131
		$31,328

Period	Cash flow[a]	Opening cost base/ principal owing[b]	Accrued gain[c]
0	$(100,000)		
1	10,000	$100,000	$10,000
2	10,000	100,000	10,000
3	41,328	100,000	10,000
4	10,000	68,672	6,867
5	10,000	65,539	6,554
6	nil	62,093	6,209
7	nil	68,302	6,830
8	nil	75,132	7,513
9	nil	82,645	8,264
10	100,000	90,909	9,091

Scenario 2

Coupon bond issued at face amount	YTM = 10% with annual compounding
Face amount = $100,000	Issued January 1, 1999
5-year term	Maturity January 1, 2004
Coupon rate payable annually = 10%	Interest for years 1-5 prepaid on January 1, 1999

Interest for	Number of years discounted	Amount
1999	1	$ 6,209
2000	2	6,830
2001	3	7,513
2002	4	8,265
2003	5	9,091
		$37,908

(Table 5.2 is concluded on the next page.)

Table 5.2 Concluded

Period	Cash flow[a]	Opening cost base/ principal owing[b]	Accrued gain[c]
0	$(62,092)[d]		
1	nil	$62,092	$ 6,209
2	nil	68,301	6,830
3	nil	75,131	7,513
4	nil	82,644	8,265
5	100,000	90,909	9,091
			$37,908

Scenario 3

Coupon bond issued at face amount
Face amount = $100,000
4-year term
Coupon rate payable annually = 40% year 1
5% year 2
5% year 3
5% year 4

Issued January 1, 1999
Maturity January 1, 2003
YTM = 7.5884% with semi-annual compounding

Compounding periods	Cash flow[a]	Opening cost base/ principal owing[b]	Accrued gain[c]
0	$(100,000)		
1	nil	$100,000	$7,588
2	40,000	107,588	8,164
3	nil	75,752	5,748
4	5,000	81,500	6,185
5	nil	82,500	6,274
6	5,000	88,960	6,751
7	nil	90,711	6,883
8	105,000	97,594	7,406

Scenario 1: [a] All cash flows are reversed for a borrower and accrued gains equal accrued losses. [b] Opening cost base/principal owing from previous period + accrued gain – cash flows received. [c] Opening cost base/principal owing × YTM.

Scenario 2: [a] All cash flows are reversed for a borrower and accrued gains equal accrued losses. [b] Opening cost base/principal owing from the previous period + accrued gain – cash flows received. [c] Opening cost base/principal owing × YTM. [d] $100,000 face amount paid – $37,908 received as prepaid interest for years 1-5.

Scenario 3: [a] All cash flows are reversed for a borrower and accrued gains equal accrued losses. [b] Opening cost base/principal owing from previous period + accrued gain – cash flows received. [c] Opening cost base/principal owing × YTM.

variation in the pattern of accrual in the case of a lengthy compounding period arises because there is no assumed reinvestment during the period, which means that expected gain and loss related to the period is spread evenly on a daily basis. Since daily compounding assumes that the accrued returns are reinvested on a daily basis, it does not result in pro rata spreading. Table 5.3 and figure 5.1 illustrate these results.

Table 5.3 Spreading of Expected Gain/Loss Under Different Compounding Assumptions

Compounding period	Cash flow[a]	Opening cost base/ principal owing[b]	Accrued gain[c]
All scenarios			
Zero-coupon bond		Issued January 1, 1999	
Face amount = $121		Maturity January 1, 2001	
2-year term		Issue price = $100	
Scenario 1			
YTM = 10% with annual compounding			
0	$(100.00)		
1		$100.00	$10.00
2	121.00	110.00	11.00
Scenario 2			
YTM = 4.881% with semi-annual compounding			
0	$(100.00)		
1		$100.00	$4.88
2		104.88	5.12
3		110.00	5.37
4	121.00	115.37	$5.63
Scenario 3			
YTM = 0.026% with daily compounding			
0	$(100.00)		
30		$100.00	$0.80
60		100.80	0.80
90		101.60	0.81
120		102.41	0.82
150		103.23	0.82
180		104.05	0.83
210		104.88	0.84
240		105.72	0.84
270		106.56	0.85
300		107.41	0.86
330		108.27	0.86
360		109.13	0.87
390		110.00	0.88
420		110.88	0.88
450		111.76	0.89
480		112.65	0.90
510		113.55	0.91
540		114.46	0.91
570		115.37	0.92
600		116.29	0.93
630		117.22	0.93
660		118.15	0.94
690		119.09	0.95
720	121.00	120.04	0.96

(Table 5.3 is concluded on the next page.)

Table 5.3 Concluded

Period	Annual compounding	Semi-annual compounding	Daily compounding
January 1999	0.83	0.81	0.80
February 1999	0.83	0.81	0.80
March 1999	0.83	0.81	0.81
April 1999	0.83	0.81	0.82
May 1999	0.83	0.81	0.82
June 1999	0.83	0.81	0.83
July 1999	0.83	0.85	0.84
August 1999	0.83	0.85	0.84
September 1999	0.83	0.85	0.85
October 1999	0.83	0.85	0.86
November 1999	0.83	0.85	0.86
December 1999	0.83	0.85	0.87
January 2000	0.92	0.89	0.88
February 2000	0.92	0.89	0.88
March 2000	0.92	0.89	0.89
April 2000	0.92	0.89	0.90
May 2000	0.92	0.89	0.91
June 2000	0.92	0.89	0.91
July 2000	0.92	0.94	0.92
August 2000	0.92	0.94	0.93
September 2000	0.92	0.94	0.93
October 2000	0.92	0.94	0.94
November 2000	0.92	0.94	0.95
December 2000	0.92	0.94	0.96
Spreading of accrued gain/loss			
Year 1	10	10	10
Year 2	11	11	11
Total	21	21	21

Note: A year is assumed to be 360 days or 12 months of 30 days each.

All scenarios: [a] All cash flows are reversed for a borrower and accrued gains equal accrued losses. [b] Opening cost base/principal owing from the previous period + accrued gain − cash flows received. [c] Opening cost base/principal owing × YTM.

Differences in the pattern of accrual that arise from different compounding assumptions are not problematic for income tax purposes provided that the period of measurement of accrued gain or loss for tax purposes is equal to or greater than the longer of two possible compounding periods. Under these conditions, the amount of accrued income or expense for tax purposes will be equal to the amount under the longer compounding assumption. Since annual accounting is used for the measurement of income or loss for tax purposes, equivalent results arise provided that the yield to maturity on a debt instrument is calculated on a minimum assumption of annual compounding. Differences between possible assumptions about the pattern of accrual may be a problem, however, if a longer compounding period straddles a taxation year.[110] This straddling occurs whenever a financial instrument is issued or acquired at a

Figure 5.1 Accrual Patterns of Unexpected Gain/Loss Under Different Compounding Assumptions

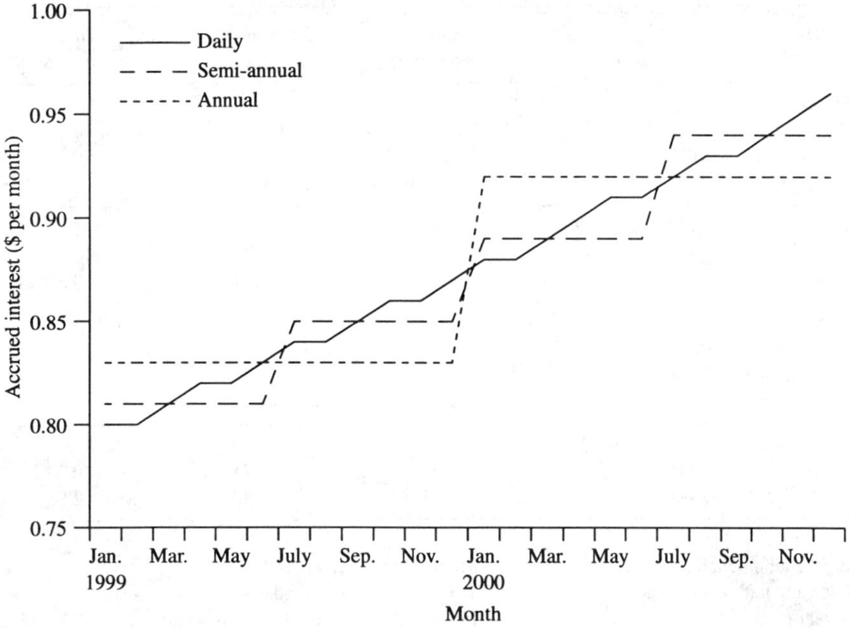

point other than the beginning of a taxation year. In this case, accrued income and expense must be reported for the portion of the accrual period that falls within the taxation year, and assumptions about the pattern of accrual that is attributable to the specified compounding period become important.[111] In the case of compounding assumptions other than daily compounding, income or expense accruing during a period that straddles a year must be spread evenly over each day in the period and recognized on the basis of the number of days that fall within the taxation year. Relative to an assumption of daily compounding, then, the assumption of a longer compounding period will either overstate or understate the accrued amounts.[112] The result depends on whether the portion of the compounding period that falls within the relevant taxation year is the earlier portion or the later one. If it is the earlier portion, the result will be an overstatement of accrued income and expense relative to the result that would occur under an assumption of daily compounding. If it is the later portion, an understatement will result. Daily compounding is desirable largely because it avoids this type of mismeasurement. Table 5.4 illustrates this point.

The specification of a compounding period is not the end of the matter. The development and application of a YTM calculation also requires the resolution of three additional issues. First, it must be determined whether discount or premium that arises on a secondary-market transfer is subject to accrual recognition by the transferee[113] and, if it is, how the amount should be incorporated in a YTM calculation as the primary accrual methodology. In general, discount

Table 5.4 Significance of Compounding Assumptions Where the Term to Maturity Straddles a Taxation Year

Taxation year	Period	Annual compounding[a]	Semi-annual compounding[b]	Daily compounding[c]
Scenario 1				
Zero-coupon bond		Issued October 1, 1999		
Face amount = $121		Maturity October 1, 2001		
2-year term		Taxation year = calendar year		
1999	Oct. 1-Dec. 31	$ 2.49	$ 2.43	$ 2.41
2000	Jan. 1-Dec. 31	10.22	10.23	10.24
2001	Jan. 1-Oct. 1	8.28	8.34	8.35
Scenario 2				
Zero-coupon bond		Issued March 1, 1999		
Face amount = $121		Maturity March 1, 2001		
2-year term		Taxation year = calendar year		
1999	Mar. 1-Dec. 31	$ 7.47	$ 7.43	$ 7.41
2000	Jan. 1-Dec. 31	10.77	10.75	10.73
2001	Jan. 1-Mar. 1	2.76	2.82	2.86
Scenario 3				
Zero-coupon bond		Maturity October 1, 2004		
Face amount = $1,000,000		Taxation year = calendar year		
5-year term		Issue price = $680,583 (8% discount rate compounded annually)		
Issued October 1, 1999				
1999	Oct. 1-Dec. 31	$ 13,612	$ 13,350	$ 13,221
2000	Jan. 1-Dec. 31	55,535	55,515	55,504
2001	Jan. 1-Dec. 31	59,978	59,956	59,945
2002	Jan. 1-Dec. 31	64,777	64,752	64,740
2003	Jan. 1-Dec. 31	69,959	69,932	69,920
2004	Jan. 1-Oct. 1	55,556	55,912	56,087
		$319,417	$319,417	$319,417
Scenario 4				
Zero-coupon bond		Maturity March 1, 2004		
Face amount = $1,000,000		Taxation year = calendar year		
5-year term		Issue price = $680,583 (8% discount rate compounded annually)		
Issued March 1, 1999				
1999	Mar. 1-Dec. 31	$ 40,835	$ 40,573	$ 40,440
2000	Jan. 1-Dec. 31	57,714	57,693	57,682
2001	Jan. 1-Dec. 31	62,331	62,308	62,296
2002	Jan. 1-Dec. 31	67,317	67,292	67,280
2003	Jan. 1-Dec. 31	72,702	72,676	72,663
2004	Jan. 1-Mar. 1	18,518	18,875	19,056
		$319,417	$319,417	$319,417

Scenarios 1 and 2: [a] YTM = 10 percent annually. [b] YTM = 4.881 percent semi-annually. [c] YTM = 0.026 percent daily.

Scenarios 3 and 4: [a] YTM = 8 percent annually. [b] YTM = 3.92 percent semi-annually. [c] YTM = 0.02 percent daily.

or premium arises when changes in the market rate of interest affect the value of an instrument that provides a fixed rate of return greater or less than the market rate.[114] Discount arises on a secondary-market transfer if the market rate is greater than the fixed rate on the instrument; the excess of the stated principal over the cost to the transferee ("the discount") ensures that the instrument provides the market rate of return. Premium arises if the market rate is less than the fixed rate on the instrument; the excess of the cost over the stated principal ensures that the instrument provides the market rate. Whether discount or premium arises on issue or on a secondary-market transfer, its amount affects the expected gain or loss and should be incorporated in the calculation of a yield to maturity.[115] The only difference between the two cases, which should not lead to any significant distinction between them, is the fact that in the case of a new issue the discount or premium will affect both the issuer's yield to maturity and the holder's, whereas in the case of a secondary-market transfer it will affect only the yield to maturity for the new holder.[116]

Some legislative regimes incorporate all discount or premium in the calculation of the yield to maturity on an instrument fairly simply by providing that the expected return subject to YTM spreading is the difference between[117] (1) the total of all payments required to be made under the instrument after its acquisition by the particular holder and (2) the cost of the instrument to the holder.[118] Since this amount is based on the instrument's cost to the particular holder, the expected return reflects any discount or premium, whether it arises on issue or on a secondary-market transfer.[119] Table 5.5 provides examples of the recognition of secondary-market discount and premium on a YTM basis. A unique requirement under this form of recognition is that the transferee must produce his own YTM calculation for the expected cash flows after an acquisition. Since the discount or premium arises on a secondary-market transfer, this calculation will differ from the calculation made on issue; accordingly, it will impose additional compliance costs. At least in the case of sophisticated investors, any argument for alleviation of these costs seems weak when it is weighed against the problems associated with the benefit of anticipated deferral that arises if the discount or premium is recognized on realization. Where secondary-market transfers are effected through financial intermediaries, it is possible to shift the compliance burden imposed by a new YTM calculation from less sophisticated investors by imposing information reporting on the intermediary.

The second issue associated with the application of the YTM method arises from the fact that a YTM calculation presupposes a specified redemption date and hence a finite term to maturity for any particular instrument. This premise presents no problems if an instrument has a single redemption date and definite term. Problems arise in the case of instruments that do not have a unique redemption date. There will be no unique redemption date

- if the holder has a right to require repayment ("retraction right" or "put option") at various times before maturity, or

Table 5.5 Application of the YTM Method on Secondary-Market Transfers

Scenario 1

Coupon bond issued at face amount	Issued January 1, 1999
Face amount = $1,000,000	Maturity January 1, 2004
Coupon rate payable annually = 8%	Secondary-market transfer on January 2, 2001
5-year term	when interest rate = 10%

Initial holder/transferor

Period	Cash flow	Opening cost base/ principal owing[a]	Accrued gain[b]	Realized gain/ loss[c]
0	$(1,000,000)			
1	80,000	$1,000,000	$80,000	
2	80,000	1,000,000	80,000	
3	950,263[d]	1,000,000		$(49,737)

Subsequent holder/transferee

Period	Cash flow	Opening cost base/ principal owing[a]	Accrued gain[b]	Realized gain/ loss
3	$(950,263)	$950,263		
	80,000		$95,026	
4	80,000	965,289	96,529	
5	1,080,000	981,818	98,182	

Scenario 2

Coupon bond issued at face amount	Issued January 1, 1999
Face amount = $1,000,000	Maturity January 1, 2004
Coupon rate payable annually = 8%	Secondary-market transfer on January 2, 2001
5-year term	when interest rate = 6%

Initial holder/transferor

Period	Cash flow	Opening cost base/ principal owing[a]	Accrued gain[b]	Realized gain/ loss[c]
0	$(1,000,000)			
1	80,000	$1,000,000	$80,000	
2	80,000	1,000,000	80,000	
3	1,053,460[d]	1,000,000		$53,460

Subsequent holder/transferee

Period	Cash flow	Opening cost base/ principal owing[a]	Accrued gain[b]	Realized gain/ loss
3	$(1,053,460)	$1,053,460		
	80,000		$63,208	
4	80,000	1,036,668	62,200	
5	1,080,000	1,018,868	61,132	

(Table 5.5 is concluded on the next page.)

Table 5.5 Concluded

Scenario 1—Initial holder/transferor: [a] Opening cost base/principal owing from previous period + accrued gain − cash flows received. [b] Opening cost base/principal owing × YTM. [c] Opening cost base/principal owing + accrued gain − cash flows received from secondary-market transferee. [d] $950,263 = present value of cash flows for periods 3-5 discounted at 10 percent rate.

Scenario 1—Subsequent holder/transferee: [a] Opening cost base/principal owing from previous period + accrued gain − cash flows received. [b] Opening cost base/principal owing × YTM.

Scenario 2—Initial holder/transferor: [a] Opening cost base/principal owing from previous period + accrued gain − cash flows received. [b] Opening cost base/principal owing × YTM. [c] Opening cost base/principal owing + accrued gain − cash flows received from secondary-market transferee. [d] Present value of cash flows for periods 3-5 discounted at 6 percent rate.

Scenario 2—Subsequent holder/transferee: [a] Opening cost base/principal owing from previous period + accrued gain − cash flows received. [b] Opening cost base/principal owing × YTM.

- if the issuer has a right of redemption ("call option") at various times before maturity, or
- if the issuer or the holder has a right to extend the maturity of an instrument beyond the date specified on issue.[120]

In any of these instances, a particular instrument will have several possible maturity dates that will produce different yields to maturity and, consequently, different patterns of accrual of expected amounts.[121] From the purely ex ante perspective on which a system of expected-return taxation is based, there is no obvious reason to regard any of the possible redemption dates, such as the first one or the last one, as being determinative.[122] In the absence of a determinative date, some legislative regimes assume accrual at the maximum rate in the case of instruments that are retractable or extendable at the option of the holder[123] and accrual at the minimum rate in the case of instruments that are redeemable or extendable at the option of the issuer.[124] These assumptions, in effect, break down a retractable, redeemable, or extendable debt instrument into a set of separate instruments, each of which matures on one of the possible redemption dates.[125] Expected gains and losses are accrued for each of these separate instruments, and recognition is extended to either the maximum amount or the minimum amount that has accrued up to the end of the taxation year. The choice of one amount or the other assumes rational economic behaviour by holders that maximizes their returns and comparable behaviour by issuers that minimizes their cost of funds. The choice of the determinative assumption depends on which party to a debt instrument has the benefit of the relevant option.

The third issue has to do with the fact that the accrual pattern produced by a YTM calculation is based on a level yield or internal rate of return.[126] In other words, it is assumed that the rate of return on an instrument is constant, whereas in fact accrued amounts for a given period vary with the frequency of compounding. To establish a more accurate accrual pattern, it is necessary to incorporate the yield curve or "term structure of interest rates," which allows the rate of return for a period to vary with the length of the instrument's term.[127] The assumption of a level yield ignores expected movements in interest rates that should, in theory, be taken into account in order to produce an accrual pattern that is consistent with the pattern expected by market participants. For example, an upward-sloping yield curve may be attributable to a risk premium that long-term lenders have demanded as compensation for fluctuations in value caused by changes in the market rate of interest.[128] Longer-term debt is more exposed than is shorter-term debt to fluctuations in value of this kind and is, therefore, riskier than shorter-term debt. Where an upward-sloping yield curve is attributable to the presence of a risk premium associated with long-term debt, the assumption of a level yield to maturity understates expected gains in the earlier years and overstates them in the later years. The inaccuracy arises because of a failure to impute interest income and expense at higher long-term rates in the earlier years (when the level rate is too low) and at lower short-term rates in the later years (when the level rate is too high).[129] Table 5.6 and figure 5.2 illustrate this effect.

The mismeasurement associated with a level-yield convention presents an obvious tax-avoidance opportunity. Suppose that a taxpayer issues a debt instrument that pays periodic interest and uses the borrowed funds to acquire a series of OID obligations with cash flows that correspond to those under the periodic borrowing. Failure to account for the term structure of interest when there is an upward-sloping yield curve results in a slight deferral of recognition of interest income on the series of OID obligations. The deferral arises because of the understatement of accrued gain in the earlier portions of the longer-term obligations. Thanks to the earlier recognition of the offsetting interest expense on the debt instrument that pays periodic interest, the deferred recognition of the interest on the OID obligations produces a pure arbitrage profit.[130]

In fact, however, there is no evidence of transactions intended to take advantage of deviation from the correct pattern of accrual; consequently, policy makers apparently do not consider this tax-avoidance opportunity to be a problem.[131] Moreover, assumptions about the reasons for the slope of the yield curve affect the nature of any mismeasurement.[132] If an upward-sloping yield curve is attributable to expectations that future interest rates will be higher, a level-yield convention tends to overstate the amount of interest in earlier years and understate interest in later years. The opposite effect occurs in the case of a comparable yield curve that is attributable to a risk premium for long-term debt.[133] The uncertainty of assumptions about the cause of the term structure of interest rates have made it easy for tax-policy makers to dismiss the yield-curve insight as one of academic interest only[134] and to accept a level-yield convention whose simplicity minimizes administrative and compliance costs.[135]

Foreign Currency Debt[136]

Over the long term, currency exchange rates reflect differences in the rate of inflation, which in turn reflect differences in interest rates.[137] Thus currency

Table 5.6 Accrual Patterns and the Term Structure of Interest Rates

All scenarios
Zero coupon bond — Issued January 1, 1999
Face amount = $1,000,000 — Maturity January 1, 2004
5-year term

Period	Forward interest rate
0	
1	$f(0)$ 8.00%
2	$f(0,1)$ 8.20%
3	$f(0,2)$ 8.40%
4	$f(0,3)$ 8.60%
5	$f(0,4)$ 8.80%

Scenario 1: Accrual pattern under level-yield assumption (annual compounding)

Period	Cash flow[a]	Opening cost base/ principal owing[b]	Accrued gain[c]	YTM
0	$(668,130)			
1		$668,130	$ 56,120	8.40%
2		724,250	60,834	8.40%
3		785,080	65,945	8.40%
4		851,029	71,483	8.40%
5	1,000,000	922,512	77,488	8.40%
			$331,870	

Scenario 2: Accrual pattern incorporating an upward-sloping yield curve (annual compounding)

Period	Cash flow[a]	Opening cost base/ principal owing[b]	Accrued gain[c]	YTM
0	$(668,130)			
1		$668,130	$ 58,795	8.80%
2		726,925	62,516	8.60%
3		789,441	66,313	8.40%
4		855,754	70,172	8.20%
5	1,000,000	925,926	74,074	8.00%
			$331,870	

Scenario 3: Accrual pattern under level-yield assumption (daily compounding)

Period	Cash flow[a]	Opening cost base/ principal owing[b]	Accrued gain[c]	YTM
0	$(668,130)			
1		$668,130	$ 56,120	8.17%
2		724,250	60,834	8.17%
3		785,080	65,945	8.17%
4		851,029	71,483	8.17%
5	1,000,000	922,512	77,488	8.17%
			$331,870	

(Table 5.6 is concluded on the next page.)

Table 5.6 Concluded

Scenario 4: Accrual pattern incorporating an upward-sloping yield curve (daily compounding)

Period	Cash flow[a]	Opening cost base/ principal owing[b]	Accrued gain[c]	YTM
0	$(668,130)			
1		$668,130	$ 58,795	8.44%
2		726,925	62,516	8.25%
3		789,441	66,313	8.07%
4		855,754	70,172	7.88%
5	1,000,000	925,926	74,074	7.70%
			$331,870	

All scenarios: [a] All cash flows are reversed for a borrower and accrued gains equal accrued losses. [b] Opening cost base/principal owing from previous period + accrued gain − cash flows received. [c] Opening cost base/principal owing × YTM.

exchange rates and interest rates tend to be closely correlated. Yet changes in spot exchange rates are not entirely reflections of changes in interest rates, and movements in the former are unpredictable in the short term.[138] In other words, the relationship between spot exchange rates and interest rates is not a causal one; gains and losses that arise because of movements in spot rates are entirely unexpected and do not present the problem of anticipated deferral. There is no reason to apply to them an accrual accounting method that is designed for expected gains and losses. This proposition applies equally to exchange gains and losses that are associated with the physical holding of foreign currency or with the assumption of a derivative position in a forward, futures, or swap contract written on foreign currency.[139] On the other hand, the financial equivalence expressed in interest-rate parity means that expected movements in exchange rates should be accounted for in the application of a YTM calculation to debt instruments denominated in a foreign currency ("foreign currency debt"). This accounting is, in fact, necessary to ensure equivalent treatment of domestic and foreign currency debt with an expected time-value return associated with an advance of funds. In this narrow instance only, exchange gains and losses present unique problems that must be dealt with in the application of the YTM method.

As was described in chapter 1,[140] interest-rate parity expresses a basic relationship between interest rates and forward currency rates that reflects arbitrage pricing conditions under which the difference between the forward and spot exchange rates for two currencies must equal the difference between interest rates for borrowings in the same currencies. This equivalence ensures that an investment in a weaker currency yields the same return as an equivalent investment in a stronger currency. In the absence of an equivalence of this kind, an opportunity to realize arbitrage profits would arise, and arbitrage traders would enter the market to seize the opportunity in a way that quickly equated the rates of return on the two currencies and restored price equilibrium. The financial equivalence expressed by interest-rate parity means that a portion of

Figure 5.2 Accrual Patterns and the Term Structure of Interest Rates

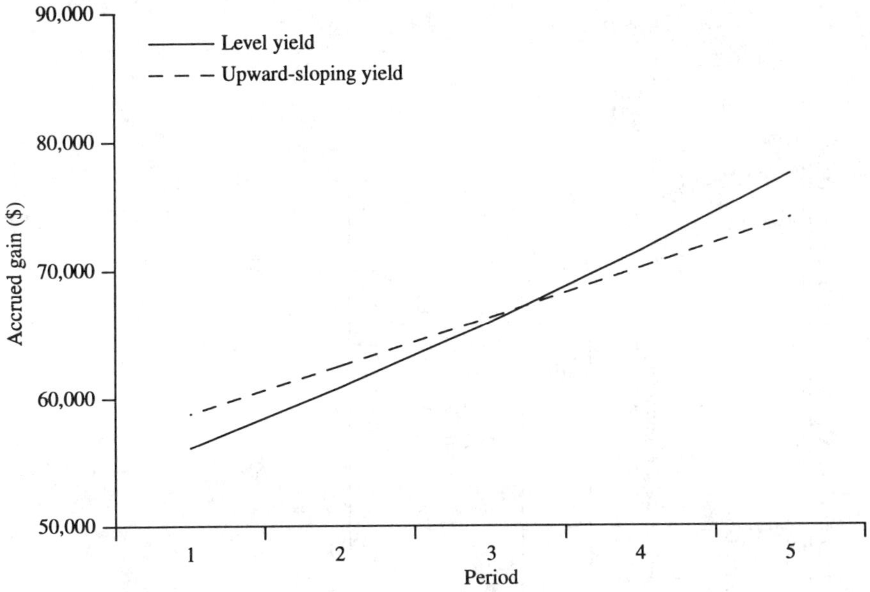

the higher interest rates associated with a weaker currency effectively compensates lenders for the expected loss in value of their loan principal. For borrowers in weaker currencies, a portion of the nominal interest payments represents a repayment of principal. The lower nominal interest payments associated with a borrowing in a stronger currency are supplemented by expected increases in the value of the loan principal. In short, the expected gain or loss associated with debt denominated in a foreign currency is a combination of the nominal interest and the expected gain or loss on the loan principal attributable to forward exchange rates. If expected gains and losses on foreign currency debt attributable to expected exchange rates are not incorporated in a YTM calculation, they will not be subject to accrual recognition.[141] In that case, foreign currency debt will not be taxed consistently with domestic debt. Lenders will have an incentive to invest in stronger currencies with expected returns that are understated for tax purposes.[142] Borrowers will have an incentive to borrow in weaker currencies with expected returns that are overstated for tax purposes.[143]

As table 5.7 shows, the significance of interest-rate parity for a system of expected-return taxation lies in the fact that from a strictly ex ante perspective foreign currency debt is the equivalent of debt denominated in the domestic currency of the taxpayer. Consistent treatment of foreign currency debt and domestic debt requires the application of expected-return taxation in the form of a YTM calculation that treats expected exchange gains and losses as interest income and expense subject to accrual recognition.[144] Unexpected exchange gains and losses may be treated as ordinary-income amounts subject to realization-

Table 5.7 Equivalence of Expected Cash Flows Associated with Foreign Currency and Domestic Debt

All scenarios

US$ bond	*Cdn.$ bond*
Issue price $100,000	Issue price $150,000
Issued January 1, 1999	Issued January 1, 1999
Maturity January 1, 2004	Maturity January 1, 2004
YTM = 5% with annual compounding	YTM = 8% with annual compounding

Exchange rates

Period	Spot rate (US$/Cdn.$)	Forward rate (US$/Cdn$)
0	0.6666666	
1	0.6481481	$f(0,1)$ 0.6481481
2	0.6301440	$f(0,2)$ 0.6301440
3	0.6126400	$f(0,3)$ 0.6126400
4	0.5956222	$f(0,4)$ 0.5956222
5	0.5790771	$f(0,5)$ 0.5790771

(Table 5.7 is continued on the next page.)

Table 5.7 Continued

	Scenario 1: Canadian holder of US$ bond								Scenario 2: Canadian holder of equivalent Cdn.$ bond		
Period	Cash flows	Expected interest payments[a]	Actual payments[b]	Opening cost base/ principal owing[c]	Closing cost base/ principal owing[d]	Expected forex gain/loss[e]	Unexpected forex gain/loss[f]	Total gain/loss[g]	Cash flows	Opening cost base/ principal owing[a]	Accrued gain/loss[b]
	US$				*Cdn.$*					*Cdn.$*	
0 ...	(100,000)[h]		(150,000)						(150,000)[c]		
1 ...	5,000	7,714	7,714	150,000	154,286	4,286	nil	12,000	7,714	150,000	12,000
2 ...	5,000	7,935	7,935	154,286	158,694	4,408	nil	12,343	7,935	154,286	12,343
3 ...	5,000	8,161	8,161	158,694	163,228	4,534	nil	12,695	8,161	158,694	12,695
4 ...	5,000	8,395	8,395	163,228	167,892	4,664	nil	13,059	8,395	163,228	13,059
5 ...	5,000	8,634	8,634	167,892			nil		8,634	167,892	13,431
	100,000		172,689			4,797		13,431			
		40,839				22,689		63,528	172,689		63,528

Scenario 1: [a] Cdn.$ contracted interest payments at forward exchange rate. [b] Cdn.$ cash flows at spot exchange rate. [c] Opening cost base/principal owing from previous period + expected forward exchange gain. [d] Closing cost base/principal owing at forward exchange rates. [e] Change in value of principal at forward exchange rates. [f] Difference between contracted cash flows at forward exchange rates and actual cash flows at spot rates. [g] Expected interest payments + expected foreign exchange gain +/– unexpected foreign exchange gain/loss. [h] All cash flows and gains/losses are reversed for a Canadian borrower.

Scenario 2: [a] Opening cost base/principal owing from previous period + accrued gain – cash flows received. [b] Opening cost base/principal owing × YTM. [c] All cash flows and gains/losses are reversed for a Canadian borrower.

(Table 5.7 is concluded on the next page.)

Table 5.7 Concluded

	Scenario 3: US holder/borrower of Cdn.$ bond								Scenario 4: US holder/borrower of equivalent US$ bond		
Period	Cash flows	Expected interest payments[a]	Actual payments[b]	Opening cost base/ principal owing[c]	Closing cost base/ principal owing[d]	Expected forex loss[e]	Unexpected forex gain/loss[f]	Total gain/loss[g]	Cash flows	Opening cost base/ principal owing[a]	Accrued gain/loss[b]
	Cdn.$				*US$*					*US$*	
0 . . .	(150,000)[h]		(100,000)						(100,000)[c]		
1 . . .	12,000	7,778	7,778	100,000	97,222	(2,778)	nil	5,000	7,778	100,000	5,000
2 . . .	12,000	7,562	7,562	97,222	94,522	(2,700)	nil	4,862	7,562	97,222	4,862
3 . . .	12,000	7,352	7,352	94,522	91,896	(2,626)	nil	4,726	7,352	94,522	4,726
4 . . .	12,000	7,147	7,147	91,896	89,343	(2,553)	nil	4,594	7,147	91,896	4,594
5 . . .	12,000	6,949	6,949	89,343		(2,482)	nil	4,467	6,949	89,343	4,467
	150,000	36,788	86,861			(13,139)		23,649	86,861		23,649

Scenario 3: [a] US$ contracted interest payments at forward exchange rates. [b] US$ cash flows at spot exchange rate. [c] Opening cost base/principal owing from previous period – expected foreign exchange loss. [d] Closing cost base/principal owing at forward exchange rates. [e] Change in value of principal at forward exchange rates. [f] Difference between contracted cash flows at forward exchange rates and actual cash flows at spot rates. [g] Expected interest payments – expected foreign exchange loss +/– unexpected foreign exchange gain/loss. [h] All cash flows and gains/losses are reversed for a US borrower.

Scenario 4: [a] Opening cost base/principal owing from previous period + accrued gain – cash flows received. [b] All cash flows and gains/losses are reversed for a US borrower.

based recognition. This result is achieved, for example, under the New Zealand accrual regime,[145] which equates the expected yield on foreign currency debt with the expected yield on a domestic currency instrument and requires the same amount to be spread on a YTM basis. Unexpected gains and losses that are attributable to movements in the spot exchange rate are recognized on realization in the same manner as unexpected gains and losses that are attributable to movements in the market rate of interest. Expected gain or loss is measured by using forward exchange rates[146] to determine the expected value in New Zealand dollars of all future cash flows, which are spread on a YTM basis over the term of the relevant foreign currency instrument.[147] Realized amounts are converted to the equivalent in New Zealand dollars at the prevailing spot rate, a transaction that gives rise to unexpected exchange gains or losses.[148]

The application of expected-return taxation to foreign currency debt[149] is illustrated in table 5.8,[150] which, with figures 5.3 and 5.4, also contrasts the treatment of foreign currency debt under a system of expected-return taxation with the realization-based recognition of expected exchange gains and losses under the accepted tax cubbyholes. The two cubbyholes relevant for foreign currency debt are (1) interest income and expense recognized on an accrual basis and (2) foreign exchange gains and losses recognized on realization.[151] Mismeasurement of income and expense under these tax cubbyholes is attributable primarily to the realization-based recognition of expected exchange gains and losses (often at reduced capital gains tax rates for taxpayers who are not traders or dealers). An acceptance of legal form as determinative in the application of the cubbyholes means that a borrower in a weak currency can deduct the full amount of nominal interest expense on an accrual basis and defer inclusion of an offsetting foreign exchange gain until repayment of the loan principal, even though that gain is entirely expected. A lender in a strong currency must include only the nominal amount of interest and can defer the inclusion of offsetting expected exchange gains. As was emphasized above, this treatment is inconsistent with the treatment of an equivalent domestic borrowing and flies in the face of the financial equivalence expressed by interest-rate parity.

Other than an expected-return approach, there are two alternatives to the application of the traditional tax cubbyholes that are commonly considered to be appropriate approaches to the taxation of foreign currency debt. One of these approaches requires the recognition of (1) nominal interest income or expense over the term of a loan translated at the relevant spot exchange rate and (2) changes in the value of the loan principal that are based on movement in the spot exchange rate from the beginning to the end of the taxation year.[152] This "retranslation basis," which is generally consistent with financial-accounting practice, is based on the assumption that the close correlation between currency exchange and interest rates means there is an interest element in exchange gains and losses that should be subject to accrual recognition.[153] As table 5.9 and figures 5.5 and 5.6 illustrate, however, the retranslation basis produces inconsistent treatment of domestic debt and foreign currency debt. It does so largely because it requires the recognition of unexpected exchange gains and losses

Table 5.8 Accrual Versus Realization-Based Recognition of Expected Gains and Losses Associated with Foreign Currency Debt

All scenarios

US$ bond	*Cdn.$ bond*
Issue price $100,000	Issue price $150,000
Issued January 1, 1999	Issued January 1, 1999
Maturity January 1, 2004	Maturity January 1, 2004
YTM = 5% with annual compounding	YTM = 8% with annual compounding

Exchange rates

Period	Spot rate (US$/Cdn.$)	Forward rate (US$/Cdn$)
0	0.6666666	
1	0.6481481	$f(0,1)$ 0.6481481
2	0.6301440	$f(0,2)$ 0.6301440
3	0.6126400	$f(0,3)$ 0.6126400
4	0.5956222	$f(0,4)$ 0.5956222
5	0.5790771	$f(0,5)$ 0.5790771

(Table 5.8 is continued on the next page.)

Table 5.8 Continued

	Canadian holder of US$ bond									
	Scenario 1: Accrual recognition/expected-return taxation				Scenario 2: Realization basis					
Period	Cash flows	Expected cash flows[a]	Opening cost base/ principal owing[b]	Accrued gain[c]	Cash flows	Expected cash flows[a]	Opening cost base/ principal owing[b]	Accrued gain[c]	Realization-based gain[d]	Total gain[e]
	US$		*Cdn.$*		*US$*			*Cdn.$*		
0	(100,000)[d]	(150,000)			(100,000)[f]	(150,000)				
1	5,000	7,714	150,000	12,000	5,000	7,714	150,000	7,714		7,714
2	5,000	7,935	154,286	12,343	5,000	7,935	154,286	7,935		7,935
3	5,000	8,161	158,694	12,695	5,000	8,161	158,694	8,161		8,161
4	5,000	8,395	163,228	13,059	5,000	8,395	163,228	8,395		8,395
5	5,000	8,634	167,892	13,431	5,000	8,634	167,892	8,634		
	100,000	172,689			100,000	172,689			22,689	31,323
				63,528				40,840	22,689	63,528

Scenario 1: [a] US$ contracted cash flows at forward exchange rates (or spot exchange rate for initial advance). [b] Opening cost base/principal owing from previous period + accrued gain – expected cash flows. [c] Cost base/principal owing × Cdn.$ YTM. [d] All cash flows and gains/losses are reversed for a Canadian borrower.

Scenario 2: [a] US$ contracted cash flows at forward exchange rates (or spot exchange rate for initial advance). [b] Opening cost base/principal owing from previous period at forward exchange rate (spot exchange rate for period 1 and initial US$ cash flow). [c] US$ contracted cash flows converted to Cdn.$ at forward exchange rates. [d] Difference between amount advanced on issue at spot exchange rate and amount received on maturity at forward exchange rate. [e] Accrued gain for period + realization-based gain for period. [f] All cash flows and gains/losses are reversed for a Canadian borrower.

(Table 5.8 is concluded on the next page.)

Table 5.8 Concluded

	US holder of Cdn.$ bond									
	Scenario 3: Accrual recognition/expected-return taxation				Scenario 4: Realization basis					
Period	Cash flows	Cash flows[a]	Opening cost base/ principal owing[b]	Accrued gain[c]	Cash flows	Cash flows[a]	Opening cost base/ principal owing[b]	Accrued gain[c]	Realization-based gain/loss[d]	Total gain/loss[e]
	Cdn.$		*US$*		*Cdn.$*			*US$*		
0	(150,000)[d]	(100,000)			(150,000)[f]	(100,000)				
1	12,000	7,778	100,000	5,000	12,000	7,778	100,000	7,778		7,778
2	12,000	7,562	97,222	4,862	12,000	7,562	97,222	7,562		7,562
3	12,000	7,352	94,522	4,726	12,000	7,352	94,522	7,352		7,352
4	12,000	7,147	91,896	4,594	12,000	7,147	91,896	7,147		7,147
5	12,000	6,949	89,343	4,467	12,000	6,949	89,343	6,949		
	150,000	86,861	86,861		150,000	86,861	86,861		(13,139)	(6,190)
				23,649				36,788	(13,139)	23,649

Scenario 3: [a] Cdn.$ contracted cash flows at forward exchange rates (or spot exchange rate for initial advance). [b] Opening cost base/principal owing from previous period + accrued gain – expected cash flows. [c] Opening cost base/principal owing × US$ YTM. [d] All cash flows and gains/losses are reversed for a US borrower.

Scenario 4: [a] Cdn.$ contracted cash flows at forward exchange rates. [b] Opening cost base/principal owing from previous period at forward exchange rate (spot exchange rate for period 1 and initial Cdn $ cash flow). [c] Cdn.$ contracted payments converted to US$ at forward exchange rates. [d] Difference between amount advanced at spot exchange rate and amount received on maturity at forward exchange rate. [e] Accrued gain for period – realization-based loss for period. [f] All cash flows and gains/losses are reversed for a US borrower.

Figure 5.3 Accrual Versus Realization-Based Recognition of Expected Gains and Losses Associated with Foreign Currency Debt

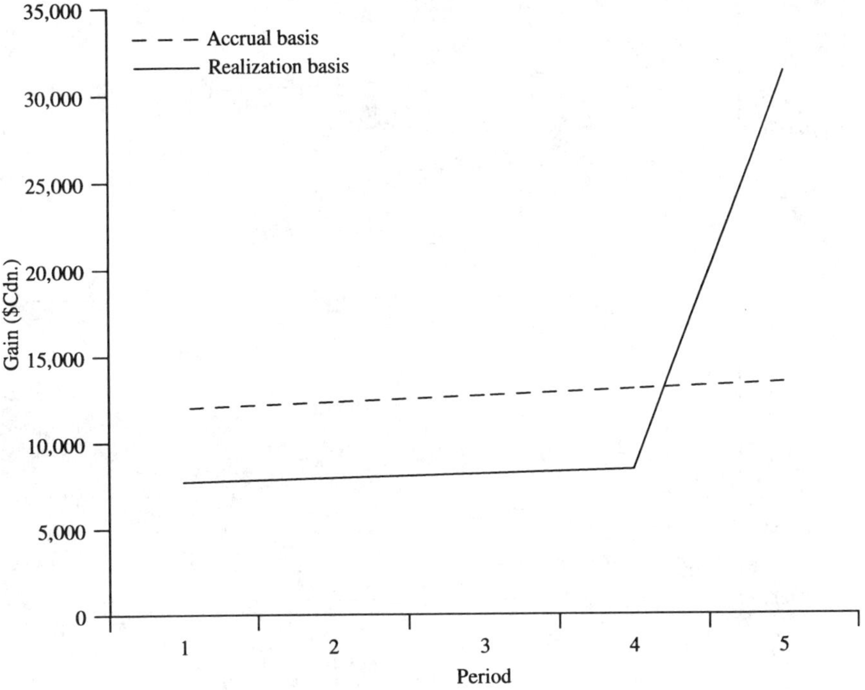

before realization on an accretion basis, whereas changes in the value of domestic debt caused by movements in interest rates are generally recognized only on realization. If one accepts the latter treatment as a standard feature of a system of expected-return taxation, there would appear to be no obvious tax-policy reason for not applying it to unexpected exchange gains and losses on foreign currency debt. Under a realization-based income tax, it will be argued below, the application of accretion taxation to all gains and losses on financial instruments is the most effective means of addressing the unanticipated deferral of unexpected gains and the selective realization of unexpected losses. Its effectiveness is greatest, however, in the case of financial instruments that can be traded at low transaction costs. Not all domestic debt falls into this category, and there is nothing about foreign currency debt to suggest that it is different in this respect. In order to address tax-avoidance opportunities and eliminate distortions in debt capital markets, it is necessary to tax foreign currency debt that cannot be traded at low transaction costs in a manner that is consistent with the taxation of comparable domestic debt. Achievement of this consistency requires adoption of the expected-return approach reflected in the New Zealand legislation, which limits accrual recognition to expected exchange gains and losses. Foreign currency debt and domestic debt that present problems of unanticipated deferral and selective realization should be equally subject to accretion taxation.[154]

Figure 5.4 Accrual Versus Realization-Based Recognition of Expected Gains and Losses Associated with Foreign Currency Debt

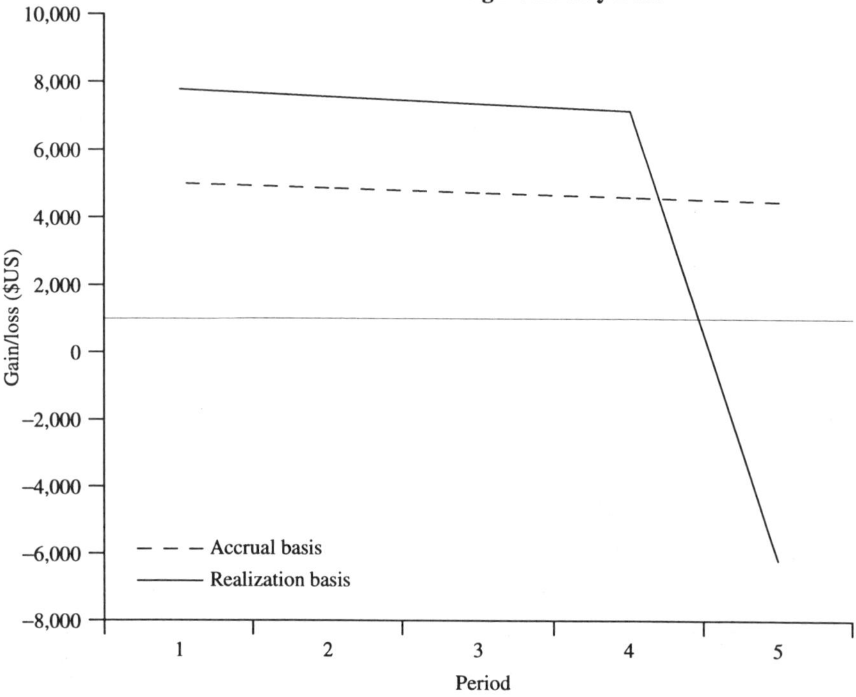

The second alternative approach to the taxation of foreign currency debt overturns the traditional cubbyholes but applies the expected-return approach only to "hedged" foreign currency debt. To achieve this end, it integrates hedged foreign debt with the offsetting derivative positions and treats the result as a synthetic domestic instrument.[155] The basis of this "integration" approach is a recognition that it is possible to replicate the cash flows associated with a domestic debt instrument by combining the cash flows associated with a foreign currency borrowing or loan and the cash flows associated with forward exchange agreements entered into for the purpose of covering future payments of interest and principal.[156] In effect, by entering into offsetting positions in derivative instruments written on the foreign currency, a borrower or a lender can ensure that the amount of any exchange gain or loss equals the expected amount reflected in forward exchange rates.[157] As table 5.10 shows, this result occurs as unexpected gains or losses on the amount of the loan principal that are attributable to movements in the spot exchange rate are offset by corresponding losses or gains on the related derivative.

By treating fully hedged foreign currency debt as a synthetic domestic instrument, the integration approach, unlike the retranslation approach, achieves some consistency in the taxation of foreign currency debt and domestic debt. In the case of unhedged (or "partially hedged") foreign currency debt, expected exchange

Table 5.9 Accrual Versus Accretion Taxation of Expected and Unexpected Gains and Losses Associated with Foreign Currency Debt

All scenarios

US$ bond	*Cdn.$ bond*
Issue price $100,000	Issue price $150,000
Issued January 1, 1999	Issued January 1, 1999
Maturity January 1, 2004	Maturity January 1, 2004
YTM = 5% with annual compounding	YTM = 8% with annual compounding

Exchange rates

Period	Spot rate (US$/Cdn.$)	Forward rate (US$/Cdn$)
0	0.6666666	
1	0.6382349	$f(0,1)$ 0.6481481
2	0.6223985	$f(0,2)$ 0.6301440
3	0.6198226	$f(0,3)$ 0.6126400
4	0.6075359	$f(0,4)$ 0.5956222
5	0.6022386	$f(0,5)$ 0.5790771

(Table 5.9 is continued on the next page.)

Table 5.9 Continued

	Canadian holder of US$ bond												
	Scenario 1: Accrual recognition/expected-return taxation							Scenario 2: Accretion taxation/retranslation basis					
Period	Cash flows	Cash flows[a]	Opening cost base/ principal owing[b]	Accrued gain[c]	Expected cash flows[d]	Realized unexpected gain/loss[e]	Total gain/ loss[f]	Cash flows	Cash flows[a]	Opening cost base/ principal owing[b]	Closing cost base/ principal owing[c]	Change in value[d]	Total gain/ loss[e]
	US$	*Cdn.$*						*US$*	*Cdn.$*				
0 . . .	(100,000)[g]	(150,000)			(150,000)			(100,000)[f]	(150,000)				
1 . . .	5,000	7,834	150,000	12,000	7,714	120	12,120	5,000	7,834	150,000	156,682	6,682	14,516
2 . . .	5,000	8,033	154,286	12,343	7,935	98	12,441	5,000	8,033	156,682	160,669	3,987	12,020
3 . . .	5,000	8,067	158,694	12,696	8,161	(94)	12,602	5,000	8,067	160,669	161,336	667	8,734
4 . . .	5,000	8,230	163,228	13,057	8,395	(165)	12,893	5,000	8,230	161,336	164,599	3,263	11,493
5 . . .	5,000	8,302	167,892	13,433	8,635	(333)		5,000	8,302	164,599			9,750
	100,000	166,047			172,689	(6,642)	6,457	100,000	166,047				
				63,529		(7,016)	56,513						56,513

Scenario 1: [a] US$ contracted cash flows at spot exchange rates. [b] Opening cost base/principal owing from previous period + accrued gain – expected cash flows. [c] Opening cost base/principal owing × Cdn.$ YTM (8% with annual compounding). [d] US$ contracted cash flows at forward exchange rates (or spot exchange rate for initial advance). [e] Difference between contracted US$ cash flows converted at spot and forward exchange rates. [f] Accrued gain for period +/– unexpected gain/loss for period. [g] All cash flows and gains/losses are reversed for a Canadian borrower.

Scenario 2: [a] US$ contracted cash flows converted at spot exchange rates. [b] Opening cost base/principal owing from end of previous period at spot exchange rate. [c] Closing cost base/principal owing at end of period at spot exchange rate. [d] Difference between opening and closing cost base/principal owing (or amount due on maturity for final payment). [e] Contracted cash flows +/– change in value of cost base/principal owing. [f] All cash flows and gains/losses are reversed for a Canadian borrower.

(Table 5.9 is concluded on the next page.)

Table 5.9 Concluded

US holder of Cdn.$ bond

Period	Scenario 3: Accrual recognition/expected-return taxation							Scenario 4: Accretion taxation/retranslation basis					
	Cash flows	Cash flows[a]	Opening cost base/ principal owing[b]	Accrued gain[c]	Expected cash flows[d]	Realized unexpected gain/loss[e]	Total gain/ loss[f]	Cash flows	Cash flows[a]	Opening cost base/ principal owing[b]	Closing cost base/ principal owing[c]	Change in value[d]	Total gain/ loss[e]
	Cdn.$			*US$*				*Cdn.$*			*US$*		
0 . . .	(150,000)[g]	(100,000)			(100,000)			(150,000)[f]	(100,000)				
1 . . .	12,000	7,659	100,000	5,000	7,778	(119)	4,881	12,000	7,659	100,000	95,735	(4,265)	3,394
2 . . .	12,000	7,469	97,222	4,862	7,562	(93)	4,769	12,000	7,469	95,735	93,360	(2,375)	5,094
3 . . .	12,000	7,438	94,522	4,726	7,352	86	4,812	12,000	7,438	93,360	92,973	(387)	7,051
4 . . .	12,000	7,290	91,896	4,594	7,147	143	4,737	12,000	7,290	92,973	91,130	(1,843)	5,447
5 . . .	12,000	7,227	89,343	4,467	6,949	278		12,000	7,227	91,130			
	150,000	90,336			86,861	3,475	8,220	150,000	90,336				6,433
				23,649		3,770	27,419						27,419

Scenario 3: [a] Cdn.$ contracted cash flows at spot exchange rates. [b] Opening cost base/principal owing from previous period + accrued gain − expected cash flows. [c] Opening cost base/principal owing × US$ YTM (5% with annual compounding). [d] Cdn.$ contracted cash flows converted at forward exchange rates (or spot exchange rate for initial advance). [e] Difference between contracted Cdn.$ cash flows converted at spot and forward exchange rates. [f] Accrued gain for period +/− unexpected gain/loss for period. [g] All cash flows and gains/losses are reversed for a US borrower.

Scenario 4: [a] Cdn.$ contracted cash flows converted at spot exchange rates. [b] Opening cost base/principal owing from end of previous period at spot exchange rate. [c] Closing cost base/principal owing at end of period at spot exchange rate. [d] Difference between opening and closing cost base/principal owing (or amount due on maturity for final payment). [e] Contracted cash flows +/− change in value of cost base/principal owing. [f] All cash flows and gains/losses are reversed for a US borrower.

Figure 5.5 Accrual Versus Accretion Taxation of Expected and Unexpected Gains and Losses Associated with Foreign Currency Debt

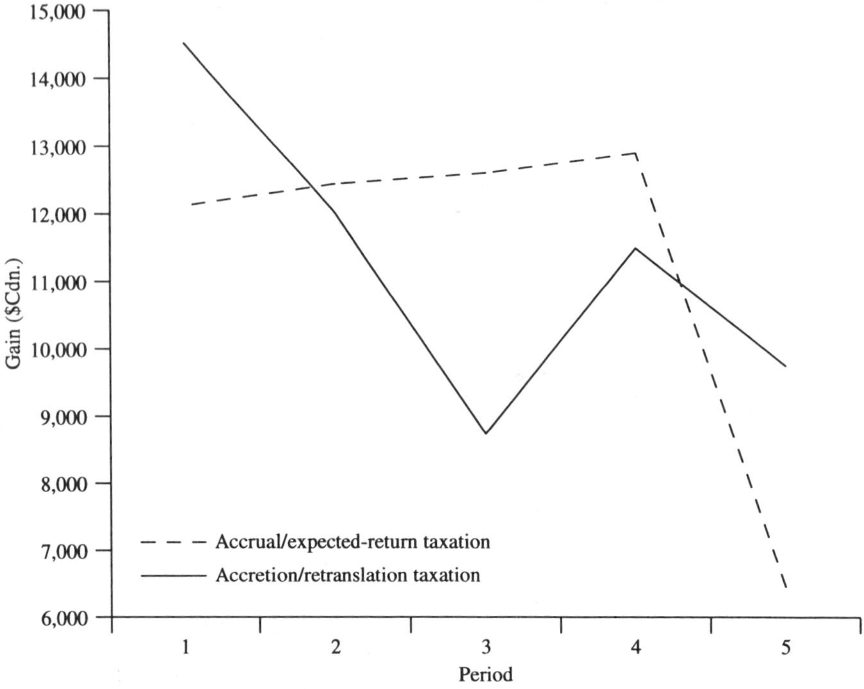

gains and losses reflected in forward rates are not treated as interest equivalents and are recognized on realization in the same way as unexpected gains and losses that are attributable to movements in the spot exchange rate.[158] This significant difference between the tax treatment of fully hedged instruments and the tax treatment of other instruments creates an important discontinuity, since it means that a fully hedged transaction and a partially hedged transaction that differ only slightly in terms of risk may result in substantially different tax consequences. By treating all foreign currency debt as the equivalent of a domestic obligation, an expected-return approach such as the one under the New Zealand accrual legislation eliminates this discontinuity and the need to define a hedged instrument as being subject to treatment as a synthetic.[159]

Indeed, since there is no obvious reason to limit this treatment to hedged foreign currency debt, the resultant discontinuity and definitional problem are entirely unnecessary.[160] Forward-rate agreements that cover future interest payments and repayments of principal simply reduce or eliminate the amount of unexpected gain or loss that will arise as a consequence of movements in the spot rate.[161] The fact that a borrowing is hedged, therefore, affects only the amount of unexpected gain or loss that is appropriately subject to realization-based recognition. Table 5.7 illustrates the simple fact that a foreign currency instrument, whether it is hedged or not, provides the same expected yield as a

Figure 5.6 Accrual Versus Accretion Taxation of Expected and Unexpected Gains and Losses Associated with Foreign Currency Debt

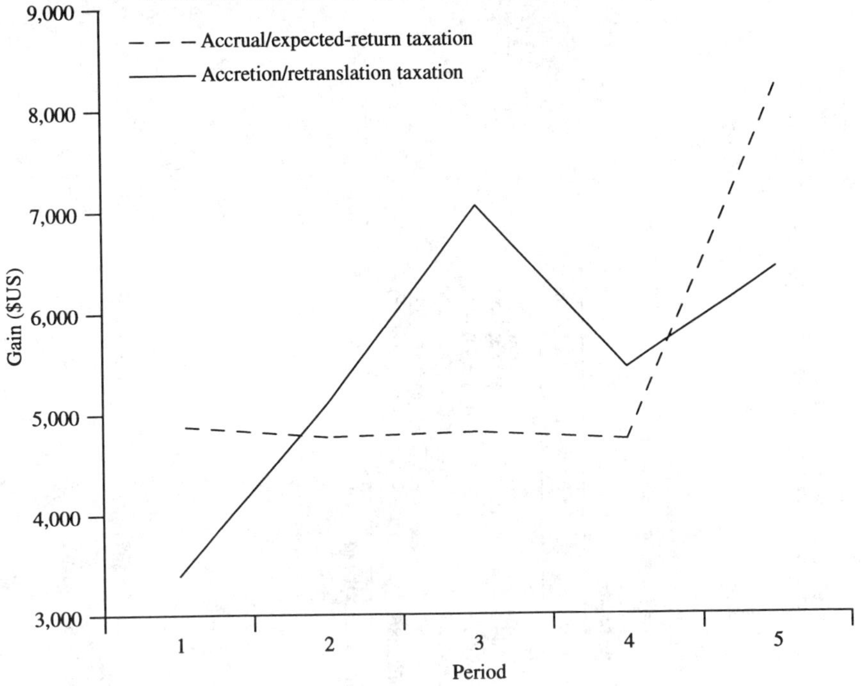

comparable domestic instrument. And whether the foreign currency instrument is hedged or not, its expected return should be subject to accrual recognition through the application of a YTM calculation on the same basis as the expected return on a comparable domestic instrument.[162]

The Role of Financial-Accounting Practice

The failure to account for the term structure of interest rates in the application of accrual methodologies[163] raises the more general question of the extent to which a system of expected-return taxation can tolerate deviations from an ideal pattern of accrual. Resolution of this issue involves some assessment, at a more general level, of the administrative and compliance costs associated with the use of a YTM calculation based on daily compounding. If this ideal is adopted for tax purposes, fundamental differences between it and financial-accounting practice are unavoidable, since the YTM calculation adopted for financial-statement purposes generally assumes some longer period of compounding.[164] Given the spectre of compliance costs that arises if taxpayers are required to use a tax-accounting method different from that used for financial-statement purposes, there is a case for providing taxpayers who are subject to an accrual regime with some form of relief from the assumption of daily

Table 5.10 Fully Hedged Foreign Currency Debt

All scenarios

US$ bond	*Cdn$ bond*
Issue price $100,000	Issue price $150,000
Issued January 1, 1999	Issued January 1, 1999
Maturity January 1, 2004	Maturity January 1, 2004
YTM = 5% with annual compounding	YTM = 8% with annual compounding

Exchange rates

Period	Spot rate (US$/Cdn.$)	Forward rate (US$/Cdn.$)
0	0.6666	
1	0.6382349	$f(0,1)$ 0.6481481
2	0.6223985	$f(0,2)$ 0.6301440
3	0.6198226	$f(0,3)$ 0.6126400
4	0.6075359	$f(0,4)$ 0.5956222
5	0.6022386	$f(0,5)$ 0.5790771

(Table 5.10 is continued on the next page.)

Table 5.10 Continued

Scenario 1: Canadian holder of US$ bond

Period	Cash flows	Cash flows[a]	Opening cost base/ principal owing[b]	Accrued gain[c]	Expected cash flows[d]	Realized unexpected gain/loss[e]	Realized unexpected gain/loss on offsetting forward[f]	Total gain/loss[g]
	US$				*Cdn.$*			
0	(100,000)[h]	(150,000)			(150,000)			
1	5,000	7,834	150,000	12,000	7,714	120	(120)	12,000
2	5,000	8,033	154,286	12,343	7,935	98	(98)	12,343
3	5,000	8,067	158,694	12,696	8,161	(94)	94	12,696
4	5,000	8,230	163,229	13,057	8,395	(165)	165	13,057
5	5,000	8,302	167,891	13,433	8,635	(333)	333	
	100,000	166,047			172,689	(6,642)	6,642	13,433
				63,529		(7,016)	7,016	63,529

[a] US$ contracted cash flows at spot exchange rates. [b] Opening cost base/principal owing from previous period + accrued gain – expected cash flows. [c] Opening cost base/principal owing × Cdn.$ YTM (8% with annual compounding). [d] US$ contracted cash flows at forward exchange rates (or spot exchange rate for initial advance). [e] Difference between US$ cash flows converted at spot and forward exchange rates. [f] Gain/loss on series of short forward contracts for sale of US$ at forward exchange rates corresponding to contracted US$ cash flows. [g] Accrued gain for period. [h] All cash flows and gains/losses are reversed for a Canadian borrower.

(Table 5.10 is concluded on the next page.)

Table 5.10 Concluded

Scenario 2: US holder of Cdn.$ bond

Period	Cash flows	Cash flows[a]	Opening cost base/ principal owing[b]	Accrued gain[c]	Expected cash flows[d]	Realized unexpected gain/loss[e]	Realized unexpected gain/loss on offsetting forward[f]	Total gain/loss[g]
	Cdn.$				*US$*			
0	(150,000)[h]	(100.000)			(100,000)			
1	12,000	7,659	100,000	5,000	7,778	(119)	119	5,000
2	12,000	7,469	97,222	4,862	7,562	(93)	93	4,862
3	12,000	7,438	94,522	4,726	7,352	86	(86)	4,726
4	12,000	7,290	91,896	4,594	7,147	143	(143)	4,594
5	12,000	7,227	89,343	4,467	6,949	278	(278)	4,467
	150,000	90,336			86,861	3,475	(3,475)	
				23,649		3,770	(3,770)	23,649

[a] Cdn.$ contracted cash flows at spot exchange rates. [b] Opening cost base/principal owing from previous period + accrued gain − expected cash flows. [c] Opening cost base/principal owing × US$ YTM (5% with annual compounding). [d] Cdn.$ contracted cash flows converted at forward exchange rates (or spot exchange rate for initial advance). [e] Difference between contracted Cdn.$ cash flows converted at spot and forward exchange rates. [f] Gain/loss on series of short forward contracts for sale of Cdn.$ at forward exchange rates corresponding to contracted Cdn.$ cash flows. [g] Accrued gain for period. [h] All cash flows and gains/losses are reversed for a US borrower.

compounding, at least where deviations from this benchmark ideal do not create significant avoidance opportunities.[165] It is not surprising, therefore, that tax-policy makers have shown a willingness to accommodate alternative accrual recognition methods, particularly if those methods are also used for financial-statement purposes.[166]

Accrual recognition methods that deviate from the application of the YTM method on a daily compounding basis fall into two general categories. One category, which is not especially problematic, includes methods that apply "straightline spreading" of expected gain or loss to a limited range of instruments for which this treatment is tolerable because the frequency of interest payments and the absence of discount or premium ensure that any anticipated deferral is limited.[167] Under straightline spreading, expected gain or loss payable periodically on a debt instrument is spread evenly over the number of days in the period to which the amounts relate.[168] Discount or premium, similarly, is spread evenly over the number of days in the term of the instrument.[169] Once the gain or loss has been allocated to particular days, it is recognized in the corresponding taxation years. Straightline spreading, therefore, is a relatively simple accrual method that is easy to administer and easy to comply with. The accrual pattern it provides, however, is much different from the pattern that the YTM method provides. This difference arises largely because straightline spreading fails to compound accrued but unpaid amounts,[170] with the result that the amount of expected gain or loss is kept constant over the term of a debt instrument. Under the YTM method, the yield is kept constant and the amount of gain or loss accrued over the term of an instrument varies as a function of the specified compounding periods. Table 5.11 and figures 5.7 and 5.8 illustrate this difference in accrual patterns. The difference tends to be most significant in the case of instruments that are issued or acquired (1) at a discount or a premium or (2) for a fixed term with periodic payments of interest and principal ("declining-principal instruments," including fixed-term annuities).[171] In the former instance, straightline spreading overstates the recognition of discount or premium in the earlier years and understates it in the later years.[172] Just the opposite effect occurs in the case of declining-principal instruments: here, straightline accrual understates the amount of expected gain or loss in earlier years and overstates the amount in later years. In the case of instruments that are issued at their face amount and that pay interest at regular intervals throughout their term, the YTM method and straightline spreading provide comparable results. Consequently, if one assumes that the use of straightline spreading minimizes compliance costs, that method can be extended, without creating significant deferral opportunities, to any instrument that (1) is issued or acquired at its face amount, (2) provides for payments of interest at regular intervals of one year or less, and (3) is redeemable on maturity for the full amount of the stated principal.[173] Instruments of this type may include both fixed-rate and floating- or variable-rate debt.[174] The same exception may be extended to discounted instruments with a term of one year or less, since the effect of any mismeasurement of the discount is limited.[175]

Table 5.11 Accrual Patterns Under Straightline Spreading Versus the YTM Method

Scenarios 1 and 2

Zero coupon bond	Issued January 1, 1999
Face amount = $1,000,000	Maturity January 1, 2004
5-year term	YTM = 8% with annual compounding

Scenario 1
Straightline accruals

Period	Cash flow[a]	Opening cost base/ principal owing[b]	Accrued gain[c]
0	$(680,583)		
1		$680,583	$ 63,883
2		744,466	63,883
3		808,349	63,883
4		872,232	63,883
5	1,000,000	936,115	63,883
			$319,417

Scenario 2
YTM method

Period	Cash flow[a]	Opening cost base/ principal owing[b]	Accrued gain[c]
0	$(680,583)		
1		$680,583	$ 54,447
2		735,030	58,802
3		793,832	63,507
4		857,339	68,587
5	1,000,000	925,926	74,074
			$319,417

Scenarios 3 and 4

Zero coupon bond	Issued October 1, 1999
Face amount = $1,000,000	Maturity October 1, 2004
5-year term	YTM = 8% with annual compounding

Scenario 3
Straightline accruals

Taxation year	Cash flow[a]	Opening cost base/ principal owing[b]	Accrued gain[c]
1999 (Oct. 1-Dec. 31)	$(680,583)	$680,583	$ 15,971
2000		696,554	63,883
2001		760,437	63,883
2002		824,320	63,883
2003		888,203	63,883
2004 (Jan. 1-Oct. 1)		952,086	47,912
			$319,417

(Table 5.11 is concluded on the next page.)

Table 5.11 Concluded

		Scenario 4 YTM Method	
1999 (Oct. 1-Dec. 31)	$(680,583)	$680,583	$ 13,612
2000		694,195	55,536
2001		749,730	59,978
2002		809,709	64,777
2003		874,486	69,959
2004 (Jan. 1-Oct. 1)	1,000,000	944,444	55,556
			$319,417

Scenarios 1 and 2: [a] All cash flows are reversed for a borrower and accrued gains equal losses. [b] Opening cost base/principal owing from previous period + accrued gain – cash flows received. [c] Opening cost base/principal owing × YTM.

Scenarios 3 and 4: [a] All cash flows are reversed for a borrower and accrued gains equal accrued losses. [b] $680,583 = present value of $1,000,000 at the end of year 5. [c] Opening cost base/ principal owing from the previous period + accrued gain – cash flows received.

The other category of deviations from a benchmark YTM is more problematic, since it raises the broader issue of the role of financial-accounting practice in providing acceptable accrual methods. This category of deviations is potentially a much wider one than the first: it includes any accrual method that is used for financial-accounting purposes, and therefore it extends to all financial instruments that are otherwise subject to the YTM method. As was argued in chapter 4,[176] this type of deviation in its extreme form eliminates all of the additional compliance costs associated with the use of separate tax-accounting standards. Reductions in compliance costs are achieved at the price of an unacceptable transfer of the function of making tax policy to the accounting profession. Indeed, this approach is not a deviation from an ideal benchmark for income tax purposes but rather an uncritical acceptance of financial accounting as that benchmark. The result is a failure to strike an acceptable balance between the goal of restraining administrative and compliance costs and other important tax-policy goals, including the goal of minimizing the benefit of anticipated deferral.[177]

As an alternative to an unqualified acceptance of financial-accounting practice, both the New Zealand accrual legislation[178] and the Australian accrual proposals[179] incorporate a compromise approach. It begins with the premise that an accrual method used for financial-statement purposes may be used for tax purposes as well, provided that it is applied consistently.[180] This presumption of acceptability is rebutted if the accrual pattern provided by an alternative to a YTM benchmark gives rise to an unacceptable level of anticipated deferral, in which case the benchmark calculation must be used. Both the New Zealand legislation and the Australian accrual proposals attempt to describe in broad terms the circumstances in which a recognition method used for financial-accounting purposes may also be used for income tax purposes, even though it

Figure 5.7 Accrual Patterns Under Straightline Spreading Versus the YTM Method

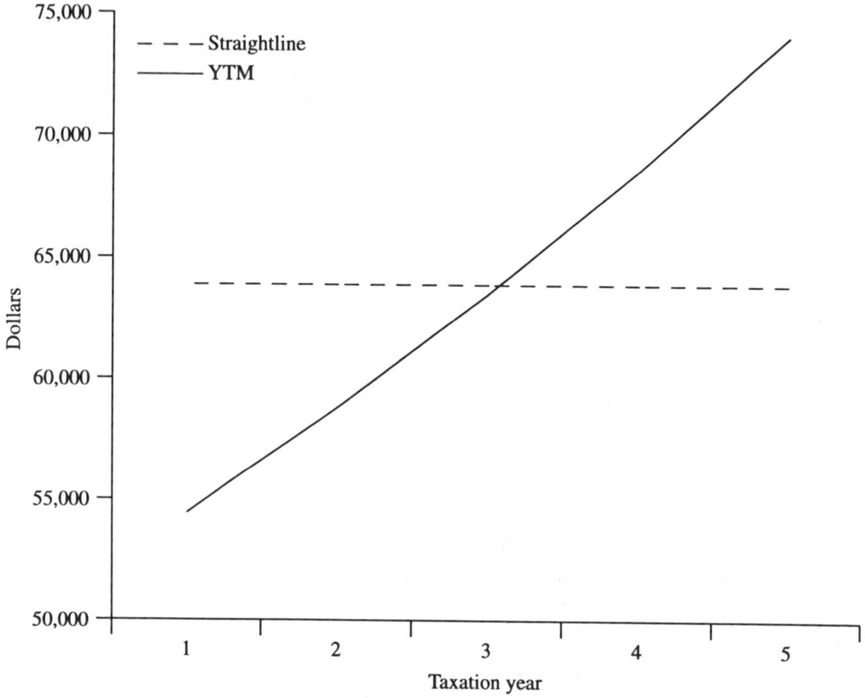

deviates from the specified benchmark. The attempt is framed in terms that purport to strike a balance between the flexibility provided by a standard of reasonableness and the certainty of a quantitative standard that provides a clearly defined line between acceptable and unacceptable deviations ("a bright-line test"). For example, the New Zealand legislation provides a general test that requires adoption of the YTM method for a particular financial arrangement unless there is an alternative method that[181]

1) has regard to the principles of accrual accounting,

2) conforms with commercially acceptable practice,

3) is adopted by the person and is or will be consistently applied in respect of all financial arrangements of the same type for financial-reporting purposes, and

4) results in the allocation to each income year of amounts that are not materially different from amounts that would be calculated under the YTM method.

The precise content of these conditions is vague and the subject of some debate.[182] The first two conditions are particularly problematic and may, in fact, add very little to the whole.[183] The more significant conditions are the third and fourth, which together amount to a reasonableness standard that permits the use of a particular financial-accounting method, provided that the resulting accrual

Figure 5.8 Accrual Patterns Under Straightline Spreading Versus the YTM Method

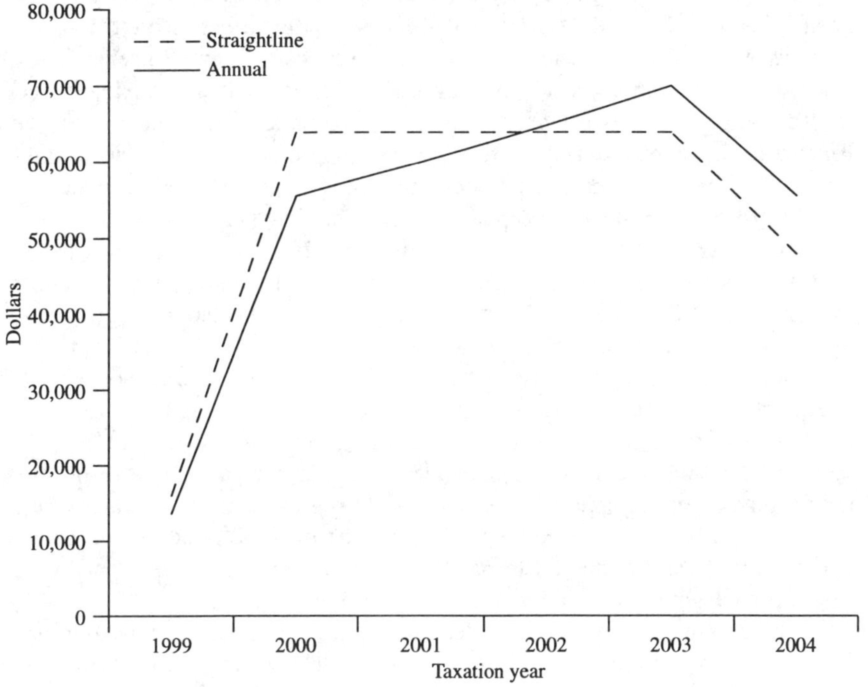

pattern does not differ "materially" from the pattern under a benchmark YTM calculation. The third condition appears to be intended to ensure that any alternative to YTM is actually used by the taxpayer for financial-accounting purposes and is not just selected for tax purposes.[184] In fact, unless an alternative tax-accounting method is also used for financial-statement purposes, there is no saving of compliance costs and the rationale for deviation from a benchmark YTM disappears.[185] The fourth condition expresses a "reasonableness standard" under which the concept of a "material difference" provides a flexible test for assessment of a particular method on the basis of factors that can be articulated over time in order to balance administrative and compliance considerations against the benefit of anticipated deferral. The Commissioner of Inland Revenue has indicated that a difference will be considered to be "materially different" if it is more than 5 percent or $500,000 of the results under a benchmark YTM (or some other specified method).[186] Although the point is not entirely clear, it appears that an alternative to YTM must pass this bright-line test if it is to be considered acceptable.[187] If the bright-line test is determinative, the benefits of a flexible standard are lost and discontinuities will arise, since some recognition methods will fall on one side of the line and some on the other side.

The Australian accrual proposals attempt to avoid the discontinuities associated with a bright-line test by combining a flexible standard of reasonableness with a defined benchmark that operates as a "safe harbour" standard for acceptable deviation.[188] The Australian proposals apparently adopted this approach on the ground that the YTM method based on daily compounding is not used for financial-accounting purposes and therefore imposes an unnecessary compliance burden.[189] Under the Australian proposals, a YTM method based on an assumption of six-month compounding is established as the benchmark accrual method.[190] The benchmark is not an exclusive test of the acceptability of a particular recognition method; rather, it deems a particular recognition method used for financial-accounting purposes to be acceptable for income tax purposes if it provides accrual results that do not deviate by more than 10 percent from the accrual results under the benchmark.[191] This standard is clearly more generous than its New Zealand counterpart, and particularly so because it places no alternative dollar limit on the amount of acceptable deviation. There is, however, no basis in principle for saying that any particular level of deviation corresponds to an acceptable level of anticipated deferral.[192] Any standard of this kind is inevitably arbitrary, and the Australian standard is used only to provide a measure of certainty. The Australian proposals, therefore, also provide a general reasonableness standard for recognition methods that do not satisfy the benchmark safe harbour.[193] This standard requires the application of a facts-and-circumstances approach that can be tailored to particular circumstances and developed over time with a degree of flexibility at the cost of some certainty.[194]

The compromise approach reflected in the New Zealand legislation and the Australian accrual proposals has an intuitive appeal, given its apparent ability to address the problem of anticipated deferral without invoking compliance costs as high as those associated with the exclusive application of the YTM method. These appearances are deceiving, however, and even the most superficial analysis shows that the effectiveness of this approach is questionable. In fact, when it is assessed in terms of a defensible tax-policy rationale, any attempt at a compromise with financial-accounting practice reveals problems that are serious enough to justify its outright rejection. To be specific, it is doubtful whether a qualified acceptance of financial-accounting practice would realize significant savings in compliance costs. This consideration is critical, since the existence of significant savings is the only defensible tax-policy basis for an acceptance of financial-accounting practice. The primary limitation on savings in compliance costs is the need to define a level of tolerable deviation from the benchmark YTM approach similar to the levels defined under the New Zealand legislation and the Australian accrual proposals. A definition is indispensable, given the undesirability of an uncritical acceptance of financial-accounting practice; yet any definition entails administrative and compliance costs that largely offset the savings from the use of accrual methods adopted for financial-accounting purposes. Any use of a bright-line standard clearly involves offsetting costs, since in that case a benchmark calculation must be made in order to ensure that the deviation does not exceed the standard. Moreover, it does not matter whether the benchmark is applied as a determinative test or as a safe harbour; the compliance costs associated with the application of the benchmark arise in either case. The alternative of a flexible standard of reasonableness does not offer a way around this problem: it entails similar administrative and compliance costs for similar reasons, and these costs too partially or wholly offset any savings that may be realized from applying a parallel tax-accounting method to the expected gain or loss on a financial instrument.

The Australian accrual proposals acknowledge the problem of offsetting compliance costs associated with the application of a benchmark safe harbour. They concede that a requirement to perform a benchmark calculation in all cases, in order to assess the acceptability of alternative accrual methods, would eliminate any savings.[195] The proposals suggest, however, that it would be possible to minimize this effect by requiring the tax administration to provide "boundary characteristics" for a range of common instruments and for methods of accounting appropriate to those instruments.[196] This approach would eliminate the need to make separate calculations for particular instruments of some types, but the savings would probably be minimal. The provision of boundary characteristics would be feasible only in the case of instruments that are relatively common, and their commonness suggests that in their case the application of the benchmark itself would entail very little additional compliance cost, even if the tax-accounting method differed from the method used for financial-accounting purposes. In any case, some important types of instruments, such as contingent-payment instruments that are either debt with embedded derivatives or derivatives with embedded debt, simply do not lend themselves to any kind of standardized approach. If the expected gain or loss associated with these instruments is subject to accrual recognition, YTM calculations must be made, and so must an assessment of the acceptability of alternative financial-accounting methods.

A compromise approach to the role of financial-accounting practice, therefore, may not provide any appreciable net savings in compliance costs. This possibility means that the policy choice is, in reality, between an uncritical acceptance of financial-accounting practice and the mandatory use of a benchmark YTM for all instruments. The former alternative may provide considerable savings in compliance costs, but only at the expense of legitimate tax-policy concerns, including the potential provision of an unacceptable level of anticipated deferral. Tax-policy makers should generally prefer the development and application of a benchmark YTM as the exclusive recognition method for expected gain and loss on all financial instruments. Given this approach, financial-accounting practice is useful primarily as an important source of information about the application of the YTM method to particular instruments. For all practical purposes, in fact, compromises with financial-accounting practice may indicate nothing more than the willingness of tax-policy makers and administrators to regard this practice as a source of recognition methods that they can adopt for tax purposes, at least to the extent that these methods do not result in a level of deferral that is unacceptable relative to the level under an ideal accrual method. Any savings in compliance costs that a compromise approach may realize are at best incidental, except perhaps in the case of the narrow range of instruments for which straightline spreading is acceptable.[197]

Realization-Based Recognition of Unexpected Gains and Losses

Chapter 3 showed that unexpected gain or loss arises when a contingency specified in a financial instrument (either explicitly or implicitly) is resolved in favour of one of the parties and the amount owing is determined. If the terms of the relevant bet are fair,[198] there is an equal probability of gain or loss when the bet is entered into, and there is no expected time-value return. In the absence of the problem of anticipated deferral, which is associated with the realization-based recognition of expected gains, the YTM method (or any other accrual method) of tax accounting is irrelevant. This simple fact leaves realization-based recognition and accretion taxation as the principal tax-accounting methods for the unexpected gain or loss associated with the bet element in financial instruments. The former method requires recognition of gain or loss when the relevant bet is resolved and the positions of the parties are settled. The latter requires the recognition of unrealized gains or losses as the passage of time reveals information that provides the position of a party with value (either positive or negative).

Because of the valuation and liquidity problems that are associated with accretion taxation,[199] policy makers may prefer to adopt a realization-based income tax, in which case realization-based recognition of unexpected gains and losses is entirely appropriate. In order to minimize tax-avoidance opportunities, however, application of the realization basis must be modified in two important respects. The more important modification concerns the related problems of unanticipated deferral of unexpected gains and selective realization of unexpected losses. As was explained in chapter 3,[200] both of these problems are associated with trading strategies that involve the manipulation of the realization requirement. In effect, realization-based recognition of unexpected gains potentially provides taxpayers with opportunities to enter into transactions that transfer the risk associated with a financial instrument without attracting a realization event for tax purposes. Deferral of the tax payable on the unexpected gain lowers the effective tax rate; the deferral is unanticipated because the taxpayer cannot anticipate ex ante the existence of a gain that he can recognize after the period in which it is expected to accrue. In short, the taxpayer must wait for the passage of time to reveal unexpected gains. The benefit of unanticipated deferral is compounded by the taxpayer's ability to selectively realize unexpected losses while deferring the recognition of offsetting unexpected gains on other instruments. Even if the net gain or loss associated with offsetting positions is nil, the selective realization of unexpected losses will produce a tax benefit if the taxpayer can deduct the losses against other income and thereby reduce tax payable. This reduction is, in effect, an interest-free loan from the government that is not repaid until the offsetting unexpected gains are realized and tax is paid on those amounts.[201]

Responses to the problem of unanticipated deferral and selective realization involve modification of the realization requirement to address potential manipulation. The traditional (and minimal) response is the adoption of a concept of realization that is based not on the receipt of cash, but on the occurrence of a transaction that gives rise to a disposition.[202] This concept of a realization event is equivalent, more or less, to the concept of "receivability" and its requirement that a taxpayer recognize an amount as income if he has an unconditional legal right to the amount.[203] Although it is more difficult to manipulate than cash-based recognition, realization that is tantamount to a "disposition transaction" is also subject to considerable manipulation. Its vulnerability arises from its dependence on the legal form of a transfer as a proxy for a transfer of the risk associated with an asset. It is possible to combine two or more instruments to transfer risk without a legal transfer, a strategy that maintains the benefit of unanticipated deferral and leaves the selective realization of losses largely unaffected.[204] The only effective responses to these problems, in fact, are limitations on the deductibility of losses and the application of accretion taxation to unexpected gains and losses. The difficulty is in selecting the appropriate response and targeting its application in a manner that addresses the problems of unanticipated deferral and selective realization without affecting the pre-tax allocation of risk or imposing undue compliance and administrative costs.

The second important modification of the realization requirement concerns periodic swap payments and, in particular, the application of either the YTM method or straightline spreading to these amounts. This approach is based on a characterization of swaps as offsetting notional loans rather than as a series of forward contracts that give rise to unexpected gains and losses. The characterization of swaps in this way permits the application of accrual recognition methods to expected gain or loss associated with the notional loans and, in effect, attempts to match the recognition of gain or loss on a swap with the recognition of gain or loss on an underlying borrowing or loan. The justification for this concept of matching is doubtful, at least in the absence of a general regime applicable to any financial instrument that is entered into as a hedge of the risk associated with another instrument or a non-financial asset. Chapter 7 will consider, and reject, the case for a regime of this kind.[205] For the purposes of the discussion below, it is assumed that specified accounting methods are to be applied to financial instruments separately, without reference to other positions. Given this assumption, any deviation from the realization-based recognition of unexpected amounts associated with swaps can be supported only as a rough response to a unique tax-avoidance opportunity that arises where counterparties disguise the prepayment of their obligations by overpaying or underpaying amounts in the earlier periods of a swap in return for underpayments or overpayments in later periods.

Price-Fixing Instruments and the Bet Element in Risky Debt

As was explained in chapter 1,[206] forwards, futures, and swaps are price-fixing financial instruments that are pure bets on a specified contingency. Because there is an equal probability of a positive or negative payoff, there is no advance of funds when the bet is entered into, and the bet has no expected value.[207] Each counterparty accepts the other's agreement to pay if the resolution of the specified contingency is unfavourable to him. Much the same characterization applies to instruments that combine an advance of funds and an associated expected return with unexpected returns and an embedded bet. For example, the value of a fixed-payment debt instrument varies with changes in the market rate of interest. Similarly, the value of a foreign currency obligation varies with changes in the spot exchange rate. Since these variations are attributable to an implicit bet on interest and currency exchange rates, they are entirely unexpected and cannot be subjected to a YTM calculation applied ex ante on issue.

The equal possibility of a gain or a loss means that unexpected increases and decreases in the value of a price-fixing instrument or a debt instrument are generally accounted for on a realization event,[208] such as settlement, redemption, or a secondary-market transfer.[209] This necessary accounting is implemented under the New Zealand legislation and the Australian accrual proposals by means of a calculation called a base price adjustment,[210] which must be made on either: (1) the sale or redemption of an instrument otherwise subject to the accrual recognition of expected gains and losses or (2) the settlement or termination of a forward, futures, or swap. In the case of debt instruments, the calculation ensures that expected gains and losses previously recognized on an accrual basis are ultimately taxable or deductible only to the extent that they are realized. In the case of price-fixing instruments, the calculation ensures that unexpected gain or loss equal to the amount receivable or payable is recognized at that time.[211] In general, therefore, a base price adjustment requires the recognition of gain to the extent that it has not been recognized in a prior taxation year. A deduction is provided to the extent that the total gain on an instrument is less than the total of all amounts recognized in prior taxation years. This result is realized by requiring the calculation of a base price adjustment equal to

- the sum of all amounts realized on a sale or redemption and all amounts received or receivable over the term of the instrument, less
- the sum of the cost of the instrument and all amounts recognized previously on an accrual basis over the term of the instrument.[212]

For the holder, a positive amount represents unexpected gain that must be included in income.[213] A negative amount represents a deductible loss.[214] An issuer, substituting the issue price of an instrument for its cost, may deduct the same positive amount as an expense arising on redemption (excess of amounts paid or payable over the issue price and prior deductions).[215] A negative amount must be recognized as unexpected gain (excess of the issue price and prior deductions over amounts paid or payable). Deductibility of the relevant amounts may be automatic, provided that all gains and losses on financial instruments are recognized in full as ordinary income. Where a distinction between capital amounts and ordinary-income amounts is maintained, deductibility should not be automatic and should be subject to any limitations that apply to it under the general income tax legislation.[216] In particular, unexpected losses attributable to a deterioration in the creditworthiness of a debtor should be deductible for the holder only to the extent that loan losses (that is, the excess of the cost of an instrument over all amounts received or receivable) are otherwise deductible as ordinary losses.[217] It is possible to realize this result generally by limiting the automatic deductibility under a base price adjustment to the overaccrual of income in prior taxation years.[218] Any remaining amount should be subject to the deductibility tests that apply to other expenses of the same kind.

It was noted above that a base price adjustment should be required where a liability is extinguished or a debt instrument is assigned. Application of this realization requirement presents some difficult definitional and measurement issues in the case of debt defeasances.[219] In general, a "debt defeasance" is any "arrangement whereby one party pays another money in return for the promise to repay over time the obligations of the first party under a particular agreement."[220] This result can be effected by either a "legal defeasance" or an "in-substance defeasance."[221] The former involves any arrangement that, as a matter of private law, results in a release of the debtor from all obligations owed to the creditor. In short, the debtor ("the defeasor") transfers all rights and obligations under a debt instrument ("the primary obligation") and has no remaining interest in the instrument. Under an in-substance defeasance, the debtor transfers the risk associated with a particular instrument but remains liable to the creditor as a matter of private law for the satisfaction of all payment and other obligations. An in-substance defeasance is commonly arranged by paying a third party ("the defeasance counterparty") an amount to assume the obligations of the defeasor under the primary obligation. Alternatively, the defeasor can set aside sufficient risk-free assets to satisfy the payment obligations under the particular debt instrument. In either case, arrangements are made to satisfy the cash flow requirements under the primary obligation, but the defeasor remains liable for the satisfaction of those requirements if the arrangements result in a shortfall.

If a defeasance is characterized as an extinguishment of the relevant instrument, a base price adjustment must be made by the defeasor and unexpected gain or loss must be brought to account.[222] This amount is essentially the difference between all amounts paid by the defeasor to either the creditor or a defeasance counterparty and the amounts received under the defeased debt instrument.[223] The defeasance counterparty should accrue as expense the difference between the amount received from the defeasor and the amount of all future payment obligations to the creditor.[224] If a defeasance is not characterized as an extinguishment of the relevant instrument, the defeasor need not perform a base price adjustment and should continue to accrue amounts under the instrument.[225] Unexpected gain or loss should not be recognized by applying a base price adjustment until the debt instrument is redeemed or settled. In effect, the defeasance creates a separate financial instrument that is equivalent to a loan between the defeasor and the defeasance counterparty.[226] The defeasance counterparty receives consideration from the defeasor in return for an agreement to pay amounts indemnifying the defeasor in respect of the primary obligation owed to the creditor. The difference between the consideration received and the payment obligations should be accrued as expense of the defeasance counterparty, and a base price adjustment should be performed only when the defeasance arrangement is closed out. The defeasor accrues income on the effective loan to the defeasance counterparty, which is offset by expense accrued on the primary obligation. Whether or not a defeasance is treated as an extinguishment, the creditor should be treated as the continuing party to the primary obligation, and a base price adjustment should be required only when that obligation is ultimately released in favour of the defeasor (in the case of an in-substance defeasance) or the defeasance counterparty (in the case of a legal defeasance).[227]

The definitional problem presented by a debt defeasance is the determination of the point at which the arrangement should be considered to have given rise to an extinguishment or realization event that necessitates a base price adjustment. This problem is no different in principle from the problem of developing a concept of a "disposition" as a realization event generally, which is discussed in more detail in chapter 7.[228] The difficulty with an in-substance defeasance is the absence of any obvious point at which it is possible to say that the degree of risk reduction is sufficient to support its characterization as an extinguishment.[229] In the absence of an appropriate bright line that minimizes discontinuities in tax treatment,[230] a reliance on legal form is a defensible alternative that provides an element of certainty in the application of the realization requirement and a base price adjustment.[231] Even if a clear bright line of this kind is chosen, however, a related measurement problem arises when only a portion of a debt instrument is legally defeased. In theory, the legal defeasance of some of the payment obligations under a debt instrument should be treated as a partial disposition of the instrument that requires a partial base price adjustment.[232] This approach necessitates the division of an instrument into two parts: the defeased portion and the remaining portion. Unexpected gain or loss associated with the former portion should be recognized only after the acquisition price has been allocated.[233] It is possible to avoid the administrative and compliance difficulties associated with the application of a partial base price adjustment by treating all legal defeasances as dispositions of the whole of an instrument, requiring a full base price adjustment.[234] The result is the application of a mark-to-market requirement for the portion of an instrument that is not defeased.[235] If unexpected gain or loss on a particular instrument is subject generally to realization-based recognition, this result is indefensible in terms of income measurement principles and can only be justified as a means of avoiding the administrative and compliance burden imposed by the more theoretically appropriate requirement of a partial base price adjustment.[236]

The Special Case of Periodic Swap Payments

Under some income tax systems, the application of realization-based recognition to unexpected gains and losses is modified significantly in the case of periodic payments under interest-rate swaps and certain other swaps. Chapter 1 noted that a swap is the equivalent of a series of cash-settled forward contracts.[237] For example, under a standard fixed-for-floating interest-rate swap, the fixed-rate payer effectively agrees to purchase a series of loans with terms defined by the payment intervals. The purchases are set for each payment date at a price equal to the fixed interest rate multiplied by the notional principal amount. The floating-rate payer effectively agrees to sell a series of loans for the same defined terms at the same price. Because the obligations of the counterparties are netted on the payment dates, the fixed-rate payer is entitled to any excess of the floating rate over the fixed rate multiplied by the notional principal, and must pay any excess of the fixed rate over the floating rate. The fixed-rate payer can achieve exactly the same result by entering into a series of cash-settled forward contracts to purchase a series of term loans on the defined payment dates at a price equal to the fixed rate.[238] On each settlement date, unexpected gain or loss arises that is based on the difference between the specified fixed rate and the prevailing floating rate for loans with a term equal to the period between payment dates. Similarly, the floating-rate payer can realize the same exposure as he would realize under a swap by entering into a series of cash-settled forward contracts to sell the same loans at the fixed-rate price. Unexpected loss or gain arises that is equal to the difference between the floating and fixed rates on the settlement dates. This functional equivalence of a swap and a series of cash-settled forwards is not unique to interest-rate swaps and holds wherever a swap provides for the settlement of periodic payments on a net basis.

Consistent tax treatment of equivalent cash flows requires the extension of the basic accounting method for cash-settled forwards to interest-based swaps and other swaps.[239] To be specific, as a series of cash-settled forwards, swaps should be subject to the realization-based recognition of unexpected gain or loss represented by the net payment that becomes receivable or payable on the payment dates. An alternative accounting method that is reflected in the income tax legislation[240] or the administrative practice in some countries[241] rejects this simple approach in favour of a characterization of the two sides (or "legs") of a swap as offsetting loans.[242] On the premise that periodic payments arise in connection with these loans, one can apply accrual accounting methods instead of the realization-based recognition of net swap payments. This approach for swaps that involve an exchange of interest payments is required, for example, under the New Zealand accrual regime.[243] The New Zealand regime treats the legs of the swap as simultaneous loans and applies the "normal" accrual rules separately to each leg, ignoring any netting of the periodic payments. In other words, it assumes the obligations under a deemed fixed-payment loan to be payable in full on the specified dates and subjects them to accrual recognition on the basis of a YTM calculation. The New Zealand regime applies the same assumption to the periodic payments under a deemed variable-rate loan, which it subjects to the specialized accrual rules that it normally applies to the cash flows associated with those instruments.[244]

The apparent rationale for this characterization and the resultant tax-accounting treatment under the New Zealand legislation is the presumed desirability of matching the recognition of swap receipts or payments with the recognition of expense or income associated with an underlying swapped position (that is, a borrowing or loan). The net result is the recognition of expense or income that would otherwise be associated with the underlying position represented by the other leg of the swap.[245] For example, an assumption of offsetting notional loans under a fixed-for-floating interest-rate swap requires the fixed-rate payer to account for the fixed-rate periodic payments as if they were expenses associated with a separate borrowing. Floating-rate periodic payments are accounted for as if they were income associated with a separate loan. To the extent that these floating-rate income amounts are matched with expenses of the fixed-rate payer on an underlying floating-rate loan, the net effect is an accounting for expenses on a fixed-rate loan on the basis of the relevant accrual methodology. The opposite result follows for the floating-rate payer.[246]

As was described in chapter 2,[247] this rationale has an intuitive appeal that is the apparent basis for the characterization of periodic swap payments on interest-based swaps as ordinary-income amounts subject to full inclusion or deduction. This treatment provides a "matched" result in the sense that the amounts of the swap payments are accounted for on the same basis (income or capital account) as the amounts of the interest obligations on an underlying loan.[248] The matching approach under the New Zealand legislation simply extends the consequences of a characterization of interest-based swaps as offsetting notional loans to the timing rules that govern the recognition of the periodic payments.

Despite any intuitive appeal it may have, the presumed desirability of matching periodic swap payments with an underlying swapped position is a questionable basis for the application of accrual accounting methods to each leg of a swap. Any accounting method that deviates from a characterization of these price-fixing instruments as a series of forward contracts giving rise to unexpected amounts is simply an example of hedge accounting, whereby the tax treatment of the cash flows associated with a particular instrument are determined with reference to another position. As chapter 7 will argue,[249] the case for the application of a hedge-accounting regime to financial instruments generally is tenuous in the context of an income tax system that requires taxpayers to account separately for the cash flows associated with particular financial instruments. Outside of the context of tax avoidance, there is no compelling policy justification for the reconstruction of certain financial instruments within a taxpayer's portfolio as a subportfolio, which is then taxed as an integrated whole. Nor is there anything unique about periodic swap payments to justify integrated treatment in their case in the absence of a general regime of integration applicable to any financial instrument that qualifies as a hedge. Indeed, there is no functional difference between a series of forward contracts that is entered into as a hedge of a borrowing or loan and a swap that provides the equivalent of a series of forwards.[250] Moreover, even if there is something unique about certain swaps that justifies their treatment as offsetting loans, this justification does not apply to swaps generally. At best, it applies only to interest-based swaps and only when the periodic payments on each leg of the swap would otherwise be subject to different accrual accounting methods for expected gains and losses.[251] Commodity, currency, and equity swaps all provide unexpected gains and losses that tend to be offset by unexpected losses or gains on an underlying position. This being the case, there is no compelling reason to alter the realization-based recognition of periodic swap payments in order to achieve a degree of matching with the accrual recognition of expected gains or losses associated with an underlying position.[252] The equivalent application of the realization basis provides offsetting recognition that is generally acceptable in the case of unexpected amounts on instruments other than swaps.

In the context of a comprehensive accrual regime that requires the separate accounting of cash flows associated with particular financial instruments, it is possible to support deviation from the realization-based recognition of periodic swap payments only as a very rough response to the unique tax-avoidance opportunity that these cash flows present. This anti-avoidance justification, however, does not require the application of the accrual methods otherwise specified for the notional loans associated with each leg of an interest-based swap. It is possible, instead, to use a generic formulaic approach to spread the periodic payments over the term of a swap.[253] In this connection, it is important to recall that the discussion to this point has assumed that forwards do not involve an advance of funds on issue. In this case, the instruments are said to be "on market" and are not prepaid. If a forward is "off market," the terms of the specified bet are unfair, since they establish a probability of resolution in favour of one counterparty. The bet has an expected value for the counterparty who benefits from its terms, and an advance of funds must be made to even up the bet.[254] The amount of the advance is essentially the present value of the difference between the price of a fair bet and the price specified under the particular forward. A forward may involve an advance of funds in other circumstances as well: under a "prepaid forward," one of the counterparties prepays one side of the bet in an amount equal to the present value of the expected amount of the specified obligation (that is, the forward price that the counterparty would be obliged to pay on settlement). As chapter 6 will discuss in more detail[255] the advance of funds under either an off-market forward or a prepaid forward presents tax-avoidance opportunities under a conventional income tax regime. These opportunities arise because it is possible

- to disguise a loan as a prepayment with an expected return equal to the difference between the amount of the payment and either (1) the difference between the price of a fair bet and the specified bet (off-market forward) or (2) the expected amount of the specified obligation (prepaid forward) and
- to accelerate the recognition of income and expense.[256]

The ideal solution here, as chapter 6 will argue,[257] is to characterize prepayments as disguised loans that are subject to accrual recognition of the expected gain or loss.[258] An alternative remedy is to defer recognition of the accelerated payments until settlement of the relevant forward. Either remedy is reasonably easy to apply if the prepayment is made under a single forward contract. If a series of forward contracts is packaged in a swap, accurate accounting of any prepayment as an embedded debt instrument requires allocation of the payment among the individual bets.[259] This allocation may be difficult, especially if the prepayments are disguised in a series of off-market bets in which underpayments or overpayments by one of the counterparties in the earlier periods of the swap are offset by overpayments or underpayments in the later periods.[260] In this case, all of the individual forwards in a series under the swap are priced off market; yet the package as a whole is on market, which means that neither counterparty is required to advance funds before the specified dates for the periodic payments.[261] The off-market pricing of forwards without explicit prepayments is most common in the case of fixed-for-floating-rate interest swaps. In this case, the failure to account for the term structure of interest rates in the context of an upward-sloping yield curve means that the fixed-rate payer effectively agrees to overpay for floating payments in the earlier periods of the swap in return for underpayments in later periods.[262]

Loan treatment of the off-market forwards in a swap requires the application of pricing models to allocate disguised prepayments to particular forwards. The allocation is necessary as the basis for the imputation of income and expense on notional principal amounts that are effectively repaid on settlement of the relevant forwards.[263] Alternatively, it is possible to use pricing models to reconstruct a swap as a series of on-market forwards, and then to reallocate any overpayments and underpayments to the appropriate contracts for recognition on their settlement.[264] Obviously, either approach imposes a considerable administrative and compliance burden.[265] This burden is no different in kind from the burden associated with the appropriate treatment of explicit prepayments. In either instance, one must use pricing models to allocate the prepayments among a series of off-market forwards. Nonetheless, explicit prepayments may be seen as indicative of a tax-avoidance purpose that warrants the administrative and compliance costs associated with loan treatment or deferred recognition.

Disguised prepayments, on the other hand, may arise innocently, as the consequence of a failure to account for the term structure of interest rates generally with either interest-based swaps or fixed-payment debt instruments.[266] Tax-policy makers can respond to disguised prepayments in any one of four ways. The first is to do nothing and permit the realization-based recognition of all periodic swap payments, even though some portion of the payment is an implicit prepayment attributable to a series of off-market forwards. The obvious problem with this approach is that it permits the use of disguised prepayments in a series of off-market forwards. This permissive approach is especially difficult to justify if specific rules have been adopted to address the problems associated with explicit prepayments. If there is no legislative response to disguised prepayments, taxpayers will be able to use them to circumvent these rules. The second possible response to disguised prepayments is to characterize all implicit prepayments associated with a series of off-market forwards as embedded loans subject to accrual treatment or deferred recognition. Since this approach would involve the complex allocative problems noted above, and the associated administrative and compliance burden, it is probably unrealistic. The third possible response, like the first, permits the realization-based recognition of all periodic swap payments but supplements this approach with an anti-avoidance rule targeted at swaps that use a series of off-market forwards to disguise prepayments.[267] As in the case of explicit prepayments, the presence of an apparent tax-avoidance purpose may justify the administrative and compliance burden associated with the identification of implicit prepayments and the adoption of pricing models in order to allocate the payments among the bets in a series of forwards. The problem with this response is that it requires the identification of a tax-avoidance purpose, a task that would inevitably involve some uncertainty in the application of the legislative response and in the related search for proxies that would indicate the presence of an avoidance purpose. Indeed, in the absence of an explicit prepayment, it is difficult to identify any particular proxy that would indicate a tax-avoidance motive. The fourth possible response is a more general one. It involves the formulaic spreading of all periodic swap payments, whether or not they give rise to disguised prepayments.

The formulaic spreading of periodic swap payments is reflected in the US regulations governing notional principal contracts (NPCs).[268] Like the New Zealand legislation, the US NPC regulations reject a characterization of swaps as a series of cash-settled forwards. This rejection extends, however, beyond interest-based swaps and applies to any swap with periodic payments. Instead of a specific accrual method that would otherwise apply to a notional loan, the NPC regulations apply a much simpler formulaic method to all periodic payments, which must be spread on a straightline basis over the number of days in the period between payment intervals.[269] Counterparties must recognize as income or expense the daily ratable portion of periodic payments in the taxation year to which the portion relates, and these amounts must be netted against all other swap payments (including non-periodic and termination payments that must be recognized in the same taxation year).[270] If a variable payment is set in arrears, the amount of the daily ratable portion related to a taxation year must be determined as if the index were set on the last day of the taxation year.[271] In the following year, when the index is set on the payment date, the counterparties must account for any difference between the actual amount allocable to the previous year on a daily ratable basis and the amount that was recognized on the basis of the prevailing index at year-end.[272] The difference is recognized as income or expense in the year in which the periodic payment becomes payable.

For the purposes of the NPC regulations, "periodic payments" are defined as "payments made or received pursuant to a notional principal contract that are payable at intervals of one year or less during the term of the contract."[273] The payments must also be based on a specified index and a single notional principal amount (or an amount that varies in the same proportion for each counterparty). This focus on all swaps with periodic payments, and not just interest-based swaps, is inconsistent with a deviation from realization-based recognition on the basis of some vague attempt to match swap payments with an underlying borrowing or loan. Indeed, application of a generic formula for the spreading of swap payments achieves an appropriate matching only if the underlying borrowing or loan is subject to the same formula.[274] Both of these aspects of the NPC regulations indicate an apparent focus (at least in part) on implicit prepayments associated with a series of off-market forwards in a swap. Although it is far from being an ideal approach,[275] formulaic spreading is an administratively simple mechanism for evening out the recognition of disguised prepayments.[276] It reduces, in a very rough manner, taxpayers' ability to manipulate the recognition of the income or expense associated with the embedding of a series of disguised prepayments for off-market forwards in the periodic payments.[277] The reduction occurs largely as a result of the spreading of periodic payments on a formulaic basis over the relevant payment intervals, which means that the particular amounts are allocated over two or more taxation years that happen to straddle the period between payment dates.[278] As will be discussed in chapter 6,[279] this approach to periodic swap payments complements rules in the US NPC regulations that govern explicit prepayments (referred to in the NPC regulations as "non-periodic payments"). The NPC regulations assume that the tax-avoidance opportunities afforded by explicit prepayments are more serious than those afforded by periodic swap payments, and they treat a swap as a combination of an embedded loan that is attributable to the prepayment and a series of on-market forwards. If the amount of a given prepayment is considered to be "significant," the associated tax-avoidance opportunities are addressed directly through treatment of the relevant amount as an embedded loan. If the amount is considered to be insignificant, deferred recognition applies. Unlike the treatment of periodic swap payments, the deferred recognition is based on an allocation of the prepayment to the particular off-market forwards that constitute the swap.

Accretion Taxation as a First-Best Response to Selective Realization

Selective Realization and the Limits of Loss Limitations

As was argued above, a comprehensive accrual regime designed to implement the core elements of expected return taxation requires the accrual recognition of expected amounts. Unexpected amounts, which do not present the avoidance opportunities that accrual recognition addresses, may be recognized on a realization basis. This basis, however, allows taxpayers to strategically trade financial instruments in order to realize unexpected losses selectively while deferring unexpected gains. A comprehensive accrual regime can respond to this tax-avoidance opportunity by incorporating one or both of two features:[280]

1) accretion recognition of all gains and losses on traded instruments and
2) limitations on the deductibility of unexpected losses on non-traded instruments.

Accretion taxation can serve a very specific (and limited) role as the first-best response to the selective realization of unexpected losses. In other words, accretion taxation is the most effective response to the problem of selective realization under a comprehensive accrual regime that is implemented in the broader context of a realization-based income tax. Chapter 3 described the relatively straightforward argument in support of this role for accretion taxation.[281] A brief review of that argument is sufficient here.

The realization requirement allows taxpayers to maximize the effective tax rate on unexpected losses by recognizing them as soon as possible; at the same time, taxpayers can reduce the effective tax rate on unexpected gains by deferring their recognition. "Straddle transactions" are the extreme case of pure tax avoidance intended to take advantage of the realization requirement through selective realization of unexpected gains and losses. In a straddle transaction, a taxpayer assumes offsetting short and long positions[282] in a particular asset, which therefore produces no net gain or loss; nevertheless, because of the accelerated recognition of the accrued loss, which maximizes the tax rate at which the loss is deducted, the transaction is profitable after tax.[283] The benefit of selective realization is not limited, however, to straddles. Even in the absence of offsetting positions, the opportunity to realize unexpected losses and defer the recognition of unexpected gains lowers the effective tax rate on instruments that have a bet element and therefore provide these amounts. Indeed, in the case of a straddle transaction, the opportunity to maximize the effective tax rate on unexpected losses while lowering the rate on unexpected gains has a value that is locked in ex ante.

Selective realization has a positive value for taxpayers provided that the income tax system permits the offset of realized losses against other income even when there may be unrealized offsetting gains. An obvious response is to eliminate this positive value by reducing the effective tax rate on unexpected losses.[284] One can achieve this result by restricting the deductibility of unexpected losses to the extent that they are offset by unrealized gains on offsetting positions.[285] Even if one can identify offsetting positions, however, the effectiveness of this response is limited to the selective realization of unexpected losses in the context of straddle transactions;[286] it fails to address the tax benefit that arises when there are no offsetting gains. The alternative is an extended loss limitation that restricts the deductibility of unexpected losses on all financial instruments to the amount of any gains on other instruments. This type of limitation takes account of the whole of a taxpayer's portfolio for loss-limitation purposes and effectively treats every position as offsetting. Although this response does eliminate the benefit of selective realization, by lowering the effective tax rate on all unexpected losses, it may generate inefficiencies by increasing the variance of after-tax returns associated with risky financial instruments.[287]

The alternative to either type of loss limitation is abandonment of the realization requirement in favour of accretion taxation.[288] Under this approach, a taxpayer who assumes a position in a risky financial instrument knows that unexpected gains and losses must be recognized as the passage of time reveals changes in the value of the position. Since the effective tax rates on unexpected gains and losses are equal to the nominal tax rate, the expected pre-tax values are undisturbed. Accretion taxation thus eliminates the benefit of selective realization in all instances without discouraging risk taking. This point is especially important if one is designing a comprehensive accrual regime that eliminates the distinction between income and capital amounts. Many income tax systems that include a realization-based capital gains tax restrict the deduction of capital losses to the amount of realized capital gains. Given a comprehensive accrual regime that eliminates the concept of capital gains and losses, an explicit response to selective realization is necessary. If accretion taxation is that response, the principal implementation issue is to ensure that the recognition method addresses the instruments that are most susceptible to strategic trading.[289]

Targeting the Application of Accretion Taxation

The value of the tax benefit from selective realization tends to be greatest in the case of assets and liabilities that[290] (1) provide a relatively high variance in possible payoffs, (2) are held or issued for a relatively long period, and (3) can be traded at low transaction costs. The first attribute is associated with risky assets and liabilities. Since the deviations in value revealed by the passage of time increase with the riskiness of the instrument, taxpayers who hold risky assets or liabilities have a greater ability than other taxpayers have to accelerate the recognition of unexpected losses and defer unexpected gains. This ability is enhanced if the asset or liability is held or issued for a long period, since the taxpayer's control over its trading, and therefore his opportunity to take advantage of a variance in returns, increases with the length of the period. Transaction costs reduce the tax benefit provided by selective realization. The lower the costs of finding purchasers and sellers, therefore, the greater the tax benefit. Not surprisingly, therefore, the tax literature[291] identifies the riskiness of an instrument (variance of returns), its term to maturity (length of holding or issue), and its liquidity (ability to trade at low transaction costs) as important conditions that facilitate strategic trading.

In order to ensure that accretion recognition addresses instruments with these three general characteristics, it is necessary to identify a point at which the riskiness of an instrument, its term, or its transaction costs make it susceptible to strategic trading and therefore an appropriate candidate for accretion recognition rather than realization-based recognition of the unexpected gains and losses that it provides.[292] In the case of the riskiness and term of an instrument, the identification of this point is highly problematic. For all practical purposes, in fact, these two characteristics should be disregarded. Differences in the risk or the term of an instrument are differences in degree only; consequently, it is difficult to define, on any defensible basis, a particular level at which either characteristic can justify the application of accretion taxation. Between the extremes of a riskless government debt instrument and the pure bets provided by forwards, futures, and swaps, there is an infinite range of instruments (including risky debt, derivatives, and shares)[293] that provide subtle differences in risk. Any attempt to define the appropriate level of risk in terms of a bright line is arbitrary and creates discontinuities in which a small change in risk can place an instrument either within or beyond accretion taxation. Similarly, the term of an instrument is a relative concept and therefore fails to provide any definitive point at which selective realization becomes sufficiently problematic to merit the application of accretion taxation. It is true that longer-term instruments provide taxpayers with greater control over the realization of gains and losses, and therefore greater opportunities for strategic trading, than do shorter-term instruments. Nevertheless, it is possible to defer unrealized gains on shorter-term instruments from one year to the next,[294] and there is no obvious reason why any particular bright line should indicate the point at which this possibility can be ignored. Indeed, as in the case of risk, any bright-line distinction between short-term and long-term instruments creates problematic discontinuities in tax treatment. One alternative to the use of a bright-line test based on the risk and term of an instrument is a vague factors approach that attempts to weigh these characteristics in the context of particular instruments without imposing the constraint of a specified boundary line between accretion taxation and realization-based recognition. This approach does avoid sharp discontinuities in tax treatment, but only at the cost of considerable uncertainty for taxpayers and tax administrators.[295]

A potentially more satisfactory approach to the definition of a boundary line between accretion recognition and realization-based recognition involves the outright rejection of the riskiness of an instrument and its term as factors that indicate opportunities for strategic trading. This approach, in effect, assumes that strategic trading occurs with all financial instruments that provide any degree of risk, irrespective of their term, and instead uses the ability to trade an instrument at low transaction costs as the determinative factor. It is possible, moreover, to reduce this factor to liquidity; that is, to require accretion recognition of unexpected gains and losses only in the case of instruments that are relatively liquid. The important difference between using liquidity as the determinative factor and using the riskiness of an instrument or its term is simply the availability in the former case of proxies that are closely related to the policy significance of the factor. In other words, it is possible to define proxies that indicate a threshold beyond which the transaction costs associated with the trading of an instrument increase significantly. Since significant differences in tax treatment are supported by significant jumps in the level of transaction costs, a bright-line distinction between instruments that are traded at relatively high transaction costs and instruments that are traded at relatively low transaction costs may not involve sharp discontinuities. If the market for a particular instrument is deep and liquid, it is easy to find potential purchasers, and the cost of effecting trading strategies intended to take advantage of the selective realization of unexpected losses is minimal. If the market is not liquid, transaction costs tend to be significant and serve as a barrier to the implementation of strategic trading.

Existing legislative regimes do not generally rely on accretion taxation as the principal response to selective realization; nor do they reflect a well-targeted approach in which liquidity serves as a proxy for instruments that can be traded strategically. For tax-policy makers, the principal concern must be the possibility that any accretion response to selective realization will be underinclusive, and that in the absence of a general capital loss limitation, or some other, comparable limitation applicable to gains and losses on financial instruments, significant opportunities for strategic trading will remain. The possible underinclusiveness of an accretion response is obviously less of a problem if it is the result of a conscious policy choice to limit accretion taxation to a narrow range of highly liquid instruments and otherwise rely on loss limitations to address the problem of strategic trading. An apparent example of this approach is the US legislation that requires taxpayers, other than traders and dealers, to apply mark-to-market reporting of gain or loss on[296] (1) exchange-traded futures contracts, (2) foreign currency contracts traded in an interbank market, and (3) exchange-traded ("listed") options other than an option on shares or a share index ("non-equity options"). This narrow application of an accretion approach leaves a broad range of instruments, including traded debt, shares, and most unlisted derivatives, open to strategic trading by taxpayers who are not traders or dealers. In the case of these taxpayers, the US legislation relies on (1) characterization of realized losses as capital amounts subject to a limitation on the deduction of such amounts generally[297] and (2) a specific loss-limitation regime applicable to straddles.[298]

Although it is far from being the best possible response to selective realization, the US legislation does at least reflect a conscious attempt to address the problem by supplementing loss limitations with a limited application of accretion taxation. In contrast, both the New Zealand accrual regime and, to a lesser extent, the Australian proposals fail to link the application of accretion taxation to the problem of selective realization. The relevant New Zealand legislation establishes a hierarchy of tax-accounting methods, in which the YTM method is the principal method for expected gains and losses.[299] Where the taxpayer cannot use that method because it is not possible to determine expected cash flows, he must either follow a determination or adopt an alternative method that conforms with financial-accounting practice.[300] In the case of taxpayers other than traders and dealers, accretion taxation (which the legislation refers to as "market valuation") is generally limited to traded futures and forward contracts for foreign exchange.[301] The only apparent rationale for this limitation is a perception that the accretion ideal is "the best comprehensive measure of income,"[302] and that the valuation problems usually invoked as a reason for not applying it disappear when there is "an active secondary market for an instrument."[303] The Australian accrual proposals apply accretion taxation to traded debt and shares, and to any derivative that is not acquired for hedging purposes.[304] This application appears to reflect a concern with selective realization, which is assumed to be most problematic in the case of debt instruments and shares that are acquired for a trading purpose. Derivatives are effectively considered to be acquired for a trading purpose if they are not acquired as a hedge of another financial instrument or a non-financial asset. The proposals do not, however, provide any explicit statement of this role for accretion taxation, and its application under the Australian proposals to traded instruments is equally consistent with an intention to approximate the accretion ideal wherever liquidity and valuation considerations are not a problem. It is possible to regard evidence of a trading purpose as a rough proxy for the absence of these conventional constraints on the application of accretion taxation generally.

Other than the creation of a somewhat confused legislative regime that may entail some administrative and compliance costs, the consequences of a failure to articulate a role for accretion taxation as a response to selective realization are not entirely clear.[305] The problem of selective realization is potentially greater if the recognition of losses on financial instruments is not subject to any limitations, but there is no clear concept in either the New Zealand legislation or the Australian proposals of accretion taxation as a response to the problem. In the absence of any clear articulation of a role of this kind for accretion taxation, its effectiveness will be entirely accidental. In other words, if there is no attempt to target accretion taxation to the instruments that provide the benefit of strategic trading, any application of that recognition method to these instruments arises fortuitously. Even so, there is no necessary reason why the range of avoidance opportunities through strategic trading should be greater than it would be if the application were deliberate. Indeed, whether accretion taxation is a response to selective realization or an attempt to apply the accretion ideal as the first-best measure of income, its application should have much the same effect. In either case, market liquidity is a functional test that indicates the appropriateness of the application of accretion taxation to particular instruments. Where accretion taxation is justified as a response to selective realization, market liquidity is an appropriate indication of low transaction costs, which allow taxpayers to trade instruments strategically. Where the accretion ideal is seen as the best measure of income, which cannot be implemented because it requires annual valuations, liquidity implies the availability of frequent price quotations, which make valuation of the relevant instruments easy.[306] In practice, however, there is an important difference between the two rationales that may produce different results. Tax-policy makers who see accretion taxation as an ideal measure of income generally may be reluctant to push the ideal too far, given the taxpayer liquidity problems caused by the requirement to pay tax in the absence of a realization event. This reluctance may be less apparent if accretion taxation is justified instead as an anti-avoidance measure that responds to opportunities for strategic trading. Whether this attitudinal perspective has any practical significance is difficult to determine.[307]

The New Zealand accrual regime is clearly underinclusive in its limitation of accretion taxation to forward contracts on foreign currency and futures contracts generally. Again, debt, shares, and other derivatives all provide opportunities for strategic trading, particularly if they are traded on an exchange or certain over-the-counter (OTC) markets. The application of accretion taxation to traded instruments is much broader under the Australian accrual proposals than it is under the New Zealand legislation, but the Australian approach fails to provide a functional test for the identification of instruments that present opportunities to trade strategically. It defines a traded derivative as a derivative that the holder does not designate as an instrument acquired for a hedging purpose. The effect of this purpose-based definition is to make the application of accretion taxation to derivatives elective. The Australian proposals classify debt and shares as either traded or non-traded instruments on the basis of a vague factors test that purports to identify a taxpayer's purpose in acquiring a particular instrument.[308] This approach is very similar to the approach that the courts in many Commonwealth countries have developed to distinguish traded assets from assets held on capital account. Thus the Australian proposals suggest that the following factors are indicative of traded debt, though no one of them is determinative:[309]

- The instrument is acquired as part of an ongoing program of buying and selling debt instruments.
- The taxpayer actively quotes two-way prices (that is, bid and offer) in relation to the instrument.
- There is an active secondary market for the instrument, so any profit or loss on the instrument is readily realizable.
- The instrument is classified as a trading instrument for financial-accounting purposes.

The use of a purpose-based test to determine the classification of debt, shares, and derivatives as traded instruments may result in underinclusiveness.[310] A taxpayer's purpose has no necessary relevance to the problem of selective realization. In fact, strategic trading is possible with many instruments that are acquired for an investment or hedging purpose, including debt issued by taxpayers for a capital-raising purpose.[311] A purpose-based test fails to subject instruments of this kind to accretion taxation even though it is possible to trade them at low transaction costs. Moreover, even if a taxpayer's purpose is somehow indicative of the presence or absence of strategic trading, a factors test cannot provide a certain identification or purpose. Instead of searching for some elusive proxy for a trading purpose, tax-policy makers should focus on factors that indicate liquidity as a proxy for low transaction costs. Liquidity (which the Australian accrual proposals identify as only one possible indication of a trading purpose) can be defined very simply in terms of the availability of markets. One can reasonably assume that any taxpayer will engage in selective realization, given the opportunity to do it at low transaction costs, if he holds instruments that are traded in active markets. The criterion of marketability provides an administrable and relatively accurate definition of the range of instruments that should be subject to accretion taxation as a response to strategic trading.

In designating the markets that provide sufficient liquidity to permit strategic trading, tax-policy makers should probably err on the side of inclusiveness. In particular, they should treat instruments that trade in a broad range of OTC markets in the same manner as exchange-traded instruments.[312] Thus the concept of "actively traded," which defines instruments that are potentially subject to the US straddle rules, includes instruments traded on domestic securities exchanges, NASDAQ, boards of trade designated as contract markets by the Commodity Futures Trading Commission (CFTC), certain foreign exchanges, interbank markets, interdealer markets, and a debt market established by broker-dealer price quotations.[313] Admittedly, an extension of accretion taxation to all instruments that are traded in these markets may result in its application even when high transaction costs present barriers to selective realization. From an efficiency perspective, this broad application of accretion taxation may not be especially problematic. It does require the valuation of instruments that are not traded in deep and liquid markets, and hence potentially serious administrative and compliance costs, but it is possible to address this problem by marking the relevant instruments to related markets.[314] The alternative is to limit accretion taxation to exchange-traded instruments, and this limitation would create opportunities to trade instruments strategically in some highly liquid OTC markets.

Exclusions and the Need for Loss Limitations

In addition to definitions of "liquid markets" and "marketable" or "traded" instruments, the use of accretion taxation as a response to selective realization requires the resolution of three secondary issues related to the scope of its application. First, tax-policy makers must decide whether they can defensibly exclude traded shares from the application of accretion taxation. Superficially, the decision is an easy one. Shares are generally riskier than debt and generally provide longer holding periods than either debt or derivatives. Traded shares, therefore, present obvious opportunities for strategic trading, and for consistency's sake accretion taxation should apply to traded debt, derivatives, and shares alike.

Like the application of expected-return taxation to non-traded shares, however, the application of accretion taxation to traded shares is complicated by the conventional use of the corporate income tax as a proxy for a shareholder-level tax on expected and unexpected gains. In fact, as chapter 6 will argue,[315] this use of the corporate income tax is the only defensible policy basis for the exclusion of shares from a comprehensive accrual regime that is designed to implement expected-return taxation. Much the same basis may be cited in support of the exclusion of traded shares from the application of accretion taxation as a response to strategic trading. Provided that the calculation of income at the corporate level accurately measures changes in the value of shares, both expected and unexpected gains are subject to tax as they are realized. Consequently, shareholders cannot selectively realize unexpected losses while deferring the recognition of unrealized gains if the latter are subject to a corporate-level income tax that does, in fact, serve as a withholding tax on shareholder gains.[316] The problem is that if a corporate income tax is to serve as a withholding tax it must rely on income measurement rules as a proxy for share gains; yet the availability of tax preferences and other problems associated with basic income measurement rules means that the calculation of corporate income invariably deviates from economic income measured as the change in share value. If the income measurement rules understate unrealized gains, shareholders will be able to trade shares strategically and thereby accelerate the recognition of unexpected losses while deferring the realization of unexpected gains until a disposition of the shares or a distribution as a dividend. Moreover, if tax-policy makers do not regard the corporate income tax as a proxy for the shareholder-level tax on share gains, the above argument for the exclusion of shares from accretion taxation does not hold, even if the income-calculation rules are a relatively accurate measure of economic income.

The principal objection to the extension of accretion taxation to traded shares is that it might have serious efficiency effects.[317] If shares are treated in the same way as any other financial instrument that is subject to a comprehensive accrual regime, the application of accretion taxation to a limited range of traded shares simply accelerates the recognition of unexpected gains and can be justified as a necessary response to strategic trading. Where a separate tax is imposed on corporate income, however, an element of double taxation arises because of a failure to integrate the corporate and shareholder-level taxes when retained earnings are reflected in the value of shares realized on a disposition in the secondary market. In other words, the limitation of imputation regimes to dividend distributions gives rise to an element of double taxation similar to the double taxation under classical corporate income tax systems. This double taxation occurs under the realization-based recognition of share gains and is only accelerated by the application of accretion taxation, which deems shares to be disposed of and reacquired at year-end for their fair market value.

In fact, however, the efficiency losses associated with this element of double taxation may not be very large. For one thing, by providing a credit for corporate income tax paid, imputation systems do provide integrated treatment of dividend distributions, which reduces the double taxation of the distributed income. If the distributed income has previously been taxed as a gain realized on a disposition of the relevant shares, a corresponding loss attributable to the dividend distribution will arise. If recognition of the loss is permitted, the amount effectively offsets the prior gain. This offset is far from complete (it arises in different taxation years, which means that taxpayers lose the time value of the tax on the prior gain and the loss may be recognized at different rates and by different taxpayers), but it reduces the incidence of double taxation to some extent.

What is perhaps more important, any double taxation that does arise because of the failure to integrate corporate and shareholder-level income taxes may not in fact be a significant source of efficiency losses. In discussing the classical corporate tax in the United States, Rudnick has argued that investors may place a premium on the liquidity provided by publicly traded shares.[318] If this is true, then optimal tax analysis may support the imposition of a higher tax burden on equity income derived from publicly traded shares than on other income.[319] In other words, since demand for traded shares may be relatively inelastic, it may be possible to subject them to higher levels of tax without affecting the allocation of capital. From an efficiency perspective, therefore, it may not matter that the application of accretion taxation to traded shares increases the double tax burden by accelerating the recognition of unexpected gains subject to tax.[320] Nonetheless, the absence of any empirical or theoretical work that attempts to model the validity of this proposition leaves tax-policy makers with a difficult judgment to make about the importance of potential revenue loss from the strategic trading of traded shares in relation to the possibility of efficiency losses from the application of accretion taxation as a first-best response. In this connection, one of the more interesting aspects of the Australian accrual proposals is their extension of accretion taxation to all traded shares, which may indicate a rejection of the case for exclusion and an acceptance of the proposition that it is necessary to apply accretion taxation at the shareholder level as a response to selective realization.

The second issue that policy makers must resolve is whether they can defensibly exclude some exchange-traded and OTC derivatives from the application of accretion taxation. A broad definition of exchange-traded and OTC instruments means that, for all practical purposes, derivatives are subject to accretion taxation. The Australian accrual proposals, which extend market-value accounting to all derivatives other than those that are acquired for hedging purposes, reflect this approach.[321] As was noted above, the extension of accretion taxation to derivatives creates obvious valuation problems and makes it necessary to mark a wide range of OTC derivatives to related markets. The associated administrative and compliance burden can be justified only by reference to the opportunities for strategic trading that would arise if accretion taxation were limited to exchange-traded futures and options. Acceptance of this justification, however, makes it essential to follow the Australian proposals in providing for the exception of derivatives that are acquired for hedging purposes.[322] The absence of a separate regime for derivatives acquired to hedge non-traded debt, shares, and non-financial assets would create obvious mismatches in the recognition of gains and losses, since the derivatives acquired for hedging purposes would be subject to accretion taxation and the hedged assets or liabilities would be subject to realization-based recognition of unexpected amounts. The difficulty for policy makers is to develop an approach that both maintains the broad application of accretion taxation as a response to selective realization and provides an administrable exception for derivatives that are acquired for hedging purposes. One possibility, which will be discussed in more detail in chapter 7,[323] is a minimal rule that would provide for realization-based recognition of unexpected gains and losses associated with qualifying hedges. Otherwise, no effort would be made to match the treatment of gains or losses on a derivative with the treatment of gains or losses on an underlying hedged item. Use of this minimal hedging regime to provide the benefit of selective realization would be prevented by limiting the recognition of realized losses to the maturity date of the relevant instrument. This measure would prevent taxpayers from accelerating the recognition of unexpected losses by designating a derivative as a hedge.

The third issue has to do with the use of loss limitations. To the extent that accretion taxation is not applied to particular instruments, policy makers must decide what role, if any, loss limitations should have in addressing strategic trading. There are three basic alternatives,[324] and the choice between them depends on the relative values that policy makers place on the need to address opportunities for selective realization and the adverse impact on risk taking that may result because restrictions on deductibility increase the after-tax amount of unexpected losses. At one extreme is the alternative of rejecting any restriction on the deductibility of realized losses and accepting the application of accretion taxation as the exclusive response to strategic trading. Provided that a taxpayer has sufficient income from financial instruments or other sources, an absence of any deductibility restrictions is tantamount to a system of loss refundability under which taxpayers receive the full after-tax value of losses. By reducing the after-tax value of both unexpected gains and unexpected losses, a system of this kind would reduce the variance of possible payoffs and the risk associated with risky instruments. This effect would be achieved, however, at the cost of making strategic trading available for instruments that were not subject to accretion taxation.

At the other extreme is the alternative of limiting the deduction of unexpected losses to the amount of any unexpected gains realized on other financial instruments.[325] This alternative would allow taxpayers to offset realized unexpected losses only against realized unexpected gains.[326] Expected amounts would be subject to accrual recognition as a response to timing-arbitrage opportunities available with those amounts. As was noted above, this approach would indeed address selective realization, but by increasing the after-tax amount of realized unexpected losses that were subject to restricted deductibility it would also discourage risk taking. The provision of a loss-carryover period, however, would at least reduce the possibility of the extreme case of unusable losses, in which the after-tax amount of losses were equal to the pre-tax amount.[327]

The third alternative is a compromise between the two extremes. It takes the form of a loss-limitation rule that applies only to straddle transactions, in which the risk associated with one position is offset by the risk associated with an opposite position. In effect, a narrowly applied loss limitation of this kind attempts to ensure that taxpayers cannot engage in the most abusive instances of strategic trading by using offsetting positions in financial instruments that are not subject to accretion taxation.[328] It realizes this result by limiting the deduction of realized loss on one position to the amount of loss, if any, in excess of the unrealized gain on the offsetting position. This approach, which is reflected in the US straddle rules, gives priority to avoiding any adverse impact on risk taking that might arise from the imposition of loss limitations on non-offsetting positions. In particular, the treatment of the offsetting positions in a straddle as a single integrated position means that the transaction is a "wash" if the loss fully offsets the corresponding gain. The net amount recognized for tax purposes is nil, which is the same pre-tax result as the one associated with the two offsetting cash flows. At the same time, the deductibility provision avoids any adverse impact on risk taking by permitting the unrestricted deduction of unexpected losses to the extent that they are not offset by unrealized gains on an offsetting position.[329]

In general, the choice between these three approaches to the recognition of unexpected losses depends on the robustness of the application of accretion taxation.[330] If a wide range of traded instruments are excluded from accretion taxation, a broad rule that limits the deduction of realized unexpected losses to the amount of realized unexpected gains may be necessary to address selective realization effectively, though at the cost of a possible adverse impact on risk taking. If accretion taxation is applied to a wide range of traded instruments, a straddle rule may be sufficient to address the worst instances of selective realization in the case of non-traded instruments. A straddle rule, however, presents enormous administrative and compliance problems, owing to the difficulty of defining offsetting positions[331] and identifying these positions within large taxpayer portfolios.[332] Moreover, where accretion taxation is adopted as the principal response to strategic trading, a loss-limitation rule should apply only to non-traded instruments that are subject to realization-based recognition of unexpected gains and losses. In this context, the application of a straddle limitation, which restricts the deduction of realized losses on one position to the amount of unrealized gains on the other, presents an additional administrative constraint, since it is necessary to value non-traded instruments for the purpose of applying the limitation.[333] A much simpler approach is to treat all financial instruments that are not subject to accretion taxation as a subportfolio made up of offsetting positions.[334] For this notional subportfolio, the principal choices for tax-policy makers are (1) unrestricted deductibility of realized losses and (2) a general limitation that restricts the deduction of realized unexpected losses to the amount of realized unexpected gains.[335]

The Limitations of a Comprehensive Accrual Regime

A comprehensive accrual regime is an imperfect, second-best alternative to the accretion ideal. Even in thoroughly developed accrual regimes, such as the ones reflected in the New Zealand legislation and proposed in Australia, problems arise because of the continued acceptance of different tax treatments for interest and dividends and the continued application of the realization requirement to non-traded shares and other non-traded financial instruments and non-financial assets. Acceptance of these constraints requires the reiteration of familiar boundaries, and also the drawing of some new ones, since differences in tax treatment on each side of these boundaries continue to be significant. As this chapter has suggested, the principal points of pressure under a comprehensive accrual regime occur in the following four areas:

- The fact that debt and derivatives are subject to different tax treatments requires some limited application of the tax technique of bifurcation to hybrid instruments that are (1) debt in form but have an embedded derivative or (2) derivatives in form but have an embedded loan. As several US commentators have pointed out, however, bifurcation is virtually impossible to apply as a general approach to the taxation of financial instruments under an income tax system that treats any of the basic building blocks of financial innovation differently from the others.[336] The almost limitless variety of financial equivalences and the sophistication needed to bifurcate complex financial instruments make bifurcation administratively problematic. In many instances, moreover, the application of different tax treatments to different components of complex financial instruments renders bifurcation inconclusive, since different combinations of the basic components may produce different tax treatments even after bifurcation.
- The distinction for tax purposes between interest and dividends requires a distinction between debt and equity that is exceedingly difficult to make once a purportedly substantive approach is adopted in place of an approach based on an acceptance of legal form. It is interesting, therefore, that the Australian accrual proposals acknowledge the uncertainty associated with a "facts and circumstances test" and its tendency to undermine the stated policy goal of determinacy for all financial instruments. The proposals' suggestion that a regulatory power develop the details of the facts and circumstances test is reminiscent of the United States' singularly unsatisfactory experience with classification regulations in the mid-1980s. After several attempts to develop an appropriate classification framework that would be applicable to financial instruments generally, the US Treasury department and the Internal Revenue Service gave up.[337] A realistic alternative is reliance on the legal form of an instrument as debt or equity for classification purposes. This reliance, however, requires the adoption of some important features of a corporate income tax as substitutes for, and complements of, some features of a comprehensive accrual regime.
- Since accretion taxation must be limited to traded financial instruments that are easily valued, it continues to be possible under a comprehensive accrual regime for taxpayers to create financial equivalences that are advantageous from a tax perspective. For example, taxpayers can create offsetting positions with financial instruments that are subject to accretion taxation and others that are subject to expected-return taxation. Similarly, taxpayers can use financial instruments that are subject to expected-return taxation to replicate other instruments that are subject to accretion taxation. These transactions are advantageous because expected-return

taxation requires the recognition of expected gains and losses on an accrual basis, whereas accretion taxation captures both expected and unexpected gains and losses. Avoidance opportunities may also be available because of rate differences among taxpayers or because an accrual regime excludes instruments held by individuals. The exclusion of non-traded shares is another weakness, one that permits taxpayers to create financial equivalences that substitute taxation of gain or loss at the investor level for taxation of income or loss at the corporate level. These avoidance opportunities can be addressed, to some extent, through specific anti-avoidance provisions that are applicable to transactions that involve synthetic replication. The impossible problem of defining the boundary between the disposition of an asset and its retention is similar in many ways to the definitional problem at the root of the debt-equity distinction and cannot be avoided. Since neither distinction has any basis in principle and both are a matter of differences in degree, boundary-drawing is necessarily an arbitrary exercise.

- A hedge-accounting regime presents serious administrative and compliance problems. Indeed, the application of an integrated tax treatment to two or more financial instruments or to a financial instrument and a non-financial asset has an intuitive appeal that tends to mask the difficult identification issues that arise under an income tax system with different tax rules for different types of instruments and assets. The problem centres on the appropriate identification of integrated positions, and in particular on the development of purpose-based identification criteria that it is possible to administer effectively. Although the Australian accrual proposals have gone a long way in developing "robust" hedging principles, the necessary details remain contentious. In many respects, the comparable identification rules developed by the accounting profession, which are reflected to some extent in the US legislation, are excessively flexible and too subjective to be administrable for income tax purposes. The contrasting approach, reflected in the New Zealand accrual regime, is the rejection of a hedging regime.

Despite these problems, a comprehensive accrual regime has strong claims as the preferable second-best alternative to the accretion ideal. It eliminates much of the tax significance of distinctions among financial instruments and many opportunities to defer anticipated gains. Some ambiguity in the position of the boundary between debt and equity and some anti-avoidance provisions that attempt to address the worst instances of synthetic replication may be justifiable as a means of introducing sufficient legal risk to deter taxpayers from exploiting the remaining tax cubbyholes unduly. Hedging rules represent a limited form of integrated treatment that may be neither necessary nor worth the considerable administrative and compliance burdens that it would entail. All of these issues are addressed in the following two chapters. Chapter 6 explores bifurcation and other approaches to the treatment of hybrid instruments that challenge the traditional boundaries between debt and derivatives and debt and equity. Chapter 7 examines integration as a technique for addressing the tax-driven use of synthetics. It also reviews, and rejects, integration as the basis of a hedging regime. In all of these problematic areas, the desirable approach is the adoption of fundamental reform measures that suppress inconsistencies and discontinuities in tax treatment by extending the underlying principles of a comprehensive accrual regime to hybrid and synthetic instruments.

6

Bifurcation and the Taxation of Hybrid Instruments

Introduction

Chapter 1 drew a distinction between the basic building-block basic financial instruments (fixed-payment debt, forwards, futures, swaps, and options) and the more complex financial instruments that are assembled from these basic instruments in the process of financial innovation. One of the general points emphasized in chapter 1 was that the return on each of the building-block instruments represents expected or unexpected gains and losses. A riskless government debt obligation, for example, provides an expected time-value return that compensates lenders for the use of their funds. Forwards, futures, and swaps, on the other hand, are pure bets that provide unexpected gain or loss determined on the resolution of a specified contingency. The counterparties do not advance any funds at the outset of the contract; each of them assumes an obligation to pay an amount if the specified contingency is not resolved in his favour. Options combine a time-value return and a bet element. In fact, all complex financial instruments, and risky debt and shares as well, are combinations of an expected time-value return and a bet element whose cash flows reflect various combinations of expected and unexpected gains and losses. Thus the fundamental tax-policy issues presented by complex instruments are identical to the issues presented by the basic building-block instruments. In each case, these issues concern the critical distinction between expected and unexpected gains and losses, a distinction that each of the preceding five chapters has emphasized in its turn.

This chapter considers the problems created by "hybrid" financial instruments, or instruments that combine an expected time-value return attributable to the advance of funds and unexpected gain or loss attributable to a bet element.[1] These instruments can take the form of a debt obligation, a derivative, or a share; their hybrid nature means that they straddle the boundaries between the conventional tax cubbyholes for (1) debt and derivatives and (2) debt and equity. By confounding the application of the distinctions that define the conventional cubbyhole system, hybrids provide taxpayers with opportunities to

- accomplish realization-based recognition of expected gains and losses and
- alter the character of expected gains and losses.

The second part of this chapter begins with a brief review of the concept of bifurcation (which was described fully in chapter 4)[2] and of the problems associated with the distinction between debt and derivatives that existing income tax systems maintain. In general, the problems associated with this distinction arise from its inappropriateness as a means of addressing two types of hybrid instruments:[3]

- derivatives with an embedded debt element and
- debt instruments with contingent payments attributable to an embedded derivative.

The balance of the second part examines the selective application of bifurcation as a technique for taxing the expected gain or loss associated with these two categories of hybrids. Derivatives with embedded debt include prepaid and off-market forwards,[4] which are similar to options in their provision of expected gain or loss associated with an advance of funds. Arguably, this gain or loss should be taxed in the same manner as the gain or loss associated with fixed-payment debt. Under most tax systems, however, the standard cubbyhole treatment for derivatives continues to prevail, and the embedded debt is mistaxed in much the same way as the debt embedded in option premiums is mistaxed. In contrast with the treatment of the embedded debt in certain derivatives, bifurcation has been applied as a tax technique for debt instruments with contingent payments attributable to embedded derivatives ("contingent debt"). The latter portion of the second part examines these contrasting approaches and demonstrates the effectiveness of an expected-return approach that depends on the concept of bifurcation but, in practice, eliminates the need for its application. The discussion throughout this part of the chapter draws on the legislative experience in the United States for the purposes of illustration. US tax-policy makers have been more aggressive than their counterparts elsewhere in employing bifurcation as a conceptual basis for legislative responses to hybrid instruments that lie across the traditional boundary between debt and derivatives.

The third part of the chapter considers the inconsistencies and discontinuities that continue to characterize the boundary between debt and derivatives even under an extensive legislative approach such as the one in the United States. Any effective legislative response to hybrid instruments that blur the distinction between debt and derivatives, it is argued, must extend the insights gained from the design of appropriate rules for the basic building-block instruments. These insights refer to the need to identify the embedded debt that is present in all financial instruments and to tax the associated expected gain or loss in the same manner as conventional debt. Bifurcation provides a useful analytical technique for the division of all financial instruments into their embedded debt element and bet element, and it is consistent with the premises underlying a system of expected-return taxation that incorporates the basic design features described in chapter 5. By refining the conventional tax cubbyholes so that they correspond more closely to the provision of expected and unexpected gains and losses associated with the basic building-block financial instruments, bifurcation can alleviate much of the pressure of financial innovation on existing income tax systems.

In essence, bifurcation is a matter of identifying the two types of gains and losses in the basic instruments and applying appropriate tax rules to each type separately.[5] An obvious model for this approach is the tax treatment of prepaid swaps and contingent debt under the US regulations. At least in theory, it is possible for a comprehensive accrual regime to extend these regulations and require the accrual recognition of expected gains and losses on all prepaid forward contracts and on the embedded debt in long-dated options that are not publicly traded or used as a hedge of another position. The US experience is also important, however, because of its focus on the need to balance an extended application of expected-return taxation against administrative and compliance constraints. The more significant constraints are the need to (1) identify the embedded debt in all hybrids and (2) determine appropriate accrual methods for expected amounts associated with contingent payments. These administrative and compliance concerns have been cited as the primary reason for the limited application of the US regulations, although it is argued here that the importance of these concerns may be overstated, particularly in relation to the problems that arise if there is only a limited scope for the imputation of interest on the embedded debt in derivatives.

The chapter concludes with a brief discussion of the comparable (and familiar) problem presented by hybrids that lie across the boundary between debt and equity. In order to determine the appropriate tax treatment of these instruments, it is necessary to consider the possibility of applying expected-return taxation to shares as a means of eliminating inconsistencies between the tax treatment of interest and the tax treatment of dividends. This application would require fundamental reform of the corporate income tax, but the standard concerns associated with that subject are not critical to the simple points made here. These wider concerns, including the desirable design features of corporate income tax systems, are the subject of an enormous literature,[6] which this chapter does not attempt to review. The discussion assumes that it would be desirable to realize the consistent treatment of debt and equity by reducing or eliminating the double taxation of dividend distributions. It focuses, instead, on the conceptual link between the taxation of the building-block financial instruments and the taxation of shares as combinations of those basic instruments.

In theory, there is nothing special about shares as financial instruments that dictate unique tax treatment in their case. The cash flows associated with shares present many of the same tax-policy issues as those associated with options, prepaid forward contracts, and contingent-debt instruments, which lie across the boundary between debt and derivatives. Shares, too, are hybrid instruments, and it is possible to apply the analytical technique of bifurcation to them in much the same way as it has been applied to derivatives with embedded debt and contingent debt with embedded derivatives. Moreover, traded shares present the same opportunity as these instruments do for manipulation of the realization-based recognition of unexpected gains and losses through strategic trading. As in the case of traded debt and derivatives, the most effective way in which to address this opportunity is through the application of accretion taxation. Nonetheless, given the longstanding acceptance of shares as being different from other financial instruments, it may be necessary, as a practical policy matter, that shares remain subject to a separate regime, one that attempts to approximate the results of a comprehensive accrual regime. Dividend imputation systems tend to serve this second-best role, though they are desirable only to the extent that practical constraints necessitate the exception of shares from the application of expected-return taxation. Given a separate corporate income tax that does not ensure the consistent taxation of interest and dividends, however, tax-avoidance opportunities will arise and tax-policy makers must respond to them by classifying particular instruments on a basis other than their legal form. These responses are ultimately without any basis in principle and should be judged only in terms of their ability to provide an effective barrier to tax-driven financial innovation that exploits the distinction between debt and equity.

The General Features of Bifurcation and the Distinction Between Debt and Derivatives

In the tax literature,[7] the term "hybrid instrument" (or "hybrid") is used to describe any financial instrument that combines (1) an expected time-value return and (2) unexpected gain or loss that is attributable to a bet element. Among the basic building-block instruments, the most obvious hybrid is the option. Options provide both a time-value return, in the form of a premium paid by the holder in advance of performance, and unexpected gain or loss, in the form of the difference between the specified exercise price and the spot price of the underlying asset on maturity. The other basic building-block instruments are either (1) pure bets that provide only unexpected gain or loss (forwards, futures, and swaps) or (2) time-value instruments that provide only expected gain or loss (riskless debt). Hybrid instruments other than options combine expected time-value returns and unexpected gain or loss by

- combining two or more of the basic building-block instruments in a single instrument or
- prepaying the bet element in a forward-based contract and thereby creating an embedded-debt instrument.

Bifurcation is conventionally understood to be the process in which a hybrid instrument is broken down into its component parts (the basic building-block instruments) and a specified tax treatment that is consistent with the recognized tax cubbyholes is applied separately to each part.[8] Bifurcation in this conventional sense raises the problem of multiple bifurcations, which has to do with the fact that it is generally possible to break down a particular instrument in more ways than one. Thus the instrument becomes two or more different sets of building-block instruments—sets that may be subject to different but, perhaps, equally valid tax treatments.[9] Bifurcation can also be understood in another (perhaps simpler) sense, and it is in this sense that it has proved to be a useful analytical technique in the taxation of hybrids. Bifurcation in this sense is simply a technique for identifying the expected time-value return in any hybrid instrument and separating it from the unexpected gain or loss attributable to a bet element. Once an appropriate identification has been made, accrual treatment is applied to the expected gain or loss as interest income and expense. By avoiding the application of the cubbyhole tax treatments to the component parts of a hybrid, this use of bifurcation minimizes the problem of multiple bifurcations. In effect, multiple bifurcations do not matter, provided that the application of accrual recognition is consistent. That is, its application to the expected gain or loss associated with a hybrid must have the same result as would its separate application to the expected gain or loss associated with each of the basic building-block instruments under any possible analysis of the hybrid into building-block instruments. Indeed, it is necessary under this approach to significantly modify the cubbyhole treatment associated with options and derivatives by assuming that expected gain or loss, which is normally associated only with debt, in fact arises whenever funds are advanced in return for a right to receive an amount in the future.[10] It does not matter whether the expected gain or loss is associated with an option, a prepaid or off-market forward,[11] a contingent-debt instrument,[12] or a share. To eliminate anticipated deferral and its associated problems, it is necessary to impute an appropriate time-value return on the advance of funds that is associated with each of these "contingent-payment" instruments. The unexpected gain or loss that arises on resolution of the specified contingencies may be recognized as ordinary income or loss on realization.

This simplistic analytical process is the underlying conceptual basis of expected-return taxation.[13] The income tax systems in most countries, however, do not apply this kind of bifurcated treatment of hybrid instruments to options, prepaid and off-market forwards, or shares. As a rule, in fact, they treat these simple instruments as being predominantly bets and tax any gain or loss only on realization,[14] although some countries require recognition of the amount of an option premium on payment unless the option is exercised and the underlying asset is physically delivered.[15] The failure to bifurcate options, in particular, causes substantial problems for the application of bifurcation and expected-return taxation as approaches to the taxation of hybrid instruments generally. In the absence of the application of these approaches to this basic building-block instrument, it becomes difficult to justify their application to more complex hybrids that contain embedded options. The alternative approach under the cubbyhole system of taxation is to characterize a particular financial instrument as being predominantly debt, equity, or a derivative and require the application of the relevant cubbyhole treatment on the basis of that characterization.[16] The inconsistencies and discontinuities that many commentators[17] describe as being characteristic of the cubbyhole approach to the taxation of financial instruments arise primarily from a failure to identify the embedded elements in hybrids and tax them separately.[18]

The following two subparts review certain legislative attempts in the United States to use bifurcation and expected-return taxation to define the tax cubbyholes for debt and derivatives. The relevance of these concepts to the equally problematic distinction between debt and equity is the subject of the last part of this chapter.[19] The first aspect of the problem of defining a boundary between debt and derivatives is the issue of the appropriate treatment of derivative instruments that provide for payments in advance of performance. As was noted above, these payments provide derivatives, which are normally pure bets, with an element of expected gain or loss, which is usually associated with fixed-payment debt.[20] The second aspect of the debt/derivative problem is the issue of the appropriate treatment of contingent-debt instruments, which appear to be predominantly debt in character but provide contingent payments that reflect an embedded bet element of the kind normally associated with options and forward contracts.

Where debt is embedded in an instrument that takes the form of a derivative, one of the parties to the contract has prepaid all, or some portion, of his part of the bet. The application of expected-return taxation in this case requires the imputation of an expected time-value return on the amount of the prepayment.[21] Where a derivative is embedded in an instrument that takes the form of a debt obligation, there is an embedded bet element that must be identified and taxed appropriately within the relevant cubbyhole. Although these two issues are easy enough to state, they have presented considerable problems for tax-policy makers. As in the case of the design of yield-to-maturity methods for the taxation of the expected gain or loss on fixed-payment debt, effective resolution of these issues requires a balance between theoretical purity and the practical constraints imposed by the administrative and compliance considerations associated with any attempt to apply expected-return taxation to the embedded debt in all financial instruments.[22] Thus US tax-policy makers have attempted to apply the dictates of expected-return taxation extensively but by no means comprehensively. The practical aspect of the US approach is reflected most obviously in legislation that taxes the embedded debt in derivatives solely in response to the existence of significant avoidance opportunities that are attributable to a failure to apply the insights of bifurcation and expected-return taxation.[23]

Taxing the Embedded Debt in Certain Derivatives

Mistaxation of the Embedded Debt in Options and Prepaid Forwards

Chapter 3[24] made the point that accrual recognition of expected gain or loss is required to eliminate "anticipated deferral" and its associated costs and tax-avoidance opportunities.[25] Expected gain or loss is conventionally attributed to debt instruments that involve an advance of funds in return for a right to receive a corresponding amount plus a fixed sum to compensate the holder for the use of the borrowed funds ("fixed-payment" or "non-contingent" debt). This time-value return ensures that the value of the debt instrument is expected to increase in increments equal to the promised compensation for the particular period (with a corresponding decrease in the net wealth of the borrower). In contrast, a cash-settled forward or futures contract is a bet between two counterparties on the future price of a specified asset.[26] One counterparty agrees to purchase, and the other agrees to sell, a specified asset at a specified price on a future date. Where the specified price represents a "fair bet," the mutual obligations of the counterparties to pay in the event of an adverse outcome are regarded as being of equal value, and no amount of funds is transferred when the contract is entered into. The contract is said to be "on market," in the sense that the forward price specified by the counterparties is the price that persons dealing at arm's length would specify for the same bet. Each counterparty has an asset and a liability of equal value and, accordingly, realizes no increase or decrease in net wealth that should be recognized for income tax purposes. A contract of this kind is a pure bet: only unexpected gain or loss arises on maturity when the bet is resolved, and the losing counterparty pays the winning counterparty the difference between the spot price of the asset and the forward price. As a series of forward contracts, swaps are the equivalent of a series of bets.

Exploitation of the distinction between debt and derivatives centres on the fact that the two types of instruments are subject to different timing rules for gains and losses. In particular, it centres on the inconsistencies that result when the expected gain or loss associated with the embedded debt in certain derivatives is taxed on a cash or realization basis.[27] Since an on-market forward contract does not involve any up-front payment, the gain or loss on the contract is entirely unexpected and therefore sufficiently different from the expected gain or loss on fixed-payment debt to justify different tax treatment. Mistaxation occurs when a loan element is introduced into a forward contract by the prepayment of some or all of the contracted obligation under the specified bet. The cash flows that arise in this case are similar to those associated with options. Like forwards and futures, cash-settled options are bets on the future price of a specified asset, with terms that are set by the exercise price under the option. In each case, the contract involves the resolution of a single contingency; that is, the price of the specified asset on the maturity date. Options differ from the other building-block financial instruments in that the holder of an option advances funds to the issuer in return for the right to purchase (call option) or sell (put option) the specified asset at the specified price. The premium is necessary to compensate the issuer for the unfair nature of the bet, which arises from the fact that the holder has acquired a right either to purchase or to sell the specified asset at the exercise price without incurring an offsetting obligation.[28] The option premium represents the present value of that right. In a sense, the holder has prepaid (or provided collateral for) his side of the bet.[29] If the difference between the spot price and the exercise price on maturity of the option is favourable to the holder, the holder will exercise the option and the issuer will have to pay that difference. If the movement in the spot price of the underlying asset is unfavourable to the holder, the option will expire unexercised and the issuer will retain the premium.

The advance of funds on the issue of an option means that the right of the holder gives rise to expected gain[30] equal to the difference between the amount of the premium and the forward price (expected value) of the option. In general, the forward price is equal to the spot price on issue plus the cost of carry to maturity.[31]

> **Example 1:** On January 1, 1996, Alvin acquires a European call option[32] from Betty for the purchase of 100 units of a commodity in two years at a price of $15 per unit. Alvin pays Betty $175 for the option.

Alvin pays Betty for the right to purchase 100 units of the commodity at $15 per unit.[33] The present value of that right is $175. At a cost of carry of 8 percent per annum, the two-year forward price (or the expected value) of that right is $204. The $29 difference between the spot price of the option and this forward price represents an expected gain to Alvin and an expected loss to Betty. In other words, the value of the call option is expected to increase by $14 at the end of year one and another $15 at the end of year two. If at the end of year two the spot price of the commodity is $18 per unit, Alvin will realize an unexpected gain of $96 (the $300 difference between the spot and exercise prices of 100 units of the commodity less the $204 expected value of the option). Betty will realize a corresponding unexpected loss. If the spot price of the commodity turns out to be $16 per unit, Alvin will realize an unexpected loss of $104 (the $100 difference between the spot and exercise prices of 100 units of the commodity less the $204 expected value of the option). Betty will realize a corresponding unexpected gain.

The European call option in example 1 is issued at an exercise price that makes it uncertain whether the relevant right to purchase or sell the underlying asset will have a value on maturity that will cause the holder to exercise it. This uncertainty disappears in the case of an option that is "deep in the money."[34] Options of this kind are issued at an exercise price that virtually ensures exercise by the holder; consequently, the holder must pay a larger premium, one that is equivalent to a loan advance. On exercise of the option and its settlement in cash, the issuer is invariably required to pay an amount that exceeds the premium. This payment repays the loan and provides the holder with an appropriate return for the use of the funds. In fact, a deep-in-the-money option resembles the combination of a loan and a long position[35] in a forward contract on the underlying asset.

> **Example 2:** On January 1, 1996, Cathy acquires a European call option from David for the purchase of 100 units of a commodity in two years at a price of $2.15 per unit. Cathy pays David $1,101.68 for the option. The two-year forward price of the commodity is $15 per unit.

Cathy effectively loans David $1,101.68 in return for a right to receive in two years the $1,285 difference between the two-year forward price of the underlying commodity and the inordinately low exercise price under the call option ($1,500 less $215). The deep-in-the-money option has an expected value of $1,285 in two years, which provides Cathy with an expected gain of $183.32 ($1,101.68 × 0.08 = $88.13 for year one and $1,189.81 × 0.08 = $95.19 for year two). This result becomes apparent if it is assumed that the spot price of the commodity in two years equals the two-year forward price of $15 per unit. In that case, Cathy will exercise the option and receive the $1,285 difference between the spot and exercise price.

In addition, however, Cathy has the equivalent of a long position in a forward contract to purchase 100 units of the commodity at the two-year forward price of $15 per unit. This position arises from her right to receive any amount by which the spot price of 100 units of the commodity exceeds $15 per unit. If the spot price of the commodity is $16 per unit, Cathy will exercise the option and receive from David the $1,385 difference between the spot price and the exercise price under the option. This amount consists of (1) repayment of the $1,101.68 option premium, (2) realization of the $183.32 expected gain on the option ($1,285 expected value less the option premium), and (3) an unexpected gain of $100 on the long forward contract. If the spot price of the commodity is less than the two-year forward price, Cathy will realize an unexpected loss equal to the difference. For example, if the spot price is $14 per unit, Cathy will exercise the option and receive the $1,185 difference between that spot price and the exercise price ($1,400 less $215). The result will be repayment of the $1,101.68 loan advance plus $83.32. Since the option had an expected value of $1,285, the $100 shortfall in the spot price results in an unexpected loss for Cathy ($183.32 expected gain less $100 shortfall = $83.32 excess of the amount received over the option premium). David will realize corresponding losses and gains.

It is also possible to realize the cash flows associated with a deep-in-the-money option by prepaying the bet under a forward contract. In fact, a fully prepaid forward contract is equivalent to the extreme case of a deep-in-the-money option that is issued with a strike price of nil.

> **Example 3:** On January 1, 1996, Ernie enters into a cash-settlement forward contract with Florence to purchase 100 units of a commodity in two years at a price of $15 per unit. Rather than pay $1,500 in two years, Ernie pays Florence, on entering into the contract, the present value of $1,500, which is $1,286 (at an assumed discount rate of 8 percent per annum). On maturity of the contract in two years, Florence will pay Ernie the spot price of 100 units of the commodity.[36]

Ernie prepays his side of the bet under the forward contract and thereby creates the equivalent of (1) a $1,286 loan to Florence at a rate of interest of 8 percent (compounded annually) and (2) the acquisition of a deep-in-the-money option to purchase 100 units of the commodity at an exercise price of zero. The expected value of Ernie's prepaid obligation in two years' time is the $1,500 expected price of 100 units of the commodity. Ernie thus expects the value of the loan to increase to $1,500 by the end of year two. The $214 difference between the amount advanced and the $1,500 forward price represents an expected gain for Ernie and an expected loss for Florence that will be realized if the spot price of the 100 units of the commodity turns out to be $15 per unit at the end of two years. In other words, the loan is expected to increase in value by $102.88 at the end of year one ($1,286 × 0.08) and by another $111.12 at the end of year two ($1,388.88 × 0.08).

If the spot price of the commodity in two years turns out to be greater than the forward price, Ernie will realize a total amount under the prepaid forward contract that is greater than the forward price; the difference between the two amounts will be an unexpected gain. For example, if the spot price of the commodity in two years is $16 per unit, Florence will have to pay Ernie $1,600 on maturity. Of that amount, $100 is unexpected gain equal to the difference between the spot and forward prices. The other $1,500 is attributable to the implicit loan and provides an expected gain of $214 ($1,500 less the $1,286 prepayment). If the spot price of the commodity turns out to be less than the forward price, Ernie will realize an unexpected loss equal to the difference. For example, if the spot price of the commodity in two years is $13 per unit, Florence will have to pay Ernie $1,300 on maturity. Of that amount, $200 is unexpected loss equal to the difference between the spot and forward prices. This amount reduces the total gain to Ernie on the prepaid forward to $14, which is the difference between the expected gain of $214 on the implicit loan and the $200 unexpected loss on maturity. In both cases, Florence will realize corresponding amounts of loss or gain.

It is also possible to make a prepayment under a forward contract in partial satisfaction of the obligation of a counterparty. Partial prepayments of this kind occur if the bet under a forward is "unfair," in which case the forward is said to be "off market."[37] The bet is "unfair" if the forward price under the contract is not equal to the market price, with the result that one of the counterparties has an advantage over the other. The mutually offsetting obligations are not of equal value, and an initial payment is required to balance the bet.

Example 4: On January 1, 1996, Galina enters into a cash-settled forward contract with Harold to purchase 100 units of a commodity in two years at a price of $14 per unit. Since the two-year forward price of the commodity is $15 per unit, Galina must pay Harold the present value of the $100 difference between the forward price under the contract and the market forward price ($85.73 at an assumed discount rate of 8 percent per annum). On maturity of the contract, Harold will pay Galina the amount, if any, by which the spot price for 100 units exceeds $14 per unit, and Galina will pay Harold the amount, if any, by which the spot price for 100 units falls short of $14 per unit.

Galina effectively loans Harold the present value of the right to receive $100 in two years. The difference between the $85.73 advanced and the expected payment of $100 represents an expected gain of $14.27. In other words, the right to receive the $100 in two years is expected to increase in value by $6.86 at the end of year one ($85.73 × 0.08) and another $7.41 at the end of year two ($92.59 × 0.08). In the unlikely event that the spot price of the commodity in year two turns out to be $15 per unit, Harold will have to pay Galina the $100 excess of that price over the contract price ($14 per unit) and Galina will realize the full amount of the $14.27 expected gain on the implicit loan, as well as repayment of the $85.73 advance. If the spot price turns out to be greater than $15 per unit, Harold will have to pay the additional excess amount, which will represent unexpected gain to Galina. If the spot price turns out to be less than $15 per unit, Galina will realize unexpected loss. If the spot price is greater than $14 but less than $15 per unit, the loss will reduce both the expected gain on the implicit loan under the off-market forward and the amount of principal to be repaid by Harold. If the spot price is less than $14 per unit, Galina will have to pay Harold the difference and thus will realize further unexpected loss.[38]

These simple examples illustrate the bifurcation of a cash-settlement option and a prepaid forward contract into (1) an embedded loan represented by the advance of funds before maturity of the contract and (2) a bet on the future price of a specified asset. Consistency of tax treatment requires characterization of the embedded loan as debt that is subject to the same treatment as fixed-payment debt. In effect, the payment under each of these derivatives in advance of performance is analogous to the advance of loan principal by a lender.[39] As in the case of fixed-payment debt issued at a discount, interest should be imputed at a rate equal to the implicit cost of carry associated with the option premium or the forward price that is prepaid under a forward contract. This imputation results in the recognition of the expected gain or loss over the term of the relevant instrument, which matures on resolution of the related bet.

In the case of a cash-settled option, this characterization means that the difference between the premium and the expected value of the option should be accrued as expected gain of the holder and expected loss of the issuer over the period between issue and maturity.[40] Thus Alvin and Betty in example 1 should accrue the $29 difference between the $175 option premium and its $204 expected value as interest income and expense over the two-year term of the option (assuming exercise on maturity); $14 would accrue in respect of the first year ($175 option premium × 0.08 implicit cost of carry) and $15 in respect of the second year ($189 × 0.08). These accrued amounts should be added to the cost base of the option for Alvin, and unexpected gain or loss should be determined as the difference between the amount received on exercise and the adjusted cost base. If the option expires unexercised, the whole of the adjusted cost base should be recognized as unexpected loss in the form of the expected value that was not realized. As the issuer of the option, Betty should realize a corresponding unexpected loss that is equal to the amount by which the payment she is required to make when the option is exercised exceeds the sum of the option premium and accrued interest expense. Conversely, she should realize as unexpected gain any amount by which the payment she must make when the option is exercised falls short of this sum.[41]

Given a similar characterization of a prepaid forward contract, the difference between the prepayment and the on-market forward price should be accrued as expected gain of the payer and expected loss of the payee.[42] Thus Ernie and Florence in example 3 should accrue the $214 difference between the on-market forward price of 100 units of the specified commodity and the amount prepaid by Ernie ($1,500 less $1,286). This expected gain should be imputed as interest over the two-year term of the forward contract; thus $102.88 ($1,286 × 0.08) should be recognized as interest income of the payer (Ernie) and interest expense of the payee (Florence) in respect of year one, and a further $111.12 should be recognized in respect of year two ($1,388.88 × 0.08). These accrued amounts should be added to the cost base of the forward contract for Ernie ($1,286 prepayment plus $214 accrued interest income), and the amount by which any payment received exceeds that cost should be recognized on maturity as unexpected gain. Any shortfall in the amount received would be recognized as unexpected loss. The payee (Florence) would realize corresponding loss and gain. An off-market forward should be subject to the same analysis to the extent that the partial prepayment is made to balance the bargain between the counterparties.

With the exception of accretion taxation (and its periodic recognition of unrealized changes in value), any tax treatment of options and prepaid forwards other than the expected-return approach described above mistaxes the embedded debt in these instruments. As several commentators have observed,[43] mistaxation is characteristic of the treatment under the standard cubbyholes. In the case of cash-settled options, the cubbyhole treatment is relatively clear but incorrect. As chapter 2 noted in the context of the Canadian and Australian income tax systems, the tendency is to adopt one of two standard treatments. The first is sometimes referred to as "wait and see taxation" or "open-transaction treatment."[44] Under this cubbyhole treatment, the cash flows associated with an option are considered to be attributable to a bet that gives rise to unexpected gain or loss only. The holder acquires a cost base in the option that is equal to the premium, and this amount is not deducted until realization, when the difference between the premium and the amount received (if any) is recognized as gain or loss. Similarly, the issuer recognizes gain equal to the amount of the premium if, and when, the option expires unexercised. Unexpected loss is realized to the extent that the amount paid when the option is exercised exceeds the premium. In this way, the whole of any gain or loss on an option is considered to be unexpected and is not taxed until realization. Interest income and expense is not imputed on the amount of the premium, which means that the expected gain or loss associated with that amount is not recognized as interest on an accrual basis during the term of the option. Open-transaction treatment, therefore, provides anticipated deferral of the expected gain or loss associated with an option premium.[45]

The second type of cubbyhole treatment does not provide the benefit of anticipated deferral but results nonetheless in the mistaxation of options. Under this cubbyhole treatment,[46] the issuer must include the amount of the premium on receipt. The holder is entitled to either an immediate corresponding deduction or a deferred deduction when the option is exercised (or expires unexercised).[47] This immediate inclusion and deduction of the present value of the forward price of the option represented by the premium has the effect of requiring the accelerated recognition of expected gain or loss. In essence, the difference between the forward price of the option and premium is taxed in advance of the accrual period on a cash flow basis, a procedure that eliminates anticipated deferral of the expected gain or loss associated with the option. This result is achieved at the cost of mistaxation, since an income tax should require recognition over the term of the option on an accrual basis.[48]

To be more particular, mistaxation occurs under this type of cubbyhole treatment in the sense that the wrong persons are taxed. Expected-return taxation requires that the holder recognize the expected gain as income on an accrual basis; the issuer should recognize the same amount as an expected loss. An immediate inclusion by the issuer and deduction by the holder of the option premium reverses this result in the same way as an immediate inclusion by the borrower and deduction by the lender of the amount of a loan advance reverses the conventional treatment of debt under an income tax (that is, no inclusion or deduction of loan proceeds). This conventional tax treatment of loans under an income tax should be extended to option premiums on the basis of the same premise—namely, that the issue of the option results in no increase or decrease in the net wealth of the parties. The amount paid by the holder (lender) is offset exactly by a valuable right in the form of the option (debt obligation), which has an expected value that is equal, in present-value terms, to the amount of the premium paid (loan proceeds).[49] Similarly, the amount received by the issuer of the option (borrower) is offset by a valuable right in the form of the option (debt obligation), which is a liability of the issuer (borrower) that has an expected value, in present-value terms, equal to the amount of the premium received (loan proceeds). A cash-basis inclusion and deduction of an option premium is an exception to the general treatment of loan transactions under an income tax, whereby the advance of loan principal is not taxed to the borrower because of his offsetting liability to repay and no deduction is provided to the lender because of his offsetting right to repayment. If the issuer and the holder were taxable at the same rates, the mistaxation would not be problematic, since any disadvantage of an accelerated income inclusion by the issuer would be offset by the benefit of accelerated deductibility by the holder.[50] Since in fact issuers and holders are not taxable at equivalent rates, the benefit of accelerated deductibility to holders will in some cases be greater than its cost to issuers.[51] The tax saving that results from asymmetry in tax rates may be shared by the parties; that is, the holder may pay a higher premium to compensate the issuer for the use of a lower tax rate. The extreme case is that of non-taxable persons, who are insensitive to the immediate income inclusion or deduction and who can facilitate transactions that attempt to "freshen expiring loss carryover accounts."[52] Any attempt to address these problems by deferring the deduction of the option premium by the holder compounds mistaxation by overtaxing the transaction.[53] This result occurs because the deferral of the deduction effectively denies a corresponding offset of the immediate inclusion by the issuer. The result is that the parties pay tax on the transaction in advance and the government enjoys the benefit of the time-value return on the prepayment.[54] Overtaxation of this kind imposes an additional transaction cost that may discourage the use of options and thus result in inefficiencies.[55]

Although the point is not entirely clear, it should be possible to extend the traditional cubbyhole treatments that apply to options to prepaid and off-market forwards.[56] The most obvious approach in this context is to characterize gain or loss as being wholly unexpected and apply realization-based recognition to the difference between the amount of the prepayment and the amount paid under the contract at maturity. This approach effectively allows the counterparty who prepays his obligation when he enters into a forward to deduct the payment on maturity, when the other counterparty makes a payment equal to the spot price of the specified asset. This result occurs because the prepayment is recognized as an expense against which the amount of gain or loss is determined on the basis of the amount paid by the other counterparty on maturity. The counterparty who receives the prepayment realizes the same amount as income in determining the corresponding loss or gain. A cash-basis inclusion and deduction allows the counterparty who prepays his obligation to deduct the amount of the prepayment immediately and recognize the whole of any receipt as unexpected gain on maturity. The counterparty who receives the prepayment must include the amount immediately and can deduct the whole of any payment made as unexpected loss on maturity.

For the same reasons as were described above in connection with the taxation of options, neither realization-based recognition nor the alternative of a cash-basis inclusion/deduction is appropriate for the expected gain or loss associated with the advance of funds under a prepaid or off-market forward. The principal difference between these approaches and the cubbyhole taxation of options is probably the lack of clarity in the application of either approach to prepayments under forward contracts.[57] The lack of clarity is attributable to the simple fact that these contracts do not appear to fit easily within any of the existing tax cubbyholes for debt or derivative instruments. In particular, the income tax legislation in many countries fails to define the concept of a debt obligation and accepts legal form as being determinative, which means that a prepaid forward must be considered to be a derivative.[58] Even for countries that require a more substantive assessment of an instrument for characterization purposes, there is the difficulty that a prepaid forward lacks a promise to repay a sum at least equal to the amount of funds advanced.[59] The lack of this characteristic may be considered to be fatal to the characterization of a prepaid forward as indebtedness.[60] Moreover, the legislative provisions and general principles that have been developed for the taxation of forward contracts within the derivative cubbyhole often seem inappropriate for prepaid forwards,[61] primarily because they fail to take into account the possibility of prepayment of the obligations of counterparties. Instead, the provisions reflect realization-based recognition of gain or loss on income or capital account, on the apparent assumption that all forward contracts are on-market and no payments are made by the counterparties until maturity. It has been suggested in this connection that the wording of some legislative provisions that require the cash-basis inclusion of amounts received for prepaid services may be applicable to prepaid forwards.[62] These provisions, however, are limited to the tax treatment of the payee.[63] In the case of the payer, the alternatives appear to be either immediate deduction of the payment as a current expense of earning income or its deferred deduction as a capital amount.[64] Chapter 2, in discussing the representative Canadian and Australian legislation,[65] made the point that these alternatives are derived not from specific legislation that governs forward contracts but rather from general principles that govern the measurement of business income.

It is possible to realize accrual recognition of expected gain or loss on the embedded debt in derivatives by imputing interest at an appropriate rate on the amount of any prepaid bets. In the absence of the adoption of this approach generally, it is extremely difficult to draw a sensible line between debt and derivatives and between their respective cubbyhole treatments. The application of expected-return taxation to derivatives has been very limited, however, since tax-policy makers and administrators have adjusted the application of the traditional tax cubbyholes solely in response to clear cases of tax avoidance, such as the use of deep-in-the-money options to disguise a loan as a derivative[66] or the use of prepayments to take advantage of cash-basis recognition.[67] This limited response reveals a hesitancy to impute interest on all prepayments. Indeed, the distinction between debt and derivatives is both unclear and largely the product of administrative practice rather than specific legislation.

A particular concern of this practice has been the treatment of the embedded loans in prepaid and off-market swaps. In general, the attempt to identify the embedded debt in a prepaid swap and treat it as indebtedness for income tax purposes is similar in concept to the attempt to distinguish between an option that is subject to taxation under the derivative cubbyhole and a deep-in-the-money option that provides an unduly expected return; that is, an expected return of the kind normally associated with fixed-payment debt. The distinction purports to limit the tax-cubbyhole treatment of swap payments to "bona fide contracts," a term that is apparently intended to exclude any transaction with the legal form of a swap but cash flow patterns that permit its characterization as a loan substitute. An extreme example is an interest-rate swap in which one of the counterparties prepays his entire fixed-rate obligations in return for a series of floating-rate payments that repay the advance with a suitable rate of return. Like the characteristics of a deep-in-the-money option, the precise characteristics of a swap that is, in substance, a loan are elusive, and the distinction between the debt cubbyhole and the derivative cubbyhole is unclear except in extreme instances.

An important exception to the general run of administrative practice is the set of notional principal contract (NPC) regulations in the United States, which apply a loan characterization to swap prepayments and certain options. As this chapter will argue more fully later,[68] the approach realized in these regulations is a useful paradigm for the taxation of non-periodic payments that are associated with the embedded debt in derivative instruments generally. Finally, a particularly contentious issue in this context is the extent to which it is possible to impute interest on a relatively broad range of instruments, given the perceived constraints imposed by administrative and compliance considerations.[69]

The Bifurcation of Swaps and the Search for Embedded Debt

Example 5: On January 1, 1996, Ivan and Jenny enter into a two-year interest-rate swap under which Ivan agrees to pay at the end of each year an amount equal to a fixed rate of interest of 8 percent on a notional principal amount of $1 million. In return for this promise, Jenny agrees to pay corresponding amounts equal to a floating rate of interest that fluctuates with the London interbank offering rate (LIBOR) on the same notional principal amount. Although the swap is on market, Ivan agrees to pay his obligations when the contract is initiated. The amount of the payment is $142,661, which is the sum of the present value of the expected obligation of $80,000 for year one and the present value of the expected obligation of $80,000 for year two.

Example 6: On January 1, 1996, Lori and Marvin enter into a two-year interest rate swap under which Lori agrees to pay at the end of each year an amount equal to a fixed rate of interest of 6 percent on a notional principal amount of $1 million. In return for this promise, Marvin agrees to pay corresponding amounts equal to a floating rate of interest that fluctuates with LIBOR on the same notional principal amount. Under an on-market swap, Lori would have been required to promise a fixed-rate payment at 8 percent. Accordingly, Lori agrees to pay the present value of the difference between the market rate of interest and the swap rate on the notional principal amount. The amount of the payment is $35,666.

As a series of cash-settled forward contracts,[70] an on-market swap represents a fair bet on the forward prices of the specified asset or index. The mutual promises of the counterparties are of equal value, and no payments arise on initiation of the contract. Thus the swap in example 5 is equivalent to a series of two on-market forward contracts, one of which matures at the end of year one and the other at the end of year two. By prepaying his obligations under the two contracts, however, Ivan achieves a result similar to the result that Ernie achieves by prepaying his obligation under the single forward contract in example 3.[71] The only difference is that Ivan's prepayment of $142,661 is the equivalent of two separate loans to Jenny. The first loan is an advance of $74,074, which is the present value of the expected $80,000 obligation at the end of year one. The second loan is an advance of $68,587, which is the present value of the expected obligation of $80,000 at the end of year two. In other words, the prepayment is allocated between the two forward contracts on the basis of the relative present values of the expected obligations of the payer. If on maturity of the two loans LIBOR exceeds the fixed rate of 8 percent, Ivan will realize expected and unexpected gains. For example, if LIBOR at the end of year one is 9 percent, Ivan will receive $90,000 from Jenny. This amount will consist of (1) repayment of the $74,074 prepayment of Ivan's one-year obligation, (2) payment of an expected gain of $5,926 (the difference between the prepayment of $74,074 and the $80,000 expected value of the obligation), and (3) an unexpected gain of $10,000 (the amount by which the payment by Jenny exceeds the expected value of the prepaid obligation). Jenny will realize corresponding expected and unexpected losses. If LIBOR is less than the 8 percent fixed rate, Ivan will realize an unexpected loss equal to the shortfall and Jenny will realize a corresponding gain.

Like an off-market forward, an off-market swap requires prepayment by one of the counterparties to balance the bargain and provide a "fair bet."[72] Thus the swap in example 6 is equivalent to a series of two forward contracts that mature respectively at the end of year one and the end of year two. Since the swap is off market, Lori must pay an amount on initiation of the contract to balance the bargain in the same way as Galina prepays an amount under the off-market forward in example 4. The principal difference is that Lori's prepayment balances the bargains under two forward contracts that constitute the swap. In effect, Lori makes two implicit loans to Marvin that together total $35,666. The first loan is an advance of $18,519, which is the present value of the right to receive $20,000 at the end of year one. The latter amount represents the difference of 200 basis points between the market rate of fixed interest and the lower rate, applied to the $1 million notional principal amount, that Lori has promised to pay under the swap. The second loan is an advance of $17,147, which is the present value of the right to receive $20,000 at the end of year two. The $35,666 prepayment, which is intended to bring the swap on market, is in effect allocated between the two forward contracts on the basis of the present value in each case of the difference between the market price and the contract price that Lori has agreed to pay under the swap. The difference between the amount advanced by Lori and the $20,000 expected payment at the end of year one is an expected gain of $1,481 ($20,000 less the $18,519 present value of the amount prepaid by Lori). In the unlikely event that LIBOR turns out to be exactly equal to the fixed market rate of 8 percent, Lori will receive $20,000 under the swap (LIBOR less the 6 percent promised fixed rate); this amount will consist of the repayment of the $18,519 embedded loan and the expected gain. Any fluctuation in LIBOR above or below that market rate will result in unexpected gain or loss for Lori and corresponding loss or gain for Marvin.

For income tax purposes, an accelerated payment under a swap presents the same issues as a prepayment under a single forward contract. The accelerated payment creates the equivalent of an embedded loan with expected gain or loss that should be taxed in the same manner as expected gain or loss associated with fixed-payment debt. To realize this treatment, one must bifurcate the instrument into its debt and derivative components and apply a different tax treatment to the unexpected gain or loss attributable to the bet element. The significant difference between a swap and a single forward contract is that the accelerated payments under a swap effectively prepay one or more of a series of bets associated with the series of forward contracts. In the case of a swap, therefore, it is necessary to allocate any prepayments among the various subcontracts.

Failure to use bifurcation in order to identify and appropriately tax the embedded debt in a prepaid swap has led to inconsistent taxation of the prepayment and hence to some notable avoidance arrangements. The most obvious avoidance strategy is the use of accelerated payments to manipulate cash-basis recognition; mischaracterization of the embedded loan is especially advantageous for a counterparty who has loss carryovers that are about to expire. On the assumption that the transaction is properly considered to be a swap, a counterparty can include the amount of the upfront payment in income and offset that inclusion with the loss carryovers. He can deduct the series of payments that are to be made in the future in order to create new losses with a fresh carryover period. The counterparty who makes the upfront payment receives the benefit of an immediate deduction that can be used to reduce tax payable on other income. In present-value terms, this saving will exceed any liability on the future payments that he receives under the swap. By altering the return on the upfront lump-sum payment, the counterparties can price the swap transaction to take into account the mutual tax advantages.[73] If the purported swap is treated as the equivalent of a disguised loan, however, the tax advantages disappear, since in that case the accelerated payment is considered to be a non-deductible capital amount for the payer and a non-taxable receipt by the payee that is repaid without any tax consequences. Only the excess amount that represents the expected time-value return is deductible and taxable.[74]

As was noted above, the most intensive legislative attempt to identify the embedded debt in certain derivatives is found in portions of the US regulations that apply to "notional principal contracts" (NPCs).[75] In general, these regulations attempt to address the unique timing concerns presented by derivatives, such as swaps and interest-rate caps and collars,[76] that provide for a series of payments on the basis of a series of bets. In accounting for prepayments under these contracts, the regulations attempt to bifurcate the serial exchanges into their debt and derivative elements and apply separate recognition rules to each. The regulations do not, however, consistently apply a loan characterization to all prepayments and impute interest for all income tax purposes. They attempt instead to draw a line between instances in which the embedded loan is significant enough to merit debt-tax treatment and instances in which it is possible to subject an accelerated payment to realization-based recognition as unexpected gain or loss. In instances of the first kind, a loan characterization is apparently necessary as a response to avoidance strategies that use a notional principal contract to disguise a loan and manipulate the realization requirement, often in an attempt to freshen loss carryovers. Otherwise, presumably, the avoidance possibilities do not merit the administrative and compliance effort involved in bifurcating a swap into its embedded debt and derivative elements and imputing interest on the former. The interesting thing is where the US regulations have drawn the line and, in particular, their use (or failure to use) a bright-line approach to the definition of the distinction between debt and derivative instruments. These matters are discussed in some detail later in the chapter.[77]

The NPC regulations define a "notional principal contract" as an instrument that provides for payments between the counterparties at designated intervals, and for determination of the amount of these payments by reference to an index or notional principal amount.[78] NPCs include swaps and interest-rate caps and floors but not forwards or other options, since the payments under the latter instruments are not calculated by reference to a notional principal amount. The timing rules under the regulations effectively require the amortization of "non-periodic" swap payments and cap or floor premiums. In the case of a swap, this result is realized by bifurcating the instrument and accounting for it as a series of cash-settled forward contracts. A cap or a collar is accounted for as a series of cash-settled options. Interest is imputed on embedded debt only if a non-periodic payment is "significant," a term that the regulations leave undefined.[79] "Non-periodic payments" are defined negatively as payments made under or for a notional principal contract that are not periodic[80] and are not "termination payments."[81] These payments include the prepayment of one obligation or more under a swap, payments for an off-market swap, premiums for an exercised option to enter into a swap (a "swaption"), and the upfront premium under a cap or floor.[82] Non-periodic payments that are "significant" are treated as an embedded loan from the payer to the payee, and the notional principal contract is treated as if it were on market.[83] To be more specific, the difference between the expected amount of an on-market obligation and the related non-periodic payment is treated as imputed interest that must be accrued as income by the payer and as expense by the payee. Both the embedded debt and imputed interest are treated as being paid over the term of the notional principal contract in level payments. Periodic amounts in excess of the loan principal and imputed interest are treated as unexpected gain or loss to be recognized on realization.

If it is assumed that the swap prepayment in example 5 is "significant," the NPC regulations provide a result that is similar to the result under the bifurcation approach described above. Under the NPC approach, Ivan is deemed to have loaned Jenny the $142,661 prepayment, which she is to repay over the term of the swap in two level payments of $80,000 each (the contracted obligations under an on-market swap for each of the two years of the contract). The discount rate of 8 percent that the counterparties used to arrive at the amount of the prepayment is applied to that amount, and income and expense of $11,413 are imputed for year one and recognized by Ivan and Jenny on an accrual basis. The $80,000 level payment for year one is allocated between the accrued interest and the loan principal to arrive at a remaining principal balance for year two of $74,074. Interest income and expense of $5,926 on that balance is imputed for year two, and this interest income and the remaining principal are deemed to constitute the second $80,000 payment. Any amount by which either payment exceeds (or falls short of) the $80,000 on-market amount is considered to be unexpected gain (or loss) that must be recognized in the year of payment. The principal difference between this approach and the bifurcation approach described above is that the former treats the prepayment as a single two-year loan payable in instalments and the latter treats it as two separate one-year loans.

Under the NPC regulations, non-periodic payments that are not "significant" must be allocated over the term of a notional principal contract and recognized in a manner that reflects their economic substance.[84] In the case of a swap, the allocation is generally made in accordance with the value of a series of cash-settled forwards written on the specified index.[85] To be more specific, the regulations appear to require the counterparties to a swap to amortize any upfront payment by treating it as a loan to be repaid over the term of the swap in a series of notional service payments. Each notional payment is equal to the corresponding off-market portion of the periodic payment. This amount is then discounted at a rate that provides a present value equal to the non-periodic payment. The portion of each notional loan service payment that is allocable to repayment of the notional principal and interest is determined by applying the discount rate to the unpaid balance of the notional loan. Notional principal payments are treated as additional periodic payments that are recognized as expense by the counterparty who made the prepayment and as income by the counterparty who received it. Thus the notional interest payments do not directly affect the calculation of income or loss. The allocation formula, however, effectively limits recognition of the upfront payment for any period to the amount by which the relevant portion of the off-market amount exceeds the imputed interest on the whole of the upfront payment that is not allocated to previous periods. The result is comparable to the amortization of the prepayment as loan principal to be repaid in level payments along with imputed interest. In this way, the regulations address the possible use of the cash-basis recognition of non-periodic payments as a means of accelerating income inclusion in order to freshen loss carryovers. If the non-periodic payments are not significant, the failure to impute interest for recognition on an accrual basis means that the expected gain or loss associated with the upfront payment is recognized when it is realized, and the benefit of anticipated deferral remains.[86]

Assume that the off-market swap in example 6 gives rise to a non-periodic payment of $35,666 that is not significant. In this case, the NPC regulations require Lori and Marvin to amortize the amount over the term of the swap in increments of $17,147 for year one and $18,519 for year two. These amounts plus accrued interest are deemed to be repaid in two level payments of $20,000 each (the expected value of the corresponding off-market payment for each of the two years of the contract). The discount rate of 8 percent that the counterparties used to arrive at the amount of the prepayment is applied to calculate notional interest income and expense of $2,853 as part of the first level payment of $20,000. The other $17,147 of that payment is deemed to be the excess of the off-market amount over the imputed interest and is allocated to year one for recognition as an additional periodic amount deductible by Lori (the counterparty who made the prepayment) and taxable to Marvin (the counterparty who received the prepayment). The remaining principal balance of \$18,519 is deemed to accrue \$1,481 of interest in year two, with the second level payment of \$20,000 repaying that interest plus the principal balance. The latter amount is in effect allocated to year two as an additional periodic amount for recognition by the counterparties. Thus Lori, as the counterparty who made the prepayment, may deduct the \$35,666 prepayment over two years, but no amount of expected gain on that prepayment is imputed as interest and recognized by her as income on an accrual basis. Marvin, as the counterparty who received the prepayment, recognizes the same prepayment as income over two years, but no amount of expected loss is imputed as interest expense that is deductible on an accrual basis.

In general, the NPC regulations do not impute interest on caps and floors.[87] The regulations are concerned primarily with the allocation of the single premium to each series of embedded options.[88] The non-periodic premium is bifurcated into a series of premiums, and the result is a series of separate cash-settled options payable on the respective settlement dates.[89] Each premium that is allocated separately may be recognized as expense and income by the holder and the issuer in the year to which the payment is allocated.[90] Open-transaction treatment is applied to the separate premiums embedded in the total premium payment for the interest-rate cap or floor. The NPC regulations originally required the imputation of interest on caps and collars that can be considered "significantly in-the-money," which were defined as any agreement that provided[91]

- a cap rate that was less than the market rate of the specified index by 25 basis points or more, or
- a floor rate that exceeded the market rate of the specified index by 25 basis points or more.

In either case, the option premium was considered to consist of a series of embedded loans allocable to the series of cash-settled options that comprised the cap or floor.[92]

Taxing the Embedded Derivatives in Contingent Debt

A failure to impute interest on an option or a prepaid forward contract creates significant problems in the taxation of debt with contingent payments attributable to an embedded bet associated with the option or prepaid forward. The term "contingent debt," in its broadest sense, refers to any financial instrument that is, in form, a debt instrument that provides for one or more payments that are dependent on specified variables; the payments are contingent in the sense that they are not fixed in amount on issue and give rise to unexpected gain or loss attributable to a bet associated with a derivative that is embedded in the debt instrument. A common example is debt with a payoff that depends on changes in the level of an index, such as the consumer price index (CPI) or a composite share price index, and the price of a specified commodity, such as gold. The changes in the level of an index or in the price of a commodity may affect either the amount of principal to be repaid or the amount of the return in the form of interest. Thus contingent debt includes any instrument that has (1) non-contingent principal and contingent interest, (2) contingent principal and non-contingent interest, or (3) contingent principal and interest.[93]

> **Example 7:** On January 1, 1998, Nathan acquires on issue a bond of Resource Inc. for $1,000. The bond matures in five years and entitles the holder to annual interest payments of $80. On maturity, the instrument pays $1,000 plus or minus the difference between $1,500 and the price of 10 common shares of Resource Inc.[94]

> **Example 8:** On January 1, 1998, Olivia acquires on issue a bond of Financial Corp. for $1,000. The bond matures in five years and entitles the holder at that time to the greater of the spot price of 10 common shares of Financial Corp. and $1,000.[95]

Each of the instruments in examples 7 and 8 can be bifurcated or disaggregated into a fixed-payment debt obligation and another building-block instrument that receive recognized tax treatment under the conventional cubbyholes. The bond in example 7 contains an embedded long forward contract on the 10 common shares of Resource Inc.; the bond in example 8 contains a European call option on the shares of Financial Corp. Nathan can replicate the bond in example 7 by acquiring separately (1) a five-year fixed-payment debt obligation that pays annual interest at 8 percent and (2) a cash-settled long forward contract on 10 common shares of Resource Inc. for $1,500 that matures in five years. If it is assumed that the forward contract is in fact available and that the forward price is on market, Nathan is not required to advance any funds and either pays or receives an amount in five years that is based on the difference between the spot and forward prices for the shares. He accrues the $400 of interest income on the separate bond over its five-year term in $80 increments. Any unexpected gain or loss on the long forward contract is recognized on maturity in five years when the payment rights under the contract are determined. Similarly, Olivia can replicate the bond in example 8 by acquiring separately (1) an original issue discount (OID) obligation that pays $1,000 in five years and (2) a cash-settled European call option on the 10 common shares of Financial Corp. If it is assumed that the discount rate is 8 percent per annum and that the exercise price under the call option is on market, Olivia pays $680 for the OID obligation and $320 for the option. She accrues the $320 expected gain ($1,000 due on maturity less the $680 issue price) on the OID obligation over its five-year term. Treatment of the option premium depends on the treatment under the relevant tax cubbyhole. Under a cash-basis approach, Olivia deducts the option premium when it is paid and the issuer includes in his income a corresponding amount. On exercise of the option, Olivia recognizes any unexpected gain represented by the amount by which the spot price of the shares of Financial Corp. exceeds the exercise price of the option, and the issuer recognizes a corresponding unexpected loss. Under an open-transaction approach, recognition of unexpected gain or loss and the option premium is deferred until exercise or maturity of the option.

Despite the apparent equivalence between these single instruments and the disaggregated positions, their tax treatment under traditional income tax principles is unclear. This uncertainty arises largely because the instruments combine the characteristics of other instruments that fit within different cubbyholes. In short, contingent-debt instruments must be classified as a whole and slotted within one of the cubbyholes for debt, equity, or derivative instruments.[96] If legal form is determinative, these hybrids can be considered debt. Concepts of debt that have been developed by the courts in some countries, however, often define debt as requiring an advance of funds in return for a right to receive a principal sum certain or other amount that can reasonably be expected to equal or exceed the amount advanced.[97] This type of substantive requirement goes beyond legal form to require an assessment of the significance of the contingencies that affect the amount of any payments. Moreover, if the contingencies depend on the performance of the business of the issuer or on changes in the value of underlying property owned by the issuer ("participating debt"), either the whole of the debt obligation or just the participating payments themselves may be characterized as equity.[98] Even if the contingencies do not support the recharacterization of a contingent-debt instrument as equity or a derivative, the rules that are applicable to fixed-payment debt do not readily apply. In particular, accrual recognition of interest income and expense tends to be based on the yield-to-maturity (YTM) method for the spreading of expected gains or losses over the term of a fixed-payment debt instrument.[99] The YTM method cannot account for amounts that depend, in whole or in part, on the resolution of contingencies after the obligation is issued. Faced with this difficulty, the courts in many countries have been willing to use the realization approach and require the recognition of contingent payments only when they are paid or when they become determinable.[100]

If it is assumed that the form and predominant characteristics of a contingent-debt instrument are sufficient to support its categorization within the debt cubbyhole, the problem that arises is how to determine the appropriate tax treatment of the contingent cash flows that are associated with the embedded derivative. Two principles can assist in making this determination. First, gain or loss realized from the holding and issuing of contingent debt should be recognized in full as ordinary income or expense.[101] Second, as with fixed-payment debt, gain or loss realized on the disposition of contingent debt in the secondary market should be considered ordinary income or loss.[102] These two principles eliminate issues of character arbitrage that are associated with the attempt to convert expected time-value returns into tax-preferred capital gains.[103] When ordinary income or loss character is assumed, the principal tax-policy issue becomes the appropriate timing rules for the recognition of the cash flows under a particular debt instrument. In this respect, three approaches are evident in certain legislative proposals and some of the tax literature:

- realization-based recognition,
- bifurcation, and
- expected-return taxation.

Realization-based recognition and bifurcation are based on an acceptance of the traditional tax cubbyholes and have generally been ineffective, largely because they provide opportunities for anticipated deferral that are attributable to a failure to impute accurately an amount of expected gain or loss. Although expected-return taxation is also based on an acceptance of the traditional tax cubbyholes, it modifies the treatment associated with options and other prepaid bets embedded in contingent debt. In effect, an expected return is imputed on the advance of funds that are otherwise attributable to these embedded derivatives, as well as the fixed-payment component of contingent debt. Various aspects of these approaches, as well as the problems associated with them, are reflected in the US regulatory regime governing the taxation of contingent debt.[104] The lengthy and intensive development of that regime produced three different sets of regulations ("the contingent-debt regulations")[105] that proposed, in turn, (1) a realization-based approach,[106] (2) a bifurcation approach,[107] and (3) a system of expected-return taxation.[108] In general, the approach reflected in the final regulations is consistent with the treatment of contingent debt under a comprehensive accrual regime that is intended to implement the dictates of expected-return taxation. Like the treatment of embedded debt in derivatives that are subject to the NPC regulations,[109] the treatment of contingent debt requires accrual recognition of any expected gain or loss associated with the embedded derivatives in a contingent-debt instrument.

Realization-Based Recognition and the Application of Bifurcation in the Context of the Tax Cubbyholes

As approaches to the taxation of contingent debt, realization-based recognition and bifurcation are linked primarily because they are applied in the context of the conventional tax cubbyholes for debt and derivatives. In its application to the cash flows associated with a contingent-debt instrument, the realization-based approach does not recognize contingent amounts as income for a holder and as expense of an issuer until the relevant contingencies are resolved and the amounts become determinable. Bifurcation requires that a contingent-debt instrument be broken down into its fixed-payment and derivative elements. The conventional tax cubbyholes applicable to the disaggregated parts are then applied to the cash flows associated with those parts. Because of their acceptance of those cubbyholes and the appropriateness of the related tax treatment for the basic building-block financial instruments, both realization-based recognition and bifurcation suffer from fundamental deficiencies that make them undesirable as approaches to the taxation of contingent debt. In particular, each approach fails to tax on an accrual basis the full amount of expected gain or loss associated with the fixed-payment debt and derivative components embedded in a contingent-debt instrument. This failure is critical because realization-based recognition of expected gain or loss eliminates the benefit (and associated problems) of the anticipated deferral of expected gain or loss only if all potential issuers are taxable at the same rates. In that case, the problems that usually arise from the provision of a deferral benefit for taxable holders are minimized by the offsetting detriment of a deferred interest deduction. The obvious problem with this state of affairs is the simple fact that, under most income tax systems, issuers and holders are taxable at different rates.[110] Indeed, the significant presence of holders and issuers who are taxable at different rates requires that expected gain or loss be recognized on an accrual basis in order to eliminate anticipated deferral and its associated opportunities for tax avoidance.

The extension of realization-based recognition to contingent debt is an extreme approach that provides the maximum amount of anticipated deferral for expected gain or loss associated with the embedded fixed-payment debt and derivative components. The application of this approach and its problems are illustrated by the experience with the first set of contingent-debt regulations released by the IRS in 1986 ("the 1986 proposals").[111] Under the proposed regulations, contingent debt was treated as an indivisible instrument and all contingent payments were recognized as interest income and expense on realization. The proposed regulations adopted a cost-recovery method of accounting for the associated cash flows by treating all non-contingent payments as non-taxable returns of principal. Accrual recognition was required only to the extent that the amount of these payments exceeded the issue price. In effect, the proposed regulations required no deduction for interest expense and no inclusion of interest income until the original investment in a contingent-debt instrument (represented by the issue price) was fully recovered. This approach applied generally in one of two situations:

- where the total non-contingent payments on a debt instrument were equal to or greater than the issue price and one or more contingent payments were not determined with reference to the value of publicly traded property ("the non-public-index contingent-interest regulations");[112] or
- where the non-contingent payments on a debt instrument were less than the issue price ("the contingent-principal regulations").[113]

Under the non-public-index contingent-interest regulations, the whole of the issue price of a contingent-debt instrument was allocated to the non-contingent payments and OID was considered to arise to the extent that the total of the non-contingent payments (the effective redemption amount) exceeded the issue price. Only this excess amount had to be accrued as interest expense of the issuer and as interest income of the holder. On resolution of the specified contingencies, the contingent payments were recognized as interest expense and income. Under the contingent-principal regulations, all non-contingent payments were treated as repayments of the issue price. To the extent that contingent payments exceeded the issue price, they were recognized as interest expense and income when they became fixed.

Compared with the conventional cubbyhole treatment of the separate issue of a fixed-payment debt instrument and a derivative providing cash flows comparable to the contingent payments, the non-public-index contingent-interest and the contingent-principal regulations provided recognition on maturity of a significant portion of the expected gain or loss associated with the embedded fixed-payment instrument. For example, the bond in example 7 would have been subject to the contingent-principal regulations because it provides total non-contingent payments of $400, which is less than the issue price. As a result, the whole of the $400 of non-contingent payments would have been considered repayments of principal, and the contingent payment due on maturity would have been treated in part as a repayment of principal and in part as a payment of interest. To be more specific, $600 of the contingent payment would have been allocated first to the remaining amount of principal (the $1,000 issue price less the $400 non-contingent interest payments), with any excess considered interest income and expense recognized on maturity of the instrument. This result is much different from that associated with the separate issue of a fixed-payment debt obligation and an on-market forward contract written on the shares of Resource Inc. With a separate issue, the $400 of interest income and expense would be recognized on an annual accrual basis and unexpected gain or loss on the forward contract would be recognized on realization (that is, on maturity of the contract).[114]

The result under the non-public-index contingent-interest regulations was not much better. If it is assumed that the contingent payments on the bond in example 8 are not determined with reference to the value of publicly traded property (the common shares of Financial Corp.), the bond would have been subject to the non-public-index contingent-interest regulations because the instrument provides a non-contingent payment that is equal to its issue price. The whole of the $1,000 issue price would have been allocated to the $1,000 non-contingent payment due on maturity, and no amount of OID would have arisen. The contingent payment due on maturity, based on the amount by which the spot price of the common shares of Financial Corp. exceeded $1,500, would have been recognized only at that time. The result would have been a significant deferral of OID that would have arisen if the bond had been bifurcated into an OID obligation issued for $680 and a European call option on the shares of Financial Corp. issued for the remaining $320 of the $1,000 issue price.

Because the realization basis reflected in the 1986 proposals would have applied to both issuers and holders of contingent debt, the deferral of expected amounts was available for both deductibility and inclusion purposes and was assumed to be neutral in its effect. The obvious problem with this assumption (that issuers and holders are taxable at comparable rates) became apparent soon after the proposed regulations were released. Certain issuers subject to zero or low effective tax rates attempted to take advantage of a lack of symmetry in tax rates and issued contingent-debt instruments to taxable holders in the United States.[115] The availability of the deferred interest deduction was irrelevant to these issuers; they were more interested in the tax advantage that could be gained by issuing contingent-debt instruments to taxable holders who valued the deferred interest inclusion and were willing to accept an expected pre-tax return lower than that offered on a comparable instrument that did not provide the benefit of anticipated deferral. In a sense, the realization basis reflected in the 1986 proposals allowed taxpayers to elect deferred or accrual treatment by using a contingent-debt instrument or a combination of fixed-payment debt and a separate forward contract or option.[116] The deferred interest deduction also represented a "tax disadvantage" for taxable issuers that was said to have "chilled the issuance of any number of economically viable transactions."[117] The disadvantage was not offset by the benefit of a deferred income inclusion for tax-exempt and non-resident investors who were potential holders of contingent debt.[118]

In a second set of proposed regulations released in 1991 ("the bifurcation regulations"),[119] the IRS attempted to eliminate a significant element of the benefit of anticipated deferral that was available under the 1986 proposals. The second proposed regulations applied bifurcation as a tax technique to achieve greater consistency in tax treatment between the issue of a contingent-debt instrument and the separate issue of the embedded components that together provided equivalent cash flows. In general, the bifurcation regulations purported to achieve this goal by identifying the component elements of a contingent-debt instrument and taxing them separately under the conventional tax cubbyholes. To the extent that the bifurcation regulations applied, a contingent-debt instrument was not treated as an indivisible instrument, and a portion of the issue price was allocated to the embedded derivatives. In effect, this approach considered a greater portion of the non-contingent payments to be expected gain or loss (and not repayment of the issue price) recognized on an accrual basis. The bifurcation regulations applied when the total non-contingent payments on a debt instrument were equal to or greater than the issue price, and one or more contingent payments were determined by reference to the value of publicly traded property. In all other cases, the realization basis under the 1986 proposals applied. When the bifurcation regulations applied, they allocated the issue price of a contingent-debt instrument between the non-contingent and contingent amounts by discounting the non-contingent payments to their present value using a discount rate equivalent to the current yields on comparable fixed-payment debt of comparable issuers. If the contingent payments were "substantially equivalent to publicly traded property" (for example, a publicly traded option), the bifurcation regulations allocated the issue price on the basis of the value of that property. The non-contingent payments were treated as a separate fixed-payment debt instrument subject to the accrual rules for interest income and expense. Contingent payments were "treated in accordance with their economic substance as payments pursuant to one or more options or other property rights." The application of the bifurcation regulations can be illustrated with the bond in example 8. Under the proposed bifurcation approach, the bond would have been split into two separate instruments: (1) an OID obligation with a redemption amount of $1,000 and an issue price of $680 (assuming an 8 percent discount rate); and (2) a European call option on the shares of Financial Corp. issued for a premium of $320 (the remaining portion of the issue price of the contingent-debt instrument taken as a whole). Both the issuer and the holder would have been required to accrue $320 of OID over the term of the instrument rather than recognize the whole of the amount on maturity. The option would have been treated as a separate instrument that gave rise to unexpected gain or loss on maturity.[120]

Despite their apparent improvement over the 1986 proposals, the bifurcation regulations attracted considerable criticism, which tended to follow one of three lines.[121] The first line of criticism focused on the inconsistent and limited scope of the application of bifurcation. In particular, the bifurcation regulations applied only when a contingent-debt instrument provided for payments that were determined by reference to the value of publicly traded property. Familiar contingent-debt instruments, such as shared appreciation mortgages and participating debt with payments based on the profitability of an issuer, would not have been bifurcated, even though the contingent payments were equivalent to an option on the relevant property.[122] Similarly, contingent-debt instruments such as the bond in example 7 would not have been bifurcated, because their issue price exceeded the total of all non-contingent payments.[123] In the absence of bifurcation in these kinds of situations, recognition of interest on the fixed-payment debt embedded in these instruments remained subject to the flawed treatment under the 1986 proposals and their provision of anticipated deferral. It was argued that the bifurcation regulations treated in significantly different ways instruments that were not all that different in their cash flow patterns. In short, the bifurcation regulations created substantial discontinuities in tax treatment on either side of the distinction between[124]

- debt with contingent payments that are determined by reference to publicly traded as opposed to non-publicly traded property, and
- debt with non-contingent payments that are equal to or greater than the issue price of the instrument and debt with non-contingent payments that are less than the issue price.

A second line of criticism focused on the vagueness of the bifurcation proposals, which depended on a concept of "economic equivalence."[125] The essence of this criticism is the familiar problem of multiple bifurcations under the cubbyhole tax system.[126] As described in chapter 1, the interrelation of the basic building-block financial instruments and their pricing allows instruments to be combined in various ways that produce equivalent cash flows.[127] This interrelation is seen most starkly in the put-call parity theorem and the various combinations of equivalent transactions that it reveals.[128] The problem is that the cubbyhole system of taxation often taxes these various combinations differently when the tax treatments specified by the cubbyholes are applied separately to the basic instruments that, in the aggregate, provide equivalent cash flows. As a result, the sum of the tax treatments of the different parts is not equal, even though they add up to the same whole.[129] The bifurcation regulations were premised on an analysis of the contingent-payment rights in a particular debt instrument as one or more options or other "economically equivalent" property rights, the tax treatment of which should be applied to the contingent payments. This principle quickly proved much easier to state in the abstract than to apply in practice and raised serious questions about the analysis of equivalence when applied to specific instruments that are more complex than simple bonds such as the ones in examples 7 and 8.[130] In other words, it was not always obvious which of several possible combinations of property rights should be chosen as the equivalent of a particular contingent-debt payment and, moreover, what the tax treatment should be even where equivalence could be identified.[131] Faced with the difficulties associated with such an analysis, the IRS was unprepared to follow through with the development of the necessary details of the bifurcation regulations.[132]

A third and more fundamental line of criticism emphasized that any effort to extend the application of the bifurcation regulations and develop the necessary details would ultimately be worthless.[133] In particular, some practitioners argued that the regulations were so flawed in their basic premises that any effort to develop the necessary details should be abandoned. This flaw was seen to be rooted in an acceptance of the standard tax cubbyholes and their treatment of the bifurcated components of a contingent-debt instrument. As was noted above, the bifurcation regulations were an improvement over realization-based recognition in that a greater portion of expected gain or loss in the form of OID would have been accrued by issuers and holders. This result generally would have approximated more closely the tax consequences of issuing and holding the embedded components of a contingent-debt instrument separately. Some critics of the bifurcation regulations asserted, however, that bifurcation resulted in an inappropriate deferral of the expected time-value return associated with options or prepaid forward contracts embedded in contingent-debt instruments.[134] In effect, the regulations would have treated the amount of the issue price of contingent debt allocated to an embedded option or forward contract in the same way as if the instruments had been issued separately from the embedded fixed-payment debt. The bifurcation of options resulted in realization-based recognition of gain or loss on maturity and, for holders and issuers who were not traders or dealers in financial instruments, characterization as a capital gain or loss.[135] The result of the bifurcation of forward contracts was much more uncertain, because in allocating a portion of the issue price to the fixed-payment component of a contingent-debt instrument, the regulations often allocated a residual amount of the issue price to an embedded forward contract. The result was the creation of a prepaid forward contract whose tax treatment was unclear.[136] In short, in the context of the conventional tax cubbyholes, bifurcation simply perpetuated the mistaxation of options and other embedded derivatives, such as prepaid forward contracts that provide expected gain or loss. Some critics of the bifurcation regulations argued that a more appropriate, and much simpler, alternative to bifurcated treatment would be one that imputes interest at the riskless rate on the whole of the issue price of a contingent-debt instrument, including embedded options and prepaid forward contracts. Under an alternative of this kind, accrued but unpaid interest is added to the cost of the instrument, and the difference between the total of all contingent payments and the adjusted cost is recognized as unexpected gain or loss on realization. This simple insight provided much of the conceptual basis for the approach reflected in the final US regulations.

Expected-Return Taxation and the Imputation of Interest on Embedded Derivatives

The application of expected-return taxation to contingent-debt instruments requires a determination of the expected gain or loss associated with both the fixed-payment debt and derivative components embedded in the instruments.[137] Like bifurcation, expected-return taxation begins, therefore, by explicitly recognizing that contingent-debt instruments consist of fixed-payment debt and one or more derivative instruments on which there may be expected gain or loss. To eliminate the benefit of anticipated deferral, expected-return taxation requires the recognition of all expected gain or loss on an accrual basis, whether the gain or loss is attributable to the fixed-payment debt or to derivative elements. When expected gain or loss is attributable to derivative elements, the issue is the same as that when instruments are derivatives in form but contain an embedded loan that arises when one of the parties prepays the expected amount of his obligation.[138] As was described above, the prepayment effectively represents the present value of the bet for the payer determined on the basis of forward prices for the relevant asset. The difference between the prepayment and the forward price is the expected gain for the payer and the expected loss for the payee that should be accrued over the term of the bet; otherwise, the prepayment will give rise to anticipated deferral.

This basic insight is, apparently, the conceptual basis of proposed regulations released by the IRS in 1994,[139] which were followed by the release of final regulations in substantially similar form in 1996 ("the final regulations").[140] In general, these regulations abandon the realization-based approach of the 1986 proposals, as well as the bifurcation approach of the 1991 regulations, and impose in their place a "non-contingent bond method" on most forms of contingent debt. Under this method, the expected amount of all contingent payments must be accrued over the relevant term. In essence, a contingent-debt instrument is treated as an indivisible instrument, and both issuers and holders must accrue interest on the whole of the issue price, even though a portion of that price may be allocable to an embedded option or prepaid forward contract on which interest would not normally accrue. The result is comparable to that of a bifurcation approach that imputes an expected return on both the embedded fixed-payment debt and derivative components of a contingent-debt instrument. Adjustments to the amount of accrued interest take into account unexpected gain or loss that is realized on resolution of the bet elements.

The non-contingent bond method described in the final regulations consists of two essential elements intended to require accrual recognition of the expected gain or loss on contingent debt. Those elements involve the determination of the expected gain or loss associated with a particular instrument and the spreading of that amount over the relevant term on the basis of a YTM calculation similar to that with fixed-payment debt.[141] First, a "comparable yield" for comparable non-contingent debt of the issuer is established on the basis of market information such as the level of subordination, the term of the particular contingent instrument, the timing of payments, and the existing market conditions.[142] The risk associated with the contingent payments or the liquidity of the instrument is not considered, and the comparable yield may not be less than an average of the US government treasury bill rate ("the applicable federal rate" or "AFR"). Accordingly, interest is imputed and must accrue in an amount at least equal to the riskless rate of return. Second, issuers must construct a projected payment schedule that takes into account the amount of all non-contingent payments and the projected amount (as of the issue date) of all contingent payments due under the instrument. The accrual of interest expense and income is determined on the basis of the projected payment schedule, which must produce a yield equal to the comparable yield. The projected payment schedule may not be revised after the issue date of the contingent-debt instrument, although it must be adjusted at the outset as necessary to reflect the comparable yield. In other words, once the projected payment schedule is constructed, a level yield is computed for the whole of a contingent-debt instrument on the basis of the projected payments, which must conform to the comparable yield.[143] That yield is multiplied by the "adjusted issue price" for an accrual period, which product must equal the amount of accrued interest expense or income in respect of the period. The "adjusted issue price" is the issue price of the whole instrument, which is determined by treating all projected payments as actually paid. Because the accrual of interest income and expense is based on the determination of a comparable yield, the purpose of the projected payment schedule is largely to determine the timing of adjustments that must be made when the amount of any contingent payments turns out to be greater than, or less than, the projected amount.[144] When contingent payments are made, both the issuer and the holder must adjust the amount of accrued expense and income to reflect the difference between the projected contingent payments and the actual payments. If the amount of any payment exceeds the accrued interest, the excess is treated as additional interest in the year of payment. If the amount of any payment is less than the projected amount, the difference between actual and projected amounts reduces accrued interest for the year of payment. If the amount of the difference is greater than the accrued interest, the remaining excess is treated as ordinary loss by the holder (ordinary gain by the issuer) to the extent of accrued interest for prior years. Through this mechanism, unexpected gain or loss attributable to the bet element in a contingent-debt instrument is recognized as ordinary income or loss on realization.[145]

In establishing the projected payment schedule, the issuer must account for all non-contingent payments and the expected value of all contingent payments. For this purpose, contingent payments are divided into two types.[146] The first type includes all contingent payments that are based on market information and that are substantially similar to a property right for which forward prices are generally available.[147] The projected amount is equal to the arm's-length quoted forward price for the substantially similar property right. If the forward price of an embedded derivative is on market, no additional amount need be projected to be paid or received as of the time of issue. In effect, any contingent payment that is ultimately paid or received is considered to be entirely unexpected and is recognized on realization. If the price for an embedded forward is off market, there will be a projected amount at the time of issue equal to the difference between the two prices. That amount effectively represents expected gain or loss and must be spread over the term of the instrument and recognized on an accrual basis. To illustrate, assume that the forward contract embedded in the bond in example 7 is on market and constitutes a property right for which forward price quotes are readily available. A payment schedule for the bond thus consists of (1) the $400 of annual interest payments, (2) the $1,000 redemption amount due on maturity, and (3) nil in respect of the forward contract. Because the forward contract is on market, the bet that it reflects is a fair one, and no amount can be projected to be paid on maturity in respect of that right.[148] If the forward price is off market (say, $1,400), the bet has an expected value of $100 (the $1,500 on-market price less the $1,400 contract price), and the holder is considered to have prepaid the present value of that expected amount ($68 at a discount rate of 8 percent) with a portion of the issue price. The $32 difference is accrued over the term of the contingent-debt instrument, as is the additional $32 of OID that is considered to have arisen on the embedded fixed-payment debt.[149]

Where a contingent-payment right is substantially similar to an exchange-traded option, the issuer must construct a forward price by compounding the spot price of the option by the applicable treasury bill rate from the date of issue to the due date of the contingent payment. The projected amount of the contingent payment is thus the spot price of the option plus the imputed expected increase in value. This approach ensures that an issuer and a holder must accrue over the term of a contingent-debt instrument both the current spot price of the embedded option and an imputed return equal to the riskless rate.[150] The spot price is treated as implicit OID on the contingent-debt instrument, and the equivalent amount of the issue price is allocated to the cost of the embedded option. The implicit cost of carry associated with an option is assumed to be the expected return, which must also be accrued over the period from the issue of the contingent-debt instrument to the time that payment of the contingent amount is due. For instance, the projected fixed payment associated with the bond in example 8 is $1,000, which gives rise to $320 of OID ($680 issue price based on a discount rate of 8 percent) that must be accrued over the five-year term. If the spot price of the embedded option is $320, the projected contingent payment associated with it is $470 (assuming a treasury bill rate of 8 percent), and the $150 excess is also accrued over the five-year term.

The second type of contingent payment for which a projected payment schedule must be constructed includes all contingent payments that are based on information that is unique to the issuer, such as dividend payments on its shares, realized profits, or share values ("participating debt").[151] The projected amount of the payment is the expected amount of the contingent payment, which must be set at an amount that produces the comparable yield. The final regulations provide that the projected amount of contingent payments based on non-market information must be adjusted first in providing a projected payment schedule that produces the comparable yield. Because these contingent payments are not based on market information, their expected amounts are the most difficult to determine accurately.

Eliminating Inconsistencies and Discontinuities Along the Boundary Between Debt and Derivatives

Significance of Administrative and Compliance Concerns

Under a comprehensive accrual regime, the distinction between debt and derivative instruments is a simple one. Interest income and expense should be imputed on any advance of funds before performance, irrespective of the form of the particular financial instrument. Imputation occurs as the result of a general requirement to accrue expected gain or loss on a YTM basis. Critical to the application of this basic principle is a wide definition of affected financial instruments, which ensures that all debt and derivatives are potentially subject to accrual treatment.[152] In particular, a definition of debt instruments that includes all instruments in which funds are advanced in return for a right to receive an amount in the future ensures that all options and derivatives with prepaid bets (prepaid and off-market forwards and swaps) are treated as debt and are subject to accrual recognition of the associated expected gain or loss.[153] A definition this wide eliminates inconsistencies in the tax treatment of fixed-payment debt and the embedded debt in derivatives, and small changes in the cash flows of different instruments do not result in disproportionately different tax treatments. Indeed, in the absence of a system of accretion taxation, the problems that arise from the attempt to distinguish between debt and derivative instruments (and to assign them to the appropriate tax cubbyholes) can be effectively addressed only through the application of expected-return taxation to the expected gain or loss associated with the embedded debt in any derivative, as well as the embedded option or prepaid forward contract in a contingent-debt instrument.

As a model for the application of expected-return taxation to derivatives with embedded debt, the NPC regulations in the United States are the most aggressive legislative attempt to use the concept of bifurcation as the basis for the imputation of interest. The US regulations governing contingent debt also make use of bifurcation in a basic way to identify embedded options and forward contracts and impute interest on the related premiums and/or prepayments of the obligations of the counterparties. Compared with an ideal accrual regime, however, each set of regulations is far from comprehensive. It is not entirely clear why there remain limitations on the application of the US regulations; there may be a perceived need to balance the administrative and compliance burden associated with a rigorous application of expected-return taxation against a desire for theoretical purity and the elimination of all inconsistencies and discontinuities.[154] For instruments that contain a debt element but that provide predominantly unexpected gains and losses associated with a dominant bet element, the administrative and compliance burden may seem too great to justify such application.[155] In the event, a range of instruments are excepted from accrual treatment, including long-dated options and prepaid forwards that are issued on a stand-alone basis and that are outside the scope of both the NPC and the contingent-debt regulations.

There is nothing unique about the application of a comprehensive accrual regime that eliminates the need to account for administrative constraints and the attendant line drawing. The same administrative and compliance concerns that have caused US tax-policy makers to hesitate in applying expected-return taxation to all advances of funds are equally relevant in the context of a comprehensive accrual regime. Theoretical purity may thus have to be compromised in order to distinguish between the debt and derivative cubbyholes in a manner similar to that under the US legislation. It is argued here, however, that the details of the perceived administrative and compliance burden associated with the extended application of expected-return taxation have not been clearly set out and may be overstated.[156] The only sensible application of expected-return taxation as a second-best approach to accretion taxation requires the identification of the embedded debt in all hybrid instruments and the imputation of interest in an amount at least equal to the riskless rate. Where administrative and compliance concerns dictate an exception to an approach of this kind, those concerns should be clearly stated and weighed carefully against the costs of the inconsistencies and discontinuities that result, as well as against the administrative and compliance costs of defining the scope of any exception to accrual treatment.

In assessing the significance of administrative and compliance concerns, it is important to distinguish two levels of analysis relevant to the application of a system of expected-return taxation along the boundary between debt and derivatives. The first level involves the decision to impute interest income or expense to the extent of the expected gain or loss associated with a defined range of hybrid instruments. This kind of "first-order" decision concerns the scope of the application of expected-return taxation to particular instruments. The second level involves various decisions regarding the technical details necessary to the application of accrual recognition of expected amounts. These "second-order" decisions concern the measurement of expected amounts and the determination of the accrual methods that implement expected-return taxation; they presuppose an acceptance of the first-order decision to extend accrual treatment to particular instruments. The decision regarding the scope of the application of expected-return taxation effectively defines the boundary between debt and derivative instruments and is the more fundamental policy decision. It is at this level of decision making that concerns about administrative and compliance burdens must be weighed carefully against the costs of the inconsistencies and discontinuities that result from making exceptions to the accrual taxation of expected gains and losses. From close examination of these administrative and compliance concerns, it is arguable that tax-policy makers should almost always err on the side of caution by extending the imputation of interest to any advance of funds before performance, irrespective of the form of the particular instrument. The alternative approach, that of excepting certain instruments from accrual recognition, also requires a definition of the boundary between debt and derivative instruments, and when a definition is called for, administrative and compliance costs inevitably arise. These costs are compounded by troublesome inconsistencies in the taxation of fixed-payment debt and the embedded debt in certain derivatives that can be used as debt substitutes.

This distinction in levels of analysis and its significance for the application of a comprehensive accrual regime are evident in the US regulations governing notional principal contracts and contingent debt. In general, the regulations reflect some important concessions to administrative constraints. In their second-order decisions regarding the design of accrual methods, however, US tax-policy makers have drawn on a range of alternatives to accommodate administrative and compliance concerns without undermining the integrity of the boundary between debt and derivatives. Some of the more obvious and important of these compromises are apparent in four broad areas.

The first area concerns the choice of a formula that reduces the expected value of contingent-debt payments to an appropriate yield to maturity. The application of expected-return taxation to any contingent payment requires a formulaic approach that imputes interest on the basis of ex ante projections of the expected value of the payments.[157] In the process, a rate of return must be applied to the whole of the issue price of a contingent-debt instrument. As do accrual regimes that apply generally to fixed-payment debt, the US contingent-debt regulations require the accrual of interest on the basis of a projection that depends on the unique characteristics of a particular instrument and the rate of return implied by those characteristics. Indeed, the US regulations require the rate of return on a contingent-debt instrument to conform to the yield on comparable fixed-payment debt of the particular issuer. An alternative approach involves the imputation of interest on the whole of the issue price of a contingent-debt instrument using the riskless interest rate.[158] Although this alternative is simpler than the approach under the US regulations, it does not require accrual recognition of any risk premium included in the projected yield on a contingent-debt instrument. This failure is inconsistent with the approach to the taxation of fixed-payment debt generally, whereby the pure time-value element and any risk premium incorporated in the fixed rate must be accrued over the term of the instrument.[159] If it is assumed that this treatment is a constant feature of income tax systems, consistency of treatment of the expected gain or loss associated with fixed-payment debt and a contingent-debt instrument requires adoption of an approach similar to that under the US regulations. Where, however, expected-return taxation cannot be applied because of difficulties in determining the expected value of contingent payments, imputation of interest at the riskless rate is preferable to realization-based recognition because the latter approach provides much greater opportunity for anticipated deferral.[160]

The second area in which US tax-policy makers have balanced practical and theoretical goals concerns the determination of the expected value of an embedded derivative that gives rise to contingent payments. In general, the US contingent-debt regulations use forward prices to determine the expected value of embedded options and forwards. As a result, a contingent-debt instrument must be bifurcated before a payment schedule can be constructed for the contingent amounts attributable to the embedded derivatives. The contingent-debt regulations, however, minimize the problem of multiple bifurcations that was seen to arise under the 1991 proposed regulations by requiring the accrual of any expected gain or loss on the embedded derivatives. The inquiry is directed instead to the identification of a bifurcation that mimics the most probable form in which the instruments would be issued separately,[161] and it is further assumed that expected gain or loss associated with the instruments would otherwise be accrued as interest income or expense. As Shuldiner has pointed out, a pure system of expected-return taxation requires the determination of the "true" expected value for the bets associated with options and forward contracts based on actual expectations regarding the price of the underlying assets.[162] Forward prices are simply a function of the spot price of an asset plus the implicit cost of carry less any expected return associated with the asset for the relevant period;[163] in no sense are they an expression of market expectations about future values, which, by definition, cannot be known. Forward prices are therefore only a proxy for expected values; yet, in "a competitive equilibrium in a risk-neutral world,"[164] forward prices and expected values are, in fact, equivalent.[165] If they were not, arbitrageurs would avail themselves of profits by purchasing a commodity forward and selling it in the spot market after taking delivery, until the forward price increased to a level that eliminated the arbitrage profits.[166] In a world of risk-averse or risk-preferring purchasers and sellers of forward contracts and options, the expected value and forward price of an asset will differ.[167] Nonetheless, it seems preferable from an administrative perspective[168] to follow the approach reflected in the US regulations and use forward prices as a convenient proxy for expected values and as a means of determining the amount of expected gain or loss associated with an embedded option or forward contract.

In this respect, it is notable that the earlier versions of the Australian accrual proposals did not advocate the use of forward prices to determine the expected values of contingent payments associated with various contingent-debt instruments.[169] In particular, the proposals for non-traded contingent debt[170] required the calculation of a yield to maturity on the basis of (1) an assumption of constant growth where contingent cash flows are referable to changes in an index or other variable, or (2) an assumption of a constant level in any other case (other than share-indexed instruments that are always subject to an assumption of constant growth). Although these assumptions are administratively convenient, they do not reflect "true" expected values and do not produce an accrual that is more accurate than one that is based on the forward prices of embedded derivatives. Indeed, assumptions about the future levels of specified indexes that are based on observations of past levels provide entirely random expected amounts. Forward prices also do not provide any indication of what future values will be, but at least they represent what market participants are willing to pay now for an entitlement to a future payment. Forward prices thus provide a market-based measure of expected values determined purely ex ante, which is the perspective underlying any attempt to accrue expected amounts on that basis. Assumptions about the level of an index provide, at best, a reasonable proxy for expected amounts that are linked to interest and inflation indexes. Any mismeasurement of expected amounts that results from a failure to use forward prices for these indexes may be offset by the benefits of adopting a simplified tax-accounting method that uses assumptions about the level of the indexes.[171] The simplification is important, because a large number of debt instruments with contingent payments are floating-rate or inflation-indexed instruments.

The third area concerns the extent to which a specified YTM calculation must be applied, without deviation, to expected amounts. At one extreme, the US contingent-debt regulations require accrual recognition on the basis of a projected payment schedule that produces the comparable yield on a fixed-payment debt instrument. There is no flexibility in the application of the YTM method once the comparable yield is determined. The Australian accrual proposals, in contrast, provide significant flexibility in establishing the parameters for applying accrual recognition of expected gains or losses on contingent debt. This flexibility follows largely from the decision to forgo the use of a comparable yield on the fixed-payment debt of a particular issuer as the determinative factor in the measurement of the expected return on a contingent obligation. In place of this standard, the Australian proposals substitute a determination of expected values of contingent payments on the basis of specified assumptions about the level of the indexes on which the payments are based. Additional flexibility is provided by the fact that the significance of the relevant assumptions is limited to their use as the basis for determining a benchmark YTM calculation within which any chosen method of accrual can deviate, provided that the deviation is within a specified standard (10 percent) for any year.[172] The problem with this flexibility under the Australian proposals is the simple fact that it is based on a benchmark that is difficult to justify, largely because of the use of the specified assumptions about the level of the relevant indexes. As was argued above, these assumptions are problematic indicators of the expected values of contingent payments, particularly when compared with the use of forward prices for the embedded derivatives in a contingent-debt instrument that provide cash flows analogous to the contingent payments. An interesting compromise between the approach under the US regulations and the Australian accrual proposals is the specification of a benchmark accrual standard that is based on a comparable yield on non-contingent debt using forward prices to determine the expected amount of contingent payments. Accrual methods can offer some flexibility by permitting limited deviation from the benchmark within a specified standard. In this way, a more theoretically defensible benchmark for accrual treatment of contingent debt can be established and, at the same time, allow some deviation from the benchmark in recognition of the difficulties in applying accrual methodologies to ex ante projections of contingent payments. This ability to deviate should be restricted and subject to anti-abuse rules in order to ensure that significant opportunities for anticipated deferral are unavailable.

The fourth area in which US tax-policy makers have sought a compromise between administrative realities and theoretical purity concerns those instruments (swaps, caps, floors, and collars) that provide a series of variable payments based on the resolution of specified contingencies. In these instances, there is a need to separate disguised loans from periodic payments that represent unexpected losses of the payer; in practice, however, it can be difficult to distinguish an amount that represents the prepayment of an obligation from other amounts that represent unexpected losses arising on the unfavourable resolution of a contingency for the payer. A related difficulty, to the extent that a payment can be identified as a prepayment, is the need to determine an appropriate payment schedule for repayment of the loan principal and the expected time-value return. A system of expected-return taxation can address these problems by requiring the allocation of prepayments on the basis of the relative fair market values of the related obligations measured using forward rates (in the case of swaps) and option-pricing models (in the case of caps, floors, and collars).[173] Once this allocation is made, payments made by the counterparties are treated as payments of accrued interest and principal to the extent of the expected amount of the related obligation. Any excess is considered unexpected gain; any shortfall is recognized as unexpected loss. Although implementing this approach is difficult, it represents a one-time burden imposed when a prepayment is made by one of the counterparties.[174] Similar issues are addressed in other areas, including the allocation of a global sale price among various assets on an asset sale.[175] In general, the US NPC regulations provide a useful and workable model for the resolution of these allocation issues with "non-periodic payments" under swaps, caps, floors, and collars.[176] To some extent, the NPC regulations alleviate the administrative and compliance burden by limiting the accrual of interest income and expense to non-periodic payments that can be considered "significant."[177] In this respect, administrative and compliance concerns do not preclude the treatment of non-periodic payments as embedded loans, where the payments are made or received by a counterparty on an assignment to a third party.[178] In that case, changes in the spot price of the referenced index or commodity can create an off-market instrument. Expected gain or loss arises for an assignee who prepays (or receives a payment) of a portion of the expected future obligations on an assignment from one of the counterparties. As with a prepayment made between counterparties who enter into an off-market instrument, the amount of that gain or loss is the difference between the expected amount of an on-market obligation and the amount of the payment. These gains or losses are comparable to the discount or premium that arises on a secondary-market transfer of fixed-payment debt and should be accrued as interest income or expense in much the same way, at least to the extent that those amounts must also be accrued when they arise on the entering into of an off-market instrument.[179]

Decisions in each of these four areas require the resolution of some important design issues in the application of a sensible regime of expected-return taxation to the embedded debt in certain derivatives and the embedded derivatives in contingent debt; yet, as was emphasized above, the relevant issues are based on the premise that expected-return taxation must be applied to expected gain or loss on the various instruments. For that reason, it was suggested that these second-order issues are not as fundamental or problematic as the first-order decision regarding the scope of the application of accrual treatment. In effect, it is assumed that a system of expected-return taxation will apply to the relevant instruments, and these second-order design issues will affect only the degree to which theoretical purity will be maintained in the application of the accrual principle. To the extent that the accrual principle is compromised in its application by administrative and compliance concerns, the benefit of anticipated deferral may be available. That benefit may be tolerable, however, because deviations involve modification of the measurement of the expected return associated with a particular instrument. In other words, because accrual taxation is still applied to expected gain or loss, any refinements in the application of accrual methods that deviate from the expected-return ideal do not amount to problematic exceptions that provide realization-based recognition for the whole of the expected gain or loss associated with the embedded debt in a derivative or the embedded derivative in a contingent-debt instrument. Before these issues can be addressed, it must be determined which instruments will be subject to expected-return taxation. This determination involves making the more fundamental decision of where to draw the boundary between the tax cubbyholes for debt and derivatives. Even in the context of this important policy decision, policy makers and administrators have tended to compromise their desire to extend debt characterization to all payments in advance of performance with an approach that maintains the realization-based recognition of gains or losses on derivatives that have an expected time-value return that is not considered significant. This approach has the important consequence of creating problematic inconsistencies and discontinuities in taxation that do not arise as starkly with the kinds of second-order design issues that were described above.

Case for the Extension of Expected-Return Taxation to Options and Prepaid Forwards

Weaknesses of a "Facts-and-Circumstances" Approach to the Boundary Between Debt and Derivatives

In defining the scope of accrual treatment, there are two approaches to the application of expected-return taxation along the boundary between debt and derivative instruments. One approach is consistent with the application of a comprehensive accrual regime[180] and involves the identification of a loan wherever funds are advanced in return for a right to receive an amount in the future. Under this approach, as was described above,[181] the cash flows associated with a particular hybrid instrument must be bifurcated into a time-value element and a bet element. Wherever funds are advanced in return for a right to receive an amount in the future, the party who advances those funds should be considered to have made a loan with an expected time-value return. Bifurcation is invoked in a simple sense as an analytical technique to identify the loan advance and the associated expected return.[182] Interest income and expense equal to the amount of the expected return should be imputed on the loan advance and recognized on an accrual basis, irrespective of the form of a particular instrument. An approach of this kind represents, therefore, the application of expected-return taxation in its extreme form to all expected gains and losses. To the extent that the cash flows under a particular financial instrument are bifurcated into their time-value and bet elements, the boundary between debt and derivative instruments is drawn on the basis of the character of those cash flows, and expected-return taxation is applied in the broadest possible manner. Realization-based recognition is limited to the bet element in any instrument and the unexpected gains or losses that arise on resolution of the specified bet.

The other approach, referred to here as a facts-and-circumstances test, is consistent with legislative and administrative practice in many countries[183] and provides much more limited scope for the accrual recognition of expected gains and losses. As Hariton has described more fully,[184] this approach involves the characterization of a particular hybrid as predominantly indebtedness or a derivative based on an assessment of the facts and circumstances associated with the issue of the instrument. Imputation of interest is limited to those instruments that have a predominantly time-value return as indicated by certain factors, including:[185]

- the variability of the associated cash flows,
- the term of the instrument,
- the presence of a guaranteed minimum return,
- a promise to repay a fixed amount,
- the relative size of any advance of funds compared with the overall transaction or instrument of which the advance is a part, and
- the legal form of an instrument.

Because a debt instrument is conventionally regarded as an instrument with minimal variation in the amount and timing of promised payments, variability of the cash flows is a critical indication of the degree of risk associated with a derivative.[186] In short, a lack of variability indicates that the time-value return, rather than a bet element, is predominant. In general, however, no one factor is determinative, and there is no defined point at which the variability of the cash flows necessarily indicates a characterization as debt or a derivative. Moreover, a facts-and-circumstances approach is an all-or-nothing proposition: the expected gain or loss associated with a hybrid is accorded either accrual or realization-based recognition on the basis of the particular instrument's characterization as either predominantly debt with a time-value return or predominantly a derivative with unexpected gain or loss attributable to a bet.

The US NPC and contingent-debt regulations are a curious combination of these two extreme approaches to the definition of the boundary between (1) debt and the application of accrual taxation and (2) derivatives and the application of realization-based recognition. In extending expected-return taxation to the embedded debt in certain notional principal contracts and the embedded derivatives in contingent debt, the regulations go beyond an approach that treats legal form as determinative or requires that the cash flows under a debt instrument be fixed in amount and timing before the instrument can be considered indebtedness for income tax purposes. Indeed, to the extent that the regulations apply, they illustrate the extent to which a system of expected-return taxation can achieve theoretical purity in its design and implementation and, at the same time, take into account some of the practical concerns in its application to instruments other than fixed-payment debt. Most important, the US regulations generally manage to eliminate the benefit of anticipated deferral that would be available with realization-based recognition of the expected gain or loss associated with options and prepaid forwards embedded in contingent-debt instruments, as well as the embedded debt created by non-periodic payments under notional principal contracts. There are, however, critical limitations on the scope of the application of the regulations, which appear to reflect a continued acceptance of a facts-and-circumstances approach and a hesitancy to extend accrual recognition to the expected return associated with any advance of funds in return for a right to receive an amount in the future.

As was described above,[187] the non-contingent bond method under the contingent-debt regulations is applied relatively broadly, extending to any contingent-debt instrument that is publicly traded or that is issued for cash or publicly traded property. This broad application is subject to two important exceptions. First, outside of several specific exclusions of particular debt instruments with contingent payments,[188] the regulations do not define the concept of a contingent-debt instrument and, therefore, leave open the definition of the boundary between debt and derivative instruments and debt and equity. In the absence of a definition of a contingent-debt instrument, the regulations assume that a particular instrument is properly classified as debt under the relevant case law.[189] Because options and prepaid forwards lack a promise to repay a sum certain equal to the advance, they are not generally considered indebtedness subject to the contingent-debt regulations.[190] In effect, the contingent nature of the loan principal means that there is no imputation of interest for options and prepaid forward contracts issued on a stand-alone basis. These instruments are also exempt from interest imputation under the NPC regulations, because the relevant payments are not determined with reference to a notional principal amount. As a result, options and prepaid forwards remain subject to the standard cubbyhole treatment for derivatives.[191] That treatment is modified to provide accrual treatment of expected gain or loss associated with embedded debt only in the case of non-periodic swap payments that are significant.[192]

Second, the contingent-debt regulations do not apply to instruments that are considered predominantly equity in nature, even though these instruments give rise to expected gain or loss associated with an embedded loan that is not otherwise subject to accrual recognition.[193] In this respect, the contingent-debt regulations contain a specific exclusion for debt that is convertible into shares of the issuer or exchangeable into shares of a corporation related to the issuer.[194] These instruments presumably continue to be considered fixed-payment debt that may, in some circumstances, be characterized as equity.[195] This exclusion means that the embedded option or prepaid forward contract in these instruments is exempt from the imputation of interest, and the amount of the option premium or prepayment is not accrued as OID.[196]

The rationale for these limitations on the application of the NPC and contingent-debt regulations is not entirely clear. The exclusion for convertible and some exchangeable debt may be intended to avoid the problem of multiple bifurcations commonly associated with these instruments. A rejection of bifurcation accepts that the accrual recognition of interest at the stated rate on the whole of the issue price of these particular instruments provides a result that is not especially problematic, at least with respect to the availability of an undue amount of anticipated deferral.[197] The maintenance of realization-based recognition for options and prepaid forwards issued on a stand-alone basis is equally difficult to explain. The offsetting effects on issuers and holders, who must accrue equivalent expected amounts as expense and income, help to explain the willingness of taxpayers to accept the application of expected-return taxation to derivative instruments that are embedded in contingent debt. Adjustments to account for unexpected gains or losses are made only when the amount of the payments differs from the expected amount. The interesting policy issue concerns the justification for the selective application of accrual recognition to the expected gain or loss associated with embedded derivatives. In short, what is it about embedded options and prepaid forwards that requires the application of accrual recognition when that recognition is not applied generally under existing income tax systems to derivatives with embedded debt? The answer may lie in the fact that accrual recognition is required only when a derivative contains a significant embedded loan. Options and prepaid forwards embedded in contingent-debt instruments are often long term and are unavailable on a stand-alone basis at acceptable transaction costs. As a result, these embedded derivatives tend to have a significant time-value return that cannot be replicated with stand-alone instruments. The short-term nature of stand-alone options and forwards may mean that the application of expected-return taxation, although theoretically defensible, would be administratively burdensome and the associated benefit of anticipated deferral would not be worth the effort to eliminate it. This is not the case with the long-term, embedded derivatives in most contingent-debt instruments, and the only sensible response is to extend the application of expected-return taxation to the significant time-value element.[198]

In a sense, therefore, these exceptions to the application of the US NPC and contingent-debt regulations can be understood as specific instances of the general case for the limited application of comprehensive accrual taxation in the face of administrative and compliance concerns. That case supposedly is based on the assumption that the application of expected-return taxation to all hybrid instruments entails practical difficulties associated with the identification of embedded debt in all such instruments. Those difficulties are said to involve administrative and compliance costs that arise from the effort to isolate the relevant debt element and measure the expected gain or loss subject to accrual treatment.[199] The costs are, in turn, said to be justified only when the term of an instrument is long and the cash flows are relatively fixed, so that the debt element is significant and the expected gain or loss can be measured with some accuracy. These administrative and compliance costs are difficult to quantify, however, which makes it difficult to assess whether they should be determinative in limiting the application of accrual treatment along the boundary between debt and derivative instruments. Indeed, perceived problems associated with the identification of embedded debt in all hybrids are not even clearly articulated. The only specific identification problems cited by most commentators[200] are those described above[201] regarding non-periodic payments under notional principal contracts (that is, swaps and interest-rate caps, floors, and collars). Furthermore, administrative and compliance costs associated with a facts-and-circumstances approach to the characterization of particular hybrids tend to be ignored or understated. Because no one factor is determinative under such an approach, there is no clear bright line for classification purposes. Characterization of a particular instrument as debt or a derivative entails administrative and compliance costs in interpreting and applying the various factors in a specific set of circumstances. These costs include the uncertainty surrounding the appropriate classification and tax treatment of a particular instrument which can distort its pricing and/or discourage its use for legitimate, non-tax purposes. Nonetheless, critics of expected-return taxation tend to focus on the practical problems of identifying embedded debt in all hybrids and tend to ignore the costs that arise in the application of a facts-and-circumstances test.[202] Even if lawyers have the necessary expertise and judgment to draw the kind of vague boundary under a facts-and-circumstances test,[203] that expertise does not eliminate the associated costs. In fact, much the same argument can be made with regard to the identification of the embedded debt in hybrids in the sense that financial engineers have the expertise and judgment required to isolate and allocate the cash flows under complex financial instruments. This allocation is critical to the pricing of instruments, and it seems naive to suggest that the parties are unaware of the nature and reason for particular payments. The important issue is whether the administrative and compliance costs of identifying the embedded debt in all hybrid instruments are greater or less than the comparable costs of interpreting and applying a facts-and-circumstances test that results in the characterization of the whole of an instrument as indebtedness or a derivative. Assertions that the former is likely to "give rise to more confusion and uncertainty"[204] than the latter are intuitive and unsupported by any quantitative assessment. Without evidence to the contrary, it seems equally plausible to argue that the administrative and compliance costs associated with either approach are roughly equivalent, particularly if the approach under the US NPC regulations is adopted and the imputation of interest is limited to non-periodic payments that are considered significant.

Perhaps most important, the all-or-nothing characterization under a facts-and-circumstances test creates inconsistencies in the taxation of expected gains and losses, as well as discontinuities whereby small changes in the cash flows under an instrument avoid or attract debt classification. As is emphasized throughout this chapter, the principal policy significance of the kinds of boundaries drawn in the US NPC and contingent-debt regulations lies in the inconsistencies and discontinuities that arise from a failure to tax consistently the expected gain or loss on all financial instruments. Tax-avoidance opportunities that are created by changes in the form of an instrument or its risk characteristics can result in realization-based recognition of expected gain or loss and the benefit of anticipated deferral. A prepaid forward contract provides an obvious example of this kind of opportunity under the US regulations that govern notional principal contracts and contingent-debt instruments. As has been noted, a prepaid forward provides an expected time-value return, but is not generally considered indebtedness subject to the contingent-debt regulations,[205] nor is it considered a notional principal contract subject to the accrual rules for non-periodic payments.[206] In some cases, a prepaid forward contract can be substituted for a contingent-debt instrument or a swap with the benefit of realization based recognition of expected gain or loss. The fundamental problem, as was emphasized earlier,[207] is the mistaxation of both options and prepaid forwards under the accepted tax cubbyholes, which fail to achieve consistency in treatment with the expected returns on more conventional forms of debt. The inconsistency allows taxpayers to substitute prepaid forwards and options for debt instruments and avoid accrual recognition of the expected gain or loss as interest income or expense. To the extent that these instruments are substitutable, taxpayers are able, in effect, to elect different tax regimes by using a prepaid forward to provide the identical cash flows associated with a combination of fixed-payment debt and an on-market forward, or by structuring options as loan equivalents. Taxpayers can also manipulate cash-basis recognition of option premiums and prepayments under forward contracts to accelerate deductions and income inclusions. In the absence of symmetrical tax rates, the tax benefit for one party to an option or prepaid forward is not offset by a corresponding detriment for the other.

Consistency in the tax treatment of debt with embedded derivatives similarly requires the characterization of all convertible and exchangeable debt as the equivalent of a fixed-payment instrument plus an embedded option or prepaid forward contract. Otherwise, recognition of some portion of the expected gain and loss associated with these embedded derivatives is deferred.[208] This deferral is difficult to justify in the context of an expected-return approach that requires the accrual recognition of the full amount of expected gain and loss associated with the embedded derivative and fixed-payment debt elements of contingent-debt instruments generally. The only way to eliminate these kinds of inconsistencies and discontinuities is, first, to identify the embedded debt in any derivative and the embedded derivative in any contingent debt. Then, accrual recognition of the expected gain or loss is required, irrespective of the form of the instrument.[209] Indeed, to the extent that comparable instruments are available on a stand-alone basis, the direct response to inconsistency in tax treatment must be an extension of accrual recognition to the combination of basic building-block instruments in any hybrid.[210] An obvious constraint on this extension is the significant presence of tax-exempt entities such as pension funds. With these investors, a comprehensive application of expected-return taxation along the boundary between debt and derivatives maximizes the amount of deductible interest expense for taxable issuers without providing offsetting taxable interest income. At least in terms of revenue concerns, however, there seems to be nothing unique about the nature of the expected gains and losses associated with convertible and exchangeable debt to suggest that deductibility on an accrual basis should be limited to fixed-payment instruments and other forms of contingent debt.[211] As a condition for the extension of a comprehensive accrual regime, revenue neutrality can be ensured by addressing the non-taxability of expected returns earned by tax-exempt investors on all debt and debt equivalents.[212]

Consistency and the Application of Expected-Return Taxation

This brief description of some of the problems associated with a limited application of accrual taxation along the boundary between debt and derivatives is not intended to suggest that the extension of a comprehensive accrual regime to the embedded debt in all hybrids, including options and prepaid forwards, is free of problems. The point is simply that the principal alternative to this approach—a facts-and-circumstances test—also presents problems that tend to be glossed over. Provided that the administrative and compliance costs are acceptable, the extension of expected-return taxation more effectively eliminates problematic inconsistencies and discontinuities. In this respect, attempts to eliminate all inconsistencies and discontinuities by applying expected-return taxation to all embedded debt in all derivatives may not be worth the effort. In a sense, the administrative and compliance concerns associated with the extension of expected-return taxation to all expected gains or losses raise the prospect of diminishing returns for a tax administration. The important policy issue is where to draw the line and limit the application of accrual treatment.[213]

As a general proposition, an accrual regime can be defensibly limited to those instances in which a particular financial instrument can be considered to serve as a debt substitute. In other instances, the complexity involved in extending expected-return taxation may require the use of other approaches that are not theoretically pure but that nonetheless provide a satisfactory response by addressing avoidance opportunities at minimal administrative and compliance costs. For example, most options that are issued on a stand-alone basis have relatively short terms and can be subjected to open-transaction treatment without providing significant deferral benefits. Moreover, to the extent that these options are publicly traded, they can be subjected to accretion taxation as a response to the problem of selective realization. A system of accretion taxation ensures that both expected and unexpected gain or loss is realized annually. Where there is also a hedging regime that governs the character and timing rules for gains and losses on derivatives used for hedging purposes, the need to impute interest on non-traded options may, in fact, be greatly overrated as a fundamental reform measure. Under these conditions, inconsistencies and discontinuities are eliminated for a substantial range of options that are

- embedded in contingent debt and subject to expected-return taxation,
- publicly traded and subject to accretion taxation, or
- used to hedge an underlying position and subject to hedge-accounting treatment.

This kind of limited approach does not address the appropriate treatment of long-dated options, deep-in-the-money options, and prepaid forwards that are issued on a stand-alone basis and are not traded or acquired as a hedge. The application of expected-return taxation to these particular hybrids can be justified on the ground that consistency with the tax treatment of debt is required. This point of comparison underlies examples 1 to 6 discussed above, where the prepayment of a bet specified in a particular derivative instrument introduced an embedded loan with an expected time-value return. An emphasis on consistency of treatment of debt and the embedded loan in a derivative assumes that the latter is substituted for the former and must be treated similarly.

A much different perspective on the goal of consistency underlies the case for a facts-and-circumstances approach to the characterization of particular instruments as indebtedness or derivatives. Under this approach, the goal is consistency in treatment of a derivative instrument and a direct investment in an underlying asset.[214] The comparison is thus between a derivative financial instrument and a direct ownership interest in the underlying property.[215] In effect, an advance of funds under a derivative is equated with a net investment in the underlying asset, which gives rise to both expected and unexpected gain or loss.

Where the underlying asset is subject to realization-based recognition of both types of gain or loss, consistency of tax treatment requires that a related derivative instrument be subjected to the same recognition rules.[216] On this premise, each of the instruments in examples 1 to 6 should be analogized with interests in the underlying assets and taxed on the same basis. An emphasis on consistency of tax treatment of a derivative instrument and a direct ownership interest in the underlying property assumes that a derivative is substituted for the ownership interest and must be taxed similarly. The only possible exception is the circumstance in which prepayment of the obligations of one of the parties to a derivative is considered significant. In that case, the embedded loan may be considered to cross an ill-defined line beyond which the debt element becomes predominant and the appropriate point of comparison becomes consistency of treatment with fixed-payment debt.[217]

This alternative perspective emphasizes the important fact that a derivative with an embedded loan straddles the boundary between financial instruments and non-financial assets, as well as the boundary between the accepted cubbyholes for debt and derivatives. The inconsistencies in tax treatment are attributable to a basic structural failure to extend expected-return taxation to non-financial assets.[218] In effect, by imputing interest on the embedded debt in a derivative instrument, a comprehensive application of expected-return taxation achieves consistency of treatment with debt, but creates inconsistency of treatment with a direct investment in an underlying asset that is subject to realization-based recognition of all gains and losses. If it is assumed that expected-return taxation will not be extended to a range of non-financial assets in the near future, tax-policy makers are left with an intractable choice. Superficially at least, it is unclear what point of comparison is appropriate for the purposes of applying accrual taxation to the expected gain or loss associated with the embedded loan in a derivative that is created when one of the parties prepays its obligations. Furthermore, there is no clear point at which the debt element can be said to become predominant, nor is there an obvious proxy that can be identified with any such point. In this context, the case for extending the application of expected-return taxation to options and prepaid forwards depends on four related propositions. Although none of these propositions is compelling on its own, together they constitute a defensible basis for emphasizing debt equivalence as the important point of comparison for the embedded loans in these instruments.

First, an emphasis on consistency of tax treatment between a derivative instrument with an embedded loan and a direct investment in the underlying asset ignores the fact that the same analogy applies equally to all financial instruments. Indeed, all financial instruments, and not just derivatives, represent a position in non-financial assets in the sense that the value of the former depends on the value of the latter. For example, the value of a fixed-payment debt instrument depends on the ability of the issuer of the instrument to service the payments with cash flows from his own assets and, thereby, represents an effective investment in those non-financial assets. As such, both fixed-payment debt and hybrid instruments provide expected and unexpected gains and losses, only with different levels of risk reflected in the variability of the associated cash flows. Although the difference between fixed-payment debt and hybrids is merely one of degree, the application of accrual taxation to the expected return on fixed-payment debt is accepted as necessary to address problems of anticipated deferral. No attempt is made to link these financial instruments with the underlying assets and realize consistency in treatment across the boundary between financial and non-financial assets. To the extent that the application of realization-based recognition to hybrid instruments (including derivatives with embedded loans) provides the benefit of anticipated deferral and the same avoidance opportunities otherwise associated with fixed-payment debt, expected gain or loss should be subject to accrual treatment, and the analogy with an investment in a non-financial asset should be rejected.

Second, all financial instruments can be used to create multiple long and short positions in a non-financial asset, yet there can be only one interest with all the incidents of ownership, which has traditionally been accepted as determinative of the distinction between financial and non-financial assets.[219] In short, only the owner of a non-financial asset is generally subject to the tax regime applicable to that asset. All other interests are considered derivative financial positions subject to the relevant cubbyhole treatment for the particular instruments. Wherever funds are advanced in return for a right to receive an amount in the future, the advance provides an expected time-value return that is equivalent to interest on debt. Consistency in treatment between instruments of this kind and the embedded debt in hybrids can be taken as an appropriate point of reference, so long as the distinction between financial and non-financial assets is defined in terms of a direct ownership interest in the latter.

Third, to the extent that an underlying asset is itself subject to accrual taxation, consistency in treatment of a derivative position with an embedded loan requires the application of accrual taxation, whether the point of comparison is a fixed-payment debt instrument or a direct investment in the underlying asset. This proposition is particularly significant with respect to derivative positions in shares. As is argued below,[220] the expected return on shares is subject to a form of accrual taxation through the application of the corporate income tax. In effect, investors who would otherwise be subject to accrual treatment are subject to the corporate tax on equity income as a proxy for the investor-level tax, particularly in those countries with dividend imputation systems. It is arguable that application of expected-return taxation to the embedded debt in a derivative position in shares achieves a rough consistency in taxation with both a direct share ownership interest and fixed-payment debt.

Fourth, the choice of the appropriate point of comparison for measuring consistency of tax treatment ultimately depends on which inconsistency is considered more problematic, assessed in terms of the substitutability of investment forms for avoidance purposes. In general, tax-policy makers have focused on consistency of taxation between financial instruments because a higher degree of substitutability at low transaction costs increases the problems of anticipated deferral and selective realization.[221] An emphasis on extending expected-return taxation to options and prepaid forwards is consistent with this assumption. In effect, it is assumed that a counterparty who prepays all or some of his obligations under a derivative instrument advances funds to the other counterparty as a debt substitute, and ownership of the relevant underlying asset is accepted as a suitable proxy for determining the boundary between financial and non-financial assets.

To some extent, an assumption of debt substitutability is borne out by recent structured financings[222] that have used long-dated options[223] and prepaid forwards.[224] In fact, the most problematic issue along the boundary between debt and derivatives is likely the tax treatment of prepaid and off-market forwards. Because these instruments are, in principle, no different from prepaid and off-market swaps that are subject to the rules governing non-periodic payments under the US NPC regulations, an obvious regulatory response is the extension of accrual treatment using the same type of approach. The extension of accrual treatment to prepaid forwards, as well as to deep-in-the money options, that are used as debt substitutes has been suggested by several US commentators[225] and apparently remains under consideration by the IRS and the US Treasury department.[226] To avoid problematic inconsistencies and discontinuities, this extended application requires the imputation of interest on all hybrids, including options, prepaid forwards, the embedded debt in notional principal contracts, and the embedded derivatives in contingent debt. In short, within the parameters of a comprehensive accrual regime that excludes shares, expected-return taxation must be applied to any advance of funds under any instrument, whether it takes the form of indebtedness or a derivative. This result can be realized most directly by requiring[227]

1) the imputation of interest on all non-traded options that are issued on a stand-alone basis or embedded in a contingent-debt instrument;

2) the application of the non-contingent bond method under the US contingent-debt regulations to non-traded prepaid forward contracts and any other non-traded instrument that is debt in form, whether it provides for (a) non-contingent principal and contingent interest, (b) fully contingent principal and non-contingent interest, (c) partially contingent principal and non-contingent interest, or (d) contingent principal and contingent interest; and

3) the application of accretion taxation to options, prepaid forwards, and contingent-debt instruments that are traded in specified markets.

All gain or loss on instruments within the third category is subject to accretion taxation as a response to the problem of selective realization. For non-traded instruments within the first category, interest can be imputed in a manner similar to that for embedded options that are subject to the US contingent-debt regulations. In effect, interest should be accrued over the term of an option by using the forward price and deeming the difference between that price and the premium to be interest.[228] Where forward prices are unavailable, interest can be imputed on the amount of an option premium using an implicit cost of carry. For non-traded instruments within the second category, interest can be accrued on the basis of a projected payment schedule for all non-contingent and contingent payments, which, in turn, provides a yield to maturity that conforms with the comparable yield on a comparable non-contingent debt instrument. The result is similar to that of requiring the accrual of interest on the full issue price of an instrument at a reasonable rate calculated with reference to the rate on comparable fixed-payment debt. Indeed, the underlying principle is nothing more than an extension of the expected-return approach to foreign currency debt that was described in chapter 5. In essence, all instruments that provide contingent payments (whether contingent interest and/or contingent principal) are treated as synthetic fixed-payment debt (non-contingent interest and principal) with a yield to maturity determined on issue on the basis of the expected amounts of all future cash flows. Interest is imputed and accrued at the yield to maturity. Unexpected gain or loss equal to the difference between actual and expected payments is recognized when payment of the promised cash flows is made at the prevailing spot prices of the relevant underlying asset. Construction of the payment schedule should take into account the expected gain and loss associated with the embedded components of a particular instrument, including options, forward contracts, and fixed-payment debt. Interest in the form of expected gain or loss is thereby accrued on these instruments, whether they are issued on a stand-alone basis or embedded in a contingent-debt instrument.[229] Because limitation of accrual treatment to instruments with non-contingent principal only creates problematic discontinuities, the fact that the principal amount of an instrument is contingent should, ideally, be irrelevant.[230] There also appears to be little reason to maintain realization-based taxation for contingent-payment instruments that are issued privately in exchange for non-publicly traded property, as is the case under the US contingent-debt regulations.[231] To the extent that it is difficult to determine an expected return for these instruments, the riskless rate plus an arbitrary percentage can be substituted. Although this approach only roughly approximates the expected return, it avoids significant discontinuities associated with a boundary between privately issued and publicly issued instruments, as well as instruments issued in exchange for traded and non-publicly traded property.

If concessions to perceived administrative and compliance concerns are considered necessary, maintenance of the cubbyholes for debt and derivatives should be adjusted in a way that ensures that the worst inconsistencies in the taxation of hybrid instruments and equivalent combinations of fixed-payment debt and derivatives are eliminated. Moreover, discontinuities should be suppressed as much as possible by minimizing the differences in tax treatment of contingent-payment instruments that are subject to accrual taxation and those instruments that are exempt from accrual taxation. These goals can be realized by limiting loan characterization and the imputation of interest to "long-term" options and prepaid forwards with "significant" non-periodic payments.[232] "Non-significant payments" can be recognized on the maturity of a single option or forward contract and amortized over the various maturity dates of a series of options or forwards, as provided under the US NPC regulations. Although this difference in the tax treatment of payments that are "significant" and "not significant" creates a new boundary and an associated discontinuity, the difference in tax treatment is minimized, which means that the importance of the discontinuity is minimized. As it is in the US NPC regulations, "not significant" can be left undefined in order to discourage tax planning by introducing sufficient friction along the boundary between significant and non-significant payments. With prepaid forwards, the significance of a prepayment can be assessed in terms of the amount of the present value of the payer's future obligations. A similar measure can be implemented for options by comparing the exercise price and premium with those under an option that is on market and issued out of the money. Alternatively (or in addition to a distinction between significant and non-significant payments), accrual treatment can be limited to options and prepaid forward contracts whose term exceeds a specified maximum.[233] In effect, realization-based recognition can be available for administrative and compliance considerations only if a particular derivative contains an embedded debt element that is not significant, and the term of the instrument does not exceed a specified maximum. Any instrument that fails to meet these two tests can be considered a debt substitute, and administrative and compliance concerns must give way to concerns over consistency of treatment of expected gains and losses. The goal is to apply expected-return taxation in an administratively feasible manner that provides a tolerably certain and appropriate tax treatment of the range of existing hybrid instruments that lie along the boundary between the cubbyholes for debt and derivatives.

Even under a system of expected-return taxation that extends to the embedded debt in all hybrids, there remain two important problems that are unrelated to inconsistencies or discontinuities otherwise attributable to administrative considerations and a perceived need to compromise on such an extension. First, the application of accrual recognition to expected gains on any contingent-payment instrument exacerbates the problem of the selective realization of unexpected losses.[234] This problem arises as expected gains are recognized on an accrual basis by holders and added to the cost base of a contingent-payment instrument. When the passage of time reveals the unfavourable resolution of the specified contingencies, holders accumulate unexpected losses that are equal to the difference between the amount of the expected gains previously recognized on an accrual basis and the amount of gains that are expected on the basis of the subsequent changes in information. Under a realization-based system for unexpected amounts, holders have an incentive to realize selectively the unexpected losses, and defer recognition of the unexpected gains, on contingent-payment instruments.

As was described in chapter 5, the problem of selective realization arises generally with all financial instruments that have a bet element that gives rise to unexpected gains and losses. For example, forwards, futures, and swaps that are on market are pure bets providing only unexpected gains and losses subject to realization-based recognition under a system of expected-return taxation. Although the problem of selective realization is conventionally associated with these instruments, fixed-payment debt that is subject to accrual recognition of the expected gain or loss also contains a bet element that gives rise to problems of selective realization when subsequent changes in interest rates affect the value of the debt instrument.[235] In particular, an increase in the market interest rate results in a decrease in the value of a previously issued fixed-rate instrument, while a decrease in the rate results in an increase in value. The decrease or increase arises as the value is less than or greater than the issue price plus accrued but unpaid interest. The problem of selective realization is thus one of degree. Under a system of expected-return taxation, it is arguable that hybrid instruments represent the worst possible problems of selective realization because they provide both (1) a time-value return associated with an embedded debt element that is absent with a pure bet, and (2) a bet element associated with the contingent payoffs that is more significant than the bet element under a fixed-payment instrument. The problem is worse than that with either a pure bet or a fixed-payment debt instrument because, unlike a pure bet, the application of accrual recognition to the expected gain associated with the embedded debt element requires the accrued amount to be added to the cost of the instrument. In this respect, the embedded debt in a hybrid is treated like fixed-payment debt, yet the two types of instruments differ in the sense that the embedded derivatives in a hybrid give rise to contingent payoffs that are much more likely to deviate from the expected amounts and, thereby, result in greater amounts of unexpected gain or loss than result with fixed-payment debt.

If realization-based recognition is applied to hybrid instruments, expected gain is not subject to accrual treatment, and unexpected loss arises only to the extent that the specified contingencies produce an amount that is less than the amount advanced under the instrument. In effect, no amount of expected gain that has previously accrued must be added to the cost of a hybrid instrument, and the problem of selective realization is reduced to any shortfall in the amount of contingent principal to be repaid. Under expected-return taxation, the cost base must be increased to equal the amount advanced plus accrued interest, which gives rise to unexpected losses when the passage of time reveals contingent payoffs that are less than this expected amount. To some extent, the US contingent-debt regulations reduce the impact of the problem of selective realization, while imposing accrual recognition on certain contingent-payment instruments. They do this by requiring the periodic recognition of unexpected gains and losses on the basis of the differences between expected payments under the projected payment schedule and the payments actually due on the resolution of the specified contingencies. This approach allows unexpected losses to be realized under the terms of an instrument without a disposition. Moreover, the US regulations avoid problems of selective realization with contingent-principal obligations by limiting accrual recognition of expected gains to holders of debt instruments with non-contingent principal. Ultimately, however, an extension of treatment similar to that suggested above must be based on an assessment that the problems associated with the substitutability of long-dated options and prepaid forwards for combinations of separately issued fixed-payment debt and derivatives are more significant than the problem of selective realization, which is compounded under a system of expected-return taxation applied to most forms of these hybrids. In this respect, it is important to emphasize that an extended application of accretion-based recognition to all traded instruments eliminates both problems, leaving only the question of the appropriate approach to non-traded options, prepaid forwards, and other hybrids. The application of superficial loss or wash-sale rules can address the most abusive instances of selective realization, in which the holder disposes of a non-traded instrument to realize an unexpected loss and subsequently reacquires the same or similar instrument. With these kinds of loss limitations in place, it is unclear whether the problem of selective realization is more problematic than that of debt substitutability, which is addressed most effectively within a realization-based income tax by extending accrual recognition to the expected gains and losses associated with long-dated options and prepaid forwards.

The second problem follows from the fact that the application of expected-return taxation along the boundary between debt and derivatives focuses exclusively on timing issues and assumes that character issues can be eliminated by recognizing all gain or loss on ordinary-income account. A comprehensive accrual regime based on the dictates of expected-return taxation does not, however, address the application of non-resident withholding tax. In particular, the characterization of all gain and loss on ordinary-income account does not go far enough in the context of withholding tax, which requires that gain or loss be specifically designated as taxable interest or non-taxable payments on derivatives.[236] Conceptually at least, this characterization issue is relatively straightforward. Provided that a hybrid instrument is not characterized as equity,[237] the expected gain or loss associated with the embedded fixed-payment debt should be treated as interest. This characterization should extend to any option, prepaid forward, or contingent-debt instrument that is considered to give rise to expected gain or loss subject to accrual recognition as interest expense and income for resident taxpayers.[238] These amounts should also be treated as interest income of non-resident holders subject to withholding tax on a cash basis.[239] If the amount of the payments exceeds the expected gain, the excess is attributable to an embedded bet element and should be subject to the withholding tax treatment provided for derivatives that are pure bets with only unexpected gain and loss.[240] If the amount of the payments is less than the expected gain, the shortfall represents unexpected loss that should reduce that gain otherwise subject to withholding tax. This approach ensures consistent taxation of interest on fixed-payment debt and the equivalent cash flows associated with the embedded debt in a hybrid that lies along the boundary between the tax cubbyholes for debt and derivatives. Inconsistent taxation based on an acceptance of a hybrid as a derivative instrument creates opportunities to substitute hybrids for fixed-payment debt and avoid the application of non-resident withholding tax in instances of pure and approximate tax avoidance.[241] These instances arise most obviously where all payments on derivatives (whether expected or unexpected) are exempt from non-resident withholding tax.

This simple prescription for the application of non-resident withholding tax raises two issues. The first concerns the creditability of source-country withholding tax in the country of residence of the holder of a hybrid instrument. This issue arises primarily where the residence country characterizes the instrument as a derivative and adheres to the standard practice of exempting from withholding tax cross-border payments on derivatives. The country of residence may not consider source-country taxation of the payments to be a creditable income tax, which can result in overtaxation of the hybrid compared with the taxation of the equivalent (and creditable) cash flows associated with a fixed-payment debt instrument.[242] The direct response to this issue is obvious. Creditability can be achieved by ensuring that the expected gain or loss associated with the embedded debt in a hybrid is characterized as interest under the domestic law of the source country and its tax treaties. Indeed, this characterization does not offend the standard practice of exempting unexpected gain on derivatives that are pure bets; non-resident withholding tax is applied only to the expected gain associated with the embedded debt in a hybrid that takes the form of a derivative. This application of bifurcation in the international context assumes, however, that source countries are sufficiently interested in protecting their withholding tax base on fixed-payment debt from erosion through the substitutability of otherwise exempt payments on derivatives. To date, there has been little evidence of the required commitment.

Even where non-resident withholding tax is applied to hybrid instruments, tax-policy makers may be concerned about tax-avoidance opportunities that are provided by an accrual-based deduction of expected losses by resident issuers. In fact, an important asymmetry arises from the accrual-based deduction by resident issuers and the cash-basis recognition of corresponding amounts by non-resident holders. Issuers can use this asymmetry to lower the cost of borrowing by substituting hybrid instruments for fixed-payment debt. The substitution can provide for holders a deferral benefit that is not matched by a corresponding detriment for accrual-based issuers. The benefit is greatest for holders of instruments that provide an expected gain that is realized some time after the period of accrual. Hybrid instruments whose payments are made at maturity generally provide the most effective combination of expected gain and deferred payments, which is most obviously associated with fixed-payment OID instruments. Other fixed-payment instruments with periodic payments of accrued interest tend to provide a closer matching of accrual-based deductions for resident issuers and cash-basis inclusions for non-resident holders. Accordingly, the deferral benefit under asymmetric recognition rules is minimized.

Where fixed-payment debt and hybrid instruments are issued to non-resident holders, a measure of symmetry can be restored most directly by deferring the deduction of expected losses to the time of payment.[243] This type of response is clearly discriminating to non-resident holders, however, and may violate non-discrimination articles in tax treaties, at least in the absence of a specific exception for such a provision. Although the non-discrimination issue can be finessed by extending deferred deductibility to instruments held by cash-basis holders, including resident individuals, this option is available only where there are exceptions for such taxpayers. As was argued in chapter 5,[244] the case for these exceptions (and the two-code approach to the taxation of financial instruments that they entail) is problematic. The only other alternative is to maintain the realization-based recognition of the expected gain and loss associated with hybrid instruments. But that alternative creates the kinds of avoidance opportunities that were described earlier.[245] In particular, an issuer who is insensitive to the availability of an accrual-based deduction can substitute a hybrid instrument for fixed-payment debt in order to provide taxable holders with realization-based recognition of expected gains. This avoidance opportunity is compounded by the ability to avoid non-resident withholding tax where a hybrid instrument is considered a derivative, and the expected gain benefits from a general exemption for cross-border payments on derivatives. The choice for tax-policy makers depends on the relative significance of consistency and symmetry as policy goals and, more specifically, on the relative significance of the range of avoidance opportunities that are created by inconsistencies and asymmetries. It was argued in chapter 3[246] that consistency is generally the more important of these two characteristics; symmetry is largely unnecessary under any system that realizes the consistent taxation of equivalent cash flows. Most important, consistency ensures that taxpayers cannot engage in timing arbitrage by assuming offsetting positions with offsetting cash flows that are taxed differently. Realization-based recognition of the expected gain and loss associated with the embedded debt in a hybrid maintains an element of inconsistency that is not necessarily offset by any gain associated with the symmetrical treatment of resident issuers and non-resident holders. Indeed, it is arguable that, in the absence of the provision of deferred deductibility for hybrid instruments issued to non-residents, consistency of treatment of expected gain and loss under a comprehensive accrual regime should be maintained at the expense of symmetry.

Bifurcation and the Boundary Between Debt and Equity

Expected-Return Taxation and the Corporate Income Tax

Historically, inconsistencies and discontinuities associated with the boundary between debt and derivatives have not been as troublesome as the similar problems created by the different taxation of interest and dividends and the boundary between debt and equity. The problems in the latter area do not arise from any uniqueness in the cash flows associated with instruments that lie along this particular boundary. In fact, the first-best response is the same as that for instruments that lie along the boundary between debt and derivatives. Shares are just another type of hybrid instrument that should, in theory, be bifurcated into an embedded loan and bet element for the purpose of applying a comprehensive accrual regime that implements the dictates of expected-return taxation. Even so, certain constraints, which are not evident along the boundary between debt and derivatives, have led to an acceptance of a separate corporate tax on equity income. This acceptance necessitates the exclusion of shares from a comprehensive accrual regime and the use of unprincipled classification approaches to address avoidance opportunities that arise from inconsistencies in the taxation of interest and dividends.

Chapter 2 took the experience in Canada and Australia as representative of the different treatment of debt and equity characteristic of the income tax legislation in many countries.[247] The most important observation in this context is that interest on corporate debt is deductible for the issuer and taxable to the investor on an accrual basis. Dividends are considered non-deductible distributions of after-tax corporate profits and must be included in the income of shareholders, often with some credit for corporate tax paid on the underlying income. To avoid multiple levels of corporate tax, dividends can usually be paid free of tax (or bearing a reduced tax rate) between resident corporations. As was indicated in chapters 2 and 3,[248] this fundamentally different treatment has been the focus of much tax planning intended to alter the character of the return on financial instruments ("character arbitrage") by

- substituting debt for equity to change the character of dividend payments to interest, or
- substituting equity for debt to change the character of interest payments to dividends.

In the former instance, taxpayers eliminate the corporate tax by substituting tax-deductible interest for dividends; in the latter instance, taxpayers reduce or eliminate the investor-level tax on interest payments. Where the particular debt and equity instruments are perfect or nearly perfect substitutes, issuers and investors can engage in pure tax avoidance with little or no sacrifice in the pattern of the associated cash flows. The perfect or near-perfect substitutability of debt and equity entails little or no efficiency costs, and only revenue loss;[249] imperfect substitutability involves some sacrifice in the desired pattern of cash flows, and some efficiency costs.[250]

The substitutability of debt and equity is attractive solely because of the inconsistency in the tax treatment of the expected return on these two instruments. Interest on debt is considered expected time-value return that can be deducted by the borrower as an expected loss, and must be included by a lender as expected gain. In contrast, dividends are assumed to be attributable primarily to the assumption of risk by shareholders, who are considered to bear the burden of the corporate-level tax on equity income. In effect, dividends are considered unexpected gains that arise on the favourable resolution of a bet on the value of the underlying assets of a corporation. This mischaracterization fails to recognize that shares also have an expected gain or loss attributable to the advance of funds. In short, shares are hybrid instruments that combine an expected time-value return with a bet on the value of the underlying corporate assets.[251] Where this value exceeds the expected value of the shares, the shareholders realize an unexpected gain; where the net value of the assets is less than the expected value of the shares, the shareholders realize an unexpected loss.

Chapter 3 described the general policy problems presented by financial instruments and the broad design features of an ideal benchmark approach that effectively addresses those problems. One aspect of that benchmark is the recognition of the functional similarity of debt and equity and the need for the identical taxation of interest and dividends. Any approach that fails to realize this goal makes the substitutability of debt and equity instruments attractive. In particular, chapter 3 emphasized that debt and equity can be seen as alternative forms of corporate instruments that differ not in kind but only in degree, measured in terms of risk.[252] Both forms of instruments provide an expected time-value return as compensation for the use of the investor's funds and a bet element representing the risk feature or variability of cash flows that produces unexpected gain or loss. In other words, all corporate investors advance funds in the expectation that they will receive a greater amount. That expected amount has both (1) a time-value element that reflects the return that is required to induce an investor to forgo current consumption, and (2) a bet element associated with the value of the underlying assets. The former corresponds to the riskless rate of return. Variability of returns associated with the latter represents the risk feature of an instrument. All debt and equity instruments with a non-trivial bet element must provide a nominal return that exceeds the riskless rate to offset the possibility of loss and equate the expected return with the riskless return. If investors are risk averse and the risk associated with a particular security is non-unique in the sense that it cannot be diversified away, issuers must induce investors to purchase the instrument by offering an expected return that exceeds the riskless rate.[253]

The embedded loan in all shares means that these financial instruments raise the exact same policy issues as those raised by the basic building-block instruments and the distinction between expected and unexpected gain or loss. In particular, expected gain or loss attributable to the advance of funds by shareholders gives rise to the problem of anticipated deferral if the expected increases and decreases in value are recognized on realization. Unexpected gain gives rise to the problem of unanticipated deferral that occurs when the accrued gain can be realized without attracting a realization event for tax purposes. Unexpected loss gives rise to the problem of selective realization that occurs when shares that have declined in value can be disposed of, while shares with an offsetting, unexpected gain can be retained and realization can be deferred. To the extent that gains are taxed preferentially as capital amounts, expected gains and losses otherwise taxable in full as dividends can be recharacterized as capital amounts realized on a disposition.

At least as an initial proposition, there is nothing unique about shares that requires deviation from the accrual principle and an exception from the application of a comprehensive accrual regime. As with the basic building-block instruments, each of the policy problems above can be addressed by extending the application of the core elements of a comprehensive accrual regime to shares, including

- the accrual recognition of expected gain and loss,
- the realization-based recognition of unexpected gain and loss,
- the application of accretion taxation to traded shares, and
- the elimination of any distinction between capital and ordinary-income amounts.

The application of a comprehensive accrual regime to shares involves the elimination of a separate tax on corporate income and the treatment of shares in a way that is roughly similar to the treatment of contingent debt under the US regulations.[254] Issuers can be provided with an accrual-based deduction of imputed interest on equity capital; shareholders can be required to recognize the same amount as taxable income. Recognition of unexpected gain or loss by shareholders can be deferred to realization, either on a disposition of the shares or on the receipt of dividends that exceed the amount of imputed interest. Furthermore, because the application of accretion taxation to traded shares involves the recognition by shareholders of all gains and losses as they arise with changes in value of the instruments, it is unnecessary to recognize separately corporate income or losses that are reflected in these values.[255]

These basic propositions appear to underlie certain proposals in the tax literature to eliminate the corporate income tax and replace it with the imputation of interest on shares.[256] Indeed, there is nothing unique about related proposals to replace existing corporate income tax systems with the accretion taxation of shares.[257] The notion follows logically from the application of the accretion ideal as a benchmark for the taxation of all financial instruments, including shares. Where liquidity and valuation concerns are considered sufficient barriers to the implementation of this ideal, a system of expected-return taxation can be applied to shares as a particular hybrid instrument comparable to options, contingent-debt, and prepaid forward contracts. In fact, consistency of tax treatment requires that an approach of this kind be extended to shares, which provide equivalent cash flows on the basis of a combination of an expected time-value return and unexpected gain and loss attributable to a bet element. Shares, however, are traditionally viewed as distinct, and their tax treatment centres on the appropriate treatment of income earned through a legal entity rather than the taxation of the cash flows associated with a financial instrument.[258] For reasons that are often unstated, the interposition of a legal entity between the holder of this particular financial instrument and the associated cash flows is seen to justify different tax treatment that focuses on the measurement of corporate income. Viewed from this different "entity perspective," proposals to replace existing corporate income tax systems with a system of either expected-return taxation or accretion taxation at the shareholder level appear radical. In fact, certain considerations render these proposals problematic and necessitate an acceptance of the corporate income tax system as distinct from a comprehensive accrual regime. The result is a commonly accepted exclusion of shares from the application of a comprehensive accrual regime or any other legislation that requires accrual recognition of expected gain or loss. This exclusion creates familiar problems associated with the need to classify financial instruments that lie along the boundary between non-equity instruments subject to a comprehensive accrual regime and shares subject to the corporate income tax system.

Several factors are commonly cited as barriers to the replacement of the corporate income tax with either expected-return or accretion taxation applied at the shareholder level.[259] The apparent acceptance of the significance of these barriers, although not entirely defensible, means that, for all practical purposes, the corporate income tax is not about to be abandoned in the short or medium term, particularly by capital-importing countries. Three factors are especially significant.

First, the application of expected-return taxation to shares requires the determination of expected gain and an appropriate imputation rate for interest based on the amount of that gain. The expected gain and the appropriate rate are difficult to determine for a broad range of shares without (1) a defined term, (2) a market that provides forward prices, and (3) comparable fixed-payment instruments from which a yield to maturity can be derived. In the absence of these features, interest on shares must generally be imputed through the use of a riskless rate or other borrowing rate that reflects an assumed cost of carry.[260] This approach is similar to that under the US contingent-debt regulations, where forward prices are not readily available for embedded options.[261] In theory, the appropriate imputation rate for shares is a risk-adjusted rate that takes into account any risk premium payable for undiversifiable risk.[262] A lesser rate based on the cost of carry means that a portion of the expected return on shares is subject to realization-based recognition, which provides the benefit of anticipated deferral.[263] This benefit can be eliminated only by taxing gains on underlying corporate assets at the corporate level.

Second, the greater variability of returns on many shares and their unlimited term accentuate liquidity problems that would arise if holders were taxable currently on expected gain. In an important sense, shares are generally seen to be riskier than other financial instruments, and this greater riskiness highlights liquidity problems associated with the payment of tax on an expected amount that may never be realized. Liquidity problems are exacerbated by the fact that the holders often do not have the same degree of control over distribution policy as they do with other financial instruments. Conversely, a failure to tax expected gain currently provides a deferral benefit where the amounts are realized at the corporate level. This problem extends to unexpected gain that exceeds the expected return, where the gain is realized at the corporate level in the form of retained earnings. Under a system of expected-return taxation applied to shares of a leveraged corporation, the realization of unexpected gain should occur whenever debt is repaid and the shareholders exercise an embedded call option on the underlying corporate assets.[264] The amount of the gain is equal to the amount by which the value of the assets exceeds the amount owing under the outstanding debt. This approach raises obvious administrative problems. Tax-policy makers tend to look, therefore, to corporate income in excess of an imputed expected return as a proxy for the realization of unexpected gain. Common shares are especially problematic in that they do not have a fixed term or maturity date that provides a point at which the bet element on the value of the underlying corporate assets can be considered to be resolved, and the associated gain realized. If gain is not realized at the shareholder level, the holders have the benefit of unanticipated deferral. The period of unanticipated deferral may be indefinite and may require curtailment. A separate tax on realized corporate income can be used to eliminate this deferral benefit and, at the same time, avoid the liquidity problems that would arise for shareholders who are subject to accrual taxation of expected gain.

Third, the imputation of deductible interest on shares, or the accretion-based taxation of all share gains or losses at the shareholder level, shifts the legal incidence of the tax from the corporate entity to the holder. This shift is problematic where the holders are non-residents or tax-exempt entities such as pension funds. When the incidence of the tax is shifted to non-resident holders, the country of residence becomes the principal taxing jurisdiction, and the capital-importing country cedes a significant portion of its source-based tax claim.[265] For small open economies, this revenue transfer makes the extension of a comprehensive accrual regime to shares untenable. The alternative approach is to deny the deductibility of imputed interest on shares held by non-residents, which may violate non-discrimination articles in tax treaties. In the domestic context, the corporate income tax also serves as a convenient tax on the share gains of tax-exempt entities and would otherwise have to be replaced with some form of direct tax levied on such entities.

The combination of these perceived problems has dictated an uneasy acceptance of the corporate income tax. It is difficult, however, to square this separate regime for share gains and losses with the application of a comprehensive accrual regime to non-equity instruments.[266] Because there is no difference in kind between the cash flows associated with shares and the cash flows associated with other hybrids, inconsistencies and sharp discontinuities in tax treatment should ideally be avoided. This goal can be realized under a separate regime for shares that is based on a view of the corporate income tax as a proxy for the shareholder-level tax on gains that would otherwise be subject to a comprehensive accrual regime. Under this view, the corporate income tax is imposed as a response to anticipated deferral; in effect, the tax is a proxy for the accrual recognition of expected gain by shareholders. The tax can also be seen as a response to unanticipated deferral that would otherwise arise on the realization of unexpected gain at the entity level that is unaccompanied by a distribution or realization event at the shareholder level.[267]

A view of the corporate income tax as a proxy for an investor-level tax on share gains appears to underlie the attempts by policy makers in some countries to reduce the differences in the tax treatment of interest and dividends (and the attendant inconsistencies and discontinuities) through the adoption of some form of imputation system that treats the entity-level tax as a withholding tax on shareholder income.[268] As was noted in chapter 3,[269] one of the general goals of these systems is the reduction or elimination of a tax bias against corporate equity that results from the application of two levels of tax on equity income distributed as non-deductible dividends. Imputation systems attempt to ensure that only the shareholder-level tax is ultimately paid on the distributed corporate income, and the tax system is roughly consistent in its treatment of debt and equity.[270] As was also described in chapter 3,[271] several structural features of imputation systems inevitably combine to undermine this result.[272] A particular problem is the need for an appropriate rate structure. Where the corporate tax rate is less than the investor-level tax rate, shareholders can enjoy the benefit of anticipated and unanticipated deferral by retaining equity income at the corporate level.[273] Debt is preferable where the combined corporate and shareholder-level taxes are greater than the investor-level tax on expected gain.[274] These problems arise most obviously where imputation credits are (1) unavailable to shareholders who receive corporate distributions in the form of capital gains on the sale of shares, and (2) denied in whole or in part for dividend distributions to certain shareholders, such as tax-exempt pension funds and non-residents. For these shareholders, all or some portion of the corporate income tax is unrelieved, which results in overtaxation as compared with the investor-level tax on gains on non-equity instruments. Moreover, even where the nominal corporate tax rate is roughly equivalent to the investor-level tax rate and full imputation credits are provided, a separate tax on corporate income is suspect as a proxy for accretion or expected-return taxation applied at the shareholder level. The effectiveness of the corporate income tax in serving as a proxy depends critically on the accuracy of income calculation rules in reflecting expected and unexpected gain and loss associated with changes in the value of outstanding shares.[275] This dependence is problematic because of the provision of tax preferences at the corporate level and the application of tax-accounting conventions in the computation of business income. Together, these preferences and conventions ensure that taxable income does not equal economic income, as measured in terms of the change in value of the underlying corporate assets. To the extent that the income calculation rules are inaccurate, a tax on corporate income is a poor proxy for either an accrual-based tax on expected gain at the investor level or a realization-based tax on unexpected gain. Inconsistencies in the taxation of interest and dividends remain, and the substitutability of debt and equity continues to be attractive as a form of character arbitrage.[276]

Indeed, tax-policy makers can be indifferent to the form of particular instruments as debt or equity only where the combined corporate and shareholder-level taxes on equity income approximate the investor-level tax on non-equity instruments subject to a system of expected-return taxation.[277] In this sense, a corporate income tax can be seen to complement a comprehensive accrual regime that would be applied to shares, were it not for the kinds of constraints indicated earlier.[278] Where the two parallel regimes realize the consistent taxation of interest and dividends, the legal form of an instrument as debt or equity can be accepted as determinative, and taxpayers can elect the treatment applicable to one or the other category.[279] This elective basis of taxation becomes problematic if inconsistencies in the taxation of interest and dividends are created by the kinds of structural features of imputation systems described above. With its unintegrated corporate and shareholder-level taxes on equity income, a classical corporate income tax represents the extreme instance of inconsistent treatment. In the context of either an integrated or classical corporate income tax, inconsistencies mean that legal form will sometimes be rejected in favour of specific responses to tax-avoidance opportunities. The responses conventionally attempt to draw the boundary between debt and equity on a basis other than legal form. In short, character arbitrage depends critically on an acceptance of the legal form of a financial instrument as debt or equity that is eligible for the relevant cubbyhole treatment. A more substantive assessment of the rights and obligations associated with a particular instrument can be invoked as the basis of a classification for tax purposes that differs from the legal form of the instrument.

Drawing the Boundary Between Debt and Equity

An acceptance of the corporate income tax necessitates the general exclusion of shares from the application of a comprehensive accrual regime.[280] In the absence of a tax on equity income that realizes a result consistent with the tax on financial instruments under an accrual regime, tax-policy makers are faced with the development of hybrids that attempt to create opportunities for pure and approximate tax avoidance. These instruments must be classified as debt or equity subject to either a system of expected-return taxation or the corporate income tax. This distinction is blurred considerably with contingent debt, prepaid forwards, and long-term options that combine an expected time-value return with a significant bet element (and attendant risk) commonly associated with traditional equity.[281] The ability to substitute these instruments for shares may even be enhanced by a comprehensive accrual regime that uses bifurcation as the conceptual basis for the extension of accrual recognition to the expected return on the embedded derivatives in debt and the embedded loans in certain derivatives.[282] An extension of accrual recognition provides a greater range of instruments with a non-trivial bet element that also contain an expected time-value return subject to accrual treatment. The certainty of an accrual deduction for the associated expected loss may enhance the ability to substitute these instruments for shares that are subject to the corporate income tax. As a result, a reliance on the legal form of an instrument as the basis for classification under the relevant cubbyholes is untenable and a "more substantive" approach is required. Although it was criticized earlier as a basis for the boundary between debt and derivatives, a factors or facts-and-circumstances test is defensible as an approach to the definition of the boundary between debt and equity. Indeed, without any principled basis for this definition, a facts-and-circumstances test can be used to constrain financial innovation that attempts to exploit the inconsistent taxation of interest and dividends.

Tax courts and policy makers have occasionally rejected as a response to avoidance opportunities an uncritical acceptance of legal form in favour of a more substantive classification of particular instruments as debt or equity. In the United States, this approach has generally been implemented through the courts.[283] The use of legislative responses in Canada and Australia was described in chapter 2 in the context of certain provisions governing preferred shares and convertible debt.[284] Whether their source is judicial or legislative, these classification efforts are based on the assumption that the whole of a particular instrument must be characterized as debt or equity.[285] No attempt is made to bifurcate an instrument into its embedded debt and bet elements and to tax the associated returns separately. In fact, as has been argued throughout this chapter, bifurcation is useful from a tax-policy perspective only when it is used to divide the cash flows associated with all financial instruments into expected returns attributable to an embedded loan and unexpected amounts attributable to a bet element. The different natures of expected and unexpected gain and loss raise different policy concerns that can be addressed with different responses. Yet the practical concerns that were noted above[286] preclude the application of a bifurcation approach to shares as the basis for extending a comprehensive system of expected-return taxation. Where bifurcation cannot be applied, an all-or-nothing classification is entirely defensible, since it is unclear what other components should be relevant in bifurcating financial instruments. In effect, it is just not clear what characteristic features of debt and equity instruments should be determinative for any bifurcation process.[287] The alternative approach, which is consistent with a failure to divide shares into an embedded debt and bet element, is to characterize the whole of a particular instrument as either debt or equity. Where an instrument is classified as debt, the whole of the associated return is excluded from the corporate income tax and is instead divided into its expected and unexpected components, which are subject to a comprehensive accrual regime. Where an instrument is classified as equity, the whole of the return is subject to the corporate income tax[288] and excluded from a comprehensive accrual regime.[289]

An all-or-nothing classification of particular instruments as debt or equity is conventionally implemented through one of two general approaches, both of which focus on legal rights and obligations as proxies for the perceived substance of an instrument.[290] One approach involves the articulation of a "bright-line" test whereby particular rights and obligations are taken as determinative. The bright line can be defined on either a quantitative or a qualitative basis. For example, proposed (and subsequently withdrawn) regulations released by the US Treasury department in 1980 attempted to classify "hybrid instruments" using a quantitative test.[291] For this purpose, "hybrid instruments" were defined as debt obligations that provide a right of conversion into shares or contingent payments.[292] These instruments were to be treated as debt if, on the issue date, the value of the debt features was greater than 50 percent of the total fair market value of the instrument.[293] The proposed regulations defined the relevant equity features as conversion and contingent-payment rights.[294] The relevant debt features were fixed interest and principal payments (fixed in amount and the time for payment) referred to as "straight-debt payments." The value of straight-debt payments, relative to the value of the equity features in the form of conversion rights or contingent payments, effectively determined the status of hybrid instruments.[295]

A qualitative bright line identifies certain factors as being determinative of the classification of an instrument as debt or equity, irrespective of the relative value of the particular rights.[296] For example, the preferred share rules in Canada[297] apply to "debt-like" shares that provide (1) a retraction or redemption right, (2) a fixed dividend or liquidation entitlement, (3) a guarantee of dividend or capital payments, or (4) a right of conversion into an instrument other than certain fully participating shares. Any of these particular rights is considered determinative of the classification of a share, regardless of their value relative to the value of the instrument as a whole.[298] An extreme version of a qualitative bright line attempts to avoid arbitrary distinctions among hybrid instruments by drawing the boundary between debt and equity at either end of a continuum of instruments. This result can be realized by restricting a particular tax treatment to fixed-payment debt or common shares.[299] For example, the accrual-based inclusion and deduction of financing charges can be limited to fixed payments that are considered interest within the restrictive legal definition described in chapter 2.[300] All other charges can be subject to dividend tax treatment. A limitation of this kind recognizes that the ideal of accrual taxation is achieved most easily with fixed amounts that represent compensation for the use of borrowed funds and that accrue on a daily basis in the sense that they can be allocated prospectively over the term of a borrowing. This strict concept is considered suitable to basic statutory rules that provide for the inclusion of interest income and the deduction of interest expense on an accrual basis. Contingent amounts are regarded as unsuitable for this treatment and can be subjected to dividend tax treatment.

The obvious problem with bright-line tests is the sharp discontinuities that they create.[301] In particular, the addition, deletion, or alteration of particular rights and obligations can produce a modest change in the risk and return profile that results in a radically different tax treatment when the instrument lies along the boundary between debt and equity. These sharp discontinuities become a focus for tax-driven financial innovation. A clear example of such discontinuities and the tax planning they create is provided by the classification regulations for hybrid instruments proposed by the US Treasury department.[302] In anticipation of the release of these regulations and their 50 percent bright-line test, investment bankers designed hybrid debt instruments bearing fixed interest and principal amounts with a value just exceeding the 50 percent threshold for classification as debt.[303] The IRS became alarmed at the prospect of debt tax treatment for these kinds of hybrid instruments with a significant equity component and responded by issuing ruling 83-98,[304] which classified an "adjustable-rate convertible note" (ARCN) as equity on the basis of a traditional factors approach.[305] Shortly after the ruling was issued, the proposed regulations were withdrawn, and no attempt has since been undertaken to classify instruments comprehensively as debt or equity.[306] Similar discontinuities arise under a qualitative bright-line test (although they are not as obvious as those that arise under a quantitative bright-line test), whereby the addition of a particular right can alter the classification of an instrument. The change in classification and tax result can be disproportionate to any change in the risk and return profile.[307]

An alternative classification approach involves a qualitative assessment of various factors that are considered indicative of debt or equity. As with the same approach along the boundary between debt and derivatives, no particular weight is attached to any one factor, and no bright line is defined. This approach is associated most commonly with that developed by US courts.[308] Indeed, there is an enormous volume of US case law concerning the classification of instruments as debt or equity, primarily for the purpose of determining the availability of the corporate interest deduction. Without articulating any organizing principle, US courts have focused on several particular rights and obligations associated with the classical forms of debt and equity, as well as certain other factors that are taken to be indicative of the underlying substance of an investment.[309] The approach was also reflected in an earlier version of the Australian accrual proposals for the classification of preferred shares and other hybrid instruments that combine rights and obligations normally associated with debt and equity.[310] Under these proposals, such instruments would be considered one type or the other on the basis of an examination of several factors, including[311]

- the nature of the repayment rights and the relevant return as fixed or contingent,
- the ability to participate in gains and losses,
- priority on winding up,
- ownership and control, and
- the legal form of an instrument.

Consistent with the approach developed by US courts, no particular weight would be attached to any of the factors, nor would any combination be determinative.[312] To facilitate the application of the classification factors, regulatory powers would be given to the Australian Taxation Office (ATO) to determine the debt or equity classification of sophisticated hybrid instruments.[313] This power is presumably patterned on the regulatory power given to the US Treasury department to develop regulations for the classification of instruments as debt or equity.[314]

In contrast to a bright-line test, a factors approach tends to suppress sharp discontinuities by avoiding any clear definition of the boundary between debt and equity or a focus on specific factors as determinative. The principal problem with this approach is the uncertain status of particular instruments that lie along what is, in essence, a moving or flexible boundary.[315] A similar approach advocated by Hariton[316] for the definition of the boundary between debt and derivatives was rejected earlier on the basis of the administrative and compliance costs that arise from the uncertainty.[317] The preferable approach, it was argued, is the extension of a first-best response that imputes an amount of interest equal to the expected return on any advance of funds, whatever the legal form. This response achieves consistency in the taxation of fixed-payment debt, contingent debt with embedded derivatives, and the embedded debt in certain derivatives. Although there are some administrative and compliance costs of identifying embedded instruments and the associated expected return, they are not demonstrably greater than the costs associated with an uncertain factors approach to the boundary between debt and derivatives. As has already been emphasized, however, adoption of the same first-best response to the embedded debt in shares is constrained by practical concerns that dictate the adoption of the corporate income tax as a proxy for a system of expected-return taxation applied to shares. Where this proxy does not result in the consistent taxation of interest and dividends, the need to draw a boundary between debt and equity is unavoidable. If it is assumed that an uncritical acceptance of legal form is undesirable, tax-policy makers are left with a choice between a bright-line and a factors approach. This choice involves an assessment of the relative significance of the sharp discontinuities under a bright-line approach and the uncertain results under a factors approach.[318]

In general, each approach is undesirable for the same basic reason. Any classification exercise involves fine distinctions in degree with no principled basis.[319] In particular, refinement of the boundary between debt and equity (and the associated tax cubbyholes) is based on the fundamentally flawed premise that there is some defining point at which an instrument can be appropriately categorized. This assumption ignores the simple fact that the difference between debt and equity instruments is not one of kind but a subtle one of degree.[320] As a hybrid instrument with an embedded debt element, a share has an expected time-value return that should, in principle, be subject to accrual recognition in the same manner as the expected return on fixed-payment debt. Wherever the boundary between debt and equity is drawn, the result is an important discontinuity, whereby small changes in cash flows cause significant changes in tax treatment. A factors test does not avoid this discontinuity, but disguises it in the sense that the boundary is uncertain and does not provide as obvious a focus for tax planning as a bright-line test does. It is perhaps in this latter respect that a factors approach may be preferable. In effect, a factors approach may constrain the unlimited substitutability of debt and equity for tax-avoidance purposes by introducing sufficient friction in the form of "legal risk."[321] As was noted in chapter 3,[322] this concept encompasses the notion that the position of a taxpayer for filing purposes may be challenged by the government and ultimately rejected by the courts. A taxpayer therefore assumes the risk that an uncertain interpretation and application of the relevant provisions in the income tax legislation may be successfully challenged by the tax administration. Given the costs of defending a challenge and the chance of defeat, the uncertainty of characterization can be an effective constraint on tax avoidance. In effect, these costs may outweigh any tax savings, particularly when they are combined with other non-tax factors, such as the impact on reported income for financial-accounting purposes,[323] which may discourage the use of debt and debt-like hybrids that give rise to deductible interest and a consequent reduction in reported earnings.[324]

This effect of uncertainty may be most significant in the cross-border context, where tax-avoidance opportunities arise with instruments that are classified inconsistently as debt under the rules of the source country of the issuer and as equity under the rules of the country of residence of the holder.[325] Where the source country provides a deduction for the interest expense of an issuer, corporate income tax in the source country is avoided. Yet the country of residence of a holder may apply its rules for shares of a non-resident corporation. Those rules typically include deferral of residence-country tax until income is repatriated as dividends. In addition, the residence country may provide relief for source-country tax on the assumption that dividends have been paid as non-deductible distributions of corporate income subject to source-country tax. The result is a cash flow that is subject only to withholding tax applicable to interest paid by a resident of the source country to a non-resident. An exemption from withholding tax may even ensure that the cash flow is exempt from source- and residence-country tax.[326] Inconsistent classifications of particular financial instruments persist because of a general failure to harmonize tax systems across countries and insist on consistent classification in a cross-border context as a condition for the availability of relief in a residence country for tax paid to a source country.[327] In the absence of greater harmonization of tax systems across countries, including the harmonization of classification, a factors approach at least enables tax administrators to account for the classification of an instrument in another jurisdiction as a factor that is relevant to its classification under the relevant domestic law. Although classification under the foreign law should in no way be determinative,[328] it can be an important factor much like the classification of an instrument for regulatory and financial-accounting purposes. A factors approach can also be supported by a thin capitalization rule that establishes a bright-line limit on the amount of debt that can be held by certain tax-exempt entities and non-resident investors as a means of avoiding the corporate-level tax through the provision of deductible interest expense. As was described in chapter 2, a rule of this kind applies even where particular instruments are classified as debt for income tax purposes after a substantive assessment of the relevant rights and obligations. That classification is effectively ignored on the assumption that a certain level of debt is, in fact, disguised equity when it is held by certain insiders, who treat the instrument as equity but prefer the tax-deductible status of interest expense because of its avoidance of the corporate income tax.[329]

Policy makers may thus embrace the uncertainty of a factors approach as a positive feature that prevents revenue loss otherwise attributable to a high degree of substitutability of instruments that results from an uncritical reliance on legal form.[330] The principal argument against the use of a factors approach to define the boundary between debt and equity centres on the same uncertainty that enables the approach to serve as an effective constraint on tax-avoidance opportunities created by the inconsistent taxation of interest and dividends.[331] In much the same way that the uncertainty may constrain the development of hybrids for tax-avoidance purposes, a factors approach can suppress the development of hybrids for non-tax reasons, which results in efficiency losses. In particular, uncertainty regarding the tax treatment of particular hybrids as debt or equity may discourage the development of instruments in ways that complete markets and constitute genuine financial innovation. The critical aspect of this argument is the assumption that a significant portion of financial innovation along the boundary between debt and equity is, in fact, genuine innovation that is not driven by tax-avoidance opportunities. It is unclear, however, whether much if any genuine innovation can be attributed to the development of hybrid instruments.[332] An admittedly casual empiricism indicates that a sizable element of innovation along the boundary between debt and equity is driven by tax and regulatory arbitrage. Moreover, even where some innovation is genuine, possible efficiency losses associated with an uncertain factors test must be weighed against the need to address revenue loss from taxpayers' substitution of instruments to take advantage of inconsistent taxation of interest and dividends. As was argued in chapter 3,[333] the substitutability of instruments may even entail efficiency losses in those instances in which instruments are imperfect substitutes in the sense that they necessitate deviation from a desired cash flow pattern to access the tax saving. To the extent that the uncertainty associated with a factors approach constrains instances of approximate tax avoidance, there may be offsetting efficiency gains.[334]

The simple point emphasized here is that it is not clear that the use of a factors approach entails net welfare gains or losses in its impact on financial innovation along the boundary between debt and equity. To conclude that a factors approach does, in fact, entail net welfare losses and should therefore be rejected requires acceptance of the proposition that financial innovation produces net welfare gains when it is unconstrained by a tax system that relies on the legal form of an instrument for classification purposes. Acceptance of this problematic proposition requires, in turn, acceptance of the notion that the benefits of genuine innovation outweigh the losses attributable to tax-driven innovation designed to take advantage of the inconsistent taxation of interest and dividends. This proposition, however, is debatable and has not been the subject of much study.[335] In the context of an income tax system that treats interest and dividends inconsistently, it is unclear how any classification process can be developed that allows genuine innovation to occur at the same time as it prevents the development of hybrids for tax-avoidance purposes.[336] Achieving both goals may well be impossible; it is more likely that a difficult choice has to be made between the relative significance of the forces that drive financial innovation along the boundary between debt and equity. To the extent that tax-avoidance opportunities are considered a dominant cause, an uncertain factors test can be used as an effective anti-avoidance device. In that case, genuine innovation must bear the costs of uncertainty, and there must be a rulings process to minimize that uncertainty, but at the expense of additional transaction costs.

7

Integration and the Taxation of Synthetics

Introduction

Chapters 1 and 2 suggested that complex financial instruments can be divided into two general categories: (1) hybrid instruments and (2) synthetics. Because they combine expected time-value returns and unexpected gains and losses in a single instrument, hybrid instruments challenge the accepted tax cubbyholes for debt and derivatives and debt and equity, which are based on the classification of a particular instrument as predominantly one type or the other. As chapter 6 described, bifurcation is a tax technique that breaks a hybrid into its debt and derivative elements for the purpose of taxing those elements separately. This approach assumes that the specific building-block instruments that are embedded in another instrument can be accurately identified, though this in fact can be a problematic exercise. Nonetheless, as chapter 6 argued, the US legislative experience provides some important examples of the usefulness of bifurcation as the basis for a workable system that can be applied to a broad range of hybrid instruments. This application is entirely consistent with a comprehensive accrual regime that is focused on the accrual recognition of expected gain or loss associated with fixed-payment debt instruments and the embedded debt in certain derivatives. Synthetics present, at least in concept, many of the same problems for the application of the tax cubbyhole approach. The context in which those problems arise, however, makes the selective application of appropriate tax techniques even more problematic than the application of bifurcation. Perhaps most important, the use of synthetics raises problems that go beyond the identification of expected gain or loss and the need to tax those amounts on an accrual basis. These problems undermine (1) the application of realization-based recognition to unexpected gains, (2) the provision of relief at the shareholder level for dividend distributions, and (3) the application of non-resident withholding tax. A comprehensive accrual regime that is focused on debt, derivatives, and debt equivalents has very little to offer as a basis for a principled response to many of the problems in these areas.

A "synthetic instrument" consists of the combination of long and short positions in legally distinct instruments that provide offsetting cash flows that, in the aggregate, replicate the cash flows associated with another single instrument within one of the tax cubbyholes for debt, derivatives, or shares.[1] A concept closely related to a "synthetic instrument" is a "synthetic transaction," which consists of long and short positions in legally distinct financial instruments that are combined in a manner that replicates the cash flows associated with a disposition or transfer of an asset (including shares). The term "synthetics" is used here to include either a synthetic instrument or a synthetic transaction. Synthetics present tax-avoidance opportunities largely because the cubbyhole approach to the treatment of financial instruments is based on an acceptance of legally distinct instruments as separate instruments subject to an appropriate cubbyhole treatment. In the absence of a general attempt to combine the instruments that comprise a synthetic and tax them as a unit, synthetics can be used to attract a tax burden equal to the sum of the taxes on the component parts that is less than the tax payable on the replicated instrument or transaction. This inconsistency in tax treatment gives rise to opportunities for pure tax avoidance, with revenue loss and little or no associated inefficiencies.

The term "integration," as it is used in the tax literature on financial instruments,[2] describes a general approach that has been applied selectively to address the tax-driven use of synthetics and to provide a workable regime for the taxation of the basic building-block instruments used for hedging purposes.[3] In this context, the term "integration" refers to any approach that combines otherwise separate instruments and taxes the sum of the associated cash flows as an integrated unit that replicates the cash flows associated with another single instrument within one of the recognized cubbyholes.[4] This result occurs even though the sum of the taxes applied to the separate instruments that comprise the synthetic under their own cubbyholes does not equal the tax on the single instrument replicated by the synthetic. In the context of "hedge tax accounting," integration refers to the attempt to alter character and timing rules for gains and losses on financial instruments that are used to alter the risk associated with an underlying asset or liability.[5] In these instances, the cash flows associated with the particular financial instrument are netted against those associated with the hedged item. The result is a net tax treatment for the hedge and hedged items that would not necessarily follow if the treatment specified by the tax cubbyholes were applied to the relevant financial instrument independent of the hedged asset or liability.

This chapter examines the application of integration as an approach to the taxation of synthetics. As a tax technique, integration has an intuitive appeal; but, as many commentators have pointed out, there are notable problems that render it no more than a short- or medium-term solution.[6] Because synthetics are, by definition, a combination of financial instruments that provide cash flows equivalent to those under a recognized single instrument, the obvious issue that integration must address is the appropriate identification of the relevant combination of instruments.[7] This issue is particularly problematic where a taxpayer has a large portfolio of instruments that provide offsetting cash flows. The application of integration thus imposes a significant administrative burden, which limits its use to selected circumstances. A similar issue arises with the application of integration to hedge transactions. First, the relevant instruments to be combined must be identified; and second, it must be determined whether there is a sufficient correlation of cash flows to justify integrated treatment. In contrast to a synthetics regime, however, a hedge accounting regime places the onus of identifying component instruments on taxpayers, who generally have an incentive to do so. No similar incentive exists with the use of synthetics for tax-avoidance purposes, and the identification problem appears to be much greater.

Given the administrative difficulty of identifying component instruments, integration is ultimately of limited use as a means of addressing inconsistencies created by the existing tax cubbyholes. The more desirable long-term approach is a rejection of the continued reliance on the existing cubbyholes in favour of fundamental reform of the taxation of the basic building-block instruments. This alternative approach must ensure that the basic instruments are taxed in a manner that equates the sum of the tax treatments of the components of a synthetic. It is often suggested that the imputation of interest on options would go a long way in achieving this desirable result and make integration unnecessary. This fundamental reform, if combined with other reforms suggested in chapters 5 and 6, can in fact eliminate much of the need for a specialized hedge-accounting regime. There would remain, however, a whole range of problems associated with the use of synthetics (1) to transfer dividends and the related tax relief, (2) to lock in unexpected gain without attracting a realization event for tax purposes, and (3) to avoid the application of non-resident withholding tax.[8] In many cases, a synthetic combines a long position in shares with short and long positions in derivatives, the result of which is a net cash flow that is not taxed appropriately by the imputation of interest on options or even by the accretion-based recognition of all gain or loss on derivatives generally. Fundamental reform of dividend taxation is required, along with the rationalization of the tax cubbyholes applicable for non-resident withholding tax purposes. Even then, the realization-based recognition of unexpected gain or loss provides opportunities to use synthetics to obtain the benefit of unanticipated deferral, which arises whenever unexpected gain can be realized without attracting a realization event for tax purposes. Among the various fundamental reform alternatives that have been suggested, only a comprehensive application of accretion taxation to all gains and losses on all financial instruments, including shares, can eliminate these avoidance opportunities. The absence of that kind of fundamental reform leaves the selective application of integration as a response to synthetics as the obvious means of preventing erosion of the revenue base.

The second part of this chapter begins with an overview of some general areas in which the use of synthetics has confounded the cubbyhole approach to the taxation of financial instruments. In the more problematic instances, synthetics have been used in tax-avoidance transactions that (1) alter the character of gains; (2) transfer tax attributes, such as dividend tax credits, associated with shares; and (3) realize unexpected gains on a tax-deferred basis. The part then presents a summary of the general features of integration as a tax technique that attempts to address the use of synthetics for avoidance purposes.

An important (and conventional) distinction is drawn between the application of integration to the tax-driven use of synthetics and the similar issues presented by hedge transactions undertaken for non-tax reasons. Despite apparent weaknesses, integration remains the only effective response to tax-avoidance opportunities created by troublesome inconsistencies in tax treatment that cannot be eliminated by limited reform of the traditional tax cubbyholes.

The third part examines the role of integration as a response to synthetics under a comprehensive accrual regime intended to implement the dictates of expected-return taxation. It is argued that a comprehensive accrual regime can alleviate many of the problems raised by synthetics in the context of the traditional tax cubbyholes. It does so by extending accretion taxation to traders and traded instruments and by requiring the accrual recognition of the expected gain or loss on the embedded debt in options and prepaid forwards and swaps. Certain problems remain, however, primarily because of the exclusion of non-traded shares and the use of imperfect corporate/shareholder tax systems for the taxation of equity income. As a result, the application of integration as a tax technique for synthetics remains necessary. The part therefore includes some general observations on the debate over the usefulness of detailed legislative responses as a means of implementing integrated treatment for the components of a synthetic. The difficulties with these kinds of responses are contrasted with a competing model, which involves a mix of narrowly targeted anti-avoidance rules, judicial anti-avoidance doctrines, and a more activist role for the courts in interpreting and applying general provisions and principles governing the taxation of financial instruments. It is argued that this debate is ultimately a sterile one. In the context of the conventional tax cubbyholes, all legislative responses are similar to the limited transactional approach of past legislative practice in most countries. The only difference is that the ad hoc transactional responses move away from the taxation of the basic building-block instruments to more complex combinations. Existing income tax systems that treat equivalent cash flows in different ways are fundamentally unsound. The application of integration as a tax technique under that kind of system inevitably results in selective, complex, and unprincipled legislation. A reliance on purportedly general principles and purpose-based rules provides only an illusion of simplicity and a "more principled" approach. At best, purpose-based rules may create enough uncertainty to deter the more abusive transactions without affecting legitimate hedge transactions.

The fourth part of this chapter describes the general features of a suggested legislative approach to the application of integration. The approach is based largely on a series of US responses to the use of synthetics for avoidance purposes. The description is not a detailed review or technical analysis; rather, it provides a sense of general trends and features reflected in these various legislative responses. For the most part, the courts have not embraced integration as a tax technique applied to synthetics.[9] The technique has been implemented, instead, in selective legislative responses that have tended to create new cubbyholes for the affected instruments. This approach is most obvious in certain US provisions, which have been emulated to a degree in anti-avoidance legislation in other jurisdictions. Indeed, under a comprehensive accrual regime that excludes shares, integration can be applied most effectively in legislation patterned on some of these US provisions. In contrast, a defensible case for the rejection of hedge accounting can be made in the context of a comprehensive accrual regime. To the extent that hedge accounting is considered necessary, tax-policy makers should adopt stringent identification requirements that ensure the designation of a financial instrument as a hedge on acquisition. Contemporaneous identification requirements permit acceptance of a taxpayer's designation, which avoids the administrative and compliance costs associated with the need to define a qualifying hedge. In short, if a taxpayer satisfies the identification requirements and designates a financial instrument as a hedge of another position, the instrument can be accepted as a hedge for income tax purposes. Even then, a comprehensive accrual regime suppresses many of the worst inconsistencies that otherwise provide a basis for the application of hedge accounting, and the consequences of hedge treatment can be very limited.

Synthetics and the Tax Cubbyholes

Synthetics and Opportunities for Tax Avoidance

Application of the tax cubbyholes based on legal form creates inconsistencies in the taxation of particular instruments or transactions and the synthetics that are intended to replicate the associated cash flows. In essence, the combination of legal form and the application of the tax cubbyholes based on that form ensures that the sum of the taxes on the component instruments that comprise a synthetic does not equal the tax payable on a single instrument or transaction replicated by the synthetic. Reliance on legal form as being determinative in the application of the tax cubbyholes is evident for both character and timing purposes. Subject to limited exceptions, such as original issue discount (OID) on a debt instrument, gain that arises on the disposition of a financial instrument is considered an unexpected amount that is recognized on realization and is characterized as a capital gain for those taxpayers who are not traders or dealers in the particular asset. Ownership of a financial instrument and/or its transfer as a matter of legal form also tends to determine (1) who is taxable on the associated cash flows and (2) when accrued gain or loss must be realized. This reliance on legal form is confounded rather easily by the use of derivative instruments to create various long and short positions[10] (1) to disguise expected amounts equivalent to interest as unexpected gain realized on the disposition of an asset,[11] (2) to transfer risk without a legal transfer, or (3) to retain risk even after a legal transfer.[12] The effectiveness of these transactions depends on the identification of equivalent cash flows that are taxed differently under the tax cubbyholes. Put-call parity and other arbitrage pricing relationships, such as futures parity and interest-rate parity,[13] reveal equivalent cash flows that are taxed inconsistently because of a reliance on legal form in an attempt to maintain the integrity of the cubbyholes.[14] In general, the tax-driven use of synthetics has involved the application of these basic relationships in specific strategies designed to take advantage of avoidance opportunities in the following four areas under the tax cubbyholes:

- characterization of gain or loss as interest or capital amounts,
- provision of dividend tax relief,
- avoidance of non-resident withholding tax, and
- realization-based recognition of unexpected gain.

Synthetics and Character Arbitrage

Synthetics can be used for tax-avoidance purposes in instances of "character arbitrage," whereby a change in the legal form of an instrument alters the tax treatment of expected gain or loss in the form of interest without altering the desired pattern of cash flows. The concept underlying character arbitrage is the same as that discussed earlier in the context of structured finance transactions[15] and hybrid instruments that combine an expected time-value return with unexpected gain or loss attributable to a bet element. Those instruments challenge the accepted tax cubbyholes and the associated boundaries between debt and derivatives and debt and equity, which are both premised on the characterization of a particular instrument as one type or the other. Character arbitrage can occur under the conventional cubbyhole approach when expected gain or loss that is otherwise taxable as interest on an accrual basis is disguised as tax-preferred dividends or unexpected amounts taxable on realization as capital amounts. Dividends and unexpected gain or loss can similarly be disguised as interest expense or income. As was described in previous chapters, this character transformation can occur where

- preferred shares are substituted for debt,
- debt is substituted for shares of a thinly capitalized corporation,
- derivative instruments are substituted for debt through prepayment of the obligations of one of the counterparties, and
- debt is substituted for shares or a derivative instrument through the provision of profit participation or other contingent-payment rights.

Although there is no necessary analytical significance to the distinction, the principal difference with character arbitrage in the context of synthetics is the use of a combination of two or more financial instruments issued separately to realize the same kind of mischaracterization that can occur with a hybrid that combines an expected time-value return and unexpected gain or loss attributable to a bet element. Legislative responses to character issues with synthetics have focused primarily on their use to disguise the expected gain that is otherwise taxable as interest as unexpected gain realized on the disposition of a financial instrument or as tax-preferred dividends. Similar character issues arise with the use of synthetics to avoid the application of non-resident withholding tax.

Interest Income Disguised as Capital Gain

The combination of long and short positions in an asset using derivatives can produce net cash flows that are equivalent to the expected time-value return on debt. When the standard tax cubbyholes based on legal form are applied, however, the combination can be characterized as a capital gain subject to realization-based recognition (often at a preferential inclusion rate). This result is inconsistent with the accrual-based recognition of interest as ordinary income.

> **Example 1:** In April 1998, Alvin acquires gold in the spot market at a price of $275 per ounce. At the same time, he enters into a futures contract to sell gold in March 1999 at a forward price of $294 per ounce.

Alvin's acquisition of a long position in gold constitutes an investment that, because of the short gold futures, provides an expected gain of $19. Provided that Alvin continues to hold his long gold position, this $19 gain will be realized on maturity of the contract when he closes out his long and short positions either by delivering the gold in settlement of the forward or by settling the contract in cash and selling gold in the spot market. An unexpected gain or loss on the short forward contract will be offset exactly by unexpected loss or gain on the long position in gold. For example, if the spot price of gold in March 1999 is $300 per ounce, Alvin will realize an unexpected loss of $6 on the short futures contract that will be offset by an unexpected gain of $6 on the long position in gold. If the spot price of gold is $290 per ounce, Alvin will realize an unexpected gain of $4 on the short futures contract that will be offset by an unexpected loss of $4 on his long position in gold. In an important sense, Alvin's return is equivalent to the expected gain realized by a taxpayer who sells an asset on an instalment basis and, on the transfer, becomes entitled to interest on the unpaid balance of the purchase price as compensation for the use of the transfer proceeds. In effect, Alvin has created a synthetic instalment sale through an application of the basic relationship between spot and forward prices, which posits that the forward price of an asset is equal to the spot price plus the cost of carry less any expected return on the asset for the relevant term.[16]

> **Example 2:** In April 1998, Betty acquires 10 shares of Aco at a price of $100 per share. At the same time, she issues a European call option to Calvin, which permits him to acquire the shares in March 1999 at an exercise price of $110 per share. Betty also acquires a European put option from Calvin, which permits her to sell the shares to him in March 1999 at the same exercise price of $110 per share.

Betty's acquisition of the shares also constitutes an investment that, because of the options, provides an expected gain of $10. The premium paid for the put is offset by the premium received for the call, leaving a $100 net investment. If the spot price of the shares on maturity of the options exceeds the exercise price, Betty will realize an unexpected loss on the call option equal to the excess. If the spot price is less than the exercise price, she will realize an unexpected gain on the put option. In either case, the unexpected loss or gain will be offset exactly by unexpected gain or loss on the underlying shares, leaving Betty with an expected gain of $10. Her investment in the shares is equivalent, therefore, to a $100 investment in a debt instrument with a redemption amount of $110 and an expected gain equal to the $10 difference. By covering the long position in shares with call and put options ("a married put and call"), Betty has replicated an OID debt instrument in a basic application of put-call parity.

Application of the tax cubbyholes based on the legal form of the separate positions created by Alvin and Betty results in the inconsistent taxation of equivalent cash flows. In Alvin's case, entering into the short futures contract does not oblige him to dispose of his long gold position. Accordingly, he cannot be considered to have disposed of that position for a long position in debt that provides interest income of $19 on maturity in March 1999.[17] If he settles the short futures contract by delivering gold, he will dispose of his position at that time and realize a gain of $19, which can be characterized as a tax-preferred capital gain, provided that Alvin is not a trader or dealer. This treatment is inconsistent with the accrual recognition of the $19 as interest income realized on a sale of the long gold position in April 1998, with cash settlement deferred to March 1999. Similarly, if Betty is not a securities trader or dealer, she can dispose of her long position in the shares on maturity of the options in March 1999 and realize a tax-preferred capital gain. That gain will be offset in part by realized loss on the call option or realized gain on the put option that will ensure a net $10 gain on the shares. This treatment is inconsistent with the accrual recognition of the $10 discount on an OID obligation that is replicated by the covered option arrangement.

Interest Income Disguised as Dividends

Application of the tax cubbyhole treatment of dividends is based on share ownership.[18] In short, dividends are generally taxable on a cash basis to the person who owns the shares as a matter of private law. As a means of reducing or eliminating the impact of the corporate-level tax on the underlying income from which dividends are paid, liability for dividend taxation may be offset, in whole or in part, by the provision of relief at the shareholder level. This relief includes an offsetting deduction for the amount of dividends received by corporate shareholders and/or the provision of imputation tax credits for other shareholders. For the most part, the approach to share ownership has been exceedingly formalistic, with the registered legal owner treated as the owner for tax purposes. Unlike the approach to the determination of ownership issues with lease transactions, courts and tax administrators in most countries generally have not assessed the risk and return characteristics of a particular arrangement to determine the ownership of shares.[19] This acceptance of legal form has necessitated specific legislative responses that reflect a more substantive determination of share ownership based on risk and return characteristics in those instances in which the combination of short and long positions in derivatives permits the effective transfer of dividend receipts and the related tax relief.

Like long positions in other assets, a long position in shares can be combined with short positions using derivatives to provide an expected return similar to that on debt. An important difference is the fact that the expected return can take the legal form of dividends received by the owner of shares rather than gain realized on the disposition of an asset. In effect, an expected gain equivalent to interest can be converted into a dividend. Inconsistency in taxation arises because of the provision of dividend tax relief at the shareholder level, which reduces the investor-level tax compared with that on an equivalent interest receipt. To the extent that certain investors such as tax-exempt pension funds and non-residents are denied this relief, the cubbyhole system provides an incentive to transfer or "rent" dividends and the attendant tax relief to taxable investors. The tax-exempt or non-resident transferor obtains the benefit of a higher expected return in the form of interest on a loan, while the taxable transferee is willing to accept a lower pre-tax return because of the higher after-tax return attributable to the dividend relief. The transfer is "synthetic" in the sense that it replicates a transfer of the risk and return usually associated with a transfer of legal ownership. The transfer of share ownership, however, is only a matter of legal form that allows the ostensible owner to claim the dividend relief. Little or no portion of the risk usually associated with share ownership is present because of the assumption of related short positions. The transaction, when assessed in terms of risk and associated cash flows, is in reality a low-risk investment in debt.[20]

Example 3: Cantaxable Inc. has $100,000 of surplus funds to invest on a 90-day basis at an annualized interest rate of 10 percent. On January 1, 1998, Cantaxable Inc. uses the funds to acquire shares of Publico from the trustee of a tax-exempt pension fund for their current value of $100,000, and agrees to transfer the shares back to the trustee at the same price on March 31, 1998. At the end of the 90-day period, Cantaxable Inc. receives a dividend on the shares of Publico equal to $2,000.

Example 4: On January 1, 1998, UStaxable Inc. acquires shares of Publico from the trustee of a pension fund for $100,000 and, at the same time, issues to the trustee a European call option on the shares exercisable on December 31, 1998 at a price of $80,000. The trustee pays a premium of $24,000 for the option.

Example 5: Doris owns 10 shares of Aco with a cost of $10 per share and a current value of $100. On January 1, 1998, she enters into a two-year swap agreement whereby she agrees to pay Bankco at the end of years 1 and 2 an amount equal to dividends paid on the 10 shares of Aco, plus any appreciation in value. In return, Bankco agrees to pay Doris the London interbank offering rate (LIBOR) on a notional principal amount equal to the current value of the 10 shares of Aco, plus any depreciation in value of the shares.

Example 3 is a simple "dividend rental arrangement" whereby Cantaxable Inc. has "rented" the dividends on the Publico shares and substituted a $2,000 tax-free intercorporate dividend for taxable interest. Because the transfer agreement requires Cantaxable Inc. to return the shares at the initial transfer price, any risk of loss or opportunity for gain remains with the pension fund. However, Cantaxable Inc. ostensibly owns the shares for the 90-day period and, therefore, is taxable on the dividend receipt, which provides a greater after-tax return than taxable interest on the surplus funds. The pension fund may receive a fee for the use of the shares, which would usually be reflected in a transfer price on the repurchase that is slightly lower than the initial transfer price. In addition, the pension fund can invest the surplus funds received from Cantaxable Inc. in short-term debt that earns a tax-free return greater than the dividend on the Publico shares. As a result, both parties to the dividend rental arrangement realize an expected after-tax return that is greater than that available in the absence of the transfer, and the government forgoes the tax revenue that would otherwise be payable on taxable interest receipts earned by Cantaxable Inc.

Examples 4 and 5 are slightly more sophisticated versions of a dividend rental arrangement. The combination of the long position in shares and the short call option in example 4 ("covered call arrangement") substantially reduces the risk otherwise associated with the long position in the shares of Publico assumed by UStaxable Inc., and provides an expected return that approximates the return associated with fixed-payment debt. In a sense, UStaxable Inc. has loaned to the pension fund the $76,000 difference between the $100,000 purchase price of the shares that it pays and the $24,000 option premium that it receives. Because the call option is "deep in the money," the pension fund is likely to exercise it on maturity one year after the share transfer. If the option is physically settled, UStaxable Inc. will receive $80,000 from the pension fund and will be assured a return equal to the sum of (1) $4,000 (that is, the difference between the $76,000 initially advanced to the pension fund and the proceeds of $80,000 received on physical settlement of the call option) and (2) all dividends received on the Publico shares during the period of ownership.

The "total return" equity swap in example 5 replicates a long position in a debt instrument that pays interest at LIBOR for the two-year term of the swap. Doris realizes this result by assuming a short position in the shares under the swap, which offsets the cash flows associated with her previously acquired long position. For the period of the swap, she eliminates all risk otherwise associated with a long position in shares, and Bankco assumes the risk associated with a long position. To Doris, the counterparty who makes the equity payments, the swap replicates the cash flows otherwise associated with a vendor-financed sale of the shares in an amount equal to their spot price. To the counterparty who receives the equity payments, the swap is equivalent to a fully leveraged purchase of the shares for the relevant period. A reliance on legal form means that Doris remains taxable on the dividends as the owner of the shares, despite any exchange of that cash flow for an expected return equivalent to interest.[21]

Avoidance of Non-Resident Withholding Tax[22]

A reliance on legal form, including a restrictive concept of share ownership, provides opportunities to avoid the application of non-resident withholding tax, which depends on the characterization of cash flows as (1) interest, (2) dividends, or (3) payments on derivatives. Amounts within the third category are generally non-taxable.[23] Cash flows within the first two categories are taxable, subject to an important exception provided by many countries for interest on portfolio debt.[24] Where interest and dividends are taxable, taxpayers can create non-taxable equivalents by combining long and short positions in debt and shares with offsetting positions in derivatives. The simpler combinations involve many of the same applications of the basic relationship between spot and forward prices (Alvin in example 1) and put-call parity (Betty in example 2) described in some of the above examples.[25] As in those examples, taxpayers can use synthetics to convert (1) interest into gain realized on the disposition of an asset, and (2) dividends into interest.

> **Example 6:** Erica is a non-resident of country Z. On January 1, 1998, she acquires $1 million worth of bonds of Publico, which is a resident of country Z. The bonds pay interest at 8 percent per annum. At the same time that Erica acquires the bonds, she enters into a one-year cash-settled forward contract to acquire 1 million shares of Publico at a forward price of $1 million.

> **Example 7:** Investment Inc. is a securities dealer and a resident of country Y. Investment Inc. owns 100 shares of Publico, another resident corporation. Fabian is a non-resident investor with a portfolio of treasury bills issued by the government of country Y. On January 1, 1998, Fabian and Investment Inc. enter into an equity swap, whereby Fabian agrees to pay Investment Inc. LIBOR on a notional principal amount equal to the spot price of the 100 shares of Publico, plus any depreciation in value of the shares. In return, Investment Inc. agrees to pay Fabian all dividends paid on the shares of Publico during the term of the swap, plus any appreciation in value.

> **Example 8:** Grace is a non-resident of country X. On January 1, 1998, she acquires 10 common shares of Research Inc., which is a resident of country X. At the same time that Grace acquires the shares, she issues a European call option to Dealerco, which is a securities dealer resident in country X. The option permits Dealerco to acquire the shares in March 1999 at an exercise price of $110 per share. Grace also acquires a European put option from Dealerco, which permits her to sell the shares in March 1999 at the same exercise price of $110 per share.

Erica has created a synthetic investment in the shares of Publico. Because the forward contract is cash settled, she will realize any unexpected gain on the shares in excess of the one-year forward price. She will also realize any unexpected loss equal to the amount by which the one-year forward price exceeds the spot price on maturity of the contract. Because the forward price of the Publico shares is equal to the spot price on January 1, 1998 plus the cost of carry less the amount of any expected dividends, Erica receives the benefit of that expected amount in the form of a reduction in the forward price. Her exposure is similar, therefore, to an acquisition of the Publico shares in the spot market on January 1, 1998.[26] However, Erica has effectively converted the expected amount of the dividends into an equivalent amount of interest on the bonds of Publico. If country Z imposes withholding tax on dividends paid to non-residents, but exempts interest on portfolio debt, Erica's synthetic investment avoids the application of that tax (assuming that her long position in the bonds of Publico qualifies as portfolio debt).[27]

Fabian realizes a similar result through the equity swap in example 7, which is an application of the same "total-return swap" in example 5 (Doris), but in a cross-border context. The swap replicates a long position in the shares of Publico, without the application of non-resident withholding tax that would otherwise apply to dividend payments. The swap provides Fabian with all dividends on the shares, along with all unexpected gain and loss attributable to changes in the spot price. Interest receipts on the long position in government treasury bills offset interest-equivalent payments on the short position under the swap, and should normally be exempt from non-resident withholding tax. As was noted above, dividend-equivalent payments on Fabian's long position in the shares of Publico under the swap are also generally exempt from withholding tax as non-taxable payments on a derivative. Accordingly, Fabian has substituted non-taxable payments on a long position under the swap for taxable dividend payments on a long position in the shares.

In contrast with examples 6 (Erica) and 7 (Fabian), in example 8 Grace has created a synthetic bond to avoid non-resident withholding tax that is otherwise applicable to interest payments. She realizes this result by substituting a long position in non-dividend-paying growth shares of Research Inc. for a long position in debt. As in example 2 (Betty), Grace combines that long position with put and call options to create a married put and call that provides an expected return of $10 equivalent to the expected return on an OID bond issued for $100 and redeemable for $110. If the spot price of the Research Inc. shares on maturity of the options exceeds $110, Grace will realize an unexpected loss under the call option that will be offset by unexpected gain on the long position in the shares. If the spot price is less than the $110 exercise price, Grace will realize an unexpected gain on the put option that will be offset by unexpected loss on the long position in the shares. The premium paid for the put is offset by the premium received for issuing the call. Because the shares of Research Inc. provide an expected return in the form of appreciation rather than dividends, Grace benefits from that expected appreciation as reflected in a forward price that is a function of the spot price on January 1, 1998 plus the cost of carry. The married put and call effectively ensures that Grace will realize the expected amount of $10 (or cost of carry) in the form of gain on the shares, not in the form of interest income on a debt instrument. Application of the standard tax cubbyholes for non-resident withholding tax based on legal form allows Grace to convert the taxable interest into non-taxable gain on the shares (assuming that the gain is not considered income sourced in country X).[28]

Synthetics and Constructive Sales

Accrual recognition under the tax cubbyholes is generally limited to expected gain or loss on debt. Unexpected gain or loss is recognized on realization, which is generally defined in terms of the "disposition" of an asset.[29] Legislative definitions of a disposition are, for the most part, based on two assumptions: first, that the essence of a disposition is the transfer of risk associated with an asset; and, second, that transfer of the ownership of an asset as a matter of private law is an accurate proxy for changes in risk. The transfer of an asset in the form of a sale is thus considered the core element of a disposition.[30] The concept is modified only in a handful of circumstances involving a limited range of assets in which a transfer of ownership is not regarded as a suitable proxy for changes in risk. For example, certain involuntary transactions, such as the expropriation, theft, destruction, and damage of an asset, are considered dispositions even though ownership is not transferred.[31] In these instances, the loss of the possession, use, and risk associated with the asset is apparently a sufficient basis for a realization event, particularly where the loss is accompanied by the receipt of insurance proceeds. In other instances, transactions such as assignments for loan security are specifically excluded from the concept of a disposition.[32] These exclusions seem to be justified on the ground that the transfer of ownership as a matter of legal form is unaccompanied by a sufficient loss of possession, use, and risk.

A basic acceptance of legal form as a proxy for changes in risk is reflected in the general approach to the application of the realization requirement in the context of financial instruments.[33] In general, ownership of debt and shares is considered indicative of the requisite assumption of risk associated with those financial instruments. Similarly, the holder of a long position in a derivative instrument is considered to own that position and assume all the associated risk. The issuer of a debt obligation and the holder of a short position in a derivative are considered to bear the burden of the payment obligations under the relevant instrument. In each case, a transfer of the legal rights and obligations associated with a particular instrument, or the closeout of an open position in a derivative, is the occasion that indicates a change in risk sufficient to support a realization event. As with assets generally, this general approach has been qualified in certain instances in which a change in the legal rights associated with debt and shares is considered substantive enough to result in a disposition. In particular, amendments of the terms and conditions can be considered to alter the associated risk in a manner that results in an exchange of an old instrument for a new instrument with significantly different cash flows.[34] Even though no legal transfer occurs, a disposition may be considered to arise on the amendment of the share or debt entitlements.[35] In other instances, the risk associated with a long or short position in an asset may be altered by the issue or acquisition of derivative positions on the asset. The risk may be altered to an extent that the holder of the position has effectively locked in an unexpected gain that will be realized when the positions are closed out. Although a transaction of this kind involves no change in the legal rights and obligations otherwise associated with the long or short position in the asset, specific legislative responses often require an integrated analysis of the open asset position and the related derivative positions, which can lead to a realization event before the positions are closed out. In short, the risk associated with the asset may be considered sufficiently altered by the derivative positions to result in a realization event on entry into those positions. At least in concept, the reasoning underlying this conclusion is similar to that underlying the characterization of certain amendments of shares and debt instruments as giving rise to a disposition. In each instance, a substantive change in risk occurs without a transfer as a matter of private law.[36] Even so, the use of derivative instruments to synthetically replicate a disposition involves a much different approach in which otherwise independent financial instruments are combined to replicate a disposition. This different factual context requires a somewhat different analytical approach under which the various components of the synthetic must be identified before it can be determined whether the risk is sufficiently altered to support a disposition.

> **Example 9:** Henry owns a block of shares of Publico, which he acquires for $25,000. On December 31, 1998, Henry sells an identical block of these shares for a price equal to their market value of $75,000. To satisfy his obligations under the sale agreement, he borrows the shares from Investmentbank, which he agrees to return on March 31, 1999. Henry also agrees to pay Investmentbank an amount equal to dividends paid on the Publico shares during the term of the loan. He posts his block of shares as collateral for his obligations.

> **Example 10:** June owns 10 shares of Publico, which she acquires for $10 per share. On December 31, 1998, when the shares have a value of $100 per share, June enters into a forward contract to sell them on January 1, 2000 for a price of $110 per share.

Henry has created a riskless long position in shares by effecting a "short sale against the box."[37] By entering into the short sale and creating offsetting long and short positions in the Publico shares, he has effectively locked in the $50,000 accrued gain and has insulated himself against future fluctuations in value. His short position arises from the short sale, and his long position arises from the continued holding of an identical block of shares that he previously acquired.[38] Although Henry is exposed to unexpected gain or loss on his open short position, any amount of unexpected gain or loss that subsequently arises is offset by unexpected loss or gain on his long position. Any increase or decrease in the amount of dividends on the shares is also offset by an increase or decrease in the required compensation payments under the securities loan. Assume, for example, that the Publico shares decline in value to $70,000. Henry can close out his short position by purchasing the requisite block in the market and returning them to Investmentbank under the securities loan. Henry will realize a gain of $5,000 on his closed-out short position that is offset exactly by a loss of $5,000 on the long position. If the shares increase in value to $80,000, Henry will realize a loss of $5,000 on his closed-out short position that is offset by a gain of $5,000 on his open long position.

Although Henry has realized the $75,000 value of his Publico shares as proceeds that he can invest for the period of the short sale, it is arguable that a strict adherence to legal form as a proxy for a disposition provides the benefit of the deferred recognition of any accrued gain. The analysis supporting this position depends on a formalistic approach to the application of the realization requirement and the cost base rules that distinguish among identical securities.[39] Critical to this analysis is the proposition that, when the short sale is entered into, Henry cannot determine his cost base because he does not know what shares will be used to close out his short position. Any gain remains uncertain and is not realized until the short sale is covered by the physical delivery of shares with a determinable cost base. In this respect, the fact that Henry retains the right to satisfy his obligation under the securities loan with shares subsequently acquired in the market negates any presumption (at least at the time of the short sale) that the identical property he holds "in the box" is, in fact, the property sold. Until identifiable shares are transferred in satisfaction of the short sale and related securities loan, a strict adherence to legal form as a proxy for a disposition means that the $50,000 accrued gain is unrealized. In effect, Henry has "monetized" that gain without attracting a realization event. The tax consequences on closeout depend largely on how Henry chooses to satisfy his obligations under the securities loan and the rules that determine the cost of identical securities. Some jurisdictions, such as the United States, provide generous rules that allow a taxpayer to identify the order in which identical securities with different cost bases are disposed of.[40] If Henry chooses to close out his short position by delivering his previously acquired block of shares, he will realize the $50,000 accrued gain only on that subsequent transfer when the cost base of those shares that are used to close out his open position is determined. If Henry chooses to satisfy his obligations by acquiring a separate but identical block of shares in the market, gain will arise only to the extent that the acquisition price of those shares is less than the proceeds of the short sale. As was noted above, structuring the transaction in this way produces unexpected gain or loss accruing after the short sale, which is offset by subsequent loss or gain on the long position in the shares. In that case, no amount of the gain accrued on the shares when the transaction is entered into is realized on the short sale against the box. In other jurisdictions, such as Canada, the application of an average cost rule for identical securities[41] reduces any deferral benefit.[42] In particular, where shares are acquired in the market to cover a short position, some of the accrued gain on previously acquired shares that are held in the box must be realized, since their lower cost base is averaged with the subsequently acquired identical shares. Deferral of accrued gain for the period of the short sale may be available, however, even where the open position is closed out by the delivery of the shares that constitute the long position with accrued gain. Deferral is available to the extent that there is some authority for the position that gain is not realized until the taxpayer chooses to close out the position and the cost base of the shares sold short becomes determinable.[43]

Constructive sales of appreciated assets can be implemented with other strategies that involve short and long positions revealed by simple applications of put-call parity and futures parity. In example 10, in a simple application of the basic relationship between spot and forward prices identical to the forward sale of gold by Alvin in example 1, June has created a synthetic debt instrument comparable to the instrument created by Betty in example 2 (using a married put and call in an application of put-call parity) and by Doris in example 5 (using a total-return equity swap). By combining a short position in the forward contract with a long position in the shares, June has effectively locked in a sale price equal to the spot value and assured herself a return equivalent to interest reflected in the forward price. In other words, she has invested the $100 spot value of the shares and assured herself of an expected gain of $10 in one year. Any unexpected gain or loss on her open long position in the shares will be offset by unexpected loss or gain on her short position in the forward contract. In terms of cash flows, she has exchanged an equity instrument with unexpected gain or loss for a fixed-payment debt instrument with expected gain equivalent to interest. On the theory that a forward sale is equivalent to a spot sale and the making of a loan, the risk associated with a long position in the shares has been effectively transferred on entry into the short forward contract. In this respect, June has assured herself of an additional $100 in proceeds for the shares in the event that she decides to close out her open short position in the forward contract by physically delivering the shares. To the extent that legal form is determinative, June does not have to realize the gain of $90 accrued on her long position in the shares until she closes out that position on physical settlement.

If Betty (example 2) and Doris (example 5) have accrued gain on their long share positions, the married put and call and the equity swap provide the same ability to monetize the gain without entering into a share transfer that results in a disposition and realization event for income tax purposes.[44] Indeed, Henry's short sale against the box in example 9 produces the same cash flows as Doris's equity swap, provided that he invests the short sale proceeds in short-term debt that pays LIBOR. In that case, Henry has effectively swapped his equity return on the shares of Publico (dividends and appreciation or depreciation for the period of the open short position) for debt that pays LIBOR. Issuing a deep-in-the money call option comparable to that in example 4 can also provide a constructive sale without a legal transfer, at least to the extent that the option is covered by a long position in the underlying asset. In that case, the issuer of the option is virtually assured that the option will be exercised and will provide a net cash flow equal to the spot value of the underlying asset plus an expected return equivalent to interest.

General Features and Application of Integration to Synthetics

As a tax technique, integration combines the long and short positions that comprise a synthetic and taxes the net cash flows as a single instrument or transaction. Legal form is ignored and the synthetic is taxed as if it were a debt instrument or sale transaction replicated by the synthetic. For example, the offsetting positions entered into by Alvin (example 1), Betty (example 2), and June (example 10) could be combined and each taxpayer treated as if they had created a synthetic debt instrument in respect of which they would be required to recognize the expected gain as interest income on an accrual basis. They could also be treated as if they had disposed of their long positions in shares and realized accrued gains on entering into the offsetting short positions. Similarly, Doris (equity swap in example 5) and Henry (short sale against the box in example 9) could be treated as if they had constructively disposed of their shares on entering into the short positions that offset the risk associated with their long positions in shares. Erica (forward purchase in example 6), Fabian (equity swap in example 7), and Grace (married put and call in example 8) could all be considered to have created synthetic instruments with associated cash flows subject to non-resident withholding tax as dividends or interest.

There is no coherent body of rules and/or general principles governing the taxation of synthetics. To the extent that rules and principles exist, they are found in a diverse collection of judicial doctrines, general legislative provisions, and selective legislative responses applicable to specific synthetics. The result is a series of transactional responses consistent with past legislative practice in many countries and the taxation of the basic building-block instruments under the accepted cubbyholes.[45] Despite this eclectic mix of responses, four broad themes can be discerned in them, and will be the focus of the discussion in the next two parts of this chapter.

First, selective legislative responses to the use of synthetics reflect a general move away from a reliance on legal form in favour of the concept of risk as an apparent indicator of the perceived substance of a synthetic. This concept appears to underlie attempts to

- recharacterize unexpected gain or loss as expected amounts equivalent to interest,
- modify the concept of ownership to deny the provision of dividend tax relief, and
- modify the application of the realization requirement to require the recognition of gain.

From a broad policy perspective, the use of the concept of risk as indicative of ownership and/or a transfer is a matter of debate and is discussed in detail in the following part. Even if that use of the concept of risk is assumed to be legitimate, it is difficult to identify the point at which the risk associated with legally distinct instruments can be said to be altered sufficiently to ignore the tax consequences that would otherwise follow from an acceptance of legal form and the application of the tax cubbyholes to the separate components of a synthetic. In this respect, a US tax practitioner has noted that the concept of a "straddle transaction" appears to have become important, at least in its broad sense of "two or more market positions that in combination substantially reduce the risk that would otherwise be associated with the positions held independently."[46] Indeed, as a general proposition, it seems accurate to state that responses to synthetics have tended to be limited to those instances in which risk has been altered in a manner characteristic of a straddle.[47] This feature is especially evident in the series of aggressive legislative responses implemented by US tax-policy makers.[48]

Second, the various responses to the tax-motivated use of synthetics depend on the identification of the legally distinct instruments that comprise a synthetic. In effect, the positions to be integrated must be identified before it can be determined whether there is a sufficient correlation to justify integrated treatment. This initial step entails administrative and compliance problems, yet it is critical to the attempt to distinguish tax-motivated uses of synthetics from commercially motivated hedge and arbitrage trading strategies. An overly broad application of legislation intended to address the use of particular synthetics for tax-avoidance purposes can adversely affect these legitimate uses of derivatives in risk-reducing and trading strategies. Tax-policy makers must somehow find proxies that accurately reflect the purpose-based premise for integrated treatment, and tax administrators must somehow find audit techniques that isolate those proxies in the context of large taxpayer portfolios. In all instances, the focus of this issue is an appropriate definition and identification of positions that are sufficiently offsetting to be integrated and taxed with reference to one another. Specific exceptions from the application of anti-avoidance legislation for certain taxpayers are sometimes used as a proxy for commercially driven uses of synthetics that are not the target of the legislation.

Third, although the concept of integration underlies all responses to synthetics, not all of those responses are identical in their effect. In fact, the effect of the application of a particular legislative response tends to differ according to the assumptions that are made about the purpose underlying the use of a synthetic. To be more particular, once the cash flows that are associated with the component instruments of the synthetic are identified, they can be integrated to determine a net result in terms of the risk and return profile provided by the replicated instrument or transaction. If the level of risk is considered to be sufficiently altered to justify a disregard of legal form, the tax treatment can be determined on the basis of the integrated result of the various positions that comprise the synthetic. As a tax technique reflected in specific legislative responses, integration can be defined in terms of its effect, which is divided into two general categories described by Weisbach as[49] (1) partial integration and (2) full integration. Partial-integration responses are far more common than full-integration responses; they deny a tax benefit associated with a synthetic but do not tax the synthetic as if it were entered into as a single, indivisible instrument or transaction. Partial integration thereby reflects a broader concept of integration that includes the taxation of one position with reference to another, without taxing the positions as a single unit.[50] In general, partial-integration responses yield harsher results that ignore attempts to ensure symmetry of tax treatment between counterparties to a synthetic instrument or transaction.[51] The responses appear intended to provide a type of tax penalty that is justified as a response to tax-motivated uses of synthetics. Obvious examples are legislative responses that deny dividend tax treatment to shareholders who have entered into offsetting positions that transfer the associated risk. In these instances (which might include the dividend rental arrangement in example 3, the covered call in example 4, and the total-return equity swap in example 5), the shareholder is considered to have transferred ownership, but only for the purpose of the provision of dividend tax relief. In more limited instances, full-integration responses attempt to tax a synthetic as if it were entered into as a single unit or transaction. This approach eliminates the tax benefit associated with a synthetic, but also ensures that there is no tax penalty compared with the alternative instrument or transaction replicated by the synthetic. For example, the US legislation governing foreign exchange gains and losses contains specific rules that treat a hedged foreign currency borrowing or loan as if it were entered into as a single US-dollar instrument.[52] Similarly, the contingent-debt regulations permit the treatment of fully hedged qualifying instruments as a synthetic fixed-payment instrument or a variable-rate debt instrument.[53] This approach seems to be premised on the view that synthetics can be used for legitimate hedging purposes that should not be discouraged by the imposition of a tax penalty.

Fourth, and perhaps most important, integration is a limited, second-best response to the tax-driven use of synthetics. The more direct response is reform of the basic tax rules that give rise to problematic inconsistencies in taxation. At least as an initial proposition, it should first be asked whether there are any reform alternatives that eliminate directly the need for integration in the taxation of synthetics. As is the case with the taxation of the basic building-block instruments, this alternative to integration involves fundamental reform of the tax cubbyholes in a manner that eliminates the inconsistencies and discontinuities that give rise to tax-avoidance opportunities in which synthetics are used. In this respect, the appropriate treatment of the tax-driven use of synthetics reflects a tension that runs throughout tax-avoidance cases generally. The effectiveness of a tax-avoidance transaction (taking a synthetic as a particular example) depends on the significance of the legal form of the relevant arrangements necessary to attract a tax treatment that is inconsistent with perceptions of the underlying economics. Regardless of the verbal formulas invoked by tax practitioners, the courts, and tax administrators, the fundamental question remains the same from a tax-avoidance perspective: when should the legal form of a transaction be respected in preference to the substantive economics? From a policy perspective, the important questions are much different. Indeed, tax-policy makers should explore the extent to which tax legislation is constrained by a need to tax on the basis of legal form and/or the availability of alternative approaches as a means of implementing taxation on the basis of economic substance, defined here as the consistent taxation of equivalent cash flows. Viewed from this perspective, the tax-driven use of synthetics is interesting only because it highlights weaknesses in the underlying cubbyhole structure of existing income tax systems that accept legal form and changes in that form as proxies for economic income and changes in economic income.[54] The tax treatment of synthetics is one area in which a dependence on legal form has come under severe strain. As a fundamental reform measure, the adoption of a system of expected-return taxation does not relieve that strain entirely, and integration remains necessary as a response to the tax-driven use of synthetics.

Role of Integration Under a Comprehensive Accrual Regime

Implications of the Realization-Based Recognition of Unexpected Gains and the Exclusion of Shares

In the attempt to implement the dictates of expected-return taxation, a comprehensive accrual regime reflects some clear, underlying principles that are consistent with the underlying economics of the cash flows associated with financial instruments. In particular, the distinction between expected and unexpected gain and loss emphasized throughout the previous chapters provides a benchmark for the design of appropriate timing and character rules. Tax-avoidance opportunities arise when income tax systems deviate from those rules and depend, instead, on legal form as a proxy for the application of character and timing rules. Complexity results when detailed legislative responses are grafted on to the general rules reflected in the accepted tax cubbyholes, which often provide inappropriate proxies for the underlying economics of the cash flows associated with particular instruments. The promise of fundamental reform under a system of expected-return taxation, however, is severely constrained in the context of synthetics. Although a system of expected-return taxation can alleviate some of the strain created by synthetics in the maintenance of the traditional tax cubbyholes, its effectiveness is limited by (1) a failure to apply accrual recognition to the expected gain on the embedded debt in shares, and (2) the application of realization-based recognition of unexpected gain and loss on a broad range of non-traded financial instruments (including shares). To the extent that a comprehensive accrual regime incorporates realization-based recognition and provides a general exclusion for shares, the problems presented by synthetics are identical to those under existing income tax systems and the application of the traditional cubbyholes. Furthermore, the dictates of a comprehensive accrual regime have no obvious relevance in the context of cross-border transactions. In the absence of any attempt to rationalize differential withholding tax rates on interest, dividends, and payments on derivatives, there remains a broad range of avoidance opportunities in which synthetics are likely to be used. These problems require the application of integration as a flawed tax technique under either the tax cubbyhole system or a comprehensive accrual regime.

As chapter 6 argued,[55] a comprehensive accrual regime that implements the dictates of expected-return taxation should, ideally, be applied to all shares and require the accrual recognition of the expected gain or loss associated with the embedded debt. This result can be realized by the imputation of interest on shares at an appropriate rate. As long as all gains and losses (both expected and unexpected) are recognized in full, a comprehensive accrual regime can eliminate the differences in tax treatment otherwise associated with the taxation of (1) ordinary income and capital amounts and (2) interest and dividends. In effect, an ideal system of expected-return taxation realizes the consistent taxation of the expected gain or loss on all financial instruments, and eliminates any incentive to convert those gains from fully taxed interest into preferentially taxed dividends or capital gains, whether through the use of a hybrid instrument or a synthetic. For example, the imputation of interest on shares would ensure that the married put and call in example 2 is taxed as a debt equivalent, with offsetting interest income and expense on the offsetting option premiums. Integration of the various positions would not be required. Similarly, the imputation of interest on shares would eliminate any incentive to disguise interest income as dividends using the dividend rental arrangement in example 3 or the covered call arrangement in example 4. In each instance, dividends would be recognized in full as received but would be taxable only if they exceed the amount of imputed interest already recognized on an accrual basis by the shareholder. In essence, dividends would be treated as a recovery of accrued interest that would be added to the cost of the shares. Unexpected gain or loss would arise to the extent that the amounts of the dividends are greater or less than the imputed interest. A similar result would occur with the equity swap in example 5. The equity payer (Doris) would recognize imputed income on the long position in the shares, with unexpected gain or loss arising on the short position under the swap. The amount of the gain or loss would equal the difference between the obligations and entitlements (the "net payment") of the equity payer under the swap.

Even under an ideal system of expected-return taxation applicable to shares, however, synthetics present avoidance opportunities associated with the realization-based recognition of unexpected gains and losses. Indeed, the critical distinction under this system is that between expected gains and losses associated with the advance of funds and unexpected gains or losses attributable to the bet element in a financial instrument. To prevent the benefit of anticipated deferral, the former are recognized on an accrual basis and the latter are recognized on realization. These timing rules mean that simple strategies, such as a short sale against the box and a forward sale, can be used to lock in accrued gains without attracting a realization event that depends on the form of a transaction as a transfer or sale. Short positions in derivatives can also be used to cover a long position in non-financial assets outside an accrual regime. As illustrated in example 1, this strategy can provide expected gain on the long position that is assured on maturity of the short position, but that is not recognized until maturity and may be eligible for a preferential capital gains tax rate. A comprehensive system of expected-return taxation that does not apply to non-financial assets cannot address this strategy, unless the long position is combined with the short position and treated as a synthetic sale that provides an expected gain equivalent to interest.

These limitations of an ideal system of expected-return taxation are compounded under an approach that excludes shares in favour of a separate corporate income tax system applicable to equity income. The problems are most pronounced where the corporate system imposes a combined corporate/shareholder tax on dividends that is different from that imposed on interest under an accrual regime. The result is an incentive to disguise one type of return for the other depending on the relative differences in tax treatment. In some instances, hybrids can be used to take advantage of the tax-avoidance opportunities; in other instances, synthetics can be used. The most obvious problems are associated with a classical corporate tax system and its two levels of tax on equity income, which provides an incentive to substitute debt for shares. In an attempt to narrow the gap in the tax treatment of interest and dividends, an imputation system involves the use of the corporate income tax as a withholding mechanism on both the expected and the unexpected gains associated with shares. Under a system of this kind, consistent treatment of interest and dividends requires the adoption of a corporate income tax rate that approximates the highest marginal personal rate and the provision of fully refundable imputation tax credits for all shareholders, including tax-exempt entities and non-residents. An advance corporate tax imposed on dividend distributions can be used to ensure that corporate tax is paid in support of the provision of imputation credits. Where revenue reasons dictate the denial of full imputation credits to particular taxpayers such as tax-exempts and non-residents, however, there is an incentive to substitute interest for dividends, sometimes through the use of synthetics. A similar incentive exists under a classical corporate income tax if an intercorporate dividend deduction is provided to avoid multiple levels of corporate tax on equity income but is unavailable to non-resident shareholders and is valueless for tax-exempts. Where credits are provided without the payment of corporate tax in support of the credit, the lower tax rate on dividends provides an incentive to disguise interest as dividends through the use of hybrid instruments such as preferred shares. In other instances, tax-exempts and non-resident corporate shareholders who do not benefit from the deduction have an incentive to transfer the tax benefit for interest income.

The only way to address both the manipulation of the realization-based recognition of unexpected amounts and the different taxation of interest and dividends is to require the accretion taxation of all gains and losses on all financial instruments and eliminate the corporate tax on equity income. For the kinds of reasons described in chapter 3,[56] this ideal remains impractical, and expected-return taxation is preferable as a second-best approach that addresses the tax-driven use of synthetics most effectively when it is extended to shares. In the context of a comprehensive accrual regime that excludes shares and retains realization-based recognition of unexpected gains and losses, there are two principal approaches that can be used in combination to address the tax-driven use of synthetics. The first approach involves the adoption of certain incremental reform measures that address some of the underlying inconsistencies that give rise to avoidance opportunities. The second approach involves the application of integration in specific legislative responses to the tax-driven use of synthetics; this approach is necessary because of the limitations on incremental reform measures.

The reform measures involved in the first approach to synthetics are incremental in that they stop short of the application of expected-return taxation to the embedded debt in shares, as well as the extension of accretion taxation to all financial instruments. They are, nonetheless, fundamental reform measures in that they attempt to eliminate the need for integration by eliminating some significant underlying inconsistencies in the tax treatment of particular cash flows. As was noted above, some of these measures, such as the refundability of imputation credits, must be implemented as part of the corporate tax system applicable to shares and equity income. Indeed, the direct response to tax-avoidance opportunities involving the substitutability of interest and dividends is reform of the corporate income tax to ensure consistent taxation of these two cash flows. For the reasons cited in chapter 6,[57] these reform measures remain as problematic, in many ways, as the extension of a system of expected-return taxation to shares. As was described in previous chapters, other incremental reforms can be implemented as part of an accrual regime. Three of the more significant measures are:

- *Limited application of accretion taxation* Accretion taxation can be applied to all gains and losses on a range of instruments that can be traded at low transaction costs.[58] This limited application of accretion taxation addresses directly the problem of selective realization of unexpected gains and losses under realization-based recognition. Accretion taxation can also be applied to all financial instruments held or issued by those taxpayers who can be considered traders or dealers.[59] This limited application of accretion taxation provides a comprehensive substitute for a hedge accounting regime otherwise required by traders or dealers, who commonly assume offsetting long and short positions. In effect, these taxpayers can be taxed on the basis of changes in the value of their whole portfolio of instruments.
- *Imputation of interest on non-traded options* To the extent that options are not subject to accretion taxation, expected gains and losses can be recognized on an accrual basis by the imputation of interest on the

amount of the option premium.[60] This limited measure eliminates the benefit of anticipated deferral otherwise available under realization-based recognition.

- *Application of expected-return taxation to all foreign currency debt* Expected-return taxation can be applied to all foreign currency borrowings and loans so that they are effectively treated as synthetic domestic instruments.[61] To obtain this result, expected foreign exchange gains and losses (measured using forward exchange rates) must be accrued as interest income and expense. Unexpected foreign exchange gains and losses must be treated as ordinary-income amounts recognized on realization.

Although these kinds of measures are an improvement over existing income tax systems and reliance on the accepted tax cubbyholes, they have obvious limitations. In particular, the third measure is useful but can address only a narrow range of synthetics.[62] As was noted in chapter 5,[63] the principal virtue of this measure is its ability to provide appropriate tax treatment for all foreign currency debt, whether or not structured as a synthetic for tax-avoidance purposes. The measure obviates, therefore, the need to define specifically the kinds of synthetic instruments to be singled out for integrated tax treatment. The other two measures—the application of accretion taxation to derivatives and the imputation of interest on options—affect a much wider range of synthetics, but do not address in any complete sense their tax-driven use. To the extent that the expected gain or loss produced by a synthetic is attributable to expected gain or loss on options, those amounts must be recognized on an accrual basis, and any benefit associated with realization-based recognition is eliminated. The benefit is reduced further to the extent that both expected and unexpected gain or loss on publicly traded options must be recognized on an accretion basis. The limitations of accretion taxation and interest imputation are most evident where short positions in derivatives are used by taxpayers who are not traders or dealers to cover a long position in an asset, such as shares, that is excluded from accrual recognition of expected gain or loss. In that case, only gain or loss on the short position is recognized on an accrual basis. Offsetting loss or gain on the long position remains subject to realization-based recognition, along with the portion of the gain that is locked in through a covered arrangement. For instance, the forward sale in example 1 remains attractive, primarily because the expected gain on the long position in gold provided by the short futures contract remains subject to realization-based recognition and possible characterization as a capital gain. Unexpected gain or loss on a traded short futures contract may be subject to accretion taxation, but any amount of gain or loss is offset by corresponding loss or gain on the long position. Because that asset remains outside the application of a comprehensive accrual regime, the expected gain is not subject to accrual recognition or characterization as an ordinary-income amount, unless the position is integrated with the short futures contract and treated as a synthetic instalment sale that arises on entry into the short futures contract.

Similarly, a comprehensive accrual regime that excludes shares does not significantly impair the tax-effectiveness of the married put and call used to cover the long position in shares in example 2. If interest is imputed on the option premiums, interest income on the issued call will be offset by interest expense on the acquired put. If the options are subject to accretion taxation, unexpected loss on the call or unexpected gain on the put (depending on movements in the spot price) will be offset by a corresponding gain or loss on the long position in shares recognized on realization. The result will be a mismatch of the offsetting amounts, along with an assured gain on the long position equivalent to interest. Although the mismatch will be detrimental where gain on the option is realized before offsetting loss on the shares, that detriment is not sufficient to negate the obvious benefit associated with realization-based recognition of the expected gain on the shares created by the synthetic. Moreover, that gain may be subject to preferential capital gain characterization simply because the shares are excluded from the application of an accrual regime. As with the forward sale, the synthetic debt created by the married put and call can be subjected to accrual recognition on ordinary-income account only if the short and long positions are integrated and treated as a debt instrument. Constructive sale strategies that use derivatives also remain unaffected by the application of accretion-based recognition to related short positions in derivatives or the imputation of interest on options. These strategies remain effective because the accrued unexpected gain on a long position in a non-financial asset or non-traded instrument remains subject to realization-based recognition.

Ultimately, therefore, synthetics present many of the same tax-avoidance opportunities under existing income tax systems based on the accepted tax cubbyholes or a comprehensive accrual regime intended to implement the dictates of a system of expected-return taxation that excludes shares. These opportunities arise to the extent that realization-based recognition is used for unexpected amounts, and a separate corporate income tax system fails to provide consistent taxation of interest and dividends. Incremental reforms such as those suggested above can alleviate, but not eliminate, the inconsistencies that are the source of tax avoidance. In this type of second-best context, integration must be used to maintain the integrity of the remaining tax cubbyholes. This reality is recognized, for example, in the Australian accrual proposals, which include a relatively brief discussion of tax-avoidance opportunities presented by synthetics in the context of a differentiated tax system and financial markets based on fundamental pricing relationships that permit the replication of basic instruments.[64] As the proposals point out, this general problem is addressed in a limited way by an expanded definition of debt subject to accrual treatment, which can include a broad range of hybrid instruments. This effort to address tax-avoidance opportunities must be supplemented, however, by specific anti-avoidance proposals intended to address the tax-driven use of synthetics in the same problematic areas under existing income tax systems based on the accepted tax cubbyholes.[65] The difficult question is how best to apply integration in a second-best context. In particular, the application of integration raises serious problems centred on the appropriate boundary between the tax-driven use of synthetics and the acquisition of offsetting short and long positions as part of a trading or hedging strategy.

Weakness of Integration as a Tax Technique: The Identification Issues

Because synthetics involve various combinations of legally distinct instruments, they appear to be more complex than hybrid instruments. That complexity may also seem to pose a greater challenge to the maintenance of the integrity of the traditional tax cubbyholes. This appearance is deceiving. As was noted above, the tax-driven use of synthetics is conceptually indistinguishable from the tax-driven use of hybrid instruments. Indeed, synthetics present the same issues as those associated with the basic building-block instruments, with hybrids, and with tax-avoidance transactions generally. Those issues concern the tax-motivated use of synthetics as just another means of taking advantage of opportunities for character arbitrage and the realization of unexpected gains in non-dispositive transactions. Synthetics differ principally in their use of a combination of two or more legally distinct instruments to replicate, at a lower tax cost, the cash flows associated with debt instruments or a dispositive transaction. However, even this difference is nothing new. The tax-driven use of synthetics involves the application of the same basic principle that underlies hedge transactions—namely, a reduction in the risk associated with a long or short position through offsetting short or long positions using derivatives. With synthetics, the result is either (1) realization of an expected cash flow equivalent to interest but taxed inconsistently (and preferentially) as a capital gain or a dividend, or (2) the ability to lock in an accrued gain without the application of the realization requirement. The same identification problems arise with synthetics as they do with hedge transactions. In short, the various elements comprising an integrated position that provides a specified cash flow must be identified and treated as a single instrument or transaction. Identification involves three different but closely related issues. Each is focused on certain aspects of the need to identify offsetting positions that are to be taxed with reference to one another under an integrated approach. The first issue concerns an appropriate definition of the types of property, financial instruments, or positions in property that are potentially offsetting. The second concerns a definition of the degree of correlation between the cash flows associated with two or more instruments or positions that is considered sufficiently offsetting to justify integration. The third issue concerns the practical audit problem that arises with large taxpayer portfolios consisting of a broad range of positions. In effect, tax administrators must be able to identify the offsetting subportfolios within a taxpayer's larger portfolio.

In each of these respects, the examples in the preceding part of this chapter were simplistic in their illustration of the fundamental nature of the problems presented by the tax-driven use of synthetics. In particular, various positions were assumed to be entered into as offsets that, because of their perfect correlation, eliminated all risk otherwise associated with a long position. This elimination replicated the cash flows associated with a fixed-payment debt instrument or a disposition transaction. The examples were misleading primarily in the sense that they glossed over the important identification issues that arise with any set of robust facts involving positions that are imperfectly correlated and/or multiple positions within a larger portfolio.

Example 11: In April 1998, George acquires a basket of shares at a total price of $275. At the same time, he enters into a futures contract to sell an index of publicly traded shares in March 1999 at a forward price of $294. The index includes some of the shares that are part of George's portfolio. Historical data indicate that for every $1.30 change in the index, the value of George's portfolio changes by $1.

Example 12: In April 1998, Halle acquires 10 shares of Aco at a price of $100 per share. At the same time, she issues a European call option to Irving, which permits her to acquire the shares in March 1999 at an exercise price of $112 per share. She also acquires a European put option from Irving, which permits her to sell the shares to him in June 1999 at an exercise price of $108 per share.

Example 13: Jenny owns 10 class A shares of Aco, which she acquired at a price of $100 per share. In April 1998, when her class A shares have a value of $110 per share, Jenny sells short 10 class B shares of Aco for $108 per share. She satisfies her obligations under the short sale by borrowing the block of class B shares from Investmentbank, which she agrees to return in July 1998.

Example 14: Kevin owns 10 shares of Aco, which he acquired at a price of $100 per share. In April 1998, when his shares have a value of $110 per share, Kevin sells short 10 shares of Bco for $108 per share. Bco is in the same business as Aco. Kevin satisfies his obligations with a securities loan from Investmentbank on the same terms as Jenny received.

Each of these examples is a simple variation of one of the previous examples, the principal difference being the imperfect offset provided by the long and short positions. Like Alvin and June and their offsetting long and short positions in examples 1 and 10, George has entered into a short futures contract that eliminates a considerable portion of the risk associated with his net investment in the share portfolio. The reduction of risk is incomplete, however, because his long and short positions are not taken with respect to identical property. Moreover, the reduction depends on the accuracy of historical data indicating a correlation in the price movements between his long and short positions that, even if accurate, is imperfect. George thus retains some risk, and has not created a synthetic instalment sale in the same manner as Alvin and June. George could realize a similar result by entering into an equity swap whereby he agrees to pay all dividends and appreciation in value of his portfolio in return for payments equal to all dividends and appreciation in the value of shares that comprise the index based on a notional value equal to the value of his portfolio. Unlike Doris in example 5, George would again transfer a significant portion, but not all, of the risk associated with his long position in the share portfolio. Similarly, Halle retains some risk associated with a range of price movements on her long position in shares. That range is effectively defined by the different exercise prices and maturities under the married options, which have been used to create a "collar" rather than the fixed return provided by the married put and call used by Betty in example 2.[66] Although a large portion of her return is an expected time-value amount, Halle is not assured of a return equal to that on a fixed-payment debt instrument. Jenny and Kevin have also entered into short sales against the box like Henry in example 8, but the shares sold short are of a different class of the same corporation (Jenny) and of a different corporation (Kevin). This difference means that the offsetting short and long positions are imperfect and do not provide an assured gain. Nonetheless, the close correlation in price movements ensures the realization of an accrued gain on the long positions in the shares.

The definition of the point at which imperfectly correlated positions should be treated as the offsetting components of a synthetic is especially troublesome for the application of integration. The tax-driven use of synthetics is not limited to instances in which perfect offsets provide a net cash flow that replicates a fixed-payment debt instrument or a disposition transaction. Approximate, rather than pure, tax-avoidance opportunities remain where risk is reduced but not eliminated. Legislative responses apparently recognize this fact by applying partial integration regimes that attempt to deny a tax benefit in instances in which risk is reduced but not eliminated. In fact, application of full integration regimes that treat a synthetic as the instrument or transaction that it replicates is the exception rather than the norm. An approach of this kind can only be applied in those instances in which perfectly correlated positions provide perfect offsets that eliminate risk completely. Any attempt, however, to implement integrated treatment beyond those instances of perfect offsets must be able to distinguish between incomplete risk reduction that is tax driven and similar strategies associated with legitimate hedge transactions and the investment principle of diversification. In addition to this issue, there are the difficult identification issues, noted above, regarding the definition of the positions that are potentially affected by what is, in essence, anti-avoidance legislation and the practical audit problem that such legislation entails.

Indeed, the primary difference between hedge transactions and synthetics is the context.[67] The former are entered into in non-tax-motivated strategies intended to reduce the risk otherwise associated with a long position in an asset or liability. The latter are entered into generally for tax-avoidance purposes and implement the kinds of broad strategies noted above. It is perhaps not surprising that the explicit tax-avoidance context associated with synthetics means that their use raises the same policy stakes as the tax-driven use of the basic building-block instruments, hybrid instruments, and tax-avoidance transactions generally. In almost every case, a synthetic is used in an attempt to take advantage of an avoidance opportunity in which the synthetic substitutes for a single instrument or transaction at a lower tax cost. The lack of any significant sacrifice in the desired pattern of cash flows means that there are virtually no inefficiencies or non-tax costs, but only revenue loss, associated with the substitution. This different context is an important distinguishing feature from hedge transactions. With a hedge, taxpayers have an incentive to identify the relevant components in order to qualify for integrated treatment of the hedge and hedged item. With synthetics, taxpayers have no similar incentive and, in fact, have an incentive to hide the particular components. Indeed, the tax-effectiveness of a synthetic depends critically on the treatment of the various components as legally distinct instruments. This different context means that the identification issue is especially problematic with synthetics. Tax-policy makers and administrators must search for proxies that indicate a tax-avoidance purpose and test for a required correlation between otherwise distinct positions. The boundary that must be determined is that between hedge transactions entered into for non-tax purposes and synthetics entered into for tax-avoidance purposes. Any response to the use of synthetics should not adversely affect the combination of long and short positions entered into by taxpayers as a hedge.

As an approach to the taxation of synthetics, integration may be implemented through one of two basic processes. Each depends on an acceptance of the existing tax cubbyholes and attempts to maintain the integrity of those cubbyholes by applying integrated treatment that ignores a strict reliance on legal form. One process is characteristic of the US approach to synthetics and involves detailed legislative responses. The other process involves a mix of purpose-based anti-avoidance rules, a reliance on general provisions and principles, and judicial anti-avoidance doctrines. The strengths and weaknesses of the general features of these two methods of implementation are examined below. The discussion focuses primarily on the different aspects of each process relevant to the attempt to address the difficult identification issues associated with the application of integration to synthetics. It is argued that detailed legislative responses to synthetics are preferable for many of the same reasons that a detailed legislative regime is preferable as an approach to the taxation of financial instruments generally. An approach of this kind is also the best way to address the identification problems, at least in the absence of fundamental reform that refines many of the existing tax cubbyholes and eliminates the need to tax a synthetic as a single instrument or transaction. Nonetheless, the distinguishing feature of synthetics is that they are often used for tax-avoidance purposes, and this fact provides some support for a selective reliance on purpose-based anti-avoidance rules.

Detailed Legislative Responses or a Reliance on General Principles and Purpose-Based Rules?

In the United States (and to a lesser extent in other countries), much of the detailed and complex legislation associated with the taxation of financial instruments is found in the various legislative responses to the tax-driven use of synthetics. It is not surprising, therefore, that the debate over the usefulness of detailed legislation tends to focus on this area for representative examples.[68] The fact that synthetics are a focus of debate is not especially significant; the debate over the appropriate approach to the taxation of synthetics is merely one instance of the more general debate over the use of detailed legislation or a reliance on general principles and purpose-based rules in the taxation of financial instruments generally. In the specific context of synthetics, the more important substantive issue concerns the relative merits of the two approaches in providing the most effective means of maintaining (1) the realization-based recognition of unexpected gains and losses and (2) the distinction between interest and dividend taxation. In this respect, chapter 4[69] argued that the debate over detailed legislation in the context of the taxation of financial instruments is sterile in that it concerns matters of process rather than substance. Whether tax-policy makers choose to rely on detailed legislation or the interpretation and application of general provisions, the same substantive issues must be addressed under the tax-cubbyhole system. In short, those issues can be addressed either through detailed legislation that has the appearance of certainty at the expense of simplicity, or through the expression of general principles and purpose-based rules that have the appearance of simplicity at the expense of certainty.[70] Either of these two general approaches can be used to address the specific problem of the taxation of synthetics. Moreover, any decision to choose one over the other involves many of the same issues concerning matters of process.

Whether integration is implemented through detailed legislation or a combination of general principles and judicial activism, its application to the tax-driven use of synthetics involves an attempt to maintain the integrity of the existing tax cubbyholes by ignoring a strict reliance on legal form. The theory underlying the use of detailed legislative responses is no different from that underlying the use of detailed income tax legislation generally. The impetus for this legislation is the tax-driven use of a particular instrument or transaction that exposes the weakness of a reliance on legal form as a proxy for economic income and changes in such income. A legislative response attempts to tax the instrument or transaction on the basis of its perceived substance and rejects the results that would otherwise be produced by the characterization of its legal form. The need for legislation arises from a basic distrust of the judiciary's ability to reach the same (appropriate) results in interpreting and applying existing provisions.[71] The distrust is especially pronounced with the tax-driven use of synthetics in jurisdictions that have a tradition of a non-activist judiciary. In those circumstances, the judiciary may be less inclined to reject a reliance on legal form and apply integrated treatment of the component parts of a synthetic based on perceptions of economic substance. Once the legislative process begins, various layers of detail are grafted on to the basic provisions in an attempt to address all possible permutations of the same basic problem in slightly different forms or structures. The result is detailed legislation that appears certain in both its application and the results that it provides. Moreover, those results are considered appropriate in the sense that they accord more closely with perceptions of economic substance. This level of certainty is achieved, however, at the cost of some complexity in expression. This complexity is manifested in rules that often seem to be arbitrary and unprincipled. In some instances, they provide nonsensical or apparently unintended results when assessed in terms of the rationale for the legislative response.[72] In other instances, it is simply unclear whether the legislation was intended to apply to a particular financial instrument or transaction.[73] Despite the volume of detail, these difficult interpretive issues arise because of an inability to anticipate all possible instruments or transactions that are potentially within a detailed legislative regime originally intended to address a given set of instruments or transactions.[74] In determining whether a particular set of detailed rules applies to these unanticipated arrangements, tax practitioners and administrators must reason by analogy from the presumably paradigm transactions that were the object of the legislation. Judgment must be exercised after account is taken of both the economic effect and the differences in legal relationships otherwise associated with two comparable transactions, one of which is clearly within the legislation and the other is not.

As an alternative to detailed legislation, the interpretation and application of general principles expressed in basic core provisions that define the tax cubbyholes can be used to determine the appropriate tax treatment of synthetics.[75] Tax practitioners, administrators, and, ultimately, the courts must develop appropriate rules on the basis of analogous cases to produce results that are sensible when assessed in terms of their economic effect and the legal form of particular instruments and transactions.[76] This approach depends on a basic trust in the ability of the judiciary, tax practitioners, and administrators to develop sensible principles with sensible results in specific circumstances. It is also based on the problematic assumptions that

- detailed legislative responses are not based on rational general principles (or, at best, that the principles quickly become lost in the details);[77]
- there are clear and discernible principles that underlie the coherent development of an income tax system;[78] and
- a reliance on general principles avoids the development of necessary detail.

Indeed, the substitution of general principles and purpose-based rules for detailed legislative regimes appears deceptively simple. Even if it is assumed that there is a clearly developed set of general principles applicable to financial instruments outside of a comprehensive accrual regime (which is not the case),[79] synthetics present the same substantive issues that must be addressed through administrative practice, the rulings process, and the courts. The rejection of detailed legislation in favour of "a more principled approach" effectively substitutes a large degree of uncertainty (and associated transaction costs) for the appearance of simplicity.[80] An obvious problem with the tax-driven use of synthetics is that tax practitioners will use that uncertainty to resolve ambiguous issues in favour of their clients, knowing that the tax administration may not be able to respond quickly and effectively.[81] The ineffectiveness may be attributable in large part to an inability to rely on the courts to produce results that deter tax-avoidance arrangements designed to manipulate a reliance on legal form as the basis for inconsistent tax treatment of equivalent cash flows. In short, a reliance on the courts to address the tax-driven use of synthetics is realistic only in those jurisdictions that have a tradition of robust anti-avoidance doctrines. To the extent that the courts in some countries have addressed this issue, they have been reluctant to adopt integration as a tax technique for synthetics.

Whatever approach is chosen, the tax-driven use of synthetics within the context of the existing tax cubbyholes can only be addressed through the application of integrated treatment. In effect, that tax technique must be applied to the component elements of a synthetic under the guise of detailed legislation or through general principles, judicial doctrines, and purpose-based rules. Complexity and uncertainty associated with the taxation of synthetics is attributable more to the difficulties in designing a principled application of integration than it is to the process or form in which that tax technique is applied. The need to address this basic application question is apparent, for example, in the general approach under the New Zealand accrual regime to the use of synthetics as a means of disguising expected gain. This approach, which seems to be expressed more in principle than in detail,[82] consists primarily of an extension of the definition of a financial arrangement to "wider financial arrangements."[83] These kinds of arrangements are defined, in essence, as any arrangement that provides an expected time-value return and that includes or comprises any combination of financial arrangements[84] or excepted financial arrangements.[85] The expected return on an arrangement of this kind is characterized as a non-capital amount that must be recognized in full as income or expense on an accrual basis. The general expression of this concept, which underlies detailed legislation governing conversion transactions in the United States,[86] appears to be relatively straightforward and, thereby, attractive to those who chafe at "the rule madness" associated with detailed responses to synthetics.[87] However, this attractiveness is deceiving. The same substantive issues addressed specifically under the detailed legislation must also be addressed under the New Zealand accrual rules. Indeed, the necessary details of the application of that legislation to synthetics must be fleshed out by tax administrators, tax practitioners, and, ultimately, the courts. The approach under the New Zealand regime is no simpler than that under the more detailed US legislation and, in fact, is much less certain in its application. It is probably accurate to state that the precise scope of the application of the concept of a wider financial arrangement is unclear and the subject of surprisingly little discussion or comment.[88] The scope issue is particularly difficult in light of

- the requirement that the component parts of a synthetic instrument include or comprise a combination of financial arrangements or excepted financial arrangements;[89] and
- the existence of a specific exception for income or loss that is solely attributable to an excepted financial arrangement that is part of a wider arrangement.[90]

The rationale underlying these two principles may be intuitively appealing and relatively simple to grasp. To the extent that income or expense arises on a component of a synthetic that would not otherwise be subject to the accrual regime, the fact that the component is a part of a synthetic should not attract the application of the regime.[91] This exception, however, should be available only if the gain or loss arises on a particular component that is independent of the synthetic. In this respect, the New Zealand legislation provides that income or expense is considered solely attributable to an excepted financial arrangement if the amount could have been expected to arise without the support of the wider financial arrangement.[92] The uncertainty presented by the associated interpretive difficulties are apparent if one considers, for example, a simple forward sale of a non-financial asset such as gold in example 1, and the married put and call in example 2. The expected gain provided by the synthetic debt instruments in these examples arises because of the combination of the derivative positions that cover a long position in gold and shares, respectively. The long position in gold is not itself a financial arrangement or an excepted financial arrangement, but it is combined with a forward contract, which is a financial arrangement, to provide an expected return equivalent to interest. The covered position, however, may not be within the concept of a wider financial arrangement, which appears to require a combination of financial or excepted financial arrangements as a condition for the application of integration. In effect, for the purposes of the application of integrated treatment, the concept of a position seems to include only long and short positions in financial arrangements or excepted financial arrangements. In contrast, the long position in shares in example 2 is itself an excepted financial arrangement that is combined with other excepted financial arrangements (the call and put options on the shares). Accordingly, the synthetic debt instrument created by the married put and call seems to be within the concept of a wider financial arrangement. Even so, because the accrual legislation does not apply to the extent that the expected gain associated with the synthetic can be considered to have arisen outside of the wider financial arrangement, it is difficult to conclude how the arrangement should be taxed. All or some of the expected gain is attributable to the gain on the long position in shares that would have arisen without the married put and call and should be excluded. The extent of the exclusion depends on the spot price of the shares on maturity of the options and its relationship with the offsetting value of either the put or the call. If the spot price of the shares exceeds the exercise price under the options, the loss on the call limits the gain to the expected amount, which may all be attributable to the value of the underlying shares and subject to characterization as a capital gain. If the spot price is less than the exercise price, the expected gain will consist, in part, of gain on the option, which may be excluded as solely attributable to an excepted arrangement. On the other hand, the gain or loss on the options and shares may be seen as linked and arising as part of the wider financial arrangement, in which case the exception for income or expense solely attributable to an excepted financial arrangement would not apply.

The point illustrated here is not a technical one intended to resolve the meaning of the concept of a wider financial arrangement under the New Zealand accrual regime. The important general conclusion is simply that it is unclear what the result is (or even should be) under the general language of the definition of a financial arrangement as applied to simple (and comparable) synthetics. Problems arise because of a difficulty in determining what positions should be integrated under the concept of a "wider financial arrangement." This determination is much more difficult with more complex positions, such as those in examples 11 to 14, involving positions that are imperfectly correlated and/or that comprise subportfolios of a taxpayer. The use of language that appears to express general principles does not avoid the need to develop details in their application. In each instance, the application of integrated treatment must be defined in terms of the kinds of positions that are considered sufficiently offsetting to be taxed with reference to one another.

This proposition is not intended to deny the obvious fact that responses to the taxation of synthetics involve a difficult balance of complexity and certainty, on the one hand, and simplicity and uncertainty, on the other.[93] The point is that the balancing should not be seen at a superficial level focused on the technical details associated with legislative responses. Rather, the balancing involves the more substantive problem of the definition of the appropriate circumstances in which integrated treatment of a synthetic should be applied. Any approach that relies on general principles and the courts simply provides a different process or forum for the development of the inevitable details that arise in applying integration as a tax technique for synthetics. Within the context of the existing tax cubbyholes, the important policy question is whether the identification problem can be addressed more effectively with detailed legislative responses or a reliance on a mix of general provisions, purpose-based anti-avoidance rules, and judicial activism. In short, it must be determined what unique aspects of either process might recommend it as a more effective way to manage the substantive difficulties associated with the application of integration. At least as an initial proposition, the answer to this question is similar to the answer to the same question posed in chapter 4 in the context of the taxation of financial instruments generally. If the taxation of synthetics presents the same substantive issues that must be addressed either through specific legislation or interpretive activism, there seems to be no reason to wait for lengthy development through the judicial process. Indeed, the ability to respond quickly and effectively through specific legislation tends to support the use of these responses as a means of implementing integrated treatment, supplemented by a reliance on the courts to fill in gaps in a particular legislative regime by reasoning from the general principles reflected in that regime. The unique aspect of synthetics is their tax-driven use and the need to limit what is essentially anti-avoidance legislation to those circumstances in which a perceived abuse arises. In this respect, it is unclear whether detailed legislative responses always provide an appropriate boundary between tax-driven uses of synthetics and legitimate hedging techniques. In fact, the use of purpose-based legislation may be effective in introducing sufficient friction to deter the use of synthetics for particular avoidance purposes without affecting commercial transactions.[94] Tax-policy makers are left with the uncomfortable need to exercise their judgment on an ad hoc basis in response to the tax-driven use of specific synthetics. In some instances, the normative and revenue stakes will be sufficiently high to require a legislative response that can be crafted in detail or left explicitly purpose-based. In other instances, the matter can be left to be resolved by tax administrators, tax practitioners, and the courts without resorting to legislation. This reliance can ensure many of the same benefits as purpose-based avoidance rules, primarily by affecting only the most abusive instances of tax avoidance. The problem is that there is often no clear normative basis for relying on non-legislative solutions in some instances and specific purpose-based legislation in others. The choice of policy instruments may be exceedingly unprincipled and merely a reflection of a reluctance to legislate and contribute to a perceived "rule madness."

It is suggested here that there are, in fact, some important general features of legislative approaches that can be followed in an attempt to ensure the most effective application of integration as a tax technique for synthetics. This approach, as described in the Australian accrual proposals[95] and reflected in certain US legislative responses to synthetics, involves the expression of anti-avoidance provisions at a relatively general level of principle described in terms of certain paradigm transactions similar to those used for illustrative purposes in part two of this chapter. An approach of this kind attempts to ensure that the broadest range of synthetics are potentially included. Specific guidance can be provided through regulations that describe the application of the general rules in particular circumstances. Many of those details must address the questions that inevitably arise concerning the boundary between a disposition and the retention of an asset and the returns on debt and equity. Because the distinction between these respective categories is an unprincipled one that involves differences in degree, any attempt to draw a boundary is necessarily an arbitrary exercise with associated discontinuities. In this respect, the US approach to synthetics provides some instructive lessons regarding the design of a model approach to the tax-driven use of synthetics in the context of a comprehensive accrual regime that extends accretion taxation to a wide range of financial instruments, but excludes shares. Many of these lessons are reflected in the comparable Australian proposals, particularly certain legislative proposals that address the use of synthetics to transfer the benefit of imputation tax credits.

A basic premise of the suggested approach to the application of integration is the recognition that the lack of fundamental principles underlying the tax cubby-holes means that detailed legislative responses to the tax-driven use of synthetics are inevitable, and even preferable to a reliance on purpose-based avoidance approaches. In particular, the general features of this legislative approach address the difficult identification issues associated with the taxation of synthetics by specifically defining the boundary between acceptable hedging and unacceptable risk reduction indicative of the tax-driven use of synthetics. That boundary is drawn generally so as to fit the specific circumstances that give rise to a need to respond to the tax-driven use of synthetics. To be more specific, responses to synthetics should be limited to those instances in which the risk associated with a long position is substantially reduced to create a debt equivalent or constructive sale. By targeting only the most problematic inconsistencies in tax treatment, this kind of restriction ensures that legitimate hedge transactions are unaffected; it can also alleviate difficult audit problems associated with the need to identify synthetics within large taxpayer portfolios.[96]

Suggested Approach to the Application of Integration

General Boundary Between Synthetics and Hedge Transactions

As is the case with hybrid instruments and the debt-equity distinction, much of the inconsistency in the various responses to synthetics is attributable to the unprincipled nature of the differences in tax treatment that give rise to avoidance opportunities and the resulting need to draw equally unprincipled distinctions. Realization-based recognition of unexpected amounts and the different taxation of interest and dividends deviate from an ideal benchmark treatment that requires the accretion taxation of all gains and losses on financial instruments as non-capital amounts. Once an income tax system moves away from that ideal for apparently practical reasons such as liquidity and valuation concerns, there are no obvious principles that suggest appropriate boundaries between (1) the characterization of returns as interest, dividends, or disposition gains and (2) a disposition transaction and the retention of ownership. As is the case with hybrid instruments and the distinction between debt and equity, perceptions of risk tend to be accepted as the basis for the determination of the character of a gain or loss and the concept of a disposition.[97] Equity is regarded as riskier than debt and is subject to the corporate income tax, rather than accrual recognition of expected gain or loss.[98] Similarly, a disposition is seen as any transaction that involves a transfer of the risk otherwise associated with an asset. Instead of an assessment of risk as the basis for the application of these critical tax distinctions, legal form is accepted as a proxy for risk. As is the case with hybrid instruments, synthetics challenge this reliance on legal form as an accurate proxy and lead to responses based on perceptions of risk associated with offsetting long and short positions in an asset.

From a tax-policy perspective, the difficulty with synthetics is the fact that risk has no normative significance under an ideal accretion tax that is designed to tax all changes in value as they arise.[99] Risk is only a measure of the variability of cash flows that, in turn, affect the pricing and value of specific financial instruments and non-financial assets.[100] Under the traditional tax cubbyholes, as well as under a comprehensive accrual regime that excludes shares, perceptions of risk are elevated to an independent significance that, in fact, determines the point at which significantly different tax treatment occurs. Those points are the sources of discontinuities in which small changes in risk result in disproportionately different tax treatment.[101] The problem with synthetics, as well as with hybrids that blur the boundary between debt and equity, is the perceived need to refine the point at which those discontinuities arise. This refinement requires a rejection of legal form and the drawing of a new boundary on the basis of perceptions of economic substance defined in terms of risk. There is, however, no obvious point at which that "more substantive" boundary should be drawn. In short, the lack of normative principles underlying the concept of a disposition and the distinction between debt and equity instruments gives rise to avoidance opportunities that taxpayers can take advantage of using synthetics (and hybrids, for that matter). Any attempt to draw boundaries, whether based on legal form or otherwise, is inevitably an arbitrary exercise.

To the extent that a reliance on legal form is rejected as the basis for the maintenance of the integrity of the tax cubbyholes, the lack of underlying principles may mean that detailed legislative responses to the tax-driven use of synthetics are inevitable, and even preferable to a reliance on purpose-based avoidance approaches.[102] In particular, legislative responses permit the relevant boundaries to be drawn with relative certainty to fit the specific circumstances that give rise to a perceived need to respond to the tax-driven use of synthetics. The point at which the particular lines are drawn will depend on views about the related policy considerations. If realization-based recognition is seen as an unwarranted exception to accretion taxation, there will be some sympathy for extending the definition of a disposition to those circumstances in which the risk associated with a long position in an asset is reduced and not just eliminated.[103] If a denial of imputation tax credits is seen as an unwarranted limitation on the alleviation of the tax burden on equity income, there will be some sympathy for providing credits to shareholders who have reduced the associated risk without eliminating it.[104] If denial is seen as a paramount policy goal motivated by revenue concerns, there will be some sympathy for adopting a strict boundary that requires full exposure to risk during a specified holding period as a condition of entitlement.

These related policy considerations are complicated by the difficult identification issues with synthetics. In fact, those issues suggest that specific legislative responses should be limited to circumstances in which the risk associated with a long position is eliminated in a manner that creates a synthetic debt instrument or a constructive sale. In effect, by targeting legislative responses to these instances of pure tax avoidance, policy makers can have some assurance that risk-reduction strategies associated with commercial hedging and trading strategies are unaffected.[105] Revenue loss can be addressed, at least in part, without the imposition of unnecessary costs. Indeed, any other approach that applies beyond instances of complete risk reduction potentially imposes tax and compliance costs that undermine the benefits that are presumed to be attributable to legitimate risk-reduction strategies. In that case, it becomes difficult to determine whether the revenue concerns associated with the prevention of the tax-driven use of synthetics justify the potentially adverse effect on legitimate risk-reduction strategies.[106] Moreover, the practical audit problem associated with the application of the integrated treatment of synthetics is much reduced when legislative responses are limited to those transactions involving offsetting positions that eliminate all, or substantially all, of the risk associated with a long position. The most effective way to address the audit problem is to impose information-reporting requirements that force taxpayers to report the details of all positions entered into as an offset of the risk associated with another position.[107] This kind of requirement becomes more acceptable from a compliance and administrative perspective when it is limited to instances of offsetting positions that eliminate, or reduce substantially, the risk otherwise associated with an uncovered position.[108] In fact, those circumstances will usually arise with structured finance transactions involving the same counterparties. These kinds of transactions tend to be structured (and/or prepackaged) for avoidance purposes and differ from risk-reduction transactions involving different counterparties and the partial transfer of risk.[109] In structured finance transactions, multiple positions are negotiated with the same counterparty in an effort to provide either (1) an overall return that approximates interest on a conventional loan transaction or (2) the proceeds of disposition on a sale. In risk-reduction transactions, multiple counterparties enter into offsetting positions that tend to be short term and unstable and are often intended to generate profits from arbitrage trading strategies focused on pricing relationships.[110] The difficult identification problems with synthetics arise, therefore, in any attempt to identify a debt equivalent or sale transaction in the context of multiple positions with multiple counterparties. In those circumstances, it is difficult to conclude that the parties entered into the positions for tax-avoidance purposes in an effort to replicate the return on a debt instrument or to realize proceeds from a sale transaction.

Legislative Responses to Synthetics

Narrowly Targeted Definitions of Synthetics

Many of the details of this general approach to the tax-driven use of synthetics are reflected in US legislation that applies integrated treatment to "conversion transactions"[111] and "constructive sales."[112] In general, both legislative responses ignore the legal form of separate financial instruments in instances of pure avoidance in which the offsetting cash flows eliminate, or reduce substantially, the risk associated with a particular position. The conversion transaction rule integrates the identified positions and recharacterizes capital gain realized on a disposition as ordinary income equivalent to interest.[113] The constructive sale provisions also integrate the identified positions and require the realization of accrued gain on a long position in a related asset. The following four elements of the legislation ensure that these results arise only in respect of the targeted transactions:

- *Offsetting positions* The concept of offsetting positions is defined largely through a description of a set of paradigm transactions that provide cash flows that are perfect or near-perfect substitutes for the cash flows associated with fixed-payment debt or the disposition of property with accrued gain. In particular, the conversion transaction rule applies to one of four different categories of transactions, each of which includes offsetting long and short positions that provide an expected return, all or substantially all of which is attributable to the time value of a taxpayer's net investment in the transaction.[114] For example, the forward sale in example 1 provides an expected return that is attributable to the time value of the net investment of the taxpayer in a long position in gold (Alvin); it is probably within the specified category that includes acquisitions of property covered by a substantially contemporaneous agreement to sell the same or substantially identical property.[115] The married put and call in example 2 could also be a conversion transaction, particularly if it were marketed or sold as producing capital gain rather than interest income.

  The constructive sale provisions[116] similarly apply to a set of four enumerated transactions that consist of offsetting positions in respect of an appreciated long position[117] in shares, debt, or partnership interests.[118] These transactions include Henry's short sale against the box in example 9,[119] as well as June's forward sale in example 10[120] and Doris's equity swap in example 5,[121] provided that the latter two transactions are entered into to cover a long position in an appreciated asset.[122]

- *Level of risk reduction* The paradigm transactions are defined in terms of the level of risk reduction that the offsetting positions must entail. This stated level is considered indicative of the tax-driven use of a synthetic instrument or transaction. In general, that level is defined in terms of the elimination of all, or substantially all, of the risk otherwise associated with a long position. Risk reduction to this degree results in cash flows that synthetically replicate the return on a fixed-payment debt instrument or the realization of proceeds (and accrued gain) on a sale.[123] In short, the legislative responses are focused on those transactions that are structured and/or marketed as avoidance arrangements assessed in terms of their equivalence with a debt instrument or a sale transaction. Application of the conversion transaction rule is limited, therefore, to the expected gain on a taxpayer's net investment in a transaction that includes offsetting positions that ensure an expected time-value return or debt equivalent.[124] This result arises because of the requirement that the acquisition of a long position be covered by a substantially contemporaneous short position in the same or similar property.[125] Alternatively, the conversion rule includes only those transactions marketed as producing capital gain treatment of the expected time-value return,[126] which would usually involve fully offsetting long and short positions.

A similar approach to the required level of risk reduction is apparent in the constructive sale provisions and their requirement that each of the enumerated transactions consist of "substantially" offsetting positions.[127] In particular: (1) a short sale against the box is included only if the offsetting positions are in the same or substantially identical property;[128] (2) an offsetting notional principal contract is subject to the provisions only if it pays all, or substantially all, of the investment yield on a long position and provides for reimbursement of all decreases in value;[129] (3) a forward contract must cover a long position by providing for delivery of a substantially fixed amount of property for a substantially fixed price;[130] and (4) a long purchase must cover an appreciated short position in the same or substantially identical property.[131]

- *Partially integrated treatment* Both the conversion transaction rule and the constructive sale provisions apply a partial integration regime that is "one-sided against the taxpayer,"[132] presumably on the defensible assumption that the relevant synthetics have been structured for avoidance purposes. The conversion transaction rule recharacterizes capital gain realized on a conversion transaction as ordinary income.[133] Where a taxpayer has created synthetic debt that produces expected loss attributable to the time-value of money, however, the legislation does not apply to convert the loss into an ordinary amount.[134] Where the constructive sale rule applies, a taxpayer is deemed to dispose of the long position in the appreciated asset for proceeds equal to fair market value,[135] and to reacquire the asset at a cost equal to those proceeds.[136] This deemed sale occurs only for the purposes of the recognition of accrued gain, with any hold period requirements beginning over again after the deemed reacquisition.[137]

- *Specific exceptions* Specific exceptions for particular taxpayers and transactions are used in an attempt to refine the application of integrated treatment and to ensure that the partial integration regime does not apply, even where there is a complete reduction in risk. In these instances, it appears to be assumed that a non-tax reason motivates the risk-reduction strategy and a complete transfer of risk is not indicative of an avoidance transaction. For example, the conversion transaction rule provides an important exception for options dealers and commodity futures traders,[138] who often enter into offsetting positions with multiple counterparties as part of an overall trading strategy intended to take advantage of arbitrage opportunities presented by pricing relationships.[139] Although the combination of positions may provide an expected return that is equivalent to interest, the likely non-tax motivation for the trading strategy tends to negate the need for the application of the conversion rule.[140] The constructive sale provisions provide exceptions for (1) non-convertible debt with non-contingent principal and fixed or variable-rate interest;[141] (2) certain short-term hedges closed before the end of the 30th day following the taxation year;[142] and (3) a forward contract to sell non-publicly traded property that settles within one year after the contract is entered into.[143] The first exception permits debt to be hedged without resulting in a constructive sale;[144] the second permits hedging against short-term volatility;[145] and the third recognizes that sales of non-traded property sometimes require a year to close.[146]

The narrowly targeted approach reflected in the US conversion transaction and constructive sale provisions differs significantly from certain other legislative responses that restrict the availability of dividend tax relief for hedged share positions. The approach in these responses also involves the identification of offsetting positions and the application of a partial integration regime to the cash flows associated with those positions. The principal difference with these other legislative responses lies in the level of risk reduction that is required to constitute a tax-driven synthetic. In effect, some of these legislative responses apply where the level of risk reduction is less than that associated with an outright sale of shares and/or the creation of a debt equivalent that is eligible for dividend tax relief. These responses are not limited, however, to instances in which interest is disguised as a tax-preferred dividend, so share hedging and trading strategies are potentially affected. This result can be justified only if the benefits that are presumed to arise from the prevention of revenue loss associated with the tax-driven use of synthetics outweigh any inefficiencies from a potentially adverse effect on legitimate transactions. As was argued above, this proposition is difficult to prove, and in the absence of proof it may be preferable to adopt a limited application of a partial integration regime.

One of the more notorious examples of an expansive application of integration is the US legislative provisions that restrict the availability of the intercorporate dividend deduction to shares that have been held "naked"[147] for at least 46 days.[148] Under these provisions, integrated treatment is applied to deny the tax-free status of intercorporate dividends if offsetting positions involve something less than complete risk reduction.[149] This restriction is reflected in two separate rules. First, a corporate shareholder is denied the dividends-received deduction if it is obliged to make related payments in substantially similar or related property.[150] Second, share ownership for the purposes of the 46-day hold period is ignored for any day during which the corporate shareholder[151]

- has an option to sell ("covered put"),
- is under a contractual obligation to sell ("covered call"), or
- has made (and not closed) a short sale of substantially identical shares or securities.

These two rules are readily understood as defensible responses to obvious avoidance opportunities that arise because of the dividends-received deduction.[152] The first addresses the avoidance opportunity that arises if a corporate shareholder is able to take both sides of offsetting transactions and generate an after-tax profit attributable to the tax-preferred status of intercorporate dividends. For example, a corporate taxpayer could acquire a long position in shares and assume an offsetting short position under an equity swap, such as that in example 5. Dividends received on the long position would be offset by compensation payments required to be made on the short position under the equity swap. For income tax purposes, however, these offsetting transactions would be profitable if the corporate shareholder could deduct the amount of the compensation payments in computing its income and were also entitled to a dividends-received deduction.[153] The US legislation eliminates this opportunity for pure avoidance by denying a deduction for intercorporate dividends where there is an offsetting obligation to make related compensation payments. In short, a corporate shareholder is denied the dividends-received deduction if the receipt is transferred to another person through the obligation to make the related payment.

The second rule addresses the familiar avoidance opportunity that arises where a corporate taxpayer acquires shares, either shortly before or shortly after the dividend date, and sells them immediately thereafter. In that case, the amount paid for the shares includes the amount of the declared or expected dividend, and the subsequent receipt compensates the corporate shareholder for a portion of the cost of the shares. Although the dividend represents a recovery of a portion of the cost, a tax benefit arises if the corporate shareholder can claim a dividends-received deduction for the amount of the cost recovery and a separate loss on the sale of the shares equal to the amount of the dividend. In short, a corporate shareholder should not be able to receive a tax-free intercorporate dividend that is intended to eliminate multiple levels of corporate tax and also be able to claim a loss attributable to a decline in value associated with the dividend payment.[154] Under the US legislation, denial of the intercorporate dividends-received deduction eliminates the tax-free status of the dividend and effectively treats it as an expected return equivalent to interest that is offset by any loss on the shares. A corporate shareholder that holds shares "naked" for the requisite period is considered to be sufficiently exposed to market risk that any abuse of the dividends-received deduction is unlikely. The US legislation differs from the similar restrictions in other countries by requiring legal ownership to be supported by economic ownership assessed in terms of the burden of the associated risk.[155] These restrictions mean that UStaxable Inc. in example 4 would be denied a dividends-received deduction, unless it can establish that it held the shares that are subject to the deep-in-the-money option for a 46-day period during which the shares were not covered by a long put option, a short call option, a short forward contract, or a short sale.

A requirement that shares be held naked for a defined period is not particularly problematic, provided that it is limited to instances in which corporate taxpayers attempt to claim both a dividends-received deduction and a loss on a long position in shares. Indeed, to the extent that the dividends-received deduction yields the same result as a tax-free recovery of cost, a corporate shareholder should be denied a second deduction for an equivalent loss on a subsequent sale.[156] A rule of this kind, however, requires some limitation on its application, beyond which it can be safely assumed that any loss is attributable to market forces (that is, changes in expectations regarding future dividend payments) and not a decline in value arising from the receipt of dividends that are reflected in the cost of the shares because of an acquisition either shortly before or after the dividend date. In defining a required holding period intended to implement this kind of limitation, it may be reasonable to require that legal ownership be supported by economic ownership in the sense of full exposure to risk, particularly where the holding period is relatively brief.[157] A requirement like this is not especially harsh where the related provision denies the deduction of a loss that is offset by the receipt of a tax-free intercorporate dividend. More problematic results arise where the related provision denies the tax-free status of intercorporate dividends on hedged positions in shares. Without the offsetting loss, there is no tax-avoidance opportunity attributable to the matching of a tax-free receipt with a tax-deductible amount.[158] The related-payment rule differs significantly, therefore, from the share-hedging rule under the US provisions in requiring that the intercorporate dividend actually be offset with a related payment that is potentially deductible. Yet, even without the offsetting loss, a corporate shareholder is denied a dividends-received deduction under the US legislation if the shares are not held naked for the 46-day period. This denial results in multiple levels of corporate tax, where dividends are paid on a long position in shares that is hedged to any extent. In the absence of an offsetting compensation payment or loss, there appears to be no reason to impose multiple levels of tax. In short, the rationale for the tax-free status of intercorporate dividends seems to apply, even though the risk otherwise associated with the long position is reduced. Avoidance of multiple levels of corporate income tax seems defensible even if the relevant shares are fully hedged.[159]

The US legislation reflects, therefore, a broad rule with potentially adverse effects for share-hedging strategies. A similar approach has been introduced (and criticized) in Australia, where proposed anti-avoidance legislation denies imputation tax credits in respect of dividends on shares "that have not been held at risk for more than an appropriate short-term period, or where the taxpayer is under an obligation to make related payments with respect to positions in substantially similar or related property."[160] Like the US legislation on which the proposed legislation is patterned, the Australian proposals potentially apply beyond those circumstances in which related compensation payments or an offsetting loss create obvious avoidance opportunities when combined with the tax-preferred receipt of dividends on a long position in shares.[161] In the absence of offsetting amounts, the approach to the definition of the tax-driven use of synthetics suggested above (and reflected in the US conversion transactions rule and constructive sale provisions) would limit the denial of imputation tax credits to those circumstances in which the risk associated with shares is eliminated or reduced to the extent that the holder has created an investment equivalent to debt. In that case, denial of imputation credits or an intercorporate dividend deduction can be justified on the basis that the cash flows are equivalent to the expected return on debt and should be taxed accordingly. Moreover, it is probably safe to assume that the transaction has been structured to replicate the return on debt and effectively transfer imputation credits from a shareholder who is unable to benefit from the attendant tax relief. Beyond those circumstances, denial of imputation credits potentially affects any hedging transaction that does not approach the level of debt equivalence, and does not otherwise create avoidance opportunities because of related compensation payments or offsetting losses.[162]

An example of a more narrowly focused approach to the denial of dividend tax relief, consistent with the general approach to synthetics suggested here, is reflected in Canadian legislation addressing dividend rental arrangements.[163] The legislation denies a dividends-received deduction for a corporate shareholder,[164] as well as a dividend tax credit for a resident individual,[165] where a dividend is received as part of a "dividend rental arrangement." The definition of the term "dividend rental arrangement" is expressly purpose-based in the sense that the main reason for entering into the arrangement must be the receipt of the dividend. In addition, the arrangement must be structured so that someone other than the recipient bears the risk of loss or enjoys the opportunity for gain or profit with respect to the relevant share in "any material respect." Although the legislation fails to provide any guidance as to this required level of risk reduction, the "purpose-based" definition of a dividend rental arrangement apparently indicates an intention to target only those transactions that are structured to effectively transfer dividend tax relief by transferring share ownership to taxpayers who are able to benefit in full. This intention is supported by the fact that arrangements of this kind are limited to those circumstances in which someone other than the shareholder bears the risk of loss and opportunity for gain in "any material respect." Indeed, this qualifying phrase seems to suggest that the concept of a dividend rental arrangement includes only those transactions in which a long share position is hedged in such a way that the associated risk is virtually eliminated, and the ostensible shareholder is left with a debt equivalent that is otherwise eligible for dividend tax relief (example 3 above).[166] The legislation is targeted, therefore, to the use of synthetics in transactions that transfer risk so as to create a debt equivalent that is eligible for dividend tax treatment solely on the basis of legal form. The legislation attempts, in effect, to address those instances of pure tax avoidance that use synthetics to create a debt equivalent out of a long position in shares, without affecting risk-reduction strategies that fall short of a standard of debt equivalence.

By limiting anti-avoidance responses to those circumstances in which risk is reduced substantially, the suggested approach to the tax treatment of synthetics is open to an important criticism—namely, narrowly targeted responses are relatively easy to avoid because of the high standard of risk reduction that must be met before an anti-synthetic rule is applied.[167] Taxpayers may be willing to retain some minimal risk and thereby fall short of the creation of a debt equivalent or a disposition transaction that would otherwise be deemed to occur on the elimination of the risk otherwise associated with a long position.[168] The non-tax costs associated with this risk retention may not be sufficient to offset the tax benefits gained from a conversion transaction, a constructive sale, or a transfer of dividend tax relief. In effect, the boundary between a tax-driven synthetic and a commercial hedge transaction is drawn so that most risk-reduction strategies are defined as falling within the latter category. Accordingly, the suggested approach creates a significant discontinuity, whereby the retention of even a low level of risk results in disproportionately better tax treatment associated with commercial hedge transactions. This perceived weakness is similar to the attempt to draw an appropriate boundary between debt and equity and the characterization of hybrid instruments as one or the other. Ultimately, the boundary will be arbitrary wherever it is drawn, and significant discontinuities will arise from small changes in risk for positions on either side of that line. In the absence of fundamental reform that eliminates differences in tax treatment which give rise to avoidance opportunities through the use of synthetics, the policy alternatives are not especially attractive. One possibility is a partial integration approach that integrates any two or more offsetting positions to create a deemed disposition or recharacterization of returns to the extent of the risk reduction.[169] The complexity associated with the application of an approach of this kind is difficult to justify, particularly as it affects legitimate hedging transactions. The alternative is to draw a boundary between hedge transactions and the tax-driven use of synthetics that provides an all-or-nothing result for risk-reduction strategies on either side. In order to avoid the imposition of excessive costs on legitimate hedge transactions, that line can be defensibly drawn at the level where risk is substantially eliminated. To prevent tax avoidance along the boundary, tax-policy makers should avoid the use of clear bright-line tests and should adopt, instead, qualitative definitions that suggest a level of complete or substantial risk reduction.[170] In this way, the precise level of risk reduction that effectively defines the tax-driven use of a synthetic is left open to a limited extent and can be supported further with purpose-based anti-avoidance provisions. Like an uncertain factors approach to the boundary between debt and equity, an approach of this kind can introduce sufficient friction to deter tax avoidance along the boundary, while limiting anti-avoidance responses to those instances in which risk is reduced substantially in a way that replicates a debt instrument or a disposition transaction.[171]

This point is illustrated most obviously by a specific issue that affects both the definition of offsetting positions and the level of risk reduction that is sufficient to identify a synthetic. The issue arises with positions in property that is not identical, but is similar enough that changes in value are positively correlated. An approach to synthetics that integrates only positions in identical property is, in fact, too restrictive and easy to avoid through offsetting positions that are positively correlated because of their substantial similarity. This fact is recognized in the US legislation limiting the availability of the dividends-received deduction. As was indicated above, the holding-period requirement is satisfied only for that period in which a long position in shares is not covered by specified short positions (put or call options, forward contract, or short sale) in "substantially identical shares or securities." In addition, the requirement is not satisfied for any period during which a corporate shareholder has diminished the risk of loss on its long position by holding one or more positions with respect to "substantially similar or related property." Both of these terms are defined in regulations[172] that effectively address the difficult identification issues presented by offsetting positions in (1) different shares of the same corporation, (2) shares of different corporations, and (3) positions in share indexes covering a taxpayer's portfolio. If the relevant shares are considered sufficiently similar, they are treated as effective substitutes whose associated risk can be reduced through offsetting positions.[173] In the first two cases, the regulations adopt an imprecise approach that suggests, without defining in detail, a high level of positive correlation. The regulations merely state that the term "substantially identical stock or securities" is to be applied according to the facts and circumstances of each case.[174] Similarly, shares of the same corporation and shares of different corporations are considered substantially similar or related property on the basis of an assessment of various factors that indicate whether the value of offsetting positions can be expected to vary inversely.[175] Sharp discontinuities on either side of the line are avoided through the general expression of the relevant standard. In the case of share portfolios and offsetting positions in share indexes, however, the regulations provide a fairly precise "common capitalization test" to determine whether the positions substantially overlap and can, thereby, be considered substantially similar or related property.[176] Under this test, a portfolio and a share index are considered to overlap substantially if at least 70 percent of the value of the portfolio consists of shares that comprise the index.[177] This arbitrary bright line was apparently chosen for reasons of administrative ease and compliance.[178] The obvious problem is that the line can be skirted rather easily through the acquisition of positions that are expected to vary inversely, yet do not overlap in the sense that the share portfolio and index comprise the defined level of identical shares. To ease the pressure on this sharp discontinuity, a purpose-based anti-avoidance rule deems certain positions to overlap even though they do not meet the common capitalization test.[179]

The Curious Case of Non-Resident Withholding Tax

A curious issue with synthetics is the failure of tax-policy makers to respond to opportunities for the avoidance of non-resident withholding tax. The general approach to synthetics applied in a domestic context in the conversion transaction and constructive sale legislation in the United States has not been applied to address erosion of the withholding tax base. In the absence of fundamental reform of the relevant tax cubbyholes, it is at least arguable that the legal attributes associated with a long or short position in an asset are sufficiently different from those associated with ownership or a sale to justify different tax treatment.[180] In effect, the fact that a payment on a derivative is determined with reference to payments on an underlying asset that would otherwise attract withholding tax has generally been rejected as an insufficient basis to tax the payments on the derivative. Exemption from non-resident withholding tax is supported primarily by the proposition that payments on derivatives are made on a gross basis (that is, ignoring related expenses) and the imposition of any tax by the country of residence of the payer would affect pricing relationships in ways that might adversely affect the use of derivatives in allocating risk efficiently.[181]

The significance of these arguments in support of the non-taxable status of payments on derivatives is diminished when long and short positions in derivatives are combined with long and short positions in debt and shares to create a synthetic that provides equivalent cash flows on a tax-exempt basis. For instance, the forward purchase of shares in example 6 does not replicate exactly the ownership of the shares, since the non-resident taxpayer (Erica) loses the benefit of any dividends paid during the term of the forward contract in excess of the expected amount on entering into the forward purchase. Similarly, the equity receiver under a total-return equity swap (examples 5 and 7) does not have all the legal rights of an owner, including the right to vote the shares. A long position in shares that is covered by a married put and call (example 8) provides an expected return that is equivalent to interest, but exposes the holder to a credit risk that is much different from that associated with the ownership of a bond. In fact, the creditworthiness of the issuer of the shares in examples 6 and 7 is replaced by the creditworthiness of the counterparty under the derivative instruments used to create the particular synthetics. The cash flows associated with these synthetics replicate, however, to a considerable extent, the cash flows associated with the ownership of shares or a debt instrument that would otherwise be subject to non-resident withholding tax. The important tax policy issue is whether the differences in the legal attributes of substitutable positions are sufficient to justify different tax treatment. For the most part, it is difficult to see why the differences should have any relevance for tax purposes. The simple question should be the same as that in the domestic context—namely, are the cash flow patterns sufficiently similar to justify consistent tax treatment? Where the patterns appear to be sufficiently similar, the synthetic should be taxed as if it were the replicated shares or debt instrument. In that case, non-resident withholding tax should be applied to what are, in form, derivative payments. The imposition of withholding tax is unlikely to have adverse pricing consequences that should concern tax-policy makers, given the presence of a tax-avoidance purpose that can safely be assumed to underlie the creation of the synthetic.

Indeed, there appears to be nothing especially unique about non-resident withholding tax to suggest that the same approach to synthetics in the domestic context cannot be applied in similar fashion.[182] The kinds of structured debt equivalents subject to the US legislation governing conversion transactions could easily be subjected to non-resident withholding tax that would otherwise apply to interest on the debt instruments replicated by the particular synthetics. Much the same concept could be extended to forward share sales and similar transactions that convert dividends into exempt interest. Swap transactions that substantially eliminate the risk associated with a long position in shares could be targeted in the same manner as constructive sales are in the US legislation. Where risk associated with a long share position is substantially eliminated, a lookthrough rule could be applied to the equity recipient, and the swap payments could be characterized as taxable dividend receipts.[183] Because the targeted transactions would be limited to the kinds of structured transactions defined in the conversion transaction and constructive sale legislation,[184] third-party withholding and information-reporting obligations could be imposed and should not present unforeseen compliance problems.[185] A tax penalty in the form of overwithholding on all payments on the component derivatives of a synthetic may even be justified, given the tax-avoidance context.

This type of approach raises again the need to distinguish the tax-motivated use of synthetics from legitimate hedging strategies. The imposition of non-resident withholding tax in the latter context may, in fact, have adverse pricing effects for economically desirable transactions. This issue is, however, exactly the same as that in the domestic context. As was argued above, tax-policy makers should draw the line with enough precision to include only those structured transactions that provide returns substantially similar to interest or dividends, as well as those that eliminate all, or substantially all, of the risk associated with a long position in shares. Even so, there appears to be a lack of commitment to withholding taxes by many governments. This fact is reflected in the extension of exemptions for interest on portfolio debt and maintenance of the exempt status of payments on derivatives. Moreover, many countries are moving to lower their withholding tax rates on dividends and even eliminate them through the provision of limited imputation tax credits to non-resident shareholders. In that context, there seems to be little political will to shore up the withholding tax base. This indifference to the use of synthetics to avoid non-resident withholding taxes contrasts sharply with the quick reaction of the US, Canadian, and Australian governments to trading in foreign tax credits that makes use of many of the same synthetic investment techniques that can be used to avoid withholding taxes.[186] Potential erosion of taxes on domestic-source income through the availability of the transferred foreign tax credits perhaps explains the quick reaction. In the absence of specific legislative responses, governments seem content to rely on credit risk, legal risk, and transaction costs to serve as effective non-tax barriers to the unconstrained avoidance of withholding taxes. These factors seem to explain why substantial amounts of revenue from withholding taxes continue to be collected. By introducing further constraints on obvious instances of pure tax avoidance, specific legislative responses to the use of synthetics in the context of non-resident withholding tax would only support the effectiveness of these non-tax barriers to unconstrained avoidance.

Hedge Accounting and a Comprehensive Accrual Regime

As was suggested above, hedge transactions present the same general issues as synthetics. The principal difference is the absence, or presence, of a tax-avoidance purpose for the assumption of offsetting positions. Where a financial instrument is acquired as a non-tax-motivated hedge of another financial instrument, non-financial asset, or liability, the application of integration matches gain or loss on the instrument with loss or gain on the underlying position. Both the character and timing of the recognition of gain or loss on the hedge can be determined with reference to loss or gain on the underlying position. Integration is partial in the sense that the offsetting positions are not taxed as a single instrument or transaction.[187] Instead, the character and timing rules otherwise applicable to gain or loss on the particular financial instrument are altered to match loss or gain on the underlying position. It is probably accurate to say that this notion of integration as the basis for hedge tax accounting is regarded favourably in the tax literature.[188] In practice, however, the development and implementation of robust hedging rules present significant administrative and compliance difficulties. Moreover, although hedge accounting has an intuitive appeal, the need for this approach in the context of a comprehensive accrual regime is problematic. Once it is accepted that income tax rules are applied to something less than the whole of the portfolio of a taxpayer, it is not obvious why the character and timing of gains and losses on a financial instrument should be taxed with reference to offsetting amounts on another position.

The deceptive appeal of hedge accounting is evident in the recent Australian proposals for a comprehensive accrual regime. The initial consultative document[189] released jointly by the Australian Taxation office (ATO) and the Treasury department rejected the adoption of hedge accounting in the context of the proposed accrual regime, primarily on the basis that derivatives are normally used to hedge financial instruments that would be subject to the same tax treatment.[190] An overwhelming number of private sector submissions pointed out that this position ignores the use of derivatives to hedge non-financial assets and shares that are subject to realization-based recognition and are eligible for capital gain or loss treatment.[191] Failure to take a hedge into account was said to result in the familiar problem of "tax fragmentation," whereby gain or loss on a matching derivative instrument is subject to accretion taxation on ordinary-income account. The lack of symmetry in the taxation of gain and loss on offsetting positions that provide a net cash flow was criticized as a significant non-neutrality that distorts the pricing of derivatives acquired for hedging purposes. In effect, the tax system was seen to apply different character and timing rules to the separate cash flows associated with offsetting positions. The result is an aggregate tax burden that exceeds the tax that would otherwise apply to those cash flows if they were taxed on a net basis. Similar problems of tax fragmentation were seen to arise under the proposed approach in the consultative document even for financial instruments acquired as a hedge of other financial instruments. For example, gain or loss on a forward-rate agreement acquired as a hedge of a borrowing was to be accounted for over the term of the agreement itself, instead of being matched with the future interest costs incurred on the related borrowing.

In response to private sector submissions, a subsequent issues paper included an extensive discussion of hedge-accounting proposals intended to realize a greater degree of "risk neutrality," which was defined as non-interference with decisions to allocate or transfer risk.[192] The issues paper described the general approach in the following terms: "When financial arrangements are entered into for hedging purposes in a differentiated tax system, this risk neutrality objective would be enhanced by changing the tax treatment of the hedge transaction from what it would otherwise be to one that is consistent with the tax treatment of the underlying position."[193] In fact, it is argued here that the position outlined in the earlier consultative document is correct, and hedge tax accounting can be defensibly rejected in the context of a comprehensive accrual regime.[194] This proposition follows from the fact that a comprehensive accrual regime suppresses most of the worst inconsistencies in the taxation of financial instruments that otherwise provide a case for hedge accounting. Except with regard to synthetics that replicate a single instrument or transaction,[195] tax-policy makers should follow the example under the New Zealand accrual legislation and resist the temptation to integrate hedged positions.[196] Where the case for hedge accounting proves to be irresistible, its application should be severely limited in the manner described below and should in no sense result in the explicit matching of gains and losses on offsetting positions.[197]

In the context of a comprehensive accrual regime, the case against hedge tax accounting begins with the recognition that the approach is a product of financial-accounting practice and its overriding focus on the need to match revenue and expenses.[198] Viewed from the perspective of the tax-policy goals that underlie the benchmark treatment of financial instruments described in chapter 3, any need to realize a comparable matching is irrelevant,[199] and a hedge tax accounting regime is unnecessary.[200] To reiterate, all financial instruments provide expected and/or unexpected gains and losses. Recognition of the full amount of both types of gains and losses avoids difficult problems of character arbitrage otherwise associated with a distinction between amounts on capital and income account.[201] To address the problem of anticipated deferral, expected gains and losses should be recognized on an accrual basis. Unexpected gains and losses do not present the problem of anticipated deferral and can be subject to realization-based recognition. These amounts, however, present problems of unanticipated deferral and selective realization. To address both problems, a comprehensive accrual regime should subject traded instruments to accretion taxation. To address selective realization for non-traded instruments, a regime may also need to include loss limitations.

Under a comprehensive accrual regime that implements these basic principles, there is no need to match gains and losses on offsetting positions in financial instruments. All types of gains and losses can be recognized on each instrument separately in a manner that is entirely defensible from a tax-policy perspective.[202] Where an income tax system deviates from these principles by, for instance, excluding non-traded shares from the application of a comprehensive accrual regime, there is a case for the adoption of integration as a tax technique. As has been illustrated in this chapter, synthetics can be used to create multiple positions that replicate the cash flows associated with a single instrument or transaction. Integration of the multiple positions ensures that they are taxed consistently with that instrument or transaction. Nonetheless, outside of these instances of synthetic replication, which are commonly entered into for tax-avoidance purposes, it is unclear whether one position in a financial instrument should be taxed with reference to another. In effect, tax-policy makers must articulate a defensible reason for altering an otherwise appropriate tax treatment assessed in terms of defined policy goals. That reason boils down to the proposition articulated in the Australian accrual proposals that a failure to tax a hedge with reference to an underlying position results in adverse pricing effects that inhibit otherwise efficient hedging strategies. The tax system may impose efficiency losses, particularly where deviations from the dictates of a comprehensive accrual regime give rise to mismatches in character and timing. Those costs must be balanced against any sacrifice in the ability to address problems of character arbitrage, anticipated deferral, unanticipated deferral, and selective realization. In a sense, it must be determined that the need to address the adverse effects of tax fragmentation is a paramount policy goal that justifies an exception from the prescribed treatment under a comprehensive accrual regime. Moreover, the need to address the problem of tax fragmentation must be seen to justify the administrative and compliance costs associated with the implementation of hedge tax accounting.[203]

The basis for these propositions in support of hedge tax accounting have not been the subject of systematic study in the context of the accepted tax cubbyholes that give rise to the worst character and timing mismatches.[204] Even if the inefficiencies that are presumed to be attributable to tax fragmentation are accepted, the case for hedge tax accounting is increasingly problematic in the context of a comprehensive accrual regime that eliminates many of the inconsistencies that are the source of mismatches.[205] Two principal features of a comprehensive accrual regime reduce considerably the problem of tax fragmentation. First, traders or dealers in financial instruments can be subject to accretion taxation of the full amount of all gains and losses. These taxpayers are taxed on the whole of their portfolios, and all inconsistencies and discontinuities in tax treatment are eliminated. Offsetting positions are essentially matched, and there is no need to integrate those positions and tax them with reference to one another. Second, all expected gains and losses on financial instruments that are issued or held by all other taxpayers are effectively matched through the application of accrual recognition of the full amount of the gains and losses. Unexpected amounts on non-traded instruments are subject to realization-based recognition and may not be matched with the recognition of expected or unexpected amounts on offsetting positions. There is, however, no compelling reason to alter realization-based recognition, since the taxpayer controls the realization event. Moreover, the gain or loss represents an increment or decrease in wealth that should be recognized as it is realized. Matching with an unrealized amount provides deferred recognition that is difficult to justify on any tax-policy basis, at least to the extent that an income tax is designed to bring to account realized gains and losses. The only possible rationale that follows from relevant tax-policy goals is the need to defer realized losses as a response to selective realization with non-traded instruments. Even in that instance, the deferral should apply only to the extent of realized losses that can be considered offset by unrealized gains on an offsetting position. The need to respond to selective realization does not require the matching of realized unexpected gains with unrealized unexpected losses as the basis for deferred recognition.

It is arguable that the only troubling asymmetry under a comprehensive accrual regime arises where a traded derivative instrument is acquired to hedge unexpected gains and losses associated with an underlying position that is subject to realization-based recognition.[206] In those circumstances, recognition of gains and losses on the derivative is often accelerated compared with recognition of offsetting losses and gains on the underlying position, and the taxpayer has no control over the timing mismatch. This asymmetry arises most obviously with a long or short position in a non-traded, fixed-payment debt instrument or a foreign currency obligation that is covered with a traded derivative. The same problem also arises with non-financial assets and non-traded shares that are excluded from the application of an accrual regime. As an initial proposition, it is unclear whether this mismatch is serious enough to warrant a response. In particular, tax-policy makers must determine that any adverse effects on the pricing of traded derivatives justifies relaxation of the application of accretion taxation as a response to the strategic trading of traded derivatives. If the answer is positive, hedge accounting should be limited to traded derivatives that are used to hedge non-traded debt and shares, as well as non-financial assets. If a particular derivative can be considered a qualifying hedge, gain or loss may be deferred to realization, without matching the amount with the recognition of gains or loss on the underlying position.[207] Furthermore, stringent designation requirements should be imposed to ensure that the hedge regime cannot be used to avoid the application of accretion taxation to traded instruments as a response to strategic trading.

To be more particular, in the context of a comprehensive accrual regime, hedge accounting need apply only to derivatives and other traded instruments that are otherwise subject to accretion taxation. Where the underlying transaction or position is another financial instrument, the character of offsetting gains and losses is not a problem; gain or loss on a hedge and an underlying transaction or position that are both financial instruments is deemed to be on income account, because both the hedge and the underlying position are subject to the dictates of a comprehensive accrual regime. For traded derivatives that are acquired as a hedge of a non-traded instrument, unexpected gain or loss can be recognized on the same realization basis that is applied to the underlying position. As was argued above, however, there is no compelling tax-policy reason to match realized gains on the hedge with unrealized losses on the underlying position and defer recognition of the former. Moreover, to prevent the use of a hedge regime to provide the benefit of selective realization, recognition of realized losses should be deferred until recognition of offsetting unrealized gains on the underlying position. In effect, the result of the application of this limited form of hedge accounting is restricted to the extension of the tax treatment for non-traded instruments to those traded instruments that are acquired as a qualifying hedge. Expected gain or loss associated with an option, a prepaid forward contract, or a prepaid swap should be subject to the same accrual recognition method as an underlying debt instrument. If both the underlying instrument and the derivative are traded instruments that are subject to accretion taxation, all gains and losses should be subject to mark-to-market reporting. In all cases, the early closeout of either a hedge or an underlying transaction should result in the cessation of hedge treatment.[208] This means that the early closeout of an underlying transaction should cause a notional disposition and reacquisition of the related hedge.[209] Subsequent gain or loss should be recognized using market-value accounting applicable to traded instruments that are not acquired for hedging purposes.

Where the underlying transaction is a non-traded share or non-financial asset, the effect of hedge treatment is similar to that with an underlying transaction that is a financial instrument. Gain or loss on a hedge is not matched with that on the underlying transaction, either in terms of timing or the character of the relevant amounts as capital or income items.[210] Instead, gain or loss is generally recognized on income account on maturity of the hedge. This treatment can be rationalized on two bases described in the Australian issues paper.[211] First, there is often no fixed realization point with a share or a non-financial asset, which means that any matching of the timing of the recognition of a realized gain or loss on a traded derivative acquired as a hedge can lead to an open-ended deferral.[212] Second, the argument for characterization of hedge gains or losses based on the underlying transaction loses much of its force once matching is abandoned for timing purposes. In particular, character matching can result in the quarantining of capital losses that are realized on the closeout of a hedge before the realization of an offsetting capital gain on the underlying transaction. As an exception to a general characterization on income account, gain realized on a hedge of a non-financial transaction or share can be considered to be on capital account where a capital loss is realized on the underlying transaction in the same year. In that case, characterization as a capital gain permits offset of the loss, which may otherwise be subject to quarantining rules that limit the deductibility of realized capital losses to the amount of realized capital gains.

These very limited consequences of hedge treatment do not eliminate the difficult identification problem that is commonly associated with the need to define a qualifying hedge transaction. In the broader context of a comprehensive accrual regime, a limited form of hedge accounting requires a definition of those circumstances in which traded instruments can be excepted from accretion taxation. In this respect, any hedge-accounting regime (including the limited version described here) is an exception to the theoretically appropriate taxation of the net income or loss from a taxpayer's portfolio assessed as a whole. The other extreme is the complete bifurcation of a taxpayer's portfolio, and the taxation of each element of the portfolio as a stand-alone transaction that provides different combinations of expected and unexpected gains and losses. Hedge accounting is a bastardized approach that approximates neither the theoretical ideal nor the extreme of complete bifurcation. As a result, the significant practical problem with hedge accounting is the choice of an appropriate subportfolio that merits integrated treatment. This choice involves an implicit first step whereby the whole of a taxpayer's portfolio is bifurcated into two parts: (1) an integrated subportfolio and (2) "everything else" that is left to be treated on a stand-alone basis.

In the absence of any other obvious factor, a taxpayer's purpose in entering into a position is generally accepted as being indicative of a hedge transaction. This purpose is effectively assumed to indicate when positions are sufficiently offsetting to require the application of integration as a response to tax fragmentation and its supposedly adverse effects on the pricing of instruments and their risk-allocation function. A purpose-based approach has two principal aspects that determine the appropriate identification of the requisite purpose. First, taxpayers should be required to designate formally a financial instrument as a hedge. In the context of large taxpayer portfolios, this minimal condition provides the tax administration with a formal statement of the requisite purpose. More important, the designation must be made prospectively on entering into the relevant position. This kind of contemporaneous designation requirement ensures that taxpayers cannot selectively invoke a hedge-accounting regime to maximize the ex post tax results. Without such a requirement, the limited hedging regime described here would permit taxpayers to avoid the impact of the application of accretion taxation to traded instruments by selectively designating as hedges those positions with accrued gain. Positions with accrued losses would not be similarly designated and would remain subject to accretion taxation. The unrealized losses could be recognized without any limitation on their deductibility, to the extent that accretion taxation is applied as a first-best response to selective realization. In effect, designation of traded instruments as a hedge on an ex post basis could be used to avoid the application of accretion taxation as a response to strategic trading.

The kinds of robust designation criteria that are required to address problems of adverse selection are apparent under the much broader hedging regulations for US tax purposes.[213] Under the US tax system, the absence of stringent identification criteria permits taxpayers selectively to realize ordinary-income treatment for losses by electing hedge accounting, and to realize capital treatment for gains by forgoing hedge accounting. A taxpayer could also selectively choose to terminate a hedge position with accrued losses in order to realize the losses in a period other than that in which the offsetting gains on the underlying position are recognized. This latter problem is one that is generally tolerated under the US income tax system, but not in the case of a hedge transaction that is considered to be closely related to an underlying transaction or position. The US regulations address these problems of adverse selection by requiring a taxpayer to identify an eligible hedge transaction prospectively. More specifically, a taxpayer must identify a hedge transaction on or before the close of the day on which the transaction is entered into, and the identification must be made on, and retained in, the taxpayer's books and records. The taxpayer must specify the hedge transaction and the underlying transaction or aggregate risk that is being hedged. Because the identification must be unambiguous, it is not sufficient that it be made for financial-accounting purposes only; identification must be made specifically for income tax purposes. A taxpayer can satisfy this requirement, however, by indicating that a transaction or class of transactions identified for financial-accounting or regulatory purposes as a hedge is also being identified for income tax purposes as a hedge. Any reasonable method of identification can be used. The identification is binding on the taxpayer with respect to any gain on a transaction, but does not conclusively determine the characterization of a loss as an ordinary loss. In the latter case, the transaction must satisfy the substantive criteria for hedge treatment. On the other hand, the absence of an appropriate identification is determinative of capital treatment, unless the taxpayer's failure to make a timely identification was inadvertent and the transaction otherwise satisfies the substantive criteria for hedge treatment. A taxpayer may not avoid ordinary-income treatment simply by failing to identify transactions that are clearly hedge transactions. In the absence of a reasonable basis for not making an identification, gain on a hedging transaction (but not loss) may be treated as ordinary income.

A second aspect of the identification problem presented by a purpose-based approach to the application of hedge tax accounting concerns the need for corroborative evidence of the statement of a taxpayer's purpose. Even if a taxpayer's designation of a financial instrument as a hedge is made prospectively, it should not be accepted uncritically, and there must be some objective evidence supporting the statement of purpose. Otherwise, the use of the designation mechanism and a hedge-accounting regime could be used to avoid the application of accretion taxation to all traded instruments, and the benefits of strategic trading would be available without restriction. The requirement of supporting evidence is usually incorporated in a definition of a minimum level of correlation in the cash flows associated with two positions.[214] Where that specified level is evident, the positions can be accepted as sufficiently offsetting to support the taxpayer's expression of purpose in a formal designation.[215] The problem with this additional identification requirement is the lack of any obvious level of correlation that indicates a hedge transaction. Indeed, beyond the extremes of no correlation and a perfect correlation, there is no particular level that should be determinative.[216] Anywhere in between these extremes, any choice is arbitrary and will create discontinuities on either side of the line. An alternative approach involves a vague definition of a required correlation that ensures a hedge-accounting regime cannot be used as a formalistic means of avoiding the application of accretion taxation to traded instruments. For example, a qualifying hedge transaction can be defined generally as the acquisition of any traded financial instrument that is intended to reduce the risk arising out of an identified transaction or position. This concept of a qualifying hedge is a relatively narrow one that is tantamount to any action adopted to reduce a specified risk. A specified risk includes the singular risk associated with one transaction or the aggregate risk associated with a number of transactions taken together. In this way, both specific and general hedges can be contemplated as qualifying hedges.[217] A more specific definition of the required level of correlation is bound to entail problematic measurement issues.

Notes

Notes to Chapter 1

1 See, for example, Charles W. Smithson, *Managing Financial Risk: A Guide to Derivative Products, Financial Engineering, and Value Maximization*, 3d ed. (New York: McGraw-Hill, 1998), 1-26; Robert C. Merton, "Financial Innovation and Economic Performance" (Winter 1992), 4 *The Continental Bank Journal of Applied Corporate Finance* 12-22, at 13; and Alfred Steinherr, *The Wild Beast of Finance* (New York: Wiley, 1998).

2 These two features of the new derivative instruments are emphasized in Bradford L. Ferguson, "The Rationales for the Rules: How To Think About Derivatives in the Tax World" (December 1994), 72 *Taxes: The Tax Magazine* 995-1026, at 995.

3 One source of impressive numbers is the International Swaps and Derivatives Association (ISDA), which conducts a semi-annual market survey of dealer activity in privately negotiated, over-the-counter (OTC) transactions in derivatives. See, for example, International Swaps and Derivatives Association, *1997 Year-End ISDA Market Survey* (New York: ISDA, 1997), which reports a notional value of US$29.035 trillion for OTC transactions in currency and interest-rate derivatives (forwards, swaps, and options) outstanding as of December 31, 1997. Other sources are the triennial survey of foreign-exchange-market activity and the semi-annual survey of derivatives usage conducted by the Bank for International Settlements. See, for example, Bank for International Settlements, *Central Bank Survey of Foreign Exchange and Derivatives Market Activity 1995* (Basel, Switzerland: BIS, May 1996), which estimates an outstanding amount of US$47.453 trillion for OTC derivatives as of March 31, 1995. The BIS survey covers OTC currency, interest-rate, equity, and commodity derivatives. As many commentators have noted, these kinds of numbers are misleadingly large (and overstate the associated risk) in that they measure only the notional amount of outstanding OTC derivatives. The amount of the cash flow obligations of the contracting parties is calculated with reference to the notional amounts and therefore is much less. Moreover, the notional amount of outstanding derivatives fails to account for "the netting effects . . . of offsetting trades." See, for example, David J. Tims, "Overview of Derivative Financial Instruments and Derivative Market Participation," in *Report of Proceedings of the Forty-Seventh Tax Conference*, 1995 Conference Report (Toronto: Canadian Tax Foundation, 1996), 28:1-9, at 28:9.

4 Charles Smithson, in an annual supplement to *Managing Financial Risk*, supra note 1, summarizes some of these survey data. See, for example, Charles W. Smithson, *Managing Financial Risk: 1998 Yearbook* (Toronto: Canadian Imperial Bank of Commerce World Markets, 1998). The most comprehensive surveys of derivatives usage by non-financial firms in Canada have been conducted by the Centre for Advanced Studies in Finance at the University of Waterloo. The results of the second survey, which covers derivatives usage in 1997, are reported by Steve Fortin, "University of Waterloo Second Survey of Canadian Derivatives Use and Hedging Activities," in *Managing Financial Risk: 1998 Yearbook*, chapter 7.

Survey data on derivatives usage in the United States have been collected by the Weiss Center for International Financial Research and The Wharton School of Business, University of Pennsylvania. The results of the Wharton survey are summarized by Richard Marston, Gregory S. Hayt, and Gordon M. Bodnar, "Derivatives as a Way of Reducing Risk," in *The Complete Finance Companion: The Latest in Financial Principles and Practice from the World's Best Finance Schools* (London: Pitman, 1998), 345-52. In Australia, derivatives usage has been surveyed by the Australian Financial Markets Association. See, for example, Australian Financial Markets Association, *1996 Australian Financial Markets Report* (Sydney: AFMA, November 1996).

5 The vast majority of exchange-traded and OTC derivatives are currency and interest-rate instruments. The most commonly used derivatives are forwards and swaps. The use of these instruments by non-financial firms for hedging purposes is greatest in the agriculture and forestry, mining and oil and gas, transportation and communication, and manufacturing sectors, because firms in these sectors tend to be more exposed to currency and interest-rate risk than firms in other sectors.

6 Respondents to the Wharton survey indicated that uncertainty surrounding the tax treatment of derivatives was a significant concern limiting their use. Tax considerations ranked, however, behind concerns about credit risk, the ability of users to assess their own risk exposure, and the financial-accounting treatment of hedge transactions. See Marston, Hayt, and Bodnar, supra note 4, at 347-48.

7 The relationship between financial innovation and the US income tax system is explored in Mark P. Gergen and Paula Schmitz, "The Influence of Tax Law on Securities Innovation in the United States: 1981-1997" (Winter 1997), 52 *Tax Law Review* 119-97.

8 The term "tax cubbyholes" was coined in Jeff Strnad, "Taxing New Financial Products: A Conceptual Framework" (May 1994), 46 *Stanford Law Review* 569-605. See also Mark P. Gergen, "Apocalypse Not?" (Summer 1995), 50 *Tax Law Review* 833-59. As Gergen notes, several early commentators recognized the cubbyhole insight. See Randall K.C. Kau, "Carving Up Assets and Liabilities—Integration or Bifurcation of Financial Instruments" (December 1990), 68 *Taxes: The Tax Magazine* 1003-14; and Edward D. Kleinbard, "Beyond Good and Evil Debt (and Debt Hedges): A Cost of Capital Allowance System" (December 1989), 67 *Taxes: The Tax Magazine* 943-61. Gergen ("Apocalypse Not?" at 833, footnote 1) describes the cubbyhole insight as "banal," but mere banality does not diminish the significance of the cubbyhole system as a stimulus and a barrier to financial innovation. Indeed, the cubbyhole insight is fundamental to some of the more sophisticated theoretical work on the taxation of financial instruments, such as that of Strnad. In the regulatory context, the attempt to fit innovative financial instruments within recognized legal categories that do not accurately reflect their economic nature has been referred to as a problem of "mapping." See Henry T.C. Hu, "Swaps, the Modern Process of Financial Innovation and the Vulnerability of the Regulatory Paradigm" (December 1989), 138 *University of Pennsylvania Law Review* 333-435. The problem of mapping arises also in the income tax context. The cash flows under derivative financial instruments must somehow be squeezed within the appropriate "tax cubbyholes," but, because they are so different from the cash flows under standard debt and equity instruments, the cubbyholes do not provide an easy fit.

9 This point is emphasized by David F. Bradford, "Fixing Realization Accounting: Symmetry, Consistency and Correctness in the Taxation of Financial Instruments" (Summer 1995), 50 *Tax Law Review* 731-85.

10 See, for example, Gergen and Schmitz, supra note 7, at 125: "we feel, like others, that the best solution to the problem of taxing securities and other investment assets lies in eliminating the corporate income tax and moving to a system under which all liquid assets with monitorable prices are taxed on a mark-to-market basis and other investment assets are taxed using an expected yield or retrospective method." See also Daniel Halperin, "Saving the Income Tax: An Agenda for Research" (November 24, 1997), 77 *Tax Notes* 967-77.

11 Gergen, supra note 8.

12 Income Tax Act, 1994 (New Zealand), as amended, part O, definition of "financial arrangement."

13 In the financial literature, the meanings of the terms "financial," "financing," and "financial transaction" are much more precise. "Financial" is equated with a "systems perspective," which involves any attempt to reduce market fragmentation and information asymmetries through the use of technology and control systems. "Financing" is equated with a "product perspective" and the development of products to eliminate market fragmentation. "Financial transaction" is equated with a "process perspective," which involves the repackaging and redistribution of risky cash flows to eliminate market fragmentation. "Market fragmentation" means "the partial separation of financial markets resulting in the same arrangements being available on different terms in the same markets, including their not being available at all. This last condition is known as 'market failure.'" See E.H. Neave, *Canada's Financial System: A Managerial Approach* (Toronto: Methuen, 1987), 401.

14 Robert Baer, "Understanding Derivatives and Financial Instruments" (December 1994), 72 *Taxes: The Tax Magazine* 929-46, at 929, argues that the term derivative, primarily as it is used in the accounting literature, "is not consistently defined or universally understood." The concept described in the text is widely accepted by writers and, in fact, captures accurately the essential nature of derivatives; that is, as financial instruments whose pricing depends on changes in the price of an underlying asset and on the interrelationship of the instruments themselves, expressed in fundamental parities. See, for example, Richard Wood, *Derivatives, Financial Innovation and Taxation*, Treasury Research Paper no. 11 (Canberra: Australian Government Publishing Service, 1996), 21-25. An explanation of these fundamental relationships and their general significance for tax-policy purposes is the principal subject of this chapter.

15 John D. Finnerty provides a comprehensive taxonomy of financial innovation. See John D. Finnerty, "An Overview of Corporate Securities Innovation" (Winter 1992), 4 *The Continental Bank Journal of Applied Corporate Finance* 23-39; John D. Finnerty, "Financial Engineering in Corporate Finance: An Overview," in Clifford W. Smith Jr. and Charles Smithson, eds., *Handbook of Financial Engineering* (New York: Harper & Row, 1990), 69-108; and John D. Finnerty, "Financial Innovation: An Overview" (Winter 1988), 17 *Financial Management* 14-33. Finnerty organizes financial innovation into three branches: (1) the development of new financial products (see the "product perspective," supra note 13); (2) the development of better financial processes (see the "system perspective," supra note 13); and (3) the development and implementation of creative solutions

to corporate finance. (In comparison, James C. Van Horne, "Of Financial Innovation and Excesses" (July 1985), 21 *The Journal of Finance* 621-31, at 621, divides financial innovation into two categories: the development of new products and the development of new processes.) Finnerty's first branch involves the development of innovative financial instruments for either consumer-type applications or corporate finance applications. Consumer-type applications generally are not as complex as corporate finance applications and are marketed directly to individuals rather than institutional investors, pension funds, and other non-financial corporations. Examples of consumer-type applications are new types of bank accounts, new forms of mutual funds, new life insurance products, and new forms of residential mortgages.

Finnerty's second branch of financial innovation involves the development of new processes that reduce the cost of financial transactions. In his view, these processes are concerned broadly with the financial system and are usually developed in response to regulatory change or improvements in technology. The three most common factors underlying their development are the desire to reduce transaction costs, the desire to reduce idle cash balances in an environment of rising interest rates, and the availability of relatively inexpensive computer technology to facilitate financial transactions. Examples are the shelf registration process for certain corporate issuers, the direct sale of securities to the public in qualified instances, and discount brokerage. In each of these cases, the innovation has resulted in lower transaction costs, the benefit of which has been passed on to the issuers or purchasers of securities. Other examples are electronic securities trading, automated teller machines, point-of-sale terminals, electronic funds transfer, a clearing-house interbank payment system, and cash-management accounts. In each of these cases, the innovation has been made possible by improvements in computer technology that have facilitated financial transactions.

Finnerty's third branch involves the development and implementation of innovative cash- and debt-management strategies and customized corporate finance structures. Examples are the development of corporate debt repurchase strategies in an environment of declining interest rates; the development of debt-forgiveness and debt-defeasance strategies; and the development of contractual and security arrangements that allocate risk and reward among shareholders and creditors on the occurrence of a fundamental change, such as a leveraged buyout or a corporate restructuring. Customized financing might also be used in the financing of a particular project or in an asset-based financing. In each of these cases, the capital structure must be engineered to suit the character of the underlying operating assets, to satisfy the demands of the shareholders and creditors, to reduce the agency costs that arise between managers and investors, or to reduce potential conflicts between shareholders and creditors. In these cases, financial innovation requires an assessment of the cash flow stream from the operating assets that are available to service fixed returns on outstanding financial assets, an adjustment of the return mix for creditors and shareholders, and the design of executive compensation arrangements that align the interests of management and shareholders.

16 This concept of financial innovation includes Finnerty's first and third branches. Creative solutions to corporate finance problems that arise on a leveraged buyout, some other restructuring, or a particular project or asset-based financing inevitably involve the repackaging of conventional cash flows in an unconventional

form. The events specified by Finnerty for the development of creative solutions in his third branch of financial innovation tend to be merely the occasion for a financially engineered response. Furthermore, many of the securities that are developed for consumer-type applications, although simpler in form than the innovative securities that are developed for corporate finance applications, involve the repackaging of conventional cash flows.

17 *Managing Financial Risk*, supra note 1. Clifford W. Smith Jr. and D. Sykes Wilford were Smithson's co-authors in the first and second editions of this text, which synthesizes the various features of the building-block approach they developed in a series of articles in the late 1980s. See also Richard D. Briffet, "An Introduction to Derivative Financial Instruments and How They Are Used," a paper prepared for conference delegates at the 49th Congress of the International Fiscal Association held in Cannes, September 17-22, 1995; Clifford W. Smith Jr. and Charles W. Smithson, "Financial Engineering: An Overview," in *Handbook of Financial Engineering*, supra note 15, 3-29, at 3-10; and Charles W. Smithson, "A LEGO Approach to Financial Engineering: An Introduction to Forwards, Futures, Swaps and Options" (Winter 1987), 4 *Midland Corporate Finance Journal* 16-28.

18 *Managing Financial Risk*, supra note 1, at 27-41. Kenneth J. Arrow, *Essays in the Theory of Risk-Bearing* (Chicago: Markham, 1971), 124, refers to the basic building blocks as "pure securities" in the sense that they provide a positive payoff on the resolution of a single contingency.

19 The common characteristics of "liabilities" for financial accounting purposes are "a present obligation of the enterprise [borrower] arising from past events [the advance of funds]" and the settlement of the obligation, "which is expected to result in an outflow . . . of resources embodying economic benefits." See, for example, Financial Accounting Standards Board (FASB), *Financial Accounting Series Discussion Memorandum: An Analysis of Issues Related to Distinguishing Between Liability and Equity Instruments and Accounting for Instruments with Characteristics of Both* (Stamford, Conn.: FASB, 1990); International Accounting Standards Committee (IASC), "Framework for the Preparation and Presentation of Financial Statements," in *International Accounting Standards* (London: IASC, 1991); and UK Accounting Standards Committee, *Exposure Draft 49* (London: ASC, 1990), as cited in Peter F. Pope and Anthony G. Puxty, "What Is Equity? New Financial Instruments in the Interstices Between Law, Accounting and Economics" (November 1991), 54 *Modern Law Review* 889-911, at 890-91. See also International Accounting Standards Committee, *Accounting for Financial Assets and Financial Liabilities* (London: IASC, March 1997), 33.

20 Smith and Smithson, supra note 17, at 3-4.

21 The concept of risk and its importance in the process of financial innovation are discussed in the text that accompanies notes 126-151 infra. See generally Richard Brealey, Stewart Myers, Gordon Sick, and Ronald Giammarino, *Principles of Corporate Finance*, 2d Canadian ed. (Toronto: McGraw-Hill Ryerson, 1993), 141-64; and Douglas R. Emery, John D. Finnerty, and John D. Stowe, *Principles of Financial Management* (Upper Saddle River, NJ: Prentice-Hall, 1998), 188-215. The term "risk premium," as it is commonly used in connection with debt obligations, is usually calculated as the difference between the yield on a particular instrument and the yield on another instrument that matures on the same date and

has the same repayment rights but carries no risk of default. See William A. Klein and John C. Coffee Jr., *Business Organization and Finance: Legal and Economic Principles*, 6th ed. (Westbury, NY: Foundation Press, 1996), 231-33. The greater return on the riskier of two instruments is often referred to as the "risk-adjusted rate" (Klein and Coffee, ibid., at 234). For debt obligations, however, the principal risk factor is change in the market rate of interest that affects the price of outstanding securities. For example, the value of a security with a fixed rate of return of 10 percent will decline if the market rate of interest rises above the fixed rate. Conversely, the value of the security will increase if the market rate falls below the fixed rate. In effect, investors require a rate of return that differs from the fixed rate on the outstanding obligation and will pay an amount for that obligation to adjust the rate of return in order to match the prevailing market rate of interest. According to conventional wisdom, investors demand an illiquidity premium as compensation for holding long-term debt, because the price of long-term debt is more exposed to changes in the market rate of return than is the price of short-term securities (Klein and Coffee, ibid., at 232). Investors' exposure to market change, however, does not always give rise to a demand for an illiquidity premium, because investors may prefer the locked-in rate available with a longer-term investment (Klein and Coffee, ibid., at 232-33). The general relationship between short- and long-term rates at any particular time can be represented graphically by the yield curve for similar debt instruments that have comparable terms to maturity. A positive sloping yield curve reflects higher interest rates for longer-term debt instruments and the resulting illiquidity premium. A negative sloping curve reflects an environment in which shorter-term rates are higher. A flat curve reflects an environment in which rates are relatively constant for all periods. For a more detailed explanation of these concepts and their importance in the valuation of debt, see Brealey et al., supra, at 591-621; and Emery, Finnerty, and Stowe, supra, at 152-66. The significance of the yield curve in the recognition of time-value returns for income tax purposes is discussed in the text that accompanies notes 122-131 in chapter 5.

22 The present value of a known future amount is calculated as

$$PV = A/(1 + r)n,$$

where PV is the present value, A is the known future amount, r is the discount rate, and n is the number of compounding periods between the present (T(0)) and the time in the future when A becomes due. For a straightforward explanation of the concept of present value and its relevance to corporate finance, see Brealey et al., supra note 21, at 11-137; and Emery, Finnerty, and Stowe, supra note 21, at 116-43.

23 Credit-extension instruments are often referred to loosely as notes, bonds, or debentures. Although these categories are not precise terms of art, they reflect, to varying degrees, the characteristics of the credit-extension instruments described above. Notes are generally short-term instruments that provide a source of funds to meet immediate cash flow needs; they are placed privately with financial institutions and their term is rarely greater than five years. Bonds provide a longer-term source of funds and are usually issued in units to investors through a trust corporation or other intermediary. Debentures are similar to bonds but differ in that they are unsecured. The credit risk associated with bonds is reduced somewhat by the bond holder's security interest in the borrower's property.

24 Descriptions of the fundamental features of the basic derivative instruments can be found in any introductory textbook or article on financial management and capital markets. The following descriptions are found in Briffet, supra note 17; and *Managing Financial Risk*, supra note 1. See also Robert W. Kolb, *Financial Derivatives*, 2d ed. (Malder, Mass.: Blackwell, 1996). Because the authors of these texts do not rely excessively on mathematical equations to explain the features of the basic derivative instruments, their discussions are clear, concise, and accessible to non-specialists. Indeed, in a useful service to their readers, the authors focus on the fundamentals of financial innovation that are necessary for an understanding of the tax, accounting, and regulatory issues. Many of the more sophisticated innovative techniques are merely extensions of these basic fundamentals.

25 See Kolb, supra note 24, at 21-31; and *Managing Financial Risk*, supra note 1, at 29-31, 54-57, 60, and 89-101.

26 The "spot price" of an asset is "the current market price." The "spot market" is "the market for cash as opposed to future delivery." See Gary L. Gastineau, *Swiss Bank Corporation's Dictionary of Financial Risk Management* (Chicago: Probus, 1992), 214.

27 Assume, for example, that a farmer and a miller would like to fix, in May, the price of wheat for delivery in September. The spot price in May is $2.00 per bushel and the forward price for delivery in September is $2.50 per bushel. By entering into a forward contract to sell wheat in September at the forward price, the farmer can fix the sale price; by holding a forward contract to purchase wheat in September, the miller can fix the purchase price. If the spot price of wheat in September is less than the forward price of $2.50 per bushel (say, $2.25), the farmer will realize a gain on the forward contract that will effectively increase his sale price of wheat to $2.50 per bushel ($2.25 per bushel received for the actual delivery of the wheat plus the $0.25 gain received on cash settlement of the forward contract). Conversely, the miller will realize a loss on the forward contract that will effectively increase his purchase price of wheat to $2.50 per bushel ($2.25 per bushel paid for the actual delivery of the wheat plus the $0.25 loss paid on cash settlement of the forward contract). If the spot price of wheat in September is greater than the forward price of $2.50 per bushel (say, $2.75), the positions of the farmer and miller will be reversed but will, again, result in a net price for the actual delivery of the wheat that is equal to the forward price. The farmer will sell his wheat for the spot price of $2.75 per bushel, but this price will be reduced to $2.50 by the $0.25 loss paid on cash settlement of the forward contract. The miller will purchase September wheat at the spot price of $2.75 per bushel, but this price will be reduced to $2.50 by the $0.25 gain received on cash settlement of the forward contract. This example is taken from Brealey et al., supra note 21, at 672-73.

28 A forward contract can be structured as an "off-market" instrument under which the forward exercise price is different from the prevailing forward-market price. Under an instrument of this kind, one party must pay the other party a lump sum on entering into the contract in order to offset the difference in prices and rebalance the contract. The amount and direction of the flow of funds depend on the amount and direction of the difference in prices. Parties to a forward contract can also prepay their obligations; in this situation, the amount of the payment is

equal to the present value of the "on-market" forward price. A forward contract issued at the forward-market price ("an on-market forward") is sometimes referred to as a "naked forward," because no payments are required when counterparties with mutual and offsetting obligations enter into the contract. Payments under off-market and prepaid forwards are equivalent to loans. In effect, these derivative instruments have an embedded debt element. The tax treatment of these instruments is discussed in the text that accompanies notes 24-42 in chapter 6. The relationship between spot and forward prices and the relationships that determine forward prices are described in the text that accompanies notes 65-74 infra.

29 The essence of a forward contract as a pure bet with only unexpected gain or loss is illustrated in the example supra note 27.

30 See Gastineau, supra note 26, at 166, who defines the OTC market as follows: "A security or other instrument that is not traded on an organized exchange or a market that is not part of an organized exchange. OTC instruments can be created with any provisions allowed by law and acceptable to counterparties. OTC markets and instruments are less closely regulated in some ways than exchange markets and instruments."

31 Briffet, supra, note 17, at 12-14; and *Managing Financial Risk*, supra note 1, at 91-96.

32 The analogy was drawn first by Fischer Black, "The Pricing of Commodity Contracts" (January/March 1976), 3 *Journal of Financial Economics* 167-79, as cited in Smithson, supra note 17, at 18.

33 *Managing Financial Risk*, supra note 1, at 1-27.

34 Steinherr, supra note 1.

35 *Managing Financial Risk*, supra note 1, at 1-27.

36 Merton H. Miller, "Financial Innovation: The Last Twenty Years and the Next" (December 1986), 21 *Journal of Financial and Quantitative Analysis* 459-71, at 463. Miller nominates the development of financial futures (that is, the exchange trading of forward contracts on financial instruments) as the single greatest financial innovation. This development began in earnest with the trading of currency futures in 1972 through the International Money Market, which was a division of the Chicago Mercantile Exchange (ibid., at 462-63).

37 *Managing Financial Risk*, supra note 1, at 1-27.

38 Ibid.

39 See Briffet, supra note 17, at 15-43; Kolb, supra note 24, at 123-31; *Managing Financial Risk*, supra note 1, at 31-34 and 140-62; and Smithson, supra note 17, at 19-21.

40 In effect, the swap payments reimburse the other counterparty for the interest obligations he has incurred on his underlying borrowing and reverse the exposures of the two parties. Another common interest-rate swap is a "basis swap," under which the parties agree to exchange payments that are based on different floating-rate indexes. An interest-rate swap can also provide for the exchange of payment streams that differ with respect to the intervals between payment dates, including the payment of interest in arrears or in advance. The differences in the timing of these payment streams mean that the amounts are paid gross rather than net between the counterparties.

41 Under a "total return equity swap," the equity payer agrees to pay all dividends and any appreciation in value of a specified block of shares. The equity receiver agrees to pay a fixed or floating rate of interest that is calculated on a notional principal amount equal to the spot price of the shares on the initiation of the swap, plus any depreciation in the value of the shares. For the equity receiver, the transaction is roughly equivalent to a leveraged acquisition of the shares.

42 Kolb, supra note 24, at 162-65; and *Managing Financial Risk*, supra note 1, at 31-34.

43 Like a forward contract, a swap may be off-market or prepaid, in which case there is an embedded debt element. See supra note 28 and the discussion of the tax treatment of these kinds of derivative instruments in the text that accompanies notes 70-72 in chapter 6.

44 The position of the counterparty who is obliged to make swap payments that are based on a floating interest rate is simply the converse of the position of the counterparty illustrated in figure 1.4.

45 For example, the dates on which the swap payments on a fixed-for-floating interest-rate swap are due may differ in order to reflect the fact that fixed-rate interest payments on an underlying borrowing are usually due semi-annually or annually, while floating-rate interest payments on an offsetting borrowing are usually due quarterly.

46 *Managing Financial Risk*, supra note 1, at 33-34 and 144-45.

47 Briffet, supra note 17, at 44-47; Kolb, supra note 24, at 73-79; *Managing Financial Risk*, supra note 1, at 34-39 and 190-95; and Smithson, supra note 17, at 21-24.

48 The basics of option pricing are reviewed in the text that accompanies notes 88-107 infra.

49 The tax treatment of options and other instruments that combine these two types of returns is discussed in chapter 6.

50 *Managing Financial Risk*, supra note 1, at 1-27.

51 Briffet, supra note 17, at 46-47.

52 Preferred shares that have a fixed participation entitlement and a priority over the common shares are equivalent to a credit-extension instrument in many respects. The significance of these equivalences for income tax purposes is discussed in chapters 3 and 6.

53 Brealey et al., supra note 21, at 522-26; Emery, Finnerty, and Stowe, supra note 21, at 258-59; and Clifford W. Smith Jr., Charles W. Smithson, and D. Sykes Wilford, "Managing Financial Risk," in *Handbook of Financial Engineering*, supra note 15, 33-68, at 50-52.

54 The point is made in Smith and Smithson, supra note 17, at 24-25.

55 Ibid.

56 Brealey et al., supra note 21, at 523-24.

57 Ibid.

58 Wood, supra note 14, at 24.

59 Ian Cooper, "The World of Futures, Forwards and Swaps," in *The Complete Finance Companion*, supra note 4, at 335-39. The term "arbitrage" is used here in

the general sense of an opportunity to purchase and sell financially equivalent positions at different prices and thereby realize riskless profits. See, for example, Gastineau, supra note 26, at 24, who describes "arbitrage" as follows: "Arbitrage: (1) Technically, arbitrage consists of purchasing a commodity or security in one market for immediate sale in another market (deterministic arbitrage). (2) Popular usage has expanded the meaning of the term to include any activity which attempts to buy a relatively underpriced item and sell a similar, relatively overpriced item, expecting to profit when the prices resume a more appropriate theoretical or historical relationship (statistical arbitrage)."

60 These basic relationships should not be confused with the much more complex and separate subject of arbitrage pricing theory (APT), a complex and involved modelling process that originates in the work of Stephen A. Ross, "The Arbitrage Theory of Capital Asset Pricing" (December 1976), 13 *Journal of Economic Theory* 341-60. APT attempts to model the return on a portfolio of assets by identifying macroeconomic factors that are sources of non-unique risk that cannot be diversified away. The risk premium associated with each asset in the portfolio should be a function of the sensitivity of the asset to the factors specified. For a brief description of APT, see Brealey et al., supra note 21, at 188-90.

61 See Wood, supra note 14, at 24: "positions in the asset, positions in the forward and positions in the option are interchangeable. This result, reflecting the fungibility of almost all derivatives, has powerful implications for tax policy."

62 Wood, ibid., at 17-18 and 21-25, summarizes these pricing relationships and the significance of their interrelation for income tax purposes.

63 The concept of risk is discussed in more detail in the text that accompanies notes 126-151 infra.

64 Wood, supra note 14, at 24, describes the interrelation as follows: "Because of the arbitrage minimising forces released by the aforementioned value and pricing interrelationships and replication possibilities, derivatives are substitutable with traditional assets and with other derivatives for many purposes. It follows that asset and derivative prices and volumes are interrelated and interlinked in a complex manner—so that any change in the price of the underlying asset is most likely to be reflected in changes in either another asset price (and/or volume) or the price (and/or volume) of another derivative, or both, ceteris paribus, having regard to the degree of risk which they contribute to the overall portfolio. Imperfections can exist due, for instance, to regulatory intervention, imperfect speculative behaviour or incomplete markets. Assuming such imperfections away, if a portfolio can be perfectly hedged its return should equal that of a risk-free security."

65 Briffet, supra note 17, at 4 and 6-8; Kolb, supra note 24, at 32-44; and *Managing Financial Risk*, supra note 1, at 57-60 and 101-13. Given the similarity of forward and futures contracts and the general relationship between spot and forward prices, the pricing of these contracts should be closely linked. There is debate in the financial economics literature over the closeness of this link and, in particular, under what if any conditions forward and futures contracts may be priced identically. See, for example, John C. Hull, *Options, Futures, and Other Derivative Securities*, 2d ed. (Englewood Cliffs, NJ: Prentice-Hall, 1993), 56-57; and the authorities cited by Wood, supra note 14, at 23.

66 Brealey et al., supra note 21, at 673.

67 Ibid.

68 To illustrate the application of the principle expressed in this formula, assume that (1) the spot price of a share index is \$314, (2) the six-month forward price is \$320.28, (3) the riskless interest rate for the six-month period of a stock index forward contract is 4 percent, and (4) the return in the form of dividends on shares that comprise the index is 2 percent for the same period. On the basis of these assumptions, a prospective purchaser of shares that comprise the index will be indifferent to an immediate purchase at the spot price or a deferred purchase at the forward price. On a deferred purchase, the purchaser will realize \$320.28 at the end of the six-month period by investing \$307.96 at the riskless interest rate at the beginning of the period. In six months, he will have \$320.28 to purchase the shares that comprise the share index. On an immediate purchase, the purchaser will invest \$314 at the beginning of the six-month period to acquire the shares. In six months he will receive \$6.28 in dividend payments, giving him a total of \$320.28. In effect, the purchaser who buys at the end of the six-month period forgoes the dividend return. The spot price minus the present value of the dividend return represents the amount that must be invested at the riskless interest rate to realize the same amount at the end of the six-month period. If the return on an immediate purchase at the spot price differed from the return on a deferred purchase at the forward price, arbitrageurs would acquire positions in the underlying asset in the market (spot or forward) that had the higher return and thereby drive up the price of the asset in that market until the returns were equalized. The six-month forward price of the share price index in the above example is thus \$320.28, or

$$314 \times \frac{(1 + 0.04)}{(1 + 0.0196)}.$$

See Brealey et al., supra note 21, at 674.

69 Ibid., at 904-9; Briffet, supra note 17, at 6-7; Emery, Finnerty, and Stowe, supra note 21, at 562-63; and *Managing Financial Risk*, supra note 1, at 60-67.

70 Multiplying both sides of the equation by *Es* reveals the relationship between spot and forward exchange rates: that is, $Ef = (1 + ir)/(1 + id) \times Es$. Assume, for example, that the spot exchange rate for Canadian/US dollars is 1/0.79 and that the one-year riskless interest rate is 4 percent on US funds and 8 percent on Canadian funds. On the basis of these assumptions, the one-year forward exchange rate is 1/0.7607, which is calculated as:

$$\textit{spot rate} \times \frac{(1 + r(\text{US\$}))t}{(1 + r(\text{Cdn.\$}))t} \quad \text{or} \quad 0.79 \times \frac{(1 + 0.04)I}{(1 + 0.08)I}$$

The relationship between spot and forward exchange rates is such that differences in interest rates in strong and weak currencies are reflected in the difference between the spot and forward exchange rates. Consequently, it is impossible for an investor to realize arbitrage profits in the form of different risk-free rates of expected return in different currencies by converting investment proceeds in a foreign currency back to his domestic currency. An investor with US\$7,900 could invest the funds at the one-year riskless interest rate and realize US\$8,216 at the end of the year. The alternative is an investment of the equivalent amount of Canadian dollars at the spot exchange rate of 1 (Cdn.\$)/0.79 (US\$)

(Cdn.$10,000) at the one-year riskless interest rate on those funds. At the end of the year, this alternative would yield Cdn.$10,800, which after conversion using the one-year forward exchange rate of 1 (US$)/0.7607 (Cdn.$), would be equal to US$8,216. Accordingly, the two investments would yield the same expected return and an investor would be indifferent to an investment in US or Canadian dollars. If one of the currencies yielded a better expected return than the other, arbitrage traders would acquire investments in that currency until the returns were equalized.

71 Briffet, supra note 17, at 8 and 18-21; and Kolb, supra note 24, at 45-56; and *Managing Financial Risk*, supra note 1, at 67-72.

72 Brealey et al., supra note 21, at 677-78; and Briffet, supra note 17, at 8.

73 Ibid.

74 Brealey et al., supra note 21, at 677. For example, if the one-year spot rate is 10 percent and the two-year spot rate is 12 percent, the one-year forward rate must be 14.04 percent, which ensures that the return realized by lending and reinvesting at the one-year rate equals the return on a two-year loan compounded annually. In this way, an investor who lends $90.91 for one year at 10 percent and then reinvests that amount, along with the return, at the one-year forward rate will realize a total return for the two years of $114.04, which is equal to the return on $90.91 loaned for two years at 12 percent compounded annually. The relationship between spot and forward prices for commodities is complicated by the fact that the forward purchaser does not incur storage costs but forgoes the convenience yield from actually possessing the commodity. See Brealey et al., ibid., at 675. In determining the forward price one must account for these two factors, as well as ensure that the forward price reflects the riskless rate of return that the purchaser can earn because of the deferred purchase. The forward price is expressed as

$$\textit{forward price} = \textit{spot price} \times \frac{(1 + rf)t}{(pv\ storage\ costs) - pv(convenience\ yield)},$$

where *rf* is the riskless rate of return for the period *t* (the term of the forward contract) and *pv* is the present value.

The present values of both the storage costs and the convenience yield cannot readily be observed independently. They can, however, be approximated by observing the difference between the spot rate and the discounted present value of the forward price. See Brealey et al., ibid., at 675. The arbitrage conditions that determine the relationship between spot and forward prices for commodities are most evident if the storage costs and the convenience yield roughly offset one another and can be ignored. In that case, it is obvious that the forward price must equal the spot price multiplied by the riskless rate of return that can be earned on funds set aside for a deferred purchase. If the forward price were lower, no one would be willing to hold the commodity itself; and if the forward price were higher, no one would be willing to hold a forward contract on the commodity. See Brealey et al., ibid., at 675.

75 An explanation of the equivalent relationships among the basic building-block instruments revealed by the put-call parity theorem and arbitrage pricing can be found in any standard text on financial management or corporate finance. See, for example, Brealey et al., ibid., at 520-21; Kolb, supra note 24, at 156-62; and

Managing Financial Risk, supra note 1, at 195-97. More sophisticated and extended applications of put-call parity can be found in Robert C. Merton, *Continuous Time Finance* (London: Basil Blackwell, 1990); and Donald J. Smith, "The Arithmetic of Financial Engineering," in *Handbook of Financial Engineering*, supra note 15, 109-25. The examples and applications of put-call parity that are used here assume, for simplicity, that the relevant assets do not pay a current yield. The principles remain the same for assets that pay a current yield, although the mathematics become more complex. See, for example, Hull, supra note 65.

76 These other factors include "legal risk" and "credit risk" and are discussed in chapter 3.

77 An investor is "long in an asset" if he owns the asset or has the right or obligation to purchase it. The investor benefits if the asset appreciates in value and loses if the asset depreciates. An investor is "short in an asset" if he has sold the asset or has the right or obligation to sell it in the future. The investor benefits if the asset depreciates in value and loses if the asset appreciates.

78 The significance of put-call parity for income tax purposes is explored in some of the tax literature. The seminal work is Alvin C. Warren Jr., "Financial Contract Innovation and Income Tax Policy" (December 1993), 107 *Harvard Law Review* 460-92. See also Australia, *Taxation of Financial Arrangements: An Issues Paper* (Canberra: Australian Government Publishing Services, 1996), chapter 15; Tom Clearwater, "The Judicial Role in Derivative Taxation: The Queen v. Shell Canada Limited and Financial Contract Economics" (1998), vol. 46, no. 6 *Canadian Tax Journal* 1212-44, at 1216-17; Glenn L.E. May, "Overview of Financial, Tax, and Accounting Principles for Derivative Financial Instruments," in the 1995 Conference Report, supra note 3, 29:1-27, at 29:16-23; Roger M. Paul, "Taxation of Financial Instruments: Towards a Conceptual Understanding of Economic Substance—An Australian Update," paper presented at the Harvard International Tax Program symposium on the Taxation of New Financial Instruments, September 28, 1996, 6-8; Charles T. Plambeck, H. David Rosenbloom, and Diane M. Ring, "General Report," in International Fiscal Association, *Cahiers de droit fiscal international*, vol. 80b, *Tax Aspects of Derivative Financial Instruments* (The Hague: Kluwer Law International, 1995), 653-90, at 669-71; and Alan Preston, "The View from the High Wire: A Treasury Perspective of Corporate Tax Issues," in Taxation Institute of Australia (Victoria Division), *Red Series Intensive Retreat: Rabbits Out of Hats—Corporate Structures and Restructures* (Melbourne: TIA, 1995), 7-8.

79 Brealey et al., supra note 21, at 520-21.

80 Put-call parity posits that the combination of the purchase of a call on a non-dividend-paying share (a share with capital appreciation only) and the purchase of a zero-coupon bond is equivalent to the combination of the purchase of a put on the share and the purchase of the share itself. In other words, an investor who lends $91 for one year at an interest rate of 10 percent (the amount due in one year equals $100) and purchases a call option on a share exercisable on maturity of the debt instrument at a price of $100 will realize the same gain or loss as an investor who purchases the share at its current market value of $91 and a put option on the shares that is exercisable in one year at a price of $100. As has already been explained using this example and an asset other than a share (see

the text that accompanies note 79), this equivalence will hold regardless of the asset value (that is, the value of the share) at the end of one year. Accordingly, it can be concluded that

$$+B\ +C = +S\ +P,$$

where $+S$ denotes the purchase of a share instead of some other asset.

81 Assume that an investor borrows $91 for one year at a riskless interest rate of 10 percent per annum and purchases an asset with the borrowed funds. If at the end of the year the value of the asset (say, $75) were less than the amount due under the borrowing, the investor would realize a net loss (say, $25). That is, the investor would own an asset with a value of $75 but would have a liability of $100. An alternative portfolio that consisted of the purchase of a call option and the sale of a put on the same asset, both of which were exercisable on the maturity date of the borrowing at a price of $100, would have an equivalent value. That is, the investor would hold a call option with a value of nil ($75 value of the underlying asset minus $100 exercise price), and would realize a ($25) loss on the exercise of the put option by the holder. On exercising the put, the investor, as the issuer of the option, would be required either to buy an asset with a value of $75 for a price of $100 or to settle the $25 value of the option in cash. If at the end of the year the value of the asset (say, $125) were greater than the amount due under the borrowing, an investor who borrowed to purchase the asset would have a positive net worth of $25. That is, the investor would own an asset with a value of $125 and would owe $100 on the related borrowing. An investor who held the alternative portfolio would realize the same positive net worth. That is, the investor would hold a call option on the asset with a value of $25 ($125 value of the underlying asset minus the $100 exercise price) and would have sold a put option with a value of nil ($100 exercise price minus the $125 value of the underlying asset) that would not be exercised by the holder. See Brealey et al., supra note 21, at 520-21.

82 These relationships can be expressed as $+A = +B\ +C\ -P$ and $+B = +A\ +P\ -C$. Similarly, long and short positions in options can be replicated as follows:

$$+P = +C\ +B\ -A,$$
$$+C = +A\ +P\ -B,$$
$$-P = -C\ -B\ +A, \text{ and}$$
$$-C = -P\ +B\ -A.$$

These equivalences mean that purchases and sales of shares (as the relevant asset), debt, and options can be combined in the following equivalent positions:

$$+S = +B\ +C\ -P \text{ or } +S = +B\ +F \text{ (since } +C\ -P = +F),$$
$$+B = +S\ -C\ +P \text{ or } +B = +S\ -F \text{ (since } -C\ +P = -F),$$
$$+C = -B\ +S\ +P,$$
$$+P = +B\ -S\ +C, \text{ and}$$
$$+C\ -P = +S\ -B \text{ or } +S\ -B = +F \text{ (since } +C\ -P = +F).$$

83 *Managing Financial Risk*, supra note 1, at 27-41.

84 Kolb, supra note 24, at 160-62.

85 See Wood, supra note 14, at 23. Assume, for example, that investor A purchases a long forward contract to acquire a commodity in one year at a forward price of

$100. The spot price of the commodity is $91 when A enters into the forward purchase. If the spot price of the commodity is greater than the forward price in one year (say, $125), A will realize a gain on the forward contract (say, $25). If the spot price is less than the forward price (say, $90), A will realize a loss ($10). An equivalent portfolio constructed by investor B consists of the combination of the acquisition of a call option on the commodity and the issue of an offsetting put, both of which are exercisable in one year at the forward price of $100. If the spot price of the commodity is $125 in one year, B will realize a $25 gain on the long call option, and the short put will expire unexercised. If the spot price is $90, B will realize a $10 loss on the short put, and the long call option will expire unexercised. The premium paid for the call option will be offset by the premium received for issuing the put. If transaction costs and credit risk are ignored, A and B should be indifferent to a choice between these alternative positions.

Because a swap is equivalent to a series of forward contracts, a swap can be similar to a collar, which involves the simultaneous purchase of a cap (the call option on future interest rates) and the sale of a floor (the put option on future interest rates). See Wood, ibid.

86 Assume, for example, that investor C sells a forward contract to acquire a commodity in one year at a forward price of $100. The spot price of the commodity is $91 when C enters into the forward sale. If the spot price of the commodity is greater than the forward price in one year (say, $125), C will realize a loss on the forward contract ($25). If the spot price is less than the forward price (say, $90), C will realize a gain (say, $10). An equivalent portfolio constructed by investor D consists of the combination of the sale of a call option on the commodity and the purchase of an offsetting put, both of which are exercisable in one year at the forward price of $100. If the spot price of the commodity is $125 in one year, D will realize a $25 loss on the short call option, and the long put will expire unexercised. If the spot price is $90, D will realize a $10 gain on the long put, and the short call option will expire unexercised. The premium received for the call option will be offset by the premium paid for issuing the put. If transaction costs and credit risk are ignored, C and D should be indifferent to a choice between these alternative positions.

87 This relationship, in turn, means that the purchase of an asset is equivalent to the combination of the purchase of a forward contract on the asset and a zero-coupon bond, or $+A = +F +B$. Conversely, the purchase of a zero-coupon bond is equivalent to the combination of the purchase of an asset and the sale of a forward contract on it, or $+A -F = +B$. The sale of a forward is also equivalent to the combination of the purchase of a zero-coupon bond and the sale of the underlying asset, or $+B -A = -C +P$, which can be written as $+B -A = -F$.

88 Fischer Black and Myron Scholes, "The Pricing of Options and Corporate Liabilities" (May-June 1973), 81 *Journal of Political Economy* 637-54. See generally Brealey et al., supra note 21, at 526-35; Emery, Finnerty, and Stowe, supra note 21, at 253-55 and 704-7; Kolb, supra note 24, at 79-118; *Managing Financial Risk*, supra note 1, at 36-39 and 195-240; and Smithson, supra note 17, at 22-23. For a particularly lucid explanation of option-pricing theory in the context of European options and an interesting application of that theory to the tax treatment of nonrecourse debt used to finance the purchase of an asset, see Charles T. Terry, "Option Pricing Theory and the Economic Incentive Analysis of Nonrecourse

Acquisition Liabilities" (Fall 1995), 12 *The American Journal of Tax Policy* 273-397, at 325-43.

89 The Black-Scholes pricing models are limited to the valuation of European options. More sophisticated models that were developed later address the pricing of American options. See *Managing Financial Risk*, supra note 1, at 214-17.

90 *Managing Financial Risk*, supra note 1, at 36-39; Brealey et al., supra note 21, at 531; and Terry, supra note 88, at 328-30.

91 Ibid.

92 Ibid.

93 Ibid.

94 *Managing Financial Risk*, supra note 1, at 39-42; Brealey et al., supra note 21, at 547-49; and Terry, supra note 88, at 336-38.

95 These same factors are relevant to the value of a put option. In fact, put-call parity provides that the value of a put on an asset at a specified exercise price is equal to the value of a call on the same asset at the same exercise price plus the present value of that exercise price minus the current market value of the asset ($+P = +C + B - A$). Because a put represents the right to sell an asset for a predetermined price, the value of the option on the exercise date will equal the amount by which the exercise price exceeds the value of the underlying asset. With a put option, the relationship between the exercise price and the value of the underlying asset is thus the inverse of that with a call option. An increase in the exercise price of a put option generally results in an increase in the value of the option; an increase in the value of the asset generally results in a decrease in the value of a put. As is the case with a call, an increase in the volatility of the price of the underlying asset increases the value of a put. Increases in the riskless interest rate and the period to maturity do not, however, necessarily lead to an increase in the value of a put. Although these increases should result in an increase in the value of a call (and hence in the value of a comparable put), they also result in a decrease in the present value of the exercise price, which has the offsetting effect of decreasing the value of a put. See Terry, supra note 88, at 335-36.

96 Terry, supra note 88, at 330-34.

97 Ibid.

98 Ibid., at 333. Similarly, the value of holding a put on an asset with extremely low price volatility should approximate the net present value of (1) receiving the discounted present value of the exercise price on issue of the option, (2) investing the receipt in a debt obligation that matures on the same date as the put and pays a return equal to the discount rate used in calculating the present value of the right to receive the exercise price, (3) using the funds received on maturity of the debt to purchase the underlying asset at its prevailing market price, and (4) selling the underlying asset to the issuer of the put for its exercise price. This equivalence can be written as $+P = B(E) - A$. See Terry, ibid., at 335-36.

99 Smith, Smithson, and Wilford, supra note 53, at 50-52.

100 The inverse relationship exists for put options.

101 *Managing Financial Risk*, supra note 1, at 36-39; Brealey et al., supra note 21, at 526-35; and Terry, supra note 88, at 336-38. The Black-Scholes pricing model is

also based on other critical assumptions, such as (1) the absence of transaction costs and market imperfections and (2) a known short-term interest rate at which borrowing and lending transactions occur.

102 Ibid. See also Briffet, supra note 17, at 45-46.

103 If the options are priced lower than the equivalent portfolio, arbitrageurs will purchase them to realize the riskless profit unavailable in the market for a combination of the purchase or sale of the relevant asset and a borrowing or lending of funds. If the options are priced higher than the equivalent portfolio, riskless profit will be available through the sale of the options. By purchasing and selling the options, arbitrageurs will increase or decrease the price in a manner that will restore price equilibrium.

104 Smith, Smithson, and Wilford, supra note 53, at 50-52.

105 Ibid.

106 Ibid.

107 *Managing Financial Risk,* supra note 1, at 218-26; and Brealey et al., supra note 21, at 533-35.

108 In the text that accompanies notes 58-107 supra.

109 Merton H. Miller, "Financial Innovation: Achievements and Prospects" (Winter 1992), 4 *The Continental Bank Journal of Applied Corporate Finance* 4-11, at 6.

110 See, for example, Peter Tufano, "Securities Innovations: A Historical and Functional Perspective" (Winter 1995), 7 *The Bank of America Journal of Applied Corporate Finance* 90-104, at 91-92 and 99-104, who provides a brief history of financial innovation in the United States. Richard Wood, "The Taxation of Debt, Equity and Hybrid Arrangements" (1999), vol. 47, no. 1 *Canadian Tax Journal* 49-80, notes that preferred shares were issued by UK corporations as early as the middle of the 16th century, and that convertible instruments were first issued in the 17th and 18th centuries.

111 Miller, supra note 109, at 6.

112 Ibid. See also Miller, supra note 36, at 470-71.

113 For representative summaries of more sophisticated equivalences among the basic building-block instruments, see also *Managing Financial Risk,* supra note 1, at 288-359; Kolb, supra note 24, at 155-203; Smith, Smithson, and Wilford, supra note 53, at 54-68; and Smithson, supra note 17, at 25-26. These authors catalogue particular equivalences and divide the process of assembling the building blocks into three broad categories. In the first category, the basic instruments are used to manage an inherent risk exposure of a corporation or other business organization. Depending on the desired risk profile, risk can be managed by a simple purchase or sale of a forward, future, swap, or option or by a combination of purchases and sales of these instruments. In the second category, the building blocks are combined in various ways to give one instrument the characteristics of another. For example, forwards and swaps can be combined to create a forward or a delayed-start swap; forwards can be given option characteristics in the form of a breakforward or range forward; swaps can be given option characteristics in the form of a floating-floor-ceiling swap or a fixed-floor-ceiling swap; two or more options can be combined and redesigned to alter the payoff profile, which is the case with

straddles, strangles, butterflies, and participations; and options can be written on forwards ("options on forward rate agreements") and swaps ("swaptions"). In the third category, the building blocks are combined to create debt instruments with embedded forwards or options. Examples of these instruments are reverse floaters and indexed dual-currency bonds.

114 Warren, supra note 78, at 460-61.

115 Paul Goris, *The Legal Aspects of Swaps* (London: Graham and Trotman, 1994), 28-29.

116 Paul, supra note 78, at 9.

117 Warren, supra note 78, at 460, identifies three categories of innovation: disaggregation, recombination, and risk reallocation. The first category includes techniques that involve the decomposition of traditional debt and shares into their constituent parts and the marketing of those parts as separate instruments. The second category includes techniques that recombine the disaggregated parts of traditional debt and shares to create new financial instruments. Warren cites as an example interest payments on debt that are based on changes in an equity index ("contingent debt"). The third category includes derivative instruments used for hedging and speculative purposes.

Goris, supra note 115, describes two general categories of financial engineering. In the first category, which he refers to as "internal financial engineering," existing instruments are repackaged as new instruments. For example, a call option on shares and a debt obligation of the issuer are repackaged as one instrument—a convertible debt obligation. In the second category, which Goris refers to as "external financial engineering," different instruments are linked to form a composite that creates an economic exposure without affecting the legal independence of the instruments. For example, an option and a debt instrument are acquired separately and remain legally distinct, but they are linked in a manner that affects the economic exposure associated with one or the other instrument.

Paul's categorization is an amalgam of Warren's and Goris's.

118 The instruments that result from combinations in this category correspond roughly to "hybrid instruments," which combine in a single instrument (1) an expected time-value return and (2) unexpected gain or loss attributable to a bet element. The combinations can be effected most readily by "embedding" a derivative in a debt instrument or "embedding" a debt instrument in a derivative. The tax treatment of "hybrids" is discussed in detail in chapter 6.

119 The instruments that result from combinations in this category correspond roughly to "synthetic instruments," which combine two or more legally distinct instruments to replicate the risk and return profile associated with another legally distinct instrument. See the text that accompanies notes 177-179 in chapter 2. The tax treatment of synthetics is discussed in chapter 7.

120 Finnerty, "An Overview of Corporate Securities Innovation," supra note 15; and Finnerty, "Financial Innovation: An Overview," supra note 15. For an earlier and more limited listing of particular innovations and their underlying causes, see Van Horne, supra note 15, at 625. Van Horne's effort follows that of William L. Silber, "The Process of Financial Innovation" (May 1983), 73 *The American Economic Review* 89-95. For examples in the Canadian Tax Foundation literature, see Daniel F. Sullivan and James P. O'Sullivan, "Recent Developments in

Corporate Financing," in *Income and Goods and Services Tax Considerations in Corporate Financing*, 1992 Corporate Management Tax Conference (Toronto: Canadian Tax Foundation, 1993), 1:1-57; Daniel F. Sullivan, "New Developments in Corporate Financing," in *Report of Proceedings of the Fortieth Tax Conference*, 1988 Conference Report (Toronto: Canadian Tax Foundation, 1989), 20:1-48; Richard E. Lint, "An Overview of Recent Developments in Canadian Corporate Financing," in *Income Tax Considerations in Corporate Financing*, 1986 Corporate Management Tax Conference (Toronto: Canadian Tax Foundation, 1986), 1-19; and Daniel F. Sullivan, "New Developments in Corporate Financing," in *Report of Proceedings of the Thirty-Fourth Tax Conference*, 1982 Conference Report (Toronto: Canadian Tax Foundation, 1983), 532-79. See also Daryll G. Waddingham, "Financial Innovation: A Brief Survey" (Spring 1992), 5 *Canadian Petroleum Tax Journal* 1-17.

121 Merton, supra note 1, at 12.

122 Ibid. See also Van Horne, supra note 15, at 621-24.

123 Merton, supra note 1, at 12.

124 Ibid.

125 Ibid. The principle of "comparative advantage" was first defined by the 19th-century economist David Ricardo. The principle underlies much of trade theory and posits that a country should specialize in the productive processes in which it enjoys a comparative advantage over other countries. The advantage is measured in terms of the opportunity cost of a productive process; that is, the cost associated with forgoing other productive processes. For an entertaining and non-technical explanation of comparative advantage, see Todd G. Buchholz, *New Ideas from Dead Economists*, rev. ed. (New York: Penguin, 1999), 70-73.

126 See Brealey et al., supra note 21, at 141-64; and Emery, Finnerty, and Stowe, supra note 21, at 190-201. See also the brief but useful explanation in Deborah L. Paul, "Another Uneasy Compromise: The Tax Treatment of Hedging in a Realization Income Tax" (1996), vol. 3, no. 1 *Florida Tax Review* 1-50, at 21-26. The term "risk," as it is used in the financial literature, may refer both to the risk that there will be a default in payment by the party who is required to make the payments ("default risk") and to the volatility risk of an asset, which is a measure of the degree of dispersion of the possible returns. See Klein and Coffee, supra note 21, at 228-30.

127 Klein and Coffee, supra note 21, at 228-34, provide a similar example to illustrate these points.

128 The assessment of risk is reflected in statistical measures that are referred to variously as "variance," "standard deviation," or "coefficient of variation."

129 As noted by Klein and Coffee, supra note 21, at 233-34, it is generally assumed that investors are risk averse and, therefore, they must be adequately compensated for bearing risk. This compensation is termed the "risk premium," which may compensate for both default and volatility risk. See Klein and Coffee, ibid., at 231-35. In general, the risk premium is the amount by which the expected return on a financial asset exceeds the return on a riskless security (for example, government debt) with a similar maturity, payment terms, and other conditions. Modern financial theory posits that investors are compensated only for risk that

cannot be diversified away by holding a portfolio of assets that have varying risk characteristics which are unrelated and which thereby provide an expected return on the portfolio assessed as a whole. Risk that is unique to an investment or asset can be diversified away, since another asset can be found with unique but opposite risk characteristics to offset that risk. Risk that is non-unique ("market risk") cannot be diversified away because it is systemic; that is, it affects all assets or investments so that an offsetting position is unavailable. See Brealey et al., supra note 21, at 141-64; Emery, Finnerty, and Stowe, supra note 21, at 188-215; and Klein and Coffee, supra note 21, at 231-35.

130 Merton, supra note 1, at 17-18; and Miller, supra note 109, at 7-8.

131 According to Finnerty, "An Overview of Corporate Securities Innovation," supra note 15, at 23, the desire to reallocate risk was the primary motive for the development of debt innovations in the late 1980s. He describes "beneficial risk reallocation" in that context as "involving the reapportioning of interest rate risk, credit risk or some other risk . . . [in a manner that] transfers risk from those who are less willing to bear it to those who are more willing to bear it, in the sense that they require a smaller yield premium to compensate them for bearing the risk."

132 Finnerty, "Financial Innovation: An Overview," supra note 15, at 18-19 and 23-25; Merton, supra note 1, at 17-18; and Miller, supra note 109, at 7-8.

133 Finnerty, "Financial Innovation: An Overview," supra note 15, at 18-19.

134 Merton, supra note 1, at 17-18.

135 Ibid.; and Miller, supra note 109, at 7-8.

136 Merton, supra note 1, at 17-18. See also *Managing Financial Risk*, supra note 1, at 45-99.

137 Merton, supra note 1, at 18; Miller, supra note 36, at 466; and Merton H. Miller, *Merton Miller on Derivatives* (New York: Wiley, 1997), 80-109.

138 Merton, supra note 1, at 14. Miller, supra note 36, at 466, observes that the development of futures trading is significant for enabling the reduction of transaction costs otherwise incurred with tailored forward contracts. Similar savings are attributable to the development of cash-settled futures on equity indexes. See Miller, ibid., at 468-70; and Miller, supra note 109, at 8-10.

139 Merton, supra note 1, at 17; Miller, supra note 109, at 7; and Miller, supra note 36, at 468-70.

140 Ibid.

141 Miller, supra note 109, at 7.

142 Ibid. Merton emphasizes that the analogy between the capital markets and an insurance mechanism is functional in that it describes "a class of contracts that performs a common function as distinguished from the class of institutions called 'insurance companies.'" See Merton, supra note 1, at 18.

143 *Managing Financial Risk*, supra note 1, at 492-517.

144 Ibid.

145 See supra note 59.

146 Kolb, supra note 24, at 155-248; and *Managing Financial Risk*, supra note 1, at 492-517.

147 *Managing Financial Risk*, supra note 1, at 1-29.

148 Miller, supra note 36, at 465-66; and Miller, supra note 109, at 5.

149 Merton, supra note 1, at 18-19. See also Sean M. O'Connor, *The Development of Financial Derivatives Markets: The Canadian Experience*, Technical Report no. 62 (Ottawa: Bank of Canada, June 1993), 5-24, for a discussion of the role of many of these same factors in the development of markets for derivatives in Canada.

150 A new instrument is said to "complete" markets when it provides investors or issuers with a risk and return profile that is otherwise unavailable. See the text that accompanies notes 174-178 infra.

151 Miller, supra note 36, at 463-71.

152 Ibid., at 460-63; and Miller, supra note 109, at 6-7. See also Van Horne, supra note 15.

153 Miller, supra note 36, at 461.

154 Ibid. See also Gastineau, supra note 26, at 25, who defines "regulatory arbitrage transactions" as "transactions designed to provide indirect access to a risk management market where one party is denied direct access by law or regulation"; Frank Partnoy, "Financial Derivatives and the Costs of Regulatory Arbitrage" (Winter 1997), 23 *The Journal of Corporation Law* 211-56, at 211, footnote 1, who describes regulatory arbitrage as involving "financial transactions designed to reduce costs or capture profit opportunities created by differential regulations or laws"; and William H. Silber, "Innovation, Competition, and New Contract Design in Futures Markets" [Summer 1981], *Journal of Futures Markets* 123-56. Merton, supra note 1, at 18, attributes much of the impetus for regulatory arbitrage to a rigid "institutional" approach to the regulation of financial markets rather than a more flexible "functional" approach. An institutional approach accepts as a given that defined categories of financial institutions will perform defined functions. Regulatory constraints attempt to further the performance of those functions. In contrast, a functional approach accepts as a given the need for the performance of a range of financial functions and posits an institutional framework that can best perform those functions. See Merton, ibid., at 20-22.

155 See E.J. Kane, "Technological and Regulatory Forces in the Developing Fusion of Financial-Services Competition" (July 1984), 39 *The Journal of Finance* 759-72; E.J. Kane, "Accelerating Inflation, Technological Innovation, and the Decreasing Effectiveness of Banking Regulation" (May 1981), 36 *The Journal of Finance* 355-67; and E.J. Kane, "Good Intentions and Unintended Evil: The Case Against Selective Credit Allocation" (February 1977), 9 *Journal of Money, Credit and Banking* 55-69.

156 Miller, supra note 36, at 462-63.

157 Finnerty, "Financial Innovation: An Overview," supra note 15, at 15, cites as an example of regulatory arbitrage in the United States the development of capital notes that are debt obligations qualifying as capital for the purposes of financial institution regulations that require a minimum capital base.

158 See *Managing Financial Risk*, supra note 1, at 140-44; Miller, supra note 109, at 6-7; and Briffet, supra note 17, at 15-16. A more detailed and complete account may be found in Satyajit Das, *Swaps and Financial Derivatives*, 2d ed. (Sydney:

Law Book, 1994), 14-17 and 52-58; and Goris, supra note 115, at 47-73. Under a typical parallel loan structure, a UK parent corporation would make a sterling-denominated loan to the UK subsidiary of a US parent corporation, which would make a US dollar loan to the US subsidiary of the UK parent. The two loans would be for the same principal amounts converted at the spot exchange rate and would have parallel interest and principal repayment terms. Although the structure provided a hedge for both parent corporations against currency exchange movements, the loans were motivated by restrictions imposed by the UK government on sterling loans made by residents to non-residents and non-sterling loans made to UK residents by non-residents. The structure ostensibly avoided those restrictions by taking the form of a US dollar loan between US residents (the US parent corporation and the US subsidiary of the UK parent) and a sterling loan between UK residents (the UK parent corporation and the UK subsidiary of the US parent). The non-complying alternative was a sterling loan directly from the UK parent to its US subsidiary and a US dollar loan from the US parent to its UK subsidiary. Two problems with parallel loans were the default risk and the balance-sheet consequences for the parent corporations. Because the loans were legally independent of one another, a default under one did not release the non-defaulting party from its obligations under the other. Moreover, the loans made by the parent corporations had to be carried on their balance sheets without any offset for the legally separate liabilities of the relevant subsidiaries as distinct entities. These problems were largely overcome by the development of swap contracts under which cash flows are netted by the parties so that the default risk is reduced to the net amount of the cash flows. The development of swap contracts also eliminated balance-sheet distortions, because an agreement to exchange cash flows is an off-balance-sheet item for financial accounting purposes.

In its original form, the interest-rate swap also provided a pure arbitrage opportunity that allowed the counterparties to a swap to arbitrage their differences in quality spreads between fixed- and floating-rate borrowings and thereby benefit from their comparative advantages in the different markets. There is evidence to indicate that this opportunity has been eliminated through arbitrage trading and a restoration of price equilibrium in quality spreads. See, for example, Das, supra, at 126-27, and the discussion in Wood, supra note 14, at 13-14. Despite its origins in regulatory arbitrage and pure arbitrage, the interest-rate swap remains viable as a low-cost risk-management instrument.

159 See, for example, Gastineau, supra note 26, at 25, who states that "tax arbitrage transactions are undertaken to share the benefit of differential tax rates or circumstances of two or more parties to a transaction." Different notions of tax arbitrage and tax avoidance are discussed in more detail in chapter 3.

160 The analogy between arbitrage trading and tax avoidance is based on the fact that the tax system provides different tax treatment for equivalent cash flows. The differences in taxation permit a taxpayer to rearrange a transaction to minimize taxes in a manner that is analogous to the realization of riskless arbitrage profits, which occurs when an arbitrageur identifies differences in price for the same or similar asset in different markets and enters into offsetting transactions to capture those differences in price as profit. The tax benefit obtained through the rearrangement of a transaction is equivalent to the riskless profit otherwise available when an asset has different prices in different markets. The analogy between arbitrage

trading and tax avoidance, however, eventually breaks down: whereas arbitrage trading inevitably restores price equilibrium, a tax-arbitrage transaction seeks the avoidance of tax equilibrium (that is, consistency in tax treatment of functionally similar transactions). See *Managing Financial Risk*, supra note 1, at 156-57.

161 Miller, supra note 36, at 461.

162 A difference in taxation of equivalent cash flows is referred to as an "inconsistency" in tax treatment. See the text that accompanies notes 2-4 in chapter 3.

163 Small changes in the pattern of cash flows (that is, the risk attributes) that result in significantly different tax treatment are referred to as "discontinuities." See the text that accompanies notes 2-4 in chapter 3.

164 The ability to take advantage of inconsistencies and discontinuities in tax treatment is limited by transaction costs, credit risk, the availability of issuers and investors with an appetite for tax-driven instruments ("tax clienteles"), and "tax law uncertainty." The last factor presents the problem of "legal risk"; that is, the costs associated with a challenge by the tax administrator of a particular interpretation of the tax law on which a tax advantage depends. These factors are common to tax planning generally and are emphasized in Myron S. Scholes and Mark A. Wolfson, *Taxes and Business Strategy: A Planning Approach* (Englewood Cliffs, NJ: Prentice-Hall, 1992), chapters 6 and 7. Gergen and Schmitz, supra note 7, explore the effect of these factors on financial innovation in the United States. They argue that tax law uncertainty has made it difficult to market public issues of innovative instruments with tax advantages. Gergen, supra note 8, emphasizes the effect of transaction costs, credit risk, and legal risk as barriers to tax-driven financial innovation.

165 Miller, supra note 36, at 461.

166 Ibid.

167 Miller, supra note 36, at 462, cites the Eurodollar market as an example of an innovation initiated by tax arbitrage in the United States. The market began as an attempt to avoid the imposition of non-resident withholding tax by the United States on interest paid by US banks. Even after the repeal of the withholding tax on interest on portfolio debt, the Eurodollar market continued to thrive. The market remains viable, as Miller notes, in part because it enables investors to escape the disclosure requirements imposed by the US Securities and Exchange Commission. Another example of financial innovation driven by tax arbitrage is the dramatic increase in the volume of zero-coupon bonds issued in the early 1980s in the United States. These instruments were issued in response to the accelerated deduction of the compound interest element available to borrowers under the straightline recognition method for the amount of the discount. The deduction became available not through specific legislation but by way of an interpretive position adopted by the Internal Revenue Service. See Finnerty, "An Overview of Corporate Securities Innovation," supra note 15, at 15 and 24; Gergen and Schmitz, supra note 7, at 139-41; and Miller, supra note 36, at 462-63.

168 Miller, supra note 36, at 461.

169 Ibid.

170 Finnerty, "Financial Innovation: An Overview," supra note 15. See also Tufano, supra note 110.

171 Finnerty, "Financial Innovation: An Overview," supra note 15, at 16.

172 Transaction costs are the expenses and costs incurred in carrying out a particular financial transaction. Finnerty, "Financial Innovation: An Overview," supra note 15, at 22, cites as an example of financial innovation that reduces transaction costs the development of an extendible note whose maturity can be extended by agreement between the issuer and the holder. The extension avoids underwriting commissions and fees that would otherwise be incurred on a repayment of an outstanding issue and its refinancing with a new issue. For a description of the development of futures trading and its reduction of transaction costs in the effort to reallocate risk, see Miller, supra note 36, at 466 and 468-70. Robert C. Merton, "Financial Innovation and the Management and Regulation of Financial Institutions" (June 1995), 19 *Journal of Banking and Finance* 461-81, at 463, states that "[t]he costs of implementing financial strategies for financial institutions using derivatives can be a tenth to a twentieth of the cost of using underlying cash markets."

173 Agency costs arise when an agent has more information than a principal and may derive personal benefit at the expense of the principal by exploiting the "information asymmetry." Costs must then be incurred to monitor or control the behaviour of the agent to prevent the potential exploitation. In the corporate context, agency costs arise for outside debt and equity investors because management usually has more information regarding the operation of the corporation. Attempts to align the interests of outside investors and management can reduce agency costs. Finnerty, "Financial Innovation: An Overview," supra note 15, at 22 and 24, cites floating-rate and rating-sensitive notes, the rates of which increase if the issuer's credit rating declines, as securities innovations that lower the cost of capital for issuers by reducing information asymmetries. Puttable-extendible notes are similarly innovative; they provide the holder with a series of put options that can be exercised if the issuer's credit rating deteriorates. The legal literature on the theory of the firm has been influenced greatly by the economic literature on principal and agent conflicts.

174 Finnerty, "An Overview of Corporate Securities Innovation," supra note 15, at 23-24; and Finnerty, "Financial Innovation: An Overview," supra note 15, at 18. Finnerty reserves the term "innovative" for finance solutions that are "non-trivial" in the sense that they provide savers and users of funds with alternatives that are otherwise unavailable. Miller, supra note 36, at 462-63, defines a "significant innovation" as an innovation that has a permanent effect that grows "even after [its] initiating force has been removed." He contrasts this kind of innovation with "transitory innovation," which disappears once the particular tax law or regulatory constraint that gave rise to the innovation is changed. See also Merton, supra note 1, at 18. Van Horne, supra note 15, at 621, argues that viable financial innovation must make a market (1) more efficient by reducing the cost of intermediation represented by the spread between the return to savers and the cost of funds to users of funds, or (2) more complete by providing a distinct marketable security for every contingency. An incomplete market is one in which the range of available securities does not span the entire universe of contingencies. In other words, there is an unsatisfied clientele for a particular security. The theory of spanning and its implications for the design of a comprehensive regime for the taxation of financial instruments are reviewed in Strnad, supra note 8, at 576-93.

175 Finnerty, "An Overview of Corporate Securities Innovation," supra note 15, at 23; and Finnerty, "Financial Innovation: An Overview," supra note 15, at 18-22.

176 Ibid.

177 Ibid. See also Merton, supra note 1, at 17-18.

178 Ibid. See also Van Horne, supra note 15, at 621-22 and 624-25; and Gergen and Schmitz, supra note 7, at 170-74. These authors observe that financial theory assumes that markets are already complete in order to derive equilibrium prices for instruments, and that innovative instruments are almost always replications of cash flow patterns provided by existing instruments. The new instruments are innovative only in the sense that, by reducing transaction and agency costs, they permit the hedging of risks and the lowering of the price of assets.

179 Finnerty, "An Overview of Corporate Securities Innovation," supra note 15, at 24; and Finnerty, "Financial Innovation: An Overview," supra note 15, at 18-22.

180 Merton, supra note 1.

181 Miller, supra note 36; and Miller, supra note 109.

182 Finnerty, "Financial Innovation: An Overview," supra note 15, at 16; and Miller, supra note 109, at 5 and 10. For an interesting and readable account of the effect of academic theory and technological developments on the US capital markets, see Peter L. Bernstein, *Capital Ideas: The Improbable Origins of Modern Wall Street* (New York: Free Press, 1992). See also the review essay by Henry T.C. Hu, "Misunderstood Derivatives: The Causes of Informational Failure and the Promise of Regulatory Incrementalism" (April 1993), 102 *The Yale Law Journal* 1457-1513; and Richard Whitley, "The Transformation of Business Finance into Financial Economics: The Roles of Academic Expansion and Changes in US Capital Markets" (1986), vol. 11, no. 2 *Accounting Organizations and Society* 171-92.

183 See Wood, supra note 14, at 11, who observes that although supply influences such as computer technology and advances in financial theory have probably played a role in the growth of the derivatives market, the literature tends to emphasize the role of demand influences such as the need for enhanced liquidity, the need to manage exposure to increased price volatility, and regulatory and tax arbitrage.

184 Van Horne, supra note 15, at 626-30. See also Charles R.P. Pouncy, "Contemporary Financial Innovation: Orthodoxy and Alternatives" (March-April 1998), 51 *SMU Law Review* 505-90, who distinguishes a dominant "neoclassical" view of financial innovation from a more critical "heterodox" or "Keynesian" view, with different implications for regulatory design.

185 Van Horne, supra note 15, at 626-27. He cites (ibid., at 626) as particular examples of innovation for its own sake: defeasance, certain interest-rate swaps, arrangements designed to segregate bond portfolios in a manner that strips money out of defined benefit pension plans, the issue by financial institutions of put options on bonds, equity-for-debt swaps, high-yield junk bonds, and leveraged buyouts. But see Peter Tufano, "Financial Innovation and First-Mover Advantages" (1989), 25 *Journal of Financial Economics* 213-40, who argues that competitive pricing and product imitation leave thin profit margins for the development and marketing of innovative instruments and compel investment bankers to innovate in order to capture market share. See also Gergen and Schmitz, supra note 7, at 137-49.

186 Van Horne, supra note 15, at 627-28; and Merton, supra note 1, at 14.

187 Merton, supra note 1, at 14. Finnerty, "Financial Innovation: An Overview," supra note 15, at 18, argues that a move away from "relationship banking" to a more competitive "transactional" approach has led to a greater emphasis on the development of new products that can be marketed to clients.

188 Merton, supra note 1, at 14. Van Horne, supra note 15, at 626-30, has difficulty explaining why ideas without substance persist and why continuing high profit margins on instruments are mistaken for genuine financial innovation. He believes that a herd instinct is a significant factor in the success of many popular innovations. Van Horne compares the faddish interest in new securities that do not constitute genuine financial innovation to a series of balloons that eventually burst. He does not see the innovation craze as a more serious financial bubble similar to past, infamous ones, such as the South Sea Company in England in the 18th century. The difference between balloons and bubbles is one of degree: both are inflated by irrational behaviour and excessive expectations, but a bubble grows much larger than a balloon and, when it finally bursts, precipitates a correspondingly greater crisis. See Van Horne, ibid., at 627-28.

189 Wood, supra note 14, at 15, citing Scott P. Mason, "The Allocation of Risk," in Dwight B. Crane, ed., *The Global Financial System: A Functional Perspective* (Boston: Harvard Business School Press, 1995), 153-95.

190 Merton, supra note 1, at 14. See also Roberta Romano, "A Thumbnail Sketch of Derivative Securities and Their Regulation" (1996), vol. 55, no. 1 *Maryland Law Review* 1-83, at 83: "Regulatory fragmentation is not inherently a problem. It may well have contributed to the impressive innovation in U.S. derivative product markets over the past decade." Van Horne, supra note 15, at 629-30, argues that the discipline of the markets is ultimately the most effective means of eliminating excessive innovation. He prefers market discipline over regulatory or accounting control, which could "choke off" the genuine innovation that completes markets and makes them more efficient. For a similar view, see Miller, *Merton Miller on Derivatives*, supra note 137, at 43-75. But see also United States, General Accounting Office, *Financial Derivatives: Actions Needed To Protect the Financial System* (Washington: USGAO, May 1994), which recommends extensive disclosure requirements and other regulatory measures to ensure that derivatives are used in a manner consistent with the prudential standards imposed on financial institutions.

191 Wood, supra note 14, at 16. Viewed from a global perspective, the result is no different from that in a closed domestic economy: that is, risk is reallocated in a more cost-effective manner without any aggregate reduction.

192 Merton, supra note 1, at 16, footnote 13.

193 Ibid.

194 Differences in tax treatment of equivalent cash flows can also have efficiency and equity consequences. See chapter 3.

195 For a discussion of the different types of tax avoidance and their policy implications for the taxation of the cash flows associated with financial instruments, see the text that accompanies notes 10-16 in chapter 3.

196 Preston, supra note 78, at 3-4. For an expression of these general goals as the basis of a comprehensive legislative regime, see Australia, *Taxation of Financial*

Arrangements: An Issues Paper (Canberra: Australian Government Publishing Services, December 1996), chapter 2.

197 Preston, supra note 78, at 3.

198 Ibid.

199 See, for example, Australia, Review of Business Taxation, *A Tax System Redesigned—More Certain, Equitable and Durable* (Canberra: Australian Government Publishing Services, July 1999), 15: "A major motivation of the reforms to the taxation of financial arrangements was to ensure that different financial instruments are taxed according to their economic substance rather than their legal form."

200 Preston, supra note 78, at 4.

201 But see Gergen and Schmitz, supra note 7, who emphasize the positive effect of tax law uncertainty as a necessary "friction" to tax-driven financial innovation in the context of an income tax system with significant inconsistencies and discontinuities in tax treatment.

202 For a brief but representative summary of this assessment of conventional income tax systems, see Australia, Review of Business Taxation, *A Platform for Consultation—Building on a Strong Foundation*, Discussion Paper 2, vol. 1 (Canberra: Australian Government Publishing Services, February 1999), chapter 5. A much less apocalyptic view of the impact of financial innovation on income tax systems is apparent in Gergen and Schmitz, supra note 7; and Gergen, supra note 8. This view forms much of the basis for the case supporting certain second-best approaches to the taxation of financial instruments. The various aspects of that case and those alternatives are developed in chapters 3 to 7.

203 See, for example, Lewis Steinberg, "Commentary" (Winter 1995), 50 *Tax Law Review* 725-29, at 725, who observes that "all assets, be they financial or real, represent nothing more than an aggregation of more or less risky cash flows, to be priced on an expected value basis and to be parceled out among participants based on their relative risk tolerances."

204 Wood, supra note 14, at 18.

205 See the text that accompanies notes 20-64 supra.

206 See the text that accompanies notes 65-107 supra.

207 See supra note 6.

Notes to Chapter 2

1 Australia, *Taxation of Financial Arrangements: An Issues Paper* (Canberra: Australian Government Publishing Services, December 1996); and Australia, *Taxation of Financial Arrangements: A Consultative Document* (Canberra: Australian Government Publishing Services, December 1993). See also Australia, Review of Business Taxation, *A Platform for Consultation—Building on a Strong Foundation: Overview of the Taxation of Investments*, Discussion Paper 2, vol. 1 (Canberra: Australian Government Publishing Services, February 1999), chapters 5-7; Australia, Review of Business Taxation, *A Tax System Redesigned—More Certain, Equitable and Durable* (Canberra: Australian Government Publishing Services, July 1999), chapter 9; and Australia, *Draft Legislation—A New Tax System*

(Income Tax Assessment) Bill 1999 (Canberra: Australian Government Publishing Services, July 1999), chapter 2, division 45.

2 The concept of "expected-return" or "expected-value" taxation as it applies to financial instruments is developed in detail in the academic literature. See Reed H. Shuldiner, "A General Approach to the Taxation of Financial Instruments" (December 1992), 71 *Texas Law Review* 243-350, and Robert H. Scarborough, "Different Rules for Different Players and Products: The Patchwork Taxation of Derivatives" (December 1994), 72 *Taxes: The Tax Magazine* 1031-49. For the application of an expected-return approach to a wide range of non-financial assets, see Noël B. Cunningham and Deborah H. Schenk, "Taxation Without Realization: A 'Revolutionary' Approach to Ownership" (Summer 1992), 47 *Tax Law Review* 725-814.

3 This term was coined in Peter F. Pope and Anthony G. Puxty, "What Is Equity? New Financial Instruments in the Interstices Between the Law, Accounting and Economics" (November 1991), 54 *Modern Law Review* 889-911, at 897. Adoption of this view for income tax purposes appears to have been less a conscious policy choice than an accidental outcome of the relevant private law and accounting practice. The historical reliance of income tax systems on accounting principles has had a probably significant, but indeterminable, role in the acceptance of the proprietary view of the corporation. This view underlies accounting practice, which is based on a simple equation (assets – liabilities = equity) that equates the corporation with the residual interest of the shareholders.

4 This simplistic classification is described in Tim Edgar, "The Classification of Corporate Securities" (1990), vol. 38, no. 5 *Canadian Tax Journal* 1141-88, at 1146-47. The tax policy significance of the functional similarity of debt and equity is reviewed in the text that accompanies notes 134-184 in chapter 3.

5 See Rick Krever and Neil Brooks, *A Capital Gains Tax for New Zealand* (Wellington, NZ: Victoria University Press for the Institute of Policy Studies, 1990), 1-3.

6 This distinction is captured in the famous "fruit and tree" metaphor described in *Ryall v. Hoare* (1923), 8 TC 521 (KB). The tree is, of course, the asset that produces the current income return in the form of the fruit. Appreciation in the value of the tree itself represents a capital amount. For an interesting genealogy of this metaphor and its incorporation in Australian income tax law, see Rick Krever, "The Ironic Legacy of Eisner v. Macomber" (1990), vol. 7, no. 2 *Australian Tax Forum* 191-206. The US Supreme Court adopted the metaphor in *Eisner v. Macomber*, 252 US 189 (1920), in order to distinguish capital gains and losses from other income and loss amounts. The court held, however, that capital gains and losses were taxable and deductible amounts under the statutory concept of income in the Internal Revenue Code. The US experience with capital gains taxation is, therefore, much different from the experience in Commonwealth countries. In effect, US courts have considered such amounts to be income or losses for income tax purposes and left it to Congress to provide preferential tax treatment. In Commonwealth countries, capital gains and losses are recognized as gains or losses for income tax purposes only under specific legislative regimes. See Krever and Brooks, supra note 5, at 8-40.

7 The case for a capital gains preference applied to financial instruments is discussed in the text that accompanies notes 185-225 in chapter 3.

8 RSC 1985, c. 1 (5th Supp.), as amended (herein referred to as "the ITA").

9 Income Tax Assessment Act 1936, as amended (herein referred to as "the ITAA").

10 ITA paragraph 20(1)(c); ITAA section 51(1). For an overview of the Australian deductibility provisions, see Trevor Hughes, "National Report—Australia," in International Fiscal Association, *Cahiers de droit fiscal international*, vol. 79a, *Deductibility of Interest and Other Financing Charges in Computing Income* (Deventer, the Netherlands: Kluwer Law and Taxation, 1994), 41-64. For a similar overview of the comparable Canadian provisions, see Brian J. Arnold and Tim Edgar, "Deductibility of Interest" (1995), vol. 43, no. 5 *Canadian Tax Journal* 1216-44.

11 The Canadian rule has been interpreted to require the deduction of interest expense by accrual taxpayers as the expense accrues on a daily basis, but only once it is incurred or becomes payable. See, for example, *MNR v. Mid-West Abrasive Co. of Canada Ltd.*, 73 DTC 5429; [1973] CTC 548 (FCTD). The comparable Australian provision has been interpreted to permit the deduction in the year that the expense is incurred; that is, once there is an unconditional legal obligation to make the payment, whether or not payment is due. See *Federal Commissioner of Taxation v. James Flood Pty. Ltd.* (1953), 88 CLR 492 (HC). But see also *Coles Myer Finance Limited v. FC of T*, 93 ATC 4214 (Full HC), where the High Court required that discounts on short-term bills of exchange and promissory notes issued by the taxpayer be amortized on a straightline basis over the term of the securities. ITAA division 16E now requires that discounts on securities with a term of 12 months or more be recognized on an annual accrual basis over the term of the relevant securities. See the text accompanying notes 49-51. Financial institutions and moneylenders can generally deduct interest expense as it accrues on a daily basis. For a discussion of the relevant cases, see *Taxation Ruling* 93/27, "Income Tax: Basis of Assessment of Interest Derived and Incurred by Financial Institutions," August 26, 1993. For a discussion of the implications of the decision in *Coles Myer Finance Limited* for the deduction of expenses on an "incurred basis," see Martin Smith, "The Timing of Deductions for Expenditure 'Incurred'" (September 1994), 1 *New Zealand Journal of Taxation Law and Policy* 22-47, at 42-47.

12 TR 93/27, supra note 11; and ITA subsections 12(3) and (4). Accrual recognition extends to both the savings element in certain life insurance policies and "declining-principal instruments," such as annuities. See ITA section 12.2. The latter instruments provide for repayment of the principal over the relevant term. Accrued interest must generally be calculated and recognized on a "yield-to-maturity" (YTM) basis, and payments must be attributed first to accrued interest. Any excess is considered to be a repayment of principal. An exception for "prescribed annuity contracts" (PACs) permits the deferred recognition of interest on a cash basis, with payments allocated between interest and principal pro rata over the term of an instrument. See generally Alan Macnaughton, "New Income Tax Rules for Holders of Life Insurance Policies and Annuities" (1983), vol. 31, no. 6 *Canadian Tax Journal* 921-41.

13 See John C. King and Robert K. O'Connor, "Taxation Aspects of Finance Transactions, Including Leasing," in *Papers Presented at the Sixth National Convention of the Taxation Institute of Australia* (Sydney: Taxation Institute of Australia, 1983), 1-102, at 32-39 and 55-58; and John C. King, "Interest" (July 1980), 15 *Taxation in Australia* 2-41, at 8-23. ITAA section 19 provides that interest shall be considered to be derived in certain circumstances even if it is not paid.

14 ITA paragraph 212(1)(b); and ITAA sections 128B(2) and (5). Both the ITA and the ITAA provide relatively narrow exceptions for interest on certain portfolio debt held by non-residents. See, for example, ITA subparagraph 212(1)(b)(vii), which exempts interest on resident corporate debt held by an arm's-length non-resident, provided the debt has a term of five years or more. See also ITAA section 128F, which exempts interest on certain publicly traded debt and widely distributed debentures ("Eurobond debt"). Chapter 3, in the text that accompanies notes 245-255, discusses the significance of an exemption from non-resident withholding tax for interest on portfolio debt in the context of the design of a benchmark approach to the taxation of financial instruments.

15 See generally, Graeme S. Cooper, Richard E. Krever, and Richard J. Vann, *Cooper, Krever and Vann's Income Taxation: Commentary and Materials*, 3d ed. (Sydney: Australian Tax Practice, 1999), 800-14.

16 Reform proposals introduced in 1998 include an advance corporation tax (ACT) on dividend distributions to ensure that corporate-level tax is paid on underlying income. Because of the imposition of the compensatory tax, shareholders would be entitled to franking credits in all cases. See Australia, *Tax Reform: Not a New Tax, a New Tax System* (Canberra: Australian Government Publishing Services, August 13, 1998) (herein referred to as "*Tax Reform*"), 116-18. Resident individuals who do not bear sufficient shareholder-level tax to absorb the credits would be entitled to a refund of the excess. Refunds would also be provided to pension funds and registered charities. For a summary of these proposals, see Simon Clark, Malcolm McLean, and Richard Vann, "Tax Reform Down Under" (August 31, 1998), 17 *Tax Notes International* 610-17, at 610-12. In *A Tax System Redesigned*, supra note 1, at 411-25, the Review of Business Taxation, which was established to review the government's reform proposals, recommends abandonment of the proposed ACT. See Richard J. Vann and Graeme Cooper, "Report of Australia's Business Tax Review and the Government's Response" (October 4, 1999), 19 *Tax Notes International* 1258-70, at 1264-65.

17 ITA subsection 82(1) and section 121. The 1998 reform proposals in Australia suggest that a proportion of the underlying corporate tax (whether mainstream or compensatory tax) on dividend distributions to non-resident portfolio investors would be effectively creditable against withholding tax; see *Tax Reform*, supra note 16, at 118. The text that accompanies notes 226-273 in chapter 3 discusses the application of non-resident withholding tax under a benchmark approach to the taxation of financial instruments. *A Tax System Redesigned*, supra note 1, at 414-16 recommends abandonment of the proposed credit consequent on abandonment of the application of the proposed ACT to dividend distributions to non-resident shareholders.

18 ITAA section 46 and ITA subsection 112(1). Under the 1998 proposals for reforming the ITAA, intercorporate dividends would be subject to the proposed compensatory tax, unless the payer and the payee were both members of a 100-percent-related resident group that elected to be taxed as a group. Otherwise, the corporate shareholder would be entitled to a franking credit that would be supported by the payment of corporate tax by the payer. The payee would be able to use the credit to offset mainstream tax on its income. The credit would allow the intercorporate dividend to pass tax-free once the payee had paid tax on the underlying income through the compensatory tax. See *Tax Reform*, supra note 16,

at 116-18. *A Tax System Redesigned*, supra note 1, at 411-13 recommends full taxability of unfranked dividends paid between resident corporations. A gross-up and credit mechanism would be adopted to prevent multiple levels of corporate tax on intercorporate dividend distributions paid out of "tax-paid income."

19 ITA paragraph 212(1)(c); and ITAA subsection 128B(1). ITAA paragraph 128B(3)(ga) exempts "fully franked dividends" (that is, dividends with full imputation credits) from withholding tax.

20 The two-thirds recognition rate applies to dispositions of property after February 27, 2000. See Canada, Notice of Ways and Means Motion To Amend the Income Tax Act, February 28, 2000, resolution 9. A three-quarters recognition rate applies generally to dispositions before February 28, 2000.

21 The relevant asset must be held for one year or longer. See generally Richard Krever, "Australian Business Tax Review's Final Report Proposes Changes to Capital Gains Taxation" (September 27, 1999), 19 *Tax Notes International* 1130-33; and Australia, Treasurer's *Press Release No. 58*, "The New Business Tax System," September 21, 1999. The preferential rate applies to assets acquired on or after October 1, 1999. For dispositions of assets before that date, capital gains and losses were recognized in full, with indexing of the cost bases of assets to eliminate the inflationary component of gains only. There was also a system of averaging whereby a gain was treated as if one-fifth of the relevant amount was realized in each of the year of disposition and the four immediately preceding years. Indexing and averaging have been eliminated generally for dispositions of capital assets by all taxpayers on or after October 1, 1999.

22 ITA subsection 10(1); and ITAA section 31. This principle, which effectively requires losses on inventory to be recognized when they accrue, is a reflection of the more general principle of accounting conservatism that attempts to avoid any overstatement of profit that might mislead users of the accounting information. Application of the lower of cost and fair market value principle is generally advantageous for taxpayers, since it permits the recognition of accrued losses on inventory even though the recognition of gains is deferred until a sale or other realization event. The definition of trading stock in ITAA section 6 has been interpreted to exclude speculative trading. Moreover, it has been proposed to exclude, in particular, intangible assets (including financial assets) from the definition. See *A Tax System Redesigned*, supra note 1, at 192-93. In contrast, the Supreme Court of Canada in *Friesen v. The Queen*, 95 DTC 5551; [1995] 2 CTC 369, held that the definition of "inventory" in ITA subsection 248(1) included land held for speculative purposes as an adventure in the nature of trade and, therefore, that the lower of cost and fair market value rule in ITA subsection 10(1) applied to allow the deduction of accrued losses. In response to that decision, the Department of Finance introduced ITA subsection 10(1.01), which requires property described in an inventory of a business that is an adventure in the nature of trade to be valued at its cost. See Canada, Department of Finance, "Realization of Losses Relating to Adventures in the Nature of Trade," *Release*, no. 95-111, December 20, 1995.

23 See ITA section 54 and ITAA section 160M for definitions of a "disposition." See also the new definition of a "disposition" proposed for ITA subsection 248(1) in Canada, Notice of Ways and Means Motion To Amend the Income Tax Act, June 5, 2000. See *Interpretation Bulletin* IT-448, "Dispositions—Changes in Terms of

Securities," June 6, 1980, for a statement of Revenue Canada's administrative position regarding the circumstances in which a change in the terms of a debt instrument or a share will give rise to a disposition. For a critique of this position, see Brian J. Arnold and David A. Ward, "Dispositions—A Critique of Revenue Canada's Interpretation" (1980), vol. 28, no. 5 *Canadian Tax Journal* 559-84.

24 ITA subsections 142.5(1) and (2).

25 Specific legislation provides certainty in the characterization of gains and losses in limited circumstances. For example, ITA subsections 142.4(4) and 142.5(1) deem gains and losses on certain shares and debt held by financial institutions to be on income account. Other taxpayers may elect to treat shares and debt of Canadian corporations on capital account. See ITA subsections 39(5) and (6). ITAA division 3B of part III, sections 82U-82ZB, deems certain foreign currency gains and losses to be ordinary-income amounts recognized generally on realization. These gains and losses include those realized on repayment of a foreign currency borrowing, on the purchase and sale of assets in a foreign currency, and on the closeout of foreign exchange hedging contracts. The provisions were justified on the ground that "there are clear economic advantages in treating foreign exchange gains and losses in respect of borrowings and loans in the same way given the economic similarity between interest payments and expected exchange rate effects over the period of a foreign-currency denominated debt contract." Chris Hurford, the minister assisting the treasurer, second reading speech, Taxation Laws Amendment Bill (no. 5), 1986, as cited in Roger Paul, "Financial Risk Management and the Taxation of Financial Products," in Rick Krever, Yuri Grbich, and Patrick Gallagher, eds., *Taxation of Corporate Debt Finance* (Melbourne: Longman, 1991), 209-38, at 221. The text that accompanies notes 128-149 in chapter 5 discusses the significance of this similarity in the design of a system of expected-return taxation. For a review of ITAA division 3B, part III, see Nabil (Bill) Orow, "Taxation Consequences of Exchange Gains and Losses in Australia" (April 1999), 5 *New Zealand Journal of Taxation Law and Policy* 48-61, at 52-58. ITA subsection 39(2) does nothing to recharacterize foreign exchange gains and losses but, instead, ensures their taxability or deductibility as capital gains and losses to the extent that they are not otherwise recognized on income account. The subsection also provides a $200 de minimis exemption for exchange gains and losses of individuals.

26 Edgar, supra note 4, at 1147.

27 See, for example, *Re Canada Deposit Insurance Corp. v. Canadian Commercial Bank* (1992), 97 DLR (4th) 385 (SCC), bankruptcy proceedings in which the court treated as debt certain instruments that were debt in form but that included some features commonly associated with equity. The Supreme Court based its characterization on an assessment of various factors indicating the apparent intention of the parties. See also *Central Capital Corp. (Re)* (1996), 27 OR (3d) 494 (CA), in which the court found that retractable preferred shares are not debt instruments providing the holders with claims that are provable in bankruptcy. See also *Dupuis Frères Ltd. v. The Minister of Customs and Excise* (1927), 1 DTC 104; [1917-27] CTC 326 (Ex. Ct.), which characterized redeemable preferred shares with a fixed dividend entitlement and the protection of a sinking fund as share capital and not borrowed capital; and *Strager Securities Limited v. MNR*, 86 DTC 1507; [1986] 2 CTC 2050 (TCC), which characterized redeemable preferred shares received as consideration for the transfer of property as share

consideration and not indebtedness eligible for a reserve deduction on an instalment sale.

28 The elements of this concept of interest and its application to particular financial instruments are addressed in several articles. See, for example, Elinore J. Richardson, David Glicksman, and Lara Friedlander, "Fundamentals of Canadian Taxation of Financial Instruments," in *Report of Proceedings of the Fifty-First Tax Conference*, 1999 Conference Report (Toronto: Canadian Tax Foundation, 2000), 5:1-57, at 5:5-10 and 5:21-32; and Stephen R. Richardson, "New Financial Instruments: A Canadian Tax Perspective," in *Income Tax and Goods and Services Tax Considerations in Corporate Financing*, 1992 Corporate Management Tax Conference (Toronto: Canadian Tax Foundation, 1993), 10:1-32, at 10:4-10 and 10:14-15. The basis for the legal definition of interest is described in Tim Edgar, "The Concept of Interest Under the Income Tax Act" (1996), vol. 44, no. 2 *Canadian Tax Journal* 277-347.

29 The most frequently cited description of these three requirements is the discussion of the concept of interest in *Halsbury's Laws of England*, 4th ed., vol. 32 (London: Butterworths, 1980), 53.

30 [1947] 3 DLR 689 (SCC), aff'd. [1949] 1 WWR 742 (PC).

31 See, for example, *Riches v. Westminster Bank, ld.*, [1947] AC 390 (HL); *Bennet v. Ogston (HM Inspector of Taxes)* (1930), 15 TC 374 (KB); *Schulze v. S.W. Bensted* (1915), 7 TC 30 (Ct. Sess.); and *Bond v. Barrow Haematite Steel Company*, [1902] 1 Ch. 353 (Ch. D.).

32 *In Re Rogers' Trusts* (1860), 62 ER 408 (Vice Ch.); *Banner v. Lowe* (1806), 33 ER 245 (Ch. D.); *Pearly v. Smith* (1745), 26 ER 952 (Ch. D.); and *Edwards v. Warwick (Countess of)* (1723), 24 ER 687 (Ch. D.).

33 See, for example, section 144 of the New South Wales Conveyancing Act 1919, as amended; and section 3 of the Ontario Apportionment Act, RSO 1990, c. A.23.

34 Edgar, supra note 28, at 287-93.

35 See, for example, *Alliance Holdings Limited v. FCT* (1981), 12 ATR 509 (NSW SC); and *Mid-West Abrasive Co.*, supra note 11.

36 See, for example, TR 93/27, supra note 11; *Taxation Determination* 92/178, October 29, 1992; "Revenue Canada Panel," in *Creative Tax Planning for Real Estate Transactions—Beyond Tax Reform and into the 1990s*, 1989 Corporate Management Tax Conference (Toronto: Canadian Tax Foundation, 1989), 8:1-59, at 8:9-11; and "Revenue Canada Round Table," in *Report of Proceedings of the Fortieth Tax Conference*, 1988 Conference Report (Toronto: Canadian Tax Foundation, 1989), 53:1-188, at 53:15.

37 These concepts and their policy significance for the income taxation of financial instruments generally are discussed further in chapter 3, in the text that accompanies notes 3-19.

38 On the authority of the decision in *Mid-West Abrasive Co.*, supra note 11, it is generally accepted that interest is deductible under ITA paragraph 20(1)(c) in the year in which the interest accrues, but only once it becomes payable.

39 *Sherway Centre Limited v. The Queen*, 96 DTC 1640; [1996] 3 CTC 2687 (TCC), rev'd. 98 DTC 6121; [1998] 2 CTC 343 (FCA), in which the court characterized participating debt payments as deductible interest; and *MNR v. Yonge-Eglinton*

Building Ltd., 74 DTC 6180; [1974] CTC 209 (FCA). But see notice of ways and means motion, supra note 23, amending ITA paragraph 20(1)(e) to deny a deduction for an amount that is contingent or dependent on the use of, or production from, property or an amount that is computed by reference to revenue, profit, cash flow, commodity price, or similar criterion. Revenue Canada does not regard *Sherway Centre Limited* as authority for the proposition that all participating payments are properly characterized as interest. Its administrative position apparently limits characterization as interest to participating payments that are intended "to reflect the prevailing rate of interest." See Richardson, Glicksman, and Friedlander, supra note 28, at 5:10-13; and Robert Couzin and Stephen S. Ruby, "The Impact of Recent Cases," in *Report of Proceedings of the Fiftieth Tax Conference*, 1998 Conference Report (Toronto: Canadian Tax Foundation, 1999), 52:1-32, at 52:10-12. Under the ITAA, participating payments are treated generally as non-deductible returns on equity. See *Commissioner of Taxation (WA) v. Boulder Perseverance Ltd.* (1937), 58 CLR 223 (HC); and Hughes, supra note 10, at 45.

40 *Redclay Holdings Limited v. The Queen*, 96 DTC 1207; [1996] 2 CTC 2347 (TCC); *Barbican Properties Inc. v. The Queen*, 97 DTC 122; [1996] 2 CTC 2615 (TCC); aff'd. 97 DTC 5008; [1997] 1 CTC 2383 (FCA); and *Sherway Centre Limited*, supra note 39. In none of these cases did the courts adequately address the question whether the contingent payments could be deducted in the year of accrual retroactively once they became payable in a subsequent year. Arguably, if contingent amounts are properly considered to be interest, they should be deductible in the year of accrual, as held in *Mid-West Abrasive Co.*, supra note 11. See C. Anne Sanderson, "Interest Relating to Limited Recourse Financing," in *Current Issues in Resource Taxation* (Toronto: Canadian Tax Foundation, 1997), tab 7, at 8.

The assumption in *Redclay Holdings* and *Barbican Properties* that the contingent payments were interest seems to be consistent with Revenue Canada's stated position that it will consider a participating payment to be interest provided (1) the amount of the payment is limited to a maximum amount determined as a fixed percentage of the outstanding principal, (2) the maximum amount reflects a commercial rate of interest for borrowings with similar credit risk, and (3) there are no other factors indicating the existence of an equity investment. See "Revenue Canada Panel," supra note 36; and *Income Tax Technical News*, no. 16, March 18, 1999. This focus on the existence of a limiting percentage effectively equates the tax treatment of participating payments with the return on income bonds. Originally developed in the 1930s to assist corporations in financial difficulty, these bonds provide a return that is calculated as a fixed percentage of the principal sum but is payable only to the extent that the borrower has realized profits in the relevant period. The return is generally treated as interest even though it arguably does not accrue on a daily basis, since it depends on the satisfaction of a contingency (the availability of profits) and is not payable solely with the passage of time. Instead, the form of the bond as a debt obligation with a fixed return appears to be the basis for the characterization of the return as interest. This conclusion was the apparent premise that led the government to amend the Income War Tax Act in 1935 to deem the return on an income bond to be a dividend. Income War Tax Act, RSC 1927, c. 97, amended by SC 1935, c. 40. The deeming provision was justified on the basis that the return was no different from dividends on preferred shares, which are not deductible for the issuer. Accordingly, any deduction by the issuer of the return on an income bond should be denied. See Canada, Senate, *Debates*, June 11, 1935, 354-55.

A similar position applies under the Australian case law, which has concluded that fixed amounts calculated as a percentage of the outstanding principal but payable solely out of profits or net income of the borrower are properly regarded as interest. See *Emu Bay Railway Co. Ltd. v. Federal Commissioner of Taxation* (1944), 71 CLR 596 (HC); and Hughes, supra note 10, at 45. The interest payments are not deductible, however, until the issuer has profits or net income and the contingency is resolved.

41 In *Sherway Centre Limited*, supra note 39, at 1641-42; 2689-91, this point was the thrust of expert evidence presented before the Tax Court on the capital markets' view of participating payments.

42 See the text that accompanies note 37.

43 In contrast with its characterization of participating payments, Revenue Canada has stated that it will consider amounts based on increases in the consumer price index to be appreciation of the principal sum of a loan and not deductible interest if the amounts are added to the principal sum on the basis of increases in the consumer price index. See, for example, the memorandum of the Financial Industries Division dated April 14, 1992, in *Window on Canadian Tax* (North York, Ont.: CCH Canadian) (looseleaf), paragraph 1845. This statement appears to be based on a rigid application of the legal definition of interest that elevates the form of these inflation-indexed amounts to the level of a determinative factor. To be brief, since amounts indexed for inflation generally take the form of accretions to the principal sum of a loan they are not referable to the principal, even though they are calculated as a percentage of it. This characterization obviously ignores the fact that all nominal interest payments include compensation for inflation-induced loss in the value of the loan principal. Indexation simply attempts to measure the amount of this compensation accurately on an ex post basis. There is thus no substantive reason why inflation-indexed amounts should not be treated as interest so long as the full amounts of nominal interest payments are treated as interest. It is difficult to conclude, however, that an amount indexed for inflation, whatever its form, accrues on a daily basis, as the legal definition of interest requires. Since indexed amounts depend on fluctuations in the consumer price index, they are not fixed from the outset of a loan and cannot therefore be calculated prospectively on a daily basis.

Unlike inflation-indexed payments, variable-rate interest payments based on a floating or prevailing market rate seem to be assumed by Revenue Canada to accrue on a daily basis. In effect, because the indexes for floating-rate payments are quoted on a daily basis, it is possible to calculate the payments daily as an increasing amount for the use of borrowed funds over the term of the borrowing. On the other hand, payments based on a commodity or equity index are arguably analogous to amounts indexed for inflation. Fluctuations in these indexes often mean that the relevant amounts may ultimately be minimal or nil. Consequently, a contingent amount based on a particular index cannot necessarily be calculated prospectively on a daily basis as an increasing amount over the term of a borrowing. Thus amounts of this kind may not be considered to accrue on a daily basis. See, for example, *Income Tax Ruling* ATR-61, "Interest Accrual Rules," August 20, 1995, which spells out the application of accrual rules for interest income, under

ITA regulation 7000, to the bonus paid on a term deposit on the basis of changes in a share index.

The failure to treat inflation-indexed amounts as interest in the same manner as the portion of nominal interest payments that compensates the lender for loss in value of the loaned funds is an example of inconsistent treatment of identical cash flows. The characterization of inflation-indexed amounts also represents a discontinuity, in that the measurement of the inflation compensation is precise whereas the measurement of compensation in the form of higher nominal interest rates is not, since the latter usually involves an estimate of anticipated inflation. There is thus a change in the risk characteristics of inflation-adjusted payments relative to those of nominal interest payments that results in a different tax treatment for the former. Other indexed payments similarly involve a change in risk characteristics because of the introduction of a contingency that substantially alters their characterization and attendant tax treatment. For an example of a legal analysis that attempts to fit indexed payments into the cubbyhole created by the application of the legal definition of interest, see Richardson, supra note 28, at 10:8-9.

44 With OID, the problem is not so much whether the amount of the discount can be considered to accrue on a daily basis. There are some strong suggestions in the non-tax case law that a discount arising on issue accrues on a daily basis, presumably because it is fixed from the outset of a borrowing and is payable with the passage of time for the use of the borrowed funds. See, for example, *AG Ont. v. Barfried Enterprises Ltd.* (1963), 42 DLR (2d) 137, at 145 (SCC). For this reason, OID can be apportioned prospectively over the term of a borrowing by using an appropriate interest rate and compounding period. An issuer can deduct OID that does not qualify as interest under ITA paragraph 20(1)(f). The deduction is available on a cash basis, but only to the extent of three-quarters of the amount of a discount that is considered "deep" (ITA subparagraph 20(1)(f)(ii)). The reduced deduction rate is provided on the assumption that the holder recognizes the discount as a capital gain at the same rate.

45 Revenue Canada has suggested that OID may not qualify as interest under the legal definition, since it is not referable to a principal sum and does not accrue on a daily basis. See "Revenue Canada Round Table," in the 1988 Conference Report, supra note 36, at 53:15; the memorandum of the Financial Industries Division dated September 9, 1994, in *Window on Canadian Tax*, supra note 43, at paragraph 3306; and the memorandum of the Financial Industries Division dated December 2, 1992, ibid., at paragraph 2484. Despite its stated reliance on the legal definition of interest, however, the department has also stated that it is willing to accept a characterization of OID as interest "depending on the facts." See John A. Calderwood, "A Revenue Canada Perspective on Offshore Funds, Commodity Straddles, and Offshore Deep Discount Bonds and Treasury Bills," in *Report of Proceedings of the Thirty-Fifth Tax Conference*, 1983 Conference Report (Toronto: Canadian Tax Foundation, 1984), 253-64, at 262; the technical interpretation of the Financial Industries Division, March 21, 1994, *Window on Canadian Tax*, supra note 43, at paragraph 2958; and the technical interpretation of the Reorganizations and Foreign Division, December 3, 1992, ibid., at paragraph 2315. This willingness appears to recognize implicitly that there is sound non-tax authority for the proposition that OID accrues on a daily basis and that it can even be considered referable to a principal sum, provided one interprets that requirement of the legal definition liberally to mean compensation for the amount of principal actually advanced,

whatever the legal form of the payments. Indeed, the often-cited UK authority on the characterization of discount as interest, *Lomax (HM Inspector of Taxes) v. Peter Dixon & Son, Ltd.* (1943), 25 TC 353 (CA), provides guidelines that, in effect, permit characterization of interest if the combination of stated periodic interest and any discount provide a market rate of return. This functional approach is similar to Revenue Canada's characterization of participating payments and attempts to eliminate inconsistencies in the tax treatment of comparable cash flows at least to the extent that they provide a time value of money return. The approach has been extended logically in a series of cases that have established an effective presumption that OID is interest if no stated interest is provided. See, for example, *Gilmour v. The Queen*, 81 DTC 5322; [1981] CTC 401, where the Federal Court—Trial Division concluded that OID on a debt obligation was deductible as interest in calculating undistributed income on hand (UIOH). The court indicated (ibid., at 5326-27; 405) that there is nothing in *Barfried Enterprises Ltd.*, supra note 44, to preclude the characterization of OID as interest. In fact, *Barfried* was cited in support of the notion that discount accrues on a daily basis. The presumption that a discount is interest if no rate of interest is otherwise stated was expressed by Lord Green MR in *Peter Dixon & Son Limited*, supra, at 367. See also *Satinder v. The Queen*, 95 DTC 5340 (FCA); *Gestion Guy Ménard Inc. et al. v. MNR*, 93 DTC 1058; [1993] 2 CTC 2793 (TCC); and *O'Neil v. MNR*, 91 DTC 692 (TCC), which characterizes the discount on Government of Canada treasury bills as interest income of the holders. This characterization follows from the fact that there is no stated interest rate on treasury bills. Instead, their sale on auction at a discount effectively defines the rate. Revenue Canada has consistently taken the position that the discount on treasury bills is interest income for the holders. See Calderwood, supra, at 262; and the technical interpretation of the Reorganization and Foreign Division, October 26, 1992, in *Window on Canadian Income Tax*, supra, at paragraph 2261.

46 ITA paragraphs 20(1)(e), (e.1), and (e.2); and ITAA section 67.

47 ITA subsection 18(9.1) and ITAA section 67A. See also ITA paragraph 20(1)(f), which provides for the limited deductibility of OID that is not considered interest. See supra note 44.

48 ITA subsection 12(9) and regulation 7000. The interest rate or internal rate of return must be kept constant over the term of the instrument (regulation 7000(5)). See generally Robert Raizenne, "Accrual of Interest Income," in the 1988 Conference Report, supra note 36, 23:1-11; and John M. Ulmer, "Taxation of Interest Income," in *Report of Proceedings of the Forty-Second Tax Conference*, 1990 Conference Report (Toronto: Canadian Tax Foundation, 1991), 8:1-30.

49 ITAA division 16E. See generally Hughes, supra note 10, at 44-45.

50 See the text that accompanies notes 87-135 in chapter 5 for a discussion of the application of the YTM method generally to expected gains and losses.

51 See the text that accompanies notes 137-151 in chapter 6 for a discussion of the application of the YTM method to contingent-payment debt.

52 ITA subsections 20(14) and 214(6)-(7.1); and ITAA section 26BB, which treats all realized gains and losses on coupon-paying debt ("traditional securities") on income account, and section 128AA. These provisions apply to prevent the deferred recognition of interest equivalents as capital payments giving rise to capital gain treatment on the transfer of a debt obligation as between resident

taxpayers and/or a non-resident transferor and a resident transferee. In the latter instance, the provisions attempt to prevent the conversion of interest subject to non-resident withholding tax into a tax-preferred capital gain on the sale of a debt obligation with accrued interest. Both the domestic and non-resident withholding tax provisions attempt to reverse the decision in *Wigmore v. Thomas Summerson & Sons, Ltd.*, [1926] 1 KB 131 (KB), which holds that the right to interest represented by unmatured interest coupons is an expectancy of interest and not interest. Accordingly, on a transfer of a debt obligation with accrued but unpaid interest that is not due and payable, the amount of proceeds attributable to the unmatured interest coupons is not interest. There is thus a significant discontinuity in tax treatment as a result of the timing of interest payments; that is, the time for payment magically transforms the nature of accrued interest. Until it is due and payable, accrued interest is only an expectancy of interest, but once it becomes due and payable accrued interest represented by matured interest coupons is, in fact, interest for income tax purposes. See, for example, *Hall v. MNR*, 70 DTC 6333; [1970] CTC 510 (Ex. Ct.); and *Puder v. MNR*, 62 DTC 555; (1962), 30 Tax ABC 219. The provisions in the ITA that address this discontinuity and reverse the decision in *Wigmore* apply only for the purposes of the recognition by the transferor of proceeds attributable to accrued but unpaid interest. The provisions do not apply to characterize the same amounts as interest expense of the transferee. See, for example, *Hudson Bay Mining and Smelting Co., Limited v. The Queen*, 96 DTC 1246 (TCC), rev'd. 99 DTC 5269 (FCA), which distinguishes secondary-market purchases according to the identity of the purchaser as either a third party or the issuer. If the purchaser is the issuer, an agreement to pay accrued interest before a payment date may be characterized as an agreement to pay interest and not as just an "expectation of interest."

53 ITA subsection 16(1); and ITAA section 262.

54 See, for example, *Groulx v. MNR*, 67 DTC 5284; [1967] CTC 422 (SCC).

55 ITA subsection 16(6) and regulation 7001.

56 ITA subsections 18(9.2)-(9.8). These provisions were introduced in response to the issue by several corporations of Canadian optional interest notes (COINs). The text that accompanies notes 103-104 in chapter 5 discusses the features of these instruments and their appropriate tax treatment.

57 Canada, Department of Finance, *Budget 2000—Budget Plan*, February 28, 2000, annex 7-7; and notice of ways and means motion, supra note 20, resolutions 28-30. A "weak-currency borrowing" involves the conversion of a borrowed currency into another currency that is used by the borrower for an eligible income-earning purpose. For deductibility purposes, the amount of interest on the converted currency is determined with reference to the amount of interest on an equivalent borrowing in the currency into which the borrowed funds are converted. The budget proposals were introduced in response to the Supreme Court of Canada decision in *Shell Canada Ltd. v. The Queen*, 99 DTC 5669; [1999], 4 CTC 313. The appropriate treatment of foreign-currency debt generally is discussed in the text that accompanies notes 128-149 in chapter 5.

58 See, for example, "Revenue Canada Forum," in *Income Tax and GST Planning for the Purchase, Sale, and Canada-US Expansion of a Business*, 1996 Corporate Management Tax Conference (Toronto: Canadian Tax Foundation, 1996), 24:1-21, question 6, at 24:7-8, which indicates that the characterization of an instrument

as debt or as equity is based on the instrument's legal form and not on its classification for financial-accounting purposes. See also Revenue Canada document no. 9615465, July 17, 1996; and Revenue Canada document no. 9530990, November 27, 1996.

59 The concept of a dividend is defined, in part, in ITA subsections 248(1) (definition of a "dividend") and 84(1)-(4.1) and in ITAA sections 6(1), 47, 108, and 109. For the most part, these statutory definitions are intended to overturn deficiencies in the private law concept applied for income tax purposes. In particular, the statutory definitions attempt to distinguish the circumstances in which a distribution to shareholders will be treated as a taxable dividend, rather than as a capital payment that gives rise to capital gain treatment on a disposition of shares or a return of capital to shareholders. The underlying premise is that the form of the investment as shares is determinative in distinguishing between interest and dividends. In other words, the form of the investment as shares means that any distribution must be either a dividend or a return of capital to shareholders.

60 See Edgar, supra note 4, at 1149-55.

61 This use extends to income bonds, the interest on which is specifically deemed to be a dividend under ITA subsection 15(3). See supra note 40. Preferred shares were generally preferred over income bonds as after-tax financing instruments largely because of uncertainties in determining the amount of profits for purposes of the statutory test in the definition of an "income bond" in ITA subsection 248(1), which limited such instruments to bonds that provided for interest payments only out of profits of the issuer. (See *Interpretation Bulletin* IT-52R4, "Income Bonds and Income Debentures," October 20, 1983, paragraphs 7-10, for Revenue Canada's stated position on the meaning of profits.) Enacted as part of the initial response to the use of preferred shares as after-tax financing instruments, the current definition of an income bond in ITA subsection 248(1) limits deemed dividend treatment to instruments issued by corporations in financial difficulty.

62 In 1979, the minister of finance reported to the House of Commons that in October 1976, according to data collected by the Office of the Inspector General of Banks, the holdings of income debentures and floating-rate preferred shares by chartered banks alone totaled $765 million. By November 16, 1978, that total had increased to $10,100 million and represented 80 percent of chartered bank holdings of Canadian corporate securities. See House of Commons, *Debates*, November 2, 1979, 899; and the testimony of W.A. Kennett, Inspector General of Banks, in Canada, House of Commons, *Minutes of Proceedings and Evidence of the Standing Committee on Finance, Trade and Economic Affairs*, 30th Parliament, 4th session, 1978, issue no. 12, November 30, 1978, 7-9 and appendix FTEA-10. In the documents tabled with the November 16, 1978 budget, it was estimated that after-tax financing through preferred shares and income bonds issued to financial institutions had cost the federal and provincial treasuries $500 million.

63 ITA subsection 248(1) definition of a "taxable preferred share."

64 ITA parts IV.1 and VI.1.

65 The distributions tax offsets the mainstream corporate income tax liability on the underlying earnings. See ITA paragraph 110(1)(k). Accordingly, taxpaying corporations that issue preferred shares are not penalized, as they were when the intercorporate deduction was denied for holders irrespective of the status of the issuer.

66 For a useful overview of ITAA section 46D, see Michael Wiley, "Main Objectives of Tax-Based Financing: Current Issues," in *Taxation of Corporate Debt Finance*, supra note 25, 69-79, at 70-73; and Tony Rumble, "Tax Linearity and the 'Too Hard Basket': A Separate Tax Regime for Innovative Financial Products," in Tony Rumble, ed., *Derivative Tax Reform* (Sydney: Prospect Media, 1997), 62-141, at 101-13.

67 "Exchangeable debt" is debt with a right of conversion into shares of a corporation other than the borrower.

68 Debt that is mandatorily convertible at a predetermined ratio is the equivalent of the combination of a debt instrument and a forward contract written on the relevant shares. See chapters 4, 6, and 7 for discussion of the tax treatment that would apply to both convertible debt and exchangeable debt under a system of expected-return taxation implemented in the form of a comprehensive accrual regime.

69 William A. Klein, "The Modern Business Organization: Bargaining Under Constraints" (July 1982), 91 *The Yale Law Journal* 1521-64, at 1536 and footnotes 46-48, argues that this difference does not explain why investors would ever prefer a convertible debt issue when they can create the financial equivalent for themselves by (1) buying shares and then borrowing against them, (2) buying shares and writing options on them, or (3) buying shares and holding debt of the issuer. The various combinations and relevant proportions can be designed to replicate any risk exposure associated with the securities of a particular issuer, including convertible debt. See also William A. Klein, "The Convertible Bond: A Peculiar Package" (January 1975), 123 *University of Pennsylvania Law Review* 547-73. One explanation for the use of convertible debt, though not the only possible explanation, is the opportunity for elimination of the corporate-level tax that may arise from the availability of a corporate interest deduction, an opportunity that will be particularly important if shareholders are taxable at rates lower than the issuer's rate and the tax value of shareholder leverage is lower than the tax value of the deduction. For a relatively non-technical discussion of the pricing of convertible debt instruments and the case for their use as "equity sweeteners" and "delayed equity," see Kjell Nyborg, "Rationale for Convertible Bonds," in *The Complete Finance Companion: The Latest in Financial Principles and Practice from the World's Best Finance Schools* (London: Pitman, 1998), 241-47; and George W. Dent, "The Role of Convertible Securities in Corporate Finance" (Winter 1996), 21 *The Journal of Corporation Law* 241-65, at 245-61. See also Brad M. Barber, "Exchangeable Debt" [Summer 1993], *Financial Management* 48-60, who argues that tax effects provide only a weak motive for the issue of exchangeable debt. Barber claims that issuers find exchangeable debt attractive as a divestment strategy under which the "negative price response" for the relevant shares is much less than it is under alternative strategies, owing in part to the repurchase guarantee offered in many issues. Barber also notes that the underwriting costs for exchangeable debt are lower than those for a secondary offering and suggests that this consideration has some undefined impact. The tax-avoidance opportunities presented by exchangeable debt are discussed in chapters 6 and 7.

70 See, for example, *Interpretation Bulletin* IT-96R6, "Options Granted by Corporations To Acquire Shares, Bonds, or Debentures and by Trusts To Acquire Trust Units," October 23, 1996, paragraph 9. For the purposes of determining the accrued return on a specified debt obligation that is not mark-to-market property held by a financial institution, ITA draft regulation 9103(1) applies where the terms of the obligation

provide the holder with the right to exchange the obligation for shares of the issuer or a related corporation. The general rule is that the conversion right is to be ignored in determining the cost of the obligation for purposes of the calculation of the accrued return. This rule is subject to an allocation requirement if the value of the conversion right is 5 percent or more of the unallocated cost. In that case, the cost of the debt obligation is deemed to be the excess of the unallocated cost over the value of the conversion right. Moreover, if a specified debt obligation provides a specified financial institution with a right to exchange the obligation for shares of a corporation other than the issuer or a corporation related to the issuer, the value of the conversion right must always be accounted for separately. These allocation rules attempt to ensure that the costs of a debt obligation allocable to a significant conversion feature are not effectively deducted in calculating the amount of the accrued return on the obligation for the purposes of the mark-to-market legislation applicable to certain shares and debt held by financial institutions.

71 ITAA division 3A. ITAA section 82SA denies the deduction of interest on convertible debt issued after January 1, 1976 unless the following specified conditions are satisfied: (1) the holder of the debt obligation must have an option to convert the obligation into shares of the issuer or another corporation, (2) shares may be issued to the holder only in pursuance of the exercise of the conversion option, (3) the conversion option may be exercised no sooner than two years after issue, (4) the conversion option may be exercised no later than the earlier of the maturity of the obligation and 10 years after issue, (5) the interest rate must be fixed throughout the term of the obligation, (6) there must be no inducement for the holder to defer exercise of the conversion option, (7) the amount payable on maturity of the obligation must not be contingent on exercise or non-exercise of the conversion option, and (8) the conversion price must be no less than the greater of the par value of the shares and 90 percent of the value of shares comparable to those available on conversion determined no later than six weeks before issue of the obligation. The denial extends to debt obligations that are convertible into shares of the issuer or exchangeable into shares of any other corporation. Convertible or exchangeable debt that provides for automatic conversion or exchange is within the concept of convertible debt covered by the provision. Interest on debt of this kind is not deductible, since the debt cannot satisfy the condition that exercise of the conversion or exchange feature occur only at the option of the holder. A similar constraint applies to debt that provides for issue of shares to a person other than the debt holder on exercise of the conversion option. See generally Hughes, supra note 10, at 46-47; and Brian Lawrence, "Convertible Notes: The Problem of Antiquated Tax Provisions" (October 1993), 2 *Taxation in Australia Red Edition* 81-87.

72 The lack of any similar provision in the ITA may be attributable to the existence of some form of dividend relief for shareholders since 1948. In contrast, the ITAA has contained a provision similar to the current section 82SA since 1976 in an apparent effort to prevent the use of convertible debt as a means of holding what is perceived to be, in substance, an equity investment while providing the issuer with an interest deduction—an arrangement that avoided the imposition of the corporate-level tax and hence the double tax on dividends that existed under the Australian classical corporate income tax until 1985. It is worth noting, however, that the introduction of imputation relief has not led to repeal of the convertible-debt provision.

73 But see *Radillo Enterprises Pty. Ltd. v. FCT*, 96 ATC 4199 (HC), in which the court indicated the kinds of collateral agreements that may be considered to fall under ITAA section 46D. The decision is discussed in Robert Allerdice, Simon Clark, and Richard Vann, "Recent Cases on Taxation of Financial Transactions in Australia" (September 2, 1996), 13 *Tax Notes International* 747-52, at 751-52; and Rumble, supra note 66, at 29-30.

74 For a comparison of Australian and Canadian thin capitalization legislation, see Tim Edgar, "The Thin Capitalization Rules: Role and Reform" (1992), vol. 40, no. 1 *Canadian Tax Journal* 1-54. See also the comprehensive review in Andrew M.C. Smith, *Tax Avoidance and Non-Resident Investors: The Case of Thin Capitalisation* (Wellington, NZ: Victoria Institute for Policy Studies, 1992). The notice of ways and means motion, supra note 20, resolution 26, proposes a number of amendments to the Canadian thin capitalization rules, including a reduction of the permissible debt-equity ratio from 3:1 to 2:1.

75 See generally Anthony J. Frost, "National Report—Australia," in International Fiscal Association, *Cahiers de droit fiscal international*, vol. 80b, *Tax Aspects of Derivative Financial Instruments* (The Hague: Kluwer Law International, 1995), 21-44; Stephen R. Richardson and David G. Broadhurst, "National Report—Canada," ibid., 119-38; Paul, supra note 25; David C. Temby, "Swaps, Options, Forwards and Futures," in Richard Krever and Yuri Grbich, eds., *Australian International Taxation: Recent Developments and Future Directions* (Sydney: Law Book, 1994), 119-53; and Dennis F. Sykora, "The Income Tax Web Surrounding Derivatives," in *Report of Proceedings of the Forty-Seventh Tax Conference*, 1995 Conference Report (Toronto: Canadian Tax Foundation, 1996), 30:1-41.

76 The term refers to the fact that the value of these instruments is derived from an underlying asset or liability.

77 The cross-border aspects of derivatives and financial instruments generally are discussed in the text that accompanies notes 226-274 in chapter 3.

78 Richardson and Broadhurst, supra note 75, at 124-25.

79 Frost, supra note 75, at 26; and Richardson and Broadhurst, supra note 75, at 125.

80 ITA subsection 248(1) definition of a "business."

81 See *Taxation Ruling* 92/3, "Income Tax: Whether Profits on Isolated Transactions Are Income," July 30, 1992 and *Taxation Ruling* 92/4, "Income Tax: Whether Losses on Isolated Transactions Are Deductible," July 30, 1992. The ATO has generally taken the position that gains from speculative trading of futures must be recognized as ordinary income. The deductibility of losses is apparently a question of fact associated with the contentious characterization of speculative trading as the carrying on of a business. The ATO has conceded that it will allow the deductibility of losses if the gains would be taxable as ordinary income on the basis of the decision in *FC of T v. The Myer Emporium Ltd.*, 87 ATC 4363 (Full HC). See Frost, supra note 75, at 27; and Temby, supra note 75, at 150.

82 Some limited administrative exceptions apply to derivatives acquired for speculative purposes. For a description of Revenue Canada's administrative position, see *Interpretation Bulletin* IT-346R, "Commodity Futures and Certain Commodities," November 20, 1978, paragraphs 6-10. Revenue Canada permits speculators to elect capital treatment for all gains and losses realized on commodity transactions and commodity futures, provided that this treatment is followed consistently

from year to year. This election is unavailable for taxpayers who (1) enter into futures and commodities transactions as part of their business operations, (2) benefit from special information regarding a particular commodity, or (3) trade in futures or commodities as their principal or sole business. Revenue Canada requires these taxpayers to report all gains and losses realized on commodity futures, interest-rate futures, and commodities themselves as ordinary-income amounts. This administrative election extends to foreign currency futures and similar transactions in foreign currency (see IT-346, paragraph 15) and apparently may extend by analogy to all forward-based contracts, whether they are publicly traded on an exchange or privately over the counter, and to option-based derivatives that are traded publicly. See *Interpretation Bulletin* IT-479R, "Transactions in Securities," February 29, 1984, paragraph 25; Richardson and Broadhurst, supra note 75, at 125-26; and Sykora, supra note 75, at 30:8. As Sykora notes (ibid., at 30:8), Revenue Canada's administrative position is particularly generous, since derivatives do not qualify as Canadian securities for the purposes of the capital account election under ITA subsection 39(4). See supra note 25.

The ATO's administrative position limits the definition of gains and losses realized by speculators to gains and loses from speculative transactions that the taxpayer entered into with a view to generating a profit and carried out in connection with its ordinary business operations. In other contexts, the ATO has characterized speculative losses as non-deductible personal amounts and, possibly, capital losses. This characterization, however, has become increasingly contentious and doubtful. Several court decisions have confirmed that gains and losses realized by speculators are ordinary-income amounts, and the ATO has recently stated the position that losses from isolated speculative transactions should normally be treated as ordinary business losses if any gains from the transactions would have been taxable.

83 These cases are reviewed in Norman C. Loveland, "Currency and Interest Rate Risk Management Strategies and Products," in the 1992 Corporate Management Tax Conference, supra note 28, 11:1-38, at 11:15-25; David G. Broadhurst, "Foreign Exchange Planning," in *Tax Planning for Canada-US and International Transactions*, 1993 Corporate Management Tax Conference (Toronto: Canadian Tax Foundation, 1994), 8:1-27; and David G. Broadhurst, "Income Tax Treatment of Foreign Exchange Forward Contracts, Swaps, and Other Hedging Transactions," in *Report of Proceedings of the Forty-First Tax Conference*, 1989 Conference Report (Toronto: Canadian Tax Foundation, 1990), 26:1-32, at 26:5-8. See also Sykora, supra note 75, at 30:10-11. The decision in *Australian National Hotels Limited v. FCT*, 88 ATC 4627 (HC) has thrown judicial acceptance of a linkage approach under the ITAA into considerable doubt. The court rejected the commissioner of taxation's position that monthly insurance premiums paid by the taxpayer to protect the principal amount of a borrowing against foreign currency exposure should be characterized as non-deductible capital payments on the basis of a linkage between the underlying borrowing on capital account and the premiums. Because of the premiums' recurrent nature and their similarity to interest expense as a cost of borrowing funds, the court determined them to be currently deductible. See Frost, supra note 75, at 26; Paul supra note 25, at 219-20; and Temby, supra note 75, at 128. ITAA division 3B applies to characterize the foreign exchange gain or loss on the underlying borrowing as an ordinary-income amount. See supra note 25.

Courts have been inconsistent in their application of the linkage approach to hedged foreign currency debt. See the Supreme Court of Canada decision in *Shell Canada Ltd.*, supra note 57 (which rejects a linkage approach that would treat a foreign currency borrowing as a synthetic domestic currency borrowing, but which approves of a linkage approach to the characterization of gain or loss on a derivative instrument used to hedge currency exchange exposure on an underlying borrowing), rev'g. 98 DTC 6177; [1998] 2 CTC 207 (FCA) (which adopts the linkage approach), rev'g. 97 DTC 395; [1997] 2 CTC 2238 (TCC) (which rejects the linkage approach); and *Canadian Pacific Limited v. The Queen*, 98 DTC 2020; [1998] 4 CTC 2023 (TCC) (which follows the FCA decision in *Shell*), aff'd. 99 DTC 5132 (FCA). The linkage approach is evident in *Whittles (HMIT) v. Uniholdings Ltd. (No. 3)*, [1995] BTC 119 (Ch. D.), rev'd. [1996] STC 914 (CA). The Federal Court of Appeal in *Canadian Pacific* granted leave to appeal to the Supreme Court of Canada under section 37.1 of the Supreme Court Act. On November 10, 1999, the Supreme Court referred the matter back to the Federal Court of Appeal to be determined in accordance with the reasons of the Supreme Court in *Shell*. See Roger Taylor, "Kiwi GAAR Hearing Delayed?" (December 28, 1999), vol. 7, no. 12 *Canadian Tax Highlights* 89-96, at 91. In a judgment delivered from the bench on February 17, 2000, the Federal Court of Appeal decided to remit the case back to the Tax Court of Canada (Bonner TCCJ) for findings of fact and a decision on whether the general anti-avoidance rule (GAAR) is applicable to one of the two borrowings of the taxpayer at issue. The minister of national revenue conceded that the decision of the Supreme Court in *Shell* was determinative of the treatment of the other borrowing in the case. The Federal Court of Appeal remitted this latter matter back to the minister for reassessment in accordance with the reasons in that decision. See Federal Court of Appeal, docket no. A-480-98, February 17, 2000.

For a comment on the decision of the Chancery Division, see David Wentzell, "Taking the Composite Transaction Approach to the Taxation of Derivatives," Current Cases feature (1996), vol. 44, no. 1 *Canadian Tax Journal* 153-56. Chapter 4, in the text that accompanies notes 14-52, and chapter 7 discuss the integration of two or more financial instruments as a tax technique. The text that accompanies notes 136-162 in chapter 5 describes a general approach to foreign currency debt under a system of expected-return taxation.

84 These cases are reviewed in Loveland, supra note 83, at 11:11-15; and Broadhurst, "Income Tax Treatment of Foreign Exchange Forward Contracts, Swaps, and Other Hedging Transactions," supra note 83, at 26:3-5. See also the Revenue Canada Issue Sheet dated December 16, 1991, in *Window on Canadian Tax*, supra note 43, at paragraph 1540. The courts have tended to conclude in these cases that a foreign exchange gain or loss recognized on an asset held in the course of trading is on income amount. In contrast, a foreign exchange gain or loss realized on the disposition of a capital asset or on the repayment of a liability related to the acquisition of a capital asset is a capital amount. In the latter instance, the liability is linked with the acquisition of a capital asset and accorded capital treatment on the basis of that linkage. Broadhurst and Richardson, supra note 75, at 127, summarize the principles arising from the case law as follows:

- A foreign exchange gain or loss that is recognized in the course of trading is on income account.

- A foreign exchange gain or loss on the disposition of an asset that is capital or on a loan that is part of the fixed capital (as opposed to circulating capital) of a business is on capital account.
- A foreign exchange gain or loss on a liability that relates to acquisition of a capital asset is on capital account.
- There may be a presumption that a long-term borrowing is part of the fixed capital of the business, even if the direct use of the proceeds is to acquire current assets.
- Foreign currency balances that result from trading activities, and are therefore initially held on income account, may become capital if specifically set aside for capital purposes.

85 The concept of a hedge in the case law seems to be based on the simple idea of a transaction in which a taxpayer that is exposed to a particular risk acquires a derivative instrument whose cash flows vary inversely with the taxpayer's exposure. Gains on the derivative partially offset losses on the underlying exposure, and losses on the derivative offset gains on the underlying. In this way, the acquisition of the derivative neutralizes the taxpayer's risk exposure and thus hedges that exposure. For example, a taxpayer with a one-year receivable denominated in a foreign currency can hedge its exposure to foreign exchange risk on the asset by selling a one-year forward or futures contract on the particular currency in the amount of the receivable. The sale of the forward or futures contract effectively locks in the exchange rate on the receivable at the one-year forward rate. Fluctuations in the spot rate that produce a foreign exchange gain on the receivable are offset by a loss on the forward or futures contract and vice versa. Because the receivable and the derivative used as a hedge are linked, the character of any gain or loss on the derivative derives from the character of gain or loss on the receivable. The two transactions, accordingly, are netted and treated as one integrated transaction. See the text that accompanies notes 187-217 in chapter 7 for a discussion of the recognition of hedge transaction for income tax purposes.

86 For example, if the receivable and the sale of the forward or futures contract, described supra note 85, are treated as independent transactions, a capital loss may arise on the receivable. Since the deductibility of capital losses is limited to the amount of realized capital gains, it would not be possible to offset this loss against any gain on the forward or futures contract if the latter is characterized as an amount on income account. This result seems overly formalistic if the taxpayer sold the derivative in order to alter risk exposure on the underlying receivable and realize a certain net gain. By matching the character of the corresponding gains and losses on the receivable and the forward or futures contract, one can net the loss on either transaction against the gain on the other.

87 See, for example, Couzin and Ruby, supra note 39, at 52:17, who indicate that Revenue Canada will determine the nature of the gain or loss on a forward exchange contract by referring to the nature of an underlying foreign currency borrowing "[w]here there is no tax advantage involved and the purpose of the acquisition of a forward exchange contract is to protect against foreign currency fluctuations on assets and liabilities." Loveland, supra note 83, at 11:27-29, draws together accounting principles and some factors arising from the Canadian case law to provide a useful list of possible "linkage criteria." Frost, supra note

75, at footnote 24, notes that the ATO has indicated in *Taxation Ruling* IT 2228, "Income Tax: Futures Transactions," December 12, 1995, paragraph 24, that it will not accept the acquisition of a futures contract as a hedge if the quantity of a commodity under the contract significantly exceeds estimated production.

88 See, for example, *Echo Bay Mines Ltd. v. The Queen*, 92 DTC 6437; [1992] 2 CTC 182 (FCTD).

89 Loveland, supra note 83, at 11:27-29.

90 Ibid., at 11:22-25 and 11:27-29.

91 Ibid., at 11:16-20.

92 Ibid., at 11:20-22.

93 Ibid.

94 See, for example, *Income Tax Ruling* ATR-4, "Exchange of Interest Rates," November 29, 1985; "Revenue Canada Round Table," in *Report of Proceedings of the Thirty-Sixth Tax Conference*, 1984 Conference Report (Toronto: Canadian Tax Foundation, 1985), question 60, at 826-27; "Swap Transactions," in *Window on Canadian Tax*, supra note 43, at paragraph 1798; and *Income Tax Ruling* IT 2050 "Income Tax: Interest-Swapping Transactions," July 13, 1983. Revenue Canada has implied in IT-346R, supra note 82, at paragraph 14, that it will adopt a linkage approach to the characterization of foreign currency futures transactions by applying the same such approach evident in the foreign exchange cases. The position is expressly limited to foreign currency futures that are part of a taxpayer's business operations.

95 See, for example IT 2228, supra note 87, where the ATO divides taxpayers into the three categories of traders, speculators, and hedgers and appears to accept a linkage approach to the characterization of gains and losses on futures contracts acquired by hedgers.

96 See the sources cited supra footnotes 82 and 83. But see also "Revenue Canada Round Table," in *Report of Proceedings of the Forty-Fifth Tax Conference*, 1993 Conference Report (Toronto: Canadian Tax Foundation, 1994), 58:1-76, question 11, at 58:6, where Revenue Canada stated that all amounts paid pursuant to an interest-rate swap will be considered to be on income account and includible or deductible in income under the general dictates of ITA section 9 that govern the computation of business income generally. The use of any underlying funds was stated to be no longer relevant to the treatment of the swap payments. This position is consistent with "Interest Rate Swap," in *Window on Canadian Tax*, supra note 43, at paragraph 3310.

97 See, for example, Frost, supra note 75, at 33-34; and Temby, supra note 75, at 133. This position has been confirmed by Revenue Canada in "Revenue Canada Round Table," supra note 96; and "Swap Transactions," in *Window on Canadian Tax*, supra note 43, at paragraph 1798.

98 Revenue Canada has implied that its approach is to match any foreign exchange gain or loss realized on the subsequent re-exchange of the principal amount of the currencies with the underlying borrowings and to characterize the gain or loss as ordinary income or capital in the same manner as the gain or loss realized on maturity of the underlying. As a result, any foreign exchange gain or loss on the re-exchange of principal should be offset by a corresponding loss or gain on

repayment of the underlying borrowing. The same result is apparently realized by ITAA division 3B, which should apply to this situation in the same way as it applies to forward foreign exchange contracts. See, however, infra note 102 and the literal reading that the ATO has given to ITAA division 3B in applying its provisions to foreign exchange gains and losses on forward currency contracts and futures contracts.

99 Although there are no publicly stated administrative positions or specific legislation, the characterization of commodity and equity swaps should presumably follow the characterization of interest-rate and currency swaps, given the equivalence of the former to a series of forward contracts on commodity or equity prices. Frost, supra note 75, at 34. Traders and financiers who enter into commodity swaps as part of their operations should also be subject to ordinary-income characterization. Since payments under a commodity swap are usually connected with the underlying business operations of a commodity producer who acquires the swap as a hedge of those operations, they will in most instances be treated as ordinary-income amounts. Payments under an equity swap may be treated as capital amounts if the swap is acquired as a hedge of an underlying position in shares held as capital assets.

100 See Sykora, supra note 75, at 30:25. See also Paul, supra note 25, at 219-20.

101 Payments under an interest-rate swap are not, however, interest within the legal definition, since they are not made for the use of money advanced by the counterparty. The payments are not, therefore, interest for non-resident withholding tax purposes or the specific provision in ITA paragraph 20(1)(c) that permits the deduction of interest expense. See Edgar, supra note 28, at 329-30; Paul, supra note 25, at 213-14; and Sykora, supra note 75, at 30:13.

102 This statement is subject to certain provisions of ITAA division 3B that deem foreign exchange gains and losses to be ordinary-income amounts rather than capital amounts. In this limited instance, therefore, the provisions eliminate the distinction between income and capital amounts. It is not entirely clear that the provisions apply satisfactorily to foreign exchange gains and losses on forward currency and futures contracts. Nevertheless, the ATO evidently ignores any technical difficulties and applies the provisions in a manner that reflects its presumed intention to treat the amounts realized on such contracts as ordinary-income amounts rather than capital amounts. This position is, in fact, consistent with the deemed ordinary-income deduction applicable to the amount of any premium paid by the holder of a foreign currency option that would otherwise be on capital account and that was acquired as "a hedging contract." See ITAA, section 82X. For this purpose, the ITAA defines a hedging contract as a contract entered into for the sole purpose of eliminating or reducing the adverse financial consequences that may result under another contract from fluctuations in currency exchange rates.

103 Frost, supra note 75, at 27; Loveland, supra note 83, at 11:29; and Sykora, supra note 75, at 30:15.

104 See the text accompanying notes 10-24 for a discussion of the application of these timing principles under the ITA and the ITAA to gains and losses on debt and shares.

105 The terms "accretion taxation" and the "accretion basis" are used here, and throughout the book, to describe recognition methods that require all changes in value,

both expected and unexpected, to be recognized as they arise or accrue. The term "accrual taxation" or the "accrual basis" is used to describe recognition methods that require only expected changes in value to be recognized as they are expected to arise or accrue. The distinction is developed fully in chapters 3, 4, and 5.

106 See, generally, B.J. Arnold, *Timing and Income Taxation: The Principles of Income Measurement for Tax Purposes*, Canadian Tax Paper no. 71 (Toronto: Canadian Tax Foundation, 1983); Stan Ross and Philip Burgess, *Income Tax: A Critical Analysis*, 2d ed. (North Ryde, NSW: LBC Information Services, 1996), chapter 8; and Rick Krever, "Tax Accounting in Australia" (April 1997), 51 *Bulletin for International Fiscal Documentation* 188-97.

107 Revenue Canada permits a taxpayer to recognize foreign exchange gains and losses on income account on either a realization basis or an accretion basis, provided that (1) the method chosen is consistent with generally accepted accounting principles (GAAP) and (2) the method is followed consistently from year to year. See *Interpretation Bulletin* IT-95R, "Foreign Exchange Gains and Losses," December 16, 1980. This administrative position reflects the decision of the Supreme Court of Canada in *Canadian General Electric Co. Ltd. v. MNR*, 61 DTC 1300; [1961] CTC 512. See also *Income Tax Technical News*, no. 14, December 9, 1998, which permits mutual funds to report gains and losses on derivatives on income account using either the realization or the accretion basis "provided all such Derivatives are accounted for using the same method consistently from year to year."

108 Frost, supra note 75, at 29-30; IT 2228, supra note 87, at paragraphs 22-26; and Sykora, supra note 75, at 30:16-17. Revenue Canada has stated that it will treat hedge costs and hedge premiums not as separate items, but as part of the gain or loss on a forward contract recognized at the time of contract fulfillment. The net amount of the gain or loss is said to be the difference between the payment made under the contract and the Canadian dollar value of the consideration received for it, where the consideration is translated into Canadian dollars at the spot rate in effect on the date of delivery. See "Revenue Canada Round Table," in the 1984 Conference Report, supra note 94, question 63, at 828-29.

109 Frost, supra note 75, at 29-30; and Sykora, supra note 75, at 30:16-17.

110 The question what constitutes a disposition or realization event is also important if a forward contract is extended ("rolled over"). See Frost, supra note 75, at 30. In particular, it must be determined whether an old contract has been disposed of and a new contract entered into, or whether the new contract is simply a continuation of the old one. The same issue arises when any debt obligation changes and depends on the significance of the changes in the relevant contracts. The primacy of the realization principle is similarly evident in the context of straddle transactions. See infra note 111.

111 Application of the realization principle to forward-rate agreements means that gain or loss is recognized generally on the settlement or maturity date and is not amortized or spread on a daily basis over the subsequent term of a borrowing that may have been hedged by the agreement. Frost, supra note 75, at 29-30. Arguably, because the margin account in futures trading is only a security arrangement, variations in that account resulting from the marking to market of futures contracts on a daily basis should be disregarded as a realization event. Frost, ibid., at 30-31;

Glenn L.E. May, "Overview of Financial, Tax, and Accounting Principles for Derivative Financial Instruments," in the 1995 Conference Report, supra note 75, 29:1-27, at 29:13-14; and Geoffrey Walker, "Speculative Commodity Futures: The Computation of Income" (1989), vol. 37, no. 4 *Canadian Tax Journal* 917-68, at 943. The Supreme Court of Canada appears to have affirmed this characterization in *The Queen v. Friedberg*, 93 DTC 5507; [1993] 2 CTC 306. In rejecting the application of the mark-to-market recognition of gains and losses on commodity futures straddles, the Supreme Court (ibid., at 5508; 306) approved of an interpretation of the realization principle that requires the closing out of an open position: "While the 'marked to market' accounting method proposed by the appellant [the minister of national revenue] may better describe the taxpayer's income position for some purposes, we are not satisfied that it can describe income for income tax purposes, nor are we satisfied that a margin account balance is the appropriate measure of realized income for tax purposes." One of the adverse effects of the Supreme Court's unqualified adoption of this principle is the tax-avoidance opportunity it leaves open for "straddle transactions," whereby a taxpayer assumes offsetting long and short positions in an asset for the sole purpose of accelerating recognition of the accrued loss associated with the losing position while deferring accrued gain associated with the winning position. *Friedberg*, in fact, involved a straddle transaction in which the taxpayer had closed out the losing legs and deferred recognition of the winning legs until the following taxation year. The Supreme Court upheld the straddle on the basis of the realization requirement, which permitted the taxpayer to recognize the losing position while deferring recognition of the winning position. Chapter 5 discusses transactions of this kind and certain legislative responses in the text that accompanies notes 284-287, 298, and 324-335.

112 Paul, supra note 25, at 213-15; and Sykora, supra note 75, at 30:15-17.

113 See *Taxation Ruling* IT 2682, "Income Tax: Payments Made Under Interest Rate Swap Contracts: Timing of Income and Deductions," May 21, 1992, paragraph 90, which applies to swaps entered into on and from May 21, 1992. See also *Taxation Determination* 93/9, "Income Tax: Operation of Section 170AA and Section 233 in Relation to the Application Provisions of Taxation Ruling IT 2682," January 21, 1993, and *Draft Ruling* EDR45, which proposes cash-basis recognition of swap payments and receipts.

114 "Straightline accruals" refers to the spreading of an amount evenly on a daily basis over the relevant term of an instrument, with allocation of income or expense to taxation years based on the number of days occurring in the particular year. The method is equivalent to "straightline amortization" of an amount.

115 IT 2682, supra note 113.

116 Frost, supra note 75, at 32-33. The ATO takes the position that mark-to-market reporting is unavailable even for financial institutions. See IT 2682, supra note 113, at paragraph 29. This approach to the timing of the recognition of interest-rate swap payments is consistent with the required recognition of discount on a straightline accruals basis imposed by the Australian courts, but its adoption is curious given that the ATO applies the same requirements only to the interest expense and income of financial institutions. For taxpayers other than financial institutions, recognition of interest-rate swap payments on a straightline accruals

basis can result in a mismatch with the recognition of interest expense on a payable or incurred basis. See Frost, supra note 75, at 32-33; and *Coles Myer Finance Limited*, supra note 11, which requires the recognition of discount on short-term bills of exchange not subject to ITAA division 16E on a straightline accruals basis. The ATO accepts that the decision applies to all taxpayers and not just financial institutions. See TR 93/27, supra note 11.

See the text that accompanies notes 223-248 in chapter 5 for a "tax-avoidance based" justification of the recognition of interest-based swap payments on a straightline accruals basis. The approach represents a rough way to address disguised prepayments in an off-market series of forwards under a swap that, in the aggregate, are on-market, so that no amounts are paid on initiation of the swap. See the text that accompanies notes 70-92 in chapter 6 for a discussion of the treatment of swap prepayments.

117 Paul, supra note 25, at 217-18; and Sykora, supra note 75, at 30:18-21.

118 IT 2682, supra note 113, at paragraph 81. The tax-avoidance opportunities presented by the application of cash-basis recognition to swap prepayments and possible legislative responses are discussed in the text that accompanies notes 24-92 in chapter 6.

119 IT 2862, supra note 113, at paragraph 81. The same timing principle should presumably apply to payments made in order to enter into or terminate a swap. See Temby, supra note 75, at 138-39. ITAA section 82KZL requires the recognition of prepaid interest, rent, and insurance premiums in the subsequent period to which the prepayments can reasonably be considered to relate. This provision, however, does not appear to require the deferred recognition of swap prepayments over the remaining term of the swap. In particular, it is questionable whether either upfront fees or swap prepayments can be considered to be made for the provision of future services by the other counterparty, as ITAA section 82KZL requires. In the case of upfront fees, the payments are arguably for entering into the swap itself and not for the right to receive future swap payments in consideration for the offsetting payment obligation of the other counterparty. In the case of swap prepayments, the relevant amount is arguably paid in order to reduce or eliminate the future obligations of the payer and not in order to acquire any future services of the payee. See Paul, supra note 25, at 231; and Temby, supra note 75, at 136-37.

Although Revenue Canada has not provided any public statement of its position on this issue, the similarity between ITA subsection 18(9) and ITAA section 82KZL could support a position similar to that of the ATO. See Sykora, supra note 75, at 30:18-20, who considers different timing results under the ITA for the recipient of a swap termination payment, results that depend on the structure of the particular transaction designed to monetize accrued swap gain. The ATO position, expressly stated to be limited to upfront swap payments under "bona fide contracts," appears to exclude swaps that substitute for other financial instruments, particularly loans. The text accompanying notes 24-92 in chapter 6 discusses the issues presented by swaps and other derivatives with embedded debt.

120 Frost, supra note 75, at 28-29; IT 2228, supra note 87, at paragraph 29 (futures contracts not trading stock); and *Draft Determination* 93/D227 (forward foreign exchange contracts not trading stock).

121 Frost, supra note 75, at 28, footnote 29.

122 ITA subsection 10(1.01).

123 See Sykora, supra note 75, at 30:23-25 for a summary of the arguments and the relevant case law. *Friedberg*, supra note 111, did not expressly address the inventory issue, since the taxpayer had realized the losses on the losing legs of his straddle transactions. Accordingly, the application of the lower of cost and fair market value rules was not at issue.

124 See Sykora, supra note 75, at 30:24.

125 Ibid.

126 ITA subsection 248(1) definition of "inventory."

127 Since derivatives provide contractual rights, they constitute property. Moreover, case law has held that inventory can include intangible property for income tax purposes. See Sykora, supra note 75, at 30:24, citing *MNR v. Curlett*, 67 DTC 5058; [1967] CTC 62 (SCC), for the proposition that a mortgage portfolio of a financial institution constitutes inventory.

128 ITA paragraph 18(1)(e). See Sykora, supra note 75, at 30:24-25.

129 Ibid.

130 Under the ITAA, the property underlying an option or a forward or futures contract becomes trading stock on hand if delivery of the physical asset occurs. See Frost, supra note 75, at 29. If the asset is on revenue account but is not trading stock (that is, if it is held for speculative purposes), the cost of acquisition under the option or the forward contract will be recognized when the asset is sold. Otherwise, accrued losses on trading stock may be recognized through the application of the lower of cost and fair market value rule.

131 ITA section 9; and ITAA section 25(1). Frost, supra note 75, at 35; and Sykora, supra note 75, at 30:25.

132 See the definition of property in ITA subsection 248(1); paragraph (a) and subparagraph (b)(iv) of the definition of a "disposition" in ITA section 54; and ITAA section 160ZZC.

133 ITA subsection 49(1) and ITAA section 160ZZC treat the issue of most options as a disposition of property with a nil cost for proceeds equal to the amount of the premium received. The statutory basis for recognition of the capital loss is not entirely clear, since there is arguably no disposition of a capital asset by the issuer of the option as required by the general capital gain provisions. In the absence of any specific deductibility rule, any payment on cash settlement could be considered a non-deductible capital outlay.

134 ITA section 49.

135 ITAA division 13 of part IIIA.

136 The most important exception to this treatment occurs in the case of an option to acquire shares or debt of a corporation issued by the corporation itself. In this case, the option premium must be recognized by the corporation as a capital gain arising on a disposition of the option on its expiry. Otherwise, the option premium is not taxable and becomes part of both the capital base of the corporation and the cost of any shares or debt acquired by the option holder on exercise. See ITA paragraph 49(1)(b) and subsection 49(2); and ITAA section 160ZZC(3A).

137 ITA subparagraph (b)(iv) of the definition of a "disposition" in section 54; and ITAA section 160ZZC.

138 ITA subsections 49(3) and (3.1).

139 ITAA sections 160ZZC(7) and (8).

140 In each case, an amended return may be filed by the option writer to reverse the taxation of the grant of the option as a separate transaction in a previous taxation year.

141 ITA section 9; and ITAA section 25(1).

142 Temby, supra note 75, at 140-41; Sykora, supra note 75, at 30:25-26; and IT-479R, supra note 82, at paragraphs 28-32.

143 *Draft Determination* 93/D62, which requires the inclusion of premiums by a financial institution on receipt and not on a deferred basis over the term of the option. See also Paul, supra note 25, at 222.

144 Although this position is expressed in the context of taxpayers that are financial institutions, the reasoning would seem to apply to other taxpayers as well.

145 IT-479R, supra note 82, at paragraphs 28-32.

146 The extent of the application of this position is unclear. In the case of a financial institution that writes a cap, floor, or collar, for example, the department has stated that the institution must include the premium on receipt but may claim a reasonable reserve in respect of the future obligations, a provision that has the effect of amortizing the premium over the term of the option. See Sykora, supra note 75, at 30:26, citing Revenue Canada document no. AC567045, January 29, 1990.

147 Frost, supra note 75, at 35.

148 ITA subsection 18(9).

149 ITAA subdivision H of division 3.

150 Temby, supra note 75, at 142-43. The ambiguities that surround the characterization of other derivatives as trading stock under the ITAA would seem to arise in the case of options as well. It would appear to be easier to characterize options as inventory under the ITA, since they are not zero-present-value assets and therefore have a cost that is reflected in the amount of the premium. That cost or value of this type of intangible property might be considered relevant to the calculation of income from a business. See supra notes 120-127.

151 Sykora, supra note 75, at 30:26 citing Revenue Canada document no. AC567045, January 29, 1990.

152 Sykora, supra note 75, at 30:27.

153 IT-479R, supra note 82, at paragraphs 28-32.

154 See, for example, Joint Committee on Taxation of the Canadian Bar Association and the Canadian Institute of Chartered Accountants, "Submission to the Minister of Finance on the Issue of Deductibility of Interest," in *Canadian Tax Reports*, Special Report no. 964, extra ed. (Don Mills, Ont.: CCH Canadian, August 1990); and Barrie M. Philp, "Is It Time To Place More Reliance on GAAP?" in *Report of Proceedings of the Forty-Third Tax Conference*, 1991 Conference Report (Toronto: Canadian Tax Foundation, 1992), 25:1-55, at 25:48-55.

155 Edgar, supra note 28, at 307-27.

156 See the text that accompanies notes 257-258, 268, and 294-299 in chapter 5 for a discussion of the treatment of straddle transactions. See the text that accompanies

notes 70-92 in chapter 6 for a discussion of the treatment of swap prepayments and deep-in-the-money options. A "deep-in-the-money option" is an option with an exercise price that virtually assures its exercise. These options require large premiums that are debt equivalents. Revenue Canada and the ATO have addressed these transactions in some of their statements of administrative practices. See the text that accompanies notes 257-258, 268, and 294-299 in chapter 5 and the text that accompanies notes 24-92 in chapter 6.

157 See the text that accompanies notes 97-179 in chapter 7.

158 Anthony J. Frost, "Taxation of Financial Transactions," in *Papers Presented at the Eleventh National Conference of the Taxation Institute of Australia* (Sydney: Taxation Institute of Australia, 1993), 103-25, at 112.

159 Ibid., at 107.

160 The problems presented by a simple convertible-debt obligation are reviewed in Edward D. Kleinbard, "Beyond Good and Evil Debt (and Debt Hedges): A Cost of Capital Allowance System" (December 1989), 67 *Taxes: The Tax Magazine* 943-61, at 947-48. See also the text that accompanies notes 36-43 in chapter 4.

161 Mark P. Gergen, "Apocalypse Not?" (Summer 1995), 50 *Tax Law Review* 833-59, at 849-50, makes a similar point, one that provides much of the basis of the case for the comprehensive accrual regime described in chapters 4 and 5: "Tax policymakers are not directly concerned with innovation; they can be satisfied if the law governs the existing set of securities tolerably well and there is not a harmful level of uncertainty regarding the tax treatment of novel securities. The implication is that tax policymakers must be satisfied if they can create and preserve continuity in taxation of the existing set of securities."

162 H. David Rosenbloom, "Source-Basis Taxation of Derivative Financial Instruments: Some Unanswered Questions" (April 1996), 50 *University of Miami Law Review* 597-615, at 600.

163 Ibid., at 597-601; see also the text that accompanies notes 24-51 in chapter 1.

164 Rosenbloom, supra note 162, at 597-601, describes this analogy.

165 Ibid.

166 Ibid.

167 Scarborough, supra note 2, discusses this insight and its implications for income tax purposes in more detail.

168 The text that accompanies notes 126-151 in chapter 1 discusses risk and its importance as a cause of financial innovation.

169 See the text that accompanies notes 58-107 in chapter 1 for a discussion of these pricing relationships.

170 In the case of common shares of a leveraged corporation, this combination provides a cash flow pattern equivalent to the one associated with a call or put option written on either the shares themselves or the underlying corporate assets. See the text that accompanies notes 52-57 in chapter 1.

171 Realized gain or loss on a debt obligation that is attributable to interest-rate risk (that is, changes in the value of a fixed-rate instrument caused by fluctuations in interest rates) may also be on either capital or ordinary-income account, depending on the purpose of the acquisition by the holder. Accrued but unpaid interest is

subject to the deeming provisions under the ITA and the ITAA that ensure its treatment as interest income to the holder even when it is realized as proceeds on a disposition of the obligation. See the text that accompanies note 52.

172 See the text that accompanies notes 60-109 in chapter 1.

173 See, for example, the sources cited in chapter 1 at note 120. See also Coopers & Lybrand, *Guide to Financial Instruments*, 3d ed. (New York: Coopers & Lybrand, 1996), which describes the essential features of both the basic building-block financial instruments and the more sophisticated instruments. The guide also includes a brief summary of the US income tax and financial-accounting treatment.

174 Alvin C. Warren Jr., "Financial Contract Innovation and Income Tax Policy" (December 1993), 107 *Harvard Law Review* 460-92.

175 See Gary L. Gastineau, *Swiss Bank Corporation's Dictionary of Financial Risk Management* (Chicago: Probus, 1992), 94-95, which describes "dynamic hedging" as "[a] technique of portfolio insurance or position risk management in which an option-like return pattern is created by increasing or reducing the position in the underlying (or forwards, futures, or options on the underlying) to simulate the delta change in value of an option position. For example, a short stock index futures position may be increased or decreased to create a synthetic put on a portfolio, producing a portfolio-type return pattern. Dynamic hedging relies on liquid, continuous markets with low to moderate transaction costs."

176 These insights appear to have significantly influenced the thinking of Australian tax-policy makers in their attempt to design a set of comprehensive accrual rules. See, for example, Alan Preston, "The View from the High Wire: A Treasury Perspective of Corporate Tax Issues," in Taxation Institute of Australia (Victoria Division), *Red Series Intensive Retreat—Rabbits Out of Hats: Corporate Structures and Restructures* (Melbourne: TIA, Victoria Division, 1995), 3-10.

177 This point is taken up in the context of bifurcation and integration as approaches to the taxation of financial instruments under a comprehensive accrual regime. See the text that accompanies notes 14-52 in chapter 4, and chapters 6 and 7.

178 The term "internal financial engineering" is used by Paul B. Goris, *The Legal Aspects of Swaps* (London: Graham and Trotman, 1994), 28-29. See the text that accompanies notes 115-118 in chapter 1.

179 Ibid.

180 See the text that accompanies notes 152-207 in chapter 1.

181 Preston, supra note 176; and Jeff Strnad, "Taxing New Financial Products: A Conceptual Framework" (May 1994), 46 *Stanford Law Review* 569-605.

182 See Bradford L. Ferguson, "The Rationales for the Rules: How To Think About Derivatives in the Tax World" (December 1994), 72 *Taxes: The Tax Magazine* 995-1026, at 996. Ferguson cites the same two goals for any income tax system that treats interest and dividends differently, provides a realization basis for the recognition of gains and losses other than interest, and distinguishes between capital amounts and ordinary-income amounts. He argues that the US approach to the taxation of financial instruments has "progressed notably in recent years" by realizing a greater degree of neutrality and more effective responses to financial innovation driven by tax arbitrage. Chapter 4 discusses this characterization of the US approach and compares that approach with those of other countries.

183 The term "accretion taxation" describes the tax recognition of unrealized changes in value, whether or not the resulting gains and losses are expected. The term "accrual" describes the recognition of expected gains and losses (whether realized or not) over the term of a financial instrument as they are expected to arise.

184 See Scarborough, supra note 2; and Shuldiner, supra note 2.

Notes to Chapter 3

1 See, for example, Jeff Strnad, "Taxing New Financial Products: A Conceptual Framework" (May 1994), 46 *Stanford Law Review* 569-605; and Alvin C. Warren Jr., "Financial Contract Innovation and Income Tax Policy" (December 1993), 107 *Harvard Law Review* 460-92. To some extent, this literature has been prompted by the perceived failure of US policy makers to

- comprehensively classify corporate instruments as debt or equity,
- address the tax treatment of contingent-payment debt by decomposing the obligations into their component parts and taxing those parts as separate instruments, and
- design a coherent legislative regime applicable to derivatives.

This perception of the US experience, however, is somewhat misleading. The ad hoc development of separate legislative regimes for categories of financial instruments provides an unfortunate appearance of incoherence and incomprehensibility. See Robert H. Scarborough, "Different Rules for Different Players and Products: The Patchwork Taxation of Derivatives" (December 1994), 72 *Taxes: The Tax Magazine* 1031-49. Although the US legislation is far from perfect, there is much in it that provides a useful model for the design of a comprehensive regime for the taxation of financial instruments under a realization-based income tax. Many of these aspects of the US legislation are, in fact, drawn on for representative lessons in the design of the approach described in chapters 5, 6, and 7 as the preferable second-best alternative to the benchmark described in this chapter.

2 Strnad, supra note 1, uses mathematical proofs to develop a conceptual framework that does much to explain the underlying causes of the difficulties encountered in the taxation of financial instruments.

3 See the text that accompanies notes 3-27 in chapter 2.

4 These differences in tax treatment characteristic of most income tax systems are referred to as "risk-based rules" in Daniel Shaviro, "Risk-Based Rules and the Taxation of Capital Income" (Summer 1995), 50 *Tax Law Review* 643-724.

5 Strnad, supra note 1, reaches this conclusion in the context of the development of an elaborate conceptual framework intended to realize both "universality" and "consistency" in the taxation of financial instruments. As was described at the end of chapter 1, "universality" is the requirement that "a tax system specify a tax treatment for every possible transaction" (Strnad, ibid., at 572). Strnad (at 573) defines "consistency" as the requirement that "every cash flow pattern has a unique tax treatment" and is taxed accordingly. Universality is said to be desirable because it minimizes uncertainty in the tax treatment of new financial instruments

and the attendant administrative and compliance costs. Consistency is said to be desirable because it eliminates the ability to repackage traditional cash flows in untraditional forms that receive more advantageous tax treatment. In essence, unique treatment of cash flows on the basis of their substantive characteristics would eliminate any incentive to expend resources in searching for a tax-preferred form of a financial instrument; moreover, the government would no longer be required to expend resources in responding to particular instruments in order to address what is otherwise an effectively elective tax system. The goal of consistency, therefore, is linked closely with the control of tax arbitrage or avoidance transactions that "defeat distinctions in the tax law . . . and tend to produce free money at government expense for well-capitalized taxpayers" (Strnad, ibid., at 573).

6 Strnad, ibid., uses the two policy goals of universality and consistency as the basis for his assessment of "bifurcation" and "integration" techniques as possible approaches to the taxation of financial instruments. As he defines these terms, bifurcation is the decomposition of a new financial instrument into its component parts, with a specified tax treatment for each part. The aggregate tax treatment of the new instrument is equal to the sum of the tax treatments of the component parts. Integration is the combination of otherwise distinct financial instruments into one aggregate instrument. The tax treatment of the aggregate cash flow is determined by the dominant characteristic of the particular combination. Strnad draws on the theory of "spanning" in the finance literature and some basic principles of linear algebra to argue that any attempt to bifurcate financial instruments into recognized categories of investments will succeed only if the tax system is linear: that is, if "the tax on any transaction equals the sum of the taxes on any collection of subtransactions that comprise that transaction" (Strnad, ibid., at 576). It is only under this condition of linearity that various possible decompositions of a given transaction will result in the same aggregate tax burden. Similarly, any attempt to integrate the different components of a portfolio and tax them as a single investment will succeed only if the tax system is continuous; that is, if transactions with nearly identical cash flows have nearly identical tax treatments. It is only under this condition of continuity that small differences in the composition of an integrated transaction do not result in disproportionately different "jumps" in tax treatment.

The necessity and the effectiveness of bifurcation and integration techniques are discussed in chapters 4, 6, and 7.

7 Michael Brooks and John Head, "Tax Avoidance: In Economics, Law and Public Choice," in Graeme S. Cooper, ed., *Tax Avoidance and the Rule of Law* (Amsterdam: IBFD Publications, 1997), 53-91, at 54-78.

8 Ibid., at 61.

9 "Horizontal equity" is used here in its traditional sense of the similar taxation of similarly situated individuals. Whether or not individuals are similarly situated is conventionally measured by pre-tax incomes. Accordingly, horizontal equity is violated when equal pre-tax incomes from two different sources are taxed differently and therefore yield different after-tax incomes. "Vertical equity" or "progressivity" too is used here in its traditional sense, as in the case of a progressive income tax system under which individuals pay proportionately more in tax as their incomes increase.

10 Brooks and Head, supra note 7, at 65.

11 See, generally, Joseph E. Stiglitz, "The General Theory of Tax Avoidance" (March 1985), 38 *National Tax Journal* 325-37; and Joseph E. Stiglitz, "Some Aspects of the Taxation of Capital Gains" (July 1983), 21 *Journal of Public Economics* 257-94, cited and reviewed in more detail by Brooks and Head, supra note 7, at 65-66. As examples of pure tax avoidance, Brooks and Head (ibid., at 65 and 77) cite straddle transactions, wash sales, and original issue discount (OID) obligations. These transactions and the responses they have drawn from Canadian and Australian tax authorities were described in chapter 2.

Strnad, supra note 1, at 573, refers to pure tax avoidance as "pure tax arbitrage," which he defines as "a series of transactions [that results] in no net cash flow but provides tax advantages." He cites as an example the matching of a long position that is subject to capital gain treatment with a short position that is subject to ordinary-income treatment. Provided that the two positions have identical cash flows, their combined cash flow is zero, but a tax advantage results from the taxpayer's ability to offset a loss on the short position against ordinary income while replacing that income with a preferentially taxed capital gain on the long position. Strnad (ibid., at 598) contrasts pure tax arbitrage with "approximate tax arbitrage," which involves a sacrifice in the desired pattern of cash flows (that is, riskiness). He cites as an example the matching of a long position that is very close to the jump point represented by a tax discontinuity with a short position exactly at that point. Although the matching of cash flows is not perfect, it can be designed to be very close to a zero net position. Approximate tax arbitrage is thus structured to take advantage of discontinuities in tax treatment. Pure tax arbitrage is structured to take advantage of inconsistent taxation of equivalent cash flows.

See also David A. Weisbach, "Tax Responses to Financial Contract Innovation" (Summer 1995), 50 *Tax Law Review* 491-544, who (at 509, footnote 46) distinguishes "pure tax arbitrage" from "normal tax arbitrage." The former is said to involve the purchase and sale of the same asset in different forms. The latter is said to involve the borrowing of funds to purchase a tax-preferred asset.

12 See Brooks and Head, supra note 7, at 71, where they state that "[T]he contrasting intuition that welfare cost falls with increasing ease of substitution between taxed and untaxed alternatives achieves policy relevance therefore only in these special 'corner cases' where the untaxed option has largely replaced the taxable activity." Capital-income taxation is unique because of the wide variety of opportunities for perfect or near-perfect substitutability that it provides. See Myron S. Scholes and Mark Wolfson, *Taxes and Business Strategy* (Englewood Cliffs, NJ: Prentice Hall, 1992), chapters 6 and 7.

13 Brooks and Head, supra note 7, at 71, conclude that pure tax avoidance entails social costs that may be very large because of the need to make up revenue losses by means of either rate increases on a narrow base, which have welfare costs, or reductions in the benefits of public expenditure.

14 For lack of a better term, the discussion in this chapter will use this modified version of Strnad's "approximate tax arbitrage" category." See supra note 11.

15 Reed H. Shuldiner, "A General Approach to the Taxation of Financial Instruments" (December 1992), 71 *Texas Law Review* 243-350, at 258, argues that a reduction in the effective tax rate on certain financial instruments that provide the benefit of deferral distorts investment decisions in two ways. First, overinvestment in the tax-preferred instrument will occur, since the after-tax yield will be

higher. Second, as the tax benefit becomes capitalized in the price of the particular instrument, the pre-tax yield will decline, which will make it less attractive for lower-bracket taxpayers. Shuldiner distinguishes "anticipated" from "unanticipated" deferral and limits these particular efficiency effects to the former. The details of this distinction and their importance for tax policy purposes are discussed infra in the text that accompanies notes 58-133.

16 The equity effects of either type of tax avoidance are much more difficult to assess. Since capital income is earned disproportionately by high-income individuals, avoidance may reduce progressivity. This effect may be particularly pronounced in the case of instances of pure tax avoidance, which do not entail any offsetting excess burden for the affected taxpayers. In the case of instances of high substitutability, reductions in progressivity may be offset, in part, by an implicit tax in the form of excess burdens. Problems of horizontal equity (that is, differences in after-tax returns for equivalent pre-tax returns) associated with avoidance may be eliminated to the extent that capital markets are perfect (that is, to the extent that there are no informational problems, transaction costs, or institutional restrictions). Given perfect markets, the pre-tax return on tax-favoured investments or financial instruments will decline as capital flows to the favoured alternative, and eventually all after-tax returns will be equal. The result will be a misallocation of resources, with attendant efficiency costs only. Information asymmetries, transaction costs, and legal restrictions, however, result in market imperfections that may lead to horizontal inequities. Furthermore, the implicit tax occasioned by tax capitalization seems to be associated most obviously with real assets that have a finite supply. Since the supply of financial instruments that taxpayers can use to replicate the characteristics of other, more highly taxed instruments is unlimited, it is not obvious that the price of these instruments will be bid up in a process that eliminates horizontal inequities. The inequities occasioned by the absence of tax capitalization may be compounded by instances of pure tax avoidance and perfect substitutability if the relevant tax-avoidance arrangements are not universally available. See Brooks and Head, supra note 7, at 60-61; and Shuldiner, supra note 15, at 262.

17 Brooks and Head, supra note 7, at 77.

18 Ibid., at 64, 74, and 77-78.

19 The concept was expressed most completely in Henry C. Simons, *Personal Income Taxation: The Definition of Income as a Problem of Fiscal Policy* (Chicago: University of Chicago Press, 1938), 50. In what is probably the most quoted passage in the tax-policy literature, Simons defined personal income as

> the algebraic sum of (1) the market value of rights exercised in consumption and (2) the change in the value of the store of property rights between the beginning and end of the period in question. In other words, it is merely the result obtained by adding consumption during the period to "wealth" at the end of the period and then subtracting "wealth" at the beginning. The *sine qua non* of income is *gain*, as our courts have recognized in their more lucid moments—and gain *to* someone during a specified time interval. Moreover, this gain may be measured and defined most easily by positing a dual objective or purpose, consumption and accumulation, each of which may be estimated in a common unit by appeal to market prices.

Simons elaborated on an idea expressed in Robert M. Haig, "The Concept of Income—Economic and Legal Aspects," in R.M. Haig, ed., *The Federal Income Tax* (New York: Columbia University Press, 1921), 7. Haig stated that "income is the money value of the net accretion to one's economic power between two points of time." It is now acknowledged, however, that the accretion concept of income underlying the Haig-Simons concept was first expressed in Georg von Schanz, "Der Einkommensbegriff und die Einkommensteuergesetze" (1896), vol. 13, no. 1 *Finanz-Archiv* 1-87. See Richard A. Musgrave, "In Defense of an Income Concept" (March 1967), 81 *Harvard Law Review* 44-62, at 47, footnote 7.

20 The Haig-Simons concept of income and, in particular, its support for the elimination of differences in tax treatment for different sources of income is the conceptual foundation of the comprehensive tax base (CTB) popularized in the Carter report. See Canada, *Report of the Royal Commission on Taxation* (Ottawa: Queen's Printer, 1966) ("the Carter report"). It is only in the last 20 years or so that the timing dictates of the Haig-Simons concept have come to the forefront, particularly in the US academic legal literature. Simons himself (supra note 19, at 127) tended to dismiss timing issues rather easily and seemed generally content with the recognition of gains and losses on realization.

21 Other common terms synonymous with accretion taxation are "market-value accounting," "market-value taxation," and "mark-to-market taxation." The term "accretion taxation" is used here to avoid confusion with "accrual recognition" in the more limited sense of the spreading of expected gains and losses over the term of a financial instrument and the recognition of such amounts as they are expected to arise. Accretion taxation requires the recognition of both expected and unexpected gains and losses as they arise.

22 H. David Rosenbloom, "Source-Basis Taxation of Derivative Financial Instruments: Some Unanswered Questions" (April 1996), 50 *University of Miami Law Review* 597-615, makes this point in connection with the taxation of derivative financial instruments, but it extends to the taxation of financial instruments generally.

23 These terms were defined in chapter 2 in the text that accompanies notes 178 and 179.

24 See also Mark P. Gergen and Paula Schmitz, "The Influence of Tax Law on Securities Innovation in the United States: 1981-1997" (Winter 1997), 52 *Tax Law Review* 119-97; and Mark P. Gergen, "Apocalypse Not?" (Summer 1995), 50 *Tax Law Review* 833-59.

25 The most complete development of the significance of this distinction as a conceptual basis for the income taxation of financial instruments is in Shuldiner, supra note 15. See also David P. Hariton, "The Taxation of Complex Financial Instruments" (Summer 1988), 43 *Tax Law Review* 731-88; and Scarborough, supra note 1.

26 But see the sources cited supra note 25, where the writers draw a clear distinction between expected and unexpected gains and losses and the different issues they present under a realization-based income tax. Much of the following material is based on their analysis, particularly that of Shuldiner, supra note 15. The distinction between expected and unexpected gains and losses also forms the underlying basis of the New Zealand accrual legislation and the comparable Australian proposals discussed in chapter 5.

27 This proposition is often presented as if the underlying rationale were self-evident. But see Jeff Strnad, "Periodicity and Accretion Taxation: Norms and Implementation" (June 1990), 99 *The Yale Law Journal* 1817-1911, at 1819, who states that "the policy proposals for implementing accretion taxation are not linked clearly or carefully to the norms that motivate choice of the accretion approach in the first place."

28 This premise holds even where realization-based recognition is justified as a tax subsidy for capital accumulation. See, for example, David M. Schizer, "Realization as Subsidy" (November 1998), 73 *New York University Law Review* 1549-1626.

29 This assumption is challenged by recent literature arguing that the ability to alter portfolios in response to tax changes means that the return on risk taking is effectively exempt under both an income tax and a cash flow consumption tax. Only the riskless return on capital may be taxed under an income tax and exempt under a cash flow tax. See Joseph Bankman and Barbara H. Fried, "Winners and Losers in the Shift to a Consumption Tax" (January 1998), 86 *The Georgetown Law Journal* 539-68; Joseph Bankman and Thomas Griffith, "Is the Debate Between an Income Tax and a Consumption Tax a Debate About Risk? Does It Matter? (Winter 1992), 47 *Tax Law Review* 377-406; Noel B. Cunningham, "The Taxation of Capital Income" (Fall 1996), 52 *Tax Law Review* 17-44; and Alvin C. Warren Jr., "How Much Capital Income Taxed Under an Income Tax Is Exempt Under a Cash Flow Tax?" (Fall 1996), 52 *Tax Law Review* 1-16. Deborah H. Schenk, "A Realization-Based Income Tax and the Taxation of Capital" (draft), reprinted in *Tax Notes Today*, October 26, 1997, 97 TNT 223-39 (electronic database), argues for an ex ante wealth tax in the form of the imputation of interest at the riskless rate of return on all assets. Her case is based on the recent literature suggesting that the return to risk is effectively exempt under a normative income tax and is only accidentally taxed under existing income tax systems to the extent that certain non-tax factors constrain shifts in portfolios necessary to exempt risky returns. Bankman and Griffith, supra, argue that the historically low rates of real returns (that is, after adjustment for inflation) make the attempt to tax even the riskless rate worthless.

30 The ex ante wealth tax suggested by Schenk, supra note 29, would be equally effective. Indeed, the expected-return approach described in this book also involves the imputation of interest as the preferable method for the taxation of expected returns under a realization-based income tax. The principal difference remains an acceptance of the continued attempt to tax the return to risk in the form of unexpected gains.

31 But see Schizer, supra note 28 (justifying the adoption of realization-based recognition as a subsidy for savings).

32 Strnad, supra note 27, makes the case for the adoption of continuous taxation of gains and losses as they arise. This approach resembles daily marking to market of all assets and liabilities and is justified by Strnad on the basis of the normative principles that he sees as underlying the case for accretion taxation generally. Annual recognition of changes in value is characterized as a deviation from the benchmark principle of continuous taxation in much the same way as realization-based recognition is seen as a deviation from annual accrual recognition. Although Strnad reviews in some detail the possible normative costs caused by the acceptance of the annual accounting requirement, it is clear as a practical matter that this standard reporting period is not about to be abandoned.

33 One commentator has referred to the Haig-Simons ideal as a religion slavishly followed by many academics. See Karla W. Simon, "Revenue or Religion? Issues and Answers on Tax Deferral" (December 1990), 68 *Taxes: The Tax Magazine* 1015-32. She emphasizes the practical considerations that inevitably reduce every income tax system to a compromised accretion-based system and make the adoption of a pure cash flow tax unlikely. These considerations have considerable significance for the appropriate taxation of financial instruments and, in particular, the case for market-value accounting of this category of assets and liabilities. Their significance follows from the fact that for practical reasons actual income tax systems will continue to be hybrids of accretion, realization, and cash flow systems. The case for market-value accounting of financial instruments must be made in the context of the application of realization-based recognition and cash flow treatment of other assets.

34 But see Jeff Strnad, "Taxation of Income from Capital" (April 1985), 37 *Stanford Law Review* 1023-1107, at 1025-34 and 1040-80; and Strnad, supra note 27, at 1860-63, who argued that the Haig-Simons ideal does not suggest any particular accounting period; indeed, one can even use it to support cash flow taxation, on the ground that the latter taxes accretions to wealth proportionately over the lifetime of a taxpayer. This argument provoked responses from other academics, who argued that the Haig-Simons concept does not support a cash flow tax. See Louis Kaplow and Alvin C. Warren Jr., "An Income Tax by Any Other Name—A Reply to Professor Strnad" (January 1986), 38 *Stanford Law Review* 399-421, at 401-12; and William D. Popkin, "Tax Ideals in the Real World: A Comment on Professor Strnad's Approach to Tax Fairness" (Winter 1986), 62 *Indiana Law Journal* 63-72. The essence of these responses was that accretions to wealth during a specified accounting period must be recognized and tax paid at the end of the period. Strnad's interpretation of the Haig-Simons concept, his critics argued, was misleading, since it treated the tax on accretions as a charge that need not be paid until the accretion is realized as gain.

The difference between these two interpretations of the Haig-Simons concept is a time-value-of-money element associated with the payment of tax as the liability arises, which is the critical element of deferral. In two rejoinders, Strnad argued, in essence, that the Haig-Simons formulation of income does not provide any criteria for the choice of a taxation period. The traditional approach to tax timing analysis has been to specify an accounting period; by definition, any deviations from the recognition of wealth increments and the payments of tax at the end of the specified period are inappropriate. See Jeff Strnad, "The Bankruptcy of Conventional Tax Timing Wisdom Is Deeper Than Semantics: A Rejoinder to Professors Kaplow and Warren" (January 1987), 39 *Stanford Law Review* 389-417, at 390-405; and Jeff Strnad, "Tax Timing and the Haig-Simons Ideal: A Rejoinder to Professor Popkin" (Winter 1986), 62 *Indiana Law Journal* 73-94. Strnad's rejoinder was followed by a further rejoinder from Kaplow and Warren. See Louis Kaplow and Alvin C. Warren Jr., "Professor Strnad's Rejoinder: Simply Semantics" (January 1987), 39 *Stanford Law Review* 419-25, at 419-22.

35 The cash flow or consumption tax has an intellectual tradition even longer than that of the accretion-based income tax, one that dates back to Thomas Hobbes, *Leviathan* (London: Dent, 1924), chapter 30; and J.S. Mill, *Principles of Political Economy* (London: J.W. Parker, 1848), book V, chapter 1, section 4. The base was championed by Irving Fisher at about the same time as Henry Simons popularized

the accretion income concept. See Irving Fisher and H. Fisher, *Constructive Income Taxation* (New York: Harper, 1942). More recent proponents include William D. Andrews, "A Consumption-Type or Cash Flow Personal Income Tax" (April 1974), 87 *Harvard Law Review* 1113-88; Institute for Fiscal Studies, *Structure and Reform of Direct Taxation: Report of a Committee Chaired by Professor J.E. Meade* (London: Allen and Unwin, 1978); Nicholas Kaldor, *An Expenditure Tax* (London: Unwin University Books, 1955); and United States, Department of the Treasury, *Blueprints for Basic Tax Reform* (Washington, DC: US Government Printing Office, 1977).

36 Dissavings in the form of borrowing proceeds must be included in income and can be deducted only to the extent that the proceeds are invested. Otherwise, the borrowing proceeds represent taxable consumption receipts. Repayments of principal and interest are deductible in all cases as non-consumption expenses.

37 Much the same result can be realized by disallowing a deduction for savings as they are accumulated and exempting the return from taxation. Under this form of cash flow taxation, the so-called yield-exemption method, neither the after-tax savings nor their return are taxed when they are withdrawn for consumption purposes. In essence, the tax that is paid on consumption under the deduction method is collected in advance under the yield-exemption method, and the two amounts of tax are equivalent in present-value terms. The equivalence holds, however, only under certain conditions. Most important, tax and interest rates must remain constant, and the deduction for savings must produce an immediate tax saving that can be invested at the same rate as the return on the original investment. See Mary Louise Fellows, "A Comprehensive Attack on Deferral" (February 1990), 88 *Michigan Law Review* 722-813, at 732-33, citing Michael Graetz, *Federal Income Taxation: Principles and Policies*, 2d ed. (Westbury, NY: Foundation Press, 1988), 388-89; and Michael Graetz, "Implementing a Progressive Consumption Tax" (June 1979), 92 *Harvard Law Review* 1575-1661, at 1602.

38 Assume that a taxpayer receives $50,000 in salary in period one. Assume also that the taxpayer is subject to a 40 percent tax rate and that the riskless rate of return on savings is 10 percent. Under an accretion-based income tax, the taxpayer would pay $20,000 in tax at the end of period one, T(0), and would have $30,000 in after-tax income to invest in, say, a two-year asset that paid the riskless rate of return, compounded annually. In period two, the asset would appreciate in value to $33,000 ($30,000 + $3,000 expected return), and the taxpayer would pay tax of $1,200 ($3,000 × 0.4) at the end of the period, T(1). In period three, the asset would appreciate in value further to $36,300 ($33,000 + $3,300), and at the end of the period, T(2), the taxpayer would receive the return on the asset and pay tax of $1,320 on the increment in value during the period ($3,300 × 0.4). At that time, it would seem the taxpayer would have an after-tax amount of $33,780 available for consumption ($30,000 at T(0) + $1,800 at T(1) + $1,980 at T(2)). In fact, however, it is necessary to reduce this amount by $72, which represents the forgone after-tax return on the $1,200 tax payment required at T(1) ($1,200 × 0.1 × 0.6). Thus the effective return available for consumption is $33,708. Under a cash flow tax, the taxpayer would receive an offsetting deduction from income for any amount that he saved in the form of the two-year asset; consequently, he would pay no tax on his $50,000 wages at T(0) if he invested the whole amount in the two-year asset. Nor would he pay tax on the

$5,000 return received at T(1) if he reinvested the return. He would pay tax of $24,200 ($60,500 × 0.4) at T(2) when he withdrew the total pre-tax amount of $60,500 ($50,000 at T(0) + $5,000 at T(1) + $5,500 at T(2)) for consumption purposes. At T(2), therefore, the taxpayer would have $36,300 available for consumption ($60,500 – $24,200).

The same result would follow under a yield-exemption approach, which would require the payment of $20,000 of tax at T(0) on the wages of $50,000. The 10 percent return at T(1) ($3,000) and T(2) ($3,300) would not be taxed, leaving $36,300 for consumption. In essence, the payment of tax of $20,000 at T(0) under the yield-exemption approach is the present value of the $24,200 tax paid at T(2) under the cash flow approach of providing a deduction for savings as accumulated and taxing them (along with the return) on withdrawal for consumption.

39 But see the sources cited supra note 29, which suggest that the difference between an income tax and a cash flow consumption tax arises only to the extent of the riskless rate of return.

40 The double tax and its distorting effect are apparent if one compares the outcome under an income tax with the outcome in a notional no-tax world. In a world of this kind, the taxpayer would have $50,000 available at T(0) to invest in the two-year asset that paid the riskless return of 10 percent. At T(1), the asset would have earned $5,000 ($50,000 × 0.1); at T(2), an additional $5,500. At T(2), therefore, the taxpayer would have $60,500 available for consumption. The value of the $60,500 at T(2) would be the same as the value of the $50,000 if it were consumed at T(0); that is, the present value of $60,500 at T(2), discounted at the 10 percent riskless rate of return) is $50,000 at T(0). This neutrality between immediate consumption and deferred consumption also holds under a consumption tax, where the choice would be between immediate consumption of $30,000 at T(0) ($50,000 × the after-tax return of 0.6) and $36,300 at T(2) ($60,500 × 0.6). The value of these choices is the same as the value that would hold in a no-tax world; in other words, the present value of the $36,300 at T(2), discounted at the 10 percent riskless rate of return is $30,000 at T(0).

41 In the example in notes 38 and 40 supra, the ratio of deferred consumption to immediate consumption under an accretion-based income tax is 33,708:30,000 or 1.12, which is less than the ratio (1.21) under either a cash flow tax or in a no-tax world.

42 Strnad, supra note 27. In the example described in notes 38 and 40, that proportion is equal to the tax rate of 40 percent.

43 To see this result, compare the relative ratios between deferred consumption and immediate consumption in the example in notes 38 and 40 supra. In a no-tax world, the ratio would be 60,500:50,000 or 1.21. Under a consumption tax, the ratio would be the same (36,300:30,000). By taxing a larger proportion of savings, an income tax reduces the value of deferred consumption relative to the value of immediate consumption. This result is highlighted in the example, where the value of immediate consumption is $30,000 after tax compared with $33,708 of deferred consumption at T(2). Given a discount rate equal to the 10 percent riskless rate of return, the present value of the latter amount at T(0) is $27,857.98.

44 This result depends critically on the sensitivity of savings to after-tax returns. In effect, the level of private savings will increase under a consumption tax if the

increased after-tax return induces individuals to save rather than consume immediately. It is possible, however, that the increased after-tax return to savings would, in fact, induce individuals to save less than they would save under an income tax, since they would need less savings to realize the same level of consumption. In any attempt to model supposed efficiency gains, therefore, the elasticity of savings is determinative. The economic evidence on this point is ambiguous.

45 See, for example, Fred D. Brown, "'Complete' Accrual Taxation" (Winter 1997), 34 *San Diego Law Review* 1559-1680; Fellows, supra footnote 37; and David A. Shakow, "Taxation Without Realization: A Proposal for Accrual Taxation" (June 1986), 134 *University of Pennsylvania Law Review* 1111-1205.

46 See, for example, Alvin C. Warren Jr., "Would a Consumption Tax Be Fairer Than an Income Tax?" (April 1980), 89 *The Yale Law Journal* 1081-1124, at 1083-93. Warren argues that the Haig-Simons concept of income simply provides a useful means of allocating the collective social product among individuals for personal tax purposes. Income in a more fundamental sense is the product of all private labour and capital in a society, which, Warren concludes, can be taxed on "the theory that a producer does not have a moral claim over the product of his capital and labour, given the role of fortuity in income distribution and the dependence of producers and consumers on other producers to create value in our society" (ibid., at 1091). The distribution of social product, therefore, is no more than a function of a collective decision. The underlying philosophical bases for an income tax as an expression of "contributive justice" and a "benefits" theory of taxation are explored in detail in Graeme S. Cooper, "Income Tax Law and Contributive Justice: Some Thoughts on Defining and Expressing a Consistent Theory of Tax Justice and Its Limitations" (1986), vol. 3, no. 3 *Australian Tax Forum* 297-332.

47 See also Mark Kelman, "Time Preference and Tax Equity" (April 1983), 35 *Stanford Law Review* 649-80, who argues that the individual who consumes immediately and the individual who saves and defers consumption are not in identical positions. Kelman develops the position that, viewed ex post, the saver is better off even though, viewed ex ante, the present value of immediate and deferred consumption is equivalent in a no-tax world. Since the saver is better off, the double tax on savings under an income tax is appropriate as a matter of equity.

This conclusion depends on views about the origin of interest and, in particular, on whether interest is better explained as a supply-side or a demand-side phenomenon. Supply-side accounts hold that interest must be provided in order to induce individuals to forgo the psychological benefits of present consumption. By this reckoning, interest simply equates immediate and deferred consumption in present-value terms, so that from an equity perspective the tax on one choice should be equivalent to the tax on the other. Demand-side accounts of interest question the psychological explanation of interest as a necessary inducement to saving and argue instead that interest is paid simply because invested capital produces a return that induces individuals to save. The inducement is unnecessary from a demand perspective, since in its absence individuals would be indifferent between consuming a dollar immediately and consuming a dollar in the future. However, if the supply of savings is less than the demand for capital by projects that pay a rate of return, then individuals must be paid a return in order to induce them to invest. That return on savings is, in effect, a windfall brought about by the demand for savings to finance capital projects. The windfall represents a return that, ex post, places the saver in a position better than that of the immediate consumer. Since deferred and immediate consumption are not equal, from an equity perspective the burden on savings should be greater. See also Warren, supra note 46, at 1102-5. The empirical bases for either account of the origin of interest is contentious.

48 See Strnad, supra note 27; and Simon, supra note 33, at 1018. These intangible benefits are a kind of imputed income that advocates of the income tax believe should be taxed for redistributive purposes. See, for example, Fellows, supra note 37, at 807-8; and Warren, supra note 46, at 1121-24. Advocates of a cash flow tax also recognize the need to tax the intangible benefits from holding wealth as a basis for support of an income tax. See, for example, Andrews, supra note 35, at 956. The benefits of future tangible consumption represented by savings or wealth are taxed under a cash flow tax when the wealth is used for consumption purposes. In effect, the consumption tax reduces the present value of future consumption by imposing a charge against savings as they accumulate. This reduction is equal to the tax rate, but it is insufficient if one believes that wealth brings intangible benefits in addition to the tangible benefits of future consumption. By taxing savings as they accumulate and requiring the contemporaneous payment of the tax, the income tax imposes an additional charge that reaches these benefits and realizes a greater measure of wealth redistribution than does the proportional reduction under a cash flow tax. See Popkin, supra note 34.

49 Strnad, supra note 27, at 1834-35 and 1846-48; Fellows, supra note 37, at 808-10; and Warren, supra note 46, at 1121-24.

50 See, for example, Andrews, supra note 35, at 1169-73.

51 Strnad, supra note 27.

52 Ibid.

53 A cash flow tax may provide efficiency gains by reducing many of the distortions that arise under an income tax. Only a wealth tax, however, could address the redistributive concerns that a cash flow tax would raise, and if the political experience of most countries is any indication the adoption of a progressive wealth tax in Canada is highly unlikely. As Fellows notes (supra note 37, at 808-9) a wealth tax would undermine the efficiency gains associated with the increase in the level of savings that would presumably occur under a cash flow tax, a consideration that makes the adoption of a wealth tax a political improbability. The political obstacles to the adoption of a cash flow tax supplemented by a wealth tax are compounded by design obstacles, such as transitional considerations and the difficulty of defining taxable consumption. See, for example, Simon, supra note 33, at 1019. The seminal article analyzing the implementation problems presented by a cash flow tax is Graetz, supra note 37.

54 Owing to the prevalence of a strictly ex ante perspective that disregards ex post results and the return to risk, the same concerns presumably preclude the adoption of the system of interest imputation suggested by Schenk, supra note 29. This point is taken up in chapter 4.

55 An accretion-based income tax is said to be preferable primarily because it imposes a greater double-tax burden on savings by taxing accumulations as they arise rather than when they are realized. Thus it reaches the intangible benefits of wealth to a greater extent than does a realization-based income tax. The latter, however,

imposes a greater burden on savings than does a cash flow tax, since it applies both to income before it is saved and to the return on the after-tax savings as it is realized. Simon, supra note 33, at 1021, refers to a realization-based income tax as the "third best" method of attempting to tax the intangible benefits derived from wealth. To see the relationship between a realization-based income tax, an accretion-based income tax, and a cash flow tax, consider again the simple example used in notes 38 and 40 supra. Under a realization-based income tax that requires the recognition of income when it is received, the taxpayer with period-one wages of $50,000 will pay tax of $20,000 at T(0). Thus he will have $30,000 left to invest in the two-year asset that pays a 10 percent riskless rate of return at the end of period three (T(2)), compounded annually at the end of period two (T(1)). At T(2), the taxpayer will receive $36,300 ($30,000 initial savings + $3,000 period-two return + $3,600 period-three return) and will pay tax of $2,520 ($6,300 × 0.4), leaving him with $33,780 for consumption purposes ($36,300 – $2,520). The ratio of deferred consumption to immediate consumption in this case is 33,780:30,000 or 1.13, which is more than the ratio under an accretion-based income tax but less than the ratio under a cash flow tax. These differences arise from two factors. First, unlike a cash flow tax, a realization-based income tax reduces the initial amount of savings accumulated in period one by the 40 percent tax rate that it applies at T(0) to the wages of $50,000. Under a cash flow tax, this amount is not taxed until T(2). The taxpayer is thus able to earn an additional $4,200 over two periods on the $20,000 in tax that he must pay at T(0) under a realization-based income tax. The after-tax amount of $2,520 ($4,200 × 0.6) at T(2) represents the difference between the after-tax returns under the two bases ($36,300 – $33,780). Second, although both an accretion income tax and a realization-based income tax require the payment of $20,000 of tax at T(0), the former taxes the period-one return of $3,000 on the two-year asset at T(1) and the latter does not tax it until T(2). Under the realization-based tax, therefore, the taxpayer is able to earn an additional $120 in period three on the $1,200 that under an accretion-based income tax he would have to pay as tax at T(1). The after-tax amount of $72 ($120 × 0.6) at T(2) represents the difference between the after-tax returns under the two bases ($33,780 – $33,708).

The ratio of deferred to immediate consumption under a realization-based income tax increases with the period of deferral but can never be equal to the ratio under a cash flow tax because of the accumulation of savings out of after-tax dollars. If the period of deferral is long enough, however, the present value of any tax on the return to savings can be low enough to ensure that a realization-based income tax approximates a yield-exemption approach to cash flow taxation, which is equivalent to a cash flow tax implemented through a deduction for savings. See the text accompanying notes 37-44 supra.

56 See, in particular, Brown, supra note 45; Fellows, supra note 37; and Shakow, supra note 45.

57 The case for a cash flow tax consists in no small part of a case against tax-policy makers for failing to implement the accretion ideal. The distortions and inequities that arise from the combination of realization, accretion, and cash flow elements under the existing system are seen as being insurmountable in the face of liquidity and valuation concerns. In this context, piecemeal introduction of accretion elements may only aggravate existing distortions and inequities or create new ones without generating benefits sufficient to outweigh them.

58 The focus here is on deferral that arises with the recognition of revenue on a realization basis. The problem of deferral created by the application of the realization basis to financial instruments is discussed infra in the text that accompanies notes 62-133.

59 See Simon, supra note 33, at 1018.

60 Simon, ibid., states that "all of the complexities of the current system that Professor Andrews cites are complexities associated with trying to achieve some degree of horizontal and vertical equity within the nonaccrual system without wholly giving up the efficiency goal in the process." To some extent, the failure to focus on equity and distributional considerations may be attributed to (1) the use of a cash flow taxation approach for the retirement savings of individuals and (2) the enormous market presence of tax-exempt retirement savings funds and financial intermediaries. For the vast majority of individuals, the dollar limits on cash flow treatment of retirement savings is more than adequate for their entire pool of savings. In fact, the limits operate as effective exemptions from income tax treatment of wealth increments in much the same way as would exemption levels under a direct wealth tax. Income tax treatment applies only to the savings pool that is left, which tends to be invested through financial intermediaries. The combination of cash flow taxation and the use of taxable intermediaries tends to obscure the equity and efficiency considerations otherwise presented by simple, direct investments that generate wealth increments for individuals.

61 Strnad, supra note 27, at 1820-21 and footnote 7.

62 Assume, once again, that a taxpayer receives $50,000 in wages in period one and is subject to a 40 percent income tax rate on that amount. At the end of period one, T(0), the taxpayer invests the $30,000 of after-tax wages in an asset that provides a 10 percent riskless return for periods two and three compounded annually at T(1) and paid at T(2). In this case, the total pre-tax return to the taxpayer is $6,300, but the after-tax return under an accretion-based income tax is $72 less than the return under a realization-based system. Under the former system, the taxpayer must spread the total return over periods two and three and pay tax at T(1) and T(2) on the allocated amount. In effect, the terms of the investment indicate that $3,000 should be allocated ex ante to period two ($30,000 × 0.1) and $3,300 to period three ($33,000 × 0.1). The taxpayer must pay $1,200 in tax on the $3,000 increment to wealth that arises in period two. In period three, the taxpayer earns $3,300 on the $33,000 ($30,000 initial capital + $3,000 period one return that is capitalized or compounded at T(1)) that is effectively reinvested in the asset and must pay tax of $1,320 on that return ($3,300 × 0.4). At T(2), the taxpayer has $33,780 after tax ($30,000 initial capital + $6,300 return for periods two and three less $2,520 of tax paid at T(2) in respect of the same periods). This return is reduced, however, by a further $72, which represents the forgone after-tax return on the $1,200 of tax ($1,200 × 0.1 × 0.6) that had to be paid at T(1) on the $3,000 return for period two. In short, because no part of the $3,000 return was paid in that period, the taxpayer must find other equity funds to satisfy the tax liability or must borrow the necessary funds. Thus there is a cost of capital in the form of either an opportunity cost or a borrowing cost, which is assumed for the sake of convenience to also be the riskless 10 percent rate of return on the investment asset. That cost on an after-tax basis ($1,200 × 0.1 × 0.6 = $72) reduces the after-tax return on the two-period investment ($3,780 – $72 = $3,708).

Relative to an accretion-based income tax, a realization-based income tax provides preferential treatment for the two-year asset paying the $6,300 return at T(2). In this case, the taxpayer does not have to pay tax at T(1), since the $3,000 return allocable to period two is not realized until T(2). As a result, the taxpayer has an additional $1,200 to invest at T(1) at an assumed rate of return of 10 percent. At T(2), the taxpayer realizes the $6,300 return on the two-period investment and must pay $2,520 in tax ($6,300 × 0.4); he is left, accordingly, with an after-tax amount of $33,780 for consumption or reinvestment ($30,000 initial capital + 3,780 after-tax return; that is, $6,300 × 0.6). The additional $72 is effectively the after-tax amount of the return of $120 earned on the $1,200 that under an accretion-based tax would have been paid as tax at T(1) on the $3,000 increment to wealth allocable to period two ($1,200 × 0.1 × 0.6). Tax of $48 must be paid on the additional return, and this tax increases the amount of tax paid by the taxpayer ($2,520 + $48 = $2,578). However, the additional tax does not compensate the government completely for the $120 that it would have received had the $1,200 of tax been paid at T(1). In short, the taxpayer must ultimately pay the $1,200 in tax, but he, and not the government, receives the 10 percent pre-tax return that the $1,200 earns between T(1) and T(2). The taxpayer is thereby able to retain the after-tax return for the period of deferral ($120 × 0.1 × 0.6).

63 The effective tax rate under a realization-based income tax is *TR*/(1 + *r*)*n*, where *TR* is the nominal tax rate, *r* is the discount rate, and *n* is the number of taxation periods. In the example in note 62 supra, the use of a realization-based income tax rather than an accretion-based income tax reduces the effective tax rate from the nominal rate of 40 percent to 36 percent (0.4/1.1), where *r* is 10 percent and *n* is 1. This reduction is expressed clearly in another analogy for deferral, tax-debt forgiveness; see Fellows, supra note 37, at 731-32. Under an accretion-based income tax, the taxpayer in the example in note 62 would be required to pay $1,200 of tax at T(1) on the $3,000 return accrued over period two. Under a realization-based income tax, the taxpayer would be required to pay the $1,200 of tax at T(2). The present value of this payment at T(1) is $1,090.91, which represents the amount that the taxpayer must set aside to have $1,200 to pay the tax at T(2). The difference of $109.09 is effectively a forgiveness of a portion of the tax debt that under an accretion-based income tax is due at T(1). The ratio of the present value of the $1,200 tax due at T(2) under a realization-based income tax to the present value of the payment due at T(1) under an accretion-based income tax is 0.90909 ($1,090.91/$1,200). If the full nominal tax rate of 40 percent requires payment of $1,200 at T(1), the payment of $1,200 at T(2) is equal to a 36 percent effective rate (40 percent × 0.90909).

64 See, for example, Fellows, supra note 37, at 731. This analogy is apparent in the difference between the effective after-tax returns under an accretion-based income tax and a realization-based income tax. This difference is equal, in the example in note 63 supra, to the after-tax return on the amount of tax that is payable on an increment to wealth if the payment is deferred until realization. The return forgone under a realization-based tax arises under a full accretion tax because the tax must be paid at T(1) even though the return accrued for period two is unrealized (a period-two return of $3,000 on the two-year asset). The realization-based income tax permits the taxpayer to earn the after-tax return on the amount of tax that would otherwise be due at T(1). In the case of the two-year asset, without

changes in market conditions, this amount is equal to $72 ($1,200 of deferred tax × 0.6). By deferring the payment of tax at T(1) on the accrued return, the government can be said to have loaned the funds to the taxpayer until payment is due on realization of the return at T(2). By not charging interest on this implicit loan, the government forgoes the market rate of return that it would otherwise have earned on the deferred tax ($1,200 × 0.1 = 120) and permits the taxpayer to earn that return. Tax paid on the return is insufficient to compensate for the opportunity cost of capital borne by the government.

Other analogies are the forgiveness of a tax debt and the exemption of the yield on the deferred taxes. See Fellows, supra note 37, at 731-33, and supra note 63.

65 Shuldiner, supra note 15, at 249, refers to undifferentiated deferral as "pure deferral." Pure deferral occurs if either expected or unexpected gain or loss is recognized on realization and realization occurs after the period in which the amount can be considered to have arisen.

Consider once again the two-year asset described in note 62 supra. If the market conditions that prevail at T(0) remain constant over the term of the investment, the asset will have a value $33,000 at T(1) and $36,300 at T(2). This value is attributable to the initial capital of $30,000 plus the $3,000 return that has accrued at T(1) and the $3,600 return that has accrued at T(2). To state the matter in another way, the value of the asset at T(0) is equal to the discounted present value of the right to receive $36,300 at T(2), compounded annually at T(1). Since the discount rate is equal to the riskless rate of return of 10 percent at T(0), the value of the asset at that time is $30,000. At T(1), the asset will have a value of $33,000, which is equal to the discounted present value of the right to receive $36,300 at T(2) (again assuming a 10 percent discount rate). At T(2), the time for payment will have arrived and the value of the asset will be equal to the $36,300 owing at that time.

If market conditions change over the term of the investment, however, these values will change. Assume, for example, that market conditions change as of T(1) so that the value of the asset is $34,000; that is, the present value of the right to receive $36,300 at T(2) is now $34,000 and not $33,000. Under an accretion-based income tax that brings to account all changes in value of an asset occurring in a taxable period, the taxpayer must pay tax on both the expected gain of $3,000 that has accrued in period two and the unexpected gain of $1,000 that has arisen because of the change in market conditions. The taxpayer is thus liable for tax of $1,600 at T(1) ($4,000 × 0.4). The cost base of the asset increases to its fair market value of $34,000 to reflect taxation of the $4,000 gain, and at T(2) further tax of $920 must be paid on a further gain of $2,300 ($2,300 × 0.4) that has accrued in period three. This gain consists of the $36,300 increase in value realized as proceeds of disposition on termination of the investment less the $34,000 cost base from T(1). The result is an after-tax amount from the investment of $33,700 ($30,000 initial capital + $6,300 gain accrued over the two-year term – $2,520 of tax paid). However, this return must be reduced by the after-tax return forgone on the $1,600 of tax that was paid at T(1) on both the $3,000 expected gain for that period and the $1,000 unexpected gain. That reduction, which is equal to $96 ($1,600 × 0.1 × 0.6), results in an after-tax return of $3,684, or $24 less than the after-tax return would have been under an accretion-based tax that recognized only expected gains as they accrued. This difference is attributable to the taxation of the $1,000 unexpected gain at T(1) rather than T(2), when it was effectively realized as part of the \$3,300 expected gain for period three. Because of the taxation of that \$1,000 gain at T(2), the taxpayer is required to forgo the after-tax return of \$24 on an additional \$400 of tax ($\$400 \times 0.1 \times 0.6 = \$24$). This amount is the difference between the after-tax return under an accretion-based income tax that recognizes only expected gains on an accrual basis and an accretion-based income tax that recognizes both expected and unexpected gains on that basis (an after-tax return of \$3,708 versus an after-tax return of \$3,684).

66 Shuldiner, supra note 15. See also Scarborough, supra note 1, who draws on Shuldiner's analytical framework.

67 Shuldiner, supra note 15, at 249-55.

68 Ibid.

69 Scarborough, supra note 1.

70 But see Hariton, supra note 25, at 784, footnote 18, who argues that the return in excess of the riskless rate is payment for the assumption of risk and not compensation for the use of money. He develops this point further in David P. Hariton, "New Rules on Bifurcating Debt—A Mistake?" (April 15, 1991), 58 *Tax Notes* 235-39. Hariton argues that the risk premium should be eligible for capital gain treatment and not be treated as interest. But see Lawrence Lokken, "New Rules on Bifurcating Contingent Debt—A Good Start" (April 29, 1991), 58 *Tax Notes* 495-504, who argues that the risk premium on contingent debt should be treated as interest in the same manner as nominal interest that includes the premium. Hariton's distinction is largely irrelevant for timing purposes. A risk premium is part of the expected return associated with a financial instrument that should be recognized on an accrual basis. Otherwise taxpayers are provided with the benefit of anticipated deferral. To the extent that the actual payoff is greater or less than the premium and any pure time-value return, the holder has realized unexpected gain or loss attributable to the successful or unsuccessful assumption of a bet, which includes the chance of default by the issuer. The character issue can be eliminated by treating all payoffs on financial instruments on income account.

71 The most common assumption is that of a constant yield. See the text that accompanies notes 126-135 in chapter 5.

72 Shuldiner, supra note 15, at 249.

73 Ibid.

74 Ibid.

75 See, for example, ibid., at 250-55.

76 This is the example described in note 65 supra.

77 Stated differently, this assumption means that the value of the bond is assumed to increase on "a constant-yield basis." See Shuldiner, supra note 15, at 251 and footnote 19.

78 Scarborough, supra note 1.

79 See Shuldiner, supra note 15, at 252-53.

80 The total after-tax return under a realization-based income tax is \$4,158 (\$6,300 unexpected gain + \$630 pre-tax return on the deferred payment – \$2,772 tax payment due at T(3)). The total after-tax return under an accretion-based tax is

$4,006.80 ([$6,300 unexpected gain – $2,520 tax payment due at T(2) = $3,780 after-tax return] + [$3,780 × 0.1 pre-tax return × 0.6 after-tax return = $226.80]). The difference between the two after-tax returns is $151.20, which is the after-tax return on the interest-free loan provided in the form of the $2,520 deferred tax payable at T(3) under a realization-based income tax.

81 This same result holds if the parties do not provide an explicit rate of return on the deferred payment of the gain. In that case, there is an implicit time-value return equal to the market discount rate, which means that the present value of the $6,300 gain determined at T(2) but paid at T(3) is $5,727.27. The implicit time-value return embedded in the $6,300 payment at T(3) is $572.73. Under an accretion-based income tax, tax of $2,290.91 must be paid at T(2) on the $5,727.27 gain. Further tax of $229.09 must be paid at T(3) on the implicit interest of $572.73. Thus the total after-tax return is $3,780 ($5,727.27 + 572.73 – $2,520 tax). Under a realization-based income tax that requires the recognition of gain only when it is received in cash, both the $5,727.27 gain and the $572.73 implicit time-value return are not taxed until T(3), when $2,520 in tax must be paid ($6,300 × 0.4 = $2,520). The total after-tax return is again $3,780, but the taxpayer under an accretion-based income tax must factor in the forgone return on the $2,290.91 of tax on the $5,727.27 gain that must be paid at T(2). This forgone return of $137.45 ($2,290.91 × 0.1 × 0.6) reduces the total after-tax return to $3,642.55 and represents the value of the deferral benefit or interest-free loan of $2,290.91 under a realization-based income tax.

82 This difference in returns and in the associated deferral is also evident in the example of the two-year bond with an expected time-value return of $6,300 described in note 65 supra. In that case, the holder also assumes the risk that market interest rates will vary over the term of the bond and affect its value. This assumption of risk is equivalent to a bet on future interest rate movements that, in the example, favoured the taxpayer and gave rise to an unexpected gain of $1,000 at T(1). See supra note 65. Under an accretion-based income tax, that gain must be recognized at T(1) as it is reflected in the increase in the value of the instrument. A realization-based income tax provides the benefit of deferred recognition when payment under the terms of the bond is made at T(2).

83 Shuldiner, supra note 15.

84 Ibid., at 258-65. See, more generally, Charlotte Crane, "Some Explicit Thinking About Implicit Taxes" (Spring 1999), 52 *SMU Law Review* 339-72.

85 Shuldiner, supra note 15, at 258.

86 As the tax benefit becomes capitalized in a higher price for the tax-favoured instruments, the pre-tax return decreases, an outcome that reduces the attractiveness of the instruments for lower-bracket taxpayers.

87 Shuldiner, supra note 15, at 261-62.

88 Ibid., at 258-59.

89 See the example described infra note 90.

90 Assume, for example, that the taxpayer in the example in the text that accompanies note 79 supra loses the coin flip and has a ($6,300) loss or liability at T(2). Under an accretion-based income tax with a 40 percent tax rate, the after-tax amount of this loss is $3,780 ($6,300 × 0.6). If the taxpayer can use the loss

immediately to reduce other taxable income, the result is a current tax saving of $2,520. Accordingly, the after-tax amount of the loss equals the $6,300 pre-tax amount less the $2,520 tax saving. Under a realization-based income tax that does not recognize the loss until payment one period later, at T(3), the present value of the same tax saving at T(2) (assuming a 10 percent discount rate) is only $2,290.91 ($2,520/1.1) and the present value of the after-tax amount of the loss increases to $4,009.09 ($6,300 – $2,290.91).

91 Consider again the example in the text that accompanies note 79 supra. If the coin flip is in the taxpayer's favour, the gain at T(2) is $6,300. Under a realization-based income tax, the gain will not be recognized until one period later at T(3), when cash is exchanged between the counterparties. If the parties provide for an interest charge at a 10 percent rate on the gain to reflect the value of deferred payment, the after-tax amount of the gain increases from $4,006.80 (the value of the after-tax gain taxed at T(2) and reinvested until T(3)) to $4,158.

92 Shuldiner, supra note 15, at 258-59.

93 Ibid., at 263.

94 See, in particular, David F. Bradford, "Fixing Realization Accounting: Symmetry, Consistency and Correctness in the Taxation of Financial Instruments" (Summer 1995), 50 *Tax Law Review* 731-85.

95 Shuldiner, supra note 15, at 255-65, recognizes the significance of these opportunities and even acknowledges the need for accretion-based recognition as the most effective response. His focus, however, is on expected-return taxation as a means of addressing the adverse consequences of anticipated deferral.

96 Bradford, supra note 94, at 739-69. See also the comments on Bradford's article in Joseph Bankman, "Commentary" (Summer 1995), 50 *Tax Law Review* 787-96; and Diane Ring, "Commentary" (Summer 1995), 50 *Tax Law Review* 797-802.

97 Supra notes 7-18 and accompanying text.

98 Bradford, supra note 94, at 739-42. For a discussion of the early development of representative strategies designed to realize opportunities for timing arbitrage under US income tax law, see Frank V. Battle Jr., "Corporate Tax Shelters, Financial Engineering and the Colgate Case" (December 1997), 75 *Taxes: The Tax Magazine* 692-705, at 693-94.

99 See the text that accompanies note 76 supra.

100 Take the same two-year bond described in the text that accompanies note 76 supra (10 percent return compounded annually at T(1) and T(2)). A taxpayer could issue a bond of this kind and use the proceeds to acquire another, identical bond. Under asymmetric rules that provide for accrual recognition of interest expense and realization-based recognition of interest income, the taxpayer can deduct $3,000 of interest expense accrued in period one at T(1) and a further $3,300 of interest expense accrued in period two at T(2). He does not have to recognize the offsetting interest income for periods one and two until realization at T(2). Given full loss offsets against other taxable income that is also subject to a 40 percent tax rate, the taxpayer can realize a tax saving of $1,200 by deducting $3,000 of the interest expense at T(1) and creating a loss that shelters the taxable income from tax. He can then reinvest the savings for one period and earn the after-tax riskless rate of return (6 percent) until T(2) ($1,200 × 0.06 = $72). At T(2), the taxpayer recognizes

$6,300 of interest income on the purchased two-year bond and deducts $3,300 of interest expense that accrued on the issued bond in period two. He pays tax of $1,200 on the net return of $3,000 ($3,000 × 0.4 = $1,200) at T(2), thus recapturing the tax on other taxable income that was forgone at T(1) because of the accelerated deduction of the $3,000 of interest expense on the issued two-year bond. The accelerated deduction, however, produces a net tax benefit of $72, which is equal to the after-tax return on the $1,200 of tax deferred from T(1) to T(2). This tax benefit provides a positive value for offsetting short and long positions in the two-year bond. The tax arbitrage profit arises solely because of the asymmetric recognition rules for interest expense and income on a two-year bond.

101 It is possible to substitute an acquisition of shares for the lending side of this transaction. A pure avoidance opportunity arises to the extent that interest on the borrowing side is deductible on an accrual basis and expected gains on the lending side (share acquisition) are recognized on realization. Instead of requiring the accrual recognition of the expected return on the shares, the conventional response has been a limitation on the deductibility of interest on borrowed funds to acquire shares. This kind of limitation has a potentially adverse impact on risk taking, and it is questionable in the context of the use of interest on borrowed money to acquire shares, given the role of the corporate income tax as a proxy for the accrual recognition of expected gains at the shareholder level. For an expression of the conventional case for limitations on the deductibility of interest and a summary of country practices, see Brian J. Arnold, "General Report," in International Fiscal Association, *Cahiers de droit fiscal international*, vol. 79b, *Deductibility of Interest and Other Financing Charges in Computing Income* (Deventer, the Netherlands: Kluwer Law and Taxation, 1994), 491-541, at 505-8. See also Brian J. Arnold and Tim Edgar, "Interest Deductibility," in Roy D. Hogg and Jack M. Mintz, eds., *The Tax Effects on the Financing of Medium and Small Public Corporations* (Kingston, Ont.: Queen's University, John Deutsch Institute for the Study of Economic Policy, 1992), 59-78, at 70-71; and Michael J. McIntyre, "Tracing Rules and the Deduction for Interest Payments: A Justification and a Critique of Recent US Tracing Rules" (Fall 1992), 39 *The Wayne Law Review* 67-120. For a contrary view, see Robert Couzin, "Discussant's Remarks," in *The Tax Effects on the Financing of Medium and Small Public Corporations*, supra, at 79-84. See also E. Seiper, "Business Tax Reform," in John Head, ed., *Changing the Tax Mix* (Sydney: Australian Tax Research Foundation, 1986), 279-314, at 289-98, describing the equilibrium effects that may offset the benefit of an unrestricted interest deduction in the context of leveraged investments in tax shelters; Joseph Bankman, "The Case Against Passive Investments: A Critical Appraisal of the Passive Loss Restrictions (November 1989), 42 *Stanford Law Review* 15-49; and Cecily W. Rock and Daniel N. Shaviro, "Passive Losses and the Improvement of Net Income Measurement" (Summer 1987), 7 *Virginia Tax Review* 1-55, for discussions of the effects of the US passive loss rules on risk taking.

102 Ring, supra note 96, at 798-99. See Shuldiner, supra note 15, at 256, footnote 43, who notes that the effective-gain tax rate as a percentage of the loss tax rate under any straddle strategy depends on the discount rate and the number of periods of deferral of the gain position in relation to the recognition of the loss side. He expresses this relationship in the following formula:

$$\textit{gain rate/loss rate} = 1/(1 + r)n,$$

where r is the discount rate, and n is the number of taxation periods of deferral.

In the example in note 100 supra, the effective-gain tax rate on the $3,000 of period-one interest income expressed as a percentage of the loss rate on the same period-one interest expense is 90.90 percent (1/[(1 + 0.1]1). The lower rate arises because of the one-period deferral of the interest income. Owing to the one-period deferral, the effective-gain tax rate—that is, the effective tax rate on the interest income—is only 36 percent (40 percent/(1 + 0.1)1). The effective tax rate on the interest expense, however, is equal to the full statutory rate, since the expense is deducted in full as it accrues. The ratio of the gain tax rate to the loss tax rate is 0.36:0.4, or 90 percent.

103 Bradford, supra note 94, at 743-47.

104 Ibid., at 748-49.

105 Ibid., at 750-53 and 759-61.

106 Ibid., at 750-53.

107 But see Gergen, "Apocalypse Not?" supra note 24, at 836-40, who emphasizes that transaction costs can be important constraints on the exploitation of tax-avoidance opportunities.

108 Bradford, supra note 94, at 759-61.

109 Bankman, supra note 96, at 789.

110 Scarborough, supra note 1, at 1045. Another possible timing arbitrage opportunity would be the issue of a two-year bond subject to accrual recognition and the use of the proceeds to acquire a periodic bond subject to realization recognition. Provided that the realization event on the periodic bond occurred after the time of accrual on the two-year bond, a fully taxable taxpayer could realize an arbitrage opportunity by taking offsetting positions with the two instruments and realizing a tax benefit through the accelerated deduction of expense on the two-year bond. Again, any disadvantage from the early recognition of revenue could be negated by having a tax-exempt counterparty hold the other side of the relevant financial instruments.

111 Bradford, supra note 94, at 759-61.

112 See the text that accompanies notes 247-279 in chapter 6 for a discussion of the extension of accrual recognition to the expected gains on shares and, in particular, the constraints that prevent an extension of this kind and the use of the corporate income tax as a proxy.

113 The value of a riskless instrument is equal to the discounted present value of the promised future payments and is, therefore, solely a function of the time value of money. This value depends on just two variables: (1) the instrument's term to maturity and (2) the riskless rate of return or market discount rate demanded by investors as the price of forgone consumption. As the time of maturity (or any periodic payment date) approaches, the value of the instrument will approach the amount of the promised payment. Accrual recognition of time-value returns serves as an accretion-based system for gains and losses in a riskless world largely because the possibility of unexpected gains and losses is eliminated. The elimination of risk means that time-value returns are the only available returns and that changes in the value of a financial instrument can only be a function of the passage of time. Changes in the riskless rate of return, however, can result in changes in the value of a riskless asset that produce unexpected gain or loss.

114 In theory, accurate measurement should take into account the term structure of interest rates, which involves the imputation of time-value returns at a rate that is not constant over the term of a financial instrument. See Joseph Bankman and William A. Klein, "Accurate Taxation of Long-Term Debt: Taking into Account the Term Structure of Interest" (Winter 1989), 44 *Tax Law Review* 335-48; and Theodore S. Sims, "Long-Term Debt, the Term Structure of Interest and the Case for Accrual Taxation" (Winter 1992), 47 *Tax Law Review* 313-75. The text that accompanies notes 126-135 in chapter 5 discusses the significance of this insight and the timing arbitrage opportunities that it reveals, given an accrual recognition system that imputes interest at a constant rate.

115 See, for example, Mark P. Gergen, "The Effects of Price Volatility and Strategic Trading Under Realization, Expected-Return and Retrospective Taxation" (Winter 1994), 49 *Tax Law Review* 209-69; and Strnad, supra note 27, at 1868-85.

116 Shuldiner, supra note 15, at 255-57, uses the term "the timing option" to describe risk arbitrage. See also Strnad, supra note 27, at 1825-30. The term was coined in the seminal work of George M. Constanides, "Capital Market Equilibrium with Personal Tax" (May 1983), 51 *Econometrica* 611-30, as cited by Strnad, ibid., at 1879; and Shuldiner, ibid., at 250, footnote 16. The value of the timing option is explored in detail in Stiglitz, supra note 11.

117 See the text that accompanies note 79 supra.

118 The expected payoff is determined by first taking the sum of the two possible outcomes and the payment entitlements they provide; that is, \$36,300 (\$42,600 × 0.5 = \$21,300 + \$30,000 × 0.5 = \$15,000). Since this return equals the expected payment obligation of the taxpayer, the expected return on the financial instrument is zero.

119 Note 102 supra provides a more detailed explanation of these tax effects.

120 Shuldiner, supra note 15, at 256. The value of instruments that provide the timing option is a function of the difference between the effective tax rates on unexpected gains and the after-tax amount of unexpected losses. In the example discussed in the text that accompanies notes 117-119 supra, the effective tax rate on an unexpected gain results in an after-tax return of \$4,009.09 and the effective tax rate on an unexpected loss results in an after-tax amount of \$3,789. One-half of this difference, or \$229.09 × 0.5 = \$114.54, represents the value of the timing option. The absolute difference between the after-tax amounts of \$229.09 must be reduced by one-half to reflect the fact that a positive payoff and a negative payoff are equally likely to occur.

121 In fact, the timing option depends on three features of an instrument: (1) its risk, (2) its term to maturity, and (3) the extent to which it may be traded at low transaction costs. See Strnad, supra note 27, at 1868-79. The text that accompanies notes 280-315 in chapter 5 discusses the significance of these features for the design of an effective response to the timing option.

122 Shuldiner, supra note 15, at 256, footnote 39. See also Reed H. Shuldiner, "Consistency and the Taxation of Financial Products" (December 1992), 70 *Taxes: The Tax Magazine* 781-92, at 786.

123 In this context, a "straddle transaction" consists of offsetting long and short positions that provide offsetting cash flows. It is a pure avoidance opportunity in the sense that although the offsetting cash flows provide a nil pre-tax return, the

tax saving associated with the accelerated recognition of the losses makes the transaction profitable.

124 See the example in the text that accompanies notes 117-120 supra for an explanation of the tax benefit that arises from the early closeout of a losing position. The principal difference between this strategy and a straddle transaction is that in the latter case the taxpayer in the example would assume not one but both sides of the bet; that is, he would enter into one financial contract under which he promised to pay $36,300 in return for the right to receive either $42,600 or $30,000, depending on the outcome of a coin flip, and offset the gain or loss under that contract by entering into an identical contract under which he would receive the right to $36,300 in return for his promise to pay either $42,600 or $30,000, depending on the outcome of a coin flip.

125 Shuldiner, supra note 15, at 257.

126 Ibid.

127 Supra notes 103-114 and accompanying text. See also Shuldiner, "Consistency and the Taxation of Financial Products," supra note 122.

128 This is the concept of consistency as used by Shuldiner, "Consistency and the Taxation of Financial Products," supra note 122.

129 See, for example, section 1092 of the Internal Revenue Code of 1986, as amended (herein referred to as "IRC"), which is discussed in the text that accompanies notes 285 and 325-336 in chapter 5.

130 Shuldiner, supra note 15, at 256.

131 For a discussion of the design of loss limitations, see Robert H. Scarborough, "Risk Diversification and the Design of Loss Limitations Under a Realization-Based Income Tax" (Spring 1993), 48 *Tax Law Review* 677-717; also see the text that accompanies notes 290-302 in chapter 5.

132 The relation between restrictions on the deductibility of losses and the risk associated with an investment was first described in Evsey Domar and Richard A. Musgrave, "Proportional Income Taxation and Risk Taking" (May 1944), 58 *Quarterly Journal of Economics* 388-422. See also Scarborough, supra note 131, for a discussion of the impact of different loss limitations on risk taking.

133 The text that accompanies notes 325-335 in chapter 5 discusses this issue in more detail.

134 See the text that accompanies notes 3-74 in chapter 2.

135 See the text that accompanies notes 3-4 in chapter 2.

136 As was noted in chapter 2 at note 13, this term is used by Peter F. Pope and Anthony G. Puxty, "What Is Equity? New Financial Instruments in the Interstices Between the Law, Accounting and Economics" (November 1991), 54 *Modern Law Review* 889-911, at 897.

137 Alvin C. Warren Jr., "The Corporate Interest Deduction: A Policy Evaluation" (July 1974), 83 *The Yale Law Journal* 1585-1619, at 1586-89.

138 The seminal work that articulates this model is Adolph A. Berle and Gardiner C. Means, *The Modern Corporation and Private Property* (New York: MacMillan, 1933).

139 For a critical review of the economic literature, see Robert Flannigan, "The Economic Structure of the Firm" (1995), vol. 33, no. 1 *Osgoode Hall Law Journal*

105-50. See also William W. Bratton Jr., "The New Economic Theory of the Firm: Critical Perspectives from History" (July 1989), 42 *Stanford Law Review* 1471-1527; William W. Bratton Jr., "The Nexus of Contracts Corporation: A Critical Appraisal" (March 1989), 74 *Cornell Law Review* 407-65; and William A. Klein, "The Modern Business Organization: Bargaining Under Constraints" (July 1982), 91 *The Yale Law Journal* 1521-64.

140 Armen A. Alchian and Harold Demsetz, "Production, Information Costs, and Economic Organization" (December 1972), 62 *The American Economic Review* 777-95; Eugene F. Fama, "Agency Problems and the Theory of the Firm" (April 1980), 88 *Journal of Political Economy* 288-307; and Michael C. Jensen and William H. Meckling, "Agency Costs and the Theory of the Firm" (October 1976), 3 *Journal of Financial Economics* 305-60. This literature is reviewed in Daniel Thornton, "A Look at Agency Theory for the Novice—Part 1" (November 1984), 117 *CA Magazine* 90-97; and ". . . Part 2" (January 1985), 118 *CA Magazine* 93-100.

141 These problems result from informational asymmetries that arise when corporate managers or insiders know more about the firm than do outside investors who hold its debt or equity. Corporate managers may benefit personally at the expense of outside investors through the enjoyment of lavish expense accounts or through suboptimal performance ("shirking"). Debt holders must also be aware of managers' opportunities to transfer wealth at their expense. Thus corporate managers might undertake high-risk projects with slight opportunities for large gains and the possibility of disastrous losses. Debt holders suffer relative to shareholders because their return is fixed. Unlike shareholders, they cannot share in the upside, but they bear a greater risk of the loss of their contributed capital. Corporate managers who hold an equity stake and whose interests, accordingly, are aligned with those of the shareholders may prefer these risky projects because of the opportunities they offer to realize an unlimited upside through leveraging of the debt holders' capital. Similar transfers may occur more directly through the borrowing of funds to pay dividends or return capital to the shareholders. Corporate managers can mitigate some of these risks and lower the cost of capital by agreeing to monitoring arrangements and limitations on their actions that are designed to align their interests with those of the investors. The simple point is that both shareholders and debt holders incur agency problems and in the absence of sufficient protection demand an increased return to compensate for the risk.

For a review of the economics literature on the principal-agency relationship in the corporate context and the relevance of that literature for the conventional distinction between debt and equity underlying tax law and financial accounting, see Pope and Puxty, supra note 136, at 900-2.

142 Some of this literature is reviewed in Pope and Puxty, ibid., at 896-99. See also Warren, supra note 137, at 1594-96. Consistently with the non-tax legal and economics literature, this strain of accounting literature reflects alternative views of the corporation based on models that characterize the enterprise as "an autonomous economic entity" operated for the benefit of a class of participants that includes both debt and equity investors, as well as suppliers, employees, and customers.

143 Warren, supra note 137, at 1592.

144 Hariton, supra note 25, at 775, states that "equity and debt are both claims upon the assets of a corporation, and both are acquired in exchange for capital. The only economic distinction between them is the variability of their returns."

145 But see Adam O. Emmerich, "Hybrid Instruments and the Debt-Equity Distinction in Corporate Taxation" (Winter 1985), 52 *The University of Chicago Law Review* 118-48, at 122, who makes the point that "it is inaccurate to characterize all shareholders as necessarily bearing more risk than all creditors. The degree of risk to which an investor is exposed, and the potential payoff that he can expect, can vary more between the bond of one company and the bond of another than between the debt and stock of the same company." See also David P. Hariton, "Distinguishing Between Equity and Debt in the New Financial Environment" (Spring 1994), 49 *Tax Law Review* 499-524, who argues that the distinction between debt and equity should be based on an assessment of the relative risk borne by holders of the securities of the same issuer.

146 Warren, supra note 137, at 1588.

147 "The creditor thus hopes to recoup an amount somewhere between zero and the promised payment. The owner [equity investor] is in the same position, except that, because his return is not limited contractually, the probability distribution governing his return has no fixed upper bound. This, however, is more a theoretical than a practical difference." Emmerich, supra note 145, at 123, footnote 24.

148 Ibid.

149 Viewed ex ante, the range of probable payoffs on an equity investment should provide an expected payoff that is at least equal to the payoff on a riskless asset. Increased volatility in the range of probable payoffs results in ex post payoffs that are either greater than or less than the expected payoff. This difference represents unexpected gain or loss. The volatility of the return on equity is attributable in large part to the fact that it is eliminated before the expected return on debt in the event that the value of the corporate assets is less than the expected payoff on the debt and equity capital combined. Conversely, the equity investors benefit from any value in excess of that payoff. Emmerich, supra note 145, at 123-24, footnote 26, observes that "[t]he entrepreneur's investment is volatile because he purchases an interest in the portion of the corporation's return that is the first to be eliminated if returns are less than expected, while he also captures all the greater-than-expected returns." The increased upside in probable payoffs compensates for the higher probability of loss and combines to provide an expected return that approximates the riskless return. If the risk associated with a particular equity investment is non-unique in the sense that it is not diversifiable or if investors are risk averse, then in order to attract investors the expected return on equity must be greater than the return on riskless debt. This excess represents the required risk premium—that is, the amount of expected return in excess of the riskless rate required to compensate investors for bearing undiversifiable risk. For the same reasons, risky debt will have the same payoff characteristics as risky equity. "Blue-chip" or virtually riskless equity will provide a nominal and expected return that is close to the riskless rate and is predominantly time-value return. See Emmerich, ibid., at 123-24.

150 See, for example, Robert A. Santangelo, "Towards Reshaping the Debt-Equity Distinction" (Winter 1997), 23 *The Journal of Corporate Taxation* 312-41, at 332, where he states the following: "Financial theory informs us that there exists no principled distinction between corporate debt and corporate stock—both represent contractual claims, the value of which vary in relation to the value of the issuer's

assets. . . . There exists a spectrum of risk and return relationships that can be offered to potential investors and, correspondingly, an equally vast spectrum of claims that can be issued. Such claims differ in degree, not in kind."

151 "Both shareholders and creditors contribute capital in the expectation that the corporation will be able to use this capital productively and return it to them along with a share of the resulting gain." Emmerich, supra note 145, at 122-23.

152 Ibid., at 123-24 and footnotes 26-27. Santangelo, supra note 150, at 337-38, observes that "the value of corporate securities reflects the return on risk-free assets and an additional return that compensates the holder for bearing some measure of nondiversifiable business risk."

153 See the text that accompanies notes 126-151 in chapter 1 for a brief review of the concept of risk and diversification.

154 See the text that accompanies notes 88-107 in chapter 1.

155 Ibid. According to Santangelo, supra note 150, at 332-33, "[w]ell accepted financial theory indicates that any set of contingent payoffs—that is, payoffs that depend on the value of some other asset—can be valued as a mixture of simple options on that asset." Because the value of debt and equity depends on the value of the underlying corporate assets, it is possible to analyze the payoffs on both types of securities as a series of simple options.

156 William A. Klein and John C. Coffee Jr., *Business Organization and Finance: Legal and Economic Principles*, 6th ed. (Westbury, NY: Foundation Press, 1996), 46-49 and 297-301, provide some useful examples that illustrate, informally and intuitively, the essence of the embedded call or put options in a leveraged corporation. The examples that follow are very similar, as are the examples in the text that accompanies notes 55-57 in chapter 1.

157 See the text that accompanies notes 52-57 in chapter 1; and Santangelo, supra note 150, at 333-35.

158 See the text that accompanies notes 55-57 in chapter 1; and Santangelo, supra note 150, at 334-36.

159 According to option-pricing theory, the combined value of a long position in a riskless asset that pays a pure time-value return and a short position in a call or put option on corporate assets is affected by (1) the value of the assets, (2) the time to maturity, (3) the specified payoff on maturity, (4) the volatility of the value of the assets, and (5) the riskless rate of return. See the text that accompanies notes 87-106 supra; and Klein and Coffee, supra note 156, at 363, where they note that "the amount that [an option holder] must pay for the option depends on the variance of the expected outcomes for the value of the firm and on the market interest rate." Depending on the relationship between these variables, a corporate debt obligation may have risk and return characteristics that approximate those of a riskless asset or ownership of the corporate assets themselves. See Santangelo, supra note 150, at 336-37. The value of the corporate debt will approximate that of a riskless asset if the value of the underlying assets is virtually certain to exceed the specified payoff on the debt. In that case, the call option on the corporate assets is certain to be exercised and the option is so deep-in-the-money that it reflects a time-value return only. The corresponding put option in the same circumstances is worthless, and all of the return on the debt is attributable solely to the time

value of money. If the value of the assets is less than the specified payoff on the outstanding corporate debt, the value of the call option and the value of the debt is equivalent to the value of the assets. The debt holders are thereby the effective owners under the corresponding put option held by the shareholders.

160 Because of the embedded option, the value of corporate debt at any particular time is the lesser of (1) the specified payoff on the debt and (2) the value of the underlying corporate assets. Pope and Puxty, supra note 136, note that this relationship is captured in the accounting equation *assets = liabilities – equity*. Rewriting the variables as V = *assets* (value), P = *liabilities* (specified payoff), and C = *equity* (value of call option) reveals that $V = P + C$. Rearranging the variables and multiplying through reveals further that $P = V - C$. If P is less than V, the embedded option will capture the residual value and the debt holders will receive P. If P is greater than V, the embedded option will be worthless and the debt holders will receive V.

161 The equations described in note 160 supra reveal that *equity = assets – liabilities*. Substituting the same values for these variables (that is, V = *assets* [value], P = *liabilities* [specified payoff], and C = *equity* [value of call option]) reveals that $C = V - P$. If V is greater than P, the embedded call option held by the shareholders will have a value equal to the difference. If V is less than P, the embedded call option will be worthless.

162 See the text that accompanies notes 60-66 and 73-74 in chapter 2.

163 Franco Modigliani and Merton H. Miller, "The Cost of Capital, Corporation Finance and the Theory of Investment" (June 1958), 48 *The American Economic Review* 261-97; and Franco Modigliani and Merton H. Miller, "Reply to Heins and Sprenkle" (September 1969), 59 *The American Economic Review* 592-95. For a summary of the Modigliani-Miller thesis and the optimal capital structure literature, see Richard Brealey, Stewart Myers, Gordon Sick, and Ronald Giammarino, *Principles of Corporate Finance*, 2d Canadian ed. (Toronto: McGraw-Hill Ryerson, 1993), chapters 17 and 18; Douglas R. Emery, John D. Finnerty, and John Stowe, *Principles of Financial Management* (Upper Saddle River, NJ: Prentice-Hall, 1998), 424-35 and 440-45; and Klein and Coffee, supra note 156, at 332-65. See also Emmerich, supra note 145, at 134-39; and Michael S. Knoll, "Taxing Prometheus: How the Corporate Interest Deduction Discourages Innovation and Risk-Taking" (1993), vol. 38, no. 5 *Villanova Law Review* 1461-1516, at 1467-85.

164 This conclusion is commonly referred to as Modigliani and Miller's "proposition one." Their related "proposition two" is described infra in note 168. In addition to the absence of taxes, two other conditions must be present for "proposition one" to hold. First, there must be no additional transaction costs associated with personal borrowing as a substitute for corporate borrowing. Second, corporate investment policy must be fixed in the sense that it is independent of the composition of the capital structure. The relevance of these two additional conditions are apparent from the discussion that accompanies notes 165-183 infra.

165 Although there is some evidence of higher transaction costs or less advantageous borrowing terms for individuals, the weight of the evidence seems to support the plausible assumption that personal debt is a close substitute for corporate debt, particularly with the ready availability of margin accounts. For a brief discussion of the kinds of considerations that are relevant to the plausibility of the assumption of perfect substitutability of corporate and personal debt, see Klein and Coffee, supra note 156, at 342-43.

166 A simple example will illustrate this equivalence. Consider an investor whose opportunities consist of the securities issued by two corporations that are identical in all respects, other than their capital structures. Both corporations own assets that are expected to yield a perpetual income stream of $15,000 annually. One of the corporations (Xco) has an all equity-capital structure of 1,000 shares. The other corporation (Yco) has a debt-equity ratio of 1:2. Interest on the debt equals $5,000 annually. If the investor chooses to purchase 10 percent of the outstanding shares of Xco, he will realize an expected return of $1,500 ($15,000 × 0.1). The alternative is an acquisition of the same proportion of the debt and shares of Yco, which will also produce an expected return of $1,500. In this case, the expected return will consist of (1) $500 of interest income, which is 10 percent of the interest on the debt of Yco ($5,000 × 0.1 = $500), and (2) $1,000 of equity income, which is 10 percent of the total equity income after the interest expense of Yco ($15,000 – $5,000 = $10,000). The two alternative investment strategies provide the same expected payoffs, and the investor realizes the same return in either case. Accordingly, the investor will not pay more for the shares of the leveraged Yco than he will pay for the shares of the unleveraged Xco, which must, therefore, have the same value and costs. See the similar example in Brealey at al., supra note 163, at 428-30.

167 Assume in the example described in note 166 supra that the investor would prefer to assume more risk than that associated with a 10 percent investment in the shares of Xco or a 10 percent investment in the debt and shares of Yco. He acquires instead a 10 percent stake in the shares of Yco, which provides an expected return of $1,000 (10 percent of the $15,000 expected return on the underlying assets less 10 percent of the $5,000 of interest expense on the outstanding corporate debt). An alternative strategy is to borrow sufficient funds to acquire 10 percent of the shares of the unleveraged Xco. If the investor can borrow on the same terms as Yco (that is, if personal debt is available as a perfect substitute for corporate debt), the expected return on this alternative investment strategy is $1,000, consisting of (1) $1,500, which is 10 percent of the return on the total equity of Xco realized through the acquisition of the 10 percent equity stake less (2) $500 of interest expense on the borrowed funds used to acquire the shares of Xco. Since the expected payoffs on these investment alternatives are equivalent, an investor will not pay a premium for the shares of a leveraged corporation and the shares of Xco and Yco must be valued equivalently. The equivalence arises because the investor is able to replicate the payoff associated with the equity return of the leveraged corporation by substituting an appropriate amount of personal borrowing for corporate borrowing and using the borrowed funds to acquire shares of the unleveraged corporation.

168 According to Modigliani and Miller's "proposition two," a necessary implication of the irrelevance of corporate debt policy is the notion that the expected return on the shares of a leveraged corporation increases with the debt-equity ratio. See Brealey et al., supra note 163, at 434-37. The increase in expected return occurs as an offset to the increase in risk borne by the shareholders of a leveraged corporation. One can derive the precise amount of the increase in the expected rate of return necessary to offset the increase in risk from Modigliani and Miller's "proposition one." In particular, because the presence of corporate debt does not affect the expected operating income of the corporation or the total market value of its securities, the presence of borrowing does not affect the expected return on

the underlying assets (rA). The only thing that it does affect is the division of the return among investors. In general, it is possible to express this division as follows:

$$rA = (D/D + E \times rD) + (E/D + E \times rE),$$

where rA is the expected return on the underlying corporate assets, D is the market value of outstanding debt, E is the market value of outstanding equity, rD is the expected return on the debt, and rE is the expected return on the equity.

Rearranging the above equation to solve for rE reveals that

$$rE = rA + D/E\,(rA - rD).$$

This equation expresses Modigliani and Miller's "proposition two" in algebraic terms. In essence, the size of the increase in the expected return on shares of a leveraged corporation that is necessary to compensate shareholders for the increase in risk depends on the spread between the expected return on the underlying corporate assets (rA) and the expected return on debt of the corporation (rD). See Brealey et al., supra note 163, at 434-35. Because investors in a leveraged corporation require an increased nominal return to compensate them for the increased risk that they bear, the increase in the expected return on the shares of a leveraged corporation does not increase the value of those shares. The increase in the nominal return is reflected instead in an increased capitalization rate.

169 To return to the example described in note 166 supra, assume that Xco and Yco are both subject to a 40 percent corporate tax on operating income of $15,000. Xco has an all-equity capital structure (1,000 shares with a value of $100,000) and therefore must pay tax of $6,000 on taxable income of $15,000 ($15,000 × 0.4). Yco has a debt-equity ratio of 1:2 (debt with a value of $33,333.33 and 666.67 shares with a value of $66,666.67) and pays $5,000 of deductible interest on the debt ($33,333.33 × 0.15). Accordingly, Yco must pay tax of $4,000 on taxable income of $10,000 ($15,000 less $5,000 deductible interest expense × 0.4). The creditors and shareholders of Yco realize an increased after-tax return of $11,000 ($15,000 less $4,000 corporate tax), whereas the shareholders of Xco receive an after-tax return of $9,000 ($15,000 less $6,000 corporate tax). The $2,000 difference is attributable to the "tax shield" provided by the corporate interest deduction: that is, the saving of $2,000 of corporate tax on $5,000 of operating income distributed as deductible interest expense rather than non-deductible dividends ($5,000 × 0.4).

170 See Brealey et al., supra note 163, at 452-56, for a description of the calculation of the value of the tax shield. The calculation is generally based on two assumptions: (1) that a given amount of corporate debt is permanent, in the sense that it will be refinanced with future debt, and (2) that the tax shield presents the same risk as the debt itself and should be discounted at the same interest rate. Given these two assumptions, one can calculate the present value (PV) of the tax shield as

$$PV = Tc\,(rDD)/rD \text{ or } PV = TcD,$$

where Tc is the corporate income tax rate, rDD is the expected interest payments, and rD is the expected return on the corporate debt.

In the example described in note 169 supra, the PV of the tax shield for the leveraged corporation Yco would be $13,333.33 (0.4 [0.15(33,333.33)/0.15)] or 0.4 × 33,333.33). Since the tax shield is a corporate asset, the value of Yco is (1) the value of the corporation if the corporation is all-equity financed and (2) the PV of the tax shield ($100,000 + $13,333.33, assuming a before-tax capitalization rate of 0.15). This value is $13,333.33 greater than that of the unleveraged corporation, Xco. If debt is used to refinance outstanding equity, the additional value represented by the tax shield accrues to the remaining shareholders. See Brealey et al., ibid., at 453-55.

171 This literature is summarized in Brealey et al., ibid., at 451-66.

172 Merton H. Miller, "Debt and Taxes" (May 1977), 32 *Journal of Finance* 261-76.

173 For a clear description of these rate relationships and the biases they supposedly create under a classical corporate income tax, see American Law Institute, *Federal Income Tax Project: Integration of the Individual and Corporate Income Taxes—Reporter's Study of Integration* (Philadelphia: ALI, March 31, 1993), 21-46. The identified biases are (1) an incentive to invest in assets other than new corporate equity; (2) an incentive to raise corporate capital by issuing debt rather than equity; (3) an incentive to retain, rather than distribute, corporate earnings; and (4) an incentive to distribute corporate earnings in non-dividend transactions. See also Scholes and Wolfson, supra note 12, at chapters 15 and 18.

174 Miller first incorporated the impact of investor-level taxes in his revision of the original Modigliani-Miller view of the tax shield and its effect on capital structure. See Miller, supra note 172. See also Joseph E. Stiglitz, "Taxation, Corporate Financial Policy and the Cost of Capital" (February 1973), 2 *Journal of Public Economics* 1-34. Miller argued that the introduction of investor-level taxes at different rates on debt and equity means that there is no optimal capital structure for a particular corporation, but only an optimal capital structure for the corporate sector generally. Development of this conclusion begins with the simplifying premise that although equity returns are taxed at the investor level they are taxed at a low or even a zero rate, primarily because of the imposition of a capital gains tax on realization. Even under this relatively strict condition, however, there is a wide range of investors, such as tax-exempt pension funds and low-bracket individuals, for whom debt is preferable simply because the investor-level tax on interest income is less than the corporate-level tax on equity income. There is also a range of investors who prefer equity because they are subject to a rate of tax on interest income that is higher than the corporate rate on equity income. These different categories of investors subject to different tax rates on debt and equity income constitute "clienteles" for the securities of particular corporations. Once the relevant relationship among rates is established, corporations issue debt until the corporate income tax saving from the interest deduction equals the investor-level tax on interest income for the marginal investor. At this point, the market is in equilibrium and there is no tax advantage associated with the issue of debt for any particular corporation, although there is an optimal debt-equity ratio for the corporate sector as a whole. Equilibrium is upset by changes in the relationship between investor-level taxes on interest income and equity income. These changes provide an opportunity for corporations to issue tax-advantaged securities; yet that advantage is quickly bargained away and equilibrium is restored as corporations alter their capital structures and investors their portfolios in order to minimize taxes.

175 The expected present value of the tax shield provided by deductible interest on corporate debt decreases as it becomes less certain that a corporation will realize taxable income sufficient to offset the interest deduction. Since increases in corporate borrowing increase this uncertainty, they generate a higher probability of realized losses and a consequent reduction in the expected present value of the

tax that is alleviated only in part by loss-carryforward provisions. This insight has two important implications for the impact of income taxes on corporate capital structure. First, the equilibrium point at which the present value of the tax shield equals the investor-level tax will be different in a world in which corporations experience losses from the equilibrium point in a world in which corporations face a constant positive rate of tax. In particular, there will be fewer corporations that can expect to take full advantage of the tax shield and for which debt will be more tax-effective than equity. As a result, the total amount of corporate debt will be less than it would be under an assumption of taxable corporations. Second, there will be clienteles for the issue of debt or equity among corporate issuers, as well as investors. In a world of this kind it does in fact matter which corporations issue debt and which issue equity, and consequently an optimal tax-effective capital structure may exist for particular corporations.

176 See, for example, Jane G. Gravelle, *Corporate Tax Integration: Issues and Options* (Washington: Library of Congress, Congressional Research Service, 1991), who estimates that in the United States the average rate on equity income is about 50 percent higher than the average effective tax rate on income from corporate debt. See also United States, Treasury Department, *Report on Integration of the Individual and Corporate Tax Systems: Taxing Business Income Once* (Washington, DC: US Government Printing Office, January 1992), chapter one.

177 This description of the tax bias in favour of debt is the commonly cited one. Thus the ALI report, supra note 173, at 22, defines the bias as "the disincentive to invest in corporate equity." As the ALI report points out (ibid., at 22), the bias is greatest if the effective corporate tax rate and the shareholder-level tax rates on dividends and capital gains on shares are equivalent. In this case, investment in new equity will always be disfavoured relative to investment in corporate debt, since shareholders must pay both the corporate income tax and either the shareholder-level dividend tax or the capital gains tax, whereas debt holders must pay only the investor-level tax on interest income and any capital gains. The bias is reduced, and possibly even reversed, if this rate relationship does not hold. In particular, there may be a tax bias in favour of new equity, even under a classical corporate income tax, if the corporate tax rate is less than the investor-level tax and the tax rate on retained earnings realized as capital gains is sufficiently low. In general, then, the degree of bias depends on the relative levels of the corporate income tax rate, the capital gains tax rate, and the investor-level tax on the return on corporate debt.

178 See, however, the ALI report, ibid., at 25-28, where it is explained that under certain conditions the bias is limited to new equity issues, even under a classical corporate income tax. In particular, a corporation that is able to finance a project with either retained earnings, new debt, or new equity will be indifferent between the first two alternatives, provided that the corporate taxes and shareholder-level taxes are equivalent. In this case, financing through retained earnings means that the corporate income tax must continue to be paid on corporate earnings but the shareholder-level tax on distributions is deferred. A distribution of retained earnings followed by the issue of new debt eliminates the corporate-level tax on earnings but results in the immediate application of the shareholder-level tax to distributions. The two effects associated with the two alternatives offset one another to equate the after-tax returns. In contrast, financing with new equity means that the corporate income tax must continue to apply to corporate earnings, whereas the

shareholder-level tax on distributions applies immediately on distribution of the retained earnings and cannot be deferred. As a result, only new equity issues attract the full effect of the two levels of tax under a classical corporate tax, and there is a disincentive for financing of this kind. For corporations without retained earnings, the choice is between a new debt issue or an equity issue.

179 See, for example, Sijbren Cnossen, "Reform and Harmonization of Company Tax Systems in the European Union," in Richard Krever, ed., *Tax Conversations: A Guide to the Key Issues in the Tax Reform Debate—Essays in Honour of John G. Head* (The Hague: Kluwer Law International, 1997), 365-415, at 376-77. Cnossen notes the bias that arises in favour of debt under dividend imputation systems because of both the non-refundability of excess credits and the greater opportunities for avoidance associated with interest income, which may not be reported and taxed at source in the same way as retained equity income.

180 See, for example, the more complete overview of this subject in Brealey et al., supra note 163, at 466-76; Emmery, Finnerty, and Stowe, supra note 163, at 435-40; and Knoll, supra note 163, at 1475-81.

181 The direct costs of financial distress that are attributable to bankruptcy proceedings are relatively easy to quantify; however, as most studies have concluded, these costs are relatively insignificant as a percentage of asset value. The pioneering study of bankruptcy costs as a percentage of asset value is Jerold B. Warner, "Bankruptcy Costs: Some Evidence" (May 1977), 32 *Journal of Finance* 337-48. The subject of Warner's study was 11 railroad bankruptcies in the United States. On average, the costs were only 5.3 percent of the value of all outstanding debt and equity of the corporations immediately before bankruptcy and only 1.4 percent of this value five years before bankruptcy. See Brealey et al., supra note 163, at 469-70; and Knoll, supra note 163, at 1476, for brief summaries of Warner's results. Knoll also cites more recent studies indicating that the direct costs of bankruptcy are insignificant.

182 For a brief summary of the indirect costs of financial distress, see Knoll, supra note 163, at 1479-80. The indirect costs are more difficult to quantify than the direct costs, but they are generally considered to be more significant. The indirect costs include the inefficiencies associated with "asset substitution" and "underinvestment," which occur because of shareholders' decisions to pursue risky investments with zero or negative present values and to forgo investments that would add value to the corporation. Perhaps more important are the indirect costs that arise from attempts by debt holders to limit the potential for gaming by shareholders, and the resultant inefficient investment decisions, in the event of financial distress. These costs commonly take the form of restrictions and covenants in debt contracts intended to prevent certain actions by corporate management that might reduce the value of the issued debt. Negotiation of these complex contracts involves legal and administrative costs, and also monitoring costs incurred to ensure that the specified restrictions are observed. Not surprisingly, the costs are effectively borne by shareholders in the form of higher nominal rates of return demanded by debt investors to compensate them for the costs. The alternative is a reduction in shareholder value, since in the absence of restrictions on the potential for gaming debt investors would discount the value of the corporation.

183 See Knoll, supra note 163, for an extensive elaboration of this efficiency loss. See also Brealey et al., supra note 163, at 475-76; and Cnossen, supra note 179, at 376-77.

184 For a thorough exposition of the theoretical and design aspects of an accretion-based corporate income tax, see Joseph M. Dodge, "A Combined Mark-to-Market and Pass-Through Corporate-Shareholder Integration Proposal" (Spring 1995), 50 *Tax Law Review* 265-372.

185 See, for example, William D. Popkin, "The Deep Structure of Capital Gains" (1983), vol. 33, no. 2 *Case Western Reserve Law Review* 153-207, who argues that the distinction between expected and unexpected gains and losses distinguishes time-value returns from risk and the bet element associated with an investment, making it possible to limit a capital gains preference to unexpected amounts as a stimulus to risk taking.

186 For a comprehensive review of these arguments, see Rick Krever and Neil Brooks, *A Capital Gains Tax for New Zealand* (Wellington, NZ: Victoria University Press for the Institute of Policy Studies, 1990), 41-86. See also Noel B. Cunningham and Deborah H. Schenk, "The Case for a Capital Gains Preference" (Spring 1993), 48 *Tax Law Review* 319-80; and John W. Lee, "Critique of Current Congressional Capital Gains Contentions" (Summer 1995), 15 *Virginia Tax Review* 1-88. See also George R. Zodrow, "Economic Analyses of Capital Gains Taxation: Realization, Revenues, Efficiency and Equity" (Spring 1993), 48 *Tax Law Review* 419-527, for review of the economics literature.

187 See the text that accompanies notes 5 and 6 in chapter 2.

188 This intuition is stated most clearly by the US Supreme Court in *Eisner v. Macomber*, 252 US 189 (1920). See the text that accompanies notes 5 and 6 in chapter 2.

189 To use the "fruit and tree" metaphor, the value of any tree is equal to the discounted present value of the fruit. The passage of time reveals changes in expectations about the harvest of fruit and, therefore, changes in the value of the tree. There is no obvious reason why a farmer who continues to own his tree and harvests his fruit should be taxed differently from a farmer who sells his tree with the fruit before the harvest. Both farmers have realized the value of the fruit as income, albeit on different occasions. This point is restricted to a definition of income as equivalent to gain and ignores subsidy-based and efficiency arguments in favour of a capital gains preference.

190 This point is emphasized by Popkin, supra note 185, who accepts as given the full taxation of expected time-value returns. He argues that a subsidy-based rationale for a capital gains preference is defensible conceptually only if it is limited to unexpected gains.

191 See the text that accompanies notes 48-56 in chapter 2.

192 The difference between the face amount of a debt obligation and the issue price (OID) represents the expected time-value return for a lender payable on maturity of the debt. This return is equivalent to the expected cash flows associated with a debt obligation issued for a face amount equal to the issue price, with provision for the payment of interest at a stated interest rate determined as a percentage of the face amount. If legal form is determinative, capital gain treatment may be available for an OID obligation if the expected return is realized as appreciation in the value of the instrument on its disposition. Similarly, on a secondary market

transfer of a debt obligation, the transfer price will typically include an amount that compensates the transferor for accrued but unpaid interest. However, because the occasion for the payment is changed to a transfer of the obligation to a person other than the issuer, the appreciation in value represented by the accrued but unpaid interest may be converted into a tax-preferred capital gain. This conversion may occur even though the appreciation is the expected return that would otherwise be taxed in full as interest income to the debt holder when it is paid by the issuer. The legislative responses described in chapter 2 address these simple instances of pure avoidance by effectively deeming the expected time-value return represented by appreciation in the value of the relevant obligations to be taxable in full as ordinary-income amounts.

193 "Costlessness" is used here in two senses. The first sense refers to the fact that the transaction costs of implementing a dividend-stripping transaction are less than the tax saving derived from the conversion of fully taxable dividends into tax-preferred capital gains. The second sense refers to the fact that the transaction involves non-arm's-length parties, so that there is no economic disposition of the shares and, therefore, no discount in the sale price to reflect the expected future dividend tax. In this sense, a dividend-stripping transaction involves none of the inefficiencies associated with an imperfect substitution of one type of investment by another, tax-preferred one. Accordingly, dividend-stripping transactions represent instances of pure tax avoidance.

194 Dividend stripping has an especially long history in Canada. See, for example, H. Heward Stikeman and Robert Couzin, "Surplus Stripping" (1995), vol. 43, no. 5 *Canadian Tax Journal* 1844-60.

195 See the text that accompanies notes 16 and 17 in chapter 7.

196 In the United States, these "conversion transactions" are the subject of legislation that is intended to treat the expected return derived from the combinations as ordinary-income amounts. See IRC section 1258, which is discussed in the text that accompanies notes 111-146 in chapter 7.

197 The efficiency losses in this case are measured primarily in terms of a sacrifice in risk and return profiles that occurs as taxpayers substitute investment in real estate for other, more desirable assets.

198 A capital gains preference is said to distort dividend payout ratios, with consequent efficiency losses. Even this proposition is the subject of considerable debate, a debate that is reflected in the "old" and "new" views of dividend taxation. For a review of the relevant literature, see John G. Head, "Company Tax Systems: From Theory to Policy," in John G. Head and Richard Krever, eds., *Company Tax Systems* (Sydney: Australian Tax Research Foundation, 1997), 1-47, at 6-7 and 9-15.

199 This trading strategy is the bare timing option discussed in the text that accompanies notes 115-133 supra.

200 Domar and Musgrave, supra note 132.

201 Shuldiner, supra note 15, at 259-61.

202 See, for example, Krever and Brooks, supra note 186, at 41-86; and Lee, supra note 186.

203 Daniel Halperin, "Commentary: A Capital Gains Preference Is Not EVEN a Second-Best Solution" (Spring 1993), 48 *Tax Law Review* 381-91, at 381. See Krever and

Brooks, supra note 186, at 51-61, for a critical examination of other arguments in favour of a capital gains preference.

204 Popkin, supra note 185.

205 In view of certain practical constraints that prevent the adoption of accretion taxation, many commentators advocate a lower capital gains tax rate as a means of mitigating the lock-in effect. See, for example, Cunningham and Schenk, supra note 186; and Richard L. Schmalbeck, "The Uneasy Case for a Lower Capital Gains Tax: Why Not the Second Best?" (July 9, 1990), 48 *Tax Notes* 195-208.

206 See, for example, Cunningham and Schenk, supra note 186; Schmalbeck, supra note 205; and Daniel N. Shaviro, "Commentary: Uneasiness and Capital Gains" (Spring 1993), 48 *Tax Law Review* 393-417.

207 Halperin, supra note 203.

208 Ibid., at 382 and 386-87.

209 Ibid., at 382. See also Krever and Brooks, supra note 186, at 79-82; Jane G. Gravelle, "The Economics of Taxing Capital Income: The Twentieth Century and Beyond," in *Tax Conversations*, supra note 179, 223-59, at 225-33; and Zodrow, supra note 186. Despite literally decades of study by economists and the development of increasingly sophisticated modelling techniques, the sensitivity of the savings rate to changes in the tax rate remains difficult to specify. The difficulty arises because it has been impossible to determine whether individuals desire a certain level of current consumption and will alter their savings rate (future consumption) in response to increases in the capital income tax rate (the so-called substitution effect) or whether they desire a certain level of savings and will simply reduce their level of current consumption in response to increases in the capital income tax rate (the so-called income effect). The existence of a link between taxes and savings is even more uncertain in the case of the narrowly based capital gains tax preference. Moreover, even if it were possible to establish a positive link between the savings rate and the tax rate, it is not at all clear that a reduction in the rate of tax on capital income would be considered desirable, given the distributional consequences of a reduction and, in particular, the greater tax burden that it would place on labour income. See Gravelle, ibid., at 251, where she notes a failure in much of the literature to account for the welfare consequences of a preferential capital gains tax rate.

210 Halperin, supra note 203, at 385-87; and Alan J. Auerbach, "Capital Gains Taxation and Tax Reform" (September 1989), 41 *National Tax Journal* 391-401.

211 See, for example, Irwin Friend, "Effects of Taxation on Financial Markets," in Joseph A. Pechman, ed., *The Promise of Tax Reform* (Englewood Cliffs, NJ: Prentice-Hall, 1985), 87-113, at 99.

212 Krever and Brooks, supra note 186, at 82-84.

213 Halperin, supra note 203, at 386-87.

214 Ibid., at 387, where the point is illustrated by the following simple example. Assume that the holder of asset A acquired it at a cost of $200 and that its value has appreciated to $300. At a tax rate of 28 percent, the holder will have $272 after realization of the $100 accrued gain on asset A. If the price of asset B is $300 (reflecting the opportunity cost of capital), the holder of asset A may prefer to continue to own $300 worth of that asset rather than $272 worth of asset B.

Provided that there are other investors who are willing to own $300 worth of asset B, the impact of the lock-in effect is reflected only in the distribution pattern of the ownership of assets A and B.

215 The substantial presence of tax-exempt investors unaffected by the lock-in effect may be more than sufficient to ensure a deep market for asset B at a price that provides an attractive cost of capital for users of funds. Moreover, investors who hold asset A can always mitigate the lock-in effect by borrowing against the appreciation on another asset to acquire asset B without any realization of accrued gain on asset A and the attendant tax.

216 Krever and Brooks, supra note 186, at 77.

217 Ibid., at 85-86.

218 Brian J. Arnold and Tim Edgar, "Selected Aspects of Capital Gains Taxation in Australia, New Zealand, the United Kingdom and the United States" (November 1995), 21 *Canadian Public Policy* S58-S76; and Krever and Brooks, supra note 186, at 8-40.

219 See, for example, Krever and Brooks, supra note 186, at 61-76.

220 This first-best response would also raise more revenue than would reducing the rate of tax on capital gains in order to induce realizations. Advocates of the latter approach tend to emphasize the prospect of increased revenue from a rate reduction without accounting for the increase in individual welfare that the lower rate would provide by allowing investors to diversify their portfolios at a presumably acceptable tax cost. See Krever and Brooks, supra note 186, at 50; and Halperin, supra note 203, at 388, where he suggests that an increase in tax rates for high-income individuals is necessary to compensate for their individual welfare gains delivered through a lower capital gains tax rate.

221 Cunningham and Schenk, supra note 186.

222 See the text that accompanies notes 120-126 in chapter 4 and the text that accompanies notes 280-314 in chapter 5.

223 Halperin, supra note 203, at 382-83.

224 Ibid., at 389-91.

225 See the text that accompanies notes 133-153 in chapter 4 for a discussion of the application of different personal tax rates to labour income and capital income, as a second-best alternative to the accretion taxation of financial instruments, in the context of the Nordic dual income tax (DIT) systems.

226 Rosenbloom, supra note 22; and Malcolm Gammie, "The Source Taxation of Derivative Financial Instruments, 'Synthetic Securities,' Financial Hedging Transactions and Similar Innovative Financial Transactions" (September/October 1999), 1 *Derivatives & Financial Instruments* 231-36.

227 Rosenbloom, supra note 22; and Gammie, supra note 226. This statement is a slight exaggeration and should be qualified. Another, equally significant, issue in the cross-border context is the classification of particular instruments as either debt or equity. As was noted in the text that accompanies notes 143-184 supra, a benchmark approach to the income tax treatment of financial instruments would ensure the equivalent taxation of debt and equity, and there would be no need to draw a boundary between them. In the absence of a benchmark system, however, the need to treat interest and dividends differently for tax purposes in both the

domestic context and the cross-border context require that a distinction be made between debt and equity. Since the general issues are identical, approaches to the debt-equity distinction in the domestic context and approaches to the same distinction in the cross-border context are discussed together in the text that accompanies notes 280-335 in chapter 6.

228 See, generally, Gregory May, "Flying on Instruments: Synthetic Investment and the Avoidance of Withholding Tax" (November 11, 1996), 13 *Tax Notes International* 1625-35. See also Reuven S. Avi-Yonah and Linda Z. Swartz, "U.S. International Tax Treatment of Financial Derivatives" (March 3, 1997), 14 *Tax Notes International* 787-96; and David G. Broadhurst, "Derivatives in International Tax Planning," in International Fiscal Association—Canadian Branch, *1997 International Tax Seminar* (Scarborough, Ont.: Carswell, 1998), 85-101, at 99-101.

229 Avi-Yonah and Swartz, supra note 228, at 796. See also May, supra note 228, at 1634, where he observes that "[a]s long as the withholding tax operates on the distinction between debt and equity, prospects for jamming objectionable derivative communications seem bleak."

230 Avi-Yonah and Swartz, supra note 228, at 795-96. Contrast this proposition with the following observation by Gammie, supra note 226, at 234: "as the effect of derivative financial instruments can usually be judged effectively only on a net (rather than gross) basis, there is little or no gain from seeking to bolster withholding taxes through imposing them on the cash flows in derivative transactions."

231 But see supra note 227, which notes the need to classify instruments as either debt or equity in order to treat them appropriately for tax purposes in both the domestic context and the cross-border context. As in the case of possible approaches to the application of withholding taxes, the various approaches to the debt-equity distinction assume an acceptance of the status quo and its distinction for tax purposes between interest and dividends. See the text that accompanies notes 247-335 in chapter 6.

232 For an excellent recent discussion of these wider issues and the status quo, see Reuven S. Avi-Yonah, "The Structure of International Taxation: A Proposal for Simplification" (May 1996), 74 *Texas Law Review* 1301-59.

233 Ibid.

234 Alternative explanations are less refined but probably closer to reality. In particular, active business income is probably taxed at source primarily because the country of source is in the best position to administer and enforce any tax, given the location of the income-earning activities in the source country. Source taxation of active business income is also attractive in the case of enterprises with business operations in several jurisdictions. Since these enterprises defy any sensible application of a concept of residency, source-based taxation is the only sensible approach. See Avi-Yonah, ibid.

235 Ibid.

236 See Robert A. Green, "The Future of Source-Based Taxation of the Income of Multinational Enterprises" (November 1993), 79 *Cornell Law Review* 18-86.

237 See generally Charles T. Plambeck, H. David Rosenbloom, and Diane Ring, "General Report," in International Fiscal Association, *Cahiers de droit fiscal international*, vol. 80b, *Tax Aspects of Derivative Financial Instruments* (Deventer, the Netherlands: Kluwer, 1995), 653-90, at 684-89.

238 Organisation for Economic Co-operation and Development, *Model Tax Convention on Income and Capital* (Paris: OECD) (looseleaf), article 7 (business profits).

239 Rosenbloom, supra note 22, at 602-3. See also Gammie, supra note 226.

240 Australia, *Taxation of Financial Arrangements: An Issues Paper* (Canberra: Australian Government Publishing Service, December 1996), 249, proposes a three-step approach to the resolution of this issue. First, a financial instrument should be categorized as being either part of an established business or an isolated transaction. Second, if there is no governing tax treaty, the full amount of any gain should be considered to be sourced in Australia if certain territorial connections are present. Third, where there is a governing tax treaty, and the financial instrument is an isolated transaction of a non-resident, income and gains not covered by a specific article should be deemed to be sourced in Australia only to the extent that economically valuable functions are performed in Australia, Australian assets are used, or risks are assumed in or allocated to Australia.

241 See, for example, *Issues Paper*, ibid., at 246-47, where it cites the location of the following activities as being indicative of a sufficient "economic nexus for income and gains to be regarded as being derived from one or more geographical sources": (1) marketing, (2) preliminary risk or credit assessment, (3) pre-contractual negotiations, (4) execution of documents, and (5) performance of support and/or prudential activities. The issues paper also cites as relevant factors the places where (1) the risk was borne, (2) the relevant payments were made or the associated payment obligation was properly borne, (3) the decision to enter into the transaction was made, and (4) the parties to the transaction reside.

242 *Issues Paper*, ibid., at 248-49, proposes that income and expense from financial instruments be deemed to have an Australian source if (1) significant functions are performed in Australia; (2) a transaction involves Australian assets or the use of such assets; (3) financial risks are assumed by or on behalf of an Australian taxpayer, or in connection with a business that is wholly or partially carried on in Australia; or (4) payments are made from Australia or are deductible in Australia.

243 This proposition is perhaps most apparent in the case of global trading of financial instruments by financial institutions and securities traders and dealers. See, for example, Plambeck, Rosenbloom, and Ring, supra note 237, at 687-88, where they note that because the operations of financial intermediaries are highly integrated these firms "face transfer pricing risk in that income-generating activities may be performed in a jurisdiction without proper remuneration in the form of taxable profits." At 688, they attribute the problem to the difficulty of identifying (1) those activities that contribute to the production of a business unit's income, (2) the value of those activities, (3) where the activities are performed, and (4) which legal vehicle the activities are attributable to. They also identify the following component functions of business units: (1) originators, marketers, and salesmen; (2) market makers and dealers; (3) risk managers, bookrunners, and proprietary traders; (4) support services; (5) capital; (6) credit analysis; and (7) management. In theory, it should be possible to measure the separate contributions of these various units on a transactional basis, but the highly integrated nature of the activities of financial intermediaries has led to the use of formulary apportionment methods. See generally Organisation for Economic Co-operation and Development (OECD), *Taxation of Global Trading of Financial Instruments: A Discussion Draft* (Paris: OECD, 1998). See also Lorraine Eden, *Taxing*

Multinationals: Transfer Pricing and Corporate Income Taxation in North America (Toronto: University of Toronto Press, 1998), 574-78; Jill Pagan and Scott Wilkie, *Transfer Pricing Strategy in a Global Economy* (Amsterdam: International Bureau of Fiscal Documentation, 1993), 131-34; and Charles T. Plambeck, "Transfer Pricing Analysis of Global Trading Operations and Procedural Alternatives" (December 1996), 74 *Taxes: The Tax Magazine* 1129-43.

244 See *Issues Paper*, supra note 240, at 251-55. Internal deals are simply transactions between a branch in one country and a head office in another or between two branches in different countries. These transactions can be in goods, services, or financial instruments in which the separate branches assume opposite positions. Recognition of a transaction as being between separate entities has the effect of allocating gain or loss on the basis of the terms of the transaction in much the same way as gain or loss is allocated in the case of transactions between affiliated corporations in different countries. The converse problem is that of "split hedging," whereby a position assumed by one branch is hedged by an offsetting position assumed by another branch. Treatment of the branches as separate entities fails to consolidate the underlying position and the hedge for sourcing purposes. For an excellent discussion of these problems and some possible responses, see Diane M. Ring, "Risk-Shifting Within a Multinational Corporation: The Incoherence of the U.S. Tax Regime" (July 1997), 38 *Boston College Law Review* 667-737.

245 See the sources cited supra note 243; and *Issues Paper*, supra note 240, at 255-61.

246 Under tax treaties that follow the OECD model, cash flows associated with financial instruments are taxable in the country of source only if (1) they are business profits attributable to a permanent establishment in the country or (2) they fall under an article that specifically permits the imposition of withholding tax on certain items, such as interest, dividends, rents, or royalties. Income or expense from a financial instrument that is an isolated transaction and unconnected with a business otherwise falls under the "gains" or "other income" articles, which provide the country of residence with exclusive taxing jurisdiction. See the OECD model tax treaty, supra note 238, at article 7 (business profits), article 10 (dividends), article 11 (interest), article 12 (royalties), article 13 (capital gains), and article 21 (other income).

247 See the description of the representative legislation in Canada and Australia in the text that accompanies notes 14 and 19 in chapter 2.

248 See, for example, the limited exception in subparagraph 212(1)(b)(vii) of the Income Tax Act, RSC 1985, c. 1 (5th Supp.), as amended (herein referred to as "ITA"); and section 128F of the Australian Income Tax Assessment Act 1936, as amended.

249 See Plambeck, Rosenbloom, and Ring, supra note 237, at 685-86. The United States achieves much the same result by deeming payments on derivatives to be sourced in the country of residence of the payee. See Rosenbloom, supra note 22. Although the exemption of payments on derivatives from non-resident withholding tax is the dominant practice, it is not the accepted treatment in all countries. See, for example, Organisation for Economic Co-operation and Development, *Taxation of New Financial Instruments* (Paris: OECD, 1994). Even in countries that use an exemption approach, source taxation may be imposed in limited circumstances. For example, Canada taxes gains of non-residents on "taxable Canadian property," which includes an option or other interest in Canadian real

estate, shares of a private corporation, and shares of a public corporation that are part of a block of 25 percent or more of an issued class owned by the non-resident. See ITA paragraph 115(1)(b). The gains are subject to Canadian-source taxation, however, only if the option or other interest is held on capital account. Furthermore, source taxation is conventionally conceded under Canada's tax treaties. See Robert Raizenne and Angelo Nikolakakis, "Taxable Canadian Property," in *Report of Proceedings of the Forty-Eighth Tax Conference*, 1996 Conference Report, vol. 2 (Toronto: Canadian Tax Foundation, 1997), 46:1-72, at 46:10-13. Revenue Canada (now the Canada Customs and Revenue Agency) has stated that it will apply non-resident withholding tax to the imputed interest element on debt disguised as asymmetrical swap payments. See Revenue Canada document no. 7-902723, April 4, 1991; and Elinore J. Richardson, David Glicksman, and Lara Friedlander, "Fundamentals of Canadian Taxation of Financial Instruments," in *Report of Proceedings of the Fifty-First Tax Conference*, 1999 Conference Report (Toronto: Canadian Tax Foundation, 2000), 5:1-57, at 5:51. This position is simply an extension of the general approach to the embedded debt in certain derivatives discussed in chapter 6. ITA subsection 260(8) may similarly impose non-resident withholding tax on interest or dividend compensation payments under a securities lending arrangement.

250 See the text that accompanies notes 22-28 in chapter 7.

251 May, supra note 228, at 1625-33. The ability to synthetically replicate debt and equity investments in order to avoid withholding tax led the then US Treasury International Tax Counsel, Cynthia Beerbower, to utter her often-quoted statement that "opportunities for synthetic investments, as opposed to real investments, are so prevalent that withholding taxes are no longer real." See (March 21, 1994), 8 *Tax Notes International* 776-80, at 779.

252 See the text that accompanies notes 22-28 in chapter 7.

253 Under a total-return equity swap, one party agrees to pay (1) a fixed percentage of a notional principal amount equal to the spot value of a specified block of shares when the parties enter into the swap and (2) any depreciation below that spot value. In return, the counterparty is entitled to an amount equal to (1) the dividends paid on the notional block of shares and (2) any appreciation in the value of the shares in excess of their spot value when the parties enter into the swap. Each of these short positions under the swap is usually hedged with a long position in treasury bills and shares.

254 Broadhurst, supra note 228, at 100-1.

255 See the text that accompanies notes 75-87 in chapter 1.

256 Broadhurst, supra note 228, at 99-100; and the text that accompanies notes 22-28 in chapter 7.

257 Rosenbloom, supra note 22, at 604-5; and Plambeck, Rosenbloom, and Ring, supra note 237, at 685, where they note that "despite the relationship between DFIs [derivative financial instruments] and underlyings, DFIs are distinct from debt, equity, and other financial instruments that involve the transfer of capital."

258 Chapter 6 discusses the appropriate treatment of the expected gain and loss associated with options.

259 Chapter 6, in the text that accompanies notes 24-92, provides a detailed discussion of the conceptual basis and the implications of this proposition.

260 Rosenbloom, supra note 22, at 611 (citing Rev. rul. 80-222, 1980-2 CB 211).

261 See, for example, Gammie, supra note 226, at 234.

262 Dividends may be subject to non-resident withholding tax and the corporate-level tax on underlying earnings on the assumption that they do have a high content of net income and are not as susceptible as debt capital is to capital flight in the face of high source-country taxation. See the text that accompanies notes 257-61 supra. Also see, for example, the closing words of ITA subparagraph 212(1)(b)(vii), which deny the withholding tax exemption for interest on portfolio debt to certain "participating payments" that are evidently considered equivalent to equity or a long position in an underlying asset.

263 Rosenbloom, supra note 22, at 610-15, analyzes possible rationales for the application under the IRC of non-resident withholding tax to some financial flows and not others.

264 Ibid., at 608: "The most important point is that a source rule is *not* a rule of taxation. It is more in the nature of a national declaration of what might be taxed on the ground that the United States has, in its unilateral view, a legitimate right to do so."

265 See, for example, Reuven S. Avi-Yonah, "Virtual Taxation: Source-Based Taxation in the Age of Derivatives," in *Proceedings of the Eighty-Ninth Annual Conference on Taxation* (Washington, DC: National Tax Association, 1997), 269-74, at 273, where he cites the example of the German attempt to impose withholding tax in 1989, which led to a massive flight of debt capital to Luxembourg and the repeal of the tax three months after its enactment.

266 Avi-Yonah and Swartz, supra note 228, at 795-96.

267 A relatively wide concept of a portfolio interest might include any interest other than a controlling interest, which might be defined in terms of the concepts of arm's length or relatedness. These concepts, in turn, might be defined generally in terms of an equity ownership threshold of more than 50 percent of any particular class of shares (taking into account the ownership interests of all persons related to or dealing at non-arm's length with the particular payer). A more restrictive test of a portfolio interest would draw the line at a much lower level of equity ownership. See, for example, Avi-Yonah and Swartz, supra note 228, at 796, where they suggest a level of equity ownership of 10 percent or more as a significant ownership interest for the purposes of a distinction between foreign direct interests and portfolio interests. Any financial flow from a resident payer to a non-resident payee with a higher level of ownership would be subject to non-resident withholding tax. "Otherwise, payments under derivatives would be sourced to the recipient and exempt from withholding."

268 Avi-Yonah, supra note 265, at 273, argues that the rationale for the exemption of interest on portfolio debt should also apply to portfolio dividends, but the existence of a positive withholding tax rate on dividends in the United States has not eliminated foreign investors from the US equity market.

269 Ibid., at 273: "It needs to be demonstrated why the equity market is so significantly different from the debt market."

270 Ibid., at 272-73. See also Reuven Avi-Yonah, "Globalization, Tax Competition and the Fiscal Crisis of the Welfare State" (May 2000), 113 *Harvard Law Review* 1573-1676.

271 See Howell H. Zee, "Taxation of Financial Capital in a Globalized Environment: The Role of Withholding Taxes" (September 1998), 51 *National Tax Journal* 587-99; and Avi-Yonah, supra note 270, at 1666-70, for a defence of withholding taxes as a backup to residence-based taxation of income from financial capital. Zee argues for withholding taxes as a response to tax evasion. He does not link their application to deductibility in the source country. His concern is with the case for withholding taxes despite any distorting effect their application on a gross basis may have. For a much different view of the effect and role of withholding taxes, see PricewaterhouseCoopers, "Canada-U.S. Treaty Interest Withholding Rates: Revenue and Policy Considerations" (May 3, 1999), 18 *Tax Notes International* 1805-35, which recommends the elimination of withholding taxes on payments of interest between Canadian and US residents. See also Julian Alworth, "Taxation and Integrated Financial Markets: The Challenges of Derivatives and Other Financial Innovations" (1998), vol. 5, no. 3 *International Tax and Public Finance* 507-34, at 526-27, where he proposes the application of a comprehensive income tax base on an exclusively residence-country basis, supplemented by extensive exchange of information between countries to address opportunities for evasion.

272 Avi-Yonah, supra note 265, at 273; and supra note 270, at 1666-70, proposes the application of withholding tax to portfolio capital on the basis of a distinction between deductible and non-deductible payments. He suggests that the problem of capital flight might be less severe for the United States, as a large capital-exporting country, than it is for other countries. Small capital-importing countries might be able to follow the US lead.

273 Avi-Yonah and Swartz, supra note 228, at 796, conclude that a withholding tax system based on a distinction between direct interests and portfolio interests "at least would ensure that the most obvious forms of using derivatives to avoid withholding taxes on stock and debt investment are countered, while not affecting the market for portfolio investment into the United States."

274 Avi-Yonah, supra note 265, at 273, suggests implementation of a system of withholding taxes based on a distinction between deductible and non-deductible payments through multilateral agreement by the OECD member countries. The European Union has proposed a uniform withholding tax of 20 percent on the gross amount of interest payments between residents of member states. See Avi-Yonah, supra note 270, at 1652-57; and Andreas Haufler, "Prospects for Co-ordination of Corporate Taxation and the Taxation of Interest Income in the EU" (June 1999), 20 *Fiscal Studies* 133-53, who argues that the limited application of the proposed withholding tax provides avoidance opportunities that reduce its effectiveness. See also Gammie, supra note 226, at 234, where he notes that non-resident withholding taxes on dividend income have fallen from 10 percent to 6.6 percent in the period 1979-1994, and that withholding taxes on interest have fallen from an average of 10 percent to 8 percent. Gammie (ibid.) points out that "[w]hat is uncertain is to what extent this decline in withholding taxes can be attributed to the use of derivatives and to what extent it can be attributed to other factors."

275 This issue, which remains problematic under any approach other than accretion taxation, is explored in more detail in the text that accompanies notes 29-44 and 111-146 in chapter 7.

276 Some of these classification problems, as addressed by past legislative responses of Australian and Canadian policy makers, are highlighted in the text that accompanies

notes 58-74 in chapter 2. For a discussion of general responses to the problem of the debt-equity distinction, see the text that accompanies notes 247-335 in chapter 6.

277 See the text that accompanies notes 4-7 and 20-24 in chapter 2 for a brief review of the representative experiences in Australia and Canada in attempting to draw a distinction between ordinary income and capital amounts.

278 See the text that accompanies notes 29-57 supra.

279 The text that accompanies notes 89-134 in chapter 4 discusses these other approaches and compares them with expected-return taxation as a desirable second-best alternative.

280 Simon, supra note 33, at 1024.

281 See Brown, supra note 45; and Shakow, supra note 45.

282 See, for example, Australia, Review of Business Taxation, *A Platform for Consultation: Building on a Strong Foundation*, Discussion Paper 2, vol. 1 (Canberra: Australian Government Publishing Services, February 1999), 147-48; Australia, Review of Business Taxation, *A Tax System Redesigned: More Certain, Equitable and Durable* (Canberra: Australian Government Publishing Services, July 1999), 337-38 and 341; and Stephen B. Land, "Defeating Deferral: A Proposal for Retrospective Taxation" (Fall 1996), 52 *Tax Law Review* 45-117, at 54-59.

283 See the text that accompanies notes 185-225 supra.

284 This type of credit is described in ALI report, supra note 173, at 90-92.

285 *Report on Integration of the Individual and Corporate Tax Systems*, supra note 176.

286 For a description of this reform option as a solution to the problem of the tax treatment of financial instruments, see Edward D. Kleinbard, "Beyond Good and Evil Debt (and Debt Hedges): A Cost of Capital Allowance System" (December 1989), 67 *Taxes: The Tax Magazine* 943-61, at 955-61; and Edward D. Kleinbard, "Equity Derivative Instruments: Financial Innovation's Newest Challenge to the Tax System" (May 1991), 69 *Texas Law Review* 1319-68, at 1361-68.

287 The articles by Kleinbard, ibid., are important exceptions to this generalization.

288 A denial of the deduction of corporate interest expense raises problems of creditability of the source-country tax by non-resident investors in their country of residence. To the extent that source-country corporate tax on non-deductible interest is not creditable, double taxation of the underlying income occurs. Conversely, the deduction of the imputed cost of equity capital raises problems of revenue loss for capital-importing countries. The text that accompanies notes 247-279 in chapter 6 discusses these problems and their significance for the application of a system of expected-return taxation to shares.

289 Strnad, supra note 1, at 605. See also Hariton, supra note 145, for a suggested approach to the maintenance of the debt-equity distinction. Hariton's approach would focus on the relative risk borne by investors, which would be assessed separately for securities of different corporate issuers.

290 Strnad, supra note 1, at 605.

291 Brooks and Head, supra note 7, at 65-66 and 71-72.

292 Ibid., at 74-78.

293 Warren, supra note 1, at 473-82.

294 See the text that accompanies notes 154-184 in chapter 2.

295 Gergen, "Apocalypse Not?" supra note 24, defines "transaction costs" as the costs of effecting an alternative financial position. He defines "credit risk" as the risk of default of a counterparty to a financial instrument. Finally, he defines "legal risk" as the risk that the validity of a financial arrangement for regulatory or tax purposes will be challenged by the government, with all the attendant costs of disputing that challenge. See also Gergen and Schmitz, supra footnote 24, who emphasize the role of tax-law uncertainty as a barrier to tax-driven financial innovation.

296 Gergen, "Apocalypse Not?" supra note 24, at 849.

297 Ibid., at 849-50.

298 This term is used by Gergen, ibid., at 853-54.

299 Ibid., at 845-55. Chapter 4 reviews the importance of this conclusion and the arguments that underlie it in discussing the case for the adoption of comprehensive accrual rules as a second-best alternative for reform.

300 Brooks and Head, supra note 7, at 71-78.

301 Ibid., at 65-66; and Gergen, "Apocalypse Not?" supra note 24, at 834-35.

302 See Hariton, supra note 25; Scarborough, supra note 1; and Shuldiner, supra note 15.

303 See Santangelo, supra note 150.

304 The best combination of theoretical and practical analysis of expected-return taxation is found in Shuldiner, supra note 15.

305 See the text that accompanies notes 48-51 in chapter 2.

306 See the articles by Kleinbard, supra note 286; and Institute for Fiscal Studies, Capital Taxes Group, *Equity for Companies: A Corporation Tax for the 1990s*, Commentary no. 26 (London: Institute for Fiscal Studies, April 1991).

Notes to Chapter 4

1 Strictly speaking, a system of expected-return taxation is limited to timing issues. As the text that accompanies footnotes 187-227 in chapter 3 argues, the need to eliminate the distinction between ordinary income and capital amounts is so fundamental that the recognition of the full amount of gain and loss is an integral part of any legislative regime that is designed to implement expected-return taxation. The remaining character issue concerns differences in the treatment of interest and dividends. See the text that accompanies notes 247-335 in chapter 6.

2 See the text that accompanies notes 58-133 in chapter 3; and Reed H. Shuldiner, "A General Approach to the Taxation of Financial Instruments" (December 1992), 71 *Texas Law Review* 243-350, at 250-53.

3 See the text that accompanies notes 66-133 in chapter 3; and Shuldiner, supra note 2, at 253-57.

4 See the text that accompanies notes 280-336 in chapter 5.

5 Ibid.

6 See, for example, in the Australian context, Anthony J. Frost, "Taxation of Financial Transactions," in *Papers Presented at the Eleventh National Convention of the Taxation Institute of Australia* (Sydney: Taxation Institute of Australia, 1993),

103-25; and, in the US context, Robert H. Scarborough, "Different Rules for Different Players and Products: The Patchwork Taxation of Derivatives" (December 1994), 72 *Taxes: The Tax Magazine* 1031-49.

7 Second-best approaches raise obvious problems that are identified by the economic theory of the "paradox of the second best." Given a specified ideal and practical constraints that prevent its realization, this theory holds that no particular approach intended to approximate the ideal is necessarily more desirable in efficiency terms than any other attempt. Although a given approach may realize welfare gains by eliminating certain distortions associated with the status quo, the fact that it is only an approximation of the ideal means that it will create new distortions and other welfare costs. It is impossible in the abstract to rank-order second-best approaches and their associated welfare costs. Some assessment and comparison of the costs of the different approaches must be undertaken. See R. Lipsey and K. Lancaster, "The General Theory of the Second Best" (1956-57), vol. 24, no. 6 *Review of Economic Studies* 11-32. The importance of the paradox of the second best for tax reform generally was originally pointed out by Boris Bittker in the context of the debate over a comprehensive income tax base. See Boris I. Bittker, "A Comprehensive Tax Base" (March 1967), 80 *Harvard Law Review* 925-85. Scarborough, supra note 6, at 1049, notes the relevance of the paradox of the second best to the taxation of financial instruments.

8 Some of these alternatives are reviewed in Alvin C. Warren Jr., "Financial Contract Innovation" (December 1993), 107 *Harvard Law Review* 460-92, at 473-83. See also Tom Clearwater, "The Judicial Role in Derivative Taxation: The Queen v. Shell Canada Limited and Financial Contract Economics" (1998), vol. 46, no. 6 *Canadian Tax Journal* 1212-44, at 1227-33; and Scarborough, supra note 6, at 1032, footnote 8. Warren (supra, at 476) describes limitations on the deductibility of expenses and losses as a possible approach to the taxation of financial instruments. The use of limitations of this kind, however, is simply one form of the integration technique in which the cash flows associated with long and short positions in different instruments are matched and offset against one another in the same taxation year.

9 See, for example, Frank V. Battle Jr., "Bifurcation of Financial Instruments" (December 1991), 69 *Taxes: The Tax Magazine* 821-33; David P. Hariton, "New Rules Bifurcating Contingent Debt—A Mistake?" (April 15, 1991), 51 *Tax Notes* 235-39; Randall K.C. Kau, "Carving Up Assets and Liabilities—Integration or Bifurcation of Financial Products" (December 1990), 68 *Taxes: The Tax Magazine* 1003-14; Edward D. Kleinbard, "Beyond Good and Evil Debt (And Debt Hedges): A Cost of Capital Allowance System" (December 1989), 67 *Taxes: The Tax Magazine* 943-61; Lawrence Lokken, "New Rules Bifurcating Contingent Debt—A Good Start" (April 29, 1991), 51 *Tax Notes* 495-504; Scarborough, supra note 6; Jeff Strnad, "Commentary: Taxing New Financial Products in a Second-Best World: Bifurcation and Integration" (Summer 1995), 50 *Tax Law Review* 545-69; and David A. Weisbach, "Tax Responses to Financial Contract Innovation" (Summer 1995), 50 *Tax Law Review* 491-544.

10 See, for example, Internal Revenue Code of 1986, as amended (herein referred to as "IRC"), section 1092 (integrated treatment of straddle transactions); section 988(d) (integration of certain hedged foreign currency transactions); and section 246(c) (integration of a position in shares and derivative instruments as the basis

for a disallowance of the intercorporate dividend deduction). Arguably, the most comprehensive provisions based on integration techniques are the hedging regulations in IRC reg. section 1.446-4.

11 Warren, supra note 8.

12 Kleinbard, supra note 9, at 947-52.

13 This use of the term "integration" should not be confused with the term's more common use to describe various techniques that "integrate" the corporate and shareholder-level income taxes.

14 See Weisbach, supra note 9, at 496-502 and 507-26, where he draws this explicit link. Weisbach uses the term "hybrids" to describe both derivative instruments that contain an embedded debt element and debt instruments that contain an embedded derivative ("contingent-payment debt").

15 Paul Goris, *The Legal Aspects of Swaps* (London: Graham and Trotman, 1994), 28-29, refers to the packaging of two or more financial instruments in a single indivisible instrument as "internal financial engineering." Chapter 6 discusses bifurcation as a technique for the tax treatment of hybrid instruments.

16 Weisbach, supra note 9, at 500-2.

17 Ibid.

18 Ibid., at 502-7 and 526-38.

19 Goris, supra note 15, at 28-29, refers to the process of creating synthetic instruments as "external financial engineering," in which two or more legally independent instruments are held or acquired in combination in order to create or alter the exposure of an investor without affecting the legal independence of the instruments. Chapter 7 discusses integration as a technique for the tax treatment of synthetics.

20 Weisbach, supra note 9, at 527, notes that the matching of character and timing of gains and losses does not ensure that the hedge and hedged items are taxed as a complete unit. He points out, for example, that hedging regimes do not permit alteration of the timing of the recognition of gain or loss on the hedged item and may produce a timing result different from the timing result that would occur if the equivalent position were acquired as a single instrument.

21 This elimination is considered to be desirable on the assumption that the additional tax otherwise payable on an unmatched position would adversely affect the pre-tax pricing of the hedge. Other examples of integration techniques are loss limitations and similar provisions that deny tax benefits to prevent potential arbitrage from the holding of offsetting provisions. Weisbach, supra note 9, at 526, refers to provisions of this kind as "partial" integration techniques, since they do not address all aspects of the offsetting positions.

22 Mark P. Gergen, "Apocalypse Not?" (Summer 1995), 50 *Tax Law Review* 833-59, at 850; and Weisbach, supra note 9, at 507-11.

23 There is no analytical significance to this common distinction. Indeed, as will be argued below, bifurcation and integration are complementary techniques that one can apply to financial instruments whether or not they are considered to fall within the categories of hybrids and synthetics. Nonetheless, the categories serve as convenient terms of reference, given how bifurcation and integration have been applied under existing income tax systems. See Gergen, supra note 22, at 845-46; and Strnad, supra note 9.

24 See, in particular, the sources cited in note 9 supra.

25 This point is explained in more detail in the text that accompanies notes 32-38 infra.

26 Kau, supra note 9; Kleinbard, supra note 9; Scarborough, supra note 6; and Weisbach, supra note 9, at 512-19. But see Glenn L.E. May, "Overview of Financial, Tax, and Accounting Principles for Derivative Financial Instruments," in *Report of Proceedings of the Forty-Seventh Tax Conference*, 1995 Conference Report (Toronto: Canadian Tax Foundation, 1996), 29:1-27, at 29:22: "While matching is a laudable principle, 'integration' is fraught with difficulties."

27 Strnad, supra note 9, at 548-53, argues that bifurcation may be preferable in a "first-best world," which he defines (ibid., at 550) as one in which "consistency and linearity is [sic] attainable." Strnad also argues (ibid., at 550-51), however, that under a tax system that contains significant non-linearities bifurcation alone cannot guarantee consistency; it must be supplemented with integration techniques in order to deal with positions that "receive a specified treatment that would result from particular decompositions."

28 Gergen, supra note 22, at 850.

29 See Strnad, supra note 9, at 548-49 and footnote 13, where he refers to "a system that combines a taxpayer's portfolio into a single position and then associates a tax treatment with that position" as "entire integration."

30 Ibid., at 561-62.

31 Ibid.

32 Ibid., at 563-69.

33 Gergen, supra note 22, at 851, uses this particular example to make much the same point about the limits of bifurcation. See also Kleinbard, supra note 9, at 947-48.

34 This approach may be required for financial accounting purposes. See, for example, Canadian Institute of Chartered Accountants (CICA), *CICA Handbook* (Toronto: CICA) (looseleaf), sections 3860.24 and A24; and May, supra note 26, at 29:9. It is possible to allocate the acquisition price of a convertible obligation by using option-pricing models to value the embedded equity option. This approach allocates the balance of the acquisition price to the fixed-payment debt instrument. The portion of the acquisition price that is allocated to the embedded option is added to contributed surplus, and no interest income or expense is imputed on the amount of the option premium. The difference between the acquisition price of the fixed-payment debt instrument and the principal due on maturity must be recognized as interest on a yield-to-maturity basis. The same treatment is reflected in New Zealand Inland Revenue *Determination* G22, "Optional Conversion Convertible Notes Denominated in New Zealand Dollars Convertible at the Option of the Holder," October 1990, for the purposes of the New Zealand accrual legislation. The core elements of that legislation (including the application of the yield-to-maturity basis for the recognition of expected gains and losses) are described in chapter 5.

35 This approach is the predominant one under many existing income tax systems. See, for example, the description of the representative Canadian and Australian experiences in the text that accompanies notes 67-72 in chapter 2; and *Interpretation Bulletin* IT-96R6, "Options Granted by Corporations To Acquire Shares, Bonds, or Debentures and by Trusts To Acquire Trust Units," October 23, 1996, paragraph 9 (which provides that bifurcation is inapplicable to convertible debt if

the embedded option is not severable and cannot be separately traded). The same general approach is applied to debt that is exchangeable into shares of a corporation other than the issuer ("exchangeable debt"). See IT-96R6, ibid.; and "Revenue Canada Round Table," in *Report of Proceedings of the Forty-Fourth Tax Conference*, 1992 Conference Report (Toronto: Canadian Tax Foundation, 1993), 54:1-75, at 54:7. For a discussion of the Canadian income tax treatment of exchangeable debt, see Timothy R. Hughes, "Income Tax Implications of the Non-Dispositive Transfer of Equity Securities" (Winter 1999), 57 *University of Toronto Faculty of Law Review* 43-81, at 66-77; and Donald H. Watkins, "Equity Exchangeable Debentures and Appreciation Rights," in *Report of Proceedings of the Forty-Fifth Tax Conference*, 1993 Conference Report (Toronto: Canadian Tax Foundation, 1994), 20:1-15, at 20:1-11.

36 The failure to allocate any amount of the acquisition price of a convertible debt obligation to the embedded equity option reduces the amount of interest income and expense that would otherwise arise in the form of OID on the fixed-payment debt. This reduction provides a result that is equivalent to netting the option premium against the OID that would be recognized over the term of the obligation if a portion of the acquisition price were allocated to the embedded option. In effect, amortization of the option premium would offset both the amount of the interest income of the holder reflected in the OID (option premium recognized as an expense) and the interest expense of the issuer (option premium recognized as income). See, generally, May, supra note 26, at 29:10-11: "embedded options are best left alone, as they naturally net the option premium against interest expense for a better matching of income and expense over the term of the convertible debt." See the text that accompanies notes 208-212 in chapter 6 for a critique of this approach and a discussion of the appropriate treatment of convertible debt obligations under a comprehensive accrual regime.

37 See, for example, Kau, supra note 9, at 1003 and 1009. Kau argues that a failure to bifurcate a convertible debt obligation results in the integrated treatment of the interest expense and option premium, which may be preferable to any results that would follow from a bifurcation approach.

38 This point is emphasized in chapter 6.

39 See, in particular, Battle, supra note 9; Kau, supra note 9; and Kleinbard, supra note 9.

40 For a discussion of put-call parity and its general significance in financial theory, see the text that accompanies notes 75-87 in chapter 1. Gergen, supra note 22, at 850, refers to the creation of a synthetic debt instrument by combining a long position in shares with a long put and a short call option on the shares as "the canonical case" for the application of integration.

41 Failure to tax the $33 expected gain on the synthetic OID bond in the same manner as the return on a conventional OID bond leaves an opportunity for pure tax avoidance, which a taxpayer can realize by issuing a conventional obligation in order to borrow funds and using the borrowed funds to acquire the synthetic position. Weisbach, supra note 9, at 502-7. If the $33 expected gain associated with the synthetic position is taxed only on realization (sale of the shares and maturity of the offsetting options), the taxpayer realizes tax savings from the accelerated accrual recognition of the offsetting $33 interest expense associated

with the short position in the conventional obligation. The tax saving arises from the current deduction against other income of the taxpayer, which is not offset fully by the taxation of the identical gain associated with the synthetic position. The difference is simply the interest-free loan that arises from the tax saving realized by the deduction against other income before recognition of the offsetting gain associated with the synthetic position. See the text that accompanies notes 66-79 in chapter 3 for a more detailed discussion of the benefit of anticipated deferral provided by the failure to tax all expected gains and losses on an accrual basis.

42 Weisbach, supra note 9, at 526-38.

43 Although the identification of embedded debt does not raise the problem of multiple bifurcations that is associated with hybrid instruments (in fact, it alleviates that problem), it involves a measure of complexity that must be weighed against any benefits realized from the taxation of the expected gains and losses on embedded debt in a manner consistent with the taxation of those on conventional debt. See Kau, supra note 9, at 1005-7.

44 Weisbach, supra note 9, at 508, footnote 45, argues that choosing one of a number of possible bifurcations is desirable as a means of minimizing tax-avoidance opportunities. He concludes that if there are *n* possible bifurcations producing *m* possible tax treatments, a failure to choose one of the bifurcations simply creates an additional arbitrage opportunity ($m + 1$). Strnad, supra note 9, at 554-55, points out, however, that it is often possible to solve the problem of multiple bifurcations by adopting an integration approach that specifies one tax treatment for the different combinations that in the aggregate produce the same cash flow. Indeed, it is possible to achieve this result by simply refusing to bifurcate an instrument that is presented, in form, as a single instrument and treating it as a single position with a tax treatment that follows from its predominant characteristics. See Kau, supra note 9, at 1009, where he cites the example of the conventional treatment of a convertible bond as a single instrument.

45 See the text that accompanies notes 78-102 in chapter 2 for a discussion of the application of a purpose-based approach to hedging transactions under the representative Canadian and Australian income tax systems. The text that accompanies notes 187-217 in chapter 7 returns to this issue and also considers integration as the basis for anti-avoidance legislation that addresses the use of synthetics.

46 Gergen, supra note 22, at 846-47, refers to this identification issue as a "monitoring" problem. That is, the tax administration must somehow acquire an effective means of identifying instruments that should be integrated. Chapter 7 discusses the issue in more detail.

47 Gergen, ibid., at 845-51.

48 Ibid., at 849-50: "Tax policymakers . . . can be satisfied if the law governs the existing set of securities tolerably well and there is not a socially harmful level of uncertainty regarding the tax treatment of novel securities."

49 See, for example, Gergen, ibid., at 850-51.

50 See, for example, Frost, supra note 6; and Barrie M. Philp, "Is It Time To Place More Reliance on GAAP?" in *Report of Proceedings of the Forty-Third Tax Conference*, 1991 Conference Report (Toronto: Canadian Tax Foundation, 1992), 25:1-55, at 25:48-55.

51 Joint Committee on Taxation of the Canadian Bar Association and the Canadian Institute of Chartered Accountants, "Submission to the Minister of Finance on the Issue of Deductibility of Interest," in *Canadian Tax Reports*, Special Report no. 964, extra ed. (Don Mills, Ont.: CCH Canadian, August 1990).

52 RSC 1985, c. 1 (5th Supp.), as amended (herein referred to as "the ITA").

53 See, for example, Gary J. Webb, "GAAP and the Canadian Income Tax Act," in *Report of Proceedings of the Forty-Ninth Tax Conference*, 1997 Conference Report (Toronto: Canadian Tax Foundation, 1998), 10:1-50, which reviews the judicial development of the relationship between GAAP and tax-accounting principles for the measurement of business income generally under the ITA.

54 See, for example, International Accounting Standards Committee (IASC), *Accounting for Financial Assets and Financial Liabilities: Discussion Paper* (London: IASC, March 1997). See also the proposals of the Australian Accounting Research Foundation (AARF), *Exposure Draft ED 59: Financial Instruments* (Melbourne: AARF, March 1993); and Australian Accounting Research Foundation, *Exposure Draft ED 65: Presentation and Disclosure of Financial Instruments* (Melbourne: AARF, June 1995). The IASC and AARF proposals are generally consistent with the standards and practices adopted by the CICA in *CICA Handbook*, supra note 34, at sections 3860.01-3860.A28 (effective for fiscal periods beginning after January 1, 1996). May, supra note 26, at 29:2-16, compares some of the financial-accounting principles described in the *CICA Handbook* with the relevant tax-accounting principles under the ITA.

55 See generally Brian J. Arnold, "Conformity Between Financial Statements and Tax Accounting" (1981), vol. 29, no. 4 *Canadian Tax Journal* 476-88, at 483-87. See also the text that accompanies notes 163-197 in chapter 5 for an examination of these perceived benefits in the specific context of the application of yield-to-maturity (YTM) calculations for the accrual recognition of expected gains and losses.

56 An obvious example of this general approach is the characterization of long-term prepaid debt instruments (Canadian optional interest notes or COINs) as debt issued for a shorter term at a discount. The characterization is based on a present-value analysis of the cash flows that is foreign to the general concepts implicit in most income tax systems. See Canadian Institute of Chartered Accountants, *Abstract EIC-22* (Toronto: CICA, January 21, 1991); and the discussion in the text that accompanies notes 100-101 in chapter 5 of ITA subsection 18(9.2), which largely reflects the financial-accounting practice. Another example of the adoption of financial-accounting practice for a limited tax-accounting purpose is the recent changes to the ITA affecting the recognition of loan losses and accrued interest on impaired loans held by financial institutions and moneylenders. See P. Mark Meredith and Janet V. Mulcaster, "Traders, Dealers, and Financial Intermediaries," in the 1997 Conference Report, supra note 53, 20:1-29, at 20:2-7.

57 The more rigorous form of conformity might be reflected in a requirement of conformity between a taxpayer's financial statements and tax returns. If more than one method was appropriate for financial-statement purposes, the method chosen for financial-statement purposes would have to be used for income tax purposes as well. See Arnold, supra note 55, at 487.

58 The appropriateness of these deviations might be determined either legislatively or through the interpretation of existing legislation by the courts. This more

permissive version of conformity would also presumably permit a taxpayer to choose among different financial-accounting practices for tax purposes. Taxpayers would therefore not be bound for tax purposes to the use of a particular accounting method in their financial statements. See Arnold, supra note 55, at 487.

59 See Arnold, ibid., at 483-87. See also Australia, *Taxation of Financial Arrangements: An Issues Paper* (Canberra: Australian Government Publishing Services, December 1996), 53-55; and Calvin Johnson, "GAAP Tax" (April 1999), 83 *Tax Notes* 425-30.

60 This point is evident from even the most superficial review of the financial-accounting standards recently developed by the CICA and incorporated in *CICA Handbook*, supra note 34, at section 3860. The comparable standards released by the Australian Accounting Research Foundation, *Exposure Draft 59: Financial Instruments*, supra note 54, proved to be extremely controversial and were withdrawn for further study.

61 See, for example, *CICA Handbook*, supra note 34. This point is made by Malcolm Gammie, "The Source Taxation of Derivative Financial Instruments, 'Synthetic Securities,' Financial Hedging Transactions and Similar Innovative Financial Transactions" (September/October 1999), 1 *Derivatives & Financial Instruments* 231-36.

62 May, supra note 26, at 29:9 and 29:16-24. For a comprehensive discussion of the financial-accounting issues presented by hedging strategies, see Harold Bierman Jr., L. Todd Johnson, and D. Scott Peterson, *Hedge Accounting: An Exploratory Study of the Underlying Issues* (Norwalk, Conn.: Financial Accounting Standards Board, 1991).

63 *CICA Handbook*, supra note 34.

64 Arnold, supra note 55, at 483-84; and Johnson, supra note 59, at 425: "Reported earnings is just a communication from management to the market related to what the stock of the corporation is worth. . . . A corporate tax base equal to changes in corporate share price, plus its dividends, would generate a sounder tax, based on better theory, and would be less sensitive to tax."

65 This point is made generally in Deborah A. Geier, "The Myth of the Matching Principle as a Tax Value" (Spring 1998), 15 *The American Journal of Tax Policy* 17-166. An acceptance of financial-accounting practice is particularly troublesome in the case of hedge transactions. For financial-accounting purposes, hedge accounting requires the matching of gain or loss on a financial instrument with loss or gain on an underlying transaction, where the financial instrument is entered into as a hedge of the underlying. See the text that accompanies notes 78-102 in chapter 2 for an account of the analogous linkage approach that Canadian and Australian courts accept in limited circumstances. The text that accompanies notes 187-217 in chapter 7 argues that hedge accounting has no relevance for tax purposes under a comprehensive accrual regime intended to implement the dictates of expected-return taxation. Integrated treatment, however, may be necessary to address the tax-driven combination of instruments to synthetically replicate another instrument.

66 Under an income tax system that requires conformity of financial- and tax-accounting practices, tax considerations, in fact, may undermine the appropriate development of the former. See Arnold, supra note 55, at 487; and Johnson, supra note 59, at 425: "If there is a 28 percent or 35 percent tax on the amount communicated, then management will find less expensive ways, around the tax toll charge, by which to communicate the worth of their stock. A shriveling of the

reporting of earnings would reduce both tax revenue and also damage the pricing mechanisms of capital markets." Arnold raises this issue in the narrower context of a requirement of conformity between the financial statements and tax returns of a taxpayer. This form of conformity is even more restrictive and problematic, since it forces the taxpayer to use for tax purposes a particular method of reporting for financial-statement purposes even if there are several equally appropriate methods for financial-statement purposes and one of the methods not chosen would also be appropriate for income tax purposes.

67 The Supreme Court of Canada recently affirmed this approach in the context of the computation of business income generally. See *Canderel Limited v. The Queen*, 98 DTC 6100; [1998] 2 CTC 35. The court ruled that financial-accounting practice is relevant, but not determinative, in the computation of business profit for income tax purposes. See Webb, supra note 53, for a review of the historical development of this position under the ITA.

68 See, for example, David A. Miller, "Reconciling Policies and Practice in the Taxation of Financial Instruments" (March 1999), 77 *Taxes: The Tax Magazine* 236-76, at 246 and 257; Steven M. Rosenthal and Mark H. Price, "FAS 133 and Tax—An Unhappy Marriage Awaiting a Counsellor" (July/August 1999), 1 *Derivatives & Financial Instruments* 216-27; Lee A. Sheppard, "Slow and Steady Progress on Corporate Tax Shelters" (July 12, 1999), 84 *Tax Notes* 191-200, at 192; and Lee A. Sheppard, "Can the Tax Law Live with FAS 133?" (February 7, 2000), 86 *Tax Notes* 732-37. Sheppard argues that the recent proposals of the Federal Accounting Standards Board in the United States should lead the income tax system to apply accretion taxation more broadly. The US financial-accounting standards require public corporations, for fiscal periods beginning after June 15, 2000, to apply mark-to-market recognition of derivatives acquired for non-hedging purposes. See Financial Accounting Standards Board (FASB), *Accounting for Derivative Instruments and Hedging Activities*, Statement of Financial Accounting Standards no. 133 (Norwalk, Conn.: FASB, June 1998) ("FAS 133"). Miller (supra, at 257) concludes that this requirement provides a reason to value the affected instruments that is independent of the need to value them for the purposes of accretion taxation and therefore minimizes the compliance burden associated with accretion taxation. He acknowledges that, even if one accepts the integrity of the relevant valuations, liquidity concerns continue to present a barrier to the adoption of accretion taxation. This separate tax-policy consideration means that accretion taxation may have to be limited in its application and that it may be necessary to reject a close correspondence between tax accounting and financial accounting even where the latter implements the accretion ideal.

69 One obvious instance of a close correlation between financial accounting and income tax accounting is the treatment of long-term prepaid debt in Canada. See supra note 56 and notes 103 and 106 in chapter 5. In many respects, the provisions of subsections 18(9.2)-(9.8) of the ITA reflect the financial-accounting practice described in CICA, *Abstract EIC-22*, supra note 56, but they also address many matters that are unique to income taxation and irrelevant for financial-accounting purposes. Thus the legislature maintained its responsibility for developing appropriate income tax rules but relied to a large extent on developed financial-accounting practice for insights into the appropriateness of the tax treatment of particular instruments.

70 See the text that accompanies notes 178-197 in chapter 5.

71 The Australian proposals put forward conformity between financial-accounting practice and tax-accounting practice, and the supposed reduction in compliance burden that it entails, as one of the advantages of the proposed regime. Australia, *Taxation of Financial Arrangements: A Consultative Document* (Canberra: Australian Government Publishing Services, December 1993), 34.

72 For a more detailed discussion of the importance of financial-accounting standards in the development of the accrual proposals, see Darrell A. Nolan, "The Financial Arrangements Code: Current Policy Deliberations," in *The 1995 Derivatives Megaconference*, at 7-9.

73 See the text that accompanies notes 179-187 in chapter 5.

74 Ibid.

75 Ibid. These norms are presumably reflected in the valuation methods used for financial-statement purposes. See, for example, FAS 133, supra note 68; and Miller, supra note 68.

76 J. Scott Wilkie, "Looking Forward into the Past: Financial Innovation and the Basic Limits of Income Taxation" (1995), vol. 43, no. 5 *Canadian Tax Journal* 1144-66. See also David P. Hariton, "The Tax Treatment of Hedged Positions in Stock: What Hath Technical Analysis Wrought?" (Summer 1995), 50 *Tax Law Review* 803-27. Hariton suggests the abandonment of detailed legislative rules ("technical analysis") in favour of the resolution of specific cases by applying general principles under a method of "logic, parallelism and judgment."

77 This approach to the taxation of financial instruments is a specific application of interpretive activism, which some commentators have advocated as an appropriate role for tax courts in interpreting and applying the provisions of income tax legislation generally. See, for example, Neil Brooks, "The Responsibility of Judges in Interpreting Tax Legislation," in Graeme Cooper, ed., *Tax Avoidance and the Rule of Law* (Amsterdam: IBFD Publications, 1997), 93-129.

78 Cass R. Sunstein, "Problems with Rules" [July 1995], *California Law Review* 953-1026, quoted in Gergen, supra note 22, at 856.

79 Gergen, supra note 22, at 856-57.

80 See, for example, Lokken, supra note 9.

81 See Louis Kaplow, "Rules Versus Standards: An Economic Analysis" (December 1992), 42 *Duke Law Journal* 557-629. Kaplow argues that, from an efficiency perspective, detailed legislative rules are the preferred means of describing the legal consequences of common transactions, since the one-time promulgation costs are likely to be less than the costs associated with the process of defining, after the fact, the details of the application of broad standards to a wide range of transactions.

82 Gergen, supra note 22, at 857. Gergen suggests that, in the US context, reliance on the rulings process as the principal resolution mechanism would require significant changes in the rulings process. For example, rulings might have to be "conditional on an instrument [sic] not later exhibiting undesirable properties." In addition, it might be necessary to impose some type of notice requirement on taxpayers who issued instruments with novel characteristics. Countries with rulings systems similar to the system in the United States would probably have to make similar changes.

83 Ibid., at 857-58.

84 Ibid.

85 See the analogy drawn by Frost, supra note 6, at 107, which is cited in the text that accompanies notes 158-159 in chapter 2.

86 Gergen, supra note 22, at 858. As was argued in chapters 2 and 3, existing legislative regimes based on the traditional tax cubbyholes create important "inconsistencies" and "discontinuities" in tax treatment, largely because of a failure to push the basic distinction between expected and unexpected gains and losses to its logical extreme as a design principle for a comprehensive legislative regime. An inconsistency occurs when equivalent cash flows are taxed differently. A discontinuity arises when a small change in the pattern of cash flows (that is, risk attributes) results in a significant change in tax treatment. Chapters 5, 6, and 7 describe the features of a comprehensive legislative approach that attempts to eliminate or minimize inconsistencies and discontinuities in tax treatment and thereby provide a critical element of conceptual coherence as the underlying basis for the necessary details of legislative rules and administrative practices. In this connection, see Deborah L. Paul, "The Sources of Tax Complexity: How Much Simplicity Can Fundamental Tax Reform Achieve?" (November 1997), 76 *North Carolina Law Review* 151-231. Paul describes three types of complexity found in legislative regimes. In her taxonomy, a "complicated" regime is characterized by "numerous detailed authorities." An "intractable" regime is characterized by difficulties in applying underlying concepts. An "incoherent" regime is characterized by "inconsistent purposes or no purposes at all." Existing legislative regimes based on the traditional tax cubbyholes tend to exhibit all three types of complexities. The most fundamental problems, however, are those that arise from conceptual incoherence and intractability. This point is emphasized in much of the general literature on tax simplification. See, for example, Graeme S. Cooper, "'A Rose Is a Flower Is a Plant': Tax Simplification South of the Equator," in the 1995 Conference Report, supra note 26, 3:1-25; and Robert Couzin, "The Process of Simplification" (1984), vol. 32, no. 3 *Canadian Tax Journal* 487-500, at 491: "But no degree of linguistic purity can bring into focus what is essentially fuzzy thinking."

87 Gergen, supra note 22, at 859. Inconsistencies and discontinuities in tax treatment are sources of complexity that Paul, supra note 86, refers to as "intractability" and "incoherence." As discussed in chapters 6 and 7, the application of different tax treatments to interest and dividends and the application of the realization requirement are two important discontinuities that are inevitable under any second-best approach. These discontinuities place pressure on the boundary lines between debt and equity and between realization and non-recognition transactions. Because these different categories have no distinguishing features that are obviously relevant from a tax-policy perspective, the associated boundaries are sources of "intractability;" that is, the underlying concepts are difficult to apply in borderline cases. Paul, ibid., at 159-61.

88 Lokken, supra note 9. An element of complexity, defined in terms of the amount of detailed interpretive authorities (for example, regulations and statements of administrative practice), is perhaps inevitable. In fact, the courts are only one source of this type of complexity. But see John Avery Jones, "Tax Law: Rules or Principles?" (August 1996), 17 *Fiscal Studies* 63-89, who makes the case for a "principled approach" to the drafting of income tax legislation generally. This

approach is characterized by the implementation of necessary technical details through the courts and administrative practice, rather than through the development of legislative rules that attempt to address all conceivable circumstances. See also John Prebble, "Should Tax Legislation Be Written from a Principles and Purpose Point of View or a Precise and Detailed Point of View?" [1998], no. 2 *British Tax Review* 112-23; and Kaplow, supra note 81, who distinguishes the use of detailed legislative rules from the use of general principles or "standards" but argues that the level of complexity depends on the substantive aspects or "content" of a particular area of law and is independent of the procedural choice of the form of the law.

The approach described in chapters 5, 6, and 7 involves the use of detailed legislative rules as the most efficient means of describing the taxation of broad categories of basic instruments and paradigm transactions. Uncertainty associated with the use of standards expressed in the form of anti-avoidance rules or general classification tests can be relied on to "police" discontinuities that remain because of certain practical constraints that limit the ability of policy makers to apply accretion taxation to all financial instruments. See David A. Weisbach, "Formalism in the Tax Law" (Summer 1999), 66 *The University of Chicago Law Review* 860-86; and David A. Weisbach, "Line Drawing, Doctrine, and Efficiency in the Tax Law" (September 1999), 84 *Cornell Law Review* 1627-81.

89 Stephen B. Land, "Defeating Deferral: A Proposal for Retrospective Taxation" (Fall 1996), 52 *Tax Law Review* 45-117, at 112: "Most taxpayers have learned to cope with the problems of current law, and prefer known to unknown evils." Karla W. Simon, "Revenue or Religion? Issues and Answers on Tax Deferral" (December 1990), 68 *Taxes: The Tax Magazine* 1015-32, at 1029-31, makes much the same point after reviewing both various academic proposals for the elimination of deferral and US congressional responses to particular instances of deferral. This preference for incremental reform is not attributable solely to the practical politics of tax reform. From a substantive policy perspective, incremental reform may be less susceptible than radical reform to unforeseen problems, thanks largely to its ability to draw on past experience and hence on familiar concepts and familiar approaches to similar policy problems. It is, therefore, better equipped to anticipate tax-avoidance opportunities and non-neutralities that present efficiency problems.

90 See, in particular, Alan J. Auerbach, "Retrospective Capital Gains Taxation" (March 1991), 81 *The American Economic Review* 167-78; Meyer W. Bucovetsky, "Inflation and the Personal Tax Base: The Capital Gains Issue" (1977), vol. 25, no. 1 *Canadian Tax Journal* 79-107; Mary Louise Fellows, "A Comprehensive Attack on Tax Deferral" (February 1990), 88 *Michigan Law Review* 722-813; John Helliwell, "The Taxation of Capital Gains" (May 1969), 2 *Canadian Journal of Economics* 314-18; and William Vickrey, "Averaging Income for Income Tax Purposes" (June 1939), 47 *Journal of Political Economy* 379-97. Much of this literature is reviewed in Matt Benge, "Capital Gains and Reform of the Tax Base," in John G. Head and Richard Krever, eds., *Taxation Towards 2000* (Sydney: Australian Tax Research Foundation, 1997), 351-89, at 374-84.

91 See the text that accompanies notes 58-65 in chapter 3.

92 Ibid. But see Land, supra note 89, who argues that deferred tax is analogous to an equity investment by the government in the particular asset held by a taxpayer.

Land's analogy underlies his proposal for a system of retrospective taxation that avoids certain of the problems commonly associated with such systems. Notes 99 and 114 infra discuss these problems and Land's alternative approach. Much the same approach is described in some of the earlier literature on retrospective taxation as the equivalent of an accretion-based capital gains tax. See Benge, supra note 90, at 374-79, who describes an "impinging-on-capital" approach that is comparable to Land's suggested approach. Indeed, some of the literature on deferral characterizes tax deferral as an equity or partnership investment by the government. See generally Christopher H. Hanna, "Demystifying Tax Deferral" (Spring 1999), 52 *SMU Law Review* 383-422.

93 The concept of retrospective taxation is developed in, for example, Cynthia Blum, "New Role for Treasury: Charging Interest on Tax Deferral Loans" (Winter 1988), 25 *Harvard Journal on Legislation* 1-111, at 27-93; Fellows, supra note 90; Stephen B. Land, "Contingent Payments and the Time Value of Money" (Winter 1987), 40 *The Tax Lawyer* 237-306, at 283-88; and Vickrey, supra note 90. A comprehensive system of expected-return taxation that applies to a broad range of assets is described in Noël B. Cunningham and Deborah H. Schenk, "Taxation Without Realization: A 'Revolutionary' Approach to Ownership" (Summer 1992), 47 *Tax Law Review* 725-814. Scarborough, supra note 6, suggests the application of this system to financial instruments and Shuldiner, supra note 2, describes this application in detail.

94 Auerbach, supra note 90, at 168.

95 Vickrey, supra note 90.

96 Vickrey subsequently extended his original concept of a cumulative averaging system for capital gains to the development of a system of lifetime averaging for income generally. See William Vickrey, "Tax Simplification Through Cumulative Averaging" (Autumn 1969), 34 *Law and Contemporary Problems* 736-68.

97 Auerbach, supra note 90, at 168.

98 Ibid.

99 See, for example, Blum, supra note 93, at 27-93; Fellows, supra note 90; and Land, supra note 93, at 283-88. To varying degrees, all of these models allocate realized gain or loss retrospectively over the term of an asset on the basis of some standard allocation method. They then impose a charge for the deferral of tax payable until realization (or a refund in the case of the deferral of a loss). But see Land, supra note 89, where he revises his earlier view of retrospective taxation and proposes a system that does not require the allocation of gain or loss or the imposition of interest-deferral charges. Land's unique and elegant approach rests on the premise that deferred tax is analogous to an equity investment by the government in the relevant asset owned by a taxpayer. The government is therefore compensated for the investment of its funds (the deferred taxes) by the rate of return earned on the particular asset, which may be more or less than the riskless rate. Given Land's analogy, retrospective taxation requires only (1) computation of the gain or loss measured ex post on realization, (2) computation of the pre-tax yield earned on an asset on the basis of the ex post gain or loss and appropriate assumptions about compounding periods, and (3) computation of the after-tax yield as a function of the pre-tax yield and appropriate tax rate. The difference between the pre-tax and after-tax yield is the tax owed by the taxpayer

(the tax refund in the case of a loss). This amount effectively compensates the government for its equity investment in the asset of the taxpayer. Note 114 infra notes the apparent advantages and disadvantages of this approach.

100 Fellows, supra note 90.

101 Auerbach, supra note 90.

102 Ibid., at 169. See also Jeff Strnad, "Periodicity and Accretion Taxation: Norms and Implementation" (July 1990), 99 *The Yale Law Journal* 1817-1911, at 1863-64. Strnad notes the problems that arise from an inability to determine the pattern of accrual and the need to make assumptions about that pattern.

103 Auerbach, supra note 90.

104 The tax rate on unexpected gains and losses is effectively zero. Since the chance that the outcome will be a gain is the same as the chance that it will be a loss, there is no net benefit or detriment associated with a zero rate, provided that a strictly ex ante perspective is maintained. This strictly ex ante perspective means that for tax purposes one may ignore the basic building-block financial instruments that are pure bets and provide only unexpected gains and losses (forwards, futures, and swaps). In contrast, all income tax systems that attempt to take ex post results into account must recognize unexpected gains and losses on these financial instruments. See, for example, Land, supra note 89, where he acknowledges this need under his proposed system of retrospective taxation and the problems it presents owing to the difficulty of calculating a yield on instruments that are pure bets.

105 The lock-in effect and the problem of selective realization arise when the rate of return is higher than the riskless rate of return that every asset can be assumed to provide. Higher or lower returns are unexpected and arise as the passage of time reveals the resolution of contingencies that determine the outcome of the implicit bets. Auerbach, supra note 90, at 169, defines a realization-based income tax as being "holding-period neutral" "if it leads each investor in an asset to require a before-tax return having a certainty-equivalent value that is not a function of the length of holding period or the asset's past pattern of returns." A realization-based income tax will exhibit this attribute only if the lock-in effect and the benefit of selective realization are eliminated. Auerbach formally proves that his system of retrospective taxation realizes this result and is thus holding-period neutral. The mathematics are quite sophisticated, but they support the intuition described in the text that lies at the basis of Auerbach's system: that is, that the lock-in effect and the benefit of selective realization disappear if unexpected gains and losses are ignored.

106 David F. Bradford, "Fixing Realization Accounting: Symmetry, Consistency and Correctness in the Taxation of Financial Instruments" (Summer 1995), 50 *Tax Law Review* 731-85.

107 Under Bradford's approach, a taxpayer would be permitted to specify at the outset of an investment both a gains realization date and the tax rate on unexpected gains and losses. See Bradford, ibid., at 762-82. Since at the outset of an investment one outcome is as likely as the other, Bradford's system would also be holding-period neutral in the sense defined by Auerbach. Given two equally likely outcomes, a taxpayer would have no incentive to specify any particular realization date or tax rate; consequently, the lock-in effect and the benefit of selective realization

would not arise. The extreme case would be the specification by a taxpayer of a zero tax rate on unexpected gains and losses. For the reasons noted above, however, this specification would be no different in its effect on the property of holding-period neutrality from the specification of some positive tax rate.

108 For detailed descriptions of the concept of anticipated deferral and the efficiency and equity concerns that it presents, see the text that accompanies notes 66-79 in chapter 3 and Shuldiner, supra note 2, at 250-55.

109 Bradford, supra note 106, supports this intuition with formal mathematical proofs. Deborah H. Schenk, "A Realization-Based Income Tax and the Taxation of Capital" (draft), reprinted in *Tax Notes Today*, October 26, 1997, 97 TNT 223-39 (electronic database), argues that the disregard of ex post results in the form of unexpected gains and losses is, in fact, normatively desirable. She bases her argument on recent literature in which it is suggested that the return to risk may be equally exempt under an income tax and a cash flow consumption tax owing to taxpayers' ability to alter portfolios in response to taxation and maintain the same expected return after tax. See chapter 3 at note 29. Schenk concludes that the return to risk is taxed only accidentally or arbitrarily—that is, only when non-tax factors constrain a taxpayer's ability to make the necessary portfolio adjustments. Since an income tax effectively taxes only the riskless rate of return, Schenk proposes an ex ante wealth tax that would be based on the imputation of interest at the riskless rate on the cost of an asset.

110 See Auerbach, supra note 90, at 168; and Warren, supra note 8, at 477-78. Vickrey, too, recognized this problem in a re-examination of his earlier proposals for a system of cumulative averaging. See Vickrey, supra note 96, at 740. Vickrey also acknowledged that systems of retrospective taxation involve complicated time-value adjustments and hence significant compliance and administrative costs. These problems tend to support the use of a modified version of expected-return taxation. See the text that accompanies notes 120-123 infra.

111 Auerbach, supra note 90, at 168, expresses this problem as follows:

> For example, if an asset has increased in value over a ten-year period, the tax rate on the realized gain needed to simulate accrual taxation would be the ordinary tax rate if the gain occurred entirely in the tenth year, but this tax rate compounded by one plus the ninth power if the entire gain occurred during the first year of ownership. Simply to assume, for tax purposes, that a realized gain accrued smoothly at a constant annual rate would not solve the problem. Assets achieving above-normal rates of return initially would still be subject to a lock-in effect, because an investor anticipating only normal returns from the asset in the future would be able to spread the accrual pattern retrospectively imputed for this gain over several years by holding on to the asset.

112 Ibid.

113 See, for example, the sources cited supra note 90.

114 See also Land, supra note 89, who correctly points out (and demonstrates through formal mathematical proofs) that his system of retrospective taxation eliminates both the lock-in effect and the problem of selective realization and is therefore holding-period neutral. The advantage of Land's proposal is that the pattern of

accrual of an asset and the holding period are irrelevant. Land's proposal, in effect, avoids the weaknesses commonly associated with systems of retrospective taxation that require rough averaging assumptions about the accrual pattern of gains and losses. The proposal depends, however, on a critical change to the underlying paradigm that is used to measure the deferral benefit addressed by conventional systems of retrospective taxation. Under that paradigm, an accretion-based income tax requires the annual recognition of gains and losses that are attributable to changes in value and the payment of tax at the end of the period in which the changes arose. By deferring payment of the tax until realization, the government effectively loans those funds to the taxpayer. Conventional systems of retrospective taxation attempt to charge (or pay in the case of losses) interest on these loans on the basis of assumptions about the amount and the duration of the loans, given the pattern of accrual. Land, instead, characterizes these loans as being analogous to equity participations but nowhere justifies normatively why this characterization is more appropriate. In fact, it is simply not clear that, under a paradigm accretion-based tax, the government would invest deferred taxes by taking an equity stake in the asset of a taxpayer. In an important sense, therefore, Land ignores the opportunity cost of capital for the government, and his analogy is suspect. His modified system of retrospective taxation is acceptable from a theoretical standpoint only if the suspect analogy can be supported as normatively appropriate.

As Land acknowledges (ibid., at 84-86), Auerbach's system of retrospective capital gains taxation realizes much the same result as his own modified system of retrospective taxation by similarly changing the common accretion paradigm and the measurement of the deferral benefit on the basis of that paradigm. Auerbach, however, alters the paradigm in a different and more justifiable way: his system requires a strictly ex ante focus that ignores unexpected gains and unexpected losses on the ground that they are the equally likely outcomes of contingencies that are tantamount to pure bets.

115 Strnad, supra note 102, at 1886, footnote 199: "The problem with this scheme [Auerbach's system of retrospective capital gains taxation] is that it ignores the wealth-related norms that justify choosing accretion taxation in the first place."

116 The problem is even worse under Auerbach's system, which assumes that taxpayers earn the riskless rate of return and taxes them accordingly even if their actual rate of return is less than the riskless rate, owing to a resolution of contingencies that results in unexpected losses measured ex post. See, for example, Land, supra note 89, at 85: "the resulting tax is not an income tax at all, and even sales of assets that, in fact, have gone down in value attract tax liability." The same result would occur under a pure system of expected-return taxation, which is the equivalent of the specification by the taxpayer of a zero tax rate under Bradford's system. In either case, there would be no offset of unexpected loss against expected gain. Full offset would occur only if the taxpayer specified a tax rate equal to the rate on expected gain or loss. A partial offset would occur if the specified rate was less than the rate on expected gain or loss but greater than zero.

117 See the text that accompanies notes 28-56 in chapter 2.

118 The text that accompanies notes 125-127 infra discusses the use of a specified convention or allocation formula and the associated problems.

119 This approach is essentially the system of expected-return taxation described by Shuldiner, supra note 2. Shuldiner, however, would modify existing legislative

regimes to extend expected-return taxation to the embedded debt in options and shares. The text that accompanies notes 247-279 in chapter 6 discusses the implications for corporate income tax systems of the extension of expected-return taxation to the embedded debt in shares.

120 Miller, supra note 68, at 257-59, argues that accretion taxation should be extended on an elective basis and that tax incentives (including reduced capital gains rates) should be provided to induce elections. Miller's proposal appears to be an effort to approximate the accretion ideal but ignores the problems identified by the paradox of the second best noted in note 7 supra. But see also David A. Weisbach, "A Partial Mark-to-Market Tax System" (Fall 1999), 53 *Tax Law Review* 95-140. Weisbach argues that the application of accretion taxation to publicly traded assets, derivatives, and debt instruments can be justified on efficiency grounds, provided that the nominal tax rate is lower than the nominal rate on assets that are subject to realization-based recognition. The lower rate would compensate for the lower effective tax rate attributable to the benefit of deferral under realization-based recognition. The more limited role for accretion taxation suggested here and in chapter 5 does at least significantly reduce the problems associated with the use of second-best solutions, since accretion taxation is, in fact, the first-best response to the limited problem of selective realization. The principal weakness of this limited approach is that it requires an appropriate definition of instruments that are affected by selective realization, one that would target the application of accretion taxation to the instruments that are most susceptible to strategic trading. See the text that accompanies notes 291-315 in chapter 5. This limited role for accretion taxation is suggested in Daniel Halperin, "Saving the Income Tax: An Agenda for Research" (November 24, 1997), 77 *Tax Notes* 967-77; Scarborough, supra footnote 6; and Richard Wood, "Taxation of Financial Arrangements: The Trading Regime," in *Economic Roundup* (Canberra: Commonwealth Treasury of Australia, Summer 1998), 69-88.

121 See Halperin, supra note 120, who recommends a modified system of expected-return taxation with these core elements. The countries include New Zealand, Australia, and possibly the United States. See the text that accompanies notes 155-174 infra.

122 Mark P. Gergen, "The Effects of Price Volatility and Strategic Trading Under Realization, Expected Return and Retrospective Taxation" (Winter 1994), 49 *Tax Law Review* 209-69.

123 The two most significant instruments in this category are non-traded debt and shares, which are invariably excepted from accretion recognition. One commentator has estimated that the ability to trade bonds strategically and thus maximize the benefit of selective realization is equivalent to the provision of an investment tax credit for bondholders equal to 5 percent of the principal advanced. See Jeff Strnad, "The Taxation of Bonds: The Tax Trading Dimension" (February 1995), 81 *Virginia Law Review* 47-116.

124 See, however, Land, supra note 89, and the brief discussion of his modified system of retrospective taxation, supra notes 99 and 114.

125 The United States, in particular, uses interest-deferral charges in selected circumstances. See, for example, Fellows, supra note 90, at 728, footnote 16; and Warren, supra note 8, at 477, footnote 65, citing IRC sections 453(l)(3) and 453A (which

impose an interest-deferral charge on the instalment-sale method used by certain taxpayers); sections 460(a)(2), (b)(2)-(3) (which impose interest-deferral charges or provide credits if the taxpayer uses the percentage-of-completion method for long-term contracts and related expenses over- or underestimated for prior taxation years); and sections 1291-1297 (which impose an interest-deferral charge on US shareholders who receive a distribution from a "passive foreign investment corporation" (PFIC) if the distribution exceeds 125 percent of the average amount received during the three preceding taxation years).

126 Under any system of retrospective taxation, the government serves as a passive lender without any control over the loans it makes. All taxpayers enjoy the same access to credit, irrespective of their creditworthiness. The significance of the option to default on taxes and interest-deferral charges is emphasized in Michael S. Knoll, "Financial Innovation, Tax Arbitrage, and Retrospective Taxation: The Problem with Passive Government Lending" (Winter 1997), 52 *Tax Law Review* 199-224. In fact, Knoll shows how taxpayers can use offsetting positions under a system of retrospective taxation to provide tax-arbitrage profits, even though a system of this kind avoids the lock-in effect and the problem of selective realization. The taxpayer generates the profits by closing out the losing positions before the offsetting winning positions. The early closeout of the losing positions generates a tax saving and interest credit that is offset by the tax liability and interest charge associated with the offsetting winning position. However, the deferred closeout can be used to default on the offsetting liability. Knoll concludes that the ability to lock in the value of the default option through "selective realization" strategies of these kinds requires the adoption of loss limitations and other anti-avoidance provisions similar to those under existing income tax systems.

127 The practical problems associated with a system of retrospective taxation are acknowledged by Land, supra note 89, at 112, where he concedes that his modified system of retrospective taxation is probably not feasible even though it addresses the lock-in effect and the problem of selective realization while taking ex post outcomes into account. As noted above, however, his system depends on a questionable change in the commonly accepted paradigm for the measurement of deferral and the role of government in providing investment funds in the form of deferred taxes. Land's system also suffers from its own unique computational complexities and problems. It requires, for instance, the calculation of pre-tax and after-tax yields, which is not possible for the basic building-block financial instruments (forwards, futures, and swaps) that are pure bets and therefore involve no advance of funds or time-value return. Land's response is the recognition of gains and losses on a portfolio basis, under which a taxpayer's gains and losses on these instruments would be offset against his returns on assets with a time-value return. In effect, the former gains and losses would adjust the yield on other assets in a taxpayer's portfolio.

See also Knoll, supra note 126, who emphasizes the significance of the option to default on deferred taxes and interest charges under systems of retrospective taxation. This option presents a different type of selective realization that requires as an additional response the adoption of loss limitations, a step that is avoidable, to some extent, under a modified system of expected-return taxation. See the text that accompanies notes 280-336 in chapter 5.

128 Fellows, supra note 90, at 764-65.

129 Ibid., at 764.

130 In theory, each payment of interest and dividends constitutes a partial disposition of the financial instrument, in which the gain or loss must be allocated to an appropriate year within the holding period. The interest-deferral charge should be applied to the difference between the amount of the payment and a portion of the cost of the instrument properly allocated to it, but only to the extent that the payment is made in a year after the year to which the relevant gain or loss is appropriately allocated. The computational complexities associated with this theoretically pure approach are obvious. The alternative is simply not to treat distributions as dispositions during an instrument's holding period unless they are substantial or arise on a legal disposition.

131 Fellows, supra note 90, at 764.

132 The text that accompanies note 130 supra has noted some of these difficult distinctions. Computational problems arise wherever an amount that is allocated retrospectively to a particular taxation year is realized after that year but before the disposition of the entire asset. An obvious example is the payment of the expected return on a debt obligation during the term of the obligation but in a taxation year after the year to which the return is allocated for accrual purposes. Technically, all cases of this kind require a separate calculation of the interest deferral charge. Benge, supra note 90, at 380-83, describes these computational complexities as being unavoidable under any application of retrospective taxation to capital assets that provide intermediate cash flows.

133 Warren, supra note 8, at 478-79. See also Shuldiner, supra note 2, at 331-35. As Warren notes (supra, at 479-82), it is possible to minimize the compliance and administrative burdens that are associated with this requirement by using a standard imputation rate as a rough proxy for the expected returns. The obvious standard rate to use for this purpose is the riskless rate of return. This rate, however, represents the lowest possible standard and fails to require the accrual recognition of the expected return on certain assets that is represented by the premium for undiversifiable risk. But see Schenk, supra note 109, who argues that the exemption of the return to risk is normatively desirable under an income tax, which should apply only to interest imputed on capital assets at the riskless rate.

134 See, for example, Benge, supra note 90, at 384-85. Benge suggests that the combination of a realization-based capital gains tax and a taxpayer-elective accretion system applied to traded shares is preferable to a comprehensive system of retrospective taxation. Benge cites the Canadian experience with indexed securities investment plans (ISIPs) as an example of a taxpayer-elective system of accretion taxation for traded securities. The ISIP legislation had only a brief shelf life and was repealed in the face of widespread taxpayer indifference. To counter this indifference, Miller, supra note 68, recommends a system of "incentivized" accretion taxation, under which the application of lower tax rates to financial instruments subject to accretion taxation would presumably encourage taxpayers to elect this treatment. It is argued here and in the text that accompanies notes 280-290 in chapter 5 that in the context of a system of expected-return taxation application of the accretion basis should be mandatory as the first-best response to the strategic trading of a defined range of financial instruments.

135 See, generally, Gustaf Lindencrona, "The Taxation of Financial Capital and the Prevention of Tax Avoidance," in *Tax Reforms in the Nordic Countries, 1973-93*

(Uppsala: Nordic Council for Tax Research, 1993), 157-71; Leif Mutén, "Dual Income Taxation: Swedish Experience," in *Towards a Dual Income Tax? Scandinavian and Austrian Experiences* (The Hague: Kluwer Law International, 1996), 7-21; Peter Birch Sørensen, "From the Global Income Tax to the Dual Income Tax: Recent Tax Reforms in the Nordic Countries" (1994), vol. 1, no. 1 *International Tax and Public Finance* 57-79; Peter Birch Sørensen, "Recent Reform Experiments in Scandinavia," in *Global Change and Transformation: Economic Essays in Honor of Karsten Larssen* (Copenhagen: Handelshojskolens Forlag, 1993), 357-76; Kari S. Tikka, "A 25% Flat Tax Rate on Capital Income: The Finnish Reaction to International Tax Competition," in *Tax Reforms in the Nordic Countries*, supra, 91-108; and Frederik Zimmer, "Capital Income and Earned Income Following the Norwegian Income Tax Reform: Is the Dual Income Tax Fair?" in *Tax Reforms in the Nordic Countries*, supra, 141-54.

136 The application of different tax rates to capital income and labour income is not an entirely fresh idea; it is based on the familiar insights of optimal tax theory, which are reviewed in the text that accompanies notes 141-144 infra. These insights have also been used to justify other forms of non-uniform income tax treatments, such as the preferential taxation of capital gains as a means to alleviate the lock-in effect. See the text that accompanies notes 185-225 in chapter 3. For a general discussion of optimal tax theory, the challenge that it presents for comprehensive tax base theory, and its application as an underlying rationale for non-uniform taxation, see Graeme S. Cooper, "An Optimal or Comprehensive Income Tax?" (1994), vol. 22, no. 3 *Federal Law Review* 414-47; and Eric M. Zolt, "The Uneasy Case for Uniform Taxation" (Summer 1996), 16 *Virginia Tax Review* 39-109.

137 The first tentative steps toward the adoption of a DIT were actually taken by the Danish government in 1987. Denmark enacted a full DIT system in incremental steps in the early 1990s. The other Nordic countries reacted by introducing DITs in the same period. See Sørensen, "From the Global Income Tax to the Dual Income Tax," supra note 135, at 60-61.

138 See the sources cited supra note 135.

139 For accounts of the representative experience in Sweden, see Lindencrona, supra note 135; and Leif Mutén, "The Swedish Experiment with a General Anti-Avoidance Rule," in *Tax Avoidance and the Rule of Law*, supra note 77, 307-24.

140 This result can be realized through dividend imputation systems that provide full credit for corporate income tax on the underlying income from which dividends are paid. Effective exemption occurs because the proportional personal tax rate on the grossed-up dividend income is generally equivalent to the corporate tax rate. See Sørensen, "From the Global Income Tax to the Dual Income Tax," supra note 135, at 61. The same result can be realized by eliminating the personal tax on dividend income.

141 The traditional critique of the dual-rate structure is that it violates canons of equity by taxing capital income at a lower rate than labour income, even though they represent equal ability to pay tax. Moreover, distributional concerns dictate that capital income be taxed more heavily, since it is generally realized in disproportionate amounts by high-income individuals. These traditional critiques and responses to them are canvassed fully in Sørensen, "From the Global Income Tax to the Dual Income Tax," supra note 135, at 61-68.

142 See, for example, Tikka, supra note 135, at 94-95; and Zimmer, supra note 135, at 142-43.

143 Sørensen, "From the Global Income Tax to the Dual Income Tax," supra note 135, at 69-70.

144 According to optimal tax theory, in the absence of monitoring and enforcement mechanisms that permit the effective taxation of highly elastic factors such as internationally mobile capital the effective tax burden must be borne by less mobile factors such as labour. Accordingly, high statutory rates of tax are illusory and a lower rate simply acknowledges the reality of the relative elasticities. See Sørensen, "From the Global Income Tax to the Dual Income Tax," supra note 135, at 69.

145 See, for example, Tikka, supra note 135, at 94; and Zimmer, supra note 135, at 143-44. The problem was particularly acute in Sweden, where all personal interest expense was generally deductible, irrespective of its use. See Peter Melz, "National Report—Sweden," in International Fiscal Association, *Cahiers de droit fiscal international*, vol. 79a, *Deductibility of Interest and Other Financing Charges in Computing Income* (Deventer, the Netherlands: Kluwer Law and Taxation, 1994), 415-29, at 415-16; Lindencrona, supra note 135, at 158; and Mutén, supra note 135, at 8-9.

146 Finland and Sweden permit the offset of a limited amount of excess interest expense against labour income. See Esa Aalto, "National Report—Finland," in *Deductibility of Interest*, supra note 145, 149-64, at 149; and Melz, supra note 145, at 416.

147 For example, the array of categories into which interest and other passive investment expenses may be slotted is not as large or as complex under the Nordic DIT systems as it is under the US system.

148 Sweden, for example, imposes a final withholding tax on interest paid by financial institutions to resident individuals and on dividends paid by resident corporations on registered shares.

149 See Aalto, supra note 146, at 152; Hugo P. Matre, "National Report—Norway," in *Deductibility of Interest*, supra note 145, 345-57, at 348-49; and Melz, supra note 145, at 419.

150 Sweden addresses this problem by requiring the amortization and deduction of prepaid interest expense on an accrual basis. See Melz, supra note 145, at 419.

151 Since interest expense is allocated among income sources on the basis of a physical-tracing approach, individuals are also able to order their borrowings to stream interest expense to non-capital income sources. This strategy is effective primarily for individuals with business income from proprietorships.

152 See the text that accompanies notes 115-133 in chapter 3 for a brief discussion of these possible inefficiencies.

153 See, for example, Zimmer, supra note 135, at 143.

154 See, for example, Peter Birch Sørensen and Kare P. Hagen, "Taxation of the Self-Employed Under a Dual-Income Tax," in *Towards a Dual Income Tax?* supra note 135, 23-67. Schenk, supra note 109, notes the same difficulty under her proposed ex ante wealth tax that taxes labour income in full and exempts unexpected gains on capital assets.

155 See chapter 2.

156 Frost, supra note 6, at 112.

157 See ibid., at 112, where Frost cites two other legislative alternatives. He describes the first as "tax[ing] income calculated on [the] Haig-Simons principle." This catchphrase seems to refer roughly to the theoretical benchmark described in chapter 3, and is dismissed by Frost as "a somewhat radical alternative." His second alternative is the "use of financial accounting statements," which apparently involves an unqualified acceptance for income tax purposes of the treatment of gain or loss on financial instruments for financial-accounting purposes. The text that accompanies notes 50-75 supra discusses and dismisses this approach as a possible second-best alternative to accretion taxation.

158 Frost, supra note 6, argues that the first three of these approaches are inadequate "long-term" alternatives to the status quo. In particular, he rejects the first and third because they ignore the fact that taxpayers other than financial institutions are frequent users of new financial instruments and are likely to experience problems, as well as benefit from tax-arbitrage opportunities, under a status quo that is based on the traditional tax cubbyholes and limited transactional responses intended to maintain the integrity of those cubbyholes. Although financial institutions are the heavier users of financial instruments, any difference between these taxpayers and non-financial institutions is one of degree and not one of kind and therefore does not justify different rules for financial institutions. Frost characterizes the second approach as an attractive short-run alternative that tends to mask its lack of fundamental guiding principles and makes consistency in the treatment of different financial instruments more difficult to achieve than does the fourth approach.

159 For example, Frost's first category of "half-page amendments" is a limited version of a code applicable to all financial instruments held or issued by financial institutions. In fact, limited application of mark-to-market reporting of certain financial instruments, whether or not dependent on the identity of the taxpayer, is often an element of concerted piecemeal amendments. Similarly, reliance on financial-accounting practices tends to be a significant feature of any attempt to devise a comprehensive code for the taxation of most financial instruments; at the very least, these principles are often used as a starting point for the recognition of gain or loss.

160 It may be more accurate to state that the above list of possible legislative approaches leaves tax-policy makers with a choice between only two significantly different alternatives: (1) a comprehensive legislative code that is applicable to a wide range of financial instruments held or issued by most taxpayers; and (2) a legislative code that is applicable to a wide range of financial instruments held or issued by a narrow range of taxpayers, usually financial institutions, that trade or deal in these instruments. The latter alternative is commonly referred to as "a two-code approach," since for taxpayers who are not financial institutions it leaves intact the application of existing core provisions originally designed for traditional financial returns. More sophisticated recognition rules that apply to a wide range of financial instruments are limited to the returns on instruments held and issued by financial institutions. Whether this "second code" should be the product of concerted piecemeal amendments or a conscious attempt to develop a comprehensive code may be no more than a question of form. In either case, financial-accounting practices are important but not determinative.

The text that accompanies notes 66-83 in chapter 5 reviews the scope of a comprehensive accrual regime, defined in terms of the taxpayers who are subject to it. The merits and shortcomings of a two-code legislative approach are discussed in that context.

161 IRC section 1275.

162 Ibid., section 1092.

163 Ibid., section 1256.

164 Ibid., section 988; and IRC reg. section 1.988-5.

165 Ibid., sections 1272 and 1273.

166 IRC reg. sections 1.1275-4 and 1.1275-6.

167 IRC section 475.

168 IRC reg. section 1.446-3.

169 IRC reg. section 1.446-4.

170 IRC section 1258.

171 IRC section 1259. Although the UK Inland Revenue has been more restrained than the US Treasury department, it has tended to follow the US lead. In the early and mid-1990s, Inland Revenue introduced very detailed regimes for foreign currency transactions, foreign currency and interest-rate contracts, and most debt obligations.

172 New Zealand Income Tax Act, 1994, as amended, subpart H of part E, sections EH A1-EH 18 (division 1 applicable generally to financial arrangements entered into on or after October 23, 1986 and before May 20, 1999); and sections EH 19-EH 59 (division 2, applicable generally to financial arrangements entered into on or after May 20, 1999).

173 *Issues Paper*, supra note 59; and *Consultative Document*, supra note 71. See also Australia, Review of Business Taxation, *A Platform for Consultation: Building on a Strong Foundation*, Discussion Paper 2, vol. 1 (Canberra: Australian Government Publishing Services, February 1999), chapters 5-7; Australia, Review of Business Taxation, *A Tax System Redesigned: More Certain, Equitable and Durable* (Canberra: Australian Government Publishing Services, July 1999), chapter 9; and Australia, *Draft Legislation: A New Tax System (Income Tax Assessment) Bill 1999* (Canberra: Australian Government Publishing Services, July 1999), chapter 2, division 45.

174 Some of the more contentious definitional issues concern the acceptance of "bifurcation" and "integration" as analytical techniques that may be used to identify disguised financial instruments as an appropriate basis of taxation. Another definitional issue that is related to the bifurcation and integration issue is the attempt to identify disguised debt and draw a distinction between debt and equity instruments. These issues are discussed in chapters 6 and 7.

Notes to Chapter 5

1 See the text that accompanies notes 185-225 in chapter 3.

2 New Zealand Income Tax Act, 1994, as amended, subpart H of part E, sections EH A1-EH 18 (division 1 applicable generally to financial arrangements entered into on or after October 23, 1986 and before May 20, 1999); and sections EH 19-EH 59

(division 2 applicable generally to financial arrangements entered into on or after May 20, 1999).

3 Australia, *Taxation of Financial Arrangements: A Consultative Document* (Canberra: Australian Government Publishing Service, December 1993); and Australia, *Taxation of Financial Arrangements: An Issues Paper* (Canberra: Australian Government Publishing Service, December 1996). See also Australia, Review of Business Taxation, *A Platform for Consultation—Building on a Strong Foundation*, Discussion Paper 2, vol. 1 (Canberra: Australian Government Publishing Service, February 1999), chapters 5-7; Australia, Review of Business Taxation, *A Tax System Redesigned: More Certain, Equitable and Durable* (Canberra: Australian Government Publishing Service, July 1999), chapter 9; and Australia, *Draft Legislation: A New Tax System (Income Tax Assessment) Bill 1999* (Canberra: Australian Government Publishing Service, July 1999), chapter 2, division 45.

4 It is interesting that, in practice, piecemeal amendments have tended to produce more consistency between the definition of financial arrangements subject to accrual treatment and the underlying policy than have comprehensive regimes. This result may be largely attributable to the fact that under the piecemeal amendment approach the definitions of the particular instruments and the specific tax-accounting methods, which implement the underlying policy, are developed together. Accordingly, the definitions of the particular instruments subject to specialized legislation tend to closely parallel the appropriate recognition methods. Because it lacks any overriding principle that is applicable to financial instruments generally, the piecemeal approach may leave gaps in the legislation. Otherwise, a concerted piecemeal approach to the taxation of financial instruments may not be significantly inferior to the development of a comprehensive accrual regime based on a general definition of a financial arrangement.

5 This matter is discussed in the text that accompanies notes 247-279 in chapter 6 as a possible approach to the discontinuities associated with the distinction for tax purposes between debt and equity and the related issue of the boundary between the two tax cubbyholes.

6 These techniques and their application are discussed in the text that accompanies notes 90-197 infra.

7 See the text that accompanies notes 36-58 infra.

8 See the text that accompanies notes 24-46 in chapter 1 for a review of the essential features of these instruments.

9 *Consultative Document*, supra note 3, at 17; and Martin A. Smith, "An Overview of the Accrual Provisions and Issues Arising Thereunder" (May 1994), 48 *Bulletin for International Fiscal Documentation* 218-35, at 220.

10 Anthony J. Frost, "Taxation of Financial Transactions," in *Papers Presented at the Eleventh National Convention of the Taxation Institute of Australia* (Sydney: Taxation Institute of Australia, 1993), 103-86, at 112. See the text that accompanies notes 154-174 in chapter 4 for a brief description of various legislative approaches, including the use of "concerted piecemeal amendments."

11 *Consultative Document*, supra note 3, at 17.

12 For example, the application of the UK legislation that governs financial instruments is limited to "qualifying contracts," which the legislation defines by reference

to the types of payments under these contracts. The scope of the US legislation that governs contingent debt, notional principal contracts (NPCs), and traded options and futures is similarly determined by definitions of each of these types of instruments.

13 It is notable that even under the wide definitional approach recommended in the *Consultative Document*, supra note 3, at 18, the Australian Taxation Office (ATO) admits that it is difficult "to describe precisely yet comprehensively all of the characteristics of every financial transaction." Consequently, the proposed Australian accrual regime would maintain a residual capacity to include or exclude specific products. The resulting approach is described as a combination of "characterization" and "specific products listing."

14 See, for example, Smith, supra note 9, at 220, where in discussing the New Zealand legislation he states the following:

> Alternatively, a very wide-ranging definition could be adopted, with the express exclusion of certain arrangements that were not to be targeted by the regime. In light of the fact that the accrual provisions were to perform an anti-avoidance role, and of the propensity of the finance industry to continually develop and construct "synthetic" instruments and arrangements with commercial, accounting and taxation benefits in mind, it is hardly surprising that the latter route was adopted. Whether that is the best alternative, however, is not beyond doubt.

15 Ibid., at 220-21, where Smith makes this point in support of a comprehensive definitional approach over an instrument-specific list.

16 A comprehensive approach based on the general characteristics of financial instruments is cited in the *Consultative Document*, supra note 3, at 18, as "the more appropriate means of achieving tax neutrality between like products and providing a tax framework within which financial markets can continue to innovate."

17 Disagreement over the underlying policy of the New Zealand legislation and its significance for the interpretation of the apparently wide definition of a "financial arrangement" is evident in the decisions of the Tax Review Authority ("the TRA") and the Court of Appeal, respectively, in *TRA Case 76* (1992), 17 TRNZ 481 and *CIR v. Dewavrin Segard (NZ) Ltd.* (1994), 18 TRNZ 509. The decisions concerned the characterization of executory contracts for sales of commodities denominated in foreign currencies. The TRA concluded that a deferred sale did not constitute a financial arrangement until the relevant contract was executed (usually, by delivery of the goods) and the vendor provided the purchaser with time to pay the sale price. Critical to this conclusion was the lack of any time value of money element until execution of a contract for sale. The TRA considered this element to be an underlying policy of the accrual regime and therefore read down the wide wording of the definition of a financial arrangement to exclude the recognition of unrealized foreign exchange gains that arose on the executory contract before delivery. In contrast, the Court of Appeal held that the wide wording of the definition included both forward currency contracts and forward sales of commodities. The court rejected any implied requirement that there be a time-value-of-money element for a transaction to be included within the definition of a financial arrangement. For a comment on the Court of Appeal decision, see (September 1994), 1 *New Zealand Journal of Taxation Law and Policy* 48-53.

18 See the discussion of the representative experiences in Canada and Australia in the text that accompanies notes 28-45 in chapter 2.

19 New Zealand Income Tax Act, 1994, as amended, section EH 14 definition of "financial arrangement." See also section EH 22, which defines a financial arrangement as

> (a) a debt or debt instrument, including a debt that arises by law;
> (b) an arrangement (that may include a debt or debt instrument or an excepted financial arrangement) under which a person receives money in consideration for a person providing money to any person
> (i) at a future time, or
> (ii) when an event occurs in the future or does not occur
> (whether or not the event occurs because notice is or is not given).

20 As Smith, supra note 9, at 221, points out, the significance of the additional inclusion of a "debt instrument" is unclear given the prior inclusion of "debt." The legislative history seems to indicate that the addition of a separate reference to "debt" was intended to ensure that undocumented arrangements were included.

21 The definition of "money" in New Zealand Income Tax Act, 1994, as amended, section OB 1, includes money's worth (whether or not convertible into money) and the right to money. Thus a financial arrangement potentially includes in-kind exchanges and is not limited to transactions in money in the strict sense.

22 For a comprehensive review of these interpretive issues, see Susan Glazebrook and Robin Oliver, *The New Zealand Accruals Regime: A Practical Guide* (Auckland: CCH New Zealand, 1989), 18-28; Anton Nannestad, "The Meaning of 'Financial Arrangement' in the Accrual Rules" (1991), vol. 35, no. 19 *Current Taxation* 35:134-46; and Smith, supra note 9, at 220-24.

23 Glazebrook and Oliver, supra note 22, at 20-27.

24 A technical difficulty with this reading is the definition's lack of a specific reference to a promise to pay money on both sides of a transaction. In particular, the second element of the definition of a financial arrangement refers only to one person, who obtains money in consideration for a promise by any person to pay money in the future. The failure to refer to the obtaining of money or a promise to pay money in consideration for a promise to pay in the future arguably suggests that money must be received initially. This interpretation is supported by the specific reference to a promise to pay money in the future, but it would exclude mutual promise contracts (forwards, futures, and swaps) from the definition of a financial arrangement. See Smith, supra note 9, at 224. The definition of a "financial arrangement" in New Zealand Income Tax Act, 1994, as amended, section EH 22, attempts to ensure the inclusion of mutual promise contracts by referring only to the receipt of money (which includes money's worth and the right to money) in consideration for the provision of money. See the new definition of a "financial arrangement," supra note 19; and New Zealand, *The Taxation of Financial Arrangements: A Discussion Document on Proposed Changes to the Accrual Rules* (Wellington, NZ: New Zealand Inland Revenue, Policy Advice Division, December 1997), 12.

25 Glazebrook and Oliver, supra note 22, at 20-27; and Smith, supra note 9, at 221. But see Nannestad, supra note 22, at 134, where he argues that the first element of the definition should be considered primary and the other two elements supplementary.

26 Glazebrook and Oliver, supra note 22, at 20-27. Since it is difficult to imagine any arrangements within the first element of the definition that are not within the second, some commentators have concluded that the first element is probably redundant. As an independent legislative concept, the broad wording of the second element means that the definition of a financial arrangement includes any debt obligation, purchase and sale agreement, debt defeasance, assignment of income, foreign currency transaction, forward or futures contract, swap, option, trade credit, annuity agreement, convertible note, guarantee agreement, letter of credit, underwriting agreement, or indemnity. See, for example, Smith, supra note 9, at 221. Smith notes that this application is supported by specific references to many of these particular arrangements in the transitional provisions, which would presumably not have been necessary if the specified arrangements were considered to be outside the definition of a financial arrangement. But see *Taxation of Financial Arrangements*, supra note 24, at 14, where it is indicated that the first element of the definition is not necessarily redundant.

27 *Consultative Document*, supra note 3, at 15; and *Issues Paper*, supra note 3, at 72-73. A fourth class consists of transactions that involve both the right to receive, or the obligation to pay, an amount in foreign currency and any physical holdings of foreign currency.

28 *Consultative Document*, supra note 3, at 15. The consultative document (ibid., at 20) makes it clear that the status of a transaction as a financial arrangement in general and as a debt arrangement in particular is to be determined when the transaction is entered into. Subsequent events would normally not affect this determination. As examples of transactions that are debt arrangements, the consultative document cites obvious ones, such as advances of money, loans, fixed-interest and variable-rate coupon securities, hire-purchase transactions, bank deposits, overdraft facilities, and other forms of credit and financial accommodation with a similar effect. This class of transactions is also intended to include discounted and deferred securities, inflation-indexed securities, annuities, perpetual notes, and debt with contingent payments.

29 *Consultative Document*, supra note 3, at 27; and *Issues Paper*, supra note 3, at 81-82 and 85. This standard concept of a derivative means that cash-settled forwards, futures, swaps, and options are within the proposed accrual regime. At least for the purpose of determining the scope of the accrual proposals, it does not matter whether a particular derivative is used for hedging interest-rate risk, exchange-rate risk, or other risk or for speculative purposes.

30 *Consultative Document*, supra note 3, at 28.

31 *Issues Paper*, supra note 3, at 28. The consultative document specifically excludes a derivative based on the value of a single commodity or equity security from the proposed accrual regime on the apparent premise that the derivative in this case is roughly equivalent to a direct investment in the underlying, which is not itself subject to accrual treatment. *Consultative Document*, supra note 3, at 15. With the introduction of hedge-accounting rules, the issues paper extends accrual treatment to all derivatives, including non-debt derivatives that are based on the value of a single commodity or equity. *Issues Paper*, supra note 3, at 72.

32 See the text that accompanies notes 18-57 in chapter 3.

33 The primary exception to this general principle is the application of market-value accounting to shares that taxpayers acquire for trading purposes. In this instance, the usually short-term nature of the shareholding is considered to be sufficient justification for the extension of accretion taxation to holders in a manner consistent with the recognition methods applicable to non-equity holdings. See *Issues Paper*, supra note 3, at 73. Market-value accounting also extends to units in unit trusts that are acquired for trading purposes.

34 See Glazebrook and Oliver, supra note 22, at 18-28; and Smith, supra note 9, at 220-24. In fact, the 1986 budget statement and the original discussion document that introduced the accrual regime focused primarily on the accrual recognition of systematic gains on debt securities. See Glazebrook and Oliver, supra note 22, at 3-6 and 17-18. The adoption of a wide definition, one that applied to all financial instruments except those that it specifically excluded, was apparently intended to prevent the avoidance that a more narrowly targeted definition might permit.

35 *Consultative Document*, supra note 3, at 15-32; and *Issues Paper*, supra note 3, at 72.

36 Consultative Committee on the Taxation of Income from Capital ("the Valabh committee"), *The Operational Aspects of the Accruals Regime* (Wellington, NZ: New Zealand Government Printer, October 1991), 10-26.

37 Ibid., at 10. A government consultative document released in October 1986 stated that the New Zealand accrual rules are intended to realize three objectives:

> - to remove deficiencies . . . which allow expenditure to be deducted before the corresponding revenue is assessable;
> - to require income and expenditure to be recognized on an accrual basis to minimize the scope for arbitrage between taxpayers on different tax rates; and
> - to minimize the additional administrative and compliance costs of the new provisions by making them compatible with accounting practices, except where this conflicts with the other objectives listed above.

See New Zealand, *Consultative Document on Accrual Tax Treatment of Income and Expenditure* (Wellington, NZ: New Zealand Government Printer, October 1986), chapter 1.

38 Valabh committee, supra note 36, at 95. The concept of a debt arrangement under the Australian accrual proposals is obviously patterned on this recommendation. See supra note 27 and accompanying text.

39 Valabh committee, supra note 36, at 14.

40 The requirement that there be a present cash flow in exchange for a future cash flow that is expected to exceed the former was designed as a proxy for this time-value element. The Valabh committee, supra note 36, at 15, believed that the use of the term "time value of money" might be too restrictive, since it could be considered to include only returns that are riskless. The recommended standard for the relative amounts of present and future cash flows presumably includes returns that are predominantly attributable to the time value of money but also have some volatility.

41 Ibid., at 14 and 16-17.

42 Ibid., at 17.

43 Ibid., at 17-18 and 95-96. The Valabh committee did not define "forward contracts for foreign exchange" and "interest-rate swaps." At least in the case of the latter term, the intention was to allow the relevant concept to develop flexibly over time in a manner consistent with market usage. Valabh committee, supra note 36, at 17. The committee also specifically included mutual promise contracts, in which money is received by one party sometime after entering into the contract in exchange for a reasonable expectation of receiving a greater amount in the future from the other party. As an example, the committee cited (ibid., at 18) an agreement for purchase and sale that provides for the transfer of the property in 3 months' time and deferral of the payment of the purchase price for a further 12 months. The inclusion was apparently necessary to preclude the argument that transactions of this kind were outside of the recommended definition simply because the property was not transferred when the parties entered into the contract. Although on-market forwards, futures, and swaps consist of mutual promises, the committee did not include them in this category of contract. The ground for this exclusion was that these derivatives involved only one cash flow, whereas the specific provision that included mutual promise contracts required the receipt of money by one party in return for a reasonable expectation that the other party would receive a greater amount in the future. Interestingly, the specific provision could have included off-market forwards and swaps. It could also have included prepaid contracts, under which one of the counterparties receives a prepayment. Even in that case, however, it would be necessary to conclude that the payer could reasonably expect to receive at some time in the future an amount greater than the amount paid.

44 This specific inclusion is apparently restricted to loans providing for fixed amounts of interest that become payable on the resolution of defined contingencies. See Valabh committee, ibid., at 18. The wording of the inclusion in the recommended definition does not appear to extend to debt with returns that are contingent in amount. The importance of this distinction is discussed in the text that accompanies notes 50-51 infra.

45 Smith, supra note 9, at 222.

46 Ibid.

47 Valabh committee, supra note 36, at 11 and 15-16. The inclusion of common items such as drycleaning contracts, multi-ride bus tickets, travellers' cheques, and employment contracts under the wide wording of the second element of the definition of a financial arrangement has always been a point of contention. Although these items often have a time-value-of-money element, they are not commonly seen as financial arrangements. Moreover, the smallness of the amounts involved in transactions of this kind tends to support their exclusion for compliance reasons. See Smith, supra note 9, at 221.

48 The argument put forward by the Valabh committee, supra note 36, at 13-14, that the list of exemptions might become inordinately long is hardly a sound reason for abandoning this alternative approach. Lengthy lists, including the recommended definition of the Valabh committee, do not appear to be especially problematic in other areas of tax legislation. Moreover, any problems that arise from the inclusion of transactions that are similar to, but not exactly the same as, exempted transactions, should not present enormous difficulties. The technical application of the accrual rules should not result in any tax effect for transactions that lack a

time-value-of-money element. If necessary, the list of exemptions can be added to from time to time in order to exclude such transactions of this kind.

49 See Smith, supra note 9, at 224, who criticizes the Valabh committee's recommended definition (and by implication the current legislative definition) as "still a conglomerate of general attributes and specific inclusions, rather than presenting any cohesive underlying policy."

50 The tax treatment of this particular type of hybrid instrument (referred to as "contingent debt") is discussed in detail in the text that accompanies notes 110-151 in chapter 6.

51 The need for consistent taxation of the expected return on fixed-payment debt and all contingent debt is illustrated by the US experience with the appropriate treatment of contingent debt. See the text that accompanies notes 110-136 in chapter 6. The Valabh committee's specific inclusion of debt with cash flows that are fixed in amount but contingent in terms of the time for payment would address only some instances in which contingencies might be introduced to avoid the application of a primary debt category.

52 Valabh committee, supra note 36, at 17-18.

53 Ibid., at 17.

54 See the text that accompanies notes 136-162 infra for a discussion of the appropriate treatment of foreign currency borrowings and loans, and exchange gains and losses generally, under a system of expected-return taxation.

55 The Valabh committee, supra note 36, at 18, included options on financial arrangements because of a perceived opportunity to use them as indirect debt investments that would otherwise be outside of the recommended definition of a financial arrangement and its requirement that there be a future cash flow that can reasonably be expected to exceed a present cash flow.

56 Recent proposals to amend the New Zealand legislation attempt to realize a greater measure of consistency between a wide definitional approach and the underlying policy of the New Zealand accrual regime by clearly establishing a hierarchy of tax-accounting methods. At the top of that hierarchy are YTM and comparable accounting methods that impose accrual recognition on expected gains and losses on debt and debt equivalents. The proposals limit accretion taxation to (1) instruments held and issued by a limited range of taxpayers (dealers in financial arrangements) and (2) a limited range of instruments held and issued by all taxpayers (futures and foreign currency contracts traded in active markets). See *The Taxation of Financial Arrangements*, supra note 24, at chapter 7; and New Zealand Income Tax Act, 1994, as amended, sections EH 33-EH 40. For a discussion of the proposals, see Andrew M.C. Smith, "New Zealand's Interest Accrual Rules: A Comprehensive Review 12 Years On" (1998), vol. 46, no. 4 *Canadian Tax Journal* 819-38.

57 The proposed definition is expressly adopted in *Issues Paper*, supra note 3, at 72 and 85.

58 The Valabh committee, supra note 36, at 14, notes that the use of the YTM method is appropriate for systematic gains on debt.

59 New Zealand Income Tax Act, 1994, as amended, sections EH 14 and EH 24 definitions of an "excepted financial arrangement." Under the definition of a

financial arrangement, an excepted financial arrangement is excluded only if it is not part of a wider financial arrangement (that is, "a synthetic instrument"). See the text that accompanies notes 82-92 in chapter 7 for a discussion of this exception. If the underlying property that is the subject of an agreement for purchase and sale is real property, "short term" means a period from the date of the agreement to the specified settlement date of no more than 93 days. In all other cases, the period is 63 days. A contract is considered an agreement for purchase and sale only if there is no option for cash settlement. For a discussion of the significance of this restriction, see the text that accompanies notes 214-217 in chapter 6.

60 *Consultative Document*, supra note 3, at 30-32, describes exclusions for shares, life insurance policies, interests in superannuation plans (including annuities issued under a superannuation plan), interests in controlled foreign corporations, short-term trade credits, short-term instalment sales of real property, and leasing transactions for plant and equipment. *Issues Paper*, supra note 3, at 71-91, generally incorporates these exclusions but limits the exclusion for shares to non-traded equity. Traded equity would be subject to market-value accounting under the proposed accrual regime. This extension is discussed in the text that accompanies notes 316-321 infra.

61 Security arrangements that insure against credit risk do not generally have an expected time-value return and are excluded from the New Zealand accrual regime. See *The Taxation of Financial Arrangements*, supra note 24, at 80-84; and *McElwee v. CIR* (1997), 18 NZTC 13,288 (HC) (a guarantee is not a financial arrangement unless it is accompanied by a guarantee fee). See also *The Queen v. Melford Developments Inc.*, 82 DTC 6281; [1982] CTC 330 (SCC) (a guarantee fee that is paid annually to a non-resident guarantor by a resident borrower is not considered to be interest for the purposes of non-resident withholding tax under ITA paragraph 212(1)(b)).

62 For example, it is unclear whether the exclusion of security arrangements under the New Zealand accrual regime (supra note 61) extends to "credit derivatives," such as total-return swaps, default swaps, and credit-linked notes. In general, these instruments insure against credit risk in much the same manner as conventional arrangements such as indemnities and guarantees. According to *The Taxation of Financial Arrangements*, supra note 24, at 82, security arrangements that are intended to insure against price risk (including exchange risk) and interest-rate risk should be subject to the accrual regime in the same manner as forward contracts generally. Credit derivatives should probably be considered financial instruments within an accrual regime only if the associated unexpected gains and losses would otherwise not be recognized on realization (that is, on resolution of the bet, which occurs when the creditworthiness of the debtor is established) as ordinary income or loss amounts. For a description of standard credit derivatives and their treatment under the IRC, see Bruce Kayle, "Will the Real Lender Stand Up? The Federal Income Tax Treatment of Credit Derivative Transactions" (Spring 1997), 50 *The Tax Lawyer* 569-615; David Z. Nirenberg and Steven L. Kopp, "Tax Treatment of Total Return Swaps, Default Swaps, and Credit-Linked Notes" (August 1997), 87 *Journal of Taxation* 1-14; and Lee A. Sheppard, "Credit Derivatives, Guarantees and the Ponies" (June 8, 1998), 79 *Tax Notes* 1220-24 ("credit derivatives can be viewed as fancy forms of guarantee"). See also Janice

C. Russell, "How Tax Principles Are Applied to Specific Derivative Products," in *Corporate Tax Minimization Strategies: Innovative Financing and Risk Management Structures* (Toronto: Strategy Institute, May 27, 1998), tab 5, at 9-18.

63 Leases are a significant example of financial transactions that are excluded because of the existence of parallel legislation. Financial leases that are equivalent to instalment sales are referred to as "specified leases" and are treated as deferred sales with interest. The Valabh committee, supra note 36, at 19 and 70-88, recommended that these leases be included within the accrual regime. New Zealand Inland Revenue has since accepted this recommendation, and financial leases are now subject to the accrual regime. See New Zealand, *Taxation (Accrual Rules and Other Remedial Matters) Bill: Commentary on the Bill* (herein referred to as "the taxation bill") (Wellington, NZ: Inland Revenue, Policy Advice Division, November 1998), 22-24. See also *A Tax System Redesigned*, supra note 3, at 369-406, which distinguishes "routine" (operating) leases from "non-routine" (financial) leases.

64 Infra notes 66-75 and accompanying text. The Valabh committee, supra note 36, at 18-22, recommended the addition of specific exclusions for (1) non-interest-bearing chequing accounts payable on demand in a foreign currency, (2) travellers' cheques and physical holdings of foreign currency, (3) partnership interests and joint ventures, (4) security arrangements and guarantees and indemnities, (5) interest-free loans, and (6) contracts for the provision of services. An unqualified exclusion for this latter category is arguably the most problematic one, because of the potential to use prepayments as disguised loans that are not subject to accrual recognition of the expected return. In principle, all prepayments for goods or services are debt arrangements on which interest income should be imputed to the payer and interest expense should be imputed to the payee. The debt is generally repaid when the specified goods or services, which have a value equal to the amount of the prepayment plus any imputed interest, are provided in the future at the specified time. Administrative and compliance considerations associated with the debt characterization of all prepayments, however, support the limiting of such characterization to long-term prepayments with significant time-value returns. The imputation of interest on prepaid forwards and swaps is discussed in the text that accompanies notes 25-94 and 235-236 infra. The approach, and its limitations, described in the context of long-term prepayments with significant time-value returns could be extended in many respects to prepayments for goods and services generally.

65 See also, in this respect, Clarissa Potter, "Mark-to-Market Taxation as the Way To Save the Income Tax—A Former Administrator's View" (Summer 1999), 33 *Valparaiso University Law Review* 879-905, at 901-5. Potter argues that taxpayer resistance to the application of accretion taxation to all publicly traded assets and liabilities means that a two-code approach is the only politically feasible approach. She would limit accretion taxation to "the types of transactions and taxpayers that generate the lion's share of the problems with realization: large corporations and high income or net-worth individuals."

66 New Zealand Income Tax Act, 1994, as amended, section EH 27. Each of the thresholds was recently increased. See the taxation bill, supra note 63, at 12-13; and New Zealand Income Tax Act, 1994, as amended, section EH 3(1). Because the annual threshold for income and expense is applied on the basis of the "absolute value" of each, there is no netting of income and expense from financial instruments issued and held by an individual.

67 New Zealand Income Tax Act, 1994, as amended, section EH 35. This threshold was recently increased from $1,000,000. See the taxation bill, supra note 63, at 15; and New Zealand Income Tax Act, 1994, as amended, section EH 1(3).

68 *Consultative Document*, supra note 3, at 30-31. The exemption in the *Consultative Document* would have been available for individuals whose holdings of financial arrangements did not exceed a specified threshold ($500,000).

69 *Issues Paper*, supra note 3, at 95. If the status of the taxpayer changes from that of a cash-basis holder to that of an accrual-basis holder or vice versa, all instruments should be deemed to be disposed of and reacquired at their fair market value. This notional disposition ensures that the appropriate recognition methods apply to gain or loss accrued to the date of the change in status. See, for example, New Zealand Income Tax Act, 1994, as amended, sections EH 3(3) and (4); and section EH 32.

70 *Issues Paper*, supra note 3, at 95-98.

71 The text that accompanies notes 110-136 in chapter 6 describes certain avoidance opportunities under a realization-based approach to the treatment of contingent debt.

72 See *Consultative Document*, supra note 3 at 31; *Issues Paper*, supra note 3, at 94; and *A Tax System Redesigned*, supra note 3, at 57. Both documents attempt to address arbitrage opportunities by denying the proposed exemption for individuals in cases in which a particular financial instrument incorporates significant deferral. See also New Zealand Income Tax Act, 1994, as amended, section EH 27(6); and section EH 3(2)(b), which empower the Commissioner of Inland Revenue to deny cash-basis status to individuals in the case of a class of financial arrangements that are designed to postpone liability to income tax.

73 See, for example, *Issues Paper*, supra note 3, at 98-100, rejecting the argument, advanced by several submissions, that large investment entities, if they are operating as investment conduits or pooling mechanisms for individuals, should be exempt from the proposed accrual regime.

74 This approach is used under subsections 12(4) and (9) of the Canadian Income Tax Act, RSC 1985, c. 1 (5th Supp.), as amended (herein referred to as "ITA"), which require the annual accrual recognition by individuals of interest income on fixed-payment debt, OID instruments, and certain contingent-debt instruments. Information-reporting requirements are imposed on financial institutions that issue the relevant instruments. See ITA regulation 201.

75 See generally David Daugaard and Tom Valentine, *Reforming the Taxation of Financial Arrangements: How Many Steps Forward?* Research Study no. 22 (Sydney: Australian Tax Research Foundation, 1995).

76 ITA sections 142.2-142.6, applicable generally to taxation years beginning after October 1994. For a description of the mark-to-market legislation, see Hugh G, Chasmar, "Securities Held by Financial Institutions," in *Report of Proceedings of the Forty-Sixth Tax Conference*, 1994 Conference Report (Toronto: Canadian Tax Foundation, 1995), 15:1-49. See also section 475 of the United States Internal Revenue Code of 1986, as amended (herein referred to as "IRC"), which applies accretion taxation to securities traders and dealers. The US mark-to-market rules are described in Edward D. Kleinbard and Thomas L. Evans, "The Role of Mark-to-Market Accounting in a Realization-Based Tax System" (December 1997), 75 *Taxes: The Tax Magazine* 788-823.

77 Thomas L. Evans, "Lower of Cost or Market Method—The Need for Reform" (September 5, 1994), 64 *Tax Notes* 1349-55; Kleinbard and Evans, supra footnote 76; and *A Tax System Redesigned*, supra note 3, at 192-93. Kleinbard and Evans recommend the exclusion of intangible assets (including financial assets) from the category of "trading stock" subject to the lower of cost and fair market value rule.

78 Kleinbard and Evans, supra note 76. See also *A Platform for Consultation*, supra note 3, at 148; and *A Tax System Redesigned*, supra note 3, at 337-38, which suggest that a taxpayer-elective mark-to-market regime would benefit "market makers," defined as taxpayers who hold both long and short positions in financial instruments. The benefit supposedly follows from the elimination of the timing mismatches and the variability of tax liabilities that occur under a realization-based system. *A Platform for Consultation* argues that this elimination would make Australian-based market makers "more competitive in international markets." See also *A Tax System Redesigned*, supra, at 338: "Financial institutions with trading desks have argued in favour of market-value treatment to improve pricing neutrality and reduce compliance costs."

79 See, for example, *A Platform for Consultation*, supra note 3, at 148: "The alternative approach to distinguishing between trading and investment activities or portfolios, namely, an approach which required only some institutions to be taxed on annual changes in market value of financial assets and liabilities, would not be sustainable because institutions are not sufficiently specialised."

80 ITA subsection 142.2(1), which defines a "financial institution" for the purposes of the mark-to-market legislation to include (1) banks, (2) trust corporations, (3) credit unions, (4) insurance corporations, (5) corporations whose principal business is the lending of funds to arm's-length persons, (6) investment dealers, and (7) certain entities controlled by one or more of these institutions. A change in status results in a deemed disposition and reacquisition of property in order to quarantine gains and losses that accrued while the holder was inside or outside the mark-to-market legislation.

81 Kleinbard and Evans, supra note 76.

82 See the text that accompanies notes 280-314 infra.

83 See the text that accompanies notes 187-217 in chapter 7.

84 New Zealand Tax Administration Act, 1994, as amended, section 90, empowers the Commissioner of Inland Revenue to issue determinations that prescribe accounting methods and their application. In addition, determinations may be used to prescribe sources of interest rate and pricing information for the application of accrual accounting methods and market-value accounting described in other determinations. See Glazebrook and Oliver, supra note 22, at 87-93; and Smith, supra note 9, at 230-31, for a description of the New Zealand determination process.

85 The legal status of the determinations is comparable to that of regulations under the income tax legislation in many other countries. In particular, the Commissioner of Inland Revenue must take into account the basic principles reflected in the legislation and cannot develop tax-accounting methods independently of those principles. What is most important, any method prescribed under a determination must result in an allocation of income and expenditure that is consistent with the tenor of the spreading provisions under the legislation, including the YTM method and market-value accounting. Adoption of hedge accounting is precluded largely because there

is a requirement in the legislation to account for income or expenditure from each financial instrument separately. A determination that is issued for a category of instrument must be followed unless an alternative accounting method provides a result that does not differ materially from the result under the specified method. In terms of their form, the determinations are similar to regulations under the US IRC. Each determination includes a statement of principle and scope, definitional provisions, a basic charging provision, and illustrative examples. A general explanation precedes the determination but does not form part of it.

86 The same general approach is suggested in *A Platform for Consultation*, supra note 3, at 160: "The principles should be clearly established in legislation, but the range of financial assets and the degrees of innovation in this area suggest that the detailed application of the approach would need to be set out in guidelines developed in consultation with industry." In practice, the development of determinations under the New Zealand legislation has not always been timely. For example, a determination governing swaps was issued nine years after enactment of the accrual legislation.

87 See the text that accompanies notes 66-79 and 96-114 in chapter 3.

88 This consistency in accrual patterns appears to underlie general references in the Australian accrual proposals to the accrual of "economic income." See *Consultative Document*, supra note 3, at 35; and *Issues Paper*, supra note 3, at 124.

89 See, for example, ITA paragraph 142.3(1)(a) and draft regulations 9102(1) and (2), which require the recognition of the "accrued return" on specified debt obligations held by financial institutions; and subsections 12(3), (4), and (9) and regulations 7000(1)(a) and (b). Regulation 7000(5) requires the annual accrual recognition of original issue discount by all holders of OID obligations and stripped securities under a minimum assumption of annual compounding. See also the Australian Income Tax Assessment Act, 1936, as amended (herein referred to as "ITAA"), division 16E; IRC sections 1272, 1273, and 1275(d) and the regulations thereunder, which govern the accrual recognition of original issue discount; and New Zealand Income Tax Act, 1994, as amended, section EH 34; section EH 1(2) and *Determination* G3, "Yield to Maturity," May 13, 1987, which require the yield-to-maturity method of accounting for income and expense over the term of a financial instrument.

90 See, for example, ITA draft regulation 9100, which defines the "total return" on a fixed-payment debt obligation subject to the mark-to-market legislation as the amount by which (1) the total of all payments (other than a fee or similar payment) required to be made by the debtor under the obligation after its acquisition by the taxpayer exceeds (2) the cost to the taxpayer of the obligation. The cost of an instrument is generally the amount advanced by the holder on issue or the amount paid by the holder on a secondary-market acquisition.

Fees for services related to a financial arrangement are not considered part of the expected return; consequently, the various accrual recognition methods under the New Zealand legislation require that the fees be spread only if they are contingent on the implementation of the arrangement. To prevent the use of service fees to disguise interest payments, the exception is limited to a maximum amount of 2 percent of the "core acquisition price" of a financial arrangement. New Zealand Income Tax Act, 1994, as amended, sections OB 1 and EH 14 definitions of "acquisition price." *The Taxation of Financial Arrangements*, supra note 24, at 103-4, proposes the elimination of the 2 percent threshold, on the assumption that non-contingent fees cannot be easily substituted for interest. See also the taxation bill, supra note 63, at 22, which would carry the proposal forward and eliminate the 2 percent limitation for non-contingent fees. Contingent fees remain subject to accrual recognition, on the assumption that they are substitutable. The Valabh committee, supra note 36, regarded with skepticism the rationale for the distinction between the two types of fees and recommended its elimination in favour of the immediate deduction of all fees, subject to a 2 percent limitation.

Consultative Document, supra note 3, at 29-30, similarly excepts all cash flows that would normally not be considered to be paid or received under a financial arrangement. These cash flows are considered to include (1) brokerage fees, (2) legal and accounting expenses of document preparation, (3) provision of professional advice in relation to a financial arrangement, (4) government charges, and (5) application fees payable whether or not a financial arrangement is entered into. See also the definition in ITA draft regulation 9100 of the "total return" on fixed-payment debt held by a financial institution. Since the definition excludes any fees or similar payment from the total of all payments under the obligation, these amounts are not subject to accrual recognition by the holder.

91 The cost of an instrument acquired on issue will generally be equal to the issue price (that is, the amount paid for the issue of the instrument). If the acquisition occurs on a secondary-market trade, the cost will generally be the amount paid to the transferor. If the interest coupons on a debt instrument are stripped from the principal and sold separately to different holders, special rules are needed to require the initial holder and "stripper" of the coupons to allocate the cost among the various portions on the basis of their respective fair market values. See, for example, IRC section 1286, which addresses the tax treatment of coupon-stripping transactions generally; Bruce Kayle, "Where Has All the Income Gone? The Mysterious Relocation of Interest and Principal in Coupon Stripping and Related Transactions" (Fall 1987), 7 *Virginia Tax Review* 303-61; ITA regulation 7000(2)(b)(i), which defines the "specified cost" of the stripped portions of a stripped bond as the present value of the relevant payments at the date of purchase; and infra note 231, which describes the application of a "full or partial base price adjustment" under the New Zealand accrual legislation on the assignment of a financial arrangement or the defeasance of a liability. An allocation rule prevents the artificial loss for the stripper that would arise if all of the cost were allocated to the principal entitlement. The stripped portions should be treated as separate obligations for each purchaser with a cost equal to the purchase price and a discount equal to the difference between that cost and the redemption amount. The inappropriate tax results attributable to a failure to allocate the cost of a debt instrument among the cash flow streams (interest coupons and right to principal repayment) are illustrated in *FC of T v. The Myer Emporium Ltd.*, 87 ATC 4363 (Full HC), where the Australian High Court found that the whole of the payment, equal to the present value of future interest payments, should be included in income of the taxpayer on assignment and that no portion of the acquisition price of the loan was to be allocated as cost base.

92 See *Consultative Document on Accrual Tax Treatment*, supra note 37, at 61, which states that "when there is a constant discount rate" of $R1$, the present value of the expected cash flows (P) payable at T under an instrument is simply

$$PV = \frac{P}{(1 + R)_t}.$$

See also *Determination* G10B, "Present Value Calculation Methods," October 24, 1990, which provides two alternative methods for calculating present values required in any other determination; and *Determination* G11A, "Present Value Based Yield to Maturity Method," October 24, 1990, which provides a present-value-based alternative to the application of the YTM method described in *Determination* G3, supra note 89.

93 These steps are summarized in *Consultative Document on Accrual Tax Treatment*, supra note 37, at 69-70. See also *Consultative Document*, supra note 3, at 39, which describes "a compounding accruals method" as a three-step procedure that involves (1) definition of the compounding period, (2) calculation of the constant yield, and (3) derivation of the accrued gains and losses in each taxation year over the term of an instrument. A similar approach, referred to as "the timing adjustment benchmark method," is described in *A Platform for Consultation*, supra note 3, at 161-63, and is referred to in *A Tax System Redesigned*, supra note 3, at 343-44. Under this method, the accrued return for a period is defined as "the closing balance" of a financial arrangement minus (1) "the opening balance" plus or minus (2) any cash flows within the period. The "opening balance" for the first period of an instrument is the initial cash flow. For subsequent periods, the opening balance is simply the closing balance from the previous period. The "closing balance" of a financial instrument is described as

$$\text{opening balance} \times (1 + IRR)n,$$

where *IRR* is the internal rate of return or the yield to maturity and *n* is the number of compounding intervals (including fractions within the relevant period).

94 Application of the YTM method to debt issued at a premium eliminates avoidance opportunities associated with the non-taxability of the amount of any premium and the deduction of the full amount of coupon payments at an above-market rate of interest. See, for example, *Interpretation Bulletin* IT-114, "Discounts, Premiums and Bonuses on Debt Obligations," August 3, 1973 (withdrawn June 10, 1994); Wayne Adams, "The General Anti-Avoidance Rule (GAAR) Committee," in *Report of Proceedings of the Forty-Seventh Tax Conference*, 1995 Conference Report (Toronto: Canadian Tax Foundation, 1996), 54:1-9, at 54:7-8; William R. Lawlor, "GAAR Challenges by Revenue Canada: An Update," in *Report of Proceedings of the Forty-Ninth Tax Conference*, 1997 Conference Report (Toronto: Canadian Tax Foundation, 1998), 6:1-11, at 6:5; and Elinore J. Richardson, David Glicksman, and Lara Friedlander, "Fundamentals of Canadian Taxation of Financial Instruments," in *Report of Proceedings of the Fifty-First Tax Conference*, 1999 Conference Report (Toronto: Canadian Tax Foundation, 2000), 5:1-58. As table 5.1 illustrates, the expected gain or loss on any instrument subject to a YTM calculation equals the difference between the amount paid for the instrument (including any premium) and the expected amount of the promised cash flows to be made in the future. Interest income and expense is recognized at the relevant market rate or yield to maturity, taking into account any premium included as part of the cost of the instrument to the holder and the amount advanced to the issuer.

95 See, for example *Determination* G3, supra note 89, which limits the application of the YTM method under the New Zealand accrual legislation to "financial

instruments where the amounts and dates are known not later than the first balance date of the issuer or holder after issue or acquisition . . . and [are] determined in New Zealand currency." See also ITA draft regulation 9100, which defines a "fixed payment obligation" for the purposes of the mark-to-market recognition rules. The definition includes a debt obligation under which the amount and timing of each payment to be made by the debtor were fixed when the holder acquired the obligation and have not changed.

96 In the case of these instruments, the choice of accounting methods for tax purposes is either realization-based recognition or accretion taxation of the unexpected gains and losses as they arise. See the text that accompanies notes 206-336 infra.

97 This proposition holds where the pure bet element under a forward or swap is prepaid, either wholly or in part. In that case, the advance of funds provides an expected return that is combined with unexpected gain or loss on the resolution of the specified contingency. See the text that accompanies notes 24-92 in chapter 6.

98 There is perhaps a lingering misconception that the YTM method cannot be applied to instruments providing contingent payments. See, for example, the taxation bill, supra note 63, at 15: "The yield to maturity method is applied if expected cashflows and payment dates for a financial arrangement are certain"; New Zealand Income Tax Act, 1994, as amended, sections EH 37 and EH 1(5), which notes that alternatives to the YTM method are available when it is "not possible" to use that method; and *A Tax System Redesigned*, supra note 3, at 341-43, which recommends the limitation of accrual recognition to gains and losses that can be characterized as "certain" in the sense that the relevant amounts are "non-contingent." An alternative method under the New Zealand legislation must (1) conform with commercially acceptable practice, (2) be adopted and applied consistently for financial reporting purposes, and (3) result in an allocation of income and expenditure that is fair and reasonable, having regard to the spreading of expected gains and losses on a YTM basis. The third requirement makes sense only if it is somehow supposed that there are instruments with expected gain or loss for which a YTM calculation is not possible. Market-value accounting and realization-based recognition cannot possibly be acceptable as alternatives to the YTM methods, since they do not systematically spread expected gain and loss over the term of an instrument. See Smith, supra note 9, at 228-29. Indeed, instruments that provide only unexpected gain and loss cannot possibly be subjected to a recognition method that approximates the results under a YTM basis, since there are no expected gains and losses that can be spread ex ante on a systematic basis. On the other hand, instruments that involve an advance of funds provide expected gain or loss, which can always be subjected to a YTM calculation; consequently, there is no need to search for alternative methods that approximate the results under the YTM method. It is difficult, therefore, to make any sense of the provision for alternative recognition methods.

99 See the text that accompanies notes 7-16 in chapter 3 for definitions and discussion of these terms. "Pure tax avoidance" is the implementation of purely paper transactions in order to arbitrage differences in tax treatment without sacrificing the desired pattern of cash flows. "Approximate tax avoidance" involves the use of alternative investments that are highly but not perfectly substitutable and therefore requires some deviation from the desired pattern of cash flows.

100 See the text that accompanies 94-112 in chapter 3.

101 This basic design issue is referred to in *Consultative Document*, supra note 3, at 39, as the first step in the application of "a compounding accruals method."

102 *A Platform for Consultation*, supra note 3, at 161-63; *Consultative Document on Accrual Tax Treatment*, supra note 37, at 82-83; and *Determination* G3, supra note 89. See also IRC reg. section 1.1273-1, which governs the recognition of OID on installment obligations. The US OID and other time-value-of-money rules that apply the YTM method to expected gains and losses are discussed in Lawrence Lokken, "The Time Value of Money Rules" (Fall 1986), 42 *Tax Law Review* 1-292, at 20-81. Under the tax-cubbyhole treatment for debt, expected gain or loss in the form of interest is deductible for the borrower and taxable to the lender. The advance of funds is a non-taxable event that does not give rise to income for the borrower or a deduction for the lender. Since the borrower's receipt of funds is offset by an obligation to repay, there is no net increase in wealth that should be subject to tax. Similarly, since the lender has exchanged one form of wealth (cash) for another (debt instrument), there is no net decrease in wealth that should give rise to a deduction. This analysis is followed again on repayment of the loan principal, which does not give rise to any tax consequences for the borrower or the lender unless some portion of the principal is forgiven. This critical distinction between the tax treatment of principal and the tax treatment of interest payments tends to be made purely on the basis of the legal form of the relevant payments.

103 A reliance on legal form in order to distinguish between deductible payments of interest and non-deductible payments of principal allows taxpayers to convert cash flows in the latter category into deductible payments of interest. One notable instance of this kind of character arbitrage occurred in the case of Canadian Optional Interest Rate Notes (COINs), a number of which were issued in Canada in the early 1990s for terms of 40 to 99 years. These transactions were modified versions of similar transactions effected in Europe. In a typical transaction, a corporation would borrow an amount of funds for, say, 99 years at annual interest of 12 percent. Under the loan agreement, the borrower would have the right to prepay interest for years 11 through 99, a right that he would exercise immediately after receipt of the loan proceeds. In terms of cash flows, this arrangement meant that the corporation borrowed the difference between the amount advanced and the present value of the future interest obligations that were prepaid. Since the present value of the obligation to repay the nominal amount of loan principal at the end of the term of the loan was nominal, the prepayment of interest resulted in a 10-year borrowing of the net proceeds. Over the 10-year term, the corporation paid stated interest at 12 percent per annum calculated on the nominal principal amount. The transaction therefore replicated the issue of an OID obligation with a redemption amount equal to the nominal principal that was payable in instalments over a 10-year term. If legal form were determinative in distinguishing between interest payments and principal payments, the full amount of the nominal interest payments would be deductible as interest, and the borrower would be allowed to deduct as interest what were, in effect, instalments of principal. A YTM approach that does not depend on the form of cash flows as interest and principal would realize the appropriate treatment by accounting for the prepayment of interest as a reduction in the cost of the instrument (the issue price). For a general discussion of COINs, see Stephen R. Richardson, "New Financial Instruments: A Canadian Perspective," in *Income Tax and Goods and*

Services Tax Considerations in Corporate Financing, 1992 Corporate Management Tax Conference (Toronto: Canadian Tax Foundation, 1993), 10:1-32, at 10:21-32; and Leif Mutén, "The Swedish Experiment with a General Anti-Avoidance Rule," in Graeme S. Cooper, ed., *Tax Avoidance and the Rule of Law* (Amsterdam: IBFD Publications, 1997), 307-24, at 311.

104 In applying the YTM method to the relevant cash flows, it may be necessary in some instances to ignore the existence of an intermediate entity that may be interposed between an issuer and investor. See, for example, Notice 97-21, 1997-1 CB 407; and IRC prop. reg. section 1.7701(1)-3, REG-104072-97, 1999-11 IRB 12, where the US Treasury department adopted this approach to address the use of "stepped-down preferred stock." Like COINs (described supra note 103), stepped-down preferred stock allowed taxable borrowers to deduct both principal and interest payments. In a simple instance of a transaction of this kind, a taxable US corporation would fund a real estate investment trust (REIT). A non-taxable investor would provide additional funds to the REIT, which would loan these funds (along with the funds contributed by the taxable corporation) to the corporate borrower. The non-taxable investor would receive preferred shares with an above-market dividend rate and a limited term, during which all interest payments on the loan to the taxable corporation would be used by the REIT to fund the dividend payments. At the end of the specified term, the dividend rate would be reduced ("stepped down") to nil, and the shares would have a nominal value. In terms of its associated cash flows, the transaction was the equivalent of a self-amortizing loan from the non-taxable investor to the taxable corporation at a market rate of interest on the funds contributed to the REIT by the investor. The interposition of the REIT, however, enabled the taxable corporation to deduct interest on the full amount of the loan from the intermediate entity. The additional interest effectively provided a deduction for the principal repayments to the non-taxable investor, who was insensitive to the full inclusion of the cash flows as dividend income. The policy of "looking through" the REIT ignores the loanback of funds from the REIT to the taxable corporation and results in a characterization of the relevant cash flows as a self-amortizing loan from the non-taxable investor to the corporation. For a brief discussion of step-down preferred stock, see Joseph Bankman, "The New Market in Corporate Tax Shelters" (June 28, 1999), 18 *Tax Notes International* 2681-2705, at 2685-86 and 2688; Lee A. Sheppard, "Treasury Steps on Step-Down Preferred" (March 3, 1997), 74 *Tax Notes* 1102-03; and United States, *The Problem of Corporate Tax Shelters: Discussion, Analysis and Legislative Proposals* (Washington, DC: US Treasury Department, July 1999), appendix A, paragraphs 394-401. The lookthrough approach is limited generally to circumstances in which (1) a conduit entity is interposed between a borrower and a lender; (2) the lender's investment in the conduit entity is "self-amortizing," in the sense that the value of the lender's interest is expected to decrease as payments are received; and (3) payments that represent a recovery of the lender's cost are made by the conduit from earnings and profits.

105 The irrelevance of the legal form of cash flows in the application of the YTM method is also evident in the approach of Revenue Canada (now the Canada Customs and Revenue Agency, or CCRA) to the accrual of expected gains on stripped bonds subject to ITA regulations 7000(1)(b) and (2)(b). See Revenue Canada document nos. 9235556, March 18, 1993 and 9206645, April 15, 1992.

106 It is possible to achieve much the same result under an approach based on the legal form of cash flows as principal and interest by deeming prepayments of interest to be repayments of principal and then calculating accrued amounts on the basis of the reduced principal. See, for example, ITA subsections 18(9.2)-(9.8), which were enacted in response to COIN transactions. The operative provision of the legislation (ITA subsection 18(9.2)) limits the amount of deductible interest in respect of taxation years following the prepayment of interest to the amount of interest calculated on the nominal loan principal less (1) the amount of the prepayment and (2) any excess of the nominal interest payments over deductible interest from previous years. The legislation is patterned generally on the financial-accounting treatment of long-term prepaid debt, which was settled in 1991 shortly before the introduction of the legislative response. See, for example, Canadian Institute of Chartered Accountants, Emerging Issues Committee, *Abstract EIC-22*, July 29, 1991, which describes the financial-accounting treatment as follows: "taken as a whole, the arrangement can be viewed as an initial borrowing to be retired, together with interest accruing thereon, through [a series] of payments. . . . The Committee reached a consensus that the prepayments of interest should be accounted for as a reduction of the outstanding amount of the obligation."

107 *Consultative Document*, supra note 3, at 35.

108 See, for example, Stephen B. Land, "Defeating Deferral: A Proposal for Retrospective Taxation" (Fall 1996), 52 *Tax Law Review* 45-117, at 73-75, which describes the significance of an assumption of continuous compounding in measuring the deferral benefit associated with realization-based recognition of gains. The logical extension of the concept of continuous compounding is the assessment of tax on a continuous basis as the theoretically appropriate taxation period. See Jeff Strnad, "Periodicity and Accretion Taxation: Norms and Implementation" (June 1990), 99 *The Yale Law Journal* 1817-1911.

109 Income tax legislation in many countries incorporates an assumption of daily compounding in the calculation of interest charges on late payments. See, for example, ITA subsection 248(11). *Consultative Document*, supra note 3, at 40, lists the following advantages of "daily compounding accruals":

> It gives a more precise measure of accrued economic income than compounding based on longer periods;
>
> there is no need for special provisions to apportion accrued gains of a period that straddles two taxation years. . . ;
>
> the required degree of precision for the calculation of the daily compounding accruals rate could be defined as a number of decimal places to be kept constant for all calculations for all taxpayers; and
>
> there would be no need to convert the daily compounding rate calculated on an annual basis into an annual rate, as is necessary when different compounding intervals are used.

110 See *A Platform for Consultation*, supra note 3, at 163: "Where the 'compounding interval' is broken by a balance date [taxation year-end], accurate calculation of the timing adjustment [accrued gain or loss] requires compounding for that broken or fractional period." In the context of the New Zealand legislation, the necessary details of this allocation process are described generally in *Determination* G1A,

"Apportionment of Income and Expenditure on a Daily Basis," December 4, 1989: "the income derived or expenditure incurred by a holder or an issuer of a financial arrangement in respect of a period shall be apportioned among the income years of the holder or issuer in which that period falls pro-rata with the number of days in the period within each income year calculated (at the option of the holder or issuer) on a 360 or 365 day basis." As the determination indicates, taxpayers may use the simplifying assumption that each year consists of 12 months of 30 days each ("the 360-day basis").

111 The compounding of interest on a daily basis has the added benefit of eliminating any need to apportion accrued gains and losses of a period that straddles two taxation years. In effect, accrued gain or loss for a taxation year is simply the sum of the accrued amounts for each day. See *Consultative Document*, supra note 3, at 40.

112 This result occurs under the New Zealand accrual legislation, since the compounding period on an instrument is the specified date for each regular payment subject only to the requirement of annual compounding if the period between payment dates is greater than one year. See *Determination* G3, supra note 89. If a compounding period straddles a taxation year, accrued amounts are spread on a straightline basis pro rata with the number of days in the period in each year. See *Determination* G11A, supra note 92.

113 The tax consequences to the transferor are discussed in the text that accompanies notes 206-218 infra.

114 Discount can also arise because of declines in the creditworthiness of a debtor, which impairs the value of a debt instrument.

115 But see IRC section 1276(a), which alters the character of market discount from capital gain to ordinary income without requiring the recognition of the discount on an accrual basis, unless the holder elects otherwise. If market discount is recognized on realization, IRC sections 1277 and 1278(b) defer the recognition of interest expense incurred on related indebtedness. Deferral of the interest deduction eliminates opportunities for realizing pure avoidance by taking offsetting positions with equivalent cash flows that are subject to different recognition rules. IRC section 171(c) permits holders to amortize bond premium over the term of an instrument. No legislative provision requires issuers to recognize any premium that arises on issue over the term of an instrument.

116 It is possible to make a defensible exception to accrual recognition in the case of secondary-market discount that arises because of a decline in the creditworthiness of a debtor. If the creditworthiness is subsequently restored, wholly or in part, an amount realized on the discount represents an unexpected gain that should generally be subject to realization-based recognition under a realization-based income tax. In effect, the transferee has assumed the winning side of a bet on future movements in the creditworthiness of the debtor. See, for example, "Revenue Canada Round Table," in *Report of Proceedings of the Fortieth Tax Conference*, 1988 Conference Report (Toronto: Canadian Tax Foundation, 1989), 53:1-188, at 53:17; and "Revenue Canada Round Table," in *Report of Proceedings of the Thirty-Ninth Tax Conference*, 1987 Conference Report (Toronto: Canadian Tax Foundation, 1988), 47:1-103, at 47:31, where it is stated that discount on a demand obligation is subject to the accrual rules in ITA regulations 7000(1)(a) and (2)(a) but it is accepted that the result is unworkable if the discount is

attributable to a decline in the creditworthiness of a debtor. The fact that a debt instrument has a fixed term or is due on demand should have no relevance to the characterization of discount as unexpected if the impairment in value is attributable to a decline in the creditworthiness of the debtor.

117 See, for example, the definition in ITA draft regulation 9100 of the "total return" (noted supra note 90) on fixed-payment debt instruments held by financial institutions subject to the mark-to-market legislation. The accrual rules in ITA regulation 7000 have not been interpreted to require the accrual of secondary-market discount on debt instruments acquired by individuals and corporations that are not financial institutions. See Robert Raizenne, "Accrual of Interest Income," in the 1988 Conference Report, supra note 116, 23:1-11, at 23:7; and John M. Ulmer, "Taxation of Interest Income," in *Report of Proceedings of the Forty-Second Tax Conference*, 1990 Conference Report (Toronto: Canadian Tax Foundation, 1991), 8:1-30, at 8:25.

118 If secondary-market discount is attributable to a decline in the creditworthiness of the debtor, expected gain should be accrued on the basis of a cost that, in turn, is based on an assumption that the value of the instrument is unimpaired. Discount attributable to the decline in value should be recognized on realization as unexpected gain. See supra note 116. This result was the outcome of the reasoning of the Supreme Court of Canada in *Antosko et al. v. The Queen*, 94 DTC 6314; [1994] 2 CTC 25.

119 This same result would occur for purchasers of stripped coupons at a discount. The difference between the amount paid for the coupon and the redemption amount would be subject to accrual recognition on the basis of a YTM calculation. See supra note 91.

120 *Consultative Document on Accrual Tax Treatment*, supra note 37, at 158.

121 Ibid., at 161. A perpetual security with no maturity date does not present this problem. A yield to maturity for an instrument of this type may be calculated on much the same basis as the YTM for an instrument with a unique redemption date. The assumption is simply that the instrument will never be redeemed. *Determination* G10B, supra note 92; and *Determination* G11A, supra note 92, provide some examples of the application to perpetual instruments of the YTM method based on present values.

122 *Consultative Document on Accrual Tax Treatment*, supra note 37, at 159.

123 Ibid., at 160. See, for example, ITA regulations 7000(2)(a)-(c.1), which require computation of interest on a compound basis, using the maximum of all rates in respect of each possible circumstance under which the interest of the holder could be redeemed or retracted; and IRC reg. section 1272-1(f).

124 *Consultative Document on Accrual Tax Treatment*, supra note 37, at 160.

125 Ibid., at 161.

126 ITA draft regulation 9102(1) refers to the YTM calculation used for accruing income and expense on specified debt obligations held by financial institutions as "the level-yield method."

127 See Joseph Bankman and William A. Klein, "Accurate Taxation of Long-Term Debt: Taking into Account the Term Structure of Interest" (Winter 1989), 44 *Tax*

Law Review 335-48. This article is the seminal account of the significance of the term structure of interest for income tax purposes and, in particular, the inaccuracy of an assumption of a level yield in the context of an upward-sloping (or downward-sloping) yield curve. See also Kayle, supra note 91, at 324-32, where he discusses the mismeasurement that can arise from a failure to account for the term structure of interest in coupon-stripping transactions; and *Consultative Document on Accrual Tax Treatment*, supra note 37, at 61, where it is noted that the YTM method is generally applied on an assumption of "a constant interest or discount rate applying to all future cash flows" but "interest rates may be expected to rise or fall in future. In that case, these expected movements in interest rates should, in principle, be taken into account in determining present values." The consultative document provides nothing more than this general observation; it does not develop the policy implications (including technical design issues) of the term structure of interest rates in any detail.

128 Bankman and Klein, supra note 127, at 336-37.

129 See *Consultative Document on Accrual Tax Treatment*, supra note 37, at 61, where it is noted that in a climate of expected movements in interest rates the present-value formula used to calculate the yield to maturity must be altered to reflect the different expected discount rates of $R1$, $R2$, etc. Given this alteration, the present-value formula for a given amount payable at T is

$$PV = \frac{P}{(1 + R1)(1 + R2) \ldots (1 + RT)}.$$

The inaccuracy in the pattern of accrual caused by the failure to alter the present-value formula to account for the term structure of interest is most problematic in the case of long-term OID obligations. Inaccuracy also arises, however, and for the same reason (albeit to a lesser extent), in the case of debt instruments that pay periodic interest. See Bankman and Klein, supra note 127, at 341-42.

130 See, for example, David A. Weisbach, "Tax Responses to Financial Contract Innovation" (Summer 1995), 50 *Tax Law Review* 491-544, at 502-3 and 542-44; and Mark P. Gergen, "Apocalypse Not?" (Summer 1995), 50 *Tax Law Review* 833-59, at 836-38. This effect is the opposite of the effect under a straightline method of spreading expected gain or loss, which tends to accelerate the recognition of discount. In the latter case, it is possible to realize tax-arbitrage profits by issuing a series of OID obligations and using the proceeds to purchase a debt instrument that provides offsetting cash flows in the form of periodic interest. The transaction is profitable only because of the accelerated recognition of the discount on the longer-term OID obligations under the straightline method. See the text that accompanies notes 167-175 infra for a discussion of the effect of the straightline method and the case for its use in limited circumstances.

131 Gergen, supra note 130, at 838, suggests that "there is no evidence that firms issue straight debt to reinvest in zeros to make the yield-curve play." He believes that transaction costs and credit risk offset any benefit from the potential tax saving. On the other hand, the early 1980s saw several large transactions in which high-rate borrowers took advantage of the accelerated recognition of original issue discount under the straightline method of accrual permitted by former IRC section 1232. In an environment of high interest rates, the advantage of accelerated recognition was extremely attractive for US corporate borrowers subject

to high tax rates, and it was not offset by a corresponding income inclusion for lenders, who tended to be tax-exempts, non-residents, and low-rate individuals. These transactions caused the US Treasury department to repeal IRC section 1232 in 1984 and require the use of the YTM method for original issue discount.

Bankman and Klein, supra note 127, at 346-47, note briefly that the revenue effects of the use of the level-yield method depend on the relative presences of low-rate and high-rate borrowers and lenders in capital markets. Since the level-yield method defers the recognition of expected gains and losses in the context of an upward-sloping yield curve, there is no tax benefit for tax-exempt lenders, such as pension funds, and high-rate borrowers are disadvantaged by the deferred recognition of interest expense. Bankman and Klein suggest that there is a reallocation of debt from high-rate to low-rate borrowers and from low-rate to high-rate lenders, but the dimensions of this effect would be difficult to determine.

132 Bankman and Klein, supra note 127, at 348, conclude that the principal difficulty presented by the term structure of interest rates is not the lack of information about that structure but, rather, the problem of identifying the reason for the shape of a particular yield curve, since that reason determines the nature of the expected increases in value of a debt instrument. The authors conclude that a mark-to-market approach is preferable because it takes into account ex post results that are measured accurately irrespective of the term structure of interest rates and its underlying causes. The text that accompanies notes 280-315 infra discusses the role of market-to-market reporting under a system of expected-return taxation.

133 Bankman and Klein, supra note 127, at 344-45. In the limited case of certain bank deposits that provide for escalating interest rates, *Consultative Document on Accrual Tax Treatment*, supra note 37, at 166-67, recommends taking into account an upward-sloping yield curve attributable to an expectations theory of interest rates. ITA regulations 7000(1)(c) and (2)(c) require holders to accrue interest at the greater of the actual rate for a year and the level-yield rate calculated on the assumption of a maximum yield. ITA regulation 7000(2)(c.1) allows the level-yield method to be used exclusively for obligations on which the interest rate is fixed on issue and never decreases. This regulation excludes, for example, guaranteed investment certificates that are issued by financial institutions and that provide escalating interest rates on the basis of the length of the holding period. See Canada, Department of Finance, "Explanatory Notes—Draft Regulations: Changes to the Accrual Rules," *Release*, no. 93-50, August 11, 1993.

134 See, for example, Kayle, supra note 91, at 314-15, where he concludes that the reduction of administrative and compliance costs associated with the use of the level-yield method is desirable in the absence of significant tax-avoidance transactions based on the term structure of interest rates.

135 But see *Issues Paper*, supra note 3, at 128, where it is noted that the assumption of a flat yield curve is not always appropriate and that a different assumption may be acceptable even if it deviates from a benchmark standard specified for tax purposes. The relationship between a benchmark of this kind and financial-accounting practice is discussed in the text that accompanies notes 176-197 infra.

136 Much of the discussion in this section is taken from Tim Edgar, "Some Lessons from the Saga of Weak-Currency Borrowings" (2000), vol. 48, no. 1 *Canadian Tax Journal* 1-34.

137 *The Taxation of Financial Arrangements*, supra note 24, at 45-46. See also *Issues Paper*, supra note 3, at 17-18 and 186-87; and *Consultative Document*, supra note 3, at 80.

138 The Valabh committee seemed to regard foreign currency transactions as substitutes for domestic debt in all cases because it perceived a general relationship between currency exchange rates and interest rates in which the latter determine the former. See Valabh committee, supra note 36, at chapter 4, 39-46. Since it was possible to use forward currency contracts to construct foreign currency transactions that the committee regarded as substitutes for domestic debt, the committee included these contracts as debt substitutes. See Valabh committee, ibid., at 17. The clearest statement of the committee's view of foreign currency transactions is the following (ibid., at 46): "A relatively comprehensive approach to foreign exchange gains and losses is a necessary element of the current policy settings with respect to the accrual regime. Any significant narrowing of the focus of the regime in this area would seem to result in a significant undermining of the policy of taxing interest or its equivalent on an accrual basis. Cross-border financial transactions explicitly or implicitly capitalise foreign currency fluctuations into interest rates and prices of financial instruments. The tax system must recognise this if it is to be consistent in its application to real-world situations. There is, therefore, only limited opportunity to narrow the focus of the accrual rules in this area."

139 *Taxation of Financial Arrangements*, supra note 24, at 47-49, where it is proposed that realization-based recognition be applied to unexpected gains and losses on all on-market forward contracts, instead of the previous accrual recognition of the difference between the spot price and the forward price.

140 See the text that accompanies notes 69-70 in chapter 1.

141 *Taxation of Financial Arrangements*, supra note 24, at 43: "In the case of foreign currency denominated instruments, it is necessary, therefore, to take into account expected movements in exchange rates, since they form as much a part of the return as do interest payments."

142 Ibid., where the following example is provided: "if a taxpayer purchases a yen denominated security which pays interest at a rate of, say, 3%, the taxpayer will generally expect the yen to appreciate over the term of the security so that the overall risk-adjusted yield is equivalent to what could have been earned on a New Zealand dollar denominated security. If the anticipated exchange gain is not accrued, the true interest income derived by the taxpayer would be understated, which would create incentives to hold financial assets denominated in 'hard' currencies."

143 Ibid., at 44. This incentive is the underlying reason for "weak-currency borrowings." In a typical weak-currency borrowing, a corporation borrows funds in a currency that is weaker than its functional currency. As part of the transaction, the corporate borrower enters into forward-rate agreements that fully hedge the expected exchange gain associated with repayment of the loan principal in the weaker currency. Although the hedged borrowing replicates a borrowing in the functional currency, the borrower is able to deduct the full amount of the nominal interest expense on an accrual basis and defer the inclusion of an offsetting foreign exchange gain until repayment of the loan principal. Given a reliance on the legal form of the cash flows, this result follows even though the amount of the gain is

fixed from the outset of the borrowing under a forward-rate agreement. Table 5.8 illustrates the different results under a realization-based recognition approach and an expected-return approach to expected exchange gains. For an extensive discussion of weak-currency borrowings and their treatment under the ITA, see Stephen S. Ruby, "Recent Financing Techniques," in *Report of Proceedings of the Forty-First Tax Conference*, 1989 Conference Report (Toronto: Canadian Tax Foundation, 1990), 27:1-46, at 27:2-33.

144 *Taxation of Financial Arrangements*, supra note 24, at 43. The Valabh committee, supra note 36, at 12: "it is consistent over time to provide the same income tax treatment in this context [that is, foreign currency debt] as is provided for other debt instruments denominated in New Zealand dollars, where domestic interest rates move."

145 *The Taxation of Financial Arrangements*, supra note 24, chapter 8, at 47-50; and *Determination* G9B, "Financial Arrangements That Are Denominated in a Currency Other than New Zealand Dollars: An Expected-Value Approach," May 1998. It is noted in *The Taxation of Financial Arrangements*, supra note 24, at 44, that this expected-return approach to foreign currency borrowings and loans was first suggested by the Valabh committee, supra note 36.

146 *The Taxation of Financial Arrangements*, supra note 24, at 45: "the best objective measure we have of expected exchange rate movements is the set of forward exchange rates"; and at 44: "We believe that advances in financial markets and information technology mean this [the lack of quoted forward rates] is no longer a constraint. Quoted forward rates are now more accessible, and where a rate is not quoted, ready access to spreadsheet software makes their calculation from interest rate information reasonably straightforward."

147 Under an expected-return approach to foreign currency debt, determination of the yield to maturity takes into account any discount calculated as the difference between (1) the amount advanced converted to domestic currency at the spot rate and (2) the face amount of the instrument converted at the forward exchange rate. But see *FC of T v. Energy Resources of Australia Limited*, 96 ATC 4536 (HC), in which the Australian High Court recognized as discount the difference between the amount advanced and the face amount of a foreign currency obligation converted at the spot rate. Failure to calculate discount using forward exchange rates results in understatement or overstatement of the expected gain or loss. Understatement arises in the case of a foreign currency obligation that is denominated in a currency that is stronger than the domestic currency. Overstatement arises in the case of a foreign currency obligation that is denominated in a weaker currency.

148 *Issues Paper*, supra note 3, at 190-91, proposes the availability of a taxpayer election to use a YTM approach to foreign currency debt. The proposed YTM approach is very different, however, from the New Zealand approach. It treats foreign currency debt as variable return instruments and provides for accrual calculations made at the end of each year for future cash flows on the basis of the spot exchange rate at year-end. The theoretical basis for this approach is unclear. It appears to confuse considerably the distinction between expected and unexpected exchange gains and losses that the New Zealand approach maintains. The confusion arises primarily from a failure to use forward exchange rates as the basis for the calculation of expected exchange gains and losses, which are critical to the application of a YTM calculation that takes into account the significance of interest-rate

parity. The proposed method also differs from the retranslation basis, since it does not require recognition of the full amount of unrealized exchange gains and losses at year-end. Indeed, the averaging effect that arises from applying the prevailing spot exchange rate to future cash flows in calculating a yield to maturity is put forward as the principal policy justification for this curious approach. The suggested approach is similar, however, to the retranslation basis in its failure to tax domestic and foreign currency debt consistently without providing any rational justification for the inconsistency. The YTM approach suggested in the issues paper is described more fully in *Consultative Document*, supra note 3, at 83-86. *A Platform for Consultation*, supra note 3, at 168 and 188-89, cites the expected-return approach under the New Zealand legislation as an alternative that provides consistent treatment of foreign currency debt and domestic debt.

149 In theory, one could also apply an expected-return approach to shares with paid-up capital denominated in a foreign currency. However, to the extent that the return on shares is subject to the corporate income tax and excepted from a YTM calculation under a comprehensive accrual regime, consistency of tax treatment dictates that "foreign currency shares" be taxed equivalently with "domestic currency shares." Under most corporate income tax systems, realization of consistent tax treatment requires that increases (both expected and unexpected) in paid-up capital attributable to movements in exchange rates be accounted for as additional capital amounts. The difference between the spot rate on issue and the spot rate on a return of capital should be treated as a dividend payment. If movements in the spot rate result in a reduction in the paid-up capital, the difference should be treated as a non-taxable premium for the issuer and a capital loss for the holder that is recognized on disposition of the shares. But see *MacMillan Bloedel Limited v. The Queen*, 97 DTC 1446; [1997] 3 CTC 3012 (TCC), aff'd. 99 DTC 5454; [1999] 3 CTC 652 (FCA), in which the court recognized exchange loss on redemption of US-dollar-denominated preferred shares as a deductible loss of the issuer. The exclusion of shares from the application of a comprehensive accrual regime and the resultant boundary between debt and equity are discussed in the text that accompanies notes 247-335 in chapter 6.

150 *The Taxation of Financial Arrangements*, supra note 24, at 46-47. Application of an expected-return approach is not limited to foreign currency debt for which interest is calculated and payable in the same currency as the principal amount advanced. "Dual-currency bonds" pay interest in one currency (often a strong currency with low interest rates) and are redeemable in a different currency (often the relatively weaker currency). Under an expected-return approach, expected gain and loss should be determined by using forward exchange rates for the two currencies. For example, Japanese investors who received yen-denominated interest payments on a yen/US-dollar dual-currency bond would accrue expected gain equal to the amount of the yen interest payments less the expected loss on the US-dollar principal amount. A US issuer would accrue expected loss equal to the yen-denominated interest payments converted to US dollars at the forward exchange rates. Unexpected gain or loss equal to the difference between the spot rate and the forward rate would be accounted for on realization (that is, on payment of the relevant cash flows). For the sake of simplicity, table 5.8 uses interest and principal payments in the same currency to illustrate the fundamental principles of the application of an expected-return approach to foreign currency debt. Although the principles are the same, the details are even more complex in the case of "mixed-

currency bonds," which provide for principal payments in two currencies and interest rates that are based on the forward exchange rates for those currencies.

151 Ruby, supra note 143.

152 See, for example, ITA paragraphs 142.3(1)(a) and (b) and draft regulations 9101(1)(c) and (2)(b) and 9104(1), which govern the recognition of foreign exchange adjustments on non-traded debt held by a financial institution. The retranslation basis was the original method adopted under the New Zealand accrual legislation for foreign currency borrowings and loans. See also former *Determination* G9A, "Financial Arrangements That Are Denominated in a Currency or Commodity Other than New Zealand Dollars," December 4, 1989; and *Issues Paper*, supra note 3, at 192, where the retranslation basis is proposed for non-traded foreign currency debt that is not used as a hedge and is not the subject of an election to apply the suggested YTM method described in the text that accompanies notes 90-135 supra. The conceptual basis for a retranslation approach is described in *Consultative Document on Accrual Tax Treatment*, supra note 37, at 118-45.

153 See, for example, Glazebrook and Oliver, supra note 22, at 130-31, where this assumption underlies their case for the adoption of the retranslation basis.

154 *The Taxation of Financial Arrangements*, supra note 24, at 44, notes that "taxpayers currently have the opportunity to realise losses on domestic debt instruments without bringing to tax unexpected increases in value. We believe similar treatment for foreign currency denominated arrangements should not pose a greater problem so long as all the expected gains are spread." See also *Issues Paper*, supra note 3, at 192 and 198-99, where the application of accretion taxation equally to traded foreign currency and domestic debt is proposed. But see *A Tax System Redesigned*, supra note 3, at 346, where the availability of the retranslation basis is recommended for "foreign-currency financial assets and liabilities." Application of the retranslation basis would be limited to changes in value that were attributable to movements in currency exchange rates. Unexpected gains and losses that were attributable to changes in interest rates and creditworthiness would continue to be subject to realization-based recognition. The suggested taxpayer election is apparently a response to submissions from the banking sector that emphasized conformity with financial-accounting treatment as a means of reducing compliance costs. If an election was not made, foreign exchange gains and losses would be subject to realization-based recognition.

155 See IRC section 988(d) and IRC reg. section 1.988-5(a)(9)(ii), which together treat a hedged foreign currency borrowing or loan as if it were entered into as a single US-dollar instrument.

156 After protracted litigation, it would appear that the judicial view in Canada does not support the treatment of a fully hedged foreign currency borrowing as a synthetic domestic borrowing. See *Shell Canada Limited v. The Queen et al.*, 99 DTC 5669; [1999] 4 CTC 313 (SCC) (in which the court adopted a formalistic characterization of a weak-currency borrowing and the related forward exchange contracts as separate transactions with distinct cash flows subject to different tax cubbyholes), rev'g. 98 DTC 6177; [1998] 2 CTC 201 (FCA) (in which the court disallowed the excess interest expense as unreasonable on the basis of the perceived "economic substance" of the integrated transactions as a synthetic domestic borrowing), rev'g. 97 DTC 395; [1997] 3 CTC 2238 (TCC) (in which the court rejected the integrated treatment of the borrowing and related forward exchange contracts). See also

Canadian Pacific Limited v. The Queen, 99 DTC 5132; [1999] 2 CTC 193 (FCA), aff'g. 98 DTC 2021; [1998] 4 CTC 2023 (TCC) (in which the court expressed sympathy with a formalistic approach that would not integrate a weak-currency borrowing and related forward contracts but considered itself bound by the FCA decision in *Shell*); and *Whittles (HMIT) v. Uniholdings Ltd. (No. 3)*, [1996] BTC 399 (CA) (in which the court rejected the integrated treatment of a strong-currency borrowing and the related forward exchange contracts and characterized the expected foreign exchange loss as a non-deductible capital amount), rev'g. [1995] BTC 119 (Ch. D). For a commentary on the Federal Court of Appeal decision in *Shell*, see Tom Clearwater, "The Judicial Role in Derivative Taxation: The Queen v. Shell Canada Limited and Financial Contract Economics" (1998), vol. 46, no. 6 *Canadian Tax Journal* 1212-44, at 1235-44. See also Glenn L.E. May, "Further Reflections on Derivative Taxation" (1999), vol. 47, no. 3 *Canadian Tax Journal* 534-43. Note 83 in chapter 2 provides a brief description of proceedings in *Canadian Pacific* following the FCA decision.

157 The simplest hedging strategy uses forward exchange contracts to offset unexpected gain or loss on an underlying foreign exchange loan or borrowing. More sophisticated (and less costly or more tax-effective) hedging strategies make use of currency swaps or offsetting loans or borrowings. See, for example, Ruby, supra note 143, who describes "Aussie/yen" weak-currency borrowings; Charles W. Smithson, *Managing Financial Risk: A Guide to Derivative Products, Financial Engineering and Value Maximization*, 3d ed. (New York: McGraw-Hill, 1998), 157-61, where he describes arbitrage of Japanese tax and regulatory authorities by US issuers of yen-denominated OID bonds; and Dennis Sykora, "The Income Tax Web Surrounding Derivatives," in the 1995 Conference Report, supra note 94, 30:1-41, at 30:28-30, where he compares the tax effectiveness under the ITA of a foreign currency borrowing that uses forward exchange contracts and a cross-currency swap.

158 In effect, no attempt is made to bifurcate exchange gains and losses into expected amounts equivalent to interest and unexpected amounts attributable to other factors that determine movements in exchange rates. The US rules, however, realize some measure of character matching by treating all foreign exchange gains and losses as ordinary-income amounts that are recognized on realization. See IRC section 988(d) and IRC reg. section 1.988-5.

159 IRC section 988(d)(2)(A) defines a qualifying "section 988 hedge transaction" as a transaction entered into in order (1) "to reduce risk of currency fluctuations with respect to property which is held or to be held by the taxpayer" or (2) "to reduce risk of currency fluctuations with respect to borrowings made or to be made, or obligations incurred or to be incurred by the taxpayer." Hedged foreign currency loans or borrowings are just one source of the definitional and identification issues that arise with synthetic and hedge transactions generally. See the text that accompanies notes 187-217 in chapter 7.

160 Revenue Canada has implied that it will not seek to deny the deduction of interest expense on the basis of the status of a particular borrowing as hedged. See Revenue Canada document no. 982994, November 19, 1998. Instead, the department states, it will limit consideration of the application of the general anti-avoidance rule in ITA section 245 to weak-currency borrowings in which the relevant funds are immediately converted into the currency required by the borrower and are not used

in a business. This position creates a different discontinuity, one that results from the need to determine whether a currency conversion is immediate and whether the funds are used in a business. Relatively small differences between two taxpayers' circumstances can result in different determinations and thus in different tax consequences. Moreover, inconsistencies in tax treatment will remain if Revenue Canada continues to maintain that the expected foreign exchange loss on a strong-currency borrowing is not interest within the restrictive legal definition of the term. These amounts are subject to realization-based recognition generally as capital losses and are not treated as additional amounts of interest that are recognized on an accrual basis. See Revenue Canada document no. 9219187, November 17, 1994.

161 If unexpected exchange gains and losses on non-traded foreign currency debt are covered by traded instruments, a mismatch can arise if the traded instruments are subject to accretion taxation for the reasons described in the text that accompanies notes 280-315 infra. In that case, a hedging regime can ensure that gains or losses on instruments entered into as a hedge of another position are subject to realization-based recognition. See *Issues Paper*, supra note 3, at 187. The text that accompanies notes 187-217 in chapter 7 discusses the case for a hedging regime and the shortcomings of that case.

162 This fact appears to be recognized in the budget proposals that limit the deduction of interest expense on weak-currency borrowings. See Canada, Department of Finance, 2000 Budget, Budget Plan, February 28, 2000, annex 7-7, notice of ways and means motion to amend the Income Tax Act, resolutions 28-30. The budget proposals are, however, much more limited in scope than the approach suggested here and, in fact, are very similar to Revenue Canada's administrative position described supra note 160. The budget proposals create a new tax cubbyhole for certain weak-currency borrowings, defined generally as indebtedness the proceeds of which are converted into another currency that is used for a qualifying income-earning purpose. The amount of otherwise deductible interest expense on some of these borrowings is limited to the amount of interest that would have been payable on an equivalent borrowing in the currency that is used for an income-earning purpose. Disallowed interest expense is taken into account in determining the amount of foreign exchange gain or loss realized on repayment of a weak-currency borrowing. Such gain or loss, as well as any gain or loss on a related hedge, is deemed to be on ordinary-income account.

The Department of Finance has presumably adopted the conversion of funds as a proxy or means of exposing a tax-avoidance motive that might otherwise be attributable to a hedged borrowing. As noted in note 160 supra, the use of this proxy avoids the discontinuities associated with a focus on hedged borrowings, but creates other discontinuities associated with applying the requirement to trace the conversion of the proceeds of a weak-currency borrowing to a currency that is ultimately used for an income-earning purpose. Moreover, because of the limited application of the budget proposals to weak-currency borrowings, there is no attempt to equate the treatment of borrowings in a stronger currency with the treatment of domestic currency debt. Similarly, the proposals are limited to the interest deductibility issue and do not address the tax treatment of lenders. Administrative and compliance considerations also seem to justify the incorporation of three significant exclusions from the application of the proposals for: (1) weak-currency borrowings in which the interest rate on the relevant borrowing is no more than 2 percentage points greater than that for an equivalent borrowing in the currency used for an income-earning purpose; (2) weak-currency borrowings in which the outstanding principal is $500,000 or less; and (3) all weak-currency borrowings of corporations whose principal business is the lending of money. To avoid computational complexities, the budget proposals do not require the amount of any deferred interest expense to reduce the outstanding principal of a weak-currency borrowing. As acknowledged by the Department of Finance, this limitation means that a borrower will continue to be able to deduct currently a limited portion of the nominal interest expense, even though that portion is offset fully by an expected exchange gain. In the examples in the text, the amount of loan principal must be reduced by the amount of nominal interest expense when paid, to the extent that the expense compensates the lender for expected losses in the value of the weaker currency. Conversely, the amount of loan principal must be increased by expected increases in the value of a stronger currency borrowing.

163 See the text that accompanies notes 126-135 supra.

164 *Issues Paper*, supra note 3, at 119, acknowledges submissions from private-sector representatives to the effect that "daily compounding accruals was not in accord with accounting methods currently in use, would be unnecessarily complex and would require tax accounting systems that would be very costly to establish and maintain." The submissions were responses to the original accrual proposals in the *Consultative Document*, supra footnote 3. See also Canada, Department of Finance, *Draft Amendments to the Income Tax Act and Explanatory Notes Relating to Securities Held by Financial Institutions* (Ottawa: the department, June 1995), which acknowledges that the YTM method applied on a daily compounding basis is rarely used by financial institutions.

165 The most obvious example is the change in approach in the Australian accrual proposals. *Consultative Document*, supra note 3, at 33-51, proposed the use of YTM on a daily compounding basis for debt instruments, but the purported compliance costs associated with the maintenance of a separate tax-accounting system led to the proposal's abandonment.

166 See, for example, *The Taxation of Financial Arrangements*, supra note 24, at 41: "The purpose of providing alternative spreading methods to those set out in the legislation or determinations is to reduce compliance costs by enabling taxpayers to use the same methods of accounting for tax and financial reporting purposes." *The Taxation of Financial Arrangements*, ibid., at 43, however, emphasizes that the purpose of the consistency requirement is to minimize taxpayers' ability to manipulate the recognition of income and expense by changing accounting methods for financial-statement purposes. Accordingly, it proposes (ibid., at 42) that taxpayers must use one accounting method for all financial arrangements of the same class and that a particular method, once chosen, cannot be changed unless there is a valid commercial reason for the change. Moreover, the Commissioner of Inland Revenue must be notified of any change and the reasons for it.

167 See *Consultative Document on Accrual Tax Treatment*, supra note 37, at 38-47; and *Consultative Document*, supra note 3, at 35-36 and 38-39.

168 *Consultative Document on Accrual Tax Treatment*, supra note 37, at 38.

169 Ibid.

170 *Consultative Document*, supra note 3, at 36.

171 Ibid.

172 See supra note 131, which discusses the US experience with the application of the straightline method to original issue discount.

173 New Zealand, *Consultative Document on Accrual Tax Treatment*, supra note 37, at 38-40. *Consultative Document*, supra note 3, at 38, suggests that the straightline method can be used "in prescribed circumstances where there is no significant deferral and the result does not materially differ from that under the daily compounding accruals method." New Zealand Income Tax Act, 1994, as amended, sections EH 35 and EH 1(3), deviates from an instrument-based approach to the application of the straightline method and permits certain persons to use this method if the total value of all their financial arrangements does not exceed a defined threshold. This approach was apparently adopted as a simplification measure. See Smith, supra note 9, at 225. The details of the use of the straightline accrual method for spreading expected gains and losses is set out in *Determination* G24, "Straight-Line Method," July 10, 1991.

174 *Consultative Document on Accrual Tax Treatment*, supra note 37, at 39-40, recommends the availability of the straightline method for "standard fixed," "floating," and "reviewable" interest-rate instruments, provided that they pay interest at a minimum of six-month intervals and are not issued at a discount or premium. A "standard fixed rate instrument" is defined as an instrument that pays periodic interest at a fixed rate. A "standard floating-rate instrument" is defined as an instrument on which (1) periodic interest is payable throughout the relevant term at intervals not exceeding six months, (2) the periodic interest is set in relation to a recognized market rate, (3) the margins around the base rate differ by no more than 0.5 percentage points between any two payment periods, and (4) there may be a specified maximum or minimum rate. A "standard reviewable-rate instrument" is defined as an instrument that provides for changes in interest rates upon review, provided that the changes are consistent with changes in market rates between the review dates. These concepts are reflected generally in *Determination* G26, "Variable Rate Financial Arrangements," January 22, 1993, which applies to "floating rate" and "reviewable rate arrangements" that pay interest at least annually. Interest is recognized, however, on a receivable and payable basis.

See also IRC reg. section 1.1275-5, which draws a sensible line between "variable-rate debt instruments" (VRDIs) and contingent debt subject to accrual recognition on a YTM basis. Under the US regulations, a VRDI is defined as any debt obligation with a fixed principal amount and interest that accrues or is paid at least annually but varies with current interest rates or the current values of publicly traded property. These requirements are generally intended to ensure that the simplified accounting approach under the VRDI regulations is limited to floating-rate debt instruments that provide little or no opportunity for deferred recognition of expected gain or loss. For the broad range of contingent debt instruments that qualify as VRDIs, interest income and expense is recognized as it is paid or accrues during a particular period. If an obligation of this kind is issued at a discount from its stated principal, the associated OID must be recognized on a YTM basis. For this limited purpose, the yield on a VRDI is determined on the assumption that variable interest is paid over the term of the instrument on the basis of a constant level of the relevant index. The VRDI regulations also apply to more complex variable instruments, such as "inverse floaters." These instruments provide for a fixed periodic return less a specified variable rate. The resulting variable return is the inverse of the specified variable rate. A VRDI that does not qualify under IRC reg. section 1.1275-5 is subject to the contingent-debt regulations. See the text that accompanies notes 137-151 in chapter 6. An instrument with variable payments that were set at intervals of more than one year or that were based on changes in a non-qualifying index would not qualify.

175 *Consultative Document on Accrual Tax Treatment*, supra note 37, at 38-39. *Determination* G26, supra note 174, requires the recognition of discount or premium on a variable-rate arrangement on a YTM basis if the amount is 2 percent or more of the average amount of principal outstanding over the term of the arrangement. Otherwise, the discount or premium may be recognized by using straightline accruals, irrespective of the term of the instrument.

176 See the text that accompanies notes 50-75 in chapter 4.

177 *Issues Paper*, supra note 3, at 120-21, cites many of the familiar reasons, described in chapter 4, why an uncritical acceptance of financial-accounting practices is unacceptable for tax purposes. These reasons include

> the unsettled nature of accounting standards in the area of financial instruments;
>
> the risk of unwarranted and uncontrolled flexibility and subjectivity associated with a reliance on general principles;
>
> the different purposes underlying the preparation of financial accounting statements; and
>
> the acceptance of deferred recognition on the basis of accounting concepts, such as materiality, prudence or conservatism.

178 New Zealand Income Tax Act, 1994, as amended, sections EH 39 and EH 1(2).

179 *A Platform for Consultation*, supra note 3, at 163-64 and 185-86; and *Issues Paper*, supra note 3, at 119-30.

180 ITA draft regulation 9102(1)(a)(ii) similarly permits a financial institution that is subject to the mark-to-market legislation to use any reasonable alternative to the level-yield method in recognizing accrued gain on a specified debt obligation, provided that the alternative is substantially similar. The Department of Finance states in the explanatory notes that an alternative method may be considered to be reasonable if it is consistent with generally accepted accounting practice.

181 New Zealand Income Tax Act, 1994, as amended, sections EH 39 and EH 1(2).

182 See Smith, supra note 9, at 225-28, for a more detailed discussion of the interpretation and application of these conditions.

183 In the absence of a specific reference to the YTM method, the content of the term "principles of accrual accounting" is unclear and may mean nothing more than a recognition method other than the cash basis. See Smith, supra note 9, at 227-28. As Smith notes, "principles of accrual accounting" is not a term of art with an accepted meaning. He argues (ibid., at 228) that the term encompasses any method "of attributing income or expenditure over the relevant period—including by reference to market valuation—as distinct from relying upon cash receipts and payments." The method most commonly equated with "accrual accounting" entails the recognition of revenue as it is "earned" and expenses as they are "incurred." This method differs from either the YTM method or market-value accounting, which involve the recognition of amounts when they have not necessarily been

earned or incurred. The adoption of the concepts of "receivable" and "payable" as the basis for the application of the realization requirement to unexpected gains and losses is discussed in the text that accompanies notes 202-204 infra. The related reference in the second condition to "commercially acceptable practice" is equally vague and may mean nothing more than that an accrual method must be acceptable for financial-accounting purposes.

184 Smith, supra note 9, at 227, notes that the condition "was intended to allow taxpayers to put forward an alternative method of their choice, but only where they also adopted it for financial accounting purposes."

185 This condition is obviously irrelevant if a taxpayer does not prepare financial accounts. In that case, the taxpayer should simply be required to use a benchmark calculation specified for tax purposes. Nonetheless, both the New Zealand legislation and the Australian accrual proposals apparently require the adoption of a method that conforms to commercial accounting practices and any specified benchmark for tax purposes. See, for example, *Determination* G12, "Accounting for a Financial Arrangement in the Absence of a Determination," November 21, 1988; Smith, supra note 9, at 230-31; and *Issues Paper*, supra note 3, at 135. For taxpayers who do not prepare financial accounts, any reference to financial-accounting practice as a source of accrual methods is difficult to understand, particularly if the rationale for a reliance on this practice is an intention to minimize the compliance burden. Only the absence of a specified method for tax purposes would seem to justify regard to financial-accounting practice in this much different context. *Taxation of Financial Arrangements*, supra note 24, at 42, proposes that a taxpayer who does not prepare financial statements should, in the absence of a determination, "use a method which is fair and reasonable, having regard to the tenor of the accrual rules."

186 New Zealand Inland Revenue *Tax Information Bulletin*, vol. 3, no. 1, July 1991. *The Taxation of Financial Arrangements*, supra note 24, at 42, proposes that an alternative method must provide results that have regard to the tenor of the spreading provisions. This standard would not be limited to the YTM benchmark and would include market-value accounting as an alternative.

187 *Tax Information Bulletin*, vol. 3, no. 1, supra note 186, qualifies application of the bright line as "subject to the circumstances of any particular case." This qualification appears to leave open the possible acceptability of an alternative recognition method, even if it does not satisfy the bright-line test of "material difference." See also New Zealand Inland Revenue *Technical Policy Circular* 88/2, October 1987, which states that the materiality of a difference in results under the straightline method "is something that needs to be considered in relation to each particular case."

188 *Issues Paper*, supra note 3, at 119-30. The issues paper, ibid., at 127-28, provides as an example of a discontinuity the case of a taxpayer with a bond portfolio that includes some secondary-market acquisitions. Depending on the extent of any discount, the straightline method might result in a deviation from the acceptable benchmark for the acquired bonds, with the result that all of the instruments in the portfolio would be subject to a YTM calculation. The "reasonableness standard" would apparently accommodate this particular situation.

189 Ibid., at 119. In contrast, the New Zealand legislation permits a taxpayer to use the period between regular payments on an instrument as the compounding period,

subject only to a requirement of annual compounding if the relevant period is more than one year. See *Determination* G3, supra note 89.

190 *Issues Paper*, supra note 3, at 124-26.

191 Ibid., at 126-29.

192 Ibid., at 126-27: "There is no particular percentage at which the difference between a taxpayer's method and the benchmark necessarily becomes inherently 'significant.' "

193 Ibid., at 123. If a particular recognition method does not fall within the acceptable 10 percent range of deviation from the benchmark YTM, the method may still be used for tax purposes if it is

> used in respect of that financial arrangement in the financial accounts of the taxpayer;
>
> consistent with generally accepted accounting principles;
>
> used consistently for both income and expenses for tax purposes; and
>
> a reasonable approximation of economic accrual.

These conditions are similar to those under the reasonableness standard described in the New Zealand legislation. See the text that accompanies notes 181-187 supra.

194 According to *Issues Paper*, supra note 3, at 121-22, the proposed standard of reasonableness would depend on an assessment that a particular recognition method used for financial-accounting purposes provided a "reasonable approximation of economic accrual," which would remain undefined. The issues paper (ibid., at 122) suggests that a method would be considered to satisfy the reasonableness standard if

> the amounts accrued under the method have due regard to the cost of the instrument as well as any discount, premium or interest previously accrued by the taxpayer on the instrument;
>
> the method reflects the concept of the time value of money, in particular the concept of compounding interest; and
>
> the method accrues the gain or loss from the instrument in a manner similar to the accrual of gain or loss that the market value tax accounting method would produce if market factors do not change over the term of the arrangement from what was expected or implied at the time the taxpayer entered into the arrangement.

195 *Issues Paper*, supra note 3, at 130.

196 Examples of "significance tables" are provided in the *Issues Paper*, ibid., at 142-46. The examples refer to simple OID obligations, interest-bearing instruments issued at their face amount, and interest-bearing instruments acquired at a discount or premium.

197 *Issues Paper*, ibid., at 142-46, indicates that application of the straightline method to these instruments would almost always produce results within the acceptable 10 percent range of deviation set out in significance tables.

198 Because an "on-market" price-fixing instrument represents a fair bet, there is no advance of funds by either counterparty. "Off-market" and "prepaid" price-fixing instruments involve an advance of funds. The text that accompanies notes 253-267 infra discusses briefly the tax-avoidance opportunities presented by explicit and

implicit prepayments, and some possible legislative responses, in the narrow context of periodic swap payments. A fuller discussion of the subject occurs in the text that accompanies notes 24-92 in chapter 6.

199 These problems are attributable to the basic tenet of accretion taxation, which is that unexpected gains and losses must be recognized before a realization event. Assets must be valued and tax paid on unexpected gains in the absence of a transaction that establishes value and generates cash flow. See the text that accompanies notes 278-280 in chapter 3.

200 See the text that accompanies notes 115-133 in chapter 3.

201 See the text that accompanies notes 88-93 in chapter 3.

202 See the text that accompanies note 23 in chapter 2 and notes 29-36 in chapter 7. *A Tax System Redesigned*, supra note 3, at 352-53, states that the "disposal principle applies when a taxpayer ceases to hold a financial asset or to be subject to a financial liability—whether wholly or in part, whether by sale, transfer, exchange, maturity, or other alienation, extinguishment, or synthetic disposal."

203 See the text that accompanies notes 104-106 in chapter 2.

204 See the text that accompanies notes 29-43 in chapter 7.

205 See the text that accompanies notes 187-217 in chapter 7.

206 See the text that accompanies notes 24-27 in chapter 1.

207 This point is acknowledged in *The Taxation of Financial Arrangements*, supra note 24, at 48, and apparently formed the basis for a change in accounting method for forwards on foreign exchange and commodities. *Determination* G14, "Forward Contracts for Foreign Exchange and Commodities," May 4, 1989, required that the difference between the spot rate and forward price under the contract be spread as discount or premium over the relevant term. At the end of a taxation year, movement in the spot rate was accounted for as gain or loss. As noted in *The Taxation of Financial Arrangements*, supra note 24, at 47, this retranslation basis was largely driven by the fact that the same treatment applied to foreign currency debt and by the need to realize consistent taxation of fully hedged foreign borrowings or loans and domestic borrowings or loans. This treatment is no longer necessary, since the treatment of foreign currency debt has been changed to require the accrual recognition of only expected foreign exchange gains and losses, as measured by forward exchange rates. See the text that accompanies note 142 supra. Gain or loss associated with on-market forwards that are not prepaid are now subject to realization-based recognition as unexpected amounts. See *Determination* G14A, "Forward Contracts for Foreign Exchange and Commodities: An Expected Value Approach," May 1998.

208 But see ITA subparagraphs 142.4(c)(ii) and (d)(ii) and draft regulation 9203, which require financial institutions to amortize all unexpected gains or losses realized on non-traded debt to the extent that the amounts are attributable to changes in the market rate of interest. The gains or losses must be amortized on a straightline basis over the remaining term of the transferred debt instrument. The apparent basis for the amortization requirement is the assumption that the proceeds will be reinvested by the financial institution at the prevailing market rate. The realized gain or loss is therefore averaged with the return on the new instrument to arrive at a rate of return that incorporates the rate on the original instrument.

This averaging or smoothing provision is an obvious exception to realization-based recognition and difficult to justify in tax-policy terms apart from a need for general averaging provisions under a steeply progressive rate structure. The fact that amortization is consistent with financial-accounting practice fails to provide any independent justification for its use for tax purposes.

209 Application of the realization principle to futures contracts means that gains and losses should be recognized when a taxpayer settles an open position by entering into an equal and opposite position with the clearing house. Daily settlement of open positions involves purely notional or formal dispositions and reacquisitions that are effected solely in order to determine margin calls and should not, therefore, be treated as realization events. See *A Tax System Redesigned*, supra note 3, at 355-56. Similarly, unexpected gain or loss should be brought to account when a forward, swap, or option is settled or transferred to another counterparty or holder. But see *A Tax System Redesigned*, ibid., at 353 and 354-55, where it is recommended, largely because of liquidity concerns, that physical settlement of a derivative not give rise to a disposition. This exception creates an important inconsistency in treatment between cash-settled and physically settled derivatives that provides opportunities for unanticipated deferral and selective realization. See, for example, Reed H. Shuldiner, "A General Approach to the Taxation of Financial Instruments" (December 1992), 71 *Texas Law Review* 243-350, at 308, where he argues that physical settlement of a forward should constitute a realization event, in which gain or loss is determined on the basis of the value of the underlying property. Any inconsistency in treatment is eliminated, however, to the extent that "traded" instruments are subject to accretion taxation for the reasons described in the text that accompanies notes 280-314 infra.

210 New Zealand Income Tax Act, 1994, as amended, sections EH 45 and EH 4; *A Platform for Consultation*, supra note 3, at 161 and 174-75; *Consultative Document*, supra note 3, at 111-13; and *Issues Paper*, supra note 3, at 223-28.

211 The reference under the New Zealand legislation to a holder and an issuer has apparently caused some confusion in the application of a base price adjustment to financial instruments other than debt. See *The Taxation of Financial Arrangements*, supra note 24, at 28-29. To eliminate this confusion, it is proposed (ibid., at 30) that the formula for a base price adjustment be changed to

$$a - b - c + d + e,$$

where a is all consideration paid to the taxpayer, b is all consideration paid by the taxpayer, c is income recognized in all previous taxation years, d is expense recognized in all previous taxation years, and e is any amounts forgiven by the taxpayer.

212 Both the New Zealand legislation and the Australian accrual proposals reflect these basic elements, but they differ in this context in one significant respect. Under New Zealand Income Tax Act, 1994, as amended, sections EH 45 and EH 4(1), forgiven amounts are generally not considered to be paid and must be accounted for as income under the base price adjustment. Sections EH 54 and EH 6 allow a limited range of taxpayers to deduct an equivalent amount as a bad debt. The Australian accrual proposals exclude forgiven amounts in respect of commercial indebtedness from the base price adjustment for both holders and issuers. Under the proposed Australian regime, the tax treatment of these amounts is addressed in separate legislation that requires use of the forgiven amount to reduce loss

carryovers and the cost base of assets of the debtor. Generally, the debtor must recognize as income the excess of the forgiven amount over these other amounts. In the case of foreign currency debt, the determination of forgiven amounts should use the spot exchange rate that prevailed when the loan was advanced (forgiven principal) or when interest payments were due (forgiven interest). See, for example, ITA paragraph 80(2)(k). For a general discussion of the taxation of forgiven amounts consistent with the treatment of other forms of discount, see Yishai Beer, "Unpacking the Cancellation of Indebtedness Income Doctrine: Towards Economic Reality-Based Taxation" (Winter 2000), 19 *Virginia Tax Review* 457-514.

213 Assume, for example, that an OID bond is issued for three years at a price of \$100 and pays \$133 on redemption. Given annual compounding, the holder accrues \$10 of income for the first year (\$100 × 0.1), \$11 for the second (\$110 × 0.1), and \$12 for the third (\$121 × 0.1). If \$133 is paid on redemption, the base price adjustment for the holder will be nil (\$133 consideration received – \$100 consideration paid + \$33 accrued interest income = 0). If the obligation is sold, before redemption, at the beginning of year 3, unexpected gain or loss can arise because of movements in the market rate of interest. For example, if the one-year market rate has declined below the rate on the OID obligation, the holder can sell the obligation at a premium of, say, \$4, or the difference between proceeds of \$125 and the \$121 cost base (\$100 consideration paid by the holder + \$21 of accrued income). In that case, the base price adjustment requires the holder to recognize the premium as unexpected gain represented by the positive amount under the calculation (\$125 consideration received – \$100 consideration paid + \$21 accrued income = \$4).

214 Assume, for example, that the holder in the example described in note 213 supra receives only \$128 on redemption. In that case, the base price adjustment would result in a negative amount of \$5 (\$128 consideration received – \$100 consideration paid + \$33 accrued income). Much the same result would occur if the negative amount arose on a secondary-market transfer.

215 For the purposes of the base price adjustment, amounts paid or payable by an issuer include bonuses and other redemption premiums, which would generally be deductible for issuers on income account on realization as unexpected losses. The same amounts would generally be recognized by holders on income account. See *Issues Paper*, supra note 3, at 226-27.

216 To the extent that accrued but unpaid and unrecognized income is included as part of the proceeds recognized on a secondary-market transaction, the base price adjustment ensures that the amount is taxable to the transferor. No special rules are required to address the taxability of accrued amounts to the time of transfer, unless there is a distinction between ordinary income and capital amounts. In that case, special rules are necessary to ensure that the accrued income cannot be converted into a capital gain on a secondary-market transfer. (See the text that accompanies note 52 in chapter 2.) The transferee assumes a cost equal to the amount paid and must perform a new YTM calculation to ensure that amounts accrued before the transfer effectively remain taxable to the transferor only. The application of the YTM calculation by the transferee ensures that amounts accrued after the transfer are taxable to the transferee. The YTM calculation for the transferee will be incorrect, however, if no allocation is made of interest that is accrued but unpaid before the transfer, since in that case the transferee will have

to account for the full amount of the expected cash flow that arises after the transfer. Accordingly, an allocation of accrued, but unpaid, interest must be made between the transferor and the transferee, who must account only for cash flows that represent accrued interest after the transfer. Interest accrued before the transfer may be treated as a non-taxable recovery of cost. See *Consultative Document on Accrual Tax Treatment*, supra note 37, at 85-93.

217 Characterization of these amounts as capital losses is appropriate if it has been decided to maintain capital-account treatment of the loan losses of taxpayers who are not in the business of moneylending. See, for example, *Issues Paper*, supra note 3, at 224-25, where it justifies this characterization on the basis of the similar capital-account treatment of losses on shares.

218 *Taxation of Financial Arrangements*, supra note 24, at 31-32. This result is realized for holders of debt obligations under ITA subsection 20(21).

219 Similar issues arise in the case of the assignment of a financial instrument by the holder. See *Taxation of Financial Arrangements*, supra note 24, at 51-62: "An assignment of income, on the other hand, occurs when persons receive money in consideration of relinquishing a future income stream to which they are otherwise entitled"; and *A Platform for Consultation*, supra note 3, at 178-79. "Asset securitizations" are notable examples of structured financings; their treatment should follow that of assignments generally under a comprehensive accrual regime. See infra notes 222, 225, and 231.

220 *Taxation of Financial Arrangements*, supra note 24, at 51. See also *A Platform for Consultation*, supra note 3, at 178-79.

221 Ibid.

222 This requirement also applies to the holder of a financial instrument on an assignment that is treated as a disposition. The assignor brings to account the difference between all amounts advanced by the assignor and all amounts received from the debtor and the assignee. The assignee accrues as income the difference between the amount paid to the assignor and the expected amount of future payments under the primary obligation from the date of the assignment. The assignee makes a basic price adjustment only when the primary obligation is subsequently transferred, settled, or redeemed.

223 *Taxation of Financial Arrangements*, supra note 24, at 55.

224 Ibid.

225 Ibid., at 56. If an assignment is not recognized as a disposition, a separate loan effectively arises between the assignor and the assignee. The assignor accrues expense on the effective loan from the assignee, which offsets accrued income on the primary obligation. The assignee accrues income on the effective loan to the assignor. The accrued amount equals the difference between the amount paid by the assignee and the expected value of the future payments on the primary obligation.

226 Ibid., at 57.

227 Ibid., at 55 and 57.

228 The definition of a realization event presents problems in the context of certain transactions that are transfers in legal form but do not result in a shift of the risk associated with a particular position. In other instances, risk may be shifted without transferring a financial instrument as a matter of private law. See, for example,

A Platform for Consultation, supra note 3, at 75-79. The text that accompanies notes 29-44 in chapter 7 discusses some of the difficulties associated with the definition of a disposition as being tantamount to a realization event.

229 The appropriate treatment of hedging and of synthetic instruments generally, which is the subject of chapter 7, depends on the same basic issue. Financial-accounting practice has failed to provide any general agreement about the point at which an in-substance defeasance transfers sufficient risk to support derecognition of the relevant liability by the defeasor. See, for example, *The Taxation of Financial Arrangements*, supra note 24, at 53, where it is noted that financial-accounting standards in New Zealand require the recognition of a debt defeasance whenever arrangements are entered into that make it "virtually certain" that the debtor will not be required "to assume the primary obligation or satisfy secondary obligations for the debt servicing requirement." See also Glenn L.E. May, "Overview of Financial, Tax, and Accounting Principles for Derivative Financial Instruments," in the 1995 Conference Report, supra note 94, 29:1-27, at 29:11, where he summarizes financial-accounting treatment of in-substance defeasances in Canada; and Financial Accounting Standards Board (FASB), *Accounting for Transfers and Servicing of Financial Assets and Extinguishment of Liabilities*, Statement of Financial Accounting Practice no. 125 (Norwalk, Conn.: FASB, June 1996), which sets out US financial-accounting standards for derecognition treatment of defeased liabilities.

230 A "discontinuity" occurs when small changes in the risk associated with a position result in disproportionately large changes in tax treatment. Thus a concept of a disposition that is based on a defined level of risk retention creates a discontinuity if the risk level just inside the bright line and the risk level just outside it result in significantly different tax treatments (that is, realization-event treatment and non-recognition treatment). Discontinuities create obvious opportunities for tax planning, some of which are discussed in chapters 6 and 7.

231 *The Taxation of Financial Arrangements*, supra note 24, at 53: "The concept of 'virtual certainty' [see supra note 229] would be a less clear boundary than the jurisprudential concept of an absolute release from obligations under an arrangement." See also *A Platform for Consultation*, supra note 3, at 179: "While there are similarities between legal and in-substance defeasances and assignments, particularly where an in-substance defeasance is with a risk-free entity [as the defeasance counterparty], it appears that there can be significant differences. On that basis, there is a case for taxing in-substance transactions as if they were two separate transactions rather than an implicit defeasance or assignment"; and *A Tax System Redesigned*, supra note 3, at 359-61. *The Taxation of Financial Arrangements*, supra note 24, at 53 notes that limiting the application of a base price adjustment to legal defeasances is consistent with the characterization of other risk-shifting arrangements, such as interest-rate swaps, as financial arrangements that are distinct from an underlying borrowing. Chapter 7 discusses instances in which two or more financial instruments may be treated as a single composite transaction.

The Taxation of Financial Arrangements, ibid., at 54, proposes the same bright-line test for the recognition of assignments as it proposes for the recognition of defeasance as realization events. In other words, only assignments as a matter of private law ("absolute assignments") would be treated as dispositions that required a base price adjustment. But see the taxation bill, supra note 63, at 6, 10 and 16; and New Zealand Income Tax Act, 1994, as amended, section EH 23(2) and the definition of a "legal defeasance" in section OB 1, which incorporate the concept of a legal defeasance used for financial-accounting purposes in New Zealand. This concept apparently includes only transactions that release the debtor from the primary obligation and that are acknowledged by the creditor or a duly appointed agent, or are established by legal judgment.

232 *The Taxation of Financial Arrangements*, supra note 24, at 60-61; and *A Platform for Consultation*, supra note 3, at 178. The same allocation issues arise in the case of the absolute assignment by the holder of a portion of the cash flows associated with a financial instrument.

233 *The Taxation of Financial Arrangements*, supra note 24, at 61, describes two approaches to the application of a partial base price adjustment to the defeased portion of a financial instrument. Under one approach, the acquisition price of the instrument is apportioned between the defeased portion and the retained portion, and accrued income or expense is assigned between the two portions for the period from the issue date to the date of the partial disposition. The other approach requires the discounting of the cash flows that are allocable to the remaining portion of the instrument on the basis of the yield to maturity for the whole instrument. The present value of these cash flows represents the issue price for a new instrument. This is the approach that should be used in applying a partial base price adjustment to coupon-stripping transactions and other partial assignments. See supra note 91.

234 *The Taxation of Financial Arrangements*, supra note 24, at 62.

235 Ibid.: "The full base price adjustment can be compared to a full mark-to-market adjustment at the time of the partial assignment or defeasance."

236 Ibid., where it is noted that it is possible to use the application of a full base price adjustment on a partial defeasance in order to realize selectively unexpected losses attributable to the retained portion of an instrument. See also *A Platform for Consultation*, supra note 3, at 178, where it is noted that application of a full base price adjustment on a partial disposition "could impact harshly on some taxpayers and for others it could facilitate the adverse selection of losses." The text that accompanies notes 280-336 infra discusses alternative approaches to the problem of the selective realization of unexpected losses and the strategic trading of financial instruments. As an alternative to the application of either a partial or full base price adjustment on a partial defeasance or assignment, *The Taxation of Financial Arrangements*, supra note 24, at 60-61, prefers accounting for a transactions of this kind as a "variation" of the relevant instrument. This characterization permits a one-time adjustment that is made by recalculating income or expense from the issue date of the instrument to the date of the partial disposition on the assumption that "the varied cash flows [have] been known since inception." Under this approach, the defeasor effectively spreads any realized loss over the term of the primary obligation. See *Determination* G25, "Variations in the Terms of a Financial Arrangement," May 28, 1992. The assignee, similarly, recognizes any realized gain over the term of the instrument that is partially assigned. Although more limited in application, this approach is similar in effect to the amortization under the ITA of unexpected gain or loss realized by financial institutions on non-traded debt. See supra note 208.

237 See the text that accompanies notes 39-46 in chapter 1.

238 Shuldiner, supra note 209, at 314-15; and Weisbach, supra note 130, at 500.

239 See, for example, the description of prevailing administrative practices under the Canadian ITA and the Australian ITAA in the text that accompanies notes 103-129 in chapter 2.

240 See the description of the legislative approach in New Zealand and the United States in the text that accompanies notes 243-252 and 268-279 infra.

241 See the description of the administrative practice under the Australian ITAA in the text that accompanies notes 94-103 in chapter 2.

242 Weisbach, supra note 130, at 499-500. See also *A Platform for Consultation*, supra note 3, at 167: "More generally, a swap could be notionally divided into two payment legs in order to determine how the timing adjustment [accrual method] is to be applied."

243 *Determination* G27, "Swaps," January 16, 1995. The determination applies to interest rate swaps, interest swaps, and currency swaps, and various combinations of the three types. It does not apply to commodity swaps, equity swaps, currency swaps that involve more than two currencies, or swaps that involve an amortization or accretion of loan principal. For the purpose of the determination, an "interest rate swap" is "any swap under which the parties agree to exchange fixed rate interest payments for floating rate interest, in the same currency, calculated with reference to a notional principal amount." An interest swap is "any swap under which the parties agree to exchange interest payments where the payments streams differ with respect to the basis upon which interest amounts are payable (such as monthly, and quarterly payment intervals, or payments in arrears or advance)." A "currency swap" is "any swap under which the parties are free to exchange a specified amount of currency, on a notional or physical basis, at an agreed rate of exchange." An "interest rate and currency swap" is simply an interest rate swap in two different currencies. An "interest and currency swap" is an interest swap in two different currencies.

244 Currency swaps that involve a spot exchange at the spot rate and a future exchange of fixed amounts on a single fixed date were subject to *Determination* G14, supra note 207, and its requirement to spread the difference between the spot rate and the contract rate over the relevant term with retranslation at the spot rate at the end of intervening taxation years. "Interest and currency swaps" and "interest rate and currency swaps" were similarly subject to the retranslation basis provided for foreign currency debt. The conceptual basis for this approach is described in *Consultative Document on Accrual Tax Treatment*, supra note 37, at 191-203. Accrual recognition of expected exchange gains and losses means that the unexpected gain or loss associated with the series of forward contracts that constitute an interest-based currency swap may be subject to realization-based recognition. See *Determination* G9B, supra note 145. But see also *Determination* G14A, supra note 207, which states that realization-based recognition for forward currency contracts is limited to currency swaps that involve exchanges of fixed amounts on a single fixed date. Periodic swap payments associated with interest-based currency swaps continue to be subject to accrual recognition on each leg of the swap, as if they were offsetting loans.

245 *Determination* G27, supra note 243: "In this way [treatment as notional offsetting loans], the appropriate recognition of income and expenditure under the swap . . .

will result from the net effect of the combination of your accounting for the two deemed loans"; and Erika W. Nijenhuis, "Taxation of Notional Principal Contracts," in Reuven S. Avi-Yonah, David B. Newman, and Diane Ring, eds., *Taxation of Financial Instruments* (Deerfield, Ill: Clark, Boardman Callaghan) (looseleaf), chapter 3, at 51, where it is noted that the matching of periodic swap entitlements and the expense associated with an underlying liability results in the recognition of an aggregate amount equal to the sum of the net swap payment or receipt and the expense on the liability; this outcome, in turn, results in the recognition of an amount equal to the expense that would be recognized if the swap and the liability were integrated into a synthetic debt instrument represented by the other leg of the swap; and Shuldiner, supra note 209, at 319-20, where it is noted that consistent taxation of long-term debt and the combination of a floating-rate instrument and a swap requires an accounting for periodic swap payments as they are paid or accrued.

246 Nijenhuis, supra note 245, at 51, footnote 8, cites the example of a taxpayer who borrows funds at a fixed rate of 7 percent and enters into a fixed-for-floating rate swap. Under this arrangement, the taxpayer receives fixed amounts equal to 7 percent of a notional principal amount equal to the borrowed funds and pays amounts on the same notional principal that are determined by reference to a floating rate. The aggregate of the taxpayer's expense on the fixed-rate loan and the net swap payment or receipt equals the amount of expense associated with a floating-rate loan on the notional principal amount.

247 See the text that accompanies notes 94-97 in chapter 2.

248 This intuitive appeal is apparently less compelling in the case of foreign exchange gains and losses. Interest-rate parity suggests that it is appropriate to characterize expected exchange gains and losses as ordinary income. Unexpected amounts that arise under a swap may be characterized as either income or capital, provided that the same characterization is extended to the offsetting amounts on an underlying borrowing or loan. The character issue is eliminated, of course, under a comprehensive accrual regime that treats all gains and losses on financial instruments as ordinary-income amounts. Their character as either expected amounts or unexpected amounts is relevant for timing purposes only.

249 See the text that accompanies notes 187-217 in chapter 7.

250 Shuldiner, supra note 209, at 314-15.

251 This proposition extends to interest-based currency swaps as the equivalent of a series of physically settled forward exchange contracts written at the forward rate implicit in the interest-rate differential. Like interest-rate swaps, currency swaps provide only unexpected gains or losses that arise on settlement, and there is no need to account for the legs of the swap as offsetting loans, assuming that unexpected gains and losses are generally subject to realization-based recognition. Treatment of the legs of a swap as offsetting loans should be limited to interest-based currency swaps in which the interest income or expense on each leg of the swap would otherwise be subject to a different accounting treatment, including different YTM calculations if each leg had a different interest payment date. This determination would be relatively simple under an expected-return approach that required taxpayers to account for all foreign currency debt as synthetic domestic instruments by accruing expected exchange gains and losses. See supra notes 136-162.

252 This argument for realization-based recognition of offsetting amounts on an underlying position is the apparent basis for the limitation of notional loan treatment under *Determination* G27, supra note 243, to the legs on interest-based swaps. In practice, it is usual to treat one leg or both legs of a swap, other than an interest-based swap, with reference to an underlying position, such as ownership of shares or a commodity, that is subject to realization-based recognition of gains and losses. See, for example, Weisbach, supra note 130, at 514, where he notes that the bifurcation of swaps into offsetting loans may work in the case of interest-rate swaps but is difficult to achieve in the case of equity or other types of swaps.

253 Weisbach, supra note 130, at 514-15.

254 See Shuldiner, supra note 209, at 290-97.

255 See the text that accompanies notes 24-69 in chapter 6.

256 The use of swap prepayments to accelerate the recognition of income is attractive as a means of freshening expiring loss carryovers. The income inclusion can be offset with the loss carryover, which is replenished when the prepaid receipt is repaid on settlement of the relevant forward contract under the swap. See the text that accompanies notes 70-74 in chapter 6.

257 See the text that accompanies notes 24-92 in chapter 6.

258 Shuldiner, supra note 209, at 290-97.

259 Ibid., at 297-303, where Shuldiner illustrates the allocation issue through a series of examples involving multiple bets. Shuldiner notes (ibid., at 303) that if there is more than one bet and a prepayment the use of pricing models is required, since it is impossible to determine the correct treatment from the terms of the bets themselves.

260 Ibid., at 303-4.

261 Ibid. Assume, for example, that the spot price of gold is $300 per ounce, the one-year forward price is $315, and the two-year forward price is $330.75. X enters into both a one-year forward contract to purchase gold at $328 per ounce and a two-year forward contract with the same counterparty to purchase gold at $317.10 per ounce. X has thus overpaid in respect of the one-year off-market forward and underpaid in respect of the two-year contract. Since the overpayment is offset by the underpayment, no amount is advanced by either counterparty and the package of forwards is on-market. If the spot price in one year is $320 per ounce, X will pay $8 under the one-year forward. For X, this cash flow is equivalent to the combination of a $5 income receipt under an on-market forward and a $13 loan in respect of the off-market two-year forward. At an assumed interest rate of 5 percent per annum, the $13 is the present value of the $13.65 difference between the $317.10 off-market rate and the $330.75 on-market rate for the second forward contract. In effect, X has paid $13 for an off-market bet with an expected value of $13.65. If the spot rate on settlement of the two-year forward is $325.25, X will receive $8.15 (the amount of the spot price of $325.25 in excess of the off-market forward price of $317.10). X will also, however, realize a loss of $5.50, or the $13.65 expected value of the off-market bet less the $8.15 receipt. The net result of the two off-market forwards is a loss of $0.50 for X (the $5 gain on the one-year forward less the $5.50 loss on the two-year forward), which is exactly the same result as would have arisen had X

entered into a series of two on-market forwards at forward prices of $315 per ounce (one-year forward) and $330.75 per ounce (two-year forward); that is, a gain of $5 on the one-year forward, or the amount of the $320 spot price in excess of the $315 forward price; and a loss of $5.50 on the two-year forward, or the amount of the forward price of $330.75 in excess of the spot price of $325.25. This result is realized even though the two forwards are off-market. X effectively accelerates recognition of a $13 prepayment in respect of the off-market two-year forward. Recognition of the prepayment turns what would have been an income receipt of $5 in respect of an on-market one-year forward into an expense of $8 paid on the settlement date of that forward.

262 Shuldiner, supra note 209, at 315-16; and Weisbach, supra note 130, at 513.

263 To revert to the example in note 261 supra, this treatment would require X to recognize income of $5 in respect of an on-market one-year forward. X would be considered to have loaned the other counterparty $13 in respect of the off-market two-year forward and would accrue income of $0.65 on the prepayment. X would, therefore, have a cost base in the two-year forward of $13.65 on settlement. Receipt of $8.15 at that time would give rise to a loss of $5.50 (the $13.65 cost base less the $8.15 receipt). Shuldiner, supra note 209, at 317-19, illustrates the same treatment by using a two-year fixed-for-floating interest-rate swap under which a level fixed rate results in an overpayment in respect of the two-year forward and an underpayment in respect of the one-year forward. The level rate results in an overpayment and an underpayment because of the presence of an upward-sloping yield curve under which the one-year forward interest rate is less than the level swap rate and the two-year forward rate is greater than that same rate. The US regulations that govern the timing of income and expense on notional principal contracts apply this treatment to non-periodic payments that are considered to be significant. See the text that accompanies notes 75-92 in chapter 6.

264 Thus the $13 prepayment for the off-market two-year forward in the example in note 261 supra would be allocated to that contract and recognized only on its settlement. X would have to recognize $5 as income in respect of an on-market one-year forward. No interest would be imputed, however, on the reallocated prepayment. The US regulations that govern the timing of income and expense on notional principal contracts apply this treatment to non-periodic payments that are not significant. See the text that accompanies notes 75-92 in chapter 6.

265 Weisbach, supra note 130, at 515.

266 Shuldiner, supra note 209, at 319-29, where he notes that consistent treatment of long-term debt and interest-rate swaps necessitates the disregard of disguised prepayments as embedded debt.

267 In this connection, Shuldiner, ibid., at 319-22, emphasizes the role of interest-rate swaps in allowing taxpayers to take advantage of the mismeasurement of expected gain or loss attributable to a failure to account for the term structure of interest with long-term debt. He notes, in particular, that a fixed-for-floating rate swap permits the floating-rate payer to replicate a leveraged acquisition of long-term, fixed-rate debt at much lower transaction costs, since the swap reduces the credit risk associated with the transaction. It is much easier and less costly, therefore, to enter into a swap with a notional principal amount than it is to enter into the back-to-back floating- and fixed-rate loans of the same amount that would be

required to arbitrage the mismeasurement in taxation of long-term debt. He suggests (ibid., at 322, footnote 332) the use of an anti-avoidance provision similar to the general rule governing notional principal contracts in the US regulations to distinguish between swaps that may be taxed consistently with long-term debt and swaps that should be subject to treatment of disguised prepayments as embedded loans. IRC reg. section 1.446-3(f) provides that the Commissioner may deviate from the general timing rules that govern income and expense on notional principal contracts if (1) a taxpayer enters into a transaction that is not a customary commercial transaction, (2) the general rules would produce a material distortion of income, and (3) the taxpayer would not have entered into the transaction in the absence of the prospect of that material distortion. Deviation from the general rules is permitted if it is necessary to deviate from them in order to reflect income clearly.

268 IRC reg. section 1.446-3. For a general discussion of the US NPC regulations, see Nijenhuis, supra note 245. IRC reg. section 1.446-(c)(1)(i) defines a "notional principal contract" as "a financial instrument that provides for the payment of amounts by one party to another at specified intervals calculated by reference to a specified index upon a notional principal amount in exchange for specified consideration or a promise to pay similar amounts." The definition includes most swaps calculated with reference to a specified index and caps, floors, and collars as a series of options. It excludes forwards and futures because the payments they yield are not calculated upon a notional principal amount. It excludes most options because they usually provide for a single payment rather than payments at specified intervals.

269 IRC reg. section 1.446-3(e)(2)(i). Taxpayers may elect to apply the straightline method on the basis of either the actual number of days in a year or a rule of convenience, such as a 360-day year that comprises 12 months of 30 days each. IRC reg. section 1.446-3(e)(3), example 2.

270 IRC reg. section 1.446-3(d).

271 IRC reg. sections 1.446-3(e)(2)(ii) and (iii).

272 Ibid.

273 IRC reg. section 1.446-3(e)(1).

274 Nijenhuis, supra note 245, at 51-52; and Weisbach, supra note 130, at 515: "swaps often are used to hedge level payments streams, such as those produced by debt instruments."

275 See Nijenhuis, supra note 245, at 50-51, where she notes that formulaic spreading of the periodic payments is neutral in relation to the timing and number of payments made during a taxation year but creates an inconsistency in treatment in the case of equivalent payments on forwards that are subject to realization-based recognition. See also Weisbach, supra note 130, at 515-16, where he describes avoidance opportunities that arise if swaps are subject to formulaic spreading instead of to characterization as a series of forwards. For example, it is possible to replicate a swap by entering into a series of forwards that is offset by an opposite position in an actual swap. The application of different accounting methods to the offsetting cash flows (realization-based recognition for the forwards and formulaic spreading for the periodic swap payments) permits accelerated recognition of losses. The anti-avoidance rule in IRC reg. section 1.446-3(f) (noted supra note 267) may apply to these and other, similar timing arbitrages.

276 Nijenhuis, supra note 245, at 51, uses the example of a one-year forward entered into by a calendar-year taxpayer on January 1, 1995 to illustrate the effect of a spreading approach. Realization-based recognition of any unexpected gain or loss on the forward means that this gain or loss is accounted for in full in the 1996 taxation year when the forward is settled (January 1, 1996). Daily ratable spreading of the periodic payments associated with the same forward contract entered into as part of a swap means that most of the gain or loss is recognized as accrued in 1995. The effect of this spreading extends to any disguised prepayment attributable to overpayments by the taxpayer associated with an off-market forward. Similarly, underpayments will effectively spread any prepayment receipts over the 1995 taxation year.

277 Formulaic spreading also achieves some degree of matching of periodic swap payments and the level payment stream associated with an underlying swapped position. The text that accompanies notes 190-218 supra considers whether there is any justification for matching outside of a general hedging regime that applies to all financial instruments. The treatment of periodic payments on NPCs may be motivated, at least in part, by a desire to match periodic swap payments with similar payments on an assumed underlying position. See Nijenhuis, supra note 245, at 51-52; and Weisbach, supra note 130, at 514-15.

278 Assume that the series of two forward contracts in the example in note 261 supra are packaged in a swap as periodic payments calculated with reference to a notional principal amount of $300 (the spot price of gold per ounce). X agrees to pay a fixed amount of $28, which is equal to the difference between the agreed forward price and the spot price. If the forward were on-market, X would have agreed to pay $15, which is the difference between the spot price and an on-market forward price determined by a cost of carry of 5 percent per annum. As was described in note 261 supra, this $13 difference in the contract price and the on-market price is an embedded loan that X pays to the other counterparty in return for an underpayment in respect of the second forward in the swap. Under the US NPC regulations, the $13 prepayment is effectively spread on a daily ratable basis over the first period of the swap. If that period straddles two or more taxation years, the prepayment is recognized on a daily ratable basis over those years, rather than being recognized in full in the year in which the settlement date occurs. Although this spreading reduces the effect of the recognition of a disguised prepayment in full on settlement, it does not come close to approximating the correct result, which, at a minimum, requires the allocation of the $13 prepayment to the next off-market forward in the series of two forwards. After this allocation, the prepayment should be recognized as the cost of acquisition of the second forward when the contract is settled in a later taxation year.

279 See the text that accompanies notes 75-92 in chapter 6.

280 The need for these two features assumes that the taxpayer is other than a trader or dealer who is subject to accretion taxation. To the extent that financial instruments issued or held by traders or dealers are not considered to be inventory, the lower-of-cost-and-fair-market-value rule for inventory on hand would not apply, and the opportunity for selective realization provided by this type of provision would be unavailable.

281 Notes 115-132 in chapter 3 and the accompanying text provide a series of examples that illustrate the value of the tax benefit associated with selective realization.

282 An investor is "long in an asset" if he owns the asset or has the right or the obligation to purchase it. An investor is "short in an asset" if he has sold the asset or has the right or the obligation to sell it in the future.

283 In their simplest forms, straddle transactions are relatively straightforward trading strategies in which taxpayers purchase and sell identical futures contracts with settlement dates that straddle the end of a taxation year. At year-end, the contract with accrued losses ("the losing leg") is closed out and the losses are realized. Accrued gains on the offsetting contract ("the winning leg") are not realized until the contract is closed out at some time after the end of the taxation year. This arrangement makes it possible to deduct the realized losses against other income and defer recognition of the offsetting gains until the following year. Taxpayers obtain the benefit of the tax saving that follows from the deduction of the losses against other income, though economically there is no net loss when the two legs are integrated and treated as offsetting transactions. In fact, a taxpayer can defer gain on a winning leg indefinitely by entering into a series of straddles that in effect use realized losses on losing legs to move recognition of the realized gain forward to subsequent years.

The tax effectiveness of a straddle depends on both a strict adherence to the realization requirement as the appropriate timing rule for the recognition of unexpected gain or loss and an acceptance of the legal form of the offsetting legs as separate financial instruments. This acceptance of legal form is apparent in the decision of the Supreme Court of Canada in *The Queen v. Friedberg*, 93 DTC 5507; [1993] 2 CTC 306, which expressly confirmed that the daily crediting or debiting of the margin accounts of taxpayers engaged in futures trading is a security arrangement only and does not constitute a realization event. In the absence of a specific legislative provision that required the netting of realized losses against unrealized gains, the court concluded, long and short positions in futures contracts should be regarded as separate financial instruments that are accounted for separately on a realization basis.

284 See Robert H. Scarborough, "Risk, Diversification and the Design of Loss Limitations Under a Realization-Based Income Tax" (Spring 1993), 48 *Tax Law Review* 677-717, for an excellent discussion of various types of deductibility restrictions and their possible effects. See also Rick Krever and Neil Brooks, *A Capital Gains Tax for New Zealand* (Wellington, NZ: Victoria University Press for the Institute of Policy Studies, 1990), 117-22, for a similar discussion of the role and design of capital loss limitations generally.

285 See, for example, IRC section 1092.

286 The absence of legislation that specifically addresses straddles has forced Revenue Canada to rely on the general anti-avoidance rule in ITA section 245 as authority for its requirement that taxpayers effectively collapse the offsetting legs of a straddle and defer the recognition of accrued losses until the recognition of accrued gains. Revenue Canada has published no statement on its application of the general anti-avoidance rule to straddles since the decision in *The Queen v. Friedberg*, supra note 283. Revenue Canada's prior position is summarized in John A. Calderwood, "A Revenue Canada Perspective on Offshore Funds, Commodity Straddles, and Offshore Deep Discount Bonds and Treasury Bills," in *Report of Proceedings of the Thirty-Fifth Tax Conference*, 1983 Conference Report (Toronto: Canadian Tax Foundation, 1984), 253-64, at 258-60. See also Peter Adamson, "Portfolio Securities

Transactions," Personal Tax Planning feature (1992), vol. 40, no. 3 *Canadian Tax Journal* 736-62, at 746-47, where he describes Revenue Canada's proposed application of former ITA section 245 to any early closeout of the losing side of a "convertible preferred hedge"; that is, a hedge whose elements are the acquisition of preferred shares that are convertible into common shares of the issuer (long share position) and a short sale of the common shares (short share position). For a thoughtful comment on the possible application of the general anti-avoidance rule to commodity straddles, see T.E. McDonnell, "GAAR and Pre-September 13, 1988 Tax Planning: Part 2—The Commodity Straddles Issue," Current Cases feature (1989), vol. 37, no. 3 *Canadian Tax Journal* 728-32. Since the transactions in *The Queen v. Friedberg* were effected before the application of the general anti-avoidance rule, the Supreme Court did not consider the issue.

The ATO has stated that it will normally deny the recognition of losses on straddle transactions on the basis that it is necessary to have regard to the overall result of the entire set of transactions implemented for avoidance purposes. See Australian Taxation Office, *Income Tax Ruling* IT 2228, "Income Tax: Futures Transactions," December 12, 1985; Roger Paul, "Financial Risk Management and the Taxation of Financial Products," in Rick Krever, Yuri Grbich, and Patrick Gallagher, eds., *Taxation of Corporate Debt Finance* (Melbourne: Longman, 1991), 209-38, at 237-38; and David C. Temby, "Swaps, Options, Forwards and Futures," in Richard Krever and Yuri Grbich, eds., *Australian International Taxation: Recent Developments and Future Directions* (Sydney: Law Book, 1994), 119-53, at 151-52. See also *A Tax System Redesigned*, supra note 3, at 362, where it is recommended that "the law make clear that legal disposals arising out of wash sales and straddles—where the dominant purpose is to obtain a tax benefit—will attract the general anti-avoidance rule."

Before the enactment of specific legislation, US courts denied recognition of realized losses on the losing legs of straddles either because the transactions were shams, in the sense that they were never implemented, or, if they were valid transactions, because the taxpayers could not show that they had entered into them with the motive of making a profit. See Frank V. Battle Jr., "Corporate Tax Shelters, Financial Engineering and the Colgate Case" (December 1997), 75 *Taxes: The Tax Magazine* 692-705, at 694-95; and Bradford L. Ferguson, "The Rationales for the Rules: How To Think About Derivatives in the Tax World" (December 1994), 72 *Taxes: The Tax Magazine* 995-1026, at 1023, footnote 140.

287 The text that accompanies notes 325-335 infra briefly discusses the role of this type of broad loss limitation in the context of accretion taxation as the principal response to strategic trading.

288 See Kleinbard and Evans, supra note 76, for a detailed discussion of the application of accretion taxation as a response to strategic trading under the US legislative regime governing financial instruments. The authors also support the application of accretion taxation to the inventory of traders and dealers, not as a response to selective realization but as a substitute for a hedging regime under a realization-based income tax. Given this rationale, accretion taxation should apply to instruments held and issued by taxpayers other than traders or dealers only where those instruments present opportunities for strategic trading. The text that accompanies notes 290-314 infra develops this targeting of the application of accretion taxation in the context of a comprehensive accrual regime that is intended to implement the dictates of expected-return taxation.

289 On this point see Potter, supra note 65, at 888-95.

290 See Mark P. Gergen, "The Effects of Price Volatility and Strategic Trading Under Realization, Expected-Return and Retrospective Taxation" (Winter 1994), 49 *Tax Law Review* 209-69; and Strnad, supra note 108, at 1868-85.

291 Scarborough, supra note 284, at 710-12.

292 Potter, supra note 65, at 891-93, emphasizes the link between the particular purpose for applying accretion taxation and the kinds of specific factors that are singled out as indicative of public trading.

293 See, for example, Jeff Strnad, "The Taxation of Bonds: The Tax Trading Dimension" (February 1995), 81 *Virginia Law Review* 47-116. Strnad characterizes the tax benefit from the strategic trading of debt as the equivalent of an investment tax credit equal to 5 percent of the cost of a portfolio.

294 Scarborough, supra note 284, at 711.

295 See Scarborough, ibid., at 710-11, where he notes that "factors tests" are unsatisfactory, since they fail to provide predictable results. Scarborough suggests the development of bright-line tests based on the general features of financial instruments that provide increased opportunities for strategic trading. The approach recommended here focuses on just one feature (low transaction costs) and the development of a bright-line test to indicate the presence of this determinative feature.

296 IRC sections 1256(a), (b), and (g).

297 IRC sections 1211 and 1212.

298 IRC section 1092. In contrast with their Canadian counterparts, US policy makers reacted early and swiftly to the marketing of commodity straddles by the tax-shelter industry in the late 1970s and early 1980s. United States, Staff of the Joint Committee on Taxation, *General Explanation of the Economic Recovery Tax Act of 1981*, 97th Cong., 1st sess. (Washington, DC: Joint Committee Print, 1981), 282-83. The legislation is nothing more than a loss-limitation rule based on the integration of offsetting positions that constitute a straddle. The basic limitation applies to "offsetting positions with respect to personal property." Recognition of realized losses is permitted only to the extent that they exceed unrealized gain on an offsetting position. The basic loss limitation is supplemented with a provision that requires the capitalization of interest and carrying charges that are related to a straddle. IRC section 263(g).

In *The Queen v. Stirling*, 85 DTC 5199; [1985] 1 CTC 275, the Federal Court of Appeal concluded that interest on borrowed funds used to acquire a long position in gold was not deductible currently and could not be capitalized. Since the taxpayer held the position on capital account, the borrowed funds could not be deducted under ITA paragraph 20(1)(c), which limits deductibility to interest on borrowed funds used to earn business or property income and not capital gains. Moreover, the court concluded that the expense was not part of the cost of the asset within the general meaning of that term for income tax and financial-accounting purposes. Accordingly, the expense could not be capitalized in the absence of a specific statutory provision permitting that treatment.

For an overview of the US straddle legislation, see Peter C. Canellos, "Limitations on Loss Recognition," in *Taxation of Financial Instruments*, supra note 245, chapter 6, at 10-17; and John J. Ensminger, "The Broad but Porous Net of the Straddle Rules: How Long Will the Fish Continue To Swim Through?" (Spring

1999), 18 *Virginia Tax Review* 709-80. A particularly curious feature of the US approach is the limitation of the application of the straddle legislation to offsetting positions in "personal property," which is defined to include only instruments that are "actively traded." As is argued here, loss limitations, such as the US straddle rules, are required only to the extent that traded instruments are not subject to accretion taxation as a response to strategic trading.

299 *Taxation of Financial Arrangements*, supra note 24, at 39; and New Zealand Income Tax Act, 1994, as amended, sections EH 33-EH 40.

300 Ibid., sections EH 38, EH 39, and EH 1(5).

301 Ibid., sections EH 36 and EH 1(6). Market valuation may be used only if (1) the Commissioner of Inland Revenue approves the relevant market or (2) the taxpayer is able to demonstrate that the prices obtained are reliable arm's-length prices. See *The Taxation of Financial Arrangements*, supra note 24, at 40. The latter condition was introduced recently in response to criticism of the requirement of approval by the commissioner, which restricted the availability of the market-valuation method. See Smith, supra note 9, at 229-30. Except in the case of forward contracts on foreign exchange and futures contracts generally, however, market-value accounting is available to a taxpayer who is not a trader or dealer only if there is no prescribed method under a determination and the adoption of market-value accounting is consistent with the tenor of the spreading provisions.

302 *The Taxation of Financial Arrangements*, supra note 24, at 39.

303 Ibid., at 40.

304 *Issues Paper*, supra note 3, at 198-99. The issues paper, ibid., at 192, includes traded foreign currency debt in the category of traded debt that the proposed accrual regime would subject to accretion taxation. Consequently, changes in the value of traded debt attributable to changes in interest rates and spot exchange rates would be accounted for on the same basis, and domestic and foreign currency debt would be taxed consistently, at least where they are traded.

305 If accretion taxation is the ideal income tax base, and if its implementation is constrained solely by liquidity and valuation considerations, it would seem to be a relatively simple matter to conclude that accretion taxation should be adopted wherever these constraints are absent. This basis for the adoption of accretion taxation in the context of a realization-based income tax raises serious "second-best" problems. See note 7 in chapter 4 for a brief description of the "paradox of the second best." A clear concept of the role of accretion taxation as a first-best response to strategic trading does not eliminate problems of the second best, but it does at least provide some basis for the measurement of the welfare gains that would result from the use of an accretion approach to address this tax-avoidance opportunity. These gains must be weighed against the effects of the distortions that may be associated with the limited application of accretion taxation. An identification and assessment of these offsetting effects is beyond the scope of this book.

306 *Taxation of Financial Arrangements*, supra note 24, at 40.

307 Valuation and liquidity concerns may continue to make tax-policy makers hesitant to impose accretion taxation even as a response to strategic trading. See, for example, *A Platform for Consultation*, supra note 3, at 148; and *A Tax System Redesigned*, supra note 3, at 337-40, where it is recommended that accretion taxation be applied on a "taxpayer-elective" basis. *A Platform for Consultation*

makes a similar recommendation on the ground that under an elective regime "no taxpayer is forced to incur valuation or cash flow problems." The mandatory accretion regime proposed here as a first-best response to strategic trading attempts to address concern about these problems by adopting a "functional approach" to the definition of affected instruments. Although the necessary definitional exercise entails some administrative and compliance costs, the problems may be no worse than those that would arise under a taxpayer-elective approach to the application of accretion taxation. In particular, the latter approach requires the articulation of eligibility criteria in order to limit taxpayer's ability to use the election to provide a form of statutory selective realization similar to the one provided by the use of the lower of cost and the fair market value rule for inventory (see the text that accompanies note 77 supra). Consequently, tax-policy makers must decide whether a taxpayer election should be available on (1) an instrument-by-instrument basis, (2) an asset class or entity basis, or (3) some combination of the two bases. See *A Platform for Consultation*, supra note 3, at 169-70; and *A Tax System Redesigned*, supra note 3, at 337, where it is recommended that a mark-to-market election be available on either an "asset-class" basis or for all instruments that are marked to market for financial-accounting purposes.

308 *Issues Paper*, supra note 3, at 198-99.

309 Ibid. The issues paper does not indicate whether the same factors would be used in determining the status of traded equity, although many of them appear to be equally applicable in that context. Two other factors (that is, the intention to hold the instrument for a short term and to dispose of it at a profit) are really just restatements of the taxpayer's purpose and should not be especially important.

310 Underinclusiveness is not as problematic in the case of derivatives that are designated as a hedge, provided that the applicable hedging regime modifies realization-based recognition to match realized losses on one position with offsetting gains on the other. See the text that accompanies notes 187-217 in chapter 7 for a discussion of hedging rules and their relationship to an accretion-based system for traded instruments. *A Platform for Consultation*, supra note 3, at 312-13, reflects a functional approach in its suggestion that the quarantining of capital losses be limited to shares and units in trusts. The application of a general loss limitation to these assets is supported on the ground that their price volatility and frequent liquidity make them susceptible to strategic trading. It is unclear how this suggestion would be integrated with a proposed purpose-based approach to the application of accretion taxation to traded shares. In fact, *A Platform for Consultation*, supra note 3, at 148, and *A Tax System Redesigned*, supra note 3, at 337-40, suggest that accretion taxation should be applied only on a taxpayer-elective basis, which necessitates the application of a loss limitation to traded shares generally.

311 This point is emphasized by Scarborough, supra note 284; and Battle, supra note 286, at 703-4. For example, the value of a fixed-rate debt instrument will change with changes in the market rate of interest. If rates decline, the value of previously issued instruments will increase, providing an unexpected loss for an issuer that can be realized by repurchasing the instruments and refinancing at the lower market rate. Much the same opportunity arises in the case of foreign currency debt, whose value changes with changes in the spot exchange rate.

312 *The Taxation of Financial Arrangements*, supra note 24, at 40, describes certain factors that indicate reliable market prices (and a sufficient degree of liquidity) and thus justify the application of accretion taxation:

> the number of participants in the market or having access to the market;
>
> the frequency of trading in the market;
>
> the existence of an appropriate regulatory body;
>
> the existence of industry standards regulating trade practices; and
>
> the accessibility of sources of information to market participants.

313 IRC reg. section 1.1092(d)-1.

314 *The Taxation of Financial Arrangements*, supra note 24, at 40: "taxpayers will be allowed to mark to related markets if there is no, or an inadequate, direct market in the instrument. Examples are over the counter options marked to a futures market, and swaps marked to the market in the indicator rates." In fact, developments in OTC markets for derivatives suggest that traditional differences between OTC and exchange-traded markets are eroding. In particular, it has been argued that the adoption of centralized netting systems and "automated trade execution" for OTC markets will virtually eliminate any structural differences between them. See Brenda Gonzalez Hermosillo, *The Microstructure of Financial Derivatives Markets: Exchange-Traded Versus Over-the-Counter*, Technical Report no. 68 (Ottawa: Bank of Canada, March 1994); and Lee A. Sheppard, "What Will Futures Market Deregulation Mean for the Code?" (July 3, 2000), 88 *Tax Notes* 19-23. These developments, however, do not necessarily eliminate or minimize the administrative and compliance burden associated with valuation difficulties. See Potter, supra note 65, at 895-901. This somewhat obvious point is illustrated by the experience of the IRS with the development of valuation software for a range of derivatives that are subject to mark-to-market reporting under IRC section 475. Development of the software was the subject of a project undertaken by the Los Alamos National Laboratory on behalf of the IRS. After consultation with industry representatives, the project was temporarily suspended. See the comments of IRS Assistant Commissioner (International) John Lyons in (December 22, 1997), 15 *Tax Notes International* 1996-97. Lyons cites budgetary constraints and the need for further consultation. Tax-policy makers must somehow determine whether the revenue loss from strategic trading is sufficient to justify the administrative and compliance burden associated with the application of accretion taxation as a first-best response.

315 See the text that accompanies notes 247-279 in chapter 6.

316 See, for example," Peter L. Swan, "The Taxation of Capital Gains When the Cash Component of Income Is Taxed" (September 1994), 30 *Abacus* 160-74. Swan argues that the conversion of expected time-value returns into capital gains is less problematic in the case of shares under corporate imputation systems, since in that case there is an incentive to distribute gains as dividends with imputation credits.

317 Peter L. Swan and Terry S. Walter, "The Impact of Deemed Realisation of Unrealised Trading Profits on the Equities Market: Response to Taxation of Financial Arrangements Issues Paper" (unpublished paper prepared for the Securities Industry Research Center of Asia Pacific, September 4, 1997). Swan and Walter argue that the elimination of realization-based recognition for traded shares under

the Australian accrual proposals would depress shares prices and result in both windfall losses for existing holders and a shift to non-traded assets exempt from accretion taxation.

318 Rebecca S. Rudnick, "Corporate Tax Integration: Liquidity of Investment" (February 27, 1989), 42 *Tax Notes* 1107-23; and Rebecca S. Rudnick, "Who Should Pay the Corporate Tax in a Flat Tax World?" (1989), vol. 39, no. 4 *Case Western Reserve Law Review* 965-1060. See also Lee A. Sheppard, "What Is Public Trading?" (April 24, 1995), 67 *Tax Notes* 443-46, who suggests that the corporate income tax is an excise tax on the privilege of public trading rather than on the provision of limited liability. Gene Steurele, "Will Corporate Taxes Survive?" (August 19, 1996), 72 *Tax Notes* 1043-44, also characterizes the corporate income tax as an excise tax on public trading.

319 See the text that accompanies notes 135-154 in chapter 4 for a brief description of optimal tax theory as the apparent theoretical basis for the dual income tax (DIT) systems adopted by the Nordic countries.

320 But see David A. Weisbach, "A Partial Mark-to-Market Tax System" (Fall 1999), 53 *Tax Law Review* 95-135, at 115-21, who suggests that integration of corporate and shareholder-level income taxes may be necessary to offset efficiency losses associated with an unintegrated corporate income tax and the application of accretion taxation to publicly traded shares.

321 *Issues Paper*, supra note 3, at 199. See also Weisbach, supra note 320, at 103-15, who argues that the substitutability of derivatives and debt instruments for short and long positions in publicly traded property requires the extension of accretion taxation to all derivatives and debt, whether traded or not. But Potter, supra note 65, at 889, footnote 38, correctly observes that Weisbach's suggested extension requires a defensible distinction between debt and debt substitutes, such as leases and prepayments for goods and services. Limitation of accretion taxation to traded instruments generally avoids this particular distinction. However, see notes 63 and 64 supra regarding the relevance of Weisbach's necessary distinction under a comprehensive accrual regime.

322 Ibid., at 147-82.

323 See the text that accompanies notes 187-217 in chapter 7.

324 See Scarborough, supra note 284, at 696-700, for a more detailed review of the three alternatives. These alternatives are in addition to "wash sale" or "superficial loss" rules that deny a deduction for losses realized on the disposition of an asset if the same or identical asset is acquired within a defined period by the same taxpayer or a related (associated) person.

325 See ibid., at 707-16, where Scarborough suggests this distinction as the basis for a general loss limitation. Scarborough does not consider what role, if any, accretion taxation should have as a response to selective realization or what role loss limitations should serve if accretion taxation is adopted.

326 Under a comprehensive accrual regime, realization of unexpected gains and losses may occur through a base price adjustment, which accounts for previously recognized expected gains and losses on a realization event. In effect, an income inclusion or expense deduction that arises under the base price adjustment represents the realization of unexpected gain or loss for the purpose of any loss limitation that depends on the distinction between these amounts. See the text

that accompanies notes 208-218 supra for a description of the mechanics of the base price adjustment.

327 Scarborough, supra note 284, at 700. Krever and Brooks, supra note 284, at 117-22, attempt to reduce any adverse impact on risk taking associated with this kind of a broad loss limitation by permitting the deduction of realized losses to the extent of (1) realized gains plus (2) the amount of unrealized gains that a taxpayer elects to recognize in order to offset the amount of the losses.

328 The US straddle legislation provides, in IRC section 1092(c), an exception for positions in personal property that are acquired as a hedge of ordinary business and financial activities.

329 To avoid obvious avoidance opportunities, a narrow loss limitation should be defined in terms of offsetting positions assumed by the same taxpayer or a related person. See Deborah H. Schenk, "Taxation of Equity Derivatives: A Partial Integration Proposal" (Summer 1995), 50 *Tax Law Review* 571-641, at 619-22; and IRC section 1092(d)(4), which deems a taxpayer to be holding positions of his spouse, other members of a consolidated corporate group, and certain partnerships and trusts for the purposes of the straddle rules. The extension of a loss-limitation rule to positions held by related persons can minimize the benefits of using straddle transactions to split income. This result occurs if realized losses are subject to limitation whenever the taxpayer or a related person holds an offsetting position, and if the deductible amount is limited to the lesser of (1) the excess of the loss over unrealized gain on offsetting positions held by the taxpayer or related persons and (2) gains realized by the taxpayer. In the absence of an extension of loss-offsetting rules to offsetting positions held by related persons, tax administrators are left to rely on anti-income splitting rules and other, less obvious approaches. See, for example, *Schultz et al. v. The Queen*, 95 DTC 5657; [1996] 2 CTC 127 (FCA), in which the court characterized straddle transactions of a husband and wife as a partnership and therefore as being subject to the requirement of proportionate recognition of gain and loss incurred by partners.

330 Weisbach, supra note 320, at 124-25.

331 Beneath the simplistic generalities described here, the US straddle rules present an almost impenetrable maze of technical detail, much of which focuses on the definition of offsetting positions in personal property. As was noted above, the rules apply to "offsetting positions with respect to personal property." For this purpose, "personal property" must be of a type that is "actively traded" (see supra note 298). A "position" in personal property is any interest in such property. Certain positions in shares may cause the shares themselves to be treated as part of a straddle. These positions include (1) an option with respect to shares or substantially identical shares or securities, (2) shares of a corporation formed or availed to take positions in personal property which offset positions taken by any shareholder; and, (3) under regulations, a position with respect to substantially similar or related property (other than shares). IRC section 1092(d)(3). IRC reg. section 1.246-5 defines when an offsetting position is considered to be "substantially similar or related property." For a discussion of these regulations, see generally Bradford L. Ferguson, George R. Goodman, and Jonathan P. Biller, "The Latest Stock Hedging Regulations" (June 26, 1995), 69 *Tax Notes* 1795-1818.

For the most part, the concept of offsetting positions under the US legislation is expressed at a general level of principle and appears to have been intentionally left vague. See Canellos, supra note 298, at 13-14. The legislation provides only that a taxpayer is considered to hold offsetting positions if those positions entail "a substantial diminution of risk of loss" in respect of one another. IRC section 1092(c)(3)(A) provides that positions are presumed to be offsetting if (1) they are in the same personal property (whether they are established in the property itself or in a contract for the property); (2) they are in the same personal property, even though the property may be in altered form; (3) they are in debt instruments of a similar maturity; (4) they are sold or marketed as offsetting positions; or (5) the aggregate margin requirement for the positions is lower than the sum of the margin requirements for both positions if the positions were held separately. IRC section 1092(c)(3)(A)(vi) provides that positions are presumed to be offsetting if there are such other factors (or satisfaction of subjective or objective tests) as the Secretary may by regulations prescribe as indicating that such positions are offsetting.

332 See, for example Canellos, supra note 298, at 14: "the IRS faces enormous problems in applying the straddle rules since it has no effective way of identifying offsetting positions without being tipped off by the taxpayer"; and Ensminger, supra note 298, at 711: "Many taxpayers are unaware of all the straddles that could be formed among their financial activities, and the IRS lacks the software sophistication that would probably be necessary to find the unreported straddles." Special disclosure rules supported by penalties for non-disclosure have been used in an attempt to address the identification problem. IRC section 1092(a)(3)(B) and former IRC section 6653(f). As Canellos notes, however, straddle issues have historically been raised on audit if (1) the taxpayer has elected to treat an offsetting position as a qualifying hedge within the exception from the straddle rules or (2) the taxpayer has designated a transaction as a hedge for financial-accounting purposes. In both instances, the IRS has notice of the offsetting nature of two or more positions and can challenge their characterization as qualifying hedges for tax purposes. The alternative is treatment as a straddle.

333 As noted supra note 331, the US straddle rules apply to "positions in personal property," which include only interests in personal property that is "actively traded." This limitation to actively traded property considerably reduces the administrative constraint associated with the need to value offsetting interests in order to determine the amount of unrealized gains for loss-limitation purposes.

334 The considerable complexity of the US straddle legislation is attributable to a need for specific rules that attempt to provide a sensible regime for mixed straddles, or straddles that consist of a leg that is subject to realization-based recognition and another leg that must be marked to market because of the status of the taxpayer as a trader or dealer or the status of the contract as an actively traded contract. As compensation for the loss of the deferral benefit provided by realization-based recognition, gain or loss on the instruments that must be marked to market is arbitrarily considered to be 60 percent long-term and 40 percent short-term capital gain or loss. No similar rule applies to the offsetting leg of a straddle that is subject to realization-based recognition. See Ferguson, supra note 286, at 1023-25.

335 Two variations of this general limitation are (1) restricted deductibility of realized losses to the extent of unrealized gains, with no restrictions on the amount of excess losses, and (2) deductibility of realized losses to the extent that a taxpayer elects to recognize unrealized gains, with no deduction for the amount of excess

losses. The first alternative adapts the concept that underlies a straddle limitation and applies it to the whole of a taxpayer's subportfolio of non-traded instruments. It provides, therefore, the advantages of a straddle limitation but avoids the difficulties associated with the need to define offsetting positions. The second alternative, suggested by Krever and Brooks, supra note 284, at 117-22, for capital gains and losses generally, alleviates some of the adverse impacts of a broad loss limitation on risk taking by permitting the recognition of unrealized gains without the incurrence of transaction costs required to effect a disposition. By limiting the deductibility of excess losses, however, this alternative places priority on the need to address strategic trading. In the context of an approach that uses accretion taxation as the principal response to strategic trading, both of these alternatives present the valuation difficulties associated with the measurement of unrealized gains on non-traded instruments.

336 See the text that accompanies notes 11-49 in chapter 4.

337 See the text that accompanies notes 280-335 in chapter 6.

Notes to Chapter 6

1 This combination is the essence of a hybrid instrument. See the text that accompanies notes 14-17 in chapter 4; and the text that accompanies note 7 infra.

2 This term is defined in the text that accompanies notes 11-12 in chapter 4; and the text that accompanies notes 8-18 infra. See also David A. Weisbach, "Tax Responses to Financial Contract Innovation" (Summer 1995), 50 *Tax Law Review* 491-544, at 496-502, who draws a link between hybrid instruments and bifurcation as a tax response.

3 Alvin C. Warren Jr., "Financial Contract Innovation and Income Tax Policy" (December 1993), 107 *Harvard Law Review* 460-92, at 483-89.

4 These terms are defined in the text that accompanies notes 36-38 infra.

5 Several commentators have made this point. See, for example, Mark P. Gergen, "Apocalypse Not?" (Summer 1995), 50 *Tax Law Review* 833-59; Robert H. Scarborough, "Different Rules for Different Players and Products: The Patchwork Taxation of Derivatives" (December 1994), 72 *Taxes: The Tax Magazine* 1031-49; Robert H. Scarborough, "Payments in Advance of Performance" (December 1991), 69 *Taxes: The Tax Magazine* 798-820; and Reed H. Shuldiner, "A General Approach to the Taxation of Financial Instruments" (December 1992), 71 *Texas Law Review* 243-350, at 308-13.

6 For an overview of various corporate income tax alternatives and the broader policy issues, see John G. Head, "Company Tax Systems: From Theory to Policy," in John G. Head and Richard Krever, eds., *Company Tax Systems* (Sydney: Australian Tax Research Foundation, 1997), 1-47. See also Richard M. Bird, *Why Tax Corporations?* Working Paper 96-2 (Ottawa: Department of Finance, Technical Committee on Business Taxation, December 1996).

7 See the text that accompanies notes 14-17 in chapter 4; and Weisbach, supra note 2, at 496-500.

8 See the text that accompanies notes 11-13 in chapter 4.

9 See the text that accompanies notes 32-39 in chapter 4, where this problem is described in the context of a convertible debt obligation.

10 Scarborough, "Payments in Advance of Performance," supra note 5; and Shuldiner, supra note 5.

11 Under these forward contracts, one of the counterparties prepays its contractual obligations or makes a payment that is intended to even out the terms of a specified bet to reflect an "on-market" instrument. See the text that accompanies notes 36-38 infra.

12 These instruments provide cash flows that depend on the resolution of specified contingencies. The "contingent payments" are attributable to an embedded derivative and give rise to unexpected gain or loss. See the text that accompanies notes 93-100 infra.

13 Scarborough, "Different Rules for Different Players and Products," supra note 5; and Shuldiner, supra note 5. See also David P. Hariton, "The Accrual of Interest on Derivative Instruments: Where Do We Go from Here?" (December 1996), 74 *Taxes: The Tax Magazine* 1011-22, at 1015-16, who refers to the imputation of interest on all advances of funds as "the modern approach" to the taxation of the embedded debt in certain derivatives. The same concept of bifurcation appears to underlie the bifurcation approach for financial-accounting purposes reflected in Financial Accounting Standards Board (FASB), *Accounting for Derivative Instruments and Hedging Activities*, Statement of Financial Accounting Standards no. 133 (Norwalk, Conn.: FASB, June 1998) ("FAS 133"). See generally Lee A. Sheppard, "Can the Tax Law Live with FAS 133?" (February 7, 2000), 86 *Tax Notes* 732-37, at 734.

14 For a discussion of the problems associated with this approach, see the text that accompanies notes 43-69 infra.

15 For a description of the representative provisions in the Canadian and Australian legislation, see, for example, the text that accompanies notes 130-153 in chapter 2. For a discussion of the problems associated with this approach, see the text that accompanies notes 46-55 infra.

16 This approach is discussed in more detail in the text that accompanies notes 66-69 and 280-336 infra.

17 See, for example, Jeff Strnad, "Taxing New Financial Products: A Conceptual Framework" (May 1994), 46 *Stanford Law Review* 569-605.

18 This failure and the specific problems that it creates along the boundary between debt and derivative instruments are discussed in the text that accompanies notes 24-69 and 247-279 infra. The tax treatment of a convertible debt obligation is an obvious example of the reluctance to bifurcate financial instruments under existing income tax systems that are based on the traditional tax cubbyholes. As was noted in chapters 2 and 4, the legislation in most countries treats a convertible debt obligation as a straight-debt instrument until conversion, with no requirement to allocate a portion of the issue price to the embedded option. Similarly, as was described in the text that accompanies notes 126-135 in chapter 5, debt instruments that provide for the periodic payment of interest in fixed and level amounts are not generally bifurcated into a series of original issue discount (OID) bonds that comprise the separate interest coupons and the corpus of the debt representing the principal repayment rights. Although bifurcation would reflect the term structure of interest rates and result in a more accurate accrual of

interest income and expense, the level-yield method for the spreading of expected gain or loss on fixed-payment debt remains the norm. In effect, the administrative and compliance burden involved in any attempt to implement a yield-to-maturity approach that reflects the term structure of interest rates has generally been considered excessive in the absence of significant tax avoidance that is designed to take advantage of any anticipated deferral benefit provided by the mismeasurement of interest accrual. See Weisbach, supra note 2, at 502-5.

19 See the text that accompanies notes 247-336 infra. The issues surrounding the boundary between debt and derivatives and debt and equity are described in the Australian accrual proposals. See Australia, *Taxation of Financial Arrangements: An Issues Paper* (Canberra: Australian Government Publishing Service, 1996), 84-91. The issues paper, however, focuses predominantly on the classification of certain hybrids as debt or equity. See also Australia, *Taxation of Financial Arrangements: A Consultative Document* (Canberra: Australian Government Publishing, December 1993), 22-32; Australia, Review of Business Taxation, *A Platform for Consultation—Building on a Strong Foundation: Overview of the Taxation of Investments*, Discussion Paper 2, vol. 1 (Canberra: Australian Government Publishing Services, February 1999), 197-204; and Australia, Review of Business Taxation, *A Tax System Redesigned: More Certain, Equitable and Durable* (Canberra: Australian Government Publishing Services, July 1999), 340-45 and 442-48.

20 Bradford L. Ferguson, "The Rationales for the Rules: How To Think About Derivatives in the Tax World" (December 1994), 72 *Taxes: The Tax Magazine* 995-1026.

21 Shuldiner, supra note 5, at 290-97.

22 See the text that accompanies notes 152-179 infra.

23 Ferguson, supra note 20, provides an excellent overview of the rationales underlying many of the US rules governing the taxation of derivatives.

24 See the text that accompanies notes 83-87 and 98-110 in chapter 3.

25 Anticipated deferral arises when expected gains or losses are recognized in a year subsequent to that in which increases or decreases in the value of the instrument are expected to occur. The deferral lowers the effective tax rate on instruments that provide the benefit. The concept of anticipated deferral is developed most completely in Shuldiner, supra note 5, at 250-55. See also David F. Bradford, "Fixing Realization Accounting: Symmetry, Consistency and Correctness in the Taxation of Financial Instruments" (Summer 1995), 50 *Tax Law Review* 731-85.

26 See the text that accompanies notes 24-38 in chapter 1.

27 As was described in the text that accompanies notes 78-82 and 115-133 in chapter 3, unexpected gain or loss associated with an on-market forward, futures, or swap contract presents the related problems of "unanticipated deferral" and "selective realization," which arise from an ability to manipulate the realization requirement to defer recognition of accrued gains and accelerate recognition of accrued losses. As was argued in the text that accompanies notes 280-336 in chapter 5, these problems can be addressed most effectively by applying a system of accretion taxation to instruments that can be traded at low transaction costs. For instruments that are not subject to accretion-based recognition, it is difficult to develop a comprehensive concept of realization that addresses completely all trading strategies designed to realize losses selectively, as well as achieve the economic equivalent of a realization transaction while avoiding recognition for tax purposes under

conventional concepts of realization. See the text that accompanies notes 29-44 in chapter 7 for a discussion of various "synthetic instruments" used to exploit this avoidance opportunity through "constructive sales."

28 Shuldiner, supra note 5, at 294-97.

29 This analogy is illustrated in detail by Shuldiner, ibid., at 290-97.

30 Scarborough, "Payments in Advance of Performance," supra note 5; and Shuldiner, supra note 5, at 308-13.

31 Shuldiner, supra note 5, at 309. The cost of carry and, therefore, the forward price is reduced by the amount of expected cash flows payable periodically on a long position in the underlying asset. See the text that accompanies notes 66-68 in chapter 1.

32 A European option is an option that can be exercised only on the specified maturity date. See the text that accompanies notes 47-49 in chapter 1. The following examples use simple European call options for illustrative purposes. The same principles apply, however, to American options that can be exercised at any time before maturity, since under reasonable assumptions these options will never be exercised before maturity and are equivalent in fact to European options. See Shuldiner, supra note 5, at 310-13. There is also nothing unique about put options that requires a different analysis.

33 Shuldiner, supra note 5, at 294-97, draws the analogy between an option and a collateralized or prepaid bet.

34 An option is considered to be "in the money" if the exercise price is such that exercise will produce a profit for the holder. If the reverse is the case, the option is said to be "out of the money."

35 An investor is considered to be long in an asset if he owns the asset or has the right or obligation to purchase it. An investor is considered to be short in an asset if he has sold the asset or has the right or obligation to sell it.

36 A common example of a prepaid forward contract used for financing purposes is a "prepaid forward sale." Under a typical arrangement, a commodity producer receives an upfront payment in return for a promise to deliver a specified amount of the commodity. The amount of the payment is a function of the quantity of production, the forward price for delivery, and a "discount factor" that is simply the notional borrowing costs associated with the cash payment. The forward sale agreement may be physically settled or cash settled on the basis of the spot price of the commodity in a referenced market. See Dennis F. Sykora, "Prepaid Forward Sales in the Oil and Gas Industry: Income Tax Issues" (1996), vol. 9, no. 1 *Canadian Petroleum Tax Journal* 99-116, at 100-1 and 108-9.

37 A forward contract that is "on market" on issue can gain value (or lose value) when the passage of time reveals changes in forward rates. If those changes are favourable to one of the counterparties, the forward contract becomes off market and can be disposed of at a gain or loss. If the contract has increased in value, the transferee will pay an amount to the transferor that ensures that the bet under the forward is a fair one, taking into account the subsequent changes in the forward rate. The payment creates an embedded debt in the same way as a prepayment on entering into a forward. Because the payment arises on a secondary-market transaction, the expected gain is equivalent to the discount created on a secondary-

market transfer of a fixed-payment debt instrument where market interest rates change. The treatment of the expected gain created by the transfer of an off-market forward before maturity is discussed infra note 38.

38 Assume, instead, that Galina and Harold enter into an on-market forward contract on January 1, 1996 at the two-year forward price of $15 per unit of the relevant commodity (100 units in total). Because of changes in the spot price and interest rates, the one-year forward price is $16 per unit on January 1, 1997. As a result, Galina's side of the two-year bet has become off market, and has an expected value at the end of one year of $100 ($1 excess of the one-year forward rate over the contract rate × 100 units). Galina can close her long position under the forward by assigning it to a third party (Gwyneth), who will pay her the present value of the $100 expected value of the contract (say, $92.60 at an assumed discount rate of 8 percent per annum). As with an off-market forward created on issue, this payment balances the bet under the contract. Gwyneth has effectively created an embedded debt element with an expected gain of $7.40 that will be realized on maturity of the forward. This expected gain should be accrued as interest income by Gwyneth, and added to the cost of her position. On maturity, she will realize unexpected gain or loss to the extent that the spot price of the commodity differs from the one-year forward price of $16 per unit. Galina should recognize the $92.60 payment on the assignment as unexpected gain. This treatment is identical to that of discount or premium that arises on a secondary-market transfer of fixed-payment debt, where changes in interest rates result in changes in the value of the instrument. See the text that accompanies notes 113-119 in chapter 5. Treatment of payments for off-market forwards as embedded loans arising on a secondary-market transfer is suggested in New Zealand, *The Taxation of Financial Arrangements: A Discussion Document on Proposed Changes to the Accrual Rules* (Wellington, NZ: New Zealand Inland Revenue, Policy Advice Division, December 1997), 49.

39 Scarborough, "Payments in Advance of Performance," supra note 5.

40 Ibid.; and Shuldiner, supra note 5, at 308-13. This treatment applies equally to American call options, which can be exercised at any time before maturity. Indeed, option-pricing theory holds that, under reasonable assumptions, an American call option will never be exercised before maturity and is equivalent, in fact, to a European option that can only be exercised on maturity. See Shuldiner, ibid., at 310-13, for a discussion of these assumptions and the case for treating American options equivalently under expected-return taxation. Exercise of an American option before maturity should be treated as a realization event similar to exercise (or a failure to exercise) on maturity.

41 Shuldiner, supra note 5, at 308.

42 *Taxation of Financial Arrangements*, supra note 38, at 48-49.

43 See, for example, Scarborough, "Payments in Advance of Performance," supra note 5; and Shuldiner, supra note 5, at 308-13.

44 This treatment is characteristic of the US cubbyhole treatment. For a defence of open-transaction treatment and a description of its underlying rationale, see Robert R. Wooton, "Mrs. Logan's Ghost: The Open Transactions Doctrine Today" (December 1993), 71 *Taxes: The Tax Magazine* 725-45. But see also Bruce Kayle, "Realization Without Taxation? The Not-So-Clear Reflection of Income

gain attributable to the tax. The interesting policy question is why that tax (and the resulting revenue gain) should be limited to particular forms of debt financing, such as convertible and exchangeable debt. See supra note 211.

213 Ferguson, supra note 20, at 1007.

214 Hariton, supra note 13, at 1012-14, emphasizes the inconsistency in tax treatment of a "current investment" and "forward investment" in an asset that is subject to realization-based recognition of all gains and losses. The inconsistency arises when a forward investment (a prepaid forward contract) is subject to accrual taxation as the equivalent of (1) a loan that provides for expected gain, plus (2) a non-prepaid forward contract that provides for unexpected gain or loss.

215 Ibid., at 1013, where Hariton draws the following comparison:

> Consider, for example, the stock of a growth corporation, Corporation X, which is trading at $100 per share today and is expected to trade at $115 per share in 3 years. A hypothetical investor, A, has $100 today. In "Case One," A simply purchases a share of Corporation X stock today and holds it for 3 years. In "Case Two," A invests the $100 in assets which do not result in tax deferral, such as U.S. Treasury Bonds which will generate $15 of income over the next three years, and simultaneously enters into a forward contract to purchase a share of X stock for $115 at the end of three years. Obviously, in Case Two, A will pay tax on $15 of income which will accrue currently over the next three years, whereas in Case One, A will not pay tax unless and until A disposes of the stock. And yet A is in the same economic position in either case. . . .
>
> How, for example, is the Treasury to deal with the case in which A gives B $100 today in exchange for the right to receive one share of Corporation X stock in three years . . . ? Should A be taxed in a manner that is consistent with Case One, or with Case Two? This is not a minor issue, considering that the relative tax deferral that is available in Case One does not end in year 3. If the Forward Contract described above is treated like Case One, A will be able to carry the $100 basis of the investment in the Forward Contract over into the Corporation X stock received.

216 A limited example of this perspective is evident in the characterization under the New Zealand accrual legislation of amounts that arise between the date that an agreement for the purchase and sale of property is entered into and the closing or settlement date. The legislation attempts to distinguish the expected time-value return from unexpected gains and losses that are attributable to movements in the spot price of the underlying property. Only the former must be accrued as income and expense. The accrual legislation draws the distinction by effectively deeming the acquisition price under the agreement to be the amount payable on settlement less an imputed interest element. See New Zealand Income Tax Act 1994, paragraph (b) of the definition of "core acquisition price" in sections OB 1 and EH 14; and Susan Glazebrook and Robin Oliver, *The New Zealand Accrual Regime—A Practical Guide* (Auckland: CCH New Zealand, 1989), 183-90. Prepayments in the form of deposits are subject to imputation of interest as debt equivalents, whether or not the interest element is disguised as part of the value of the underlying property. *Taxation of Financial Arrangements*, supra note 38, at 97.

from an Option To Acquire Property" (Winter 1993), 48 *Tax Law Review* 233-80, who questions the doctrinal and policy basis for the application of open-transaction treatment to the issuer of an option.

45 Shuldiner, supra note 5, at 309-10.

46 For a description of the Canadian and Australian provisions that reflect various elements of this approach to options, see the text that accompanies notes 130-153 in chapter 2. For a criticism of the Canadian approach and the case for open-transaction treatment as a preferable alternative, see Mark P. Meredith, "Current Problems and Future Directions in Derivatives Taxation," in *Report of Proceedings of the Forty-Sixth Tax Conference*, 1994 Conference Report (Toronto: Canadian Tax Foundation, 1995), 18:1-21; and Glenn L.E. May, "Overview of Financial, Tax, and Accounting Principles for Derivative Financial Instruments," in *Report of Proceedings of the Forty-Seventh Tax Conference*, 1995 Conference Report (Toronto: Canadian Tax Foundation, 1996), 29:1-27, at 29:15. But see Kayle, supra note 44, for the case against open-transaction treatment and a discussion of alternative approaches, including the immediate inclusion of the option premium by issuers.

47 Recognition of the option premium over the term of a particular instrument on an amortized basis represents a compromise approach that combines immediate recognition with open-transaction treatment. See Kayle, supra note 44, at 276-77; and May, supra note 46, at 29:20, who suggests that amortization of the premium allocable to the equity option embedded in a convertible debt instrument provides a desirable matching of income and expense over the term of the instrument. As Shuldiner, supra note 5, at 297, points out, amortization is defensible only if an asset is expected to depreciate in value, which is not the case with an option. Indeed, an option is expected to increase in value in an amount equal to the difference between its spot and forward prices. See the text that accompanies notes 88-107 in chapter 1. Shuldiner (at 337-39) argues that the persistent perception that an option declines in value systematically with the passage of time is based on a misperception of the nature of option pricing. In particular, observed differences in the price (that is, premiums) for short- and long-term options, which are otherwise identical, are attributable to the fact that with a long-term option there can be greater variability in the price of the underlying asset. Because the value of an option cannot go below zero, greater variability in the price of an underlying asset provides greater opportunity for unexpected gains. Accordingly, the price of an option (the amount of the premium) will generally increase with the term and the opportunity for greater variability in the price of the underlying asset. This fact does not mean, however, that the value of a particular option with a defined term decreases systematically over time.

48 The treatment of options under this second cubbyhole is similar to the taxation of loans under a consumption tax, whereby the loan proceeds are included in the income of a borrower to the extent that the proceeds are used for personal consumption. Interest expense and the amount of the loan proceeds are deductible when paid. The lender may deduct the amount of the loan and must include interest income and the repayment of the principal when received, at least to the extent that the amounts are used for personal consumption. See J. Clifton Fleming Jr., "The Deceptively Disparate Treatment of Business and Investment Interest Expense Under a Cash-Flow Consumption Tax and a Schanz-Haig-Simons Income Tax" (1997), vol. 3, no. 8 *Florida Tax Review* 544-61.

49 Shuldiner, supra note 5, at 296. See also Calvin Johnson, "Taxing the Income from Writing Options" (October 14, 1996), 73 *Tax Notes* 203-20, at 203, who suggests that the issue of an option by a person who does not hold the underlying property is equivalent to a borrowing transaction "in which the detriment of the cash the issuer receives is fully offset by the cash the taxpayer expects to pay out."

50 The consumption tax treatment of loans is effectively applied to the expected gain or loss on the option premium. To the extent that the amount paid on maturity exceeds the premium, the amount of the expected loss can be deducted by the issuer (borrower) and is taxable to the holder (lender). See Fleming, supra note 48.

51 Shuldiner, supra note 5, at 296.

52 Ibid. An obvious specific example is a foreign currency option under which the issuer agrees to pay the holder the difference between the domestic equivalent of a stated amount of foreign currency converted at the spot rate on exercise less the domestic equivalent converted at the stated exercise price under the option. The immediate deduction of the premium payment by the taxable holder is not offset by an income inclusion by the issuer, who may use expiring loss carryovers to render the inclusion non-taxable. On exercise of the option, inclusion of subsequent gain by the holder results in a tax liability with a present value that is less than the earlier deduction of the premium payment. The issuer can deduct the corresponding loss to effectively "freshen" the loss carryovers that were otherwise about to expire. See Roger Paul, "Financial Risk Management and the Taxation of Financial Products," in Rick Krever, Yuri Grbich, and Patrick Gallagher, eds., *Taxation of Corporate Debt Finance* (Melbourne: Longman, 1991), 209-38, at 236; and Shuldiner, supra note 5, at 296, footnote 233. These kinds of "loss-freshening transactions" have been implemented using "box spreads" and "option boxes," whereby taxpayers combine various long and short positions in derivatives. The combinations have involved prepaid forwards and/or options to create an accelerated income inclusion for a taxpayer with expiring losses. The inclusion is subsequently offset by a payment on an offsetting position. The subsequent payment generally equals the amount of the expiring loss plus a rate of return that reflects the cost of carry or riskless interest rate. See Ferguson, supra note 20, at 998-99. The use of swap prepayments for the same purpose is discussed in the text that accompanies notes 73-75 infra.

53 Shuldiner, supra note 5, at 296.

54 Ibid.

55 Ibid.

56 For an excellent "cubbyhole analysis" of the taxation of prepaid forwards under the Income Tax Act, RSC 1985, c. 1 (5th Supp.), as amended (herein referred to as "the ITA"), see Sykora, supra note 36, at 101-8. Sykora (ibid., at 104-5) contrasts the apparently ambiguous application of the traditional cubbyholes to prepaid forwards with the relatively settled treatment of equivalent "gold loans." Under a typical gold loan, a financial institution lends a quantity of gold to a producer, who immediately sells the gold in the spot market for cash. The producer must repay the loan by delivering the same quantity of gold in a series of instalments corresponding to the repayment of principal and interest on a loan, which bears a low rate of stated interest that reflects only credit risk and the riskless interest rate. There is no element of compensation for expected declines in the value of loan principal otherwise attributable to inflation. This element is unnecessary,

because of the promise to repay loan principal by physically delivering gold, which itself provides protection from inflation. Revenue Canada (now the Canada Customs and Revenue Agency) has generally treated gold loans as indebtedness, with interest income and expense recognized on an accrual basis at the stated rates. Unexpected gain or loss on the forward sale of the specified quantity of gold that must be delivered in satisfaction of the loan principal can be deferred and matched with the recognition of gain or loss on the producer's production, where the forward sale effectively hedges such production. This position reverses the department's earlier position, which required the recognition of unrealized gains and losses on the notional principal balance by retranslating the value of a producer's outstanding obligation at the end of each taxation year on the basis of changes in the spot price. The department's more recent position is consistent with the financial-accounting practice. See Sykora, ibid., for a more detailed discussion of this treatment and Revenue Canada's administrative position. But see also Australian Taxation Office (ATO), *Taxation Ruling* 92/5, "Income Tax: "Gold Loans and Forward Sales Agreements," August 27, 1992, which describes the ATO's administrative position requiring the realization-based recognition by gold producers of expected and unexpected amounts on gold loans.

The proposed taxation of prepaid forwards suggested in the text that accompanies notes 214-233 infra is generally consistent with the taxation of the equivalent cash flows under gold loans. Prepaid forwards require the imputation of interest at appropriate rates that measure the expected gain or loss that must be recognized on an accrual basis. Gold loans provide a portion of that rate in the form of a stated rate. Unexpected gain or loss on the forward sale of the underlying commodity can be recognized on realization, unless the instrument is traded or entered into as a hedge. In the case of a trade, the gain or loss can be subjected to accretion taxation as a response to selective realization. In the case of a hedge, a hedge-accounting regime can provide matched recognition with gain or loss on production of the underlying commodity. See the text that accompanies notes 187-217 in chapter 7. Under a comprehensive accrual regime that is intended to implement the dictates of expected-return taxation, however, interest on a gold loan should be imputed using forward prices. This approach provides for the imputation of interest at a rate higher than the stated interest rate. The higher imputation rate ensures that expected gains on the underlying loan principal that are attributable to expected changes in the value of gold are recognized as interest on an accrual basis. This treatment is consistent with the accrual recognition of compensation for expected declines in the value of loan principal, where that compensation is incorporated in nominal interest rates. The amount of imputed interest should be added to the cost of the gold loan for the issuer and holder, which will produce unexpected gains or losses on repayment of the gold loan only to the extent that the spot price differs from that cost. By requiring the accrual recognition of expected gain or loss at the stated interest rate under a gold loan, Revenue Canada's approach to the application of the traditional tax cubbyholes permits a portion of the expected gains and losses to be taxed on realization much as weak currency loans are taxed. See, generally, the text that accompanies notes 136-162 in chapter 5 regarding the proposed treatment of foreign exchange gains and losses on foreign currency debt under a system of expected-return taxation. This treatment should be extended to gold loans and other prepaid forwards to ensure the accrual recognition of the full amount of expected gains and losses.

57 Weisbach, supra note 2, at 498-99.

58 Sykora, supra note 36.

59 Ferguson, supra note 20, at 1008.

60 See, for example, Gregory May, "National Report—United States," in International Fiscal Association, *Cahiers de droit fiscal international*, vol. 80b, *Tax Aspects of Derivative Financial Instruments* (The Hague: Kluwer Law International, 1995), 615-47, at 621, footnote 23, who cites *Mapco, Inc. v. United States*, 556 F.2d 1107 (Ct. Cl. 1977) and *Estate of Stranahan v. Commissioner*, 472 F.2d 867 (6th Cir. 1973) regarding the possible characterization of a prepaid forward contract as indebtedness for US income tax purposes. See also Timothy R. Hughes, "Income Tax Implications of the Non-Dispositive Transfer of Equity Securities" (Winter 1999), 57 *University of Toronto Faculty of Law Review* 43-81, at 70, who argues that debt exchangeable into shares of a corporation other than the issuer ("exchangeable debt") may not give rise to interest income and expense for Canadian income tax purposes, because the amount due on maturity is contingent on the spot price of the underlying shares, which may be less than the amount advanced.

61 Sykora, supra note 36; and Weisbach, supra note 2, at 498-99.

62 Weisbach, supra note 2, at 498-99.

63 Ibid.

64 Sykora, supra note 36, and Weisbach, supra note 2, at 498-99. Where a prepaid forward contract is embedded in an exchangeable debt instrument (see supra note 60), Revenue Canada permits the issuer to deduct unexpected loss on the forward (the amount by which the spot price of the underlying shares exceeds the issue price of the debt instrument) as a discount. If the discount is considered "deep," the deduction is available on a cash basis and at a three-quarters recognition rate (ITA subparagraph 20(1)(f)(ii)). Unexpected gain that is equal to the amount by which the issue price exceeds the spot price of the underlying shares must be accounted for as forgiven loan principal that reduces the loss carryovers of the issuer and/or must be included in income at the inclusion rate for capital gains. The holder must generally recognize the corresponding gain and loss amounts on realization (exchange of the debt instrument or redemption).

65 See the text that accompanies notes 78-129 in chapter 2.

66 Dennis F. Sykora, "The Income Tax Web Surrounding Derivatives," in the 1995 Conference Report, supra note 46, at 30:27-28; and Paul, supra note 52, at 236.

67 For a brief description of common types of option-based transactions used to "freshen" expiring loss carryovers, see supra note 52 and the accompanying text. See also the text that accompanies notes 73-75 infra for a description of the use of swap prepayments to realize the same accelerated income inclusion and deferred deduction necessary to freshen expiring losses.

68 See the text that accompanies notes 213-233 infra.

69 See the text that accompanies notes 152-179 infra.

70 See the text that accompanies note 42 in chapter 1.

71 Because the prepaid swap is equivalent to a series of prepaid forward contracts, a "swap facility" can be used instead of a prepaid forward sale as a financing mechanism for a commodity producer. In return for the prepayment of the fixed

forward price of a notional amount of commodity, a producer will typically agree to make periodic payments under a swap facility equal to the spot price on settlement. In effect, the producer takes the floating side of the swap and the lender takes the fixed side. Prepayment of the fixed obligations by the lender are repaid with the floating-price obligations of the producer. See Sykora, supra note 36, at 109-10; and Sykora, supra note 66, at 30:33-37.

72 Such payments under an interest-rate swap are sometimes referred to as a "yield adjustment fee." See H. Peter Nesvold, "Interest Rate Swaps: The Taxation of Trading Places" (February 1998), 76 *Taxes: The Tax Magazine* 25-33, at 28. As Nesvold notes (ibid., at 28), these payments can be structured "to include a 'backloaded' payment, which is merely a yield adjustment fee that is paid toward the end of the swap agreement's life."

73 For a discussion of the representative Australian experience with these "loss freshening transactions," see Paul, supra note 52, at 229-35. For a description of the comparable US experience, which apparently led to the development of the regulations governing the timing of the recognition of non-periodic swap payments described in the text that accompanies notes 75-92 infra, see Ferguson, supra note 20, at 1006, footnote 59.

74 The statutory basis for this substantive approach to characterization of an accelerated swap is questionable and is discussed in Paul, supra note 52, at 229-35; and David C. Temby, "Swaps, Options, Forwards and Futures," in Richard Krever and Yuri Grbich, eds., *Australian International Taxation: Recent Developments and Future Directions* (Sydney: Law Book, 1994), 119-53, at 135-38. The most obvious approach would be to treat the disguised loan as a qualified security within the accrual provisions of division 16E of the Australian Income Tax Assessment Act, 1936 (herein referred to as "the ITAA"). However, the ATO has not expressed a public opinion on this issue. See Anthony J. Frost, "National Report—Australia," in *Tax Aspects of Derivative Financial Instruments*, supra note 60, 21-44; and Paul, supra note 52, at 230-31. Before the enactment of a regulatory response, the IRS took the position that it would disallow the cash-basis inclusion of swap prepayments because recognition would materially distort income. See Notice 89-21, 1989-1 CB 651; and Ferguson, supra note 20, at 1006, footnote 59.

75 Internal Revenue Code of 1986, as amended (herein referred to as "the IRC"), reg. section 1.446-3. For a brief description, see Ferguson, supra note 20, at 1005-7; and May, supra note 60, at 621-23. For a more detailed description, see Erika Nijenhuis, "Notional Principal Contracts," in Reuven S. Avi-Yonah, David B. Newman, and Diane M. Ring, eds., *Taxation of Financial Instruments* (Deerfield, Ill.: Clark Boardman Callaghan), (looseleaf), chapter 3, at 53-71.

76 An interest-rate cap or floor is a series of call or put options on interest rates issued in consideration of a single, upfront premium that covers all the options. See the text that accompanies note 51 in chapter 1.

77 See the text that accompanies notes 152-155 infra.

78 IRC reg. section 1.446-3(c)(1). The payment must be in exchange for specified consideration from the other counterparty or a promise to pay similar amounts.

79 Examples in the notional principal contract regulations suggest that a non-periodic payment that represents less than 10 percent of the present value of the obligations of a fixed-rate payer is not considered significant. An initial non-periodic

payment representing 40 percent of the present value of the fixed-rate payments is considered significant. See IRC reg. section 1.446-3(g)(6), examples 2 and 3.

80 "Periodic payments" are defined as amounts that are payable at intervals of no more than one year throughout the term of a notional principal contract. IRC reg. section 1.446-3(e)(1). These payments are spread ratably on a straightline basis over the year to which they can be considered to relate and are recognized on an accrual basis. IRC reg. section 1.446-3(e)(2)(i). The ratable portion must be recognized in the year of accrual even if it is payable at some time after the end of the year. Variable-rate payments are generally accounted for on the basis of the prevailing rate at year-end, and adjustments between the accrual rate and the prevailing rate on the payment date are accounted for in the year of payment. IRC reg. section 1.446-3(e)(2)(ii). The timing principles for payments under swaps generally are discussed in the text that accompanies notes 237-279 in chapter 5.

81 IRC reg. section 1.446-3(f)(1). A "termination payment" includes an amount paid or received to extinguish or assign any portion of a notional principal contract. IRC reg. section 1.446-3(h)(1). These payments are generally recognized on realization by the assigning parties, who extinguish their interests. IRC reg. section 1.446-3(h)(2).

82 IRC reg. section 1.446-3(f)(1).

83 IRC reg. section 1.446-3(g)(4).

84 IRC reg. section 1.446-3(f)(2)(i): "all taxpayers, regardless of their method of accounting, must recognize the ratable daily portion of a non-periodic payment for the taxable year to which that portion relates." See also May, supra note 46, at 29:16, who notes the similarity of treatment of non-significant payments under the US NPC regulations and Revenue Canada's administrative position regarding the recognition under ITA section 9 of cap premiums paid between banks. This administrative position is described in the text that accompanies 130-153 in chapter 2.

85 IRC reg. section 1.446-3(f)(2)(ii). Taxpayers are also provided with an alternative allocation method based on "the level-payment method." See IRC reg. section 1.446-3(f)(2)(iii)(A). Under this method, an annuity formula can be used to convert the non-periodic payments into a series of level payments over the term of a swap. The formula is applied to the present value of the non-periodic payments using the discount rate used by the counterparties to calculate the non-periodic payment. See Nesvold, supra note 72, at 28. As with an allocation using the value of a series of cash-settled forward contracts, the non-periodic payments are divided into principal and interest components. The principal component is recognized as periodic payments under the swap; the interest component is used only to amortize the principal payments over the term of the swap and is not recognized explicitly as interest income and expense.

86 Ferguson, supra note 20, at 1007, footnotes 61 and 62.

87 For a description of the application of expected-return taxation to interest-rate caps and collars, see Shuldiner, supra note 5, at 323-26. The approach to accrual-based recognition is identical to that for options generally. The unique aspect of caps and collars is the need to allocate the single premium to the series of cash-settled options for the purposes of determining expected gain or loss. This allocation question is addressed by the US regulations. See infra note 90.

88 IRC reg. section 1.446-3(f)(2)(iv) and (4).

89 Ibid.

90 The allocation is generally made on the basis of the option pricing used by the parties to determine the amount of the single premium. If this method is unreasonable, the IRS will substitute a different allocation using option-pricing models such as the Black-Scholes formula. IRC reg. section 1.446-3(f)(4). For a brief discussion of option pricing, see the text that accompanies notes 89-108 in chapter 1.

91 IRC reg. sections 1.446-3(f)(2)(iv) and 1.446-3(g)(5). The US Treasury department has since reserved on the treatment of caps and floors that are significantly in the money.

92 The amount of imputed interest for a taxation year was to equal to the lesser of "[t]he amount of the premium allocated to the relevant year and recognized in that year under the allocation rules for cap and floor premiums multiplied by the discount rate used to price the cap or floor compounded from the date the premium was paid to the earlier of the maturity date or the end of the taxation year; and the net income or deduction from the cap or floor for the relevant taxation year determined without regard to the imputed interest."

93 See David F. Levy, "Towards Equal Tax Treatment of Economically Equivalent Financial Instruments: Proposals for Taxing Prepaid Forward Contracts, Equity Swaps, and Certain Contingent Debt Instruments" (1997), vol. 3, no. 8 *Florida Tax Review* 471-543, at 492-95.

94 Common examples of contingent-debt instruments with non-contingent interest and contingent principal are (1) gold notes, (2) debt exchangeable for common shares (DECs), (3) preference equity redemption cumulative stock (PERCS), (4) exchangeable preferred income shares (EPICS), (5) equity-linked notes (ELKs), (6) principal-exchange rate linked securities (PERLS), and (7) prepaid forward sales (including gold loans). Gold notes are issued for cash equal to the spot price of gold and provide non-contingent interest payments that are payable periodically, along with a principal payment that is based on the change in the spot price of gold from issue to maturity. DECs are issued for cash equal to the spot price of referenced common shares held by the issuer and provide non-contingent interest payments payable periodically. The holder is entitled to an amount on maturity calculated with reference to the spot price of the referenced shares, which may be settled in cash or by the delivery of the shares. See Lee A. Sheppard, "Sand Castles of Debt and Equity Classification" (August 31, 1998), 80 *Tax Notes* 997-1002; and Hughes, supra note 60, at 66-77. PERCS pay periodic non-contingent amounts (referred to as "dividends"), and there is a mandatory conversion on maturity into the common shares of the issuer at a conversion ratio that is determined by the spot price of those shares. See Lee A. Sheppard, "Constructive Dividends on PERCS: Section 305 Stock Distributions" (March 2, 1992), 54 *Tax Notes* 1053-55. EPICS also pay periodic non-contingent amounts (also referred to as "dividends"), and the issuer has the option on maturity to repay the principal amount of the instrument in cash or to force the holder to accept the issue of a defined number of common shares of the issuer. See Ira Akselrad and Robert S. Bernstein, "Instruments, Techniques and Transactions" (Autumn 1994), 21 *Journal of Corporate Taxation* 283-90, at 283-85. ELKs are also issued in cash equal to the spot price of referenced common shares and pay periodic non-contingent interest. On maturity, the holder is entitled to receive the spot price of the referenced share up to a maximum percentage of the issue price (say, 135 percent). Like an EPIC, an ELK

thus contains a cap on the upside potential that the investor may realize. Some DECs have been issued with similar upside limitations. See Lee A. Sheppard, "Things That Go Bump in the Portfolio" (September 13, 1993), 60 *Tax Notes* 1423-27. PERLS pay interest in the same currency in which the principal amount of the debt instrument is denominated (say, Canadian dollars). The holder, however, is entitled on maturity to an amount that is based on movements in the exchange rate between that currency and another specified currency (say, US dollars).

Despite the differences in detail, these instruments share the same basic features. The combination of non-contingent interest and contingent principal means that the holder has a "collateralized forward purchase agreement" (a prepaid forward contract or a prepaid forward sale), which in some instances is capped. From the issuer's perspective, the cash flows associated with these contingent-debt instruments are equivalent to a prepaid forward sale or the combination of a fixed-payment debt instrument and an on-market forward contract. See the text that accompanies notes 36-38 supra for a description of prepaid forwards; and supra note 56 for a description of gold loans as a particular type of prepaid forward sale.

95 This type of contingent-debt instrument is sometimes referred to as "linked debt," because it combines a non-contingent principal amount with contingent interest based on movements in the spot price of a commodity. Common examples include (1) stock-index growth notes (SIGNs) and (2) liquid-yield option notes (LYONs). In return for an advance of funds, the holder of a SIGN is entitled to receive on maturity the repayment of the amount advanced plus a return based on the appreciation of a specified share index, such as Standard and Poor's (S&P) 500 share index. In return for an advance of funds, the holder of a LYON is entitled to receive a greater fixed amount on maturity. In addition, the holder has the right to exchange the LYON at any time for an amount equal to the spot price of a specified block of shares. A SIGN and a LYON are thus the equivalent of an OID bond with an embedded call option on the referenced index or specified shares. For a discussion of linked-debt instruments generally under the ITA, see Stephen R. Richardson, "New Financial Instruments: A Canadian Tax Perspective," in *Income Tax and Goods and Services Tax Considerations in Corporate Financing*, 1992 Corporate Management Tax Conference (Toronto: Canadian Tax Foundation, 1993), 10:1-32, at 10:2-12; and Stephen R. Richardson, "Current Developments in Debt Financing: A Canadian Tax Perspective," in *Report of Proceedings of the Fortieth Tax Conference*, 1988 Conference Report (Toronto: Canadian Tax Foundation, 1989), 22:1-32, at 22:19-29.

In some instances, contingent payments associated with an embedded option can be tied to the principal amount. For example, indexed currency option notes (ICONs or "heaven and hell bonds") pay interest in the same currency in which the principal amount of the instrument is denominated, but provide the holder with an option to require payment on redemption in another currency. These bonds are thus the equivalent of fixed-payment coupon bonds issued at a discount plus an embedded currency option. The amount of the discount equals the premium for the call option, which is written on the specified currency in which payment can be demanded by the holder. In other instances, an embedded call option can be provided in the form of a conversion feature that is based on the price of specified commodities. For example, gold notes have been issued with a conversion feature that entitles the holder to common shares of the issuer determined by reference to increases or decreases in the spot price of gold. See Judith

E. Harris, "Commodity-Linked Debt: The TVX Gold-Linked Convertible Notes," in *Current Issues in Corporate Finance*, 1997 Corporate Management Tax Conference (Toronto: Canadian Tax Foundation, 1998), 6:1-10, who discusses the tax treatment under the ITA of the TVX Gold Inc. issue of convertible gold notes. Because the holder is entitled to a non-contingent principal amount plus accrued interest in the event of failure to exercise the conversion feature, convertible gold notes are equivalent to a fixed-payment debt instrument plus a call option on common shares of the issuer.

96 Ferguson, supra note 20, at 1008. See also David P. Hariton, "Taxation of Contingent Debt Instruments," in *Taxation of Financial Instruments*, supra note 75, chapter 2A, at 11-12. As Hariton indicates, the US regulations governing the taxation of contingent debt suggest that it is possible for an instrument to be considered debt even though there is no promise of repayment of the issue price or no minimum payment.

97 This requirement is particularly evident under the US case law. See Ferguson, supra note 20, at 1008. Canadian courts have tended to avoid any assessment of the substantive characteristics of an instrument and have accepted legal form as determinative. See the text that accompanies notes 28-45 in chapter 2.

98 Ferguson, supra note 20, at 1008. Canadian courts have had difficulty characterizing contingent payments associated with participating debt (that is, debt with cash flows dependent on profits of the issuer or other factors unique to the issuer) as deductible interest. See the text that accompanies notes 39-43 in chapter 2. In *The Queen v. Sherway Centre Limited*, 98 DTC 6121; [1998] 2 CTC 343, the Federal Court of Appeal overturned the Tax Court of Canada decision (96 DTC 1640; [1996] 3 CTC 2687) and characterized the participating payments as deductible interest expense.

99 See the text that accompanies notes 87-135 in chapter 5.

100 For deductibility purposes, the decision in *Sherway Centre Limited*, supra note 98, appears to establish a wait-and-see approach: that is, participating payments are not deductible as interest until the relevant contingencies are resolved and the amount of the payments is determined. But see division 16E of the ITAA, which requires a yield-to-maturity calculation on certain debt instruments based on projections of the amount of contingent payments for deductibility and inclusion purposes. The comparable Canadian provision in ITA, regulation 7000(2), applies solely to holders for income inclusion purposes.

101 This is the approach adopted, for example, under the New Zealand accrual regime and the Australian accrual proposals. The US regulations governing contingent debt reflect the same approach. See IRC reg. section 1.1275-4; and Hariton, "Taxation of Contingent Debt Instruments," supra note 96, at 20-22.

102 See the text that accompanies notes 206-208 in chapter 5 regarding the New Zealand accrual legislation and the Australian accrual proposals. This is also the approach under the US contingent-debt regulations. See Hariton, "Taxation of Contingent Debt Instruments," supra note 96, at 25-27. As with the New Zealand legislation, any loss recognized by a holder is considered ordinary loss only to the extent of accrued but unpaid interest. The excess is treated as a capital loss. The restriction prevents the deduction of loan losses as ordinary losses by holders who are not in the business of moneylending.

103 For example, characterization of contingent-debt payments as ordinary income can be easily avoided if an instrument can be sold immediately before the payment date for proceeds that represent the value of the expected payment, but are treated as capital gain simply because they are realized on a secondary-market trade. Ordinary-income treatment of all gain or loss on contingent debt avoids this character arbitrage. See Edward D. Kleinbard, S. Douglas Borisky, and Rekha Vemireddy, "Proposed Regulations Affecting Contingent Payment Debt Obligations" (January 30, 1995), 66 *Tax Notes* 723-34, at 730. The issue is the same as that with the realization of accrued but unpaid interest as proceeds of disposition on the sale of fixed-payment debt. See the text that accompanies note 52 in chapter 2 for a description of the representative Canadian and Australian provisions that ensure that contingent-debt payments are characterized as interest income to the extent of the accrued interest. The US contingent-debt regulations, however, go beyond such provisions to characterize amounts in excess of the expected time-value return as ordinary income in all instances. Although the same characterization is not applied to fixed-payment debt, it is arguable that the problem is the availability of capital-account treatment for these instruments. Above-market rates of return are taxed as interest when fixed-payment debt is held to maturity, but are taxed as capital gain if the instrument is sold in a secondary-market trade. This characterization holds even though the gain that exceeds accrued but unpaid interest is the discounted present value of the same expected cash flow. The gain arises only because of changes in the market rate of interest and discount rates. See Kleinbard, Borisky, and Vemireddy, ibid., at 730. But see David P. Hariton, "The Accrual of Interest on Derivative Instruments," supra note 13; and David P. Hariton, "Contingent Debt: Putting the Pieces Together" (March 1, 1993), 58 *Tax Notes* 1231-43, who argues that capital gain treatment should be extended to contingent payments that exceed the accrued expected return. Hariton accepts the capital-account treatment of unexpected gain or loss on fixed-payment debt attributable to changes in interest rates and prefers that consistency of taxation be realized by extending that treatment to the unexpected gain on contingent-debt payments. Unexpected losses would, however, be treated as ordinary losses if they offset previously accrued expected gains.

104 That development began with the grant in 1984 to the Internal Revenue Service (IRS) of regulatory authority to address the taxation of contingent debt.

105 A fourth set of regulations was released in January 1993 but was never formally published and was subsequently withdrawn as part of a cleaning of all pending regulations at the request of the newly elected Clinton administration. These proposed regulations provided for a combination of recognition methods that reflected some elements of a system of expected-return taxation. See, generally, Ferguson, supra note 20, at 1010; David C. Garlock, "A Primer in the New Proposed (Almost) Regulations for Contingent Debt Instruments" (March 1, 1993), 58 *Tax Notes* 1225-30; and Hariton, "Contingent Debt: Putting the Pieces Together," supra note 103.

106 IRC prop. reg. sections 1.1275-4(e) and (f).

107 IRC prop. reg. sections 1.1275-4(g).

108 IRC reg. section 1.1275-4.

109 See the text that accompanies notes 75-92 supra.

110 See the text that accompanies notes 108-114 in chapter 3; and Bradford, supra note 25, at 759-62.

111 For brief descriptions of these proposed regulations, see Ferguson, supra note 20, at 1009-10; and Shuldiner, supra note 5, at 327-30.

112 IRC prop. reg. section 1.1275-4(e).

113 IRC prop. reg. section 1.1275-4(f).

114 This result is much different from that associated with the separate issue of fixed-payment debt and a cash-settled forward contract on the shares of Resource Inc. In that case, the $400 of interest expense and income would be recognized on an annual accrual basis.

115 The most notorious example was the issue in 1991 of SIGNs by the Austrian government. These contingent-debt instruments entitled the holder to a payment on maturity in 1996 equal to the greater of (1) the principal amount of a note and (2) the principal amount plus the percentage appreciation in the S&P 500 Composite Price Index from issue to maturity. See Weisbach, supra note 2, at 501, footnote 33.

116 Weisbach, ibid., at 516-17.

117 David P. Hariton, "New Rules Bifurcating Contingent Debt—A Mistake?" (April 15, 1991), 58 *Tax Notes* 235-39, at 237.

118 Ibid.

119 IRC prop. reg. section 1.1275-4(g). For a description of these withdrawn proposals, see Hariton, supra note 117; and Lawrence Lokken, "New Rules Bifurcating Contingent Debt—A Good Start" (April 29, 1991), 58 *Tax Notes* 495-504.

120 In jurisdictions that apply a tax cubbyhole for options similar to that in Canada and Australia, bifurcated treatment results in immediate recognition of the amount allocated to the option premium. On issue of a contingent-debt instrument, the amount of the option premium is recognized as expense and income, unless the option is a call option written on the shares of the issuer (inclusion for the issuer only if the option expires unexercised) and/or the option is physically settled (the amount of the option premium recognized as part of the price for the underlying property).

121 See, in particular, Hariton, supra note 117.

122 Ibid., at 235. See also Ferguson, supra note 20, at 1009.

123 The bifurcation regulations provided the IRS with the power to apply bifurcated treatment if the difference between the amount of the non-contingent payments and the issue price of a contingent-debt instrument was insubstantial.

124 American Bar Association Tax Section, "Report on Amendments to Proposed Regulation Section 1.1275-4: Proposed Regulations Regarding Certain Contingent Debt Instruments Under the Original Issue Discount Rules" (December 9, 1991), 53 *Tax Notes* 1187-1204; Hariton, supra note 117, at 235 and 238; and Ferguson, supra note 20, at 1009-10.

125 See, for example, Frank V. Battle Jr., "Bifurcation and Financial Instruments" (December 1991), 69 *Taxes: The Tax Magazine* 821-33; and Hariton, supra note 117, at 237.

126 See the text that accompanies notes 32-39 in chapter 4.

127 See the text that accompanies notes 58-107 in chapter 1.

128 For a description of the put-call parity theorem and its significance in the arbitrage pricing of the basic building-block financial instruments, see the text that accompanies notes 75-87 in chapter 1. The essence of the tax-policy problem presented by the broad range of equivalences expressed in put-call parity is suggested by Douglas R. Emery, John D. Finnerty, and John Stowe, *Principles of Financial Management* (Upper Saddle River, NJ: Prentice-Hall, 1998), 253, where they describe such equivalences in the following terms: "Put-call parity is interesting, but it can also be confusing. Every situation that can be described in terms of a call option has a parallel description using a put option. In this book, we try to use the description that seems easiest to see in a situation. However, because a situation can always be described in terms of either a call or put option, we sometimes talk about the 'optionality' in the situation."

129 See the text that accompanies notes 33-38 in chapter 4, where this proposition is illustrated with the simple example of a convertible debt obligation. See also Hariton, supra note 117, at 237, who cites a synthetic position in shares (as revealed by put-call parity) as an example of the problem of the concept of economic equivalence under the bifurcation regulations. This paradigmatic position is noted elsewhere in this book (the text that accompanies notes 79-80 in chapter 1 and the text that accompanies notes 39-42 in chapter 4); it is created by taking a long position in a fixed-payment debt instrument that is issued at a price equal to the spot price of the relevant shares, and combining that position with a long call option and short put on the shares written at exercise prices that are equal to the issue price of the bond and the spot price of the shares. As Hariton (ibid., at 237) asks, "should interest on the bond be recharacterized as a dividend, since the exposure of the holder is economically equivalent to a long position in the shares?"

130 Hariton, ibid., at 237.

131 Ibid., at 237-38, where Hariton describes the details of these kinds of issues in the following terms: "Even if we can determine to what contingent payments are 'economically equivalent,' that will not tell us how they should be taxed. The example in the proposed regulations is by far the simplest case. What happens when contingent payments become fixed over the life of the instrument, rather than solely at maturity? What happens when their amount is determined by the price of more than one item of publicly-traded property? What happens when their amount is determined by reference to components which are 'economically equivalent' to publicly-traded property, but only when taken together?"

132 Kirk Van Brunt, "Contingent Payment Debt Instruments—A Light at the End of the Tunnel" (July 1995), 73 *Taxes: The Tax Magazine* 365-84, at 366-67.

133 See, for example, Hariton, supra note 117, at 237-39.

134 See, for example, Hariton, supra note 13, at 1014-15, where he distinguishes "the narrower fixed payment approach" under the bifurcation regulations from a broader approach under which interest is accrued on the full amount of a loan at an objective rate. The fixed-payment approach under the bifurcation regulations is narrower in the sense that the regulations shrunk the initial amount of a loan by discounting the fixed payments to their present value and accruing the difference as interest. Under the broader fixed-payment approach described by Hariton, the initial amount of a loan would be determined as the lesser of the issue price and the aggregate of the fixed payments. Interest would be imputed on this full amount

of the loan. The result would be similar to that under the final contingent-debt regulations.

135 See Van Brunt, supra note 132, at 366, who cites a report of the New York State Bar Association that criticizes the bifurcation regulations for character mismatches arising from capital gain or loss treatment of an embedded option and ordinary income or loss on the fixed-payment component of a contingent-debt instrument.

136 Weisbach, supra note 2, at 517 and 519. Consider, for instance, the bond in example 7, which provides non-contingent payments of only $400 and is issued for $1,000. Accordingly, the 1986 proposals applied instead of the bifurcation regulations. As Weisbach points out (ibid., at 517), however, the bifurcation regulations would have applied whenever the total of the fixed-interest payments and the minimum amount under an embedded forward contract is greater than the issue price. Assume, for instance, that the bond in example 7 provides for a payment of $1,000 plus or minus the difference between $200 and the price of Bco shares (Weisbach's example ibid., at 517). In that case, the bifurcation regulations would have applied (assuming also that the shares of Bco are publicly traded property). The amount of the non-contingent payments would then be $1,200 ($400 of interest payments plus an $800 minimum payment on maturity if the shares of Bco prove to be worthless), which is greater than the issue price. Under the bifurcation regulations, this $1,200 would have been discounted at a reasonable yield on a comparable debt instrument (assume 8 percent) to its present value of $1,111.11. The other $88.89 of the issue price would be allocated to the embedded forward contract, which would result in the creation of a prepaid forward contract, for which there is no known tax treatment.

137 For the clearest exposition of this proposition, see Shuldiner, supra note 5, at 327-31.

138 See the text that accompanies notes 36-38 supra.

139 See, generally, Kleinbard, Borisky, and Vemireddy, supra note 103; and Van Brunt, supra note 132.

140 See, generally, Hariton, supra note 96; Edward D. Kleinbard, Erika W. Nijenhuis, and Rekha Vemireddy, "Final Tax Regulations Governing Contingent Payment Debt Obligations" (July 22, 1996), 72 *Tax Notes* 499-515; David S. Miller, "A Look at the Final Contingent Payment Debt Instrument Regs" (July 22, 1996), 72 *Tax Notes* 489-98; and Daniel Shefter, "A Brief Intro to the Contingent Payment Debt Instrument Regs" (July 22, 1996), 72 *Tax Notes* 479-87.

141 See the text that accompanies notes 87-135 in chapter 5.

142 In establishing a comparable yield, the issuer must first determine whether it has hedged the contingent obligation or, if not, whether such a hedge is available. If the issuer has hedged the obligation, the comparable yield is the yield provided by a synthetic instrument consisting of the contingent obligation and the hedge. In all cases, the comparable yield must be a fixed rate that remains constant over the term of a contingent-debt instrument. See Kleinbard, Nijenhuis, and Vemireddy, supra note 140, at 507.

143 Ibid., at 508. As the authors note, a more straightforward approach would be to determine the comparable yield and then solve for the projected payments that would produce that yield. The final regulations require, instead, that the projected

payment schedule be established independently and then adjusted to conform to the comparable yield.

144 Ibid., at 507.

145 This principle extends to gain or loss realized on the sale, exchange, or disposition of a contingent-debt instrument. Gain is treated as ordinary income, and loss is treated as a non-capital loss to the extent of previous interest inclusions. An investor who acquires a contingent-debt instrument from an existing holder for a price that is different from the adjusted issue price must allocate the difference over the remaining term of the instrument. The allocation must be made to either remaining interest accruals or projected contingent payments and is recognized as ordinary gain in the case of acquisition discount and ordinary loss in the case of acquisition premium. These allocations ensure that changes in the expected value of projected payments that are realized on a secondary-market transfer are amortized and recognized by the transferee over the remaining term of the instrument.

146 The final regulations do not define a "contingent payment," other than to exclude certain payments such as those based on "remote" and "incidental" contingencies. A contingency is considered "remote" if the likelihood of its occurring is remote. A contingency is considered "incidental" if the change in the expected amount of a payment affected by the contingency is insignificant. No bright-line test is provided for the concepts of "remoteness" and "significance." A payment is also not considered contingent if it may be impaired solely by insolvency or default.

147 "Objective market information" does not include information that is unique to the issuer or a related person or information that is within the control of the issuer or a related person. See Hariton, supra note 96, at 17, who cites as examples of non-market information "the issuer's dividends, profits or stock value."

148 Kleinbard, Borisky, and Vemireddy, supra note 103, at 727.

149 Ibid., at 728-29.

150 Ibid., at 728.

151 Hariton, supra note 96, at 17.

152 For a description of the wide definition of a financial arrangement that is subject to accrual recognition under the New Zealand accrual legislation and the comparable Australian proposals, see the text that accompanies notes 18-35 in chapter 5.

153 *Taxation of Financial Arrangements*, supra footnote 38, at 12-17.

154 For an expression of this position as an important limitation on the comprehensive application of accrual recognition of expected gains and losses, see, for example, Hariton, supra note 13.

155 See, for example, *A Tax System Redesigned*, supra note 19, at 341-43, which suggests that accrual recognition be limited to instruments with gains and losses that are sufficiently "certain."

156 See, for example, May, supra note 46, at 29:22, who suggests that the complexity of the US contingent-debt regulations requires caution on the part of tax-policy makers in the search for consistent treatment of expected returns and the symmetrical treatment of issuers and investors. May prefers the "rough justice" provided under the Canadian cubbyhole approach, which denies the deduction of interest that is "too contingent" and requires accrual recognition by holders of a limited

range of "interest-like" returns. See the text that accompanies notes 48-51 in chapter 2. A similar approach is reflected in *A Tax System Redesigned*, supra note 19, at 341-43, and the proposal to limit accrual recognition to "certain" returns, which would be defined legislatively at a level of general principle. This type of approach tends to understate the administrative and compliance burden associated with the necessary definition of returns that are "too contingent" for deductibility purposes and those that are sufficiently "interest-like" to be subjected to accrual recognition. Moreover, as May acknowledges, the asymmetry for issuers and holders tends to limit the market for contingent debt to tax-exempt issuers, who are insensitive to the deductibility consequences, and tax-exempt holders, who are insensitive to the accrual recognition of comparable income amounts. This market fragmentation may have efficiency consequences.

157 Warren, supra note 3, at 479.

158 Hariton, supra note 117, at 237-39; and David P. Hariton, "The Taxation of Complex Financial Instruments" (Summer 1988), 43 *Tax Law Review* 731-88. See, generally, Warren, supra note 3, at 479-81, who describes the imputation of interest at a standard rate as an approach to the treatment of all financial instruments with an expected time-value return.

159 Lokken, supra note 119. The portion of the stated fixed rate that compensates the lender for erosion of the value of the loan principal that is due to the impact of inflation is also recognized as interest income and expense. Shares may have unique features that make the choice of an interest imputation rate more problematic in the application of expected-return taxation to the embedded debt. These features may even dictate the exclusion of shares from a comprehensive accrual regime. See the text that accompanies notes 247-279 infra.

160 See, for example, Noël B. Cunningham and Deborah H. Schenk, "Taxation Without Realization: A 'Revolutionary' Approach to Ownership" (Summer 1992), 47 *Tax Law Review* 725-814, who suggest the imputation of interest at the riskless rate on the premise that all assets can be assumed to generate at least that amount in expected gain and loss. With contingent-debt instruments that are issued privately in exchange for non-publicly traded property, the US contingent-debt regulations apply a much more generous wait-and-see approach, similar to that of the 1986 proposed regulations. These instruments are bifurcated into their non-contingent and contingent components, and interest accrues on the former. Contingent payments are treated as repayments of principal to the extent of the present value of the payments on issue, and any excess is treated as interest expense or income when paid. IRC reg. section 1.1275-4(b). Non-publicly traded property commonly includes real estate and shares of a private corporation. See Hariton, supra note 96, at 33.

161 Weisbach, supra note 2, at 519.

162 Shuldiner, supra note 5, at 305.

163 See the text that accompanies notes 65-68 in chapter 1.

164 Shuldiner, supra note 5, at 305.

165 Ibid.

166 Ibid. See also the text that accompanies note 65 in chapter 1.

167 Shuldiner, supra note 5, at 305, who argues that risk-averse purchasers will be willing to pay a premium over the forward price and risk-averse sellers will be willing to accept a discount.

168 Ibid. See also *Taxation of Financial Arrangements*, supra note 38, at 43-50, which recommends the use of forward prices to determine the expected gains and losses on foreign currency debt. The treatment of foreign currency debt under a system of expected-return taxation is described in the text that accompanies notes 136-162 in chapter 5.

169 *Issues Paper*, supra note 19, at 132-33. In the absence of a determination governing the treatment of contingent debt generally, the New Zealand accrual regime leaves the timing principles for contingent-debt instruments largely to financial-accounting practice. For a discussion of the relevance of financial-accounting practice under the New Zealand legislation, see the text that accompanies notes 178-187 in chapter 5. A similar approach is reflected in ITA subsection 142.3(1) and draft regulation 9102, which apply in the determination of the accrued return on specified debt obligations, other than fixed-payment obligations, held by financial institutions.

170 *Issues Paper*, supra note 19, at 132-33. These assumptions are applied to contingent debt under division 16E of the ITAA. See the text that accompanies notes 49-51 in chapter 2. The approach described in the issues paper and the ITAA is, in fact, more defensible than the approach under ITA regulation 7000(2)(d), which requires certain contingent payments to be accrued on an assumption that the specified contingencies are resolved in favour of the holder, and the maximum amount of interest that could become payable under the instrument in respect of a taxation year becomes payable in that year. This assumption effectively requires the accrual of unexpected amounts. But see Revenue Canada document no. 9719753, discussed in *Window on Canadian Tax* (North York, Ont.: CCH Canadian) (looseleaf), paragraph 4935. Revenue Canada took the position that there is no maximum amount of interest payable in each of the first four years of an instrument with a five-year term and, therefore, no requirement to accrue interest income if the return was based on the level of a specified index five business days before maturity.

171 For a review of some of these simplified methods for variable-rate debt instruments (VRDIs), see the text that accompanies notes 174-175 in chapter 5.

172 The rationale for the adoption of this benchmark standard and the details of its application are discussed in the text that accompanies notes 188-194 in chapter 5.

173 Shuldiner, supra note 5, at 297-304, illustrates this point with a series of multiple bets.

174 Ibid., at 303.

175 Ibid.

176 See the text that accompanies notes 75-92 supra.

177 See the text that accompanies notes 75-92 supra. For a discussion of the use of a distinction between significant and non-significant payments generally as the basis for a boundary between debt and derivatives under a comprehensive accrual regime, see the text that accompanies notes 232-233 infra.

178 The US NPC regulations require a non-assigning party (including the assignee) to amortize gain or loss over the remaining term of a notional principal contract.

An assignee who makes a "termination payment," however, must treat it as a non-periodic payment subject to the rules governing embedded loans associated with significant and non-significant payments. A "termination payment" includes an amount paid or received to extinguish or assign any portion of a notional principal contract.

179 For a discussion of the accrual treatment of discount or premium on a secondary-market transfer of fixed-payment debt, see the text that accompanies notes 113-119 in chapter 5. The US contingent-debt regulations realize a similar result on a secondary-market transfer of contingent debt with embedded derivatives. In effect, the difference between the amount paid for an instrument and its cost base (the issue price plus accrued but unpaid amounts) must be amortized over the remaining term of the instrument, and recognized as interest income or expense by the transferee.

180 Hariton, supra note 13, at 1015-16, refers to the comprehensive application of expected-return taxation as "the modern approach" to the characterization of instruments as indebtedness or a derivative. He describes this approach as consisting of two basic elements: (1) the finding of a debtor-creditor relationship whenever money is advanced in return for a right to receive an amount in the future, and (2) the imputation of interest on the amount of the advance.

181 See the text that accompanies notes 24-42 supra.

182 This simplistic concept of bifurcation is the apparent basis for the extension of accrual treatment to the expected gain or loss associated with prepaid forward contracts, as suggested in *Taxation of Financial Arrangements*, supra note 38, at 47-49.

183 A facts-and-circumstances test is more commonly associated with the definition of the boundary between debt and equity. See the text that accompanies notes 280-336 infra. The test described here in the context of the boundary between debt and derivatives is similar in its general features to that described, and approved of, (at least in part), in *A Tax System Redesigned*, supra note 19, at 341-43, which distinguishes instruments with predominantly certain returns from those with predominantly uncertain returns.

184 Hariton, supra note 13, at 1016-17. Hariton uses the label "traditional approach" for a facts-and-circumstances test. His label obviously refers to the fact that a facts-and-circumstances test has traditionally been used by US courts, tax-policy makers, and tax administrators in drawing the boundary between debt and derivatives.

185 Ibid., at 1016.

186 Ibid.

187 See the text that accompanies notes 137-151 supra.

188 These specific exclusions include (1) VRDIs; (2) non-VRDIs with fixed yields but uncertain payment schedules; and (3) non-VRDIs with payments that are fixed in amount but whose timing depends on specified contingencies, including the exercise or failure to exercise a call (issuer) or put (holder) option. In these cases, simplified accounting methods can be applied for the recognition of the contingent payments, either because the contingencies are resolved periodically (VRDI) or the contingencies do not affect the yield. See the text that accompanies notes 174-175 in chapter 5; and Hariton, supra note 96, at 4-11.

189 See Ferguson, supra note 20, at 1008; and Hariton, supra note 96, at 11-12.

190 The characterization of a prepaid forward as contingent-payment debt is problematic because a prepaid forward does not provide for a return of the issue price or any minimum payment and, accordingly, does not satisfy the requirement under US case law that an instrument include a promise to pay a certain sum on maturity. See supra note 60. Under this reading of the relevant case law, any instrument that provides a contingent amount of principal may not be considered indebtedness within the contingent-debt regulations, even though the cash flows associated with the instrument are equivalent to those associated with the combination of a fixed-payment debt instrument and an on-market forward. See, for example, Kleinbard, Nijenhuis, and Vemireddy, supra note 140, at 502. But see Ferguson, supra note 20, at 1008, who suggests that there is some "theoretical appeal" in the debt classification of an instrument with contingent principal; and Hariton, supra note 96, at 12, who points out that the contingent-debt regulations imply that it is possible for an instrument to be characterized as debt even though it does not promise a return of principal or a minimum payment.

191 But see Boris Bittker and James Eustice, *Federal Income Taxation of Corporations and Shareholders*, 6th ed. (Boston: Warren, Gorham & Lamont, 1994), at paragraph 4.03[2][g], who conclude that contingent-principal instruments are properly classified as equity; and Sheppard, "Things That Go Bump in the Portfolio," supra note 94, who suggests that prepaid forwards, such as DECs, ELKs, and PERCs (described supra note 94) should be classified as equity for US tax purposes. For a discussion of approaches to the classification of hybrids that lie along the boundary between debt and equity, see the text that accompanies notes 280-336 infra.

192 See the text that accompanies notes 75-92 supra.

193 For a discussion of the constraints that prevent the application of a comprehensive accrual regime to shares and the difficult boundary between debt and equity instruments that is an inevitable consequence of an exclusion for shares, see the text that accompanies notes 247-279 infra.

194 IRC reg. section 1.1275-4(4). The exclusion applies to debt that is convertible into shares of the issuer and debt that is exchangeable for shares of a person related to the issuer. The exclusion for convertible debt includes debt with a conversion right that can be settled in cash.

195 See James S. Eustice, "Debt-Like Equity and Equity-Like Debt: Treasury's Anti-Hybrid Proposals" (June 17, 1996), 71 *Tax Notes* 1657-78, at 1672, who describes some recent US Treasury department proposals for the characterization of certain convertible debt as equity.

196 See the text that accompanies note 150 supra.

197 See the text that accompanies notes 35-37 in chapter 4, where it is observed that the failure to bifurcate convertible debt results in the effective amortization of the embedded option premium against the OID that would otherwise arise on an allocation of the issue price for the instrument to the option. The suggestion that the integrated treatment of the OID and option premium embedded in a convertible-debt instrument may be preferable to the results of the application of bifurcation is made in Randall K.C. Kau, "Carving Up Assets and Liabilities—Integration or Bifurcation of Financial Products" (December 1990), 68 *Taxes: The Tax Magazine* 1003-14, at 1003 and 1009. May, supra note 46, at 29:10, argues that the significant presence of tax-exempt investors such as pension funds presents a

revenue problem that necessitates the rejection of the bifurcation of convertible debt. In effect, bifurcation would create more deductible interest that is not necessarily offset by taxable interest income of the holders. In a sense, amortization of the option premium serves as an implicit tax on the OID that would otherwise arise on a bifurcation. This revenue concern is discussed in the text that accompanies notes 210-211 infra.

198 One explanation for the issue of contingent debt is that investors are unable to acquire a comparable embedded derivative on a stand-alone basis. Regulatory arbitrage may also be a factor, with institutional investors acquiring, for example, commodity-linked debt that avoids the application of restrictions on direct investments in commodities. See Ferguson, supra note 20, at 1007, footnote 64.

199 Hariton, supra note 13, at 1015.

200 Ibid. Hariton states that the "absence of any fixed payments makes it even more difficult to determine when there is a net financial investment within the terms of a contract calling for bilateral payments." At footnote 23, Hariton describes the problem using the following example: "In other words, if A turns out to make net payments to B during the earlier years of the life of the agreement, how will we know whether these net payments reflect economic losses attributable to unanticipated changes in the values of relevant indexes, or rather anticipated investments by A in a contract with B which are properly treated as loans? And if we do conclude that there are loans, how will we know when and to what extent they have been repaid?"

201 See the text that accompanies notes 173-179 supra.

202 Hariton, supra note 13, at 1016-17.

203 Ibid. Hariton states: "Lawyers are trained to draw lines based on judgment, and experience suggests that arbitrary bright lines do not necessarily provide for more satisfactory results."

204 Ibid.

205 See the text that accompanies notes 187-190 supra.

206 See the text that accompanies notes 191-192 supra.

207 See the text that accompanies notes 43-69 supra.

208 Failure to recognize the discount by allocating a portion of the issue price to the option premium also means that non-resident withholding tax otherwise applicable to interest (and OID as equivalent to interest) can be avoided through the use of convertible debt. See David G. Broadhurst, "Derivatives in International Tax Planning," in International Fiscal Association—Canadian Branch, *1997 International Tax Seminar* (Scarborough, Ont.: Carswell, 1998), 85-101, at 100-1.

209 See, for example, *A Platform for Consultation*, supra note 19, at 176-77, where it is stated: "Neutrality between convertible and converting instruments and other forms of debt and equity requires that the notional debt element be treated similarly to other debt instruments and that the notional equity option be treated similarly to other equity options." The New Zealand accrual regime achieves a measure of consistent treatment of equity options, fixed-payment debt, and convertible debt. A portion of the issue price of a debt instrument that is convertible into shares of the issuer at the option of the holder must be allocated to the embedded equity option, and the resulting discount on the fixed-payment debt

component is subject to accrual recognition. See New Zealand Inland Revenue, *Determination* G22, "Optional Conversion Convertible Notes Denominated in New Zealand Dollars Convertible at the Option of the Holder," October 1990. The expected gain associated with the embedded equity option is exempt from the accrual regime in the same manner as equity options issued on a stand-alone basis. A more complete bifurcation is adopted with mandatory convertible notes that are treated as a combination of either (1) a fixed-payment debt instrument and a long on-market forward contract written on the related shares, or (2) a fixed-payment debt instrument and a long prepaid forward contract written on the related shares. Expected gain associated with a prepaid forward is apparently subject to accrual recognition as a debt equivalent. See New Zealand Inland Revenue, *Determination* G5C, "Mandatory Conversion Convertible Notes," March 1994.

210 May, supra note 46, at 29:10, who points out that issuers can create deductible interest expense by issuing separately an equity option and a fixed-payment debt instrument that would otherwise be packaged together in a convertible instrument.

211 See, for example, Thomas E. McDonnell, *Tax-Exempt Organizations and the Financing of Taxable Businesses*, Working Paper 97-9 (Ottawa: Department of Finance, Technical Committee on Business Taxation, November 1997), who notes that the use of income trusts to recapitalize taxable corporations with interest-bearing debt is only one example of a financing structure that is intended to take advantage of the general tax bias in favour of debt held by tax-exempts. See also James Pesando and Thomas A. Wilson, *Tax-Exempts and Corporate Capital Structure: An Analysis of Efficiency and Revenue Implications*, Working Paper 97-10 (Ottawa: Department of Finance, Technical Committee on Business Taxation, October 1997), who note that there may be inefficiencies attributable to agency costs associated with royalty and income trust structures. To address revenue erosion, McDonnell, supra, suggests that one possible approach is a "domestic thin capitalization rule," such as that in IRC section 163(j), which limits the deductibility of interest on corporate debt held by tax exempts. He does not suggest, however, that there is anything unique about income trusts or other forms of debt financing (including convertible and exchangeable debt) that could properly restrict such a limitation to particular types of interest expense.

212 In fact, a failure to accrue the full amount of expected gain and loss on convertible and exchangeable debt is equivalent to an implicit tax for tax-exempt holders, who may prefer other contingent-debt instruments that are subject to accrual recognition under a system of expected-return taxation. To the extent that marginal investors are tax-exempt entities, the implicit tax may distort the demand for convertible and exchangeable debt, which may give rise to efficiency losses associated with pricing effects. The effect is just the opposite for taxable holders who may prefer the deferred recognition of a portion of the expected gain associated with convertible and exchangeable debt that is not subject to bifurcated treatment. See the text that accompanies note 194 supra. But see Pesando and Wilson, supra note 211, who argue that a traditional finance view holds that a tax bias in favour of debt only ensures tax clienteles for corporate debt and equity, and that there are no associated efficiency costs, provided that tax-exempt holders are inframarginal investors. Where the tax effect is reversed (that is, convertible and exchangeable debt bear an implicit tax), there may be no efficiency losses, but only revenue

217 Hariton, supra note 13, at 1013, draws a distinction in the treatment of cash-settled and physically settled prepaid forward contracts. Gain or loss on the latter would be deferred until a disposition of the underlying asset that is acquired under the contract, with any prepayment accounted for in the cost of acquisition. Settlement would not be treated as a recognition event because of the absence of a cash transaction. Gain or loss on a cash-settled prepaid forward would be recognized on settlement on the theory that the contract is equivalent to the acquisition of the underlying asset in the spot market and its forward sale. Hariton argues, however, that there is no basis for treating unexpected gain or loss as interest income or expense. Moreover, although characterization as ordinary income would be extended to expected gain or loss, recognition would be deferred until cash settlement, unless the embedded debt in a prepaid forward is significant enough to be characterized as debt. See also *Taxation of Financial Arrangements*, supra note 38, at 100, which recommends that the exclusion of unexpected gains and losses on agreements for purchase and sale of property with deferred payment terms be limited to physically settled contracts. The availability of a cash-settlement option "is an indication that the property is being used as a pricing index," which means that the agreement should be treated as a forward contract and that all gains and losses should be subject to the accrual legislation.

218 Inconsistencies are not limited to a failure to require the accrual of all expected gain and loss. For example, derivatives have been used in Canada in the context of certain deferred income plans as a means of replicating exposure to foreign assets without offending ITA restrictions on the level of foreign assets that the plans are allowed to hold. The avoidance opportunity arises because of a failure to treat the relevant derivative positions as the equivalent ownership interest in the underlying asset. In effect, there is no general attempt to look through the identity of Canadian counterparties and treat the positions of particular plans in a manner consistent with a direct ownership interest in the underlying asset that is the subject of derivative instruments. See Elinore J. Richardson, David Glicksman, and Lara Friedlander, "Fundamentals of Canadian Taxation of Financial Instruments," in *Report of Proceedings of the Fifty-First Tax Conference*, 1999 Conference Report (Toronto: Canadian Tax Foundation, 2000), 5:1-57, at 5:17-18. Treatment of a derivative position as equivalent to a position in the underlying asset can also have implications for the characterization of gain or loss on the derivative as derived from (1) a foreign or domestic source or (2) passive investment or a business. For a discussion of some of these characterization issues in the US context, see Willard B. Taylor and Diana L. Wollman, "Why Can't We Get Along? Finding Consistent Solutions to the Treatment of Derivatives and Other Problems" (Fall 1999), 53 *The Tax Lawyer* 95-127, at 95-110 and 113-18.

219 See, for example, Edward D. Kleinbard, "Risky and Riskless Positions in Securities" (December 1993), 71 *Taxes: The Tax Magazine* 783-99, at 786-87, who notes that the fungibility of publicly traded securities means that there can be many long and short positions but only one owner. The significance of this point for the analysis of the tax treatment of synthetic instruments is discussed in chapter 7.

220 See the text that accompanies notes 247-279 infra.

221 See the discussion in chapter 3 of the different forms of tax avoidance and the case for the application of accretion taxation to financial instruments.

222 The term "structured financing" is used here to mean any "financing technique in which financial assets . . . are pooled and converted into capital market instruments." Lewis R. Steinberg, "Selected Issues in the Taxation of Swaps, Structured Finance and Other Financial Products" (1993), vol. 1, no. 5 *Florida Tax Review* 263-306, at 264, footnote 5. These transactions include "asset securitizations" and are comparable in concept to "disaggregation transactions," whereby "traditional financial contracts, such as stocks and bonds have been disaggregated into their constituent parts and separately marketed." Warren, supra note 3, at 460.

223 For example, in 1996, the US Securities and Exchange Commission approved the trading of "long-term equity options" (LEAPs) and "buy-write options unitary derivatives" (BOUNDs). LEAPs and BOUNDs are essentially disaggregated equity, with LEAPs representing the appreciation in the shares and BOUNDs representing the dividend entitlement. LEAPs are long-dated American call options written on the specified shares. They provide the holder with exposure to appreciation in value of the shares in excess of the exercise price over a relatively long period. BOUNDs are long-dated European options representing the right to dividends declared on the specified shares. The holder is also entitled to cash in the amount of the exercise price if the value of the shares on maturity exceeds that price. If the value of the shares is less than the exercise price, the holder receives the shares. For a discussion of the treatment of LEAPs and BOUNDs under the Code, see Matthew Huggins, "The Probable Tax Treatment of LEAPs and BOUNDs" (June 24, 1996), 71 *Tax Notes* 1807-15.

"Endowment warrants" are another example of long-dated, deep-in-the money options that are equivalent to an agreement for the purchase and sale of specified shares, with a deposit payable by the holder. See Roger Paul, "Taxation of Financial Instruments: Towards a Conceptual Understanding of Economic Substance—An Australian Update," unpublished paper presented at the Harvard International Tax Program symposium on the International Taxation of New Financial Instruments, September 28, 1996, at appendix four; and Alan W. Schwartz, "PEACs and SPECs and Special Warrants," in *Report of Proceedings of the Forty-Fifth Tax Conference*, 1993 Conference Report (Toronto: Canadian Tax Foundation, 1994), 17:1-8. The outstanding amount under a warrant is equal to the spot price of the referenced shares on issue less the warrant premium. This amount increases over the term of the warrant with reference to a short-term interest rate, and decreases by the amount of dividends on the referenced shares. If the outstanding amount decreases to zero before maturity, the holder receives the shares and has no further payment obligations. If the outstanding amount is positive on maturity, the holder may pay the amount and receive the shares. The deposit or option premium is forfeited if the spot price of the referenced shares on maturity is less than the outstanding amount, and the holder does not exercise the warrants.

Low-exercise price options (LEPOs) are deep-in-the money share options that are traded on the Australian stock exchange and are equivalent to a prepaid forward contract with a zero strike price. See Paul, ibid., at appendix three.

224 See supra note 94 for a brief description of some examples, including DECs, PRIDEs, TRUPs, and gold notes. For a discussion of the tax treatment of these instruments under the IRC, see Sheppard, "Sand Castles of Debt Classification," supra note 94; Lee A. Sheppard, "Debt Versus Equity: A Package Deal" (June 10, 1996), 71 *Tax Notes* 1435-39; and Sheppard, "Things That Go Bump in the

Portfolio," supra note 94. See also Levy, supra note 93; Sykora, supra note 66, at 30:33-37; and Sykora, supra note 36.

225 See, for example, Levy, supra note 93, who recommends the extension of the US contingent-debt regulations to gold notes and prepaid forwards; and David Miller, "Reconciling Policies and Practice in the Taxation of Financial Instruments" (March 1999), 77 *Taxes: The Tax Magazine* 236-76, at 260 and 262, who recommends the extension of interest accrual rules to prepaid forwards and deep-in-the-money options in a first stage of reform, followed by the adoption of interest accrual rules for all options that are not otherwise subject to accretion taxation; Scarborough, "Different Rules for Different Players and Products," supra note 5, who recommends the application of expected-return taxation to all contingent-payment securities, irrespective of their form; and Lee A. Sheppard, "Clear Reflection for Contingent Payment Securities" (March 4, 1996), 70 *Tax Notes* 1411-13, who states: "Any reasonable set of rules would require current accrual of income by the holder at an economically realistic rate of return without asking questions about the classification of the security." Sheppard (ibid., at 1411) argues that the US Treasury department has the power to enact the necessary regulations under IRC section 446 and its requirement that any accounting method result in the clear reflection of income.

226 In 1993, the IRS announced its intention to address the treatment of derivatives with off-market pricing in comprehensive regulations. See TD 8491, 1993-2 CB 215. Although no regulations have been released, the IRS remains committed to some form of imputation of interest on prepaid forward contracts. An extension of accrual recognition to these derivative instruments will apparently be incorporated in a longer-term project to design a set of successor regulations to the existing NPC regulations. See Lee A. Sheppard, "Financial Transactions Committee Looks at Coming Guidance" (May 10, 1999), 83 *Tax Notes* 783. *Taxation of Financial Arrangements*, supra note 38, at 47-49, similarly proposed the extension of accrual recognition to the expected gain or loss associated with the embedded debt in all prepaid forwards.

227 This approach differs from that proposed by Hariton, supra note 13, at 1022, where he suggests maintaining a facts-and-circumstances test to determine the character of a derivative with embedded debt. Even where a debt classification is applied, Hariton recommends limiting the amount of interest income and expense to the amount of the expected gain or loss. Unexpected gain or loss that arises on the resolution of specified contingencies would continue to be subject to treatment as capital gain or loss. Hariton's approach leads him to suggest the following agenda for the US Treasury department:

> (a) "drop the other shoe" insofar as the contingent debt regulations are concerned, generally treating differences between projected and actual payments as giving rise to capital gains and losses rather than to adjustments to the aggregate amount of interest accrual;
>
> (b) stop finding loans embedded within the terms of equity swaps, commodity swaps and similar derivative contracts (although it should continue to find them in interest rate swaps, where the underlying payments under the swaps are generally equivalent to payments on fixed or floating-rate debt instruments);

(c) likewise drop the proposed project to accrue interest on forward contracts and deep-in-the-money options; and

(d) provide more "soft" guidance (i.e., rulings dealing with specific transactions, rather than bright-line regulations) to help taxpayers determine when a relatively long-term derivative investment which has been documented as a swap, a forward contract, an option or some other transaction should be treated as a loan for federal income tax purposes.

228 In principle, accrual recognition should be extended to the difference between an amount paid for a non-traded option on a secondary-market transfer and its forward price or expected value at the time of the transfer. See supra note 38 regarding the comparable treatment of off-market forwards on a secondary-market transfer.

229 See supra note 38 regarding the extension of accrual treatment to the expected gain on embedded debt that arises on a secondary-market transfer of an off-market forward. Such an extension is required to support the application of debt tax treatment to prepaid and off-market forwards created on issue. See also supra notes 145 and 179 regarding the same treatment of the expected gain arising on a secondary-market transfer when the relevant derivative is embedded in a contingent-debt instrument.

230 A failure to extend the logic of an expected-return approach to debt with contingent principal also has consequences for information reporting under an accrual regime that otherwise purports to require the accrual recognition of interest income on variable principal instruments. See, for example, Revenue Canada document no. 9633886, December 12, 1996, discussed in *Window on Canadian Tax*, supra note 170, at paragraph 4502, where Revenue Canada indicates that information reporting of interest income in the year of accrual is not required when interest is based on a variable principal amount that is determined in a subsequent year.

231 Supra note 160.

232 See, for example, New Zealand Income Tax Act, 1994, paragraph (l) of the definition of an "excepted financial arrangement" in section EH 14 and paragraph (q) of the same definition in subsection EH 24(1), excluding from the accrual legislation "short-term options" (63 days or less between the issue and settlement dates where the underlying asset is property other than real property and 93 days where the underlying asset is real property). Options for the purchase and sale of property (other than a financial arrangement or a foreign currency) are considered "specified options" and are subject to the imputation of interest as agreements of purchase and sale. See supra notes 216-217. This treatment is limited generally to options that are physically settled. Although cash-settled options are financial arrangements, the expected gain or loss does not appear to be subject to accrual recognition. As with gain or loss on cash-settled forwards and swaps, gain or loss on cash-settled options is apparently considered entirely unexpected and subject to realization-based recognition as ordinary income or loss under the accrual legislation. Traded options and futures may be subject to accretion taxation. See the text that accompanies notes 280-314 in chapter 5.

233 See, for example, Lee A. Sheppard, "Borrowing All the Way to a Constructive Sale" (August 9, 1999), 84 *Tax Notes* 816-20, at 817, who argues that interest should be imputed on LEAPs and other long-term options with a significant time-

value-of-money element. The New Zealand accrual legislation takes a rougher, and more limited, approach. "Variable-principal instruments," which are defined to include a limited range of demand deposits, are considered excepted financial arrangements if they are issued at par and the total of their principal amounts outstanding does not exceed $50,000 at any time during a taxation year. See New Zealand Income Tax Act, 1994, paragraph (u) of the definition of an "excepted financial arrangement" in subsection EH 24(1).

234 See Deborah H. Schenk, "A Realization-Based Income Tax and the Taxation of Capital" (draft), reprinted in *Tax Notes Today*, October 26, 1997, 97 TNT 223-39 (electronic database); and Shuldiner, supra note 5, at 284, footnote 181.

235 The same problem arises with foreign currency debt and changes in the value of such instruments attributable to changes in spot exchange rates. See the text that accompanies notes 136-162 in chapter 5.

236 See the text that accompanies notes 245-248 in chapter 3; and Revenue Canada document no. 9508605, November 24, 1995, where Revenue Canada states that it is the intent of the ITA that an amount required to be accrued as interest under subsection 12(9) and regulation 7000(2) should be subject to non-resident withholding tax as interest when paid. Characterization as interest should extend as well to expected currency exchange gains and losses that are accrued as interest under a system of expected-return taxation. See the text that accompanies notes 136-162 in chapter 5; and Julian S. Alworth, "Taxation and Integrated Financial Markets: The Challenges of Derivatives and Other Financial Innovations" (1998), vol. 5, no. 3 *International Tax and Public Finance* 507-34, at 517, who suggests that non-resident withholding tax should be applied to the interest element of foreign currency debt calculated as the difference between the spot exchange rate on issue and the forward exchange rates corresponding to the series of promised cash flows.

237 See the text that accompanies notes 280-336 infra. To the extent that a hybrid instrument is considered equity, cross-border cash flows should be subject to the non-resident withholding tax on dividends.

238 The same characterization should, in principle, apply to OID arising on convertible and exchangeable debt that is bifurcated into a combination of a fixed-payment debt instrument and either (1) an embedded equity option or (2) a forward contract. See Broadhurst, supra note 208, at 101.

239 For example, Revenue Canada has adopted this proposition with imputed interest on certain swap prepayments disguised as loans. See Revenue Canada document no. 7-902723, April 4, 1991; and Richardson, Glicksman, and Friedlander, supra note 218, at 5:51. Characterization as interest income should extend to the availability of any exemption for interest on portfolio debt. In effect, the embedded debt instrument in a hybrid could be characterized as a portfolio or direct investment using the same approach to fixed-payment debt instruments. If no exemption is available, all interest should be subject to non-resident withholding tax. See, for example, Reuven S. Avi-Yonah, "Memo to Congress: It's Time To Repeal the US Portfolio Interest Exemption" (December 7, 1998), 17 *Tax Notes International* 1817-26, who recommends the repeal of the portfolio interest exemption in the United States and its replacement with a non-resident withholding tax system that serves as a backup to residence-country taxation of capital income. Bifurcated treatment avoids the characterization of contingent payments as wholly ineligible

for exemption. See, for example, the closing words in ITA subparagraph 212(1)(b), which deny the portfolio-interest exemption for all amounts that are contingent or dependent on the production or use of property in Canada, or that are computed with reference to revenue, profit, cash flow, commodity price, or dividends paid. Although these amounts can be considered "equity-like" in the sense that they provide the possibility for unexpected gains, the expected gain associated with the advance of funds under a contingent-debt instrument is equivalent to interest. Consistency of treatment with fixed-payment debt suggests that the same withholding tax treatment should be applied to the extent of the amount of the expected gain.

240 Most countries, as standard practice, exempt payments on derivatives from non-resident withholding tax. See the text that accompanies notes 246-249 in chapter 3. On the basis of that practice, unexpected gains in excess of the expected gain associated with a hybrid should also be exempt. But see Avi-Yonah, supra note 239; and Reuven S. Avi-Yonah, "Virtual Taxation: Source-Based Taxation in the Age of Derivatives," in *Proceedings of the Eighty-Ninth Annual Conference on Taxation* (Washington, DC: National Tax Association and Tax Institute of America, 1997), 269-74, who suggests that non-resident withholding tax should be applied to any financial cash flow if the amount is deductible in the calculation of income in the source country and not otherwise subject to source-country taxation.

241 See Gregory May, "Flying on Instruments: Synthetic Investment and the Avoidance of Withholding Tax" (November 11, 1996), 13 *Tax Notes International* 1625-35, at 1631-32, who uses an example involving the substitution of a prepaid forward sale of gold for a debt financing otherwise subject to withholding tax.

242 This point is emphasized in Bruce A. Elvin, "The Recharacterization of Cross-Border Interest Rate Swaps: Tax Consequences and Beyond" (1995), vol. 2, no. 11 *Florida Tax Review* 631-72.

243 Sheppard, supra note 225, at 1412, suggests that the US Treasury was at one time considering the extension of accrual recognition of the expected gain by holders of long-dated options and prepaid forward contracts, while maintaining realization-based recognition for issuers. Although symmetrical treatment of holders and issuers is not a necessary tax-policy goal, Sheppard (ibid., at 1412) argues that "asymmetrical rules breed disrespect for the tax law, even if their targets are very sophisticated people who do not have a lot of respect for the tax law in the first place." Asymmetrical treatment of holders and issuers is one of the critical elements of the 7000 regulations under the ITA and the treatment of contingent debt under those regulations. Many of the concerns that have led to the maintenance of asymmetry by the Department of Finance presumably motivated the US Treasury to consider a similar approach. A fundamental concern is the potential revenue erosion resulting from an extension of accrual-based recognition of expected losses on contingent debt by issuers, with cash-basis recognition by non-resident holders subject only to withholding tax. The same concerns have not prevented US policy makers from extending accrual recognition to contingent debt. See the text that accompanies notes 137-151 supra. Presumably, the concern with long-dated options and prepaid forwards was that payments could be deferred to maturity. Contingent-debt instruments with embedded derivatives usually provide an element of periodic payments.

244 See the text that accompanies notes 66-83 in chapter 5.

245 See the text that accompanies notes 110-118 supra.

246 See the text that accompanies notes 103-114 in chapter 3.

247 See the text that accompanies notes 8-19 in chapter 2.

248 See the text that accompanies notes 60-74 in chapter 2; and the text that accompanies notes 162-184 in chapter 3.

249 See the text that accompanies notes 162-184 in chapter 3.

250 Ibid.

251 This characterization extends equally to equity interests in unincorporated organizational forms that are analogous to shares. These interests include partnership interests and beneficial interests in trusts that provide a comparable combination of expected and unexpected gains and losses.

252 See the text that accompanies notes 143-161 in chapter 3.

253 As described in the text that accompanies notes 154-161 in chapter 3, the functional similarity of debt and equity is supported by option-pricing theory. In effect, corporate debt holders can be seen as the owners of the underlying corporate assets, with the shareholders holding a call or put option on those assets. The debt holders earn an expected time-value return on the underlying assets and bear a degree of risk that depends on the outcome of the specified contingencies that determine the ex post value of the corporate assets and the embedded option. The shareholders hold only the call (or the corresponding put option) and realize any unexpected gain or loss that arises because of the difference between the value of the particular assets at maturity of the debt and the exercise price under the embedded option, which is equal to the required payoff on the debt. The embedded option in a share, however, also has an expected time-value return that gives rise to expected gain or loss in the same manner as options generally. In effect, the embedded-debt element in an option is also embedded in a share as the equivalent of an option. A system of expected-return taxation requires accrual recognition of this expected gain or loss, with realization-based recognition limited to unexpected gain or loss arising on maturity.

254 See the text that accompanies notes 137-151 supra.

255 See the text that accompanies notes 318-320 in chapter 5.

256 See, for example, Julia T. Boltar, "Corporate Taxation and the Interest-Dividend Dilemma" (August 1996), 113 *The South African Law Journal* 455-71, who recommends deduction of dividend payments in calculating income of the corporate payer; Institute for Fiscal Studies, Capital Taxes Group, *Equity for Companies: A Corporation Tax for the 1990s*, Commentary no. 26 (London: Institute for Fiscal Studies, April 1991), which recommends "an allowance for corporate equity" ("ACE" system) that provides a corporate interest deduction for the imputed expected return on equity; Edward D. Kleinbard, "Beyond Good and Evil Debt (and Debt Hedges): A Cost of Capital Allowance System" (December 1989), 67 *Taxes: The Tax Magazine* 943-61, at 955-61; Edward D. Kleinbard, "Equity Derivative Instruments: Financial Innovation's Newest Challenge to the Tax System" (May 1991), 69 *Texas Law Review* 1319-68, at 1361-68, who recommends "a cost of capital" ("COCA" system) that provides a corporate interest deduction equal to the imputed cost of all corporate capital; and Norman H. Lane, "A Theory of the Tax Base: The Exchange Model" (1984), 3 *American Journal of Tax Policy* 1-113, at 51-66, who discusses the normative basis for the imputation of interest on corporate equity.

The ACE system differs from a system of expected-return taxation in that the imputed return on equity is deductible for corporate issuers and exempt for holders. The ACE system is intended to implement the consumption tax treatment of the normal rate of return on corporate equity capital. In effect, corporate equity capital is accumulated out of after-tax earnings, and the normal rate of return is exempt from further taxation. The portion of the return that exceeds the normal rate is subject to tax at both the corporate and shareholder levels. In this respect, the ACE system represents a non-distortive tax on "economic rents," recommended by many economists as a model for reform of the corporate income tax. See Head, supra note 6.

Kleinbard's COCA system also entails a deduction for the imputed cost of corporate capital, with taxation at the investor level on realization of any gains or losses. Kleinbard generally fails to provide a normative basis for this approach and asserts only that the use of an arbitrary imputation rate is preferable to the deductibility of nominal interest expense, which does not reflect the cost of capital. He accepts a separation of the accrual-based deduction of an imputed cost of capital by issuers from the realization-based recognition of gains by investors on the apparent basis that there is a separation of identity and interests. Even if one accepts the existence of such a separation, it is unclear what normative basis this separation provides for Kleinbard's COCA system.

As described in the text that accompanies notes 254-256 supra, the application of a system of expected-return taxation to shares is a simple proposition in the context of an income tax; it requires the accrual recognition of expected gain by shareholders and the deductibility of the same amounts at the corporate level. Unexpected gains and losses can be recognized by shareholders on realization. The acceptance of an income tax as normatively desirable is discussed in the text that accompanies notes 29-57 in chapter 3. It is assumed that the issues associated with the taxation of financial instruments and the available responses arise in the context of an income tax.

257 See, for example, Joseph M. Dodge, "A Combined Mark-to-Market and Pass-Through Corporate-Shareholder Integration Proposal" (Spring 1995), 50 *Tax Law Review* 265-372. An earlier, less detailed, proposal is provided in Victor Thuronyi, "The Taxation of Corporate Income—A Proposal for Reform" (Spring 1983), 2 *The American Journal of Tax Policy* 109-45. In fact, the literature on the accretion-based taxation of shares extends back to the proposal of David Slawson, "Taxing as Ordinary Income the Appreciation of Publicly Held Stock" (March 1967), 76 *The Yale Law Journal* 623-76; and the proposals of the Canadian Department of Finance for the accretion-based taxation of publicly traded shares every five years. See E.J. Benson, *Proposals for Tax Reform* (the white paper) (Ottawa: Queen's Printer, 1969), 40-41, who proposed the deemed realization of accrued gains and losses on shares of public corporations every five years.

258 See Dodge, supra note 257, at 293: "Previous integration proposals are all based on the obsolete and unnecessary view that the problem is how to tax the net income of the entity."

259 These factors are reviewed in Bird, supra note 6; and Head, supra note 6.

260 Cunningham and Schenk, supra note 160.

261 See the text that accompanies note 151 supra.

262 Recent consumption tax literature suggests that the importance of the choice of an imputation rate may be exaggerated. In general, an imputation rate is problematic only to the extent that it includes both the riskless rate and any premium for undiversifiable risk. If taxpayers can freely adjust their investment portfolios in response to taxation, only the normal or riskless rate of return may be exempted under a consumption tax and taxed under an income tax. The same proposition may extend to the risk premium for undiversifiable risk. See Joseph Bankman and Barbara H. Fried, "Winners and Losers in the Shift to a Consumption Tax" (January 1998), 86 *The Georgetown Law Journal* 539-68; Joseph Bankman and Thomas Griffith, "Is the Debate Between an Income Tax and a Consumption Tax a Debate About Risk? Does It Matter?" (Winter 1992), 47 *Tax Law Review* 377-406; and Alvin C. Warren Jr., "How Much Capital Income Taxed Under an Income Tax Is Exempt Under a Cash Flow Tax?" (Fall 1996), 52 *Tax Law Review* 1-16. Schenk, supra note 234, argues that the imputation of interest at the riskless rate on all capital assets (including shares) is normatively desirable, since the return to risk is taxed only accidentally under an income tax when non-tax factors constrain the ability to alter portfolios appropriately in response to the tax.

263 The problem is compounded under the Nordic dual income tax (DIT) systems, which apply a lower rate of tax on capital income. See the text that accompanies notes 135-154 in chapter 4. The lower rate means that an imputed return on equity capital must be determined for small businesses, both incorporated and unincorporated, that combine the capital and labour inputs of the participants. In effect, an imputed return operates as an upper limit on the ability to disguise labour returns as capital income. The use of an imputed return also allows the lower rate on capital income to be extended to unincorporated firms. For a discussion of these difficulties and the approaches adopted in the Nordic countries, see Peter Birch Sørensen, "From the Global Income Tax to the Dual Income Tax: Recent Tax Reforms in the Nordic Countries" (1994), vol. 1, no. 1 *International Tax and Public Finance* 57-79; and Peter B. Sørensen and Kare P. Hagen, "Taxation of the Self-Employed Under a Dual Income Tax," in *Towards a Dual Income Tax? Scandinavian and Austrian Experiences* (The Hague: Kluwer Law International, 1996), 23-67.

264 See the text that accompanies notes 154-161 in chapter 3 regarding the equivalence of (1) shares of a leveraged corporation and (2) a sale of the underlying assets combined with the acquisition of a call option on those assets.

265 This shift in jurisdiction assumes that capital-exporting countries would reciprocate by imposing a system of expected-return taxation on their resident shareholders. Such a move would involve the elimination of the deferral benefit provided in respect of active business income earned through foreign corporations. The effect on cross-border cash flows would be more complicated if some countries move to a system of expected-return taxation for shares and others maintain the status quo. See, generally, Malcolm Gammie, "Reforming Corporate Taxation: An Evaluation of the United States Treasury Integration Proposals and Other Corporate Tax Systems in an International Context—Part I" [1993], no. 2 *British Tax Review* 148-73, at 157-73; and John Isaac, "A Comment on the Viability of the Allowance for Corporate Equity" (August 1997), 18 *Fiscal Studies* 303-18, at 314-17, who discusses the international implications of an ACE system. The consumption tax character of the ACE system means that the impact on accepted international

norms is even more profound than the application of a system of expected-return taxation to shares in the context of an income tax.

266 But see United States Treasury Department, *Report on Integration of the Individual and Corporate Tax Systems: Taxing Business Income Once* (Washington: US Government Printing Office, January 1992), which achieves the consistent taxation of interest and dividends by denying the deductibility of both forms of cash flows for corporate issuers and exempting the returns from taxation at the investor level. Accordingly, dividends and interest would only be subject to the corporate-level tax under the proposed comprehensive business income tax (CBIT). Other than the realization of the consistent taxation of interest and dividends, there is no normative reason to extend the proxy tax treatment of equity income under the corporate income tax to the gains on non-equity instruments, which should be subject to a comprehensive accrual regime at the investor level. Indeed, none of the practical constraints that suggest the use of a corporate income tax as a proxy for the application of a system of expected-return taxation at the shareholder level appear to apply to non-equity instruments. In this respect, the CBIT regime recommended by the US Treasury fails to indicate how options and the basic price-fixing derivatives should be treated. In short, it is unclear whether the expected gains on the former would be treated in the same manner as interest and dividends. The treatment of unexpected gains and losses on both types of instruments is equally unclear.

The denial of the deductibility of corporate interest expense is a notion that was proposed much earlier in Alvin C. Warren Jr., "The Corporate Interest Deduction: A Policy Evaluation" (July 1974), 83 *The Yale Law Journal* 1585-1619. As a purely practical matter, the adoption of a CBIT by small capital-importing countries is especially problematic. In particular, the additional source-country tax on debt returns is unlikely to be accepted by capital-exporting countries and may be denied creditability under the foreign tax credit systems of resident countries. The ostensible basis for denial would be that the corporate tax attributable to the non-deductibility of interest is not an "income tax." See Bird, supra note 6, at 7-8. The same normative and practical problems arise with certain proposals to deny the corporate interest deduction and provide imputation tax credits on interest distributions. The increased source-country tax burden on interest is unlikely to be accepted by capital-exporting countries. Some of the Nordic DITs avoid these problems by maintaining the corporate interest deduction and applying the corporate income tax on equity income either as a final tax (exemption at the shareholder level) or as a withholding tax (imputation approach). See the text that accompanies note 140 in chapter 4.

267 For unincorporated associations such as partnerships and trusts, the benefit of anticipated and unanticipated deferral is addressed by treating the association as a conduit and requiring partners and beneficiaries to recognize their share of income or loss as it is earned or incurred. An alternative approach deems these associations to be corporations and subjects the holders of equity interests to the same corporate income tax system applicable to shareholders. See, for example, Australia, *Tax Reform: Not a New Tax, a New Tax System* (Canberra: Australian Government Publishing Services, August 13, 1998), at 113-24, which proposes the treatment of business trusts as corporations subject to a reformed imputation system. For a recent proposal to extend conduit treatment to certain corporations,

see Dodge, supra note 257. See also Jeffrey L. Kwall, "Taxing Private Enterprise in the New Millennium" (Winter 1998), 51 *The Tax Lawyer* 229-78, who recommends a combination of conduit treatment and a single entity-level tax on the income of private enterprises categorized according to the complexity of their capital structures.

268 See, generally, Peter A. Harris, *Corporate/Shareholder Income Taxation and Allocating Taxing Rights Between Countries: A Comparison of Imputation Systems* (Amsterdam: IBFD Publications, 1996), 561-790, who summarizes the details of imputations systems in various countries.

269 See the text that accompanies notes 176-179 in chapter 3.

270 A similar result can be realized by substituting the corporate income tax as a final tax on equity income in place of taxation at the shareholder level. Dividends and gains realized on the disposition of shares can then be exempted from shareholder-level taxation. For a description of this type of approach, which has been adopted by some of the Nordic countries, see the text that accompanies notes 135-154 in chapter 4.

271 See the text that accompanies notes 176-179 in chapter 3.

272 Application of the corporate income tax as a final tax on equity income is not immune from many of the same structural features that give rise to inconsistencies in the taxation of interest and dividends. See the text that accompanies notes 273-279 infra.

273 To the extent that the corporate tax is substituted for the shareholder-level tax, a lower corporate rate provides an absolute tax saving and not just the benefit of deferral.

274 Under a system that uses the corporate income tax as a final tax on equity income, a preference for debt arises most obviously for non-taxable investors who can substitute tax-deductible interest payments for dividends. The same preference holds for non-resident investors who are subject only to withholding tax on interest payments. To the extent that the interest is payable on portfolio debt, withholding tax may also be waived.

275 See, for example, Joseph Bankman, "A Market-Value Based Corporate Income Tax" (September 11, 1995), 68 *Tax Notes* 1347-53; Calvin Johnson, "GAAP Tax" (April 19, 1999), 83 *Tax Notes* 425-30; and Michael S. Knoll, "An Accretion Corporate Income Tax" (November 1996), 49 *Stanford Law Review* 1-43, who recommends the replacement of the corporate-level tax on income with a corporate-level tax applied to changes in the value of outstanding securities plus distributions.

276 The failure to apply expected-return taxation to shares also provides opportunities for timing arbitrage associated with the leveraged acquisition of shares. Expected loss on the borrowing is subject to accrual recognition, while expected gain on the shares is subject to the corporate income tax, which may fail to tax that gain on an accrual basis. This avoidance opportunity has prompted calls for restrictions on the interest deduction. See the text that accompanies note 101 in chapter 3.

277 A reliance on the legal form of an instrument as a share is generally determinative of exempt status under the accrual regime. Glazebrook and Oliver, supra note 216, at 135-52. Only a limited range of debentures with equity features are treated as "shares," which are defined to include an interest in the capital of a corporation and

this limited set of debentures. See New Zealand Income Tax Act, 1994, section OB 1 definition of a "share." This reliance on legal form is defensible because of a comprehensive imputation system for equity income that realizes a degree of consistency in the taxation of interest and dividends. See infra note 279.

278 This point is alluded to in Tim Edgar, "The Debt-Equity Distinction and the Taxation of Financial Instruments: Past Practice and Future Directions in Australia and Canada," in John G. Head and Richard Krever, eds., *Taxation Towards 2000* (Sydney: Australian Tax Research Foundation, 1997), 293-335; and Richard Wood, "The Taxation of Debt, Equity and Hybrid Arrangements" (1999), vol. 47, no. 1 *Canadian Tax Journal* 49-80.

279 This result is reflected most clearly under the New Zealand Income Tax Act, 1994, which implements an imputation system for corporate equity income that generally approximates the investor-level tax on non-equity instruments under the accrual legislation. An advance corporate tax on dividend distributions ensures that corporate tax is paid in support of imputation credits. Consistency in the taxation of interest and dividends is enhanced by the taxable status of pension funds, which receive full imputation credits, and the provision of imputation credits to non-resident portfolio investors in a manner that ensures that a portion of the underlying corporate tax remains creditable in the country of residence of the shareholder. See Harris, supra note 268, at 701-18. A similar approach has been proposed in Australia where pension funds are taxable at a special low rate and may be eligible for a refund of excess imputation credits. See *Tax Reform: Not a New Tax, a New Tax System*, supra note 267, at 118-19.

The relatively well-developed imputation system for equity income is the apparent basis for a general acceptance by New Zealand Inland Revenue of legal form as determinative of the classification of instruments along the boundary between debt and equity. See, for example, *Taxation of Financial Arrangements*, supra note 38, at 17, where a factors approach to the definition of the boundary is rejected, and at 27, where the rejection is supported as follows: "Many commentators have come to the view that the only solution to the difficulty with this boundary [between debt and equity instruments] . . . is to remove the distinction altogether and tax all equity on an accrual basis. We do not consider this to be a viable proposition. . . . We have a well developed imputation system for the taxation of equity and do not propose to interfere with that."

280 For a discussion of the application of accretion taxation to traded instruments, including shares, as a response to strategic trading intended to provide the benefit of selective realization, see the text that accompanies notes 280-320 in chapter 5.

281 See, for example, Matthew P. Haskins, "Can the IRS Maintain the Debt-Equity Distinction in the Face of Structured Notes?" (Summer 1995), 32 *Harvard Journal on Legislation* 525-44, who argues that contingent debt with embedded derivatives ("structured notes") cannot be classified on any principled basis as debt or equity. Equity characterization is supported generally by the contingent principal amount and the ability of the issuer to require the holder to accept repayment in shares rather than cash. Debt classification is supported by a characterization of the instruments as a combination of fixed-payment debt and an embedded derivative, such as a call option or on-market forward contract. See also Lee A. Sheppard, "Rethinking DECS, and New Ways To Carve Out Debt" (April 19, 1999), 83 *Tax Notes* 347-52; and Lee A. Sheppard, "Can Corporate Issuers Dial Up an Overstated Interest

Deduction?" (January 31, 2000), 86 *Tax Notes* 587-91, who criticizes the application of the US contingent-debt regulations to different combinations of fixed-payment debt and long-dated, deep-in-the-money options issued in the form of structured notes that could be characterized as equity.

282 For a discussion of the treatment of these instruments under the US contingent-debt regulations and a comprehensive accrual regime intended to implement the dictates of expected-return taxation, see the text that accompanies notes 137-151 and 213-233 supra.

283 The most exhaustive review of the US case law remains William T. Plumb, "The Federal Income Tax Significance of Corporate Debt: A Critical Analysis" (March 1971), 26 *Tax Law Review* 369-640. For an interesting empirical analysis of some of the case law, see Paul J. Robertson, Zoel Daughtrey, and Daryl V. Burckel, "Debt or Equity? An Empirical Analysis of Tax Court Classification During the Period 1955-1987" (May 7, 1990), 47 *Tax Notes* 707-16.

284 See the text that accompanies notes 57-72 in chapter 2.

285 *A Platform for Consultation*, supra note 19, at 200, refers to such an approach as "a blanket approach" in contrast to a bifurcation approach, under which an instrument is split into its debt and equity components.

286 See the text that accompanies notes 259-265 supra.

287 In its attempt to distinguish debt and equity, financial-accounting practice is based on the incorrect premise that shares are a fundamental building-block instrument that can be bifurcated from a hybrid instrument and accounted for separately. It is argued here that shares are themselves hybrids in the more fundamental sense that they contain an embedded loan and a bet element. It is not entirely clear what attributes distinguish equity in a manner that allows some portion of a hybrid instrument to be accounted for as equity. In fact, the usefulness of bifurcation in this context appears to be limited largely to the bifurcation of convertible debt into a straight-debt instrument and an embedded equity option. Certain preferred shares are accounted for as debt and are not bifurcated in any sense of that term. See, for example, Canadian Institute of Chartered Accountants (CICA), *CICA Handbook* (Toronto: CICA) (looseleaf), section 3860. Because of its incorrect premise, the concept of bifurcation used in financial-accounting practice is of limited usefulness for income tax purposes and is rejected here as the basis for any sensible distinction between debt and equity instruments.

288 A possible exception to this "blanket" treatment of equity is preferred shares convertible into debt or common shares. To the extent that equity options (whether issued on a stand-alone basis or embedded in a contingent-debt instrument) are subject to the imputation of interest under a comprehensive accrual regime, the embedded option in a convertible preferred share should be separated from the rest of the instrument and subjected to the same treatment. See *A Platform for Consultation*, supra note 19, at 176-77. If equity options are excepted from accrual treatment (presumably on the assumption that the expected return is subject to the corporate income tax), there is no need to bifurcate a preferred share that is convertible into one or more common shares. In that instance, no interest is imputed on the embedded equity option and no OID is recognized on the preferred share (assuming that the share is characterized as equity). The same rationale would not apply to the non-equity option embedded in a preferred share that is convertible

into debt; nor to convertible and exchangeable debt. See the text that accompanies notes 193-198 and 208-212 supra regarding the bifurcation of these particular types of contingent-debt instruments and the imputation of interest on embedded equity options.

289 But see Wood, supra note 278, who suggests "a dual bifurcation" approach, whereby cash flows would be divided into "anticipatable" and "unanticipatable" amounts. The former would be recognized on an accrual basis. Realization-based recognition would be available for the latter. A second bifurcation would be used to characterize periodic cash flows as either dividends or interest. The bifurcation would be based on definitions of these terms and would depend on an assessment of the relative proportions of debt and equity features of a particular instrument. The result would be a sliding scale that attempts to reduce the discontinuities along the boundary between debt and equity by altering the dividend and interest character of periodic cash flows based on the proportionate amount of debt and equity features. Wood acknowledges the administrative and compliance problems with the proposal. In particular, a factors approach would have to be used to identify debt and equity features and quantify those features with relative values as the basis for the characterization of periodic cash flows. The underlying problem is, of course, the fundamentally unprincipled nature of the distinction. In the absence of the identical taxation of interest and dividends, a boundary between debt and equity must be drawn at some point on the basis of perceptions of the variability of the relevant cash flows. As Wood acknowledges, his approach reduces sharp discontinuities associated with bright-line tests, but cannot eliminate those discontinuities in the context of the inconsistent taxation of interest and dividends. Wood's dual-bifurcation approach appears to be the type of bifurcation described as a possible approach to the debt-equity distinction in *A Platform for Consultation*, supra note 19, at 200.

290 Wood, supra note 278, at 58-63.

291 United States, Treasury Department, Notice of Proposed Rulemaking, 45 Fed. Reg. 18,957 (1980). The proposed regulations were revised twice over the two years following their release and before their withdrawal. The Treasury department was provided with the power to issue classification regulations in the Tax Reform Act of 1969, Pub. L. no. 91-172, section 415, adding IRC section 385.

292 IRC prop. reg. section 1.385-3. IRC prop. reg. section 1.385-3(c) defined an "instrument" to include "any bond, note, debenture or similar written evidence of indebtedness." IRC prop. reg. section 1.385-3(d) defined an obligation as an interest in a corporation that is treated as indebtedness under the relevant non-tax law. No definition of a "right of conversion" was provided. Even the slightest possibility of conversion into equity pursuant to the terms of a debt obligation may have been sufficient to support the classification of an instrument as a "hybrid instrument." See Roger B. Madison, "The Deductibility of 'Interest' on Hybrid Securities" (Spring 1986), 39 *The Tax Lawyer* 465-517, at 486.

IRC prop. reg. section 1.385-5(d)(1) defined a "contingent payment" as "any payment other than a fixed payment of principal or interest." An interest payment was considered fixed if (1) it was payable at a definitely ascertainable rate on a definitely ascertainable day and (2) the right to receive the payment could not be impaired without the holder's consent. A principal payment was considered fixed if (1) it was payable on demand or due on definitely ascertainable dates and (2) the right to receive the payment could not be impaired without the holder's consent. See IRC prop. reg. sections 1.385-5(d)(2) and (3). A variable amount of interest or principal was considered definitely ascertainable as long as it was determined according to an external standard beyond the control of the issuer and was not related to the success or failure of the issuer's business. IRC prop. reg. section 1.385-5(d)(4).

293 IRC prop. reg. section 1.385-5(a). The proposed regulations recognized possible valuation difficulties and provided that the honest selection of an inappropriately low discount rate for fixed payments would not result in an equity classification if the payments discounted at an appropriate rate made up at least 45 percent of the total value. IRC prop. reg. section 1.385-5(c).

294 IRC prop. reg. section 1.385-5(b).

295 IRC prop. reg. sections 1.385-5(a) and (d)(2).

296 See *A Platform for Consultation*, supra note 19, at 202; and *A Tax System Redesigned*, supra note 19, at 445-48, which recommends a reliance on legal form but would extend debt classification to any instrument that is equity in form if it provides a "contractually guaranteed return of the original investment." For instruments with a term of 20 years or less, the original investment would be considered "contractually guaranteed" if the nominal amount of all non-contingent payments equal or exceed the principal or face value of the instrument. For all other instruments, the same test would be applied on a present-value basis.

297 See the text that accompanies notes 62-65 in chapter 2. The relevant shares are not treated as debt for tax purposes, but are generally subject to a distributions tax that ensures payment of a certain level of corporate tax in support of the provision of dividend relief.

298 The proposed US Treasury regulations adopted a similar approach with preferred shares. IRC prop. reg. section 1.385-10. With "preferred stock," the proposed regulations began by designating as equity all securities that are shares in form and that do not provide fixed dividend or capital repayment rights. Preferred stock that provides either or both types of fixed rights was considered an "instrument" potentially eligible for debt classification. The scope for this classification was relatively narrow, however, because the proposed regulations defined fixed payments to be only those payments that, when due, cannot be impaired without the holder's consent. Although preferred-share payments are fixed in time and amount, they are usually payable at the discretion of the board of directors of the issuer, only out of corporate profits, or only if any payment would not render the issuer insolvent. It appears that, under any of these conditions, preferred-share payments could be impaired, when due, without the holder's consent and would thus be considered contingent. Moreover, preferred stock, even if considered an instrument, was to be classified as debt only if the rules applicable to hybrid instruments or disguised equity would classify it as debt. In this respect, the proposed regulations provided a safe harbour that ensured equity classification by isolating additional formal terms thought to be indicative of equity. Under the safe harbour, preferred stock was considered equity if (1) it was labelled as preferred stock and treated as such under non-tax law, (2) any redemption payment was reasonable in relation to the issue price, (3) dividend payments were contingent (payable only out of earned surplus or at the discretion of the board of

directors), (4) capital repayments or dividend payments could not be made if doing so would render the corporation insolvent or unable to meet its liabilities as they became due, (5) default in making capital repayments or dividend payments did not entitle the holders to accelerate capital repayments, and (6) the preferred stock had a minimum term of 10 years. (In the case of preferred stock that provided for mandatory redemption over a period of years, the term was determined using the weighted average of the redemption payments.)

Because the proposed regulations were intended to classify hybrids as debt or equity for all purposes of the IRC, the Treasury department had to choose between extending the corporate interest deduction to preferred shares as debt and providing the dividends-received deduction to such instruments as shares. By limiting debt classification to a limited range of preferred shares, the Treasury department chose the latter alternative.

299 See Adam O. Emmerich, "Hybrid Instruments and the Debt-Equity Distinction in Corporate Taxation" (Winter 1985), 52 *The University of Chicago Law Review* 118-48. "Fixed-payment debt" in its classical form provides holders with a fixed return that is payable irrespective of the existence of corporate profits, as well as the right to receive a return of the amount advanced at specified times. "Common shares" are classical equity instruments in the sense that they provide holders with an unlimited right to participate in corporate profits, but bear the risk of a variable return that depends on the existence and extent of corporate profits. Holders of common shares also have no right to receive a return of the amount advanced or the benefits of any guarantees.

This distinction between the traditional forms of debt and equity appears to be the basis for the distinction under the Australian accrual proposals. See, for example, *Consultative Document*, supra note 19, at 23, which rationalizes the distinction on the ground that the payment of dividends on common shares is discretionary, with no obligation on the issuer to redeem the shares prior to maturity. Accordingly, the holder has no entitlement against the issuer to a future amount, which is the essence of the proposed "debt test."

300 See Tim Edgar, "The Classification of Corporate Securities for Income Tax Purposes" (1990), vol. 38, no. 5 *Canadian Tax Journal* 1141-88.

301 But see Robert A. Santangelo, "Towards Reshaping the Debt-Equity Distinction" (Winter 1997), 23 *The Journal of Corporate Taxation* 312-41, at 340-41, who suggests using a bright-line test based on a defined level of risk that would be measured quantitatively. Santangelo ignores the unsatisfactory experience with a similar approach under the proposed Treasury regulations and, in particular, the problems with the sharp discontinuities that are inevitable.

302 Supra note 291.

303 The most famous of these issues was a (US) $45 million private placement of adjustable-rate convertible notes (ARCNs). The notes bore interest at a below-market rate, with an additional amount payable based on dividends paid on common shares of the issuer. The notes also carried a right of conversion into common shares of the issuer at the then-market price of the shares. The investment bankers underwriting the issue estimated that the debt features of the ARCNs made up 55 percent of their total value. As a result, the ARCNs received debt classification under the proposed Treasury regulations, even though they contained a significant equity element. See Madison, supra note 292, at 484-85.

304 Rev. rul. 83-98, 1983-2 CB 40.

305 The terms of the ARCN that was the subject of the ruling were similar to those described supra note 303. For a detailed discussion of the ruling, see Madison, supra note 292, at 492-94.

306 IRC section 385.

307 Wood, supra note 278. *A Tax System Redesigned*, supra note 19, at 445-48, attempts to address the worst discontinuities associated with its recommended focus on "non-contingent principal payments" by disregarding contingencies that are "immaterially remote or artificial." See supra note 296 regarding the proposed "debt test."

308 Supra note 283.

309 See, for example, Notice 94-47, 1994-1 CB 357, which lists the following factors as relevant to a classification of an instrument as debt or equity: (1) an unreasonably long maturity; (2) an ability to repay the instrument's principal with the issuer's stock; (3) whether there is an unconditional promise on the part of the issuer to pay a sum certain on demand or at a fixed maturity date that is in the reasonably foreseeable future; (4) whether holders of the instruments have the right to enforce payment of principal and interest; (5) whether the rights of the holders of the instruments are subordinate to rights of general creditors; (6) whether the instruments give the holders the right to participate in the management of the issuer; (7) whether the issuer is thinly capitalized; (8) whether there is identity between the holders of the instruments and stockholders of the issuer; (9) the label placed on the instruments by the parties; and (10) whether the instruments are intended to be treated as debt or equity for non-tax purposes, including regulatory, rating agency, or financial-accounting purposes. The notice stipulates that "[n]o particular factor is conclusive in making the determination of whether an instrument constitutes debt or equity. The weight given to any factor depends upon all the facts and circumstances and the overall effect of an instrument's debt and equity features must be taken into account."

310 *Issues Paper*, supra note 19, at 74-80. See also *A Platform for Consultation*, supra note 19, at 201. But see *A Tax System Redesigned*, supra note 19, at 445-48, which recommends abandoning a multi-factors approach in favour of a focus on non-contingent payments as determinative of the classification of certain equity instruments as debt.

311 *Issues Paper*, supra note 19, at 76-80. Other factors include (1) automatic redemption, or redemption at the option of the holder; (2) the provision of security and/or guarantees, including a letter of credit; (3) a put option to sell shares at a predetermined price; (4) relatively large amounts of retained earnings available for distribution; and (5) the classification of the instrument for regulatory and financial-accounting purposes, provided that the classification is based on factors similar to those relevant to its classification for tax purposes.

312 Ibid., at 76: "The precise weight to be given to the following factors in the operation of the debt test would depend on the particular facts and circumstances."

313 Ibid., at 86. The issues paper (ibid., at 90) cites some typical preferred shares as examples of the possible application of the classification factors. Debt classification is suggested for preferred shares that (1) are redeemable and provide cumulative dividends; (2) are retractable at the option of the holder; and (3) provide

fixed, cumulative dividends. Equity classification would be maintained for perpetual preferred shares with fixed, non-cumulative dividends. Perpetual debt would be treated as debt provided that (1) a fixed rate of return is stipulated; (2) the rate of return is comparable to that on debt of issuers with comparable credit ratings; (3) interest is not contingent on profits of the issuer or dividend payments and is not cumulative; (4) the instrument does not participate in losses and is not convertible into equity at an amount less than the loan advance; and (5) the instrument takes the legal form of indebtedness. See also Sheppard, "Things That Go Bump in the Portfolio," supra note 94, at 1426-27, who suggests that long-term and perpetual debt can be classified as debt for tax purposes based on the limited volatility of the promised cash flows rather than a focus on the term to maturity (or lack of it).

314 Supra note 291. IRC section 385(b) sets out the following five factors that any regulations may include: (1) whether there is a written unconditional promise to pay on demand or on a specified date a sum certain in money in return for adequate consideration in money or money's worth; (2) whether there is subordination to or preference over any indebtedness of the issuer; (3) the ratio of debt to equity of the issuer; (4) whether there is convertibility into shares of the issuer; and (5) the relationship between holdings of shares of the issuer and the instrument in question.

315 Ibid.

316 Hariton, supra note 13.

317 See the text that accompanies notes 183-212 supra.

318 In this respect, it is unclear whether the dual-bifurcation approach suggested by Wood, supra note 278 (and described supra note 289) is more effective than a traditional factors approach, since his second bifurcation ultimately depends on a quantitative assessment of those factors. By drawing a moving boundary, the traditional approach may achieve much the same effect as a dual bifurcation in the sense that sharp discontinuities in tax treatment are avoided. Administrative and compliance costs may even be lower because of the relative familiarity of the traditional factors approach.

319 See David A. Weisbach, "Line Drawing, Doctrine, and Efficiency in the Tax Law" (September 1999), 84 *Cornell Law Review* 1627-81, at 1637-39. See also Emmerich, supra note 299, who argues that any attempt at classification should be assessed in terms of three criteria: (1) recognition of the functional similarity of debt and equity, (2) effectiveness in addressing tax planning centred on the different tax treatment accorded interest and dividends, and (3) ease of application; Hariton, "The Taxation of Complex Financial Instruments," supra note 158, at 775; Haskins, supra note 281; Paul Robertson and Daryl V. Burckel, "When Is Debt Synonymous with Equity? Recent Developments in the Classification of Hybrid Securities" (October 1988), 66 *Taxes: The Tax Magazine* 784-90; and Santangelo, supra note 301. The lack of any principled basis for a definition of the boundary between debt and equity is acknowledged in *Issues Paper*, supra note 19, at 75: "In financial terms there is sometimes little or no principled distinction between debt and equity."

320 Some commentators have suggested refinements of the various factors to reflect more accurately market practices and valuation techniques. See, for example, Santangelo, supra note 301, at 315-23, who suggests the use of the "weighted average time until cash flow payment" as a more accurate measure of the term of

an instrument. Refinements of the factors that are assumed to be indicative of a classification as debt or equity ultimately fail to realize an approach that is principled. The classification of an instrument as debt or equity is an assessment of the relative level of risk, with no obvious defining factor or threshold. See David P. Hariton, "Distinguishing Between Equity and Debt in the New Financial Environment" (Spring 1994), 49 *Tax Law Review* 499-524, at 521: "What debt versus equity analysis really seeks to determine is whether a given class of investors participates in the profits and risks of the corporate enterprise as compared to other classes of investors in the same enterprise."

321 Gergen, supra note 5, at 836-40.

322 See the text that accompanies note 295 in chapter 3; and Gergen, supra note 5, at 839.

323 Mark Wolfson, "Effect of Ownership and Control on Tax and Financial Reporting Income" (1993), vol. 22, no. 3 *Economic Notes* 318-22. The reduction in reported earnings for financial-accounting purposes may mean that a corporation is willing to pay taxes on equity returns. This effect is much reduced, however, with closely held corporations, where the common identity of the managers and shareholders minimizes or eliminates any sensitivity to the impact on reported earnings. In that case, the substitutability of debt, equity, and hybrids for tax purposes is largely unaffected by the impact on reported earnings. Even in the case of public corporations, this impact is reduced if a hybrid instrument is classified as equity for financial-accounting purposes. See Johnson, supra note 275, who argues that corporate management and the accounting profession can always find alternatives to reported earnings as a means to communicate information about share value.

324 An ideal instrument is one that is classified as equity for regulatory and financial reporting purposes but debt for income tax purposes. An example of this type of hybrid is "monthly income preferred securities" (MIPs), a number of which have been issued by US corporations. The instruments generally have favourable credit rating and balance-sheet treatment and are arguably indebtedness for US income tax purposes. A typical MIP structure involves the establishment of a special-purpose entity by a US corporation ("the borrower"). Investors subscribe for preferred interests in the special-purpose entity, with promised monthly distributions of income (the MIPs). The special-purpose entity lends the invested funds to the borrower on arm's-length terms. The loan is usually issued for a 30-year term and is subordinated. Interest is payable semi-annually and must be distributed by the special-purpose entity to the holders of the MIPs. The borrower has the right to defer interest payments for a maximum period of 5 years, during which dividends cannot be paid on its shares. In the event of default, the holders of the MIPs have the right to take control of the loan, accelerate repayment of the principal, and enforce their rights as creditors. The special-purpose entity has the right to renew the borrowing for an additional 20 years on satisfaction of certain conditions. After 50 years, the loan proceeds must be distributed to the holders of the MIPs; alternatively, in some cases, the holders are entitled to repayment through the issue of a fixed amount of shares of the borrower. Various MIP structures and their US income tax treatment are described in Akselrad and Bernstein, supra note 94, at 287-88; Hariton, supra note 320, at 517-21; John Reid, "MIPs Besieged: Solutions in Search of a Problem" (December 1, 1997), 76 *Tax Notes* 1057-68; and Lee A. Sheppard, "Toward Straightforward Section 385 Guidance" (November 7, 1994),

65 *Tax Notes* 664-70. See also Douglas A. Canon, "Income Trusts: The Interest (Deduction) Continues—A Review of Westshore Terminals Income Fund and Superior Propane Income Fund," in the 1997 Corporate Management Tax Conference, supra note 95, 4:1-28, at 4:8-10, who discusses the debt or equity classification of MIP-type instruments issued as part of certain income trust structures.

Trust preferred stock (TRUPS) and preferred redeemable increased dividend equity securities (PRIDES) are the latest version of MIPs. TRUPS and PRIDES consist of a preferred security similar to those under the typical MIP structure. They differ, however, in the provision to holders of a purchase contract with respect to perpetual preferred shares of the issuer. The purchase contract requires the holder to accept the shares of the issuer in lieu of repayment of the principal amount in cash. Under certain conditions, the issuer can accelerate this purchase contract before maturity of the preferred securities, while the holder has the right to settle the contract in cash or separate the preferred security from the purchase contract by posting collateral. As with DECs (described supra note 94), the cash flows associated with TRUPS and PRIDES are equivalent to a prepaid forward contract on the perpetual preferred shares of the issuer. Issuers have attempted to achieve a classification of TRUPS and PRIDES as equity for regulatory purposes (tier 1 bank capital) and debt for US income tax purposes.

MIPs were the subject of Notice 94-47, supra note 309. The US Treasury department considered the MIPs to be equity primarily on the basis of their subordination, the length of the relevant terms, and the repayment in a fixed amount of shares of the borrower. But see IRS Technical Advice Memorandum (TAM) 199910046, November 16, 1998; and Lee A. Sheppard, "Giving and Taking on Corporate Tax Shelters" (March 29, 1999), 82 *Tax Notes* 1894-97, at 1896-97. It is arguable that TRUPS and PRIDES are equity on the basis of the contingent nature of the principal amount and/or the ability of the issuers to require holders to accept repayment in the form of perpetual preferred shares of the issuers. Classification as debt is supported by a bifurcation of the hybrids into fixed-payment debt and a non-prepaid forward contract on the relevant shares. This bifurcation is supported further by the separation of the purchase contract, which can be settled in cash by a holder. See Sheppard, "Sand Castles of Debt Classification," supra note 94; and Sheppard, "Debt Versus Equity: A Package Deal," supra note 224. See also Santangelo, supra note 301, at 325-26, who supports a debt classification of EPICS (described supra footnote 94) on the basis that these hybrids are a combination of a self-amortizing, fixed-payment debt instrument and a call option on shares of the issuer with a limited upside.

325 See, for example, Glenn L.E. May, "Further Reflections on Derivative Taxation" (1999), vol. 47, no. 3 *Canadian Tax Journal* 534-43, at 543, footnote 41, who suggests that cross-border arbitrage of the distinction between debt and equity is where the "real action" is found.

326 The results of inconsistent classification are not one-sided in favour of taxpayers. Double taxation may arise where a source country classifies an instrument as equity and the country of residence of the holder classifies the same instrument as debt. In that instance, the source country imposes corporate income tax on the relevant cash flows as if they were equity distributions, while the residence country denies the relief otherwise available for source-country taxes on such distributions. See May, ibid.

327 See Philip R. West, "Foreign Tax Law in U.S. International Taxation: The Search for Standards" (1996), vol. 3, no. 4 *Florida Tax Review* 147-85, at 182-84.

328 West, ibid., argues that foreign law should be relevant where it is used in "a factual sense" to determine whether a standard under US (domestic) law is satisfied.

329 The approach to the classification of apparent debt does not have to be a quantitative bright-line test. For example, a qualitative bright line was applied under the proposed Treasury regulations in the classification of straight-debt instruments as disguised equity. The proposals required an assessment of a taxpayer's relative holdings of debt and equity of a particular issuer. Instruments that were debt under a factors approach could be reclassified as equity only if the instruments were held in rough proportion to any equity holdings of the particular taxpayer. In effect, proportional holdings created a presumption that a shareholder would treat apparent debt as an extension of the equity stake in the issuer. Although it constituted a necessary threshold, a finding of proportional holdings did not lead to the classification of apparent debt as equity. The presumption had to be supported by one of eight other factors: (1) inadequate capitalization of the issuer; (2) the lack of a reasonable interest rate or original issue discount; (3) demand obligations that did not provide a reasonable interest rate; (4) issue of an obligation for an amount not equal to its fair market value; (5) failure by the issuer to make interest payments when due and a failure by the lender to pursue its rights with the ordinary diligence of independent creditors; (6) failure by the issuer to make capital repayments within 90 days of the due dates, and a failure by the lender to pursue its remedies with the ordinary diligence of independent creditors; (7) failure to make interest payments on demand instruments; and (8) agreement to a substantive alteration of the debt obligations, in which case the obligations were treated as newly issued. These factors appeared to be designed to ensure the existence of arm's-length terms or arm's-length enforcement of any payment obligations.

330 See Mark P. Gergen and Paula Schmitz, "The Influence of Tax Law on Securities Innovation in the United States: 1981-1997" (Winter 1997), 52 *Tax Law Review* 119-97; Sheppard, "Debt Versus Equity: A Package Deal," supra note 224; and Sheppard, "Things That Go Bump in the Portfolio," supra note 94. For an attempt to rationalize a factors approach, see Hariton, supra note 320, at 522: "The real question, then, is not how many debt characteristics does the instrument possess, but rather to what extent does the instrument insulate the investor from the risks and rewards of the issuer's business." Hariton suggests the following questions as organizing principles for a factors approach intended to determine the relative risks borne by holders of securities of the same issuer: (1) How much equity capital supports the investor's rights? (2) How much debt capital is senior to it? (3) To what extent will the investor participate in the issuer's profits? and (4) What rights, if any, will the equity still have if the lender loses money?

331 See, for example, Edward D. Kleinbard, "Lee Sheppard's Misguided Attack on MIPs," *Tax Notes Today*, June 8, 1998, 98 TNT 109-88 (electronic database): "Investors and prospective issuers alike deserve some clarity about the taxation of [MIPs], so that investment decisions are made without the costly miasma of tax uncertainty," as cited by Miller, supra note 225, at 267, footnote 106; and *A Tax System Redesigned*, supra note 19, at 446-47: "The proposed approach minimises uncertainty at the border between debt and equity by focusing on a single determinative factor . . . more importance is attached to the provision of certainty

than on precisely where the distinction between membership interests (equity) and non-membership interests (debt) is drawn."

332 See, for example, John D. Finnerty, "An Overview of Corporate Securities Innovation" (Winter 1992), *The Continental Bank Journal of Corporate Finance* 23-39; John D. Finnerty, "Financial Innovation: An Overview" (Winter 1988), 17 *Financial Management* 14-33; and Gergen and Schmitz, supra note 330.

333 See the text that accompanies notes 162-183 in chapter 3.

334 See Weisbach, supra note 319, who argues that tax-law boundaries, including the distinction between debt and equity, should be drawn on the basis of efficiency considerations.

335 But see Gergen and Schmitz, supra note 330, who suggest that an uncertain factors approach is desirable as a constraint on tax-driven innovation along the boundary between debt and equity. For a review of some of the literature on the causes, benefits, and costs of financial innovation generally, see the text that accompanies notes 108-195 in chapter 1. None of that literature focuses on the more specific issue of the relative significance of tax-driven versus genuine innovation along the boundary between debt and equity. Weisbach, supra note 319, at 1669-63 and 1673-75, describes a general theoretical framework for drawing the boundary between debt and equity. His framework is derived from the insights of optimal tax theory and the efficiency implications of any particular boundary. In the context of the debt-equity distinction, Weisbach argues that efficiency considerations lead to the following proposition: that any particular instrument should be taxed like its closest substitute, although considerations of substitutability and deadweight losses suggest that a debt classification should generally be preferred under a classical corporate tax regime.

336 One possibility is the dual-bifurcation approach suggested by Wood, supra note 278. A factors approach provides policy makers with the flexibility to move the boundary between debt and equity on the basis of an assessment of the efficiency effects associated with the classification of a particular instrument. See Weisbach, supra note 319, at 1673-74, who argues that efficiency considerations may suggest that MIPs should be taxed as debt, although policy makers require empirical studies to determine the net effects that depend on (1) whether MIPs substitute for equity or debt, and (2) whether issuers can find alternative instruments to substitute debt for equity.

Notes to Chapter 7

1 David A. Weisbach, "Tax Responses to Financial Contract Innovation" (Summer 1995), 50 *Tax Law Review* 491-544. See also Australia, *Taxation of Financial Arrangements: An Issues Paper* (Canberra: Australian Government Publishing Service, December 1996), chapter 15, at 230.

2 The term should not be confused with its more common usage as a label for various approaches designed to integrate the corporate and shareholder-level taxes on distributed corporate income. See Edward D. Kleinbard, "Equity Derivative Instruments: Financial Innovation's Newest Challenge to the Tax System" (December 1991), 69 *Texas Law Review* 1319-68, at 1365, footnote 135.

3 Weisbach, supra note 1, at 502-7 and 526-38. See also Randall K.C. Kau, "Carving Up Assets and Liabilities—Integration or Bifurcation of Financial Products" (December 1990), 68 *Taxes: The Tax Magazine* 1003-14; Kleinbard, supra note 2; and Edward D. Kleinbard, "Beyond Good and Evil Debt (and Debt Hedges): A Cost of Capital Allowance System" (December 1989), 67 *Taxes: The Tax Magazine* 943-61.

4 Weisbach, supra note 1, at 527, refers to this approach as "full integration," which he distinguishes from "partial integration." The distinction is described in the text that accompanies notes 49-53 infra.

5 Ibid., at 527-28. Weisbach describes hedge accounting as a particular type of "partial integration." For a description of Weisbach's definition of the term, see the text that accompanies notes 187-217 infra.

6 See, for example, Mark P. Gergen, "Apocalypse Not?" (Summer 1995), 50 *Tax Law Review* 833-59, at 845-55.

7 For a brief discussion of this issue compared with the identification issue involved with the application of bifurcation, see the text that accompanies notes 32-49 in chapter 4. The issue is discussed at greater length in the text that accompanies notes 66-67 and 95-110 infra.

8 See, generally, *Issues Paper*, supra note 1, at 232-36.

9 But see *Whittles (HMIT) v. Uniholdings Ltd. (No. 3)*, [1995] BTC 119 (Ch. D); and *The Queen v. Shell Canada Limited*, 98 DTC 6177; [1998] 2 CTC 207 (FCA), where foreign currency borrowings were integrated with related hedging transactions and were effectively treated as synthetic domestic currency borrowings. Both decisions were overturned on appeal and integrated treatment was rejected as the basis for taxation as a synthetic. See [1996] BTC 399 (CA); and 99 DTC 5669; [1999] 4 CTC 313 (SCC). Integration as a tax technique should be distinguished from the closely related but different judicial doctrine of "step transaction." Under the latter, steps in a composite transaction may be ignored and the tax consequences applied to the remaining transactions. In the result, however, those transactions are taxed separately and the tax treatment of the composite is equal to the sum of the treatments for the remaining parts. Integration combines various financial instruments and simply ignores the tax treatment that would otherwise apply to the instruments separately. The combination of instruments is taxed in the same manner as the single instrument that it replicates, which means that the tax treatment of the various component parts is altered and is not necessarily equal to the sum of the treatments applied to the individual parts. See Kleinbard, supra note 2, at 1357-61; and Weisbach, supra note 1, at 526-27, who distinguishes full and partial integration.

10 An investor is "long in an asset" if he owns the asset or has the right or obligation to purchase it. The investor benefits if the asset appreciates in value and loses if the asset depreciates in value. Conversely, an investor is "short in an asset" if he has sold the asset or has the right or obligation to sell in the future. The investor benefits if the asset depreciates in value and loses if the asset appreciates in value.

11 In other instances, payments that take the form of interest are treated as tax-deductible expected losses even though they are equivalent to non-deductible repayments of principal. See notes 103 and 106 in chapter 5 regarding the treatment of "long-term prepaid debt" and the text that accompanies notes 136-162

regarding the treatment of "weak-currency borrowings" under a comprehensive accrual regime.

12 See Edward D. Kleinbard, "Risky and Riskless Positions in Securities" (December 1993), 71 *Taxes: The Tax Magazine* 783-99, at 786-87, who notes that the fungibility of publicly traded securities means that there can be many long and short positions but only one owner.

13 These arbitrage pricing relationships are described in the text that accompanies notes 58-107 in chapter 1.

14 *Issues Paper*, supra note 1, at 229; and Richard Wood, "Taxation of Financial Arrangements—Arbitrage Opportunities and Policy Design," in Tony Rumble, ed., *Derivative Tax Reform* (Sydney: Prospect Media, 1997), 53-61. One of the more notable examples of this proposition is provided by a US tax practitioner who lists 13 different ways to raise borrowed funds at a fixed interest rate for a specified term, all with different income tax consequences. See Kau, supra note 3, at 1004-5. Almost all of his examples are simple and more sophisticated applications of put-call parity whereby the cash flows associated with a synthetic position are equivalent to a borrowing at a fixed interest rate for a specified term; yet they are generally taxed only on realization and possibly as capital amounts, in contrast with the accrual recognition of interest in full as a current expense of the borrower and ordinary income of the issuer. In particular, Kau lists the following examples of transactions that replicate the cash flows under a loan at a fixed US$ rate (assuming that market conditions permit the replication): (1) the purchase of US$ fixed-rate debt; (2) the purchase of US$ floating-rate debt and a swap into fixed-rate debt; (3) a reverse repurchase agreement on US Treasury securities; (4) a short sale of securities, a forward purchase contract, and a term investment of the proceeds from the short sale; (5) a forward conversion transaction involving the purchase of shares, the issue of a non-exchange-traded call, and the purchase of a non-exchange-traded put at the same exercise price; (6) the same forward conversion transaction as in (5) using exchange-traded options other than foreign currency options; (7) the same forward conversion transaction as in (5) using commodities and a short position in regulated futures contracts; (8) the same forward conversion transaction as in (5) where the underlying property is foreign currency; (9) an option box conversion, similar to (4), but in which all positions consist of options, either exchange-traded or not; (10) the purchase of foreign-currency-denominated debt and simultaneous entry into a currency swap; (11) the purchase of foreign-currency-denominated debt and simultaneous entry into a regulated futures contract on the foreign currency; (12) the purchase of foreign-currency-denominated debt, the issue of a call on foreign currency, and the purchase of a put on the currency; and (13) the purchase of a commodity-indexed debt and simultaneous entry into a forward contract on underlying currency. Kau claims to have stopped at 13 only because of an irrational affinity for that number.

15 See note 222 in chapter 6, which defines this term as any "financing technique in which financial assets . . . are pooled and converted into capital market instruments." Lewis R. Steinberg, "Selected Issues in the Taxation of Swaps, Structured Finance and Other Financial Products" (1993), vol. 1, no. 5 *Florida Tax Review* 263-306, at 264, footnote 5.

16 See the text that accompanies notes 66-68 in chapter 1. A common version of this transaction is the issue of debt exchangeable into shares of another corporation

held by the issuer. See note 94 in chapter 6. As chapter 6 argued, interest should be imputed on these instruments either as prepaid forward contracts or the combination of fixed-payment debt and an embedded on-market forward written on the underlying shares. Unexpected gain or loss should be recognized on realization (that is, the physical or cash settlement of the exchange feature). Exchangeable debt and other variations of the forward sale in example 1 raise the additional issue whether the acquisition of an offsetting short position constitutes a disposition of the open long position in the particular asset with accrued gain. See the text that accompanies notes 29-44 and 97-146 infra.

17 See, for example, *CIR v. Dewavrin Segard (NZ) Ltd.* (1994), 18 TRNZ 509 (CA), which held that the acquisition of a short position in wool futures contracts to cover a long wool position of the taxpayer was not a purchase and sale agreement with an interest element.

18 See, for example, the description of the representative legislation in Canada and Australia in the text that accompanies notes 15-19 in chapter 2.

19 Kleinbard, supra note 12, at 785-86.

20 Bradford L. Ferguson, "The Rationales for the Rules: How To Think About Derivatives in the Tax World" (December 1994), 72 *Taxes: The Tax Magazine* 995-1026, at 1019.

21 The character and source of the swap payments is uncertain. Because there are no borrowed funds between the counterparties, the swap payments cannot be considered interest within traditional legal concepts. Moreover, without ownership of the shares, the equity payee cannot be considered to receive dividends from the equity payer. See Timothy R. Hughes, "Income Tax Implications of Non-Dispositive Transfers of Equity Securities" (Winter 1999), 57 *University of Toronto Law Review* 43-81, at 77-81; Edward D. Kleinbard and Erika W. Nijenhuis, "Short Sales and Short Sale Principles in Contemporary Application," in New York University, *Proceedings of the Fifty-Third Institute on Federal Taxation* (New York: Matthew Bender, 1995), chapter 17; and Kleinbard, supra note 2, at 1330-48, who discusses the application of traditional concepts under US tax law to equity-index swaps. But see Stephen F. Cappelli and Robert A. Santangelo, "Thinking About the Corporate Tax Base: Certain Capital Market Transactions" (Fall 1996), 50 *The Tax Lawyer* 65-71, at 68-69, who note that the deduction of dividend-equivalent payments by an equity payer under an equity swap allows a corporate issuer to create tax-deductible dividend payments by assuming a short position in its own shares and securing the obligations of the equity receiver with a long position in US treasury securities.

22 See, generally, Reuven S. Avi-Yonah, "Virtual Taxation: Source-Based Taxation in the Age of Derivatives," in *Proceedings of the Eighty-Ninth Annual Conference on Taxation* (Washington, DC: National Tax Association and Tax Institute of America, 1997), 269-74; David G. Broadhurst, "Derivatives in International Tax Planning," in International Fiscal Association—Canadian Branch, *1997 International Tax Seminar* (Scarborough, Ont.: Carswell, 1998), 85-101, at 99-101; Gregory May, "Flying on Instruments: Synthetic Investment and the Avoidance of Withholding Tax" (November 11, 1996), 13 *Tax Notes International* 1625-35; and Myron S. Scholes and Mark A. Wolfson, *Taxes and Business Strategy: A Planning Approach* (Englewood Cliffs, NJ: Prentice-Hall, 1992), 415-25.

23 See the text that accompanies notes 246-249 in chapter 3.

24 See the text that accompanies note 248 in chapter 3.

25 For a series of more complex examples that build on the basic concepts described in the text, see May, supra note 22; and Scholes and Wolfson, supra note 22.

26 Erica's exposure is not identical to an acquisition in the spot market. If Publico pays dividends in excess of the expected amount, Erica will not realize the benefit of that unexpected excess. See Avi-Yonah, supra note 22, at 271. If, however, the amount of dividends is less than the expected amount, she may bear the unexpected loss to the extent that the shortfall is a loss at the corporate level and not just a function of a decision to retain earnings for reinvestment. This shortfall should be reflected in the spot price on maturity of the forward contract, resulting in an unexpected loss for Erica.

27 Restrictive exemptions for portfolio debt make this synthetic investment ineffective. For example, Income Tax Act, RSC 1985, c. 1 (5th Supp.), as amended (herein referred to as "the ITA"), subparagraph 212(1)(b)(vii) requires a minimum term of five years before arm's-length debt can qualify for exemption. As a result, Erica would have to acquire a five-year bond of Publico and a five-year forward or a series of one-year forwards. The former may be unavailable and the latter may not provide the desired exposure. In particular, changes in discount rates and the amount of expected dividends on the Publico shares may mean that the new long positions in the forward contracts do not match the interest rate on the long position in the bonds. Indeed, the bond will be issued at a five-year rate and the series of forwards rolled over at one-year rates. A broad exemption for portfolio debt allows the indefinite avoidance of withholding tax. For instance, Erica could close out her synthetic investment at the end of each year and enter into a new one for as long as she pleases. See Avi-Yonah, supra note 22, at 271.

28 The standard sourcing rule in the OECD model tax treaty ensures non-taxability of share gains by the source country. See Organisation for Economic Co-operation and Development, *Model Tax Convention on Income and on Capital* (Paris: OECD) (looseleaf), article 13.

29 For a description of the representative legislation in Canada and Australia, see the text that accompanies notes 22-24 in chapter 2.

30 See, for example, the definition of a "disposition" in ITA section 54 and the new definition of a "disposition" proposed for ITA subsection 248(1) in Canada, Department of Finance, Notice of Ways and Means Motion To Amend the Income Tax Act, June 5, 2000. The definition includes any transaction that gives rise to "proceeds of disposition," which is defined in paragraph (a) to include a sale or any transaction that entitles a taxpayer to proceeds.

31 Paragraphs (b)-(f) of the definition of "proceeds of disposition" in ITA section 54.

32 Paragraph (d) of the definition of a "disposition" in ITA section 54; and paragraph (j) of the proposed definition of a "disposition" in ITA subsection 248(1).

33 See the text that accompanies notes 103-129 in chapter 2.

34 See, for example, *Interpretation Bulletin* IT-448, "Dispositions—Changes in Terms of Securities," June 6, 1980. For a critique of the position of Revenue Canada (now the Canada Customs and Revenue Agency or CCRA) and the case for a reliance on legal form, see Brian J. Arnold and David A. Ward, "Dispositions—A

Critique of Revenue Canada's Interpretation" (1980), vol. 28, no. 5 *Canadian Tax Journal* 559-84.

35 A similar issue arises with share value shifts and, in particular, whether the effective transfer of value that occurs when new shareholders are allowed to subscribe for shares at a bargain price should constitute a transfer by existing shareholders even though there is no transfer as a matter of legal form. For a discussion of the different approaches to this issue in Australia, Canada, and the United Kingdom, see Gordon Longhouse, "Policy, Pragmatism and Doctrine in the Taxation of Share Value Shifts" (March 1998), 27 *Australian Tax Review* 4-13. Australia and the United Kingdom have specific legislation that addresses transactions like these; Canada does not. The case law is not entirely clear on the disposition issue. See, for example, *The Queen v. Kieboom*, 92 DTC 6382; [1992] 2 CTC 59 (FCA), in which there was no disposition without a transfer but there was possible taxation as a benefit conferred on the new shareholder; and *FCT v. Peabody*, 94 ATC 4663; (1994), 28 ATR 344 (HC).

36 See Alan L. Feld, "When Fungible Portfolio Assets Meet: A Problem of Tax Recognition" (Winter 1991), 44 *The Tax Lawyer* 409-43.

37 These transactions and the term used to describe them are largely unique to the United States for the reasons described in the text that accompanies notes 38-43 infra. The "box" refers to the safety deposit box in which the taxpayer holds his shares that are sold short. See Kleinbard, supra note 12, at 788-92. Kleinbard (ibid., at 790) refers to a short sale against the box as "a pure creature of tax law" that is implemented solely for tax purposes and, in particular, realization of the benefit of deferral.

38 A short sale against the box differs from a conventional short sale by virtue of the seller's offsetting short and long positions in the appreciated shares. Under both a conventional short sale and a short sale against the box, there are two principal tax issues sometimes addressed in specific legislation. The first concerns whether the legal transfer by the lender gives rise to a realization event, even though the lender retains all risk because of its long position under the loan. The second issue concerns the character of dividend compensation payments made by the short seller under the securities loan. Specific legislation governing securities lending arrangements generally provides that the transfer of borrowed securities between arm's-length parties to a securities lending arrangement is not a disposition. Dividend compensation payments are generally deemed to be dividends received by the securities lender from the borrower, who is denied an offsetting deduction. Both rules recognize the risky position maintained by securities lenders, who are treated as if they still owned the loaned securities. Non-deductibility of dividend compensation payments for the short seller prevents tax-arbitrage opportunities that would arise if the short seller held identical shares and could also claim a dividends-received deduction. See ITA section 260; Internal Revenue Code of 1986, as amended (herein referred to as "IRC"), section 1058; and IRC section 246(c)(1), which denies the offsetting dividends-received deduction for a short seller who makes dividend compensation payments. A short sale against the box raises the additional issue whether the short seller should be considered to dispose of its long position in appreciated shares.

39 For an excellent review of the formalistic US rules that give rise to the short sale against the box as a tax-avoidance technique, see Peter L. Faber, Andrea S. Kramer,

and William R. Pomierski, "The Ownership and Disposition of Property: New Rules for Old Problems" (December 1997), 75 *Taxes: The Tax Magazine* 768-87; Kleinbard, supra note 12, at 788-92; and Kleinbard and Nijenhuis, supra note 21.

40 Feld, supra note 36, at 441-43.

41 See, for example, ITA section 47. But see also *Income Tax Technical News*, no. 19, June 16, 2000, which provides a last-in, first-out exception for certain shares acquired on the exercise of an employee stock option subject to ITA section 7.

42 Hughes, supra note 21, at 63-66. Section 9511 of the Revenue Reconciliation Bill of 1996 (the revenue title of President Clinton's 1997 balanced budget proposal, released on March 19, 1996) proposed an average cost base rule for identical securities that would eliminate the ability to identify the particular securities sold. In the absence of an identification, a first-in, first-out rule has been applied under IRC reg. sections 1.1012-1(c)(2)-(7). See Kleinbard, supra note 12, at 787-88; and Lee A. Sheppard, "Borrowing All the Way to a Constructive Sale" (August 9, 1999), 84 *Tax Notes* 816-20, at 817, who argues that constructive sale strategies in the United States could be addressed by the adoption of an averaging rule to determine the cost base of identical financial instruments.

43 See, for example, Revenue Canada document no. 9244305, June 10, 1993, where Revenue Canada states: "In normal situations, where the short seller continues to have a financial obligation to bear the cost of replacing the borrowed shares, realization of income is considered to occur at the time the short position is closed and the obligation has been met, thus, permitting the calculation of the amount of the income from the completed transaction."

The closing words of the definition of a "securities lending arrangement" in ITA subsection 260(1) exclude any arrangement one of the main purposes of which may reasonably be considered to be the avoidance or deferral of the inclusion in income of any gain or profit with respect to the loaned security. This wording may mean that the securities lending provisions would not apply to a short against the box by a Canadian taxpayer, with the result that a securities loan could result in a disposition for the lender. Hughes, supra note 21, at 60-63.

44 In a popular variation of this constructive sale strategy, corporate executives have used equity swaps as a low-cost means of monetizing an appreciated long position in call options written on shares of their employers ("employee stock options"). In terms of its fundamentals, the strategy involves nothing more than the substitution of the stock option for Doris's long position in shares in example 2. By swapping the return on the underlying shares for a fixed return or a return based on a share index, Doris can monetize (without attracting a realization event) the appreciation in value of her long position in the stock options, which is derived from appreciation in the underlying shares. The associated cash flows are equivalent to a sale of the options and an investment of the proceeds in debt or a diversified equity portfolio. See Steven A. Bank, "Devaluing Reform: The Derivatives Market and Executive Compensation" (Spring/Summer 1995), 7 *DePaul Business Law Journal* 301-32; Lee A. Sheppard, "Equity Swaps as an Executive Tax Shelter" (October 17, 1994), 65 *Tax Notes* 266-71; and Dennis F. Sykora, "The Income Tax Web Surrounding Derivatives," in *Report of Proceedings of the Forty-Seventh Tax Conference*, 1995 Conference Report (Toronto: Canadian Tax Foundation, 1996), 30:1-41, at 30:38-40. More complex variations of the same strategy involve forward sales of employee stock options and the use of compound options (that

is, the issue of an option written on another option), including the creation of a married put and call on an employee stock option. See Bank, supra, at 323.

45 For a description of the representative experiences in Canada and Australia, see chapter 2.

46 Ferguson, supra note 20, at 1013. See the text that accompanies notes 98-114 in chapter 3; and the text that accompanies notes 328-335 in chapter 5 regarding the tax-policy problems presented by straddle transactions generally and the appropriate response under a comprehensive accrual regime.

47 See Ferguson, supra note 20, at 1013, who argues that the concept of a straddle transaction underlies many of the specific legislative responses to synthetics in the United States.

48 Some of these responses are discussed in the text that accompanies notes 112-159 infra.

49 Weisbach, supra note 1, at 526-28.

50 Ibid., at 528.

51 See also *Issues Paper*, supra note 1, at 236, which notes the asymmetry in tax treatment of counterparties to positions that comprise a synthetic subject to anti-avoidance proposals.

52 For a discussion of the treatment of foreign currency debt under a comprehensive accrual regime and the more limited approach under the US legislation, see the text that accompanies notes 136-162 in chapter 5.

53 IRC reg. section 1.1275-6. For a discussion of the US regulations governing contingent-debt instruments, see the text that accompanies notes 137-151 in chapter 6.

54 Neil Brooks, "The Responsibility of Judges in Interpreting Tax Legislation," in Graeme S. Cooper, ed., *Tax Avoidance and the Rule of Law* (Amsterdam: IBFD Publications, 1997), 93-129, at 94-95. This general point is emphasized in a comment on the decision of the Australian High Court in *FC of T v. Spotless Services Limited & Anor*, 96 ATC 5201 (Full HC), which considered the application of the general anti-avoidance rule in part IVA of the Australian Income Tax Assessment Act, 1936 (herein referred to as "ITAA"). See Richard Krever, "The Ghost of the Duke of Westminster Laid to Rest in Australia?" Current Cases feature (1997), vol. 45, no. 1 *Canadian Tax Journal* 122-30. See also Australia, Review of Business Taxation, *A Tax System Redesigned: More Certain, Equitable and Durable* (Canberra: Australian Government Publishing Service, July 1999), 242-45, which emphasizes the need for structural reform as the preferred response to tax-avoidance transactions.

55 See the text that accompanies notes 247-258 in chapter 6.

56 See the text that accompanies notes 278-281 in chapter 3.

57 See the text that accompanies notes 259-279 in chapter 6.

58 See the text that accompanies notes 280-314 in chapter 5.

59 See the text that accompanies notes 76-83 in chapter 5.

60 See the text that accompanies notes 222-231 in chapter 6.

61 See the text that accompanies notes 136-162 in chapter 5.

62 Those synthetics are foreign currency borrowings and loans hedged with forward currency contracts.

63 See the text that accompanies notes 136-162 in chapter 5.

64 *Issues Paper*, supra note 1, at chapter 15.

65 Ibid., 232-36.

66 In fact, Halle has created a synthetic contingent-debt instrument, with contingent payments attributable to her risk exposure within the range defined by the different exercise prices under the collar. See Gergen, supra note 6, at 846, footnote 49; and Weisbach, supra note 1, at 531-32.

67 *Issues Paper*, supra note 1, at 231.

68 See, for example, David P. Hariton, "The Tax Treatment of Hedged Positions in Stock: What Hath Technical Analysis Wrought?" (Summer 1995), 50 *Tax Law Review* 803-27.

69 See the text that accompanies notes 76-88 in chapter 4.

70 See, for example, Louis Kaplow, "Rules Versus Standards: An Economic Analysis" (December 1992), 42 *Duke Law Journal* 557-629, who argues that the content of the law remains the same, with the important policy choice centred on matters of process: that is, whether to use detailed legislative rules that determine legal results ex ante or to use general standards that require a determination of the details of the law after actions are taken. Kaplow's general point, in the context of the New Zealand accrual regime, is emphasized by John Prebble, "Should Tax Law Be Written from a Principles and Purpose Point of View or a Precise and Detailed Point of View?" [1998], no. 2 *British Tax Review* 112-23, at 119-20. As described in chapter 5 and noted by Prebble, the accrual legislation is relatively simple in expression and brief. The basic principle is the accrual recognition of expected gain or loss on financial arrangements through the application of the yield-to-maturity (YTM) recognition method. This general expression avoids much of the inevitable detail involved in determining the boundaries of the concept of a financial arrangement subject to accrual treatment and the application of the YTM method to the cash flows associated with particular instruments. The resolution of these matters is not avoided, however, through the general expression of principles in the legislation and must be worked out either in specific regulations or through administrative practice and the decisions of the courts. In other words, the use of detailed legislation or general principles is a debate over matters of form, which involves a judgment regarding the relative advantages and disadvantages of the apparent certainty and complexity associated with the former approach and the apparent simplicity and uncertainty associated with the latter.

71 John Avery Jones, "Tax Law: Rules or Principles?" (August 1996), 17 *Fiscal Studies* 63-89, at 69-75. But see also Kaplow, supra note 70, who argues that detailed legislative rules are preferable, from an efficiency perspective, to address common transactions that are entered into frequently. The preference is attributable to the fact that the promulgation costs are a one-time expense that is likely to be less than the costs associated with the need to define the application of general standards to a wide range of particular transactions.

72 An obvious example of the unintended effect of detailed legislative responses to synthetics is the Canadian legislation addressing the tax treatment of Canadian optional interest notes (COINs). See notes 103 and 106 in chapter 5. Revenue Canada has taken the position that only the simple interest portion of an OID

obligation can be deducted on an accrual basis. The deduction of compound interest generally is limited under ITA paragraph 20(1)(d) to a cash basis. Accordingly, OID is deductible only on a simple-compound basis rather than a full accrual basis under the YTM method (actuarial method). See, for example, "Revenue Canada Round Table," in *Report of Proceedings of the Fortieth Tax Conference*, 1988 Conference Report (Toronto: Canadian Tax Foundation, 1989), 53:1-188, at 53:15. This approach has made the issue of OID obligations unattractive for taxable issuers. Shortly after the release of the draft legislation limiting the deduction of interest on prepaid debt, tax practitioners recognized that the legislation (ITA subsection 18(9.2)) can be applied to permit effectively the deduction of the simple and compound interest elements of OID using the YTM method. Although this result is apparently unintended as a matter of tax policy, a taxpayer can achieve this result by issuing a debt obligation with a stated rate of interest and then prepaying the interest. See Stephen R. Richardson, "New Financial Instruments: A Canadian Tax Perspective," in *Income Tax and Goods and Services Tax Considerations in Corporate Financing*, 1992 Corporate Management Tax Conference (Toronto: Canadian Tax Foundation, 1993), 10:1-32, at 10:12-27 and 10:31-32. Despite the enactment of subsection 18(9.2), it is understood that Revenue Canada continues to require the deduction of OID using the simple-compound method. Taxpayers who wish to deduct the full amount of OID on an accrual basis must issue an obligation that, in form, has a stated rate of interest, and then prepay the interest. This formalistic approach to the interpretation and application of subsection 18(9.2) may be appealing because it provides a result that is defensible as a matter of policy but that conflicts with other basic provisions of the ITA.

73 For example, there has always been some debate over the application of securities lending legislation, such as that in ITA section 260, to sale-purchase agreements such as securities repurchase arrangements ("repos"). See Kleinbard, supra note 12, at 797-99. Under a repo, the owner of shares or debt exchanges the securities temporarily for cash and agrees to repay that amount plus interest (or a lending premium) for the return of the same or similar securities. Repos are thus a combination of a secured loan and a securities lending transaction, particularly in the case of a "special repo," under which specifically identified securities must be returned and other securities cannot be substituted. Repos are not identical to securities loans, however, either in their purpose or structure. Because the Canadian legislation governing securities lending arrangements does not specifically exclude repos, Revenue Canada has allowed these transactions to be treated as securities loans. Accordingly, repos do not give rise to dispositions of the securities, either because of the application of the securities lending legislation or because they are secured money loans that do not give rise to a disposition associated with the posting of collateral. See Revenue Canada, Internal Memorandum, "An Audit Perspective of Capital Markets Tax Implications," Revenue Canada document no. 902723, April 4, 1991; and Hughes, supra note 21, at 55.

74 See, for example, Avery Jones, supra note 71, at 64-65, who argues that more detail does not necessarily provide certainty, because it is impossible to anticipate all potential circumstances to which legislation must provide an answer.

75 It is not always clear what "general principles" are and how they differ from rules reflected in detailed legislation. The difference appears to be one of degree associated with the specificity of legislation. See the text that accompanies notes

76-88 in chapter 4. Avery Jones, supra note 71, at 75, has attempted to articulate the distinction in the following terms (footnotes omitted):

> Could our tax legislation be rewritten so that it would be construed in accordance with principles rather than containing nothing but rules trying unsuccessfully to cover every eventuality? Ronald Dworkin makes the distinction, which I think we are searching for here, between rules and principles. The distinction is that rules are applicable in an all-or-nothing fashion, whereas principles are not. Principles can have exceptions; can conflict with one another; can, for example, apply only when conduct is reasonable; and they can give guidance about how to deal with the points not expressly covered by the law. Rules do not conflict with each other (if they do, one of them must give and become a subsidiary rule). Principles do not conflict with rules. If a rule is clear, the rule applies and that is the end of it, even though it is an exception to the principle and therefore in conflict with it.

Under the tax cubbyholes, the relevant principles would be accrual versus realization-based recognition, capital gain versus ordinary-income treatment, and taxation as interest or dividends. As was argued in chapters 3 and 4, the problem with these supposed principles is that they require distinctions that are not supported by the underlying economics of various cash flows and, therefore, give rise to avoidance opportunities. It is not entirely clear how such unprincipled principles can be applied in preference to detailed rules that attempt to maintain the necessary distinctions. This point is discussed in the text that accompanies notes 93-109 infra in the specific context of synthetics. The same point is made generally by Prebble, supra note 70.

76 Hariton, supra note 68, at 824, who refers to this reasoning process as a reliance on "logic, parallelism and judgment" rather than technical analysis associated with the application of detailed rules.

77 But see Avery Jones, supra note 71, at 75: "But the real use for the principle is to determine what the rule means in the first place (and hopefully to reduce the amount of detail required in stating the rule)."

78 In the context of the taxation of financial instruments under the existing cubbyholes, this assumption is challenged in chapters 3 and 4, which describe the case for a comprehensive legislative regime intended to implement the principle of expected-return taxation.

79 See chapters 2 and 3 for an examination of the tax cubbyholes and their inconsistency with an ideal benchmark approach to the taxation of financial instruments.

80 Gergen, supra note 6, at 856-57. See also Kaplow, supra note 70.

81 Ibid.

82 See New Zealand, *Taxation (Accrual Rules and Other Remedial Matters) Bill: Commentary on the Bill* (Wellington, NZ: Inland Revenue, Policy Advice Division, November 1998), 11: "A consequence of the broad definition of 'financial arrangement' is that groups of inter-related financial arrangements which may not be financial arrangements on their own may fall within the definition. Inter-related arrangements are those in which there is a degree of interdependency between the transactions. It is appropriate that they be covered by the rules if they have the same effect as debt instruments or debt substitutes."

83 Income Tax Act, 1994 (New Zealand), sections EH 14 and EH 22(1) definitions of a "financial arrangement." The two definitions are relevant for the purposes of two similar, but discrete, sets of accrual rules applicable for different periods. See note 2 in chapter 5.

84 Ibid., paragraph (a) of the definition of a "financial arrangement" in sections EH 14 and EH 22(1) includes debt instruments. The wide wording of paragraph (b) in either definition includes options and mutual promises, such as forwards, futures, and swaps.

85 Ibid., the definition of an "excepted financial arrangement" in sections EH 14 and EH 24(1) sets out a list of excepted transactions that might otherwise be within the definition of a financial arrangement. Specific exceptions are provided for shares and options on shares (paragraph (d) of the definition in section EH 14 and paragraph (o) of the definition in section EH 22(1)).

86 This legislation is discussed in the text that accompanies notes 111-146 infra.

87 This term is coined by Richard Vann, "Improving Tax Law Improvement: An International Perspective" (1995), vol. 12, no. 2 *Australian Tax Forum* 193-246, at 222.

88 New Zealand Inland Revenue, *Taxation of Financial Arrangements: A Discussion Document on Proposed Changes to the Accrual Rules* (Wellington, NZ: Inland Revenue, Policy Advice Division, December 1997), chapter 5.

89 Income Tax Act, 1994 (New Zealand), section EH 14 definition of "financial arrangement" and section EH 22(3).

90 Ibid., sections EH 2 and EH 23.

91 See *Taxation of Financial Arrangements*, supra note 88, at 25, which observes that the concept of a wider financial arrangement is necessary to address the use of synthetics to avoid the accrual rules, but the exclusion of excepted financial arrangements that are part of a wider arrangement is necessary to preserve the general distinction between the two types of arrangements.

92 Income Tax Act, 1994 (New Zealand), sections EH 2 and EH 23. See *Taxation of Financial Arrangements*, supra note 88, at 26-28, which describes various approaches to the interpretation of the meaning of expense or income solely attributable to an excepted financial arrangement. The discussion document proposes an approach that separates the excepted financial arrangement component of a wider financial arrangement by

> using pricing or valuation rules. We propose that if the terms and conditions (including consideration paid for the excepted financial arrangement) on which the excepted financial arrangement are issued are such that it would stand alone on those terms and conditions, it can properly be said that the return on that excepted financial arrangement is solely attributable to the excepted financial arrangement. However, if those terms are dependent on the issue of the wider financial arrangement, the return cannot be said to be solely attributable to the excepted financial arrangement.

This test would exclude the return on the married put and call, provided that the options were priced in the same manner as they would have been on a stand-alone basis independent of the synthetic. The exclusion appears to hold even though the options provide perfectly offsetting cash flows that result in an expected return that is equivalent to debt when combined with the long position in shares. The basis for integrated treatment does not seem to be the correlation of the offsetting cash flows, but rather their alteration as part of a synthetic as reflected in the pricing of the relevant instruments. In describing the proposed test for determining when an amount can be considered solely attributable to an excepted financial arrangement, the New Zealand discussion document draws an analogy with convertible debt and its bifurcation into a fixed-payment debt and option component by valuing the expected cash flows associated with each component. See *Taxation of Financial Arrangements*, ibid., at 26. Once the convertible debt is bifurcated, gain or loss on the embedded share option is considered an amount solely attributable to an excepted financial arrangement. The analogy does not work, however, where all the positions that comprise a synthetic are excepted financial arrangements (for example, shares covered by a married put and call), and tax administrators are not just trying to isolate the expected return on an excepted financial arrangement that is a component of a synthetic. In fact, the essence of many synthetics is the combination of unexpected gains and losses associated with independent financial instruments to produce a "synthetic" expected return. After consultation with private sector representatives, New Zealand Inland Revenue ultimately rejected the proposal in the discussion document, citing "uncertainties" that it might entail. See supra note 82, at 11.

93 See *Issues Paper*, supra note 1, at 231, which suggests the use of general provisions to address synthetics, with the necessary details being developed in regulations.

94 See, for example, David A. Weisbach, "Formalism in Tax Law" (Summer 1999), 66 *The University of Chicago Law Review* 860-86, who argues that purpose-based anti-avoidance rules are an effective means of suppressing discontinuities that are the focus of tax-driven or "uncommon" transactions.

95 *Issues Paper*, supra note 1, at 229-36.

96 For example, the implementation of structured transactions intended to eliminate risk typically involves positions of substantial value in order to justify the transaction costs and requires the provision of comparable security for the benefit of the accommodation counterparty. See Gergen, supra note 6, at 842; and John Braddock, "Zero Cost Collars" (November 1997), 10 *RISK* 50-51, who observes that an investor, to qualify for a "zero-cost collar," needs $2 million in shares of a public corporation with a price per share of $10 or more.

97 See, for example, Daniel N. Shaviro, "Risk-Based Rules and the Taxation of Capital Income" (Summer 1995), 50 *Tax Law Review* 643-724, who argues that the source of different tax treatments and associated avoidance opportunities is a reliance on perceptions regarding risk and the identification of differences in legal rights and obligations as accurate indicators of changes in risk.

98 See the text that accompanies notes 3-4 and 26-27 in chapter 2 and the text that accompanies notes 247-279 in chapter 6.

99 This point is most obvious with share-hedging strategies and the application of realization-based recognition based on an assessment of risk as the basis for the determination of the point at which a disposition can be said to occur. There is simply no clear normative basis for drawing the boundary between a disposition and the retention of an asset based on the level of risk associated with a particular position. See Deborah L. Paul, "Another Uneasy Compromise: The Treatment of

Hedging in a Realization Income Tax" (1996), vol. 3, no. 1 *Florida Tax Review* 1-50. But see David A. Weisbach, "Line Drawing, Doctrine, and Efficiency in the Tax Law" (September 1999), 84 *Cornell Law Review* 1627-81, at 1655-63 and 1672-73, who argues that the lack of a clear normative basis for the distinction between a realization transaction and non-recognition means that the distinction should be drawn on the basis of efficiency considerations. In particular, a transaction that falls between selling and holding an asset should be taxed in the same manner as its closest substitute, but should not be taxed too severely (that is, treated as a disposition) if there are other substitutes that taxpayers can access with associated efficiency costs.

100 See, for example, Lewis R. Steinberg, "Commentary" (Summer 1995), 50 *Tax Law Review* 725-29, at 725: "all assets, be they financial or real, represent nothing more than an aggregation of more or less risky cash flows, to be priced on an expected value basis and to be parcelled out among participants based on their relative risk tolerances."

101 Shaviro, supra note 97.

102 Prebble, supra note 70. See also John Prebble, "Ectopia, Formalism and Anti-Avoidance Rules in Income Tax Law," in W. Krawietz, N. MacCormick, and G.H. von Wright, eds., *Prescriptive Formality and Normative Rationality in Modern Legal Systems* (Berlin: Duncker and Humblot, 1994), 367-83; and John Prebble, "Why Is Tax Law Incomprehensible?" [1994], no. 4 *British Tax Review* 380-93.

103 See, for example, Calvin H. Johnson, "Taxing the Income from Writing Options" (October 14, 1996), 73 *Tax Notes* 203-20, who recommends partial gain recognition on writing a covered option; and Deborah H. Schenk, "Taxation of Equity Derivatives: A Partial Proposal" (Summer 1995) 50 *Tax Law Review* 571-641, who recommends partial gain recognition to the extent that risk of loss is reduced under a share-hedging strategy.

104 See, for example, Tony Rumble, "Tax Linearity and the 'Too Hard Basket': A Separate Tax Regime for Innovative Financial Products," in *Derivative Tax Reform*, supra note 14, at 62-120, who criticizes Australian proposals to deny imputation tax credits in respect of certain hedged positions in shares.

105 Gergen, supra note 6, at 855; and Rumble, supra note 104.

106 *A Tax System Redesigned*, supra note 54, at 364: "The cost to the revenue from not introducing tax rules to cope with synthetic arrangements is difficult to estimate." For a general review of the efficiency considerations associated with reforms of realization-based recognition, see Daniel N. Shaviro, "An Efficiency Analysis of Realization and Recognition Rules Under the Federal Income Tax" (Fall 1992), 48 *Tax Law Review* 1-68. See also Johnson, supra note 103; and Schenk, supra note 103, who argues that equity and efficiency considerations support an extension of realization-based recognition to risk-reduction strategies that reduce, but do not eliminate, all risk associated with a particular position. But see David A. Weisbach, "Should a Short Sale Against the Box Be a Realization Event?" (September 1997), 50 *National Tax Journal* 495-506, who argues that net welfare gains from the US constructive sale provisions are unclear and depend on the effects of various types of share trading.

107 Schenk, supra note 103, at 613.

108 Gergen, supra note 6, at 847-48. See also *A Tax System Redesigned*, supra note 54, at 364: "On balance, the Review considers that some targeted measures are an appropriate response, with their effectiveness and scope to be monitored regularly." But see Weisbach, supra note 106, who argues that administrative and compliance costs associated with the application of the US constructive sale rule probably outweigh any efficiency gains.

109 See Ferguson, supra note 20, at 1016-17, who draws a distinction between structured synthetics that are tax-driven and hedging strategies that are not. See also Gergen, supra note 6, at 842, footnote 35, who observes that counterparties to structured equity swaps usually require substantial assets, other than pledged shares, as security for the obligations of the equity payer.

110 Ferguson, supra note 20, at 1016-17. These kinds of factors can be taken to indicate the close substitutability of a particular transaction for another transaction with a defined tax treatment. The close substitutability means that, from an efficiency perspective, the two transactions should be taxed consistently, unless there are other substitutes for the synthetic transactions that would involve even greater efficiency losses. See Weisbach, supra note 99.

111 IRC section 1258 enacted by the Omnibus Budget Reconciliation Act of 1993, Pub. L. no. 103-66, enacted on August 10, 1993.

112 IRC section 1259 enacted by the Taxpayer Relief Act of 1997, Pub. L. no. 105-34, enacted on August 5, 1997. See, generally, William M. Paul, "Constructive Sales Under New Section 1259" (September 15, 1997), 76 *Tax Notes* 1467-79; and David M. Schizer, "Hedging Under Section 1259" (July 20, 1998), 80 *Tax Notes* 345-56.

113 *Issues Paper*, supra note 1, at 235-36, includes a proposal for the integrated treatment of synthetic debt similar to the US conversion rule. See also *A Tax System Redesigned*, supra note 54, at 362-64, which proposes deemed disposition and reacquisition of an open position where a taxpayer enters into an arrangement that effectively converts an uncertain return into a certain return for more than a continuous 12-month period. The certain return associated with the synthetic arrangement would be subject to accrual recognition. A more general approach to this same issue is reflected in the New Zealand accrual legislation and is discussed in the text that accompanies notes 82-92 supra.

114 IRC section 1258(c)(1). The two principal categories of transactions are (1) acquisitions of property covered by a substantially contemporaneous agreement to sell the same or substantially identical property, and (2) transactions that are marketed or sold as producing capital gain treatment of the required time-value return. IRC sections 1258(c)(2)(A) and (C). The other two categories of transactions are (1) a straddle within the meaning of IRC section 1092, but modified to include stock as personal property for the purpose of the definition of a "straddle," and (2) any other transaction specified in Treasury regulations. IRC sections 1258(c)(2)(B) and (D)). No regulations have been released.

Issues Paper, supra note 1, at 235-36, would treat any arrangement with a term in excess of a specified period as a financial arrangement subject to the accrual regime where the effect of the arrangement provides a taxpayer with the right to a payment that exceeds the value of a related underlying asset at the time of entering into the arrangement. A more specific rule would apply to the amount of disguised interest represented by the amount by which the proceeds of disposition exceed the value of an asset.

115 IRC section 1258(c)(2)(A).

116 See also the similar proposal in *Issues Paper*, supra note 1, at 232-34.

117 IRC section 1258(b)(1) defines an appreciated position generally as any position that would produce gain if the position were sold, assigned, or otherwise terminated at its fair market value. A "position" means an interest, including a futures or forward contract, short sale, or option. IRC section 1258(b)(3).

118 Those transactions are (1) a short sale of the same or substantially identical property (a short sale against the box), (2) a notional principal contract (swap) that pays all or substantially all of the investment yield and that provides for reimbursement of all decreases in value of the relevant property (an "offsetting notional principal contract"), (3) a forward contract that provides for delivery of a substantially fixed amount of property for a substantially fixed price, and (4) a long purchase of the same or substantially identical property that is the subject of an appreciated short position. IRC sections 1259(c)(1)(A)-(D). The legislation also includes a residual category of transactions "that have substantially the same effect" as the enumerated transactions. IRC section 1259(c)(1)(E). The specific inclusions under this category are to be developed in regulations, which presumably should target transactions that substantially eliminate the risk of loss and opportunity for gain on a long position in an appreciated asset. See, for example, S. rep. no. 105-33, 105th Cong., 1st sess., indicating (ibid., at 126): "It is anticipated that the Treasury will use the provision's authority to treat as constructive sales other financial transactions that, like those specified in the provisions, have the effect of eliminating all or substantially all of the taxpayer's risk of loss and opportunity for income or gain with respect to the appreciated financial position."

For a description of some instruments and trading strategies that are designed to avoid the application of the constructive sale rule and may be included in the residual category to be developed under the Treasury department's regulatory power, see infra note 168.

119 IRC section 1259(c)(1)(A) (a short sale against the box).

120 IRC section 1259(c)(1)(C) (a forward sale).

121 IRC section 1259(c)(1)(B) (an offsetting notional principal contract).

122 Although the synthetic debt instrument created by the married put and call in example 2 is not included in any of the four enumerated categories, there is a residual category that covers all transactions "that have substantially the same effect" as the enumerated transactions. IRC section 1259(c)(1)(E). No regulations describing this residual category have been released yet. To the extent that the covered options are written on a long position in shares, the married put and call is an obvious candidate for inclusion. Other options-based strategies, such as "zero-cost collars," are more problematic. See infra note 168; and Schizer, supra note 112, at 356, who observes that hedging strategies that use options are not within the enumerated transactions and are expected to be subject to the constructive sale rule only prospectively under the regulatory power, except in certain cases to prevent abuse.

123 S. rep. 105-33, supra note 118, at 126, which states that the US constructive sale rule "requires reduction of both risk of loss and opportunity for gain."

124 The requirement of a net investment in a transaction excludes transactions that consist only of on-market forward contracts with no advance of funds. See Ferguson,

supra note 20, at 1015. Similarly, although an option involves an advance of funds, the expected return is probably not certain enough to satisfy the time-value standard (ibid., at 1015). It is not clear, however, that this standard would exclude certain "deep-in-the-money options" that are virtually assured of exercise and provide a predominant time-value return (ibid., at 1016). A prepaid forward contract, which is equivalent to a deep-in-the-money option with a zero strike price, might be included as a conversion transaction, although there remains a significant element of unexpected gain or loss. See the text that accompanies notes 34-42 in chapter 6. In any of these cases, the transactions would be included only if they were marketed or sold as producing capital gain treatment of the required time-value return. See IRC section 1258(c)(2)(C).

125 IRC section 1258(c)(2)(A).

126 IRC section 1258(c)(2)(C).

127 Under the original legislative proposal, a constructive sale was defined generally as any transaction that "substantially eliminates the risk of loss and opportunity for gain" on appreciated shares, debt, or a partnership interest held by a taxpayer. That general definition was replaced in the final legislation with the set of four enumerated transactions. The constructive sale provisions were introduced largely in response to a much-publicized short sale against the box by the Lauder family. The Lauder transaction was not limited to deferral but was also intended to eliminate capital gains tax on shares of the Estée Lauder Company. This result would be realized by borrowing the shares sold short from family members with no intent to return them. Under the IRC, the short seller would dispose of the shares held in the box on death for proceeds equal to their cost base, and the beneficiaries would receive the benefit of a stepped-up cost base equal to the fair market value at that time. See, generally, Daniel Shefter, "Tax Proposals on 'Short Against the Box' and Other Hedging Transactions" (January 29, 1996), 70 *Tax Notes* 581-88, who commented on draft legislation released in advance of the March 1996 proposals; Lee A. Sheppard, "Fixes To Ensure That Tax Is Paid on Capital Gains" (December 4, 1995), 69 *Tax Notes* 1165-68; and Sheryl Stratton, "Treasury Targets Capital Gains Tax-Deferral Strategies" (January 22, 1996), 70 *Tax Notes* 347-49.

The comparable proposal for constructive sales described in *Issues Paper*, supra note 1, at 233, would apply where a taxpayer enters into an arrangement that "substantially removes the opportunities for gain and the risk of loss" from an asset with an accrued gain.

128 IRC section 1259(c)(1)(A).

129 IRC section 1259(c)(1)(B).

130 IRC section 1259(c)(1)(C).

131 IRC section 1259(c)(1)(D).

132 Ferguson, supra note 20, at 1017.

133 IRC section 1258(a). The amount of the recharacterized gain is limited to the amount of interest that would have accrued on the taxpayer's net investment for the relevant period at a rate equal to 120 percent of the applicable federal rate (AFR). IRC section 1258(b)(1).

134 The conversion rule affects only the character of the expected gain. Accrual-based recognition is not required and the expected gain thus remains subject to realization-based recognition.

135 IRC section 1259(a)(1).

136 IRC section 1259(a)(2)(A).

137 IRC section 1259(a)(2)(B). A taxpayer retains, however, the ability to designate which of several identical properties are subject to the deemed disposition where he enters into a hedge that covers only some of the properties. See IRC section 1259(e)(3).

In contrast, *Issues Paper*, supra note 1, at 232-34, provides that the constructive sale proposal would be applied to portfolios of homogenous assets on a first-in, first-out basis where only a portion of the risk is neutralized.

138 IRC section 1258(d)(5).

139 Ferguson, supra note 20, at 1017.

140 *Issues Paper*, supra note 1, at 235-36, provides specific exceptions from its comparable conversion proposal for short-term arrangements less than a specified period (12 months).

141 IRC section 1259(b)(2). "Qualifying variable-rate debt" is limited to debt with interest that varies according to certain indexes such as LIBOR.

142 IRC section 1259(c)(3). To maintain eligibility for the exception, the taxpayer generally cannot sell or hedge the appreciated asset within 60 days after closing the short-term hedge. There is a further exception where the taxpayer enters into a second, short-term hedge to protect against market risk. See Schizer, supra note 112, at 348, footnote 31.

143 IRC section 1259(c)(2).

144 Schizer, supra note 112, at 347-48.

145 Ibid., at 348-49. The comparable constructive sale proposal in *Issues Paper*, supra note 1, at 232-34, excludes the acquisition of an offsetting position with a term of less than 12 months, provided that the taxpayer can document at the time of the acquisition that there was no intention to dispose of a related asset at or around the time of the maturity of the derivative. If a disposition does occur, any realized gain plus an imputed amount of interest would be taxed as if the disposition occurred on the acquisition of the derivative.

146 Schizer, supra note 112, at 349.

147 Hariton, supra note 68, at 813.

148 IRC section 246(c). For a general description of the US limitations, see Peter C. Canellos, "Limitations on Loss Recognition," in *Taxation of Financial Instruments* (Deerfield, Ill.: Clark, Boardman Callaghan) (looseleaf), chapter 6, at 12-22.

149 The 46-day holding period is extended to 91 days in the case of certain preferred shares. IRC section 246(c)(1).

150 IRC section 246(c)(1)(B).

151 IRC section 246(c)(1)(A).

152 Ferguson, supra note 20, at 1019-20.

153 A similar opportunity for pure avoidance arises if a corporate shareholder can enter into a short sale against the box and deduct both (1) dividends received on the long position covered by the short sale and (2) dividend compensation payments made under a securities loan used to cover the short position. See Ferguson, supra note 20, at 1020.

154 See, for example, the "dividend stop-loss rules" in ITA subsections 112(3)-(5.6). The two basic rules applicable to corporate shareholders reduce the amount of any loss realized on shares by the amount of any deductible intercorporate dividends received before the disposition, unless (1) the corporate shareholder and non-arm's-length persons did not own more than 5 percent of the shares of the relevant class at the time a dividend was received, and (2) the corporate shareholder owned the share throughout the 365-day period that ended immediately before the disposition.

155 The dividend stop-loss rules under the ITA require only that shares be owned for the required period, without any qualification regarding exposure to market risk.

156 This is the effect under the dividend stop-loss rules under the ITA. See supra note 154.

157 The 46-day holding period under the US legislation is much shorter, for example, than the 365-day requirement under the comparable stop-loss rules under the ITA.

158 Ferguson, supra note 20, at 1020.

159 Ibid.

160 *Issues Paper*, supra note 1, at 234-35. The proposal in the issues paper was developed further in two press releases by the Australian Treasury department. See Australia, *Treasurer's Press Release* no. 47, "Measures To Prevent Trading in Franking Credits," May 13, 1997; and *Treasurer's Press Release* no. 89, "Budget Measures To Prevent Trading in Franking Credits: Outcome of Consultations," August 8, 1997. For a critical discussion of the original proposals released on May 13, 1997, see Rumble, supra note 104.

161 In their original form the Australian proposals were patterned largely on the US legislation restricting the availability of the dividends-received deduction. In particular, the Australian proposals required that a shareholder hold a share "at risk" for at least a 45-day period around the dividend date to be entitled to imputation tax credits. This at-risk standard was defined at 70 percent of the value of an exposed long position in the relevant shares. Any reduction of the risk of loss below this standard would result in tolling of the hold period for the number of days during which the standard was unsatisfied. As with the US legislation limiting the availability of the dividends-received deduction, a 90-day hold period was proposed for certain preferred shares.

162 In response to significant criticism that emphasized the adverse effect of its imputation credit proposals on share-hedging strategies, the Australian Treasury department modified the restrictions in *Treasurer's Press Release* no. 89, supra note 160, in order (1) to provide certain specified exceptions from the original proposal and (2) refine the risk-reduction standard to require, instead, the maintenance of a minimum net equity exposure based on the financial measure "delta," which takes into account both the opportunity for profit and the risk of loss. The combination of the exceptions and a more refined determination of risk reduction alleviated some of the concerns regarding the adverse effects of the proposal. In general, the revised proposal requires a taxpayer to maintain a delta of 0.3 for the minimum holding period. For this purpose, a delta of 1 is allocated to the relevant share and the deltas of derivatives held or issued in combination with the share are added or subtracted as appropriate. The two most important exceptions permit retail investors and pension funds to claim a maximum amount of imputation credits without application of the holding-period requirement. *A Tax System*

Redesigned, supra note 54, at 227-50, subsequently recommended that the 45-day rule be replaced with a more limited 15-day rule and that the exemption threshold for small transactions be increased from $2,000 to $5,000.

163 ITA subsections 82(1) and 112(2.3) and the definition of a "dividend rental arrangement" in subsection 248(1). For an overview of the legislation, see Gabriel J. Hayos, "Security Lending and Dividend Rentals: What They Are and the Tax Implications," in *Report of Proceedings of the Forty-First Tax Conference*, 1989 Conference Report (Toronto: Canadian Tax Foundation, 1990), 25:1-18, at 25:14-16. New Zealand Inland Revenue has adopted a similar "purpose-based" approach. See Income Tax Act (1994), section GC22, which denies dividend imputation credits where shares are issued or sold as part of an arrangement to obtain a tax advantage. But see also *A Tax System Redesigned*, supra note 54, at 48, which suggests that reliance on a purpose-based general anti-avoidance rule to address imputation credit trading could result in an annual revenue cost of $300 to $400 million for the Australian treasury.

164 ITA subsection 112(2.3).

165 ITA subsection 82(1).

166 Apparently, any agreement that the shares are to be transferred back by the recipient at their value at the time of the initial transfer is regarded as a sufficient indication of risk retention by someone else. See Canada, Department of Finance, 1989 Budget, Draft Legislation and Explanatory Notes: Securities Lending, April 26, 1989.

167 See, generally, Weisbach, supra note 94; Schenk, supra note 103; and Schizer, supra note 112, at 351-56, who describes various hedging strategies that potentially avoid the US constructive sale provisions because of the required level of risk reduction. Schenk, supra note 103, at 619-22, observes that any integration approach that depends on the definition of offsetting positions must extend to positions assumed by a taxpayer and a defined range of persons related to the taxpayer.

168 Some notable examples of this kind of strategy intended to avoid the application of the US constructive sale rule are (1) zero-cost collars, (2) exchangeable debt, and (3) "premium equity participating securities" (PEPS). Under a zero-cost collar, a taxpayer with a long position in appreciated shares issues a call and purchases a put on the shares for equal premiums (hence the "zero-cost" label). Unlike a married put and call, the exercise prices of the options differ with a zero-cost collar. The difference provides a price range within which the taxpayer is exposed to sufficient risk to avoid the level of required risk reduction under the constructive sale rule. The taxpayer can monetize the long position in the shares by acquiring low-cost financing secured against the collar. See Braddock, supra note 96; Schizer, supra note 112, at 356; and Sheppard, supra note 42, at 817-18. As the equivalent of a fixed-payment debt instrument and an embedded on-market forward contract written on a long position in shares of a corporation other than the issuer, exchangeable debt usually eliminates the risk associated with that position. Certain issues of debt exchangeable into common shares (DECS), however, have been structured so that the issuer retains sufficient upside appreciation to avoid the application of the constructive sale rule. See Schizer, supra note 112; and Sheppard, supra note 42, at 818-19. Another version of exchangeable debt (referred to as "PHONES") is equivalent to the issue of a fixed-payment debt

instrument and a long-dated, deep-in-the-money call option on referenced shares held by the issuer. In a typical issue, the holder of a PHONES is entitled to a below-market rate of interest plus dividends paid on the referenced shares and may, on maturity of the instrument, receive the greater of (1) the issue price of the PHONES (equal to the spot price of the referenced shares on issue) and (2) the spot price of the referenced shares on maturity. Because the issuer retains the risk of loss on the referenced shares, the constructive sale rule may not apply. See Lee A. Sheppard, "Rethinking DECS, and New Ways To Carve Out Debt" (April 19, 1999), 83 *Tax Notes* 347-52, at 349-50; and Lee A. Sheppard, "Can Corporate Issuers Dial Up an Overstated Interest Deduction?" (January 31, 2000), 86 *Tax Notes* 587-91, at 590-91, who argues that the retention of the risk of loss by the issuer of PHONES is insignificant in light of their 30- to 60-year terms. PEPS are, in form, unsecured debt instruments, issued for a price equal to the spot price of referenced shares held by the issuer. PEPS have a limited term (commonly 5 years) and pay interest at a below-market rate. On maturity of the instrument, the holder is entitled to cash equal to the spot price of the referenced shares. PEPS also provide the issuer with a redemption option during the later portions of the term of the security. The option is equivalent to a call option with payment terms that permit the issuer to retain a portion of any appreciation in the referenced shares. Accordingly, the PEPS can be characterized as the equivalent of a cash-settled collar issued on the underlying shares. It is arguable that PEPS, like DECs, are outside of the constructive sale rule, because the issuer retains a portion of the equity upside sufficient to support the conclusion that all, or substantially all, of the risk associated with a long position in the referenced shares has not been eliminated. Like PHONES, PEPS are considered contingent debt within the US contingent-debt regulations and thereby subject to imputation of interest on the embedded options (non-contingent principal amount). See the text that accompanies notes 137-151 in chapter 6. A number of issues of PEPS were floated, however, before the effective date for the application of the contingent-debt regulations. For a summary of PEPS and their treatment under the US tax rules, see Lee A. Sheppard, "Adding PEP to the Constructive Sale Debate" (March 18, 1996), 70 *Tax Notes* 1592-96.

169 Schenk, supra note 103; and Sheppard, "Adding PEP," supra note 168.

170 See, for example, Weisbach, supra note 94; and Glenn L.E. May, "Overview of Financial, Tax, and Accounting Principles for Derivative Financial Instruments," in the 1995 Conference Report, supra note 44, 29:1-27, at 29:26: "Narrowly prescribed rules create automatic tax biases, and these can often be used against the government."

171 An approach of this kind may provide efficiency gains by affecting instances of imperfect substitutability of transactions with the associated non-tax costs. The efficiency gains can be maximized by (1) taxing transactions that are close substitutes equivalently and (2) deterring the use of alternative substitutes through standards-based anti-avoidance rules that attempt to suppress the resulting discontinuity. See Weisbach, supra note 94; and Weisbach, supra note 99.

172 IRC reg. sections 1.246-3 and 1.246-5. For a discussion of the share-hedging regulations defining the scope of the term "substantially similar or related property," see Bradford L. Ferguson, George R. Goodman, and Jonathan P. Biller, "The Latest Stock Hedging Regulations" (June 26, 1995), 69 *Tax Notes* 1795-1818.

173 The Australian proposals restricting the availability of imputation credits rely on the delta measure to correlate long and short positions in shares. The measure does not, however, determine the initial question of when two positions should be integrated for the purpose of applying the delta measure. This issue is addressed in the US regulations defining the scope of the concepts of "substantially identical securities" and "substantially similar or related property."

174 IRC reg. section 1.246-3(c)(2).

175 IRC reg. section 1.246-5(b)(1) provides that property is considered substantially similar or related to shares if:

> (i) The fair market values of the stock and the property primarily reflect the performance of—
>
> (A) A single firm or enterprise;
>
> (B) The same industry or industries; or
>
> (C) The same economic factor or factors such as (but not limited to) interest rates, commodity prices, or foreign-currency exchange rates; and
>
> (ii) Changes in the fair market value of the stock are reasonably expected to approximate, directly or inversely, changes in the fair market value of the property, a fraction of the fair market value of the property, or a multiple of the fair market value of the property.

See also IRC reg. section 1.246-5(c)(2)(ii), which lists the following transactions as examples in which the taxpayer has diminished risk of loss by holding substantially similar or related property:

> (A) a short sale of common stock while holding convertible preferred stock of the same issuer and the price changes of the convertible preferred stock and the common stock are related;
>
> (B) a short sale of a convertible debenture while holding convertible preferred stock into which the debenture is convertible or common stock; or
>
> (C) a short sale of convertible preferred stock while holding common stock.

176 IRC reg. section 1.246-5(c)(1). An index is effectively defined as a "portfolio," which is a position that relates to at least 20 different shares.

177 IRC reg. section 1.246-5(c)(1)(iii)(B). This 70 percent test is apparently the source of the same standard used to measure the at-risk position of a shareholder under the original Australian proposals addressing transfers of imputation credits. See supra note 160.

178 See also the comparable bright lines using the delta measure under the Australian proposals, supra note 160, which applies generally for the purposes of defining the requisite level of risk for all share positions.

179 IRC reg. section 1.246-5(c)(1)(vi), which applies if (1) changes in the value of the portfolio are reasonably expected to track changes in the value of a taxpayer's holdings, and (2) the position is acquired or held as part of a plan, a principal purpose of which is to obtain tax savings that are significantly in excess of the expected economic profits from the plan.

180 For a discussion of these kinds of differences in the context of an equity swap, see, for example, Kleinbard, supra note 2. See also David P. Hariton, "Equity

Swaps, New Regulations, and Ed Kleinbard's Article" (September 2, 1991), 53 *Tax Notes* 1221-23.

181 See the text that accompanies notes 260-263 in chapter 3.

182 See, for example, May, supra footnote 22, at 1633-35.

183 Avi-Yonah, supra note 22, at 270-71. But see David P. Hariton, "Withholding on Cross-Border Stock Loans and Other Equity Derivatives" (December 1994), 72 *Taxes: The Tax Magazine* 1050-60, at 1058-59, who argues that withholding tax should not be imposed on dividend-equivalent payments, since a non-resident equity receiver under an equity swap holds the equivalent of a leveraged investment in shares of a resident corporation and has no net equity capital invested in the source country. Hariton characterizes the imposition of withholding tax on cross-border substitute or equity derivative payments on a gross basis as effectively treating the non-resident as if they held unleveraged equity positions. In fact, the imposition of non-resident withholding tax on the gross amount of dividend payments does treat the non-resident who owns the shares as if the ownership was unleveraged. Consistent treatment of this position and an equivalent long position under a swap or securities loan requires the imposition of non-resident withholding tax on the gross amount of dividend-equivalent payments. An attempt to realize consistency in the application of non-resident withholding tax to dividends and dividend-substitute payments under securities loans underlies the imposition of withholding tax to the latter payments under ITA subsection 260(8); and IRC reg. sections 1.861-3(a)(6), 1.864-5(b)(2)(ii), 1.871-7(b)(2), 1.881-2(b)(2), and 1.894-1(c), TD 8735, 1997-2 CB 72, which provides that dividend-substitute payments on securities loans and repos have the same source and character as payments on the underlying securities for withholding tax purposes. For a discussion of the US regulations and a critique of their possible extension to equity swaps, see New York State Bar Association, "Withholding Tax on Substitute and Derivative Dividend Payments Received by Foreigners" (June 29, 1998), 79 *Tax Notes* 1749-59.

184 See, for example, New York State Bar Association, supra note 183, which generally follows Hariton's analysis (supra note 183) in distinguishing a securities loan from an equity swap for the purposes of the application of non-resident withholding tax. (Hariton is the principal author of the report.) The distinction is drawn on the basis that a securities loan involves a net inbound investment in the source country (withholding tax is thereby considered appropriate), while an equity swap does not (withholding tax is thereby considered inappropriate). On the assumption that this distinction provides a defensible benchmark treatment, the report suggests that the imposition of withholding tax on dividend-equivalent payments under an equity swap should be limited to certain structured transactions "in which an equity swap replaces the actual ownership of US equities." These transactions typically involve the documentation of a securities loan as an equity swap plus a loan to a resident swap counterparty. See also Cappelli and Santangelo, supra note 21, at 71, who argue that the characterization of share-hedging transactions as synthetic equity involves a consideration "when, as an economic matter, capital should be considered to be sufficiently dedicated to corporate enterprise to be subject to a second-level of tax."

185 May, supra note 22, at 1635.

186 Transactions using derivatives to create synthetics that effectively transfer the benefit of foreign tax credits are somewhat similar to dividend rental arrangements

and other transactions intended to transfer the benefit of imputation tax credits. See the text that accompanies note 21 supra. Foreign tax credit transactions first surfaced in the United States and prompted a joint response by Treasury and the IRS in Notice 98-5, 1998-3 IRB 49. See Lee A. Sheppard, "Applying the Smell Test to Foreign Tax Credits" (January 5, 1998), 71 *Tax Notes* 8-15. The Canadian Department of Finance followed with a comparable response in Canada, Department of Finance, 1998 Budget, Budget Plan, Notice of Ways and Means Motion To Amend the Income Tax Act, February 24, 1998, resolutions 46 and 47. The budget resolutions have been carried forward in ITA subsections 126(4.1)-(4.4). By targeting particular paradigm transactions, the proposed provisions reflect many of the features of the approach to synthetics suggested in this chapter. See also Australia, *Treasurer's Press Release* no. 078, "Tax Avoidance: Foreign Tax Credit Schemes," August 13, 1998, which suggests that the general anti-avoidance rule under the ITAA should be extended specifically to transactions intended to transfer excess foreign tax credits.

187 Weisbach, supra note 1, at 527-28.

188 This favourable view of integration is evident in some of the early US literature criticizing bifurcation as a tax technique and generally extolling the virtues of hedge tax treatment. See, for example, Frank V. Battle Jr., "Bifurcation of Financial Instruments" (December 1991), 69 *Taxes: The Tax Magazine* 821-31; Kau, supra note 3; and Kleinbard, "Beyond Good and Evil Debt (and Debt Hedges)," supra note 3. For a more recent, critical view of the US hedging rules, see Paul M. Schmidt, "The Hedging Rules: Clarity or Confusion?" (August 26, 1996), 71 *Tax Notes* 1169-85.

189 Australia, *Taxation of Financial Arrangements: A Consultative Document* (Canberra: Australian Government Publishing Service, December 1993).

190 Ibid., at 53-57.

191 See, generally, Roger Paul, "Risk Neutrality Within a Differentiated Tax System," in *Derivative Tax Reform*, supra note 14, 11-24, at 11-17.

192 *Issues Paper*, supra note 1, at 147-82.

193 Ibid., at 147.

194 It is interesting that Australia, Review of Business Taxation, *A Platform for Consultation—Building a Strong Foundation*, Discussion Paper 2, vol. 1 (Canberra: Australian Government Publishing Service, February 1999), 170-73, appears to acknowledge the theoretical and practical difficulties associated with any sort of comprehensive hedging regime. Indeed, this later discussion paper released by the Australian Review of Business Taxation reflects a position that is close to that originally proposed by the government in *Consultative Document*, supra note 189.

195 These exceptions could include a fully hedged foreign currency debt, a contingent-debt instrument, and any other combination that replicates a single instrument, whether or not the synthetic is created for tax-avoidance purposes.

196 The principal exception under the New Zealand accrual legislation is the treatment of interest-rate and other interest-based swaps. In this limited case, the treatment of the offsetting positions under the swap as notional loans provides a type of hedge accounting where the counterparty has an offsetting position in an underlying borrowing. See the text that accompanies notes 240-248 in chapter 5.

197 But see May, supra note 170, at 29:23-27, who suggests a limited hedging regime to clarify uncertainty created by Canadian case law regarding the application of a "linkage approach" to the characterization of gain and loss on a hedge transaction and the underlying asset or liability. See also *A Tax System Redesigned*, supra note 54, at 346-53, where the Australian Review of Business Taxation altered its earlier position in *A Platform for Consultation*, supra note 194, at 170-73, and recommended the adoption of a purpose-based hedge-accounting regime in two limited instances: (1) internal hedge transactions entered into between domestic business units of the same entity ("internal hedging"), and (2) certain hedge transactions entered into by gold producers. By recognizing internal hedge transactions entered into between the "trading" and "investment" desks of a financial institution, the proposed internal hedge regime effectively extends realization-based recognition to the designated portion of the portfolio of the trading desk otherwise subject to accretion taxation. The relevant portion is defined by being matched with an offsetting position of the investment desk subject to realization-based recognition. The matching is evidenced by the internal transaction entered into by the different divisions of the same entity. The exception for certain hedge transactions entered into by gold producers is a limited example of the kind of hedge regime that is criticized here—that is, gain or loss on the hedge would be matched with that on the underlying position and recognition deferred until recognition of gain or loss on the underlying position. The proposed internal hedge regime is a limited example of the more general approach to hedging transactions recommended here—that is, the availability of realization-based recognition for gain or loss on traded derivatives otherwise subject to accretion taxation, if the derivative is entered into as a hedge of an underlying position subject to realization-based recognition.

198 For a comprehensive critique of the relevance of the matching principle and the relevance of financial-accounting practice generally in the calculation of business income for tax purposes, see Deborah A. Geier, "The Myth of the Matching Principle as a Tax Value" (Spring 1998), 15 *The American Journal of Tax Policy* 17-166. The case for the rejection of hedge accounting treatment of financial instruments is a specific application of Geier's general critique.

199 Matching is required for tax-policy purposes when an instrument that provides expected gain or loss is subject to realization-based recognition. In that case, a taxpayer can assume a short position in an instrument subject to accrual recognition of expected loss, and use the proceeds to acquire a long position in the instrument that provides realization-based recognition of expected gain. In the absence of accrual recognition of the expected gain on the long position, a rule limiting the deductibility of the expected loss to the amount of realized gain addresses the pure tax-avoidance opportunity that would otherwise be available through the assumption of these offsetting positions. A limitation like this depends on the integration and matching of gain and loss on the offsetting positions. See the text that accompanies notes 108-114 in chapter 3. Matching may also be used to address straddle transactions that are implemented to provide the benefit of selective realization. See the text that accompanies notes 324-335 in chapter 5.

200 This proposition assumes that offsetting positions are entered into by the same taxpayer and within the same taxing jurisdiction. If this assumption does not hold, there may be a case for matching the positions, but only in the sense of consolidating

them within the same corporate group, including for the purpose of resolving issues surrounding the taxing jurisdiction of residence and source countries. Those issues do not alter in any way the character and timing principles for the recognition of financial cash flows developed in chapter 3. Those principles should not be altered in the sense commonly associated with a hedge tax accounting regime. For an excellent discussion of these unrelated jurisdictional problems, see Diane M. Ring, "Risk-Shifting Within a Multinational Corporation: The Incoherence of the U.S. Tax Regime" (July 1997), 38 *Boston College Law Review* 667-737.

201 The question of character matching sometimes goes beyond the basic distinction between capital and income accounts. In particular, the existence of legislative provisions that apply preferential treatment for gain or loss associated with a particular asset requires a determination of the character of offsetting loss or gain on a hedge. See, for example, *Echo Bay Mines Ltd. v. The Queen*, 92 DTC 6437; [1992] 2 CTC 182 (FCTD), in which the court characterized gain or loss on derivatives entered into for hedging purposes as "resource income or loss" for the purpose of the resource allowance under the ITA. Elimination of the distinction between capital and income amounts for financial instruments does not address the need for a limited hedging regime for these other kinds of character issues.

202 See, for example, *Consultative Document*, supra note 189, at 55, which states that the economic substance of a financial instrument is not altered by the fact that the instrument is entered into as a hedge.

203 Ibid., at 56, which emphasizes the administrative and compliance costs associated with the need to identify a hedge transaction that can take various forms and depends on the intent of a taxpayer.

204 The conventional view in the finance literature holds that hedging can increase the value of a firm by, in part, reducing taxes through the "smoothing" of taxable income. See, for example, Charles W. Smithson, *Managing Financial Risk: A Guide to Derivative Products, Financial Engineering, and Value Maximization*, 3d ed. (New York: McGraw-Hill, 1998), 492-517; Richard Wood, *Derivatives, Financial Innovation and Taxation*, Treasury Research Paper no. 11 (Canberra: Australian Government Publishing Service, 1996), 11-12; and John R. Graham and Clifford W. Smith Jr., "Tax Incentives To Hedge" (December 1999), 54 *Journal of Finance* 2241-62. This literature is silent regarding the impact, if any, of tax fragmentation on the pricing of derivatives.

205 *Consultative Document*, supra note 189, at 57: "In any event, the case for special rules is weakened by the proposed scope of the accruals tax system."

206 *Issues Paper*, supra note 1, at 157-62.

207 Another alternative, which is almost universally ignored in the tax literature, focuses on the non-traded underlying asset and alters its tax treatment to require accretion recognition of all gains and losses on ordinary-income account consistent with the treatment of a traded derivative acquired as a hedge. See, for example, Steven M. Rosenthal and Mark H. Price, "FAS 133 and Tax—An Unhappy Marriage Awaiting a Counsellor" (July/August 1999), 1 *Derivatives & Financial Instruments* 216-27, at 227, who suggest that an underlying asset be marked to market for tax purposes in those circumstances in which financial accounting requires this approach.

208 *Issues Paper*, supra note 1, at 161-62.

209 Ibid., at 162.

210 Ibid., at 161-63.

211 Ibid.

212 *Issues Paper*, ibid., at 163-64, proposed an exception for hedges of the purchase price of depreciable capital equipment denominated in a foreign currency. Because the price of the underlying purchase in this instance is recognized systematically through the depreciation mechanism, foreign exchange gain or loss on a related hedge can be incorporated in the calculation of the capital cost of the equipment. For the reasons stated above, however, it is unclear whether realized gains and losses should be matched with the capital costs, even where those costs are recognized on a systematic basis.

213 The US hedging regulations are found in IRC reg. sections 1.1221-2 (character of gain or loss); and 1.446-4 (timing rules for the recognition of gain or loss). The US hedging regulations were introduced in 1994 to deal primarily with the troublesome characterization of hedge gains and losses. The timing issue was more or less an afterthought or secondary consideration. For years, the leading authority on the characterization issue was *Corn Products Refining Corp. v. Com.*, 350 US 46 (1955). The US Supreme Court in that case considered the application of IRC section 1221 to gains on corn futures transactions entered into by the taxpayer, a corn manufacturer. Section 1221 provides that an asset is considered capital in nature unless it is within one of the following categories:

- inventory;
- depreciable property and real estate used in a trade or business;
- copyrights, literary, musical, and artistic compositions, and letters or memoranda resulting from the personal efforts of a taxpayer;
- accounts receivable acquired in the ordinary course of a business of providing services or the sale of inventory; and
- certain government publications.

The Supreme Court in *Corn Products* rejected the taxpayer's argument that gains from the disposition of the corn futures did not fall within any of the specified exclusions in section 1221 and should be considered capital in nature. Instead, the court concluded that Congress intended that gains and losses from "everyday operations" be recognized as ordinary gains and losses. This conclusion apparently extended to the taxpayer's corn futures trading and was accepted as authority in subsequent cases for ordinary-income treatment for all assets acquired with a business purpose. In *Arkansas Best Corp. v. Com.*, 485 US 212 (1988), however, the Supreme Court concluded that the reasoning in *Corn Products* was limited to property acquired as inventory and did not extend to the taxpayer's acquisition of bank shares in an effort to protect its business reputation. This decision created considerable doubt regarding the ordinary income or loss characterization of gains or losses on transactions entered into in the ordinary course of business as hedges of business assets and liabilities. The confusion was not eased by the Tax Court decision in *Federal National Mortgage Association*, 100 TC 514 (1993). Without the protection of the broad characterization approach articulated in *Corn Products*, taxpayers were left with possible capital loss treatment on transactions effected as hedges of business assets and liabilities. IRC reg. section 1.1221-2(a)(1) addresses the characterization issue by providing that a "capital asset" within section 1221 does not include property that is part of a hedging transaction.

US policy makers apparently accepted that the linkage approach underlying the character regulations can suitably be extended to the recognition of gain or loss on eligible hedging transactions. The timing regulations provide a series of very general rules and principles that attempt to require the matching of the timing of gain or loss on a hedge with that on an underlying transaction. The rules consist of a general rule and a set of special rules applicable in defined circumstances; they apply to eligible hedge transactions as defined in IRC reg. section 1.1221-2(b) (described above) and take precedence over any other timing rule under the Code, subject to certain exceptions. The general timing rule in IRC reg. section 1.446-4(a) provides that the method of accounting used by a taxpayer must clearly reflect income, and to do so the method must reasonably match the timing of income, deduction, gain, or loss from the hedge transaction with the timing applicable to the same items in respect of the identified underlying position. The only specific guidance regarding this vague standard consists of the unenlightening proposition that the realization basis may clearly reflect income where, for example, the hedge and the underlying position are disposed of in the same taxation year. The regulations state, however, that the realization requirement will usually not satisfy the clear reflection of income standard for hedge transactions. In this respect, IRC reg. section 1.446-4(c) recognizes that there may be different recognition methods that satisfy the stated standard. Taxpayers are permitted to choose one of a number of methods, provided that it is applied consistently to similar hedge transactions. The chosen method cannot be changed without the consent of the IRS.

For an overview of the US hedging regulations, see Richard M. Lipton, "IRS Issues New Regulations on Hedging Transactions" (January 1994), 72 *Taxes: The Tax Magazine* 3-12.

214 See, for example, *Issues Paper*, supra note 1, at 155, which proposes that two positions must be inversely correlated to qualify for hedge treatment. Financial Accounting Standards Board (FASB), *Accounting for Derivative Instruments and Hedging Activities*, Statement of Financial Accounting Standards no. 133 (Norwalk, Conn.: FASB, June 1998), limits a qualifying "fair value hedge" to a hedge of an exposure to changes in value of an asset or liability that is "highly effective." This standard has been defined to require that the hedge offset 85 to 125 percent of the change in value of the underlying asset or liability.

215 See, for example, Lee A. Sheppard, "Can the Tax Law Live with FAS 133?" (February 7, 2000), 86 *Tax Notes* 732-37, at 735-36, who criticizes the US hedge regulations for the lack of a risk-reduction test to support a taxpayer's designation of a transaction as a hedge.

216 Paul, supra note 191.

217 In the case of general hedges, *Issues Paper*, supra note 1, at 164-66, proposes a breakdown of the related underlying transactions and positions into two different components: (1) underlying financial instruments and (2) non-financial transactions. The appropriate hedge-accounting methods are applied to the net risk attributable to these separate components. Where the underlying transactions are solely non-financial assets, the accounting approach proposed for the transactions must be applied to the net risk addressed by the general hedge. Where the underlying transactions are solely financial instruments, a hedge-accounting method must be

adopted for the portfolio that reasonably approximates the hedge-accounting rules otherwise applicable to specific hedges of the relevant financial instruments. In an assessment of the net risk addressed by general hedges, the effect of "natural hedges" is always taken into account. These hedges occur naturally in the sense that two transactions that are not entered into for hedging purposes provide an offset of the risk associated with each other.

These kinds of complexities associated with general hedges and other, more sophisticated hedging strategies are generally avoided under the limited approach suggested here. All that would be required under the suggested approach is a sufficient correlation with realization-based financial instruments, shares, or non-financial assets to justify the application of the same realization basis to traded instruments acquired as a hedge. The breakdown of an underlying position may be necessary where traded financial instruments are acquired as a general hedge of a portfolio that consists of non-traded instruments and/or non-financial assets and other traded instruments subject to accretion taxation.

Glossary

American option An option that can be exercised at any time before maturity.

Arbitrage The realization of riskless gain through the purchase of a commodity or financial instrument in one market for immediate sale in another.

Arbitrage pricing theory A model of financial instrument and portfolio behaviour that is based on the proposition that the expected return on any asset is a linear combination of various factors.

At-the-money option An option that is written on an asset with a spot price equal to the strike price under the option.

Bermuda option An option that can be exercised only on specified dates before maturity.

Black-Scholes equation The basic formula that is used to price an option.

Break forward An option on a forward contract.

Butterfly spread An option-trading strategy that involves the simultaneous issue and purchase of call options with different maturity dates and strike prices.

Call option An option to purchase an asset at a specified price.

Call premium The price of a call option.

Cap A provision in a debt contract or a stand-alone option that provides a ceiling on interest rates.

Capital asset pricing model (CAPM) A pricing model that identifies the equilibrium rates of expected return on all risky assets measured through the covariance with a market portfolio.

Cash settlement The practice of settling futures and option contracts in cash rather than by delivery of the underlying asset.

Collar The combination of a cap and a floor. A collar is typically used to restrict the range of interest rates under a floating-rate debt instrument.

Commercial paper Short-term unsecured promissory notes that are issued by corporations with high credit ratings.

Commodity swap An exchange of fixed for variable payments that are based on a notional amount of a specified commodity.

Common shares Shares that entitle the holders to participate fully and ratably in corporate assets that are left after all prior claims are paid.

Convertible bond A debt instrument that can be converted into shares of the issuer corporation.

Coupon The voucher attached to bonds that is exchangeable for cash on interest payment dates.

Covered option The acquisition of an asset that is the subject of an option.

Credit-extension instrument A present obligation of a borrower that arises from past events, the settlement of which is expected to result in an outflow of cash.

Credit risk The risk that a borrower will default on its obligations.

Cross-currency swap A swap in which each side or leg is denominated in a different currency.

Cross rate The exchange rate for two currencies.

Debenture An unsecured bond that is typically issued for a term of 15 years or more.

Deep discount bond A bond that is issued with a very low (or no) coupon and sells at a price well below its stated face amount due on maturity.

Default risk The chance that a borrower will not pay interest and/or principal.

Deliverable instrument An underlying financial instrument that is the subject of a forward contract to be delivered in the future at a specified price.

Derivative A financial instrument that derives its value from changes in the value of another asset or instrument.

Discount The difference between the sale price and the face amount of a debt instrument.

Discount rate The rate that is used to calculate the present value of expected cash flows.

Embedded option An option that is incorporated in the payment terms associated with another financial instrument, such as a bond.

Equity swap An exchange of payments that are based on a notional amount of shares or a share index.

Eurodollar loan A loan transacted outside of the United States that pays interest and principal in US dollars.

Eurodollars US dollars that are held in banks outside of the United States and used to settle international transactions.

European option An option that can be exercised only on the specified maturity date.

Exchangeable debt A debt instrument that can be converted into shares of a corporation other than the issuer.

Exchange rate The price at which one currency can be exchanged for another.

Exercise price The price at which the holder of an option can buy (a call option) or sell (a put option) the underlying asset. The exercise price is also referred to as "the strike price."

Expiration date The maturity date of an option.

Face amount The stated amount that is due under a debt obligation on maturity.

Fixed-for-floating swap The exchange of fixed for floating interest payments that are based on a notional principal amount denominated in the same currency.

Fixed-payment debt instrument A financial instrument under which all cash flows and payment dates are known at the time the instrument is issued.

Floating-rate debt A debt instrument that has an adjustable coupon payment or interest rate.

Floor A provision in a debt contract or a stand-alone option that provides a lower limit on the interest rate.

Forward contract An agreement that calls for future delivery of an asset at a specified price.

Forward exchange rate The exchange rate expressed today for an exchange of two currencies at a future date.

Forward-rate agreement An agreement to exchange on a specified future date the difference between the spot rate of interest and an agreed fixed rate.

Forward trade An agreement to buy or sell based on exchange rates established today for settlement in the future.

Futures contract A forward contract that is traded on an exchange with standardized specifications, including maturity date, commodity characteristics, and settlement procedure.

Futures parity The proposition that the combination of long and short positions in call and put options is equivalent to a long or short position in a forward contract.

Hedging The assumption of a long or short position in an asset or liability to offset the exposure to risk associated with an opposite or correlated position.

In-the-money option An option whose exercise would result in a gain (assuming that the option premium is ignored).

Interest-based swap An exchange of cash flows that are based on interest rates.

Interest rate The price paid for borrowing money.

Interest-rate parity The proposition that the difference between the forward exchange rate and the spot exchange rate for two currencies must offset the difference in interest rates for loans in those currencies.

Interest-rate risk The exposure to changes in the value of a debt instrument that are due to changes in interest rates.

Internal rate of return The interest rate that equates the present value of a future stream of payments with the cost of the investment.

Leverage The use of debt in the capital structure of a corporation.

London interbank offering rate (LIBOR) The interest rate at which the most creditworthy international banks dealing in the London market are willing to lend to each other.

Long hedge The acquisition of a forward or futures contract to protect against increases in the price of an asset.

Long position An excess of purchases over sales of an asset.

Marked to market The daily settlement of positions in futures contracts.

Market portfolio A value-weighted index of all securities that comprise a market.

Maturity date The date on which the last payment on a financial instrument is due.

Money market The market for debt instruments that have short-term maturities of one year or less.

Mortgage-backed securities Financial instruments that are secured by a mortgage on the real property of the borrower.

Naked An unhedged long or short position in a financial instrument.

Nominal interest rate The stated interest rate unadjusted for inflation.

Note An unsecured debt instrument that has a term of 15 years or less.

Notional principal amount The principal amount on which swap payments are based.

Off-market forward or swap A forward or swap contract under which the specified forward price differs from the forward price in the spot market.

Option A right to purchase or sell an asset for a specified price at a specified date or dates.

Option on futures A contract that provides the right to buy or sell a futures contract within a specified period.

Original issue discount (OID) The difference between the face amount of a debt instrument and the amount advanced to the issuer.

Out-of-the-money option An option whose exercise would not be profitable.

Over-the-counter (OTC) An instrument that is not traded on an organized exchange.

Prepaid forward or swap A forward or swap contract under which one of the parties to the contract prepays the amount of its future obligation.

Present value The current value of future cash flows discounted at a specified rate.

Principal The face amount of a debt instrument exclusive of any premium or interest. Also referred to as the "face amount" or "par value."

Put-call parity The proposition that the cash flows associated with the combination of a long position in an asset and a put option written on the asset are equivalent to a long position in a debt instrument and a call option written on the asset.

Put option An option to sell an asset at a specified price.

Range forward The combination of a long and a short position in an option issued at different strike prices that provide a "range."

Redemption The extinguishment of an instrument through a cash payment by the issuer.

Risk premium The promised return on an asset in addition to the risk-free rate.

S&P 500 Standard and Poor's composite index of shares.

Secondary market The market for the purchase and sale of issued financial instruments.

Short hedge The sale of a forward or futures contract to protect against decreases in the price of an asset.

Short position An excess of sales of an asset over purchases.

Spot exchange rate The exchange rate for two currencies for immediate delivery.

Spot interest rate The interest rate on a loan that is made today.

Spot market The market for immediate as opposed to future delivery of a commodity or financial instrument.

Spot price The price for an asset in the spot market.

Straddle The assumption of offsetting short and long positions in an asset whereby gain on one position is offset by loss on the other.

Strike price The price at which an option can be exercised.

Swap A contract that provides for an exchange of payments that are based on a notional principal amount.

Swaption An option to enter into or cancel an interest-rate swap in the future.

Systematic risk Any risk that affects a large number of assets to varying degrees. Also called "market risk."

Term structure of interest rates The pattern of interest rates on riskless debt instruments with different terms to maturity.

Term to maturity The term of a financial instrument or the period during which the instrument can be exercised or converted into cash or an underlying position.

Time value of money The amount that must be paid in the future for the use of funds in the present.

Treasury bill (T-bill) A debt instrument that is issued by a government at a discount with a term of one year or less.

Underlying The subject of a forward, futures, swap, or option contract.

Variation margin The cash transfer that takes place at the end of each trading day in a futures market after long and short positions are marked to market.

Warrant An option to purchase shares of an issuer at a specified price for a specified period.

Yield-to-maturity (YTM) The discount rate that produces the present value of expected cash flows.

Zero-coupon bond A bond without an interest coupon that pays only the face amount at maturity.

Selected Bibliography

Adamson, Peter. "Portfolio Securities Transactions." Personal Tax Planning feature. (1992), vol. 40, no. 3 *Canadian Tax Journal* 736-62.

Allgood, David R. "Recent Developments in Asset-Backed Securitization." In *Report of Proceedings of the Forty-Fifth Tax Conference*, 1993 Conference Report, 16:1-15. Toronto: Canadian Tax Foundation, 1994.

Alworth, Julian S. "Taxation and Integrated Financial Markets: The Challenges of Derivatives and Other Financial Innovations." (1998), vol. 5, no. 3 *International Tax and Public Finance* 507-34.

American Bar Association Section of Taxation Committees on Financial Transactions, Tax-Exempt Financing, and Foreign Activities of US Taxpayers. "Report on Proposed Regulations Regarding Debt Instruments with Contingent Payments." (Winter 1996), 49 *The Tax Lawyer* 195-239.

American Bar Association Section of Taxation Committee on Financial Transactions Task Force of the Interest Rate Agreements Subcommittee. "Report on Selected Aspects of Interest Rate Caps, Floors, and Collars." (Fall 1991), 44 *The Tax Lawyer* 1075-1122.

Augustyn, Francene M. "Tax Treatment of Notional Principal Contracts and Financial Products." (December 11, 1989), 45 *Tax Notes* 1353-61.

Australia. *Taxation of Financial Arrangements: A Consultative Document*. Canberra: Australian Government Publishing Services, December 1993.

———. *Taxation of Financial Arrangements: An Issues Paper*. Canberra: Australian Government Publishing Services, December 1996.

Australia, Review of Business Taxation. *A Platform for Consultation—Building on a Strong Foundation*. Discussion Paper 2, volume I, chapters 5-7. Canberra: Australian Government Publishing Services, February 1999.

———. *A Tax System Redesigned—More Certain, Equitable and Durable*. Chapter 9. Canberra: Australian Government Publishing Services, July 1999.

Avi-Yonah, Reuven S. "Virtual Taxation: Source-Based Taxation in the Age of Derivatives." In *Proceedings of the Eighty-Ninth Annual Conference*, 269-74. Washington, DC: National Tax Association and Tax Institute of America, 1997.

Avi-Yonah, Reuven S. and Linda Z. Swartz. "US International Tax Treatment of Financial Derivatives." (March 3, 1997), 14 *Tax Notes International* 787-96.

Avi-Yonah, Reuven S., David B. Newman, and Diane M. Ring, eds. *Taxation of Financial Instruments*. Deerfield, Ill.: Clark Boardman Callaghan, looseleaf.

Baer, Robert. "Understanding Derivatives and Financial Instruments." (December 1994), 72 *Taxes: The Tax Magazine* 929-46.

Bank, Steven A. "Devaluing Reform: The Derivatives Market and Executive Compensation." (Spring/Summer 1995), 7 *DePaul Business Law Journal* 301-32.

Bankman, Joseph and William A. Klein. "Accurate Taxation of Long-Term Debt: Taking into Account the Term Structure of Interest." (Winter 1989), 44 *Tax Law Review* 335-48.

Battle, Frank V., Jr. "Bifurcation of Financial Instruments." (December 1991), 69 *Taxes: The Tax Magazine* 821-33.

———. "Corporate Tax Shelters, Financial Engineering and the Colgate Case." (December 1997), 75 *Taxes: The Tax Magazine* 692-705.

Beck, Fiona and Jeff Tyler. "Taxation of Financial Transactions: Aspects of the New Zealand Accrual Regime." Unpublished paper presented at Canberra, Australia, November 19, 1991.

Beer, Yishai. "The Taxation of Interest Swaps and the Financial Services Charge: Toward a Consistent Approach." (1994), 1 *Florida Tax Review* 729-43.

Boltar, Julia T. "Corporate Taxation and the Interest-Dividend Dilemma." (August 1996), 113 *The South African Law Journal* 455-71.

Bradburne, Jeremy, Nicholas Noble, and Geoffrey Pennells. *Butterworths International Taxation of Financial Instruments and Transactions*, 2d ed. London: Butterworths, 1994.

Bradford, David F. "Fixing Realization Accounting: Symmetry, Consistency and Correctness in the Taxation of Financial Instruments." (Summer 1995), 50 *Tax Law Review* 731-85.

Brean, Donald J.S. "The Redemption of Convertible Preferred Shares: The Implications of Terms and Conditions." (1985), vol. 33, no. 5 *Canadian Tax Journal* 957-82.

Broadhurst, David G. "Derivatives in International Tax Planning." In International Fiscal Association—Canadian Branch, *1997 International Tax Seminar*, 85-101. Scarborough, Ont.: Carswell, 1998.

———. "Income Tax Treatment of Foreign Exchange Forward Contracts, Swaps, and Other Hedging Transactions." In *Report of Proceedings of the Forty-First Tax Conference*, 1989 Conference Report, 26:1-32. Toronto: Canadian Tax Foundation, 1990.

Brown, Fred B. "'Complete' Accrual Taxation." (Winter 1997), 33 *San Diego Law Review* 1559-1680.

Bureau of National Affairs. *Tax Management Financial Products Report.* Washington: BNA, 1996-present (looseleaf journal providing twice-monthly reports on the taxation of financial instruments in the United States and selected other countries).

Burger, George. "International Aspects of the Taxation of Discounted Securities." (1987), vol. 35, no. 5 *Canadian Tax Journal* 1131-60.

Caginalp, Oggie, Peter J. Connors, and R. Arnold Handler. "Section 475 After the 1997 Act and Final (?) Regs—The Makeover Continues." (August 25, 1997), 77 *Tax Notes* 1071-97.

Calderwood, John A. "A Revenue Canada Perspective on Offshore Funds, Commodity Straddles, and Offshore Deep Discount Bonds and Treasury Bills." In *Report of Proceedings of the Thirty-Fifth Tax Conference*, 1983 Conference Report, 253-64. Toronto: Canadian Tax Foundation, 1984.

Campbell, Niels. "Are the Accrual Rules Practical?" Paper presented at the 1992 Corporate Tax Reform Summit, Auckland, New Zealand, July 1-2, 1992.

———. "An Update on the Accrual Rules: Negotiating the Obstacles." Paper presented at the 1992 Corporate Tax Reform Summit, Auckland, New Zealand, July 1-2, 1992.

Carlisle, Linda E., Jeffrey A. Quinn, and Mark P. Howe. "Commodities and Financial Futures: Proposed IRS Rules for Notional Principal Contracts." (Winter 1992), 9 *Journal of Taxation of Investments* 169-80.

Carmody, Michael. "An Address by Michael Carmody, Commissioner of Taxation." The Metway Bank Bob Nicol Memorial Lecture, Brisbane, Australia September 20, 1995.

Cartusciello, Michael T. "Coping with IRS Guidance on Notional Principal Contracts." (January 1990), 72 *The Journal of Taxation* 24-33.

Clearwater, Tom. "The Judicial Role in Derivative Taxation: The Queen v. Shell Canada Limited and Financial Contract Economics." (1988), vol. 46, no. 6 *Canadian Tax Journal* 1212-44.

Conlon, Steven D., Vincent M. Aquilino, and Dale S. Collinson. "Tax Law Fundamentals of Tax-Exempt Derivatives." (April 20, 1992), 55 *Tax Notes* 381-97.

Couzin, Robert. "The Fiscal Gryphon: Some Recent Hybrids." In *Report of Proceedings of the Forty-Eighth Tax Conference*, 1996 Conference Report, 15:1-22. Toronto: Canadian Tax Foundation, 1997.

Craig, Christopher L. "The Appropriate Income Tax Treatment for the Assignment of Notional Principal Contracts." (Spring 1992), 36 *Saint Louis University Law Journal* 797-815.

Cunningham, Noël B. and Deborah H. Schenk. "Taxation Without Realization: A 'Revolutionary' Approach to Ownership." (Summer 1992), 47 *Tax Law Review* 725-814.

Daugaard, David and Tom Valentine. *Reforming the Taxation of Financial Arrangements: How Many Steps Forward?* Research Study no. 22. Sydney: Australian Tax Research Foundation, 1995.

Deak, Daniel. "The Taxation of Financial Derivatives in Emerging Financial Markets: The Hungarian Experience." (August/September 1997), 51 *Bulletin for International Fiscal Documentation* 377-86.

Dolan, Kevin and Carolyn DuPuy. "Equity Derivatives: Principles and Practice." (Fall 1995), 15 *Virginia Tax Review* 161-209.

Edgar, Tim. "The Classification of Corporate Securities for Income Tax Purposes." (1990), vol. 38, no. 5 *Canadian Tax Journal* 1141-88.

———. "The Debt-Equity Distinction and the Taxation of Financial Instruments: Past Practice and Future Directions in Australia and Canada." In John G. Head and Richard Krever, eds., *Taxation Towards 2000*, 293-335. Sydney: Australian Tax Research Foundation, 1997.

———. "Some Lessons from the Saga of Weak-Currency Borrowings." (2000), vol. 48, no. 1 *Canadian Tax Journal* 1-34.

———. "The Tax Treatment of Interest and Financing Charges in a World of Financial Innovation: Where Should We Be Going?" In *Current Issues in Corporate Finance*, Corporate Management Tax Conference 1997, 10:1-57. Toronto: Canadian Tax Foundation, 1998.

Elvin, Bruce A. "The Recharacterization of Cross-Border Interest Rate Swaps: Tax Consequences and Beyond." (1995), vol. 2, no. 11 *Florida Tax Review* 631-72.

Emmerich, Adam O. "Hybrid Instruments and the Debt-Equity Distinction in Corporate Taxation." (Winter 1985), 52 *The University of Chicago Law Review* 118-48.

Ensminger, John J. "The Broad but Porous Net of the Straddle Rules: How Long Will the Fish Continue To Swim Through?" (Spring 1999), 18 *Virginia Tax Review* 709-80.

Eustice, James S. "Debt-Like Equity and Equity-Like Debt: Treasury's Anti-Hybrid Proposals." (June 17, 1996), 71 *Tax Notes* 1657-78.

Farwell, Peter M. "Taxation of Hedging Transactions." In *Report of Proceedings of the Thirty-Fourth Tax Conference*, 1982 Conference Report, 653-55. Toronto: Canadian Tax Foundation, 1983.

Feld, Alan L. "When Fungible Portfolio Assets Meet: A Problem of Tax Recognition." (Winter 1991), 44 *The Tax Lawyer* 409-43.

Feldgarden, Robert. "Time Value of Money Principles Still Giving the Tax Court Trouble." (March 6, 1995), 66 *Tax Notes* 1471-73.

Fellows, Mary Louise. "A Comprehensive Attack on Deferral." (February 1990), 88 *Michigan Law Review* 722-811.

Ferguson, Bradford L. "The Rationales for the Rules: How To Think About Derivatives in the Tax World." (December 1994), 72 *Taxes: The Tax Magazine* 995-1026.

Ferguson, Bradford L., George R. Goodman, and Jonathan P. Biller. "The Latest Stock Hedging Regulations." (June 26, 1995), 69 *Tax Notes* 1795-1818.

Fichtenbaum, Mark. "The Forms of Equity Investments Produce Disparate Tax Effects." (Autumn 1996), 14 *Journal of Taxation of Investments* 12-19.

Flynn, Gordon W. "Creative Equity Financing." In *Report of Proceedings of the Thirty-Fourth Tax Conference*, 1982 Conference Report, 615-35. Toronto: Canadian Tax Foundation, 1983.

Freeman, Louis S. and Richard M. Lipton. "Tax Consequences of Business and Investment-Driven Derivatives." (December 1994), 72 *Taxes: The Tax Magazine* 947-94.

Freeman, Ross D. and Dixie D. Martin. "Income Tax Considerations in Swap Transactions." (Fall 1990), 3 *Canadian Petroleum Tax Journal* 33-49.

Frost, Anthony J. "Taxation of Financial Transactions." In *Papers Presented at the Eleventh National Conference of the Taxation Institute of Australia*, 103-125. Sydney: Taxation Institute of Australia, 1993.

Frost, Anthony J. and Chris Catt. "Taxation of Financial Arrangements: An Issues Paper." (February 19, 1997), special issue no. 6 *Weekly Tax Bulletin: Australian Tax Practice* 118-39.

Gammie, Malcolm. "The Source Taxation of Derivative Financial Instruments, 'Synthetic Securities,' Financial Hedging Transactions and Similar Innovative Financial Transactions." (September/October 1999), 1 *Derivatives and Financial Instruments* 231-36.

Garlock, David C. "A Primer in the New Proposed (Almost) Regulations for Contingent Debt Instruments." (March 1, 1993), 58 *Tax Notes* 1225-30.

Gergen, Mark P. "Apocalypse Not?" (Summer 1995), 50 *Tax Law Review* 833-59.

———. "The Effects of Price Volatility and Strategic Trading Under Realization, Expected Return and Retrospective Taxation." (Winter 1994), 49 *Tax Law Review* 209-69.

Gergen, Mark P. and Paula Schmitz. "The Influence of Tax Law on Securities Innovation in the United States: 1981-1997." (Winter 1997), 52 *Tax Law Review* 119-97.

Glazebrook, Susan. "The Accruals Regime: An Update." The 1988 Tax Update, Institute for International Research Conference, Auckland, April 27-28, 1988.

———. "Financial Arrangements." Paper presented at the 1995 Tax Conference, New Zealand Society of Accountants, September 29-30, 1995.

Glazebrook, Susan and Robin Oliver. *The New Zealand Accruals Regime: A Practical Guide*. Auckland: CCH New Zealand, 1989.

Glazebrook, Susan and Brian Walworth. "Impact of the Accrual Regime on Areas of Key Concern to Corporate Planners." 1991 Corporate Tax Update, Institute for International Research Conference, Auckland, 1991.

Halperin, Daniel I. "Interest in Disguise: Taxing the 'Time Value of Money.'" (January 1986), 95 *The Yale Law Journal* 506-52.

Hariton, David P. "The Accrual of Interest on Derivative Instruments: Where Do We Go from Here?" (December 1996), 74 *Taxes: The Tax Magazine* 1011-22.

———. "Contingent Debt: Putting the Pieces Together." (March 1, 1993), 58 *Tax Notes* 1231-43.

———. "Distinguishing Between Equity and Debt in the New Financial Environment." (Spring 1994), 49 *Tax Law Review* 499-524.

———. "New Rules on Bifurcating Debt—A Mistake?" (April 15, 1991), 51 *Tax Notes* 235-39.

———. "The Tax Treatment of Hedged Positions in Stock: What Hath Technical Analysis Wrought?" (Summer 1995), 50 *Tax Law Review* 803-27.

———. "The Taxation of Complex Financial Instruments." (Summer 1988), 43 *Tax Law Review* 731-88.

———. "Withholding on Cross-Border Stock Loans and Other Equity Derivatives." (December 1994), 72 *Taxes: The Tax Magazine* 1050-60.

Haskins, Matthew P. "Can the IRS Maintain the Debt-Equity Distinction in the Face of Structured Notes?" (Summer 1995), 32 *Harvard Journal on Legislation* 525-44.

Herrera, Paul and Debra M. Davis. "Taxation of Financial Products: Some Practical Guidelines." (Fall 1990), 16 *International Tax Journal* 303-22.

Hertz, Frank, John MacArthur, Barry Riddell, and Bruce Weinrib. "Taxation of Hedging Transactions: Final and Proposed Regs Leave Many Unanswered Questions." (September 19, 1994), 64 *Tax Notes* 1597-1613.

Homan, Laura A. "The Section 988(d) Hedging Rules: Room To Expand Integration Treatment." (Summer 1993), 46 *The Tax Lawyer* 887-921.

Howell, George C. III and Cameron N. Cosby. "Exotic Coupon Stripping: A Voyage to the Frontier Between Debt and Option." (Spring 1993), 12 *Virginia Tax Review* 531-60.

Huggins, Matthew. "The Probable Tax Treatment of LEAPs and BOUNDs." (June 24, 1996), 71 *Tax Notes* 1807-15.

Hughes, Timothy R. "Income Tax Implications of the Non-Dispositive Transfer of Equity Securities." (Winter 1999), 57 *University of Toronto Faculty of Law Review* 43-81.

Hutchison, Stuart and Susan Glazebrook. "The Accruals Legislation." (1988), 32 *New Zealand Current Taxation* 1-77.

International Bureau for Fiscal Documentation. *Derivatives and Financial Instruments*. Amsterdam: IBFD Publications BV, 1999-present (bi-monthly journal providing articles, country reports, and case studies on the taxation of derivatives and financial instruments).

International Fiscal Association. *Cahiers de droit fiscal international*, vol. 79b, *Deductibility of Interest*. Deventer, The Netherlands: Kluwer Law and Taxation, 1994.

———. *Cahiers de droit fiscal international*, vol. 80b, *Tax Aspects of Derivative Financial Instruments*. The Hague: Kluwer Law International, 1995.

Jacobs, Otto H. and Jurgen Haun. "Financial Derivatives in International Tax Law—A Treatment of Certain Key Considerations." [1995], no. 8-9 *Intertax* 405-20.

Johnson, Calvin H. "Taxing the Income from Writing Options." (October 14, 1996), 73 *Tax Notes* 203-20.

Johnson, Elizabeth J. "Equity Financings." In *Report of Proceedings of the Forty-Sixth Tax Conference*, 1994 Conference Report, 5:1-16. Toronto: Canadian Tax Foundation, 1995.

Kau, Randall K.C. "Carving Up Assets and Liabilities—Integration or Bifurcation of Financial Instruments." (December 1990), 68 *Taxes: The Tax Magazine* 1003-14.

Kayle, Bruce. "Realization Without Taxation? The Not-So-Clear Reflection of Income from an Option To Acquire Property." (Winter 1993), 48 *Tax Law Review* 233-80.

———. "Where Has All the Income Gone? The Mysterious Relocation of Interest and Principal in Coupon Stripping and Related Transactions." (Fall 1987), 7 *Virginia Tax Review* 303-61.

———. "Will the Real Lender Please Stand Up? The Federal Income Tax Treatment of Credit Derivative Transactions." (Summer 1997), 50 *The Tax Lawyer* 569-615.

Keyes, Kevin M. *Federal Taxation of Financial Instruments and Transactions.* Boston: Warren, Gorham & Lamont, 1997.

Kleinbard, Edward D. "Beyond Good and Evil Debt (and Debt Hedges): A Cost of Capital Allowance System." (December 1989), 67 *Taxes: The Tax Magazine* 943-61.

———. "Equity Derivative Instruments: Financial Innovation's Newest Challenge to the Tax System." (May 1991), 69 *Texas Law Review* 1319-68.

———. "Risky and Riskless Positions in Securities." (December 1993), 71 *Taxes: The Tax Magazine* 783-99.

Kleinbard, Edward D., S. Douglas Borisky, and Rekha Vemireddy. "Proposed Regulations Affecting Contingent Payment Debt Obligations." (January 30, 1995), 66 *Tax Notes* 723-34.

Kleinbard, Edward D. and Thomas H. Evans. "The Role of Mark-to-Market Accounting in a Realization-Based Tax System." (December 1997), 75 *Taxes: The Tax Magazine* 788-823.

Kleinbard, Edward D., Erika W. Nijenhuis, and Rekha Vemireddy. "Final Tax Regulations Governing Contingent Payment Debt Obligations." (July 22, 1996), 72 *Tax Notes* 499-515.

Knoll, Michael S. "Financial Innovation, Tax Arbitrage, and Retrospective Taxation: The Problem with Passive Government Lending." (Winter 1997), 52 *Tax Law Review* 199-224.

———. "Taxing Prometheus: How the Corporate Interest Deduction Discourages Innovation and Risk-Taking." (1993), vol. 38, no. 5 *Villanova Law Review* 1461-1516.

Kolbrenner, Scott M. "Derivatives Design and Taxation." (Fall 1995), 15 *Virginia Tax Review* 211-81.

Kramer, Andrea S. *Financial Products—Taxation Regulation and Design.* New York: Wiley, 1991.

Land, Stephen B. "Contingent Payments and the Time Value of Money." (Winter 1987), 40 *The Tax Lawyer* 237-306.

———. "Defeating Deferral: A Proposal for Retrospective Taxation." (Fall 1996), 52 *Tax Law Review* 45-117.

Levy, David F. "Towards Equal Tax Treatment of Economically Equivalent Financial Instruments: Proposals for Taxing Prepaid Forward Contracts, Equity Swaps, and Certain Contingent Debt Instruments." (1997), vol. 3, no. 8 *Florida Tax Review* 471-543.

Lokken, Lawrence. "New Rules on Bifurcating Contingent Debt—A Good Start." (April 29, 1991), 58 *Tax Notes* 495-504.

———. "The Time Value of Money Rules." (Fall 1986), 42 *Tax Law Review* 1-292.

Loveland, Norman C. "Currency and Interest Rate Risk Management Strategies and Products." In *Income Tax and Goods and Services Tax Considerations in Corporate Financing*, 1992 Corporate Management Tax Conference, 11:1-38. Toronto: Canadian Tax Foundation, 1993.

Madison, Roger B. "The Deductibility of 'Interest' on Hybrid Securities." (Spring 1986), 39 *The Tax Lawyer* 465-517.

Martin, Denham. "Accrual Rules-Practical Problems." Paper presented at the Joint Tax Conference, New Zealand Society of Accountants and the New Zealand Law Society, October 1991.

May, Glenn L.E. "Further Reflections on Derivative Taxation." (1999), vol. 47, no. 3 *Canadian Tax Journal* 534-43.

———. "Overview of Financial, Tax, and Accounting Principles for Derivative Financial Instruments." In *Report of Proceedings of the Forty-Seventh Tax Conference*, 1995 Conference Report, 29:1-27. Toronto: Canadian Tax Foundation, 1996.

May, Gregory. "Flying on Instruments: Synthetic Investment and the Avoidance of Withholding Tax." (November 11, 1996), 13 *Tax Notes International* 1625-35.

———. "Taxing Derivative Contracts." (Winter 1995), 12 *Journal of Taxation of Investments* 115-29.

———. "The U.S. Taxation of Derivative Contracts." (September 25, 1995), 68 *Tax Notes* 1629-37.

Meredith, P. Mark. "Current Problems and Future Directions in Derivatives Taxation." In *Report of Proceedings of the Thirty-Sixth Tax Conference*, 1994 Conference Report, 18:1-21. Toronto: Canadian Tax Foundation, 1995.

Michielse, Geersten, ed. *Tax Treatment of Financial Instruments: A Survey of France, Germany, the Netherlands and the United Kingdom*. The Hague: Kluwer Law International, 1996.

Miller, David A. "Reconciling Policies and Practice in the Taxation of Financial Instruments." (March 1999), 77 *Taxes: The Tax Magazine* 236-76.

Miller, David S. "A Look at the Final Contingent Payment Debt Instrument Regs." (July 22, 1996), 72 *Tax Notes* 489-98.

———. "Taxpayers' Ability To Avoid Tax Ownership: Current Law and Future Prospects." (Winter 1998), 51 *The Tax Lawyer* 279-349.

Nannestad, Anton. "The Meaning of 'Financial Arrangement' in the Accrual Rules." (1991), vol. 35, no. 19 *Current Taxation* 35:134-46.

———. "The Meaning of 'Financial Arrangement' in the Accrual Rules—Part B." (1991), 35 *Current Taxation* 142-46.

Nesvold, H. Peter. "Interest Rate Swaps: The Taxation of Trading Places." (February 1998), 76 *Taxes: The Tax Magazine* 25-33.

New York State Bar Association. "Withholding Tax on Substitute and Derivative Dividend Payments Received by Foreigners." (June 29, 1998), 79 *Tax Notes* 1749-58.

New York State Bar Association Tax Section (Principal Draftsman David S. Miller). "Notional Principal Contract Character and Timing Issues." (June 8, 1998), 79 *Tax Notes* 1303-36.

New York State Bar Association Tax Section and Members of the American Bar Association Tax Section (Principal Draftsman David P. Hariton). "Report and Recommendation for the Treatment of Contingent Payment Debt Instruments Under Proposed Regulation 1.1275-4." (December 6, 1993), 61 *Tax Notes* 1241-63.

New York State Bar Association (Principal Draftsman Donald Schapiro). "Recommendations for Proposed Tax Straddle Regulations Under Sections 1092 and 1256." (May 28, 1984), 23 *Tax Notes* 973-91.

New Zealand. *Consultative Document on Accrual Tax Treatment of Income and Expenditure*. Wellington: New Zealand Government Printer, October 1986.

———. *Operational Aspects of the Accruals Regime*. Wellington: New Zealand Government Printer, October 1991.

———. *Report of the Consultative Committee on Accrual Tax Treatment of Income and Expenditure*. Wellington: New Zealand Government Printer, April 1987.

———. *Taxation (Accrual Rules and Other Remedial Matters) Bill: Commentary on the Bill*. Wellington: Inland Revenue, Policy Advice Division, November 1998.

———. *The Taxation of Financial Arrangements: A Discussion Document on Proposed Changes to the Accrual Rules*. Wellington: Inland Revenue, Policy Advice Division, December 1997.

Nirenberg, David Z. and Steven L. Kopp. "Tax Treatment of Total Return Swaps, Default Swaps, and Credit-Linked Notes." (August 1997), 87 *Journal of Taxation* 1-14.

Nolan, D.A. "The Financial Arrangements Code: Current Policy Deliberations." *The 1995 Derivatives Megaconference*, August 28, 1995.

Norman, Peter J. "Debt Dividends: The Test Case." (August 1996), 5(1) *Taxation in Australia (Red Edition)* 10-18.

Oestreicher, Andreas and Jurgen Haun. "Implications of the International Use Interest-Rate Derivatives." (Summer 1998), 24 *International Tax Journal* 12-47.

Organisation for Economic Co-operation and Development. *Taxation of New Financial Instruments*. Paris: OECD, 1994.

Patterson, David and Casey Plunket. "Corporate Tax Conference 1993: Financial Instruments." Paper prepared for the Institute for International Research, February 18, 1993.

———. "Off Balance Sheet Financial Instruments: Tax Issues." Paper presented at the Accounting and Tax for Advanced Financial Instruments Conference, May 14, 1992.

Paul, Deborah L. "Another Uneasy Compromise: The Tax Treatment of Hedging in a Realization Income Tax." (1996), vol. 3, no. 1 *Florida Tax Review* 1-50.

Paul, Roger M. "Financial Risk Management and the Taxation of Financial Products." In Rick Krever, Yuri Grbich, and Patrick Gallagher, eds., *Taxation of Corporate Debt Finance*, 209-38. Melbourne: Longman, 1991.

———. "Taxation of Financial Instruments: Towards a Conceptual Understanding of Economic Substance—An Australian Update." Paper presented at the Harvard International Tax Program symposium on the Taxation of New Financial Instruments, September 28, 1996.

Paul, William M. "Constructive Sales Under New Section 1259." (September 15, 1997), 76 *Tax Notes* 1467-79.

Penn, Oren S. "Withholding Tax Issues in Cross-Border Equity Swaps: The Dividend Problem." (October 11, 1993), 7 *Tax Notes International* 917-33.

Piatoff, Mindy S. "Tax and Financial Accounting for Notional Principal Contracts." (Winter 1996), 13 *Journal of Taxation of Investments* 99-117.

Pope, Peter F. and Anthony G. Puxty. "What Is Equity? New Financial Instruments in the Interstices Between Law, Accounting and Economics." (November 1991), 54 *Modern Law Review* 889-911.

Potter, Clarissa. "Mark-to-Market Taxation as a Way To Save the Income Tax Act—A Former Administrator's View." (Summer 1999), 33 *Valparaiso University Law Review* 879-905.

Preston, Alan. "The View from the High Wire: A Treasury Perspective of Corporate Tax Issues." In Taxation Institute of Australia (Victoria Division), *Red Series Intensive Retreat: Rabbits Out of Hats—Corporate Structures and Restructures*. Melbourne: TIA, 1995.

Raizenne, Robert. "Accrual of Interest Income." In *Report of Proceedings of the Fortieth Tax Conference*, 1988 Conference Report, 23:1-11. Toronto: Canadian Tax Foundation, 1989.

Reed, Philippa. "The Accruals Rules—Recent Developments." International Institute of Research-Corporate Tax Update, March 17, 1996.

Reid, John. "MIPs Besieged: Solutions in Search of a Problem." (December 1, 1997), 76 *Tax Notes* 1057-68.

Reinhold, Richard L. "Tax Issues in Equity Swap Transactions." (November 23, 1992), 57 *Tax Notes* 1179-83.

Richardson, Elinore J. "Currency Swaps—A Canadian Perspective." International Tax Planning feature. (1984), vol. 32, no. 2 *Canadian Tax Journal* 345-61.

Richardson, Elinore J., David Glicksman, and Lara Friedlander. "Fundamentals of Canadian Taxation of Financial Instruments." In *Report of Proceedings of the Fifty-First Tax Conference*, 1999 Conference Report, 5:1-57. Toronto: Canadian Tax Foundation, 2000.

Richardson, Stephen R. "Current Developments in Debt Financing: A Canadian Tax Perspective." In *Report of Proceedings of the Fortieth Tax Conference*, 1988 Conference Report, 22:1-32. Toronto: Canadian Tax Foundation, 1989.

———. "New Financial Instruments: A Canadian Tax Perspective." In *Income Tax and Goods and Services Tax Considerations in Corporate Financing*, 1992 Corporate Management Tax Conference, 10:1-32. Toronto: Canadian Tax Foundation, 1993.

Ring, Diane M. "Risk-Shifting Within a Multinational Corporation: The Incoherence of the US Tax Regime." (July 1997), 38 *Boston College Law Review* 667-737.

Rosenberg, Menachem. "Interaction of the Final OID Regs on Contingent Payment Debt and the Instalment Rules." (February 1997), 86 *Journal of Taxation* 69-74.

Rosenbloom, H. David. "Source-Basis Taxation of Derivative Financial Instruments: Some Unanswered Questions." (April 1996), 50 *University of Miami Law Review* 597-615.

Rosenthal, Steven M. and Mark H. Price. "FAS 133 and Tax—An Unhappy Marriage Awaiting a Counsellor." (July/August 1999), 1 *Derivatives & Financial Instruments* 216-27.

———. "Time To Reconcile Tax and Accounting for Derivatives." (August 9, 1999), 84 *Tax Notes* 895-908.

Ruby, Stephen S. "Recent Financing Techniques." In *Report of Proceedings of the Forty-First Tax Conference*, 1989 Conference Report, 27:1-46. Toronto: Canadian Tax Foundation, 1990.

Rumble, Tony. "Beyond One Dimensional Tax Laws: Lessons from the Australian Experiment with Related Stock and Derivative Position and Integration." (1998), vol. 14, no. 2 *Australian Tax Forum* 179-249.

———. "Synthetic Equity: A Tax-Efficient Approach." (1998), vol. 14, no. 4 *Australian Tax Forum* 383-454.

Rumble, Tony, ed. *Derivative Tax Reform*. Sydney: Prospect Media, 1997.

Rusman, Jared M. "Equity Swaps and Post-Transaction Continuity of Interest." (July 1, 1996), 72 *Tax Notes* 113-17.

Santangelo, Robert A. "Towards Reshaping the Debt-Equity Distinction." (Winter 1997), 23 *The Journal of Corporate Taxation* 312-41.

Scace, Arthur R.A. and Michael G. Quigley. "New Developments in Debt Financing." In *Report of Proceedings of the Thirty-Fourth Tax Conference*, 1982 Conference Report, 579-615. Toronto: Canadian Tax Foundation, 1983.

———. "Zero-Coupon Obligations, Stripped Bonds, and Defeasance—An Update." (1984), vol. 32, no. 4 *Canadian Tax Journal* 689-705.

Scarborough, Robert H. "Different Rules for Different Players and Products: The Patchwork Taxation of Derivatives." (December 1994), 72 *Taxes: The Tax Magazine* 1031-49.

———. "Payments in Advance of Performance." (December 1991), 69 *Taxes: The Tax Magazine* 798-820.

———. "Risk Diversification and the Design of Loss Limitations Under a Realization-Based Income Tax." (Spring 1993), 48 *Tax Law Review* 677-717.

Schafer, Joel. "Income Access Shares." In *Report of Proceedings of the Forty-Fifth Tax Conference*, 1993 Conference Report, 18:1-18. Toronto: Canadian Tax Foundation, 1994.

Schenk, Deborah H. "Taxation of Equity Derivatives: A Partial Integration Proposal." (Summer 1995), 50 *Tax Law Review* 571-641.

Schizer, David M. "Hedging Under Section 1259." (July 20, 1998), 80 *Tax Notes* 345-54.

Schmidt, Paul M. "The Hedging Rules: Clarity or Confusion?" (August 26, 1996), 72 *Tax Notes* 1169-85.

Schnek, Morris. "Accounting and Tax Aspects of Risk Management." In *Report of Proceedings of the Thirty-Sixth Tax Conference*, 1984 Conference Report, 699-714. Toronto: Canadian Tax Foundation, 1985.

Schwartz, Alan M. "PEACs and SPECs and Special Warrants." In *Report of Proceedings of the Forty-Fifth Tax Conference*, 1993 Conference Report, 17:1-8. Toronto: Canadian Tax Foundation, 1994.

Shakow, David A. "Taxation Without Realization: A Proposal for Accrual Taxation." (June 1986), 134 *University of Pennsylvania Law Review* 1111-1205.

Shaviro, Daniel. "Risk-Based Rules and the Taxation of Capital Income." (Summer 1995), 50 *Tax Law Review* 643-724.

Shefter, Daniel. "A Brief Intro to the Contingent Payment Debt Instrument Regs." (July 22, 1996), 72 *Tax Notes* 479-87.

Shefter, Daniel A. "Section 1274, Convertibles, and the Phantom OID Conundrum." (March 6, 1995), 67 *Tax Notes* 1459-64.

Shuldiner, Reed. "Consistency and the Taxation of Financial Products." (December 1992), 70 *Taxes: The Tax Magazine* 781-92.

———. "A General Approach to the Taxation of Financial Instruments." (December 1992), 71 *Texas Law Review* 243-350.

Simon, Karla W. "Revenue or Religion? Issues and Answers on Tax Deferral." (December 1990), 68 *Taxes: The Tax Magazine* 1015-32.

Sims, Theodore S. "Long-Term Debt, the Term Structure of Interest and the Case for Accrual Taxation." (Winter 1992), 47 *Tax Law Review* 313-75.

Smith, Andrew M.C. "New Zealand's Interest Accrual Rules: A Comprehensive Review 12 Years On." (1998), vol. 46, no. 4 *Canadian Tax Journal* 819-38.

Smith, David W. "Recent Transactions: Debt." In *Report of Proceedings of the Forty-Fifth Tax Conference*, 1993 Conference Report, 19:1-24. Toronto: Canadian Tax Foundation, 1994.

Smith, Martin. "An Overview of the Accrual Provisions and Issues Arising Thereunder." (May 1994), 48 *Bulletin for International Fiscal Documentation* 218-35.

———. "The Timing of Deductions for Expenditure 'Incurred.'" (September 1994), 1 *New Zealand Journal of Taxation Law and Policy* 22-47.

Solway, Richard J. and Paul J.R. Bothamley. "Treasury Centers, Hybrid Instruments, and Foreign Currency Strategies." (February 12, 1996), 70 *Tax Notes* 883-91.

Southern, David. "The Taxation of Derivatives." [1998], no. 4 *British Tax Review* 348-63.

Speed, Robin. "Foreign Currency and the Proposed Accruals Tax System." (September 1994), 23 *Australian Tax Review* 125-34.

Spindler, Robert J. "Derivatives in Evolution." In *Report of Proceedings of the Forty-Seventh Tax Conference*, 1995 Conference Report, 26:1-13. Toronto: Canadian Tax Foundation, 1996.

———. "New Investment Products." In *Report of Proceedings of the Forty-Fourth Tax Conference*, 1992 Conference Report, 19:1-21. Toronto: Canadian Tax Foundation, 1993.

Steinberg, Lewis R. "Selected Issues in the Taxation of Swaps, Structured Finance and Other Financial Products." (1993), vol. 1, no. 5 *Florida Tax Review* 263-306.

Strnad, Jeff. "The Taxation of Bonds: The Tax Trading Dimension." (February 1995), 81 *Virginia Law Review* 47-116.

———. "Taxing New Financial Products: A Conceptual Framework." (May 1994), 46 *Stanford Law Review* 569-605.

Strother, R.C. "Income Tax Treatment of Financing Charges." In *Income Tax Considerations in Corporate Financing*, 1986 Corporate Tax Management Conference, 81-139. Toronto: Canadian Tax Foundation, 1986.

Surdell, Steven M. "Analyzing Equity-Linked Investments After Reform Proposals." (June 10, 1996), 71 *Tax Notes* 1525-36.

Sykora, Dennis F. "The Income Tax Web Surrounding Derivatives." In *Report of Proceedings of the Forty-Seventh Tax Conference*, 1995 Conference Report, 30:1-41. Toronto: Canadian Tax Foundation, 1996.

———. "Prepaid Forward Sales in the Oil and Gas Industry: Income Tax Issues." (1996), vol. 9, no. 1 *Canadian Petroleum Tax Journal* 99-116.

Taylor, Willard B. and Diane L. Wollman. "Why Can't We All Just Get Along: Finding Consistent Solutions to the Treatment of Derivatives and Other Problems." (Fall 1999), 53 *The Tax Lawyer* 95-127.

Temby, David C. "Swaps, Options, Forwards and Futures." In Richard Krever and Yuri Grbich, eds., *Australian International Taxation: Recent Developments and Future Directions*, 119-53. Sydney: Law Book, 1994.

Ulmer, John M. "Taxation of Interest Income." In *Report of Proceedings of the Forty-Second Tax Conference*, 1990 Conference Report, 8:1-30. Toronto: Canadian Tax Foundation, 1991.

United Kingdom, Inland Revenue. *The Taxation of Gilts and Bonds—A Consultative Document*. London: Inland Revenue, May 1995.

Upfold, Robert. "Taxation of Financial Arrangements: The New Approach." Paper presented at the Joint QLD/NSW Convention, Taxation Institute of Australia, April 15-16, 1994.

Van Brunt, Kirk. "Contingent Payment Debt Instruments—A Light at the End of the Tunnel." (July 1995), 73 *Taxes: The Tax Magazine* 365-84.

Waddingham, Daryll G. "Financial Innovation: A Brief Survey." (Spring 1992), 5 *Canadian Petroleum Tax Journal* 1-17.

Walker, Geoffrey. "Speculative Commodity Futures: The Computation of Income." (1989), vol. 37, no. 4 *Canadian Tax Journal* 917-68.

Warren, Alvin C., Jr. "Financial Contract Innovation and Income Tax Policy." (December 1993), 107 *Harvard Law Review* 460-92.

Watkins, Donald H. "Equity Exchangeable Debentures and Appreciation Rights." In *Report of Proceedings of the Forty-Fifth Tax Conference*, 1993 Conference Report, 20:1-15. Toronto: Canadian Tax Foundation, 1994.

Weisbach, David A. "A Partial Mark-to-Market System." (Fall 1999), 53 *Tax Law Review* 95-135.

———. "Should a Short Sale Against the Box Be a Realization Event?" (September 1997), 50 *National Tax Journal* 495-506.

———. "Tax Responses to Financial Contract Innovation." (Summer 1995), 50 *Tax Law Review* 491-544.

Wilkie, J. Scott. "Looking Forward into the Past: Financial Innovation and the Basic Limits of Income Taxation." (1995), vol. 42, no. 5 *Canadian Tax Journal* 1144-1166.

Wilson, James R. "Exchangeable Preferred Shares." The Taxation of Corporate Reorganizations feature. (1983), vol. 31, no. 2 *Canadian Tax Journal* 274-91.

Wood, Richard. *Derivatives, Financial Innovation and Taxation*. Treasury Research Paper no. 11. Canberra: Australian Government Publishing Service, 1996.

———. "The Taxation of Debt, Equity and Hybrid Arrangements." (1999), vol. 47, no. 1 *Canadian Tax Journal* 49-80.

———. "Taxation of Financial Arrangements—The Trading Regime." In *Economic Roundup*, 69-88. Canberra: Commonwealth Treasury of Australia, Summer 1998.

———. "The Taxation of Hybrid Financial Arrangements." In *Economic Roundup*, 73-87. Canberra: Commonwealth Treasury of Australia, Autumn 1999.

———. "Taxation of Returns to Financial Capital: Main Themes." (2000), vol. 16, no. 3 *Australian Tax Forum* (forthcoming).

Woods, Judith M. "Dividend Access Shares." The Taxation of Corporate Reorganizations feature. (1991), vol. 39, no. 3 *Canadian Tax Journal* 709-24.

Index